P9-APS-312

# Fodor's 2011

# PARIS

Fodor's Travel Publications   New York, Toronto, London, Sydney, Auckland
**www.fodors.com**

# Be a Fodor's Correspondent

Your opinion matters. It matters to us. It matters to your fellow Fodor's travelers, too. And we'd like to hear it. In fact, we need to hear it.

When you share your experiences and opinions, you become an active member of the Fodor's community. That means we'll not only use your feedback to make our books better, but we'll publish your names and comments whenever possible. Throughout our guides, look for "Word of Mouth," excerpts of your unvarnished feedback.

Here's how you can help improve Fodor's for all of us.

**Tell us when we're right.** We rely on local writers to give you an insider's perspective. But our writers and staff editors—who are the best in the business—depend on you. Your positive feedback is a vote to renew our recommendations for the next edition.

**Tell us when we're wrong.** We're proud that we update most of our guides every year. But we're not perfect. Things change. Hotels cut services. Museums change hours. Charming cafés lose charm. If our writer didn't quite capture the essence of a place, tell us how you'd do it differently. If any of our descriptions are inaccurate or inadequate, we'll incorporate your changes in the next edition and will correct factual errors at fodors.com immediately.

**Tell us what to include.** You probably have had fantastic travel experiences that aren't yet in Fodor's. Why not share them with a community of like-minded travelers? Maybe you chanced upon a beach or bistro or B&B that you don't want to keep to yourself. Tell us why we should include it. And share your discoveries and experiences with everyone directly at fodors.com. Your input may lead us to add a new listing or highlight a place we cover with a "Highly Recommended" star or with our highest rating, "Fodor's Choice."

Give us your opinion instantly at our feedback center at www.fodors.com/feedback. You may also e-mail editors@fodors.com with the subject line "Paris Editor." Or send your nominations, comments, and complaints by mail to Paris Editor, Fodor's, 1745 Broadway, New York, NY 10019.

You and travelers like you are the heart of the Fodor's community. Make our community richer by sharing your experiences. Be a Fodor's correspondent.

Bon Voyage!

Tim Jarrell, Publisher

# FODOR'S PARIS 2011

**Editor:** Caroline Trefler

**Editorial Contributors:** Jennifer Ditsler-Ladonne, Linda Hervieux, Rosa Jackson, Mary Papenfuss, Heather Stimmler-Hall

**Production Editor:** Jennifer DePrima
**Maps & Illustrations:** Mark Stroud, Henry Colomb, and David Lindroth, *cartographers;* Bob Blake, Rebecca Baer, *map editors;* William Wu, *information graphics*
**Design:** Fabrizio La Rocca, *creative director;* Guido Caroti, Siobhan O'Hare, *art directors;* Tina Malaney, Chie Ushio, Ann McBride, Jessica Walsh, *designers;* Melanie Marin, *senior picture editor*
**Cover Photo** (River Seine): Jon Arnold/age Fotostock
**Production Manager:** Amanda Bullock

ISBN 978–1–4000–0459–1

ISSN 0149–1288

## SPECIAL SALES

This book is available at special discounts for bulk purchases for sales promotions or premiums. Special editions, including personalized covers, excerpts of existing books, and corporate imprints, can be created in large quantities for special needs. For more information, write to Special Markets/Premium Sales, 1745 Broadway, MD 6-2, New York, New York 10019, or e-mail specialmarkets@randomhouse.com.

## AN IMPORTANT TIP & AN INVITATION

Although all prices, opening times, and other details in this book are based on information supplied to us at press time, changes occur all the time in the travel world, and Fodor's cannot accept responsibility for facts that become outdated or for inadvertent errors or omissions. So **always confirm information when it matters,** especially if you're making a detour to visit a specific place. Your experiences—positive and negative—matter to us. If we have missed or misstated something, **please write to us.** We follow up on all suggestions. Contact the Paris editor at editors@fodors.com or c/o Fodor's at 1745 Broadway, New York, NY 10019.

PRINTED IN SINGAPORE

10 9 8 7 6 5 4 3 2 1

# CONTENTS

## Fodor's Features

# ABOUT
# THIS BOOK

## Our Ratings

Sometimes you find terrific travel experiences and sometimes they just find you. But usually the burden is on you to select the right combination of experiences. That's where our ratings come in.

As travelers we've all discovered a place so wonderful that its worthiness is obvious. And sometimes that place is so experiential that superlatives don't do it justice: you just have to be there to know. These sights, properties, and experiences get our highest rating, **Fodor's Choice**, indicated by orange stars throughout this book.

Black stars highlight sights and properties we deem **Highly Recommended**, places that our writers, editors, and readers praise again and again for consistency and excellence.

By default, there's another category: any place we include in this book is by definition worth your time, unless we say otherwise. And we will.

Disagree with any of our choices? Care to nominate a place or suggest that we rate one more highly? Visit our feedback center at www.fodors.com/feedback.

## Budget Well

Hotel and restaurant price categories from ¢ to $$$$ are defined in the opening pages of the respective chapters. For attractions, we always give standard adult admission fees; reductions are usually available for children, students, and senior citizens. Want to pay with plastic? **AE, DC, MC, V** following restaurant and hotel listings indicate if American Express, Diners Club, MasterCard, and Visa are accepted.

## Hotels

Hotels have private bath, phone, TV, and air-conditioning and operate on the European Plan (aka EP, meaning without meals), unless we specify that they use the Continental Plan (CP, with a Continental breakfast), Breakfast Plan (BP, with a full breakfast), or Modified American Plan (MAP, with breakfast and dinner) or are all-inclusive (AI, including all meals and most activities). We always list facilities but not whether you'll be charged an extra fee to use them, so when pricing accommodations, find out what's included.

## Restaurants

Unless we state otherwise, restaurants are open for lunch and dinner daily. We mention dress only when there's a specific requirement and reservations only when they're essential or not accepted—it's always best to book ahead.

| Listings | |
|---|---|
| ★ | Fodor's Choice |
| ★ | Highly recommended |
| ✉ | Physical address |
| ✛ | Directions or Map coordinates |
| 🕮 | Mailing address |
| ☎ | Telephone |
| 🖷 | Fax |
| ⊕ | On the Web |
| ✎ | E-mail |
| 🎟 | Admission fee |
| ☉ | Open/closed times |
| Ⓜ | Metro stations |
| ⊟ | Credit cards |
| **Hotels & Restaurants** | |
| 🏨 | Hotel |
| 🛏 | Number of rooms |
| 🛎 | Facilities |
| ❍ | Meal plans |
| ✕ | Restaurant |
| 🔖 | Reservations |
| 🎩 | Dress code |
| ↖ | Smoking |
| 🍸 | BYOB |
| **Outdoors** | |
| 🏌 | Golf |
| ⛺ | Camping |
| **Other** | |
| ✆ | Family-friendly |
| ⇨ | See also |
| ✉ | Branch address |
| ☞ | Take note |

# Experience Paris

# 1

# PARIS TODAY

*Bienvenue à Paris*! Or, welcome to Paris! Although it may seem as if time stands still in this city—with its romantic, old buildings, and elegant 19th-century parks and squares—there's an undercurrent of small but significant changes happening here that might not be immediately obvious.

## Today's Paris . . .

**. . . is cleaner.** Parisians breathe a little easier today as the city moves toward a more eco-friendly lifestyle. And while the image of intellectual sitting in a café, cigarette in hand, may have been as much a part of the French identity as wine and cheese, that all changed in 2008, when the French government enacted a nationwide smoking ban inside all public buildings, including hotels, restaurants, and bars. Surprisingly, smokers seem to be following along with the new rules, opting to puff away on the café sidewalk terraces where it's still allowed. The city is also cutting down on smog pollution with its popular Vélib municipal bikes (see the "Bicycling in Paris" box in Chapter 3); additional pedestrian, bus, and cycling lanes; and the extension of the metro and tram network. Paris even looks cleaner, thanks to a city-wide policy of scrubbing clean building and landmark facades, and the gradual replacement of paved streets with more scenic cobblestones.

**. . . is friendlier.** One area where fraternité has evolved is with French service: although North Americans, raised on the principle that the customer is always right, may find servers and store clerks a bit curt (and not always so efficient), Paris has become friendlier than it once was. This can be chalked up to necessity, as the service industry scrambled to compete for tourism dollars after the post-9/11 slump in business, and many of Paris's waiters have discovered that happy American tourists tip better than unhappy ones—even when the 15% service fee is already included in the bill. That's not to say that service is delivered with a smile everywhere; it never hurts to learn a few French phrases, which will almost always reward you with warmer welcomes.

**. . . is open in August and on Sundays.** As recently as five years ago, Paris was still largely deserted in August when the locals fled to the countryside and beaches, leaving a wake of closed shops and restaurants. Today the city is very much alive throughout the summer, with outdoor music festivals, the beach along the Seine

## WHAT'S HOT IN PARIS NOW

The latest trend you probably haven't heard of is supposed to be a secret, but news about the latest **speakeasy-style bars and restaurants**—with anonymous entrances, private-club-like atmosphere, and hidden fumoirs for smokers—is hard to keep down. If you want to get in on the action, try asking the locals when you're out for drink at the Experimental Cocktail Club (see the *Nightlife* chapter) or elsewhere.

■ Paris has embraced the modern **burlesque scene** with regular shows at Le Bellevilloise and Casino de Paris, featuring local and international stars like Dita von Teese. There are also several professionals offering classes to teach the right moves, and boutiques specializing in sultry and saucy striptease wardrobes.

that is Paris Plage, and perhaps even budget constraints keeping more Parisians in town. While the August exodus was never official policy, the "closed on Sunday" was part of French law until 2009, when the government decided that allowing shops to stay open daily would boost the economy and employment. The Marais is still probably the liveliest place to go on Sunday, but other neighborhoods aren't the ghost towns they once were.

**. . . is becoming more globalized.** It's what the French call *mondialisation, en français*, and it's happening in Paris, as international chains and country-specific favorites are slowly seeping into Parisian culture. There are now more than 34 Starbucks in the city, including the location under the Pyramide in the Louvre—where you can also find one of Paris's many McDonald's outposts. You can also find some of the more familiar American brands in Paris supermarkets, like Skippy's peanut butter and Oreo cookies, if you're jonesing for a familiar taste. And as if there isn't enough challenge to the traditional café, the Italian-owned gelato chain Amorino has opened several more shops in Paris after the runaway success of their Ile St-Louis gelateria—just a few feet from the

famous French Berthillon ice-cream shop. Of course, we suggest trying both: compare and contrast!

**. . . is less paralyzed by strikes.** It might be hard to believe in the wake of a major 2009 museum strike that shut the Centre Georges Pompidou, the Arc de Triomphe, the Musée Rodin, Sainte-Chapelle Cathedral, and the Musée d'Orsay, and an air traffic controllers strike in early 2010 but in some respects the city is less at the mercy of strikes. It was once common for strike action in Paris to completely close down the entire metro for days or even weeks at a time. But laws passed in 2007 assure minimum service for all urban public transportation networks as well as 48 hours' notice before any strike actions You may have to wait longer and cram into buses and trains with the disgruntled commuters, but at least you're no longer completely stranded.

■ **Green** continues to gain currency in Paris, which is now home to a dozen organic fast-food chains and juice bars, several eco-label certified hotels, and the widespread availability of ethical, fair-trade, and organic products at every supermarket chain and open-air market.

■ **Street art** continues to to shake free of its illicit reputation, with shows in Paris galleries, the Palais de Tokyo, and a "live" event by the French graffiti artists Monsieur André at the Grand Palais, as well as the 2009 legalization of "Chez Robert, Electron Libre," the famous art squat on the Rue de Rivoli.

# PARIS PLANNER

## Getting Around

Paris is without question best explored on foot, and thanks to Baron Haussmann's mid-19th-century redesign, the City of Light is a compact wonder of wide boulevards, gracious parks, and leafy squares. When you want a lift, though, public transportation is easy and inexpensive. The métro (subway) goes just about everywhere you're going for €1.60 a ride (a carnet, or "pack" of 10 tickets, is €11.60); tickets also work on buses and trams, and the RER train line within Paris.

Paris is divided into 20 *arrondissements* (or neighborhoods) spiraling out from the center of the city. The numbers reveal the neighborhood's location and its age, the 1er arrondissement at the city's heart being the oldest. The arrondissements in central Paris—the 1er to 8e—are the most visited.

It's worth picking up a copy of *Paris Pratique*, the essential map guide, available at newsstands and bookstores.

## Saving Time and Money

Paris is one of the world's most visited cities—with crowds to prove it—so it pays to be prepared. Buy tickets online when you can: most cultural centers and museums offer advance-ticket sales, and the small service fee you'll pay is worth the time saved waiting in line. Investigate alternative entrances at popular sites (there are three at the Louvre, for example), and check when rates are reduced, often during once-a-week late openings. Also, national museums are free the first Sunday of each month. There are many within Paris, including the Louvre, Musée d'Orsay, and Centre Pompidou.

A Paris Museum Pass can save you money if you're planning serious sightseeing, but it might be even more valuable because it allows you to bypass the lines. It's sold at the destinations it covers and at airports, major métro stations, and the tourism office in the Carrousel du Louvre (two-, four-, or six-day passes are €32, €48, and €64, respectively; for more info visit www.parismuseumpass.com).

Stick to the omnipresent ATMs for the best exchange rates; exchanging cash at your hotel or in a store is never going to be to your advantage.

## Hours

Paris is by no means a 24/7 city, so planning your days beforehand can save you aggravation. Museums are closed one day a week, usually Tuesday, and most stay open late at least one night each week, which is also the least crowded time to visit. Store hours are generally 10 AM to 7:30 PM, though smaller shops may not open until 11 AM, only to close for several hours during the afternoon. Retailers now have the option of doing business on Sunday, although your best bets are department stores, the shops along the Champs-Élysées, the Carrousel du Louvre, and around the Marais, where most boutiques open at 2 PM.

## Eating Out

Restaurants follow French mealtimes, serving lunch from noon to 2:30 PM and dinner from 7:30 or 8 PM on. Some cafés serve food all day long. Always reserve a table for dinner, as top restaurants book up months in advance. When it comes to the check, you must ask for it (it's considered rude to bring it unbidden). In cafés you'll get a register receipt with your order. *Servis* (gratuity) is always included in the bill, but it's good form to leave something extra if you're satisfied with the service: a few cents for drinks, €1 for lunch, €3 at dinner, leave 5% of the bill only in higher-end restaurants.

## What to Wear

When it comes to clothing, the standard French look is dressier than the American equivalent. Athletic clothes are reserved for sports. Sneakers are not usually worn by adults but if you pack yours, keep them for daytime only. Neat jeans are acceptable everywhere except at higher-end restaurants; check to see whether there's a dress code.

## When to Go

The City of Light is magical all year round, but it's particularly gorgeous in June, when the long days (the sun doesn't set until 10 PM) stretch sightseeing hours and make it ideal to linger in the cafés.

Winter can be dark and chilly, but it's also the best time to find cheap airfares and hotel deals.

April in Paris, despite what the song says, is often rainy.

Summer is the most popular (and expensive) season. Keep in mind that, like some other European cities, some shops and restaurants close in August for several weeks, though there are still plenty of fun things to do, like free open-air movies and concerts, and the popular *Paris Plage,* the "beach" on the right bank of the Seine.

September is gorgeous, with temperate weather, saner airfares, and cultural events timed for the *rentrée* (or return), signifying the end of summer vacation. In the third weekend in September, scores of national buildings that are normally closed to the public open for visits during the annual Journées du Patrimoine (Patrimony Days).

## Paris Etiquette

The Parisian reputation for rudeness is undeserved. In fact, Parisians are sticklers for politesse and exchanging formal greetings is the rule. Informal American-style manners are considered impolite. Beginning an exchange with a simple "Do you speak English?" will get you on the right foot. Learning a few key French words will take you far. Offer a hearty *bonjour* (bohn-zhoor) when walking into a shop or café and an *au revoir* (o ruh-vwahr) when leaving, even if nobody seems to be listening (a chorus may reply). When speaking to a woman over age 16, use *madame* (ma-dam), literally "my lady." For a young woman or girl, use *mademoiselle* (mad-mwa-zel). A man of any age goes by *monsieur* (murh-syur). Always say please, *s'il vous plaît* (seel-voo-play), and thank you, *merci* (mehr-see).

## Paris Temps

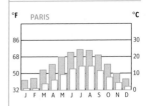

# WHAT'S WHERE

*The following numbers refer to chapters.*

**2 Ile de la Cité and Ile St-Louis.** Also known as "the Islands," although they're just a few quick steps from the "mainland," the Ile de la Cité and Ile St-Louis are the heart of Paris. This is where you can find Notre-Dame and Sainte-Chapelle.

**3 The Tour Eiffel and Invalides.** With the Eiffel Tower and Champs de Mars, and the Seine nearby, there are many lovely strolls that give you striking views of Paris's ultimate monument.

**4 The Champs-Élysées.** The Champs-Élysées and Arc de Triomphe attract the tourists, but there are also several excellent museums here, well worth checking out.

**5 The Faubourg St-Honoré.** The Faubourg, with its well-established shops and cafés, has always been chic, and probably always will be.

**6 The Grands Boulevards.** Use the Opéra Garnier as your orientation landmark and set out to do some power shopping. There are some intriguing small museums in the neighborhood, too.

**7 Montmartre.** Like a small village within a big city, Montmartre feels distinctly separate from the rest of Paris—but it's prime tourist territory, with Sacré-Coeur as its main attraction.

**8 Le Marais.** Le Marais, what used to be Paris's Jewish neighborhood, is now one of the city's hippest destinations. While away the afternoon at the Place des Vosges or shop to your heart's content.

**9 Canal St-Martin, Bastille, and Oberkampf.** If it's new and happening in Paris, this is where you can find it: trendy restaurants, funky galleries, and cutting-edge boutiques are popping up everywhere.

**10 The Quartier Latin.** Leave yourself lots of time to wander the Latin Quarter, known for its vibrant student life.

**11 St-Germain.** Fabulous cafés and the Musée d'Orsay are here, but make sure you also leave yourself time to wander the Jardin du Luxembourg.

**12 Montparnasse.** Once the haunt of writers and artists—Picasso and Hemingway included—this neighborhood is now known for its contemporary-art scene as well as the Catacombs.

**13 Western Paris.** The Bois de Boulogne and the Musée Marmottan Monet are two great reasons to trek out here.

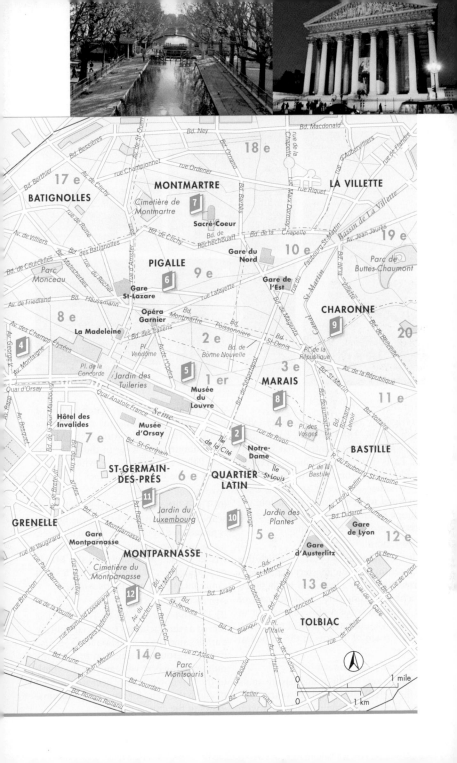

# PARIS
# TOP ATTRACTIONS

### Eiffel Tower

**(A)** Originally built as a temporary exhibition for the 1889 World's Fair, today there's no other monument that symbolizes Paris better than Gustave Eiffel's world-famous Iron Lady. It's breathtaking, whether you see it sparkling from your hotel window after dark or join the millions of annual visitors to brave the glass elevator trip to the top.

### Notre-Dame

**(B)** It took almost 200 years to finish this 12th-century Gothic masterpiece immortalized by Victor Hugo and his fictional hunchback. Climb the spiral staircase of the bell towers for a close-up gander at the gargoyles, or have a peek at relics such as the Crown of Thorns in the cathedral treasury.

### Jardin du Luxembourg

**(C)** This is one of the prime leisure spots on the Left Bank for urban-weary Parisians. Relax in a reclining park chair with a picnic lunch or a book, watch a game of *boules* while the kids enjoy a marionette show, or visit an exhibition at the Musée Luxembourg in a wing of the 17th-century Palais de Luxembourg, which is now home to the Paris Senate.

### Jardin des Tuileries

**(D)** The 17th-century formal French landscape of these gardens behind the Louvre is punctuated by contemporary sculptures, a café, and two noteworthy museums: the Musée du Jeu de Paume and the Musée de l'Orangerie. In summer there's a small amusement park and Ferris wheel.

### Arc de Triomphe

**(E)** The 164-foot-tall Arc de Triomphe has served as the backdrop to official military parades since its completion in 1836. Use the underground passageway to reach the monument, where you can visit the Tomb of the Unknown Soldier beneath the arch or climb the stairs for amazing panoramic views of the city.

## Musée d'Orsay

(F) After a stunted lifespan as a train station constructed for the 1900 World's Fair, this beautiful Belle Époque building is filled with Art Nouveau objects, Impressionist paintings, vintage photography, and realist sculptures. Don't miss the scale model of the Opéra Garnier or the views of the Seine from the grand ballroom now housing the museum's restaurant.

## Opéra Garnier

(G) Opulent, stunning, and magnificently over-the-top, Charles Garnier's opera house is one of the outstanding jewels of the Second Empire. Its illustrious marble staircase and ruby-red box seats have been featured in films from *Dangerous Liaisons* to *Marie-Antoinette*, and its backstage corridors are famously haunted by the Phantom of the Opera.

## Centre Pompidou

(H) The Pompidou Centre's groundbreaking "inside-out" design is still visually shocking (it opened in 1977) this is also the top destination for modern-art lovers in Paris.

## Sacré-Coeur

(I) This wedding-cake white basilica dominates Montmartre's hilltop. Most visitors are content with the views overlooking the city from the basilica stairs, but ambitious sight seekers can climb to the bell tower for an even higher vantage point.

## Musée du Louvre

(J) The grandest museum in the world was just a humble fortress in the 12th century, but grew in size and prestige as a sumptuous royal palace until the French Revolution gave it a new lease on life as home to the Republic's art collection. Don't miss the big three—*Mona Lisa, Winged Victory,* and *Venus de Milo.*

# PARIS LIKE A LOCAL

To appreciate the City of Light as the locals do, you can start by learning some of the daily rituals of Paris life. These simple, fun pleasures will quickly get you into the swing of being Parisian.

### Shop Like a Parisian

Parisians prefer the boisterous atmosphere of bustling street markets to the drab *supermarchés*. Even if you're just buying picnic fixings, you can follow suit. For a full listing of Paris's markets, check out the city hall Web site at ⊕ *www.paris.fr*, but these are some of our faves.

**Le Marché d'Aligre,** just off the Rue du Faubourg St-Antoine beyond the Opéra Bastille, dates back to the 18th century. Open Tuesday through Sunday, the market has fruit, vegetables, cheese, meat, fish, and poultry, as well as a host of other products. The best selection is on the weekend. And if flea markets are your thing, Paris has three that can satisfy any bargain hunter. At **Les Puces de Montreuil** (Saturday, Sunday, and Monday, 9 AM to 7:30 PM, métro Porte de Montreuil) dig through the heaps of old clothes until you make a find, probably for less than €3. **Les Puces des Vanves** (weekends, 9 AM to 7:30 PM, métro Porte de Vanves; Avenue de le Porte de Vanves and Rue Marc Sangnier) is two in one: in the morning, collectors revel among old furniture, stamps, postcards, and almost everything else imaginable; in the afternoon, merchants of new and vintage clothing take over. **Les Puces de St-Ouen** (Saturday, Sunday, and Monday, 9 AM to 7:30 PM, métro Clignancourt), otherwise known as the Clignancourt flea market, is a little more expensive, but a real treasure trove. Bypass the noisy stands near the métro in favor of the buildings beyond the elevated highway, where antiques dealers and vintage-clothing boutiques provide a

real blast from the past. You might not *need* to buy flowers, but the flower markets are lovely for wandering, and you can cheer up a budget hotel room with a few daisies in a water glass. Try one of the **Les Marchés aux Fleurs**: at Place de la Madeleine (Tuesday to Sunday, 8 AM to 7:30 PM), Place des Ternes (Tuesday to Sunday, 8 AM to 7:30 PM), or Place Lépine (Monday to Saturday, 8 AM to 7:30 PM, with the bird market Sunday morning).

### Drink Coffee Like a Parisian

Le café in Paris isn't simply a drink that begins the day: it's a way of life. Though Parisians do stop at the counter to order a quick *café expresse, bien serré, s'il vous plaît* ("good and strong, please"), more often people treat the café as an extension of their apartments, with laptops precariously balanced, cell phones ringing, and business being done; in Paris the café is the place to work, read, and chat with friends, any time of the day. Think of Simone de Beauvoir, who spent more time at the **Café de Flore** (✉ *172 bd. St-Germain, 6ᵉ* ☎ *01–45–48–55–26*) than in her chilly apartment. Choose a café with a patio or good windows for people-watching, or pause at the nearest counter, and you're in for a dose of Parisian café culture. Most locals have their own favorites, and we've listed some of our top choices on the neighborhood Getting Oriented pages; you're bound to find your own preferred haunt(s).

### Walk Like a Parisian

Paris was made for wandering, and the French have coined a lovely word for a person who wanders the streets: *le flâneur,* one who strolls or loiters, usually without a destination in mind. In Paris the streets beckon, leading you past monuments, down narrow alleyways, through arches,

and into hidden squares. As a flâneur, you can become attuned to the city's rhythm and, no matter how aimlessly you stroll, chances are you'll end up somewhere magical. Some of our suggestions for wandering are along the Seine, into the poetic streets of **St-Germain,** or into the tangled lanes around the **Bastille** and **Canal St-Martin** area. Strolling is a favorite Sunday pastime for the locals—but you're on vacation, so you can be a flâneur any day of the week.

## Eat Baguettes Like a Parisian

The Tour Eiffel might be the most famous symbol of Paris, but perhaps the true banner of France is the *baguette*, the long, caramel-color bread brandished at every meal. Locals take inordinate pride at finding the best *baguette* in the neighborhood. To find a worthy *boulangerie*—a bakery that specializes in bread, as opposed to a *pâtisserie*, specializing in pastries—look for a line outside on weekend mornings. Three faves in Paris are **Arnaud Delmontel** (✉ *39 rue des Martys* ☎ *01–48–78–29–33*), **Jean-Pierre Cohier** (✉ *270 rue du Faubourg St-Honoré* ☎ *01–42–27–45–26*), and **Boulanger de Monge** (✉ *123 rue Monge* ☎ *01–43–37–54–20*). Note that some *boulangeries* follow the traditional three-step customer service protocol: first you place your order at the counter and receive a receipt; then you pay at the *caisse* and get your receipt stamped; finally, you return to the first counter to exchange the stamped receipt for your package of edible art. As you're leaving the bakery, do as many Parisians do—nibble the end of the crust to taste the bread while it's still warm.

## Eat Pastries Like a Parisian

High prices are making luxury all the more elusive in Paris, but there's one indulgence most people can still afford, at least occasionally—fine pastries. As you can see when you stop in at any of Paris's extraordinary *pâtisseries* (pastry shops), a whole different and wonderful array of French treats await. Tops on our list are the deliciously airy and intense *macarons*—nothing like the heavy American macaroons you might be familiar with. **Ladurée** (✉ *16 rue Royale, 8ᵉ* ☎ *01–42–60–21–79*) claims to have invented these ganache-filled cookies, but two Left Bank *pâtissiers* also have particularly devoted fans of their *macarons*: the flavors at **Gérard Mulot** (✉ *76 rue de Seine, 6ᵉ* ☎ *01–43–26–85–77*) include pistachio, caramel, and terrific orange-cinnamon, and **Pierre Hermé** (✉ *72 rue Bonaparte, 6ᵉ* ☎ *01–43–54–47–77*) has exotic ones like peach-saffron, olive oil, and white truffle. The classic opera pastry—almond cake layered with chocolate and coffee cream—can be found at **Lenôtre** (✉ *61 rue Lecourbe, 15ᵉ* ☎ *01–42–73–20–97*), but devotees also flock to the fine-food emporium **Fauchon** (✉ *26 pl. de la Madeleine, 8ᵉ* ☎ *01–47–42–60–11*). Another traditional pastry is the *mont-blanc,* a mini-mountain of chestnut puree capped with whipped cream, best rendered by **Jean-Paul Hévin** (✉ *3 rue Vavin, 6ᵉ* ☎ *01–43–54–09–85*). And those really in the know watch for anything from the Tokyo-born **Sadaharu Aoki** (✉ *35 rue Vaugirard, 6ᵉ* ☎ *01–45–44–48–90*); look for his green-tea madeleines and black-sesame éclairs. Many of the sweet spots mentioned here have multiple locations; only the original store is listed.

# PARIS WITH KIDS

Paris is often promoted as an adult destination, but there's no shortage of children's activities to keep the young 'uns busy, not to mention that many of the city's top attractions have carousels parked outside them in summer. Make sure to buy a *Pariscope* (found at most newsstands) and check the *enfants* section for current children's events. In addition to what's listed below, sites of particular interest to children are marked with a rubber-ducky icon.

## Museums

Paris has a number of museums that cater to the young, and the young at heart. They're a great place to occupy restless minds, especially if the weather is bad. The **Cité des Sciences et de l'Industrie** (the Museum of Science and Industry), at the Parc de la Villette, is an enormous science center, and the children's area is divided into two main sections: one for children from 3 to 5 years of age; another for those from 5 to 12. Interactive exhibits allow kids to do everything from building a house and comparing their body to that of a favorite animal, to learning about communications systems throughout history, from the tom-tom to the satellite. The **Musée de la Poupée** (the Doll Museum) is a cozy museum in the heart of Le Marais, with a collection of more than 500 dolls dating back to the 1800s, complete with costumes, furniture, and accessories. Labels might be in French, but they're not really the point anyway, and the museum features a "Doll Hospital," where "sick" dolls and plush toys come to be repaired; the doctor is in on Thursday, but free estimates are offered throughout the week. The **Palais de la Découverte** (the Palace of Discovery) has high-definition, 3-D exhibits covering everything from chemistry, biology, and physics, to the weather, so

there's bound to be some interesting dinner conversation when the day is done. Many of the displays are in French, but that doesn't stop most kids from having a blast; hands down, the choice between this and the Louvre is a no-brainer.

## Sites and Shows

A zoo is usually a good bet to get the kids' attention—although you might want to keep in mind that most European zoos aren't as spacious as American zoos. The **Ménagerie** at the Jardin des Plantes is an urban zoo dating from 1794 and home to more than 240 mammals, 400 birds, 270 reptiles, and a number of insects. The huge **Parc Zoologique,** in the Bois de Vincennes, is the largest zoo in Paris, although parts are closed for renovation; the bonus of taking the métro out here, though, is the park's two lakes, both with rentable rowboats. When it comes to spectacles, what child would pass up the circus? There are several in the city (see the *Performing Arts* chapter), and the **Cirque de Paris** has a special feature called a "Day at the Circus"—your kids (and you) can learn some basics like juggling and tightrope walking, then you can lunch with the artists and see a performance in the afternoon. Less interactive are **Les Guignols,** French puppet shows: the original Guignol was a marionette character created by Laurent Mourguet, supposedly in his own likeness, celebrating life, love, and wine. Today the shows are primarily aimed at children, and are found in open-air theaters throughout the city in the warmer months. Check out the Champs-Élysées, Parc Montsouris, Buttes Chaumont, Jardin du Luxembourg, and the Parc Floral in the Bois de Vincennes. Even if they don't understand French, kids are usually riveted. Of course, the best sight in Paris is the city itself, and a

**boat ride** on the Seine is a must for everyone. It's the perfect way to see the sights, rest weary feet, and, depending on which option you choose, lunch or dinner may be part of the treat.

### Expending Energy

Most kids are thrilled (at least more than the grown-ups) at the prospect of climbing innumerable stairs to be rewarded with cool views: the **Eiffel Tower** is the quintessential Paris climb, but **Notre-Dame** gets extra points for the gargoyles, and the **Arc de Triomphe** is a good bet, since it's at the end of the Champs-Élysées. When it comes to open spaces for running around, Paris has lots of park options, with extra attractions in summer when kids can work off steam on the trampolines or ride ponies at the **Jardin des Tuileries**. The **Jardin du Luxembourg** has a playground and a pond where kids can rent miniature boats, and the **Bois de Boulogne** has a zoo, rowboats, bumper cars, and lots of wide-open spaces. Ice-skating is seasonal but always a thrill, and from mid-December through February, several outdoor Paris sites are turned into spectacular ice-skating rinks with Christmas lights, music, and instructors. The rinks are free to the public; skate rental for adults costs €5. The main rink is at **Place de l'Hôtel de Ville** (the square in front of City Hall).

### Underground Paris

There's something about exploring underground that seems to fascinate kids, at least the older ones. **Les Egouts**, the Paris sewer system, has a certain gross factor but isn't actually that disgusting. Keep in mind, though, that the smell is definitely ranker in the summer months. At the **Catacombs**, in Montparnasse, dark tunnels filled with bones are spookily titillating—at least for those not prone to nightmares. For some

cheap underground entertainment without the ick factor, the **métro** itself can be its own sort of adventure, complete with fascinating station art such as the submarine decor at Arts-et-Metiers, the colorful Parisian timeline murals at Tuileries, or the Egyptian statues of the Louvre-Rivoli station. A good tip: the Météor (Line 14) is the only driverless métro that lets you sit at the very front; it's hard to resist the feeling that you're driving.

### And for Treats

All that fun will no doubt bring on an appetite, and there's no shortage of special places to stop for a snack in Paris. **Angelina** (⊠ *226 rue de Rivoli*), near the Jardin des Tuileries, is world famous for its hot chocolate—deliciously thick and yummy, unlike what American children are usually used to. **Berthillon**, renowned for its decadent ice cream, has outposts around town, including on the Ile St-Louis—though the **Amorino** gelaterias give it a run for its money. And when in need, a pâtisserie selling chocolate croissants is never hard to find. French children adore the pastel clouds of *meringue* (which resemble hardened whipped-cream puffs) that decorate almost every bakery's window, and there are all sorts of cookies to tempt a smile from a tired tot.

# GREAT WALK: ARTISTS AND WRITERS OF THE LEFT BANK

Some of the greatest artists and writers of the 20th century were attracted to winding streets and bustling boulevards of Paris's Left Bank between the end of WWI and the social upheavals of the 1960s, and you can still walk the streets where they lived and worked.

## Winding Streets of the Quartier Latin

The streets around **Place de la Contrescarpe** have hardly changed since they were immortalized in Hemingway's *Moveable Feast*. He lived at 74 rue Cardinal Lemoine (down the street from James Joyce at #71) and worked at 39 rue Descartes. George Orwell lived nearby, at 6 rue Pot de Fer, while writing *Down and Out in Paris and London*. The famous bookshop **Shakespeare & Co.** prospers in a medieval house at 37 rue de la Bûcherie; many of the Beat Generation writers who frequented it in the '60s, like Burroughs, Ginsberg, and Kerouak, stayed in the Hôtel de Vieux Paris, aka the "Beat Hotel," at 9 rue Gît-le-Coeur. Pablo Picasso perfected his cubist style at 7 rue des Grands Augustins from 1936 to 1955.

## The Heyday of St-Germain-des-Près

Follow Rue St-André-des-Arts and Rue de Seine to Rue Jacob, home to American writers like Djuna Barnes, who stayed at the Hôtel d'Angleterre at #44. On the corner of Rue Bonaparte is Le Pré aux Clercs, where Hemingway and Fitzgerald shared many a drink. Henry Miller lived up the street at 24 rue Bonaparte and later at #36. Pass the home of Jean-Paul Sartre at #42 to the square that now bears his and Simone de Beauvoir's names. Along noisy Boulevard St-Germain are the **Deux Magots, Café de Flore**, and **Brasserie Lipp**, legendary establishments frequented by the couple as well as Faulkner, Camus, Apollinaire, André Gide, Giacometti, Cocteau, Duras, Hemingway, Fitzgerald, and André Breton. Bookshops like **La Hune** still give the area intellectual character despite the proliferation of fashion boutiques.

## Odéon and Luxembourg Gardens

At 12 rue de l'Odéon a plaque commemorating Sylvia Beach's publication of James Joyce's *Ulysses* marks the original location of Shakespeare & Co., which closed in 1944. On Rue de Vaugirard, Faulkner lived at #42 and Fitzgerald and his wife Zelda at #58. Man Ray's studio is still intact at #2 bis, rue Ferou. Hemingway lived at #6 with Hadley for a year, writing often about the **Luxembourg Gardens**.

## Montparnasse

Leaving the Luxembourg Gardens, follow Rue du Fleurus, where Gertrude Stein and Alice B. Toklas lived at #27, entertaining artists and writers such as Picasso, Matisse, Erik Satie, and *New Yorker* correspondent Janet Flanner. Stein's friends Ezra Pound and Hemingway—who moved a lot—lived nearby on Rue Notre-Dame des Champs (at #70 and #113, respectively), near Boulevard Montparnasse, the expat epicenter a decade before St-Germain held that distinction. Some of the establishments still here are **Closerie des Lilas** (#171), **Le Sélect** (#99), **Le Dôme** (#18), **La Rotonde** (#105), and **La Coupole** (#102), where Modigliani, Dali, Samuel Beckett, Colette, and Miro rubbed shoulders. Rue Delambre leads to the **Cimetière du Montparnasse**, the final resting place for many of the illustrious names of the Left Bank, including publishers Hachette and Larousse; artists Man Ray, Kiki de Montparnasse, Brancusi, and Brassaï; and writers like Baudelaire, Ionesco, Sartre et Beauvoir, Beckett, and Duras.

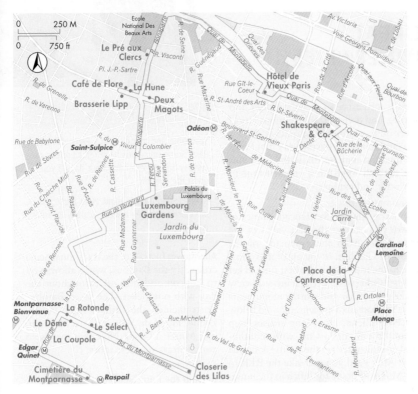

| Highlights | The historic decor of La Coupole, the picturesque winding streets of the Quartier Latin, the historic charm of Shakespeare & Co. |
|---|---|
| Where to Start | Place de la Contrescarpe, at the top of the Montaigne St-Geneviève; take métro 10 to Cardinal Lemoine or métro 7 to Place Monge for a less steep incline. |
| Length | 5.25 km (3.2 mi); duration approximately 2.5–3 hours without stops. |
| Where to End | At the Cimetère du Montparnasse, just east of the Tour du Montparnasse, next to métro Edgar Quinet (Line 6) and métro Raspail (lines 4, 6). |
| Best Time to Go | Any time of day when you can see all of the sights in daylight. |
| Worst Time to Go | Being entirely outside, it's not a good idea to do when it's raining or very cold. |
| Editor's Choice | Artistic detour to the Musée du Montparnasse (✉ 21 av. du Maine Ⓜ Montparnasse or Falguière), the Musée Zadkine (✉ 100 bis rue d'Assas Ⓜ Notre-Dame-des-Champs), or the Musée du Luxembourg (✉ 19 rue de Vaugirard Ⓜ Odéon or St-Sulpice). |

# GREAT ITINERARIES

Paris is a treasure of neighborhoods and history, and a visit to this glorious city is never quite as simple as a quick look at a few landmarks. These one-day itineraries are mix and match: follow the ones that intrigue you—and leave yourself time to just walk and explore.

## Monumental Paris

Begin your day at the Trocadéro métro, where you can get the best views of the Tour Eiffel from the esplanade of the Palais de Chaillot. If you absolutely must ride to the top, now is the best time to get in line. Otherwise, get a Seine-side view of the city's other noteworthy monuments from the Bateaux Parisiens, moored below the Pont d'Iéna. Hour-long cruises loop around the Ile de la Cité, with multilingual commentary on the sights along the way. Afterward you can take the RER to the Musée d'Orsay for lunch in the museum's Belle Époque dining room before tackling the late-19th-century works of art. Then it's a short walk to the imposing Hôtel des Invalides, the French military museum built as a retirement home for wounded soldiers under Louis XIV. The emperor Napoléon Bonaparte rests beneath the golden dome. If the weather's nice, have tea next door in the sculpture gardens of the Musée Rodin (entrance to the gardens €1). If your feet are still happy, cross the gilded Pont Tsar Alexandre III to the Champs-Élysées, passing the Belle Époque art palaces known as the Grand et Petit Palais. You can take Bus 73 from the Assemblée Nationale across the bridge to the Place de la Concorde and all the way up the Avenue des Champs-Élysées to the Arc de Triomphe. Open until 11 PM, its panoramic viewing platform is ideal for admiring the City of Light.

**Alternative:** Instead of the traditional Seine cruise, try the Batobus, which allows you to hop on and hop off throughout the day with one ticket. The seven Batobus ports include the Eiffel Tower, Notre-Dame, Hôtel de Ville, Louvre Museum, and Musée d'Orsay. Note that there's no commentary on these tours.

## Old Paris

Start at the Pont Neuf for excellent views off the western tip of the Ile de la Cité, then explore the island's magnificent architectural heritage, including the Conciergerie, Sainte-Chapelle, and Notre-Dame. The brave can climb the corkscrew staircase to the towers for a gargoyle's-eye view of the city. Then detour to the neighboring Ile St-Louis for lunch before heading into the medieval labyrinth of the Quartier Latin: its most valuable treasures are preserved in the Cluny Musée National du Moyen-Age, including the reconstructed ruins of 2nd-century Gallo-Roman steam baths. At the summit of the hill above the Sorbonne university is the imposing Panthéon, a monument (and mausoleum) of French heroes. Don't miss the exquisite Eglise St-Etienne-du-Mont next door, where the relics of the city's patron Saint Geneviève are displayed. Follow the Rue Descartes to the Rue Mouffetard for a *café crème* on one of the oldest market

streets in Paris. If the sun's still shining, visit the Gallo-Roman Arènes de Lutèce.

**Alternative:** A different look at the Quartier Latin (Old Paris) can include a visit to the sleek Institute du Monde Arabe, then a relaxing afternoon at the authentic steam baths and tearoom of the nearby Mosquée de Paris.

## Royal Paris

Begin at the Place de la Concorde, where an Egyptian obelisk replaces the guillotine where Louis XVI and Marie-Antoinette met their bloody fate during the French Revolution, then escape the traffic in the formal Jardin des Tuileries, which once belonged to the 16th-century Tuileries Palace, destroyed during the Paris Commune of 1871. Pass through the small Arc du Carrousel to the modern glass pyramid that serves as the main entrance to the Louvre, the world's grandest museum, once a 12th-century fortress. When you've built up an appetite, cross the street to the peaceful gardens of the Palais Royal for lunch at a café beneath the stone arcades. From here take métro Line 1 to station St-Paul. To the south you can find the Hôtel de Sens, home to King Henry IV's feisty ex-wife Queen Marguerite, and one of the few surviving examples of late-medieval architecture. Around the corner on Rue Charlemagne is a preserved section of the city's 12th-century fortifications built by King Philippe-Augustus. Cross the busy Rue St-Antoine to Le Marais and enter the Hôtel de Sully, a fine example of the elegant private mansions built here by aristocrats in the early 17th century. Pass through the gardens to the doorway on the right, which leads to the lovely symmetrical town houses of the Place des Vosges, designed by King Henry IV. Many of the old aristocratic mansions in Le Marais have been turned into museums, including the Musée Carnavalet and the Musée Picasso.

## Power-Shopping Paris

Get an early start to avoid crowds at Au Printemps and Galeries-Lafayette, two of the city's grandest historic department stores conveniently side by side behind the Opéra Garnier. Refuel at the Place de la Madeleine, where gourmet food boutiques such as Hédiard and Fauchon offer light deli foods for shoppers on the move. If the luxury boutiques on the Rue Royale aren't rich enough for you, head down the Rue du Faubourg St-Honoré and the Avenue Montaigne (via Avenue Matignon), where the exclusive couture houses of Chanel, Dior, Hermès, and Yves St-Laurent hold court. ■ TIP→ If you plan on spending more than €175 in one store, bring your passport to get the détaxe forms for your Value Added Tax rebate. Department stores are closed on Sunday, but open late on Thursday. Most small boutiques are closed Sunday and Monday. Le Marais and the Champs-Élysées are the best bets for shopping on Sunday.

**Alternative:** For a more genteel shopping experience, head to the Left Bank's chic Bon Marché department store, then work your way through the fashion and home decor boutiques around the Eglise St-Sulpice and St-Germain-des-Prés. Shops get less expensive between métro Odéon and the Quartier Latin.

# HANDS-ON PARIS

Sometimes, it's not enough to see the sights, shop the boutiques, and sample the regional delicacies: there is the compulsion to really immerse yourself. Taking part in some of Paris's quintessential experiences will allow you to learn more about French culture, and you'll get to meet and mingle with locals and like-minded travelers, creating a far more enriching trip to Paris, whether it's your first or fortieth visit! Below are some experiences that we recommend.

## Food

Nothing is more French than fine wine and gourmet cuisine. So why not enjoy them hands-on, with cooking classes to perfect your *magret de canard* (duck breast) or to master the art of the soufflé. There are many options, from full-day courses in a Parisian home (in English) that include a market tour, to quick lunch lessons with the locals where everyone dines together afterward. In English except as noted: **Paule Caillat's Promenades Gourmandes** (☎ 01–48–04–56–84 ⊕ www.promenadesgourmandes.com). **Food Unites the World** (☎ 01–45–00–08–31 ⊕ www.foodunitestheworld.com). **Marguerite's Elegant Home Cooking** (☎ 01–42–04–74–00 ⊕ www.elegantcooking.com). **Les Coulisses du Chef** (☎ 01–40–26–14–00 ⊕ www.coursdecuisineparis.com). **Atéliers des Chefs** (⊕ www.atelierdeschefs.com), group classes in French.

## Wine

And it's no secret that appreciating your wine is greatly enhanced when you know what you're drinking and where it came from. Wine-tasting classes range from fun and casual lessons in English for absolute beginners to more formal dégustations of the finest vintages by seasoned sommeliers. There's something to fit all budgets and experience levels. **O-Château** (☎ 01–44–73–97–80 or 0–800–801–148 toll-free in France ⊕ www.o-chateau.com) does wine-tasting lessons in English, vineyard tours, and Champagne cruises on the Seine. **Legrand Filles & Fils** (☎ 01–42–60–07–12–12 ⊕ www.caves-legrand.com) conducts Tuesday night Soirées Dégustation with a bilingual presentation of carefully chosen wines. **Wine Dinners** (☎ 01–41–83–80–46 ⊕ www.wine-dinners.com) is a French group hosted by bilingual François Audouze; it organizes gourmet meals (in Michelin-starred restaurants) with a selection of 10 wines.

## 21st-century Salons

Parisian salons—where a select group of connoisseurs gathered in a private home to discuss the artistic, literary, political, and philosophical ideas of the time—flourished in past centuries. They're back, in English, and open to anyone who calls to reserve a place. It's an experience not to be missed, and a great way to meet interesting people. **Jim Haynes** (☎ 01–43–27–17–67) hosts an international crowd for Sunday night dinner: informal "standing room only" affairs in his converted artist atelier. **Patricia Laplante-Collins** (☎ 01–43–26–12–88 ⊕ www.parissoirees.com/aboutsoirees.html) has guest speakers at her twice-weekly dinners on the Ile St-Louis, including writers, artists, chefs, or other personalities. **Dinnertime = Talktime** (☎ 01–43–25–86–55 ⊕ language.meetup.com/59/) is a weekly language gathering hosted in a Quartier Latin home by Michael and Veronique. Guests enjoy a buffet dinner while mingling, with half the evening reserved for French conversation, the other half in another language (usually English).

# MAKING THE MOST OF YOUR EUROS

Paris has never been cheap and we know you're going to be looking for some tips on how not to break the bank. Who better to ask than travelers on www.Fodors.com Travel Talk forums?

## Get Around Wisely

■ TIP➜ Paris is definitely a walking city—take the opportunity to learn the word flâneur (one who strolls)—but when your feet get tired, take the métro or bus instead of a taxi.

"We bought a book at a newspaper stand that had all of the bus routes in it. Very easy to use and it saved us so much time. We also bought the carnet of tickets at metro station. Metro is also great but we wanted to see things outside." —Tdudette

## Think with Your Stomach

■ TIP➜ There are so many ways to eat well in Paris but still save money: eat picnics, spend your restaurant euros at lunch instead of dinner, have your latté at the counter instead of at a table. You'll save money and probably have a more authentic Parisian experience, too.

"Never buy bottle water at a restaurant: ask for tap water. Lots of savings there." —4totravel

"I would second the suggestion to 'reste au comptoir' in a cafe, vs. sitting at a table. You will save a few coins, and it's a great experience." —petitepois

"There are a number of sandwich shops that sell wonderful sandwiches (goat cheese, tomato, lettuce, and a variety of meats) for takeout for about 4 euros. Pick one up and have a picnic in the park." —FrankS

"I think my big meals of the day will be late lunches and the plat du jour, but most certainly I will go to a couple of nice dinners, within reason." —mahya

■ TIP➜ Save money on lodging. Why not rent an apartment instead of shelling out large sums on a hotel (see the "Apartment rentals" feature in the Where to Stay chapter)? The built-in perk is the money you'll save if you use the kitchen—even just for breakfast. And if you do opt for a hotel, choose your neighborhood with budget in mind.

"I was in Paris last year and had a short-term apartment rental. For us, it was the absolute perfect choice. Having a mini-kitchen and Internet access in the apartment was fantastic. There was a small grocery store only a half block away, so we were able to save money by making our own breakfasts, picnic lunches, and some dinners." —likembrave

"People will get much more for their money by staying away from the exact center of the city. It is all very well to want to see the Eiffel Tower from your hotel window or to be a 5-minute walk from the Louvre or Notre-Dame, but that adds a lot of money to the travel expenses." —kerouac

■ TIP➜ Note that the jury's still out on whether a Museum Pass will save you money—but everyone agrees it'll save you time because with it, you don't have to wait in lines.

"A two-day pass will cost you 30€. If you plan on visiting more than 3 or 4 places in the two days, you will break even. Even if you don't break even, (in my opinion) the advantage is you get to skip the long lines." —Dejais

# FREE AND ALMOST FREE

It's easy to break the bank in Paris, but those acquainted with the city know where to find the free (or almost free) stuff. Here are some tips.

## Free Art

Thanks to the City of Paris's dedication to promoting culture, access to the permanent collections in the city's municipal museums is free, so you can learn about the city's rich history, the characters who contribute to its aura of romance, and the warriors who fought for France's liberation—all without dropping a cent. Setting the example, the **Hôtel de Ville** de Paris (City Hall) in Le Marais regularly runs several expositions at a time, most of which focus on French artists. Past expos have included the "Life of Edith Piaf" and the works of photographers Wally Ronis and Robert Doisneau. The **Maison Européene de la Photographie**, also in Le Marais, is a favorite among flashbulb-poppers and amateur photography buffs alike— and every Wednesday evening, from 5 to 8, this museum opens its doors free of charge. Expositions can cover everything from the history of the camera and the evolution of printing, to selections from some of the world's most famous photographers. It's a perfect prelude to cocktail hour. The **Musée Carnavalet**—yup, this is in Le Marais also, near Place des Vosges—puts Paris's history on display with a collection of old signs, relics from bars and cafés, paintings of what the city looked like before it was fully developed (Montmartre was all farmland!), and old keepsakes and letters. It's an excellent place to get a feel for Paris past and present. More free art throughout the year can be found at the **Maison de Balzac**, the **Maison de Victor Hugo**, **Musée d'Art Moderne de la Ville de Paris**, and the **Petit Palais**, also known as the **Musée des Beaux-Arts de la Ville de Paris**.

## Free Music

For free classical music in an ethereal setting, many of Paris's churches host free or almost-free concerts at lunchtime and in the evening. For popular venues like **Sainte-Chapelle**, reserve well in advance. Flyers are posted around the city and outside the churches, or check weekly events listings. Also free are l'Heure Musicale, medieval music concerts at the **Musée du Moyen-Age** every Friday at 12:30 and Saturday at 4, between October and July. In summer and fall there are free concerts in the city's parks, including the **Jardin des Luxembourg** (classical music), **Parc de la Villette** (world music and jazz), and the **Parc Floral** in the Bois de Vincennes (classical and jazz). During **Paris Plage**, in late summer, there are free nightly pop and rock concerts on the quays of the Seine. When the weather's nice, you're also likely to find would-be, wannabe, and even a few real musicians along the quai of the **Canal St-Martin**, or in the **Place des Vosges**, guitars in hand for spontaneous song.

## Free Serenity

If the hustle and bustle of Paris is getting to you, opt for a free session of **Qi gong** at the **Parc des Buttes-Chaumont** in the $19^e$ arrondissement. Every day at 9 AM instructor Thoi Tin Cau leads classes, free of charge, at 7 rue Botzaris, métro Botzaris, on the patch of grass in the middle of the park. Parisians also like to recharge their batteries with an afternoon **catnap** in one of the handy reclined chairs scattered throughout the city's gardens. This is the cheapest option for relaxation, reading, and postcard writing—just make sure your possessions are secure if you're actually going to grab some shut-eye.

Perennial favorites for parking yourself, or weary companions, are the **Jardin des Luxembourg** and the **Jardin du Tuileries,** but one of the most serene venues, buffered from the traffic by the arcaded shops, is the garden at the **Palais Royal,** not far from the Louvre. Any perch along the Seine will also do in a pinch if the busy streets are getting to you: it's amazing how serene a spot by the water can be, so close to the frenetic workings of the city, especially if you find yourself on the incomparably charming **Ile de la Cité.**

## Cheap Souvenirs

Perfect for yourself or friends back home, what souvenir retails for just about €0.10 each? The postcard, of course. Go retro (snail mail!) and send some quintessential scenery home with a "J'aime Paris" scribbled on the back, or just bring back a little packet of choice images. For the best prices, check out the news kiosks along Rue de Rivoli and the Grands Boulevards, or visit the bookstore **Mona Lisait** (✉ *9 rue St-Martin, 4ᵉ* ☎*01–42–74–03–02*). For more unusual cards, visit the **Librairie Serge Plantureux** (✉ *4 Galerie Vivienne, 2ᵉ* ☎*01–53–29–92–00*), north of the Palais Royal. **Mondial Art** (✉ *10 rue St-André des Arts, 6ᵉ* ☎*01–55–42–19–00*) has racks of stylish choices, including cards quoting famous French authors. Keep an eye out for vintage postcards, too, sold by the *bouquinistes* along the Seine and by collectors inside Passage des Panoramas. You can buy stamps at any *tabac* as well as at post offices.

## (Almost) Free Sightseeing Tours

Imagine passing the Louvre as part of your daily commute. Some of the city's public bus routes are fantastically scenic; hop on the right one and you can get a great tour for just €1.70—sans squawking commentary. The **No. 29** route reaches from the Gare St-Lazare, past the Opéra Garnier, to the heart of Le Marais, crossing the Place des Vosges before ending up at the Bastille. This is one of the few lines that runs primarily on small streets, not major arteries. Hop the **No. 69** bus at the Champ de Mars (by the Tour Eiffel) and ride through parts of the Quartier Latin, across the bridge to the Rive Droite near the Louvre, and on to the Bastille. The **No. 72** bus follows the Seine from the Hôtel de Ville west past the Louvre and most of the big-name Rive Droite sights, also giving you views of the Rive Gauche, including the Tour Eiffel. Bus **No. 73** is the only line that goes along the Avenue des Champs-Élysées, from the Arc de Triomphe through the Place de la Condorde and ending at Musée d'Orsay.

## Free Wine (Tastings)

Here's a tip for getting tipsy: wine stores sometimes offer free or inexpensive wine tastings, generally on the weekends. Check out **La Dernière Goutte** (✉ *6 rue de Bourbon le Château, 6ᵉ* ☎*01–46–29–11–62*) and the prestigious **Caves Taillevent** (✉ *199 rue du Faubourg St-Honore, 8ᵉ* ☎*01–45–61–14–09*) on Saturday afternoons. **La Cave du Panthéon** (✉ *174 rue Saint-Jacques, 5ᵉ* ☎*01–46–33–90–35*), touted for its conviviality, is another destination where wine lovers congregate on Saturday afternoons to learn about—and indulge in—their favorite beverage. If you're lucky, the winemaker hailing from the featured winery of the day may be among those taking part in the tasting.

# PARIS MUSEUMS, AN OVERVIEW

There's no shortage of museums in Paris, so it's a good idea to make a plan. This overview includes all the museums listed elsewhere in the book; check the index for full listings.

## Major Museums

Ambitious art goers will focus on the Big Three—the **Louvre**, the **Musée d'Orsay**, and **Centre Georges Pompidou**. The Louvre's collection spans from about 7000 BC until 1848, and has its own Big Three: the *Mona Lisa*, the *Venus de Milo*, and *Winged Victory*. The d'Orsay's collection picks up where the Louvre's leaves off and continues until 1914. The Pompidou has art from the early 20th century to the present.

## One-Man Shows

Three major must-sees are **Musée Rodin**, with its lovely sculpture garden; **Musée Picasso**; and **Musée Marmottan Monet**. There's also **Musée Gustave Moreau, Musée Delacroix, Musée Zadkine**, and **Musée Maillol**. Dalí enthusiasts will appreciate **Espace Salvador Dalí**, while French chanson fans shouldn't miss the tiny **Edith Piaf Museum**.

## House Museums

A house museum is two treats in one: the art, and the house itself. **Maison de Victor Hugo** and **Maison de Balzac** are the former homes of writers. **Musée Jacquemart-André** has an intriguing collection of Italian art, and **Musée Nissim de Camondo** has decorative art, mostly from the 18th century. **Musée de la Vie Romantique**, dedicated to the novelist George Sand, was the elegant town house of Dutch-born painter Ary Scheffer, and **Musée Cognacq-Jay** was the home of Ernest Cognacq, founder of the now closed *La Samaritaine* department store. The **Palais Galliera** opens for exhibits on costume and clothing design.

## Contemporary Art

Excellent venues for modern art include the **Palais de Tokyo** and **Musée d'Art Moderne de la Ville de Paris**. There's also **Fondation Cartier pour l'art contemporain** for emerging artists' work, and **La Maison Rouge**, which shows private collections. The **Pinacothèque de Paris** is a private museum dedicated solely to temporary exhibits.

## French History

**Musée National du Moyen-Age** has the well-known tapestry *Lady and the Unicorn*. **Musée d'Art et d'Histoire du Judaïsme** documents Jewish history in France. For Parisian history, don't miss **Musée Carnevalet**. Montmartre has its own museum, **Musée de Montmartre**, and the history of one of Paris's most-visited churches can be absorbed at **Musée de Notre-Dame** (although the church's archaeological crypt is more interesting). The new **Cité de l'Architecture et du Patrimoine** presents a history of French architecture, and maritime history is the subject of the **Musée de la Marine** (both are in the Palais Chaillot). The **Musée de la Légion d'Honneur** is an exploration of French and foreign military decoration, and the **Musée de l'Armée**, at the Hotel des Invalides, is a phenomenal military museum. There's also the **Musée Jean-Moulin** in the Jardin Atlantique, focusing on the life of the famous leader of the French Resistance. The **Musée de la Monnaies**, in the Hôtel des Monnaies (the mint), is impressive for its coin collection.

## Best for Kids

Kids love the hands-on science and technology displays at **Cité des Sciences et de l'Industrie** and the **Musée de la Musique**, both in Parc de la Villette. The **Grande Galerie d'Evolution** and **Musée de la Chasse et de la Nature** have stuffed animals in natural

surroundings. The **Palais de la Découverte**, a planetarium, and **Musée Grévin**, a wax museum, are perennial faves. The fabulous **Musée des Art et Metiers** has neat scientific instruments and inventions. For doll lovers, there's the **Musée de la Poupée**.

## Photography and Design

For a mix of photographs from different artists, your best bet is the **Maison Européenne de la Photographie**. **Fondation Henri Cartier-Bresson** features works by the well-known French photographer in a building that was also his atelier. The **Musée du Jeu de Paume**, in the Tuileries, showcases modern photography exhibits. For modern design, the **Fondation Le Corbusier** is well worth the trip to the western edge of the city. The **Fondation Pierre Bergé-Yves Saint Laurent** is the designer's atelier as well as an archive and gallery of his work. For architecture, sit in on a workshop (in French) at the **Maison de l'architecture d'Ile de France-Les Recollets**. For those interested in urban planning, visit the free **Pavillion de l'Arsenal** to see the miniature models of Paris neighborhoods. The **Musée des Arts Decoratifs** inside **Les Arts Décoratifs** (which includes **Musée de la Publicité** and **Musée de la Mode**) has one of the world's greatest decorative-art collections.

## African, Asian, and Islamic Art

There are two places in town to see Asian art: the **Musée Guimet** is not to be missed and the **Musée Cernuschi** is a small house museum that holds the personal Asian art collection of Enrico Cernuschi. For Arab and Islamic art and architecture, visit the impressive **Institut du Monde Arabe,** and for African art, try **Musée Dapper**. The **Musée du Quai Branly** features African, Asian, and Oceanic art.

## Etc.

Some museums aren't easily classified. The **Musée de l'Erotisme** is a seven-story building dedicated to everything associated with erotic fantasy, the **Manufacture des Gobelins** traces the history of weaving and tapestry, and the **Musée de l'Art Naïf Max-Fourny**, inside Halle St-Pierre, focuses on folk art, and *art brut* (raw art). **Maison de Baccarat** has gorgeous glass creations, and **Maison de Radio France** presents the history of French radio. The **Musée du Vin** is a history of wine making, that also has wine tastings; the **Musée du Parfum rue Scribe** is dedicated to the art of perfume. **La Musée de la Prefecture de Police** is, you guessed it, a museum of the Paris police. The **Musée de l'Orangerie** is a stunning setting for Monet's *Water Lilies*.

## Art Galleries

You can find several contemporary-art galleries near the Centre Georges Pompidou, the Musée Picasso, and the Bastille Opéra. The city's hottest avant-garde art scene is on and around the Rue Vieille du Temple in the north Marais. Around St-Germain and the Place des Vosges the galleries are more traditional; works by old masters and established modern artists dominate the galleries around Rue du Faubourg St-Honoré and Avenue Matignon. Carré Rive Gauche, around Rue du Bac in St-Germain, has dozens of art and antiques galleries on its narrow streets.

The **Association des Galeries** (⊕ *www.associationdesgaleries.org*) lists exhibits in more than 100 galleries through the city. **Paris-art.com** (⊕ *www.paris-art.com*) focuses on contemporary art, with reviews, exhibition calendars, and interviews, in French only.

# ROMANTIC PARIS

It isn't hard to stumble across a romantic moment in Paris. Couples kiss on park benches, dine by candlelight in cozy neighborhood bistros, and walk arm-in-arm in the rain.

At the top of our list for romantic moments is a trip to the top of the quintessential Paris monument, the **Eiffel Tower.** You get extra points for making a reservation at the elegant (and pricey) Jules Verne restaurant, which lets you bypass the crowds for a VIP elevator ride. And if your sweetheart isn't with you in Paris, you can send a soulful missive from the Tower's exclusive mailbox; it'll arrive with the Eiffel Tower postmark.

If seeing the Eiffel Tower in the skyline is part of your romantic vision, there are choice spots throughout Paris from which to gaze upon it. Montmartre's **Sacré-Coeur,** the second-highest point in the city (after the Tower itself), has breathtaking vistas, as well as a lovely green space to throw down a blanket and snuggle. Or head to the top of **Center Georges Pompidou** for a glass of champagne at the restaurant while gazing out at the Tower and the silvery Parisian rooftops. Although somewhat more prosaic, don't rule out **Au Printemps**'s top-floor terrace for views: the café atop the department store has stunning 360-degree panoramas.

Speaking of shopping, some of the world's best lingerie can be found in Paris; wear it for romance, but enjoy shopping for it, too. Department stores have entire floors dedicated to underthings, and there are fabulous boutiques throughout the city where you can find styles and materials to suit every personality and budget.

Romance in Paris? Well, there's always something sexy about a hotel room, but why does it seem that Paris hotels have a little something extra? It might be the gorgeous old buildings and the unique, often family-owned, accommodations. Or maybe it's the history—the ghost of Oscar Wilde or Henry Miller wandering through what used to be a *pavillon d'amour?* At any rate, it seems to us that if you're going to splurge on luxury accommodations, Paris is the place to do it.

Big spending, of course, isn't always necessary, no matter what you're up to. An expensive meal is one thing, but snacking at a corner crêperie can be just as romantic as a sit-down dinner. Indeed, a picnic by the Seine, or at one of the marvelous *jardins* (gardens) is one of the ultimate romantic, and generally inexpensive, Parisian experiences (unless you buy a €2,000 bottle of Château Lafite to wash it down). Feed your love with bites of chocolate and cheese in the manicured **Jardin du Luxembourg** or at the intimate **Place des Vosges.**

If art fuels your passions, Paris is home to romantic museums aplenty—for starters, visit the **Musée Rodin** and its elegant gardens, and make sure to see the sculpture of *The Kiss.*

If you just love to stroll, hand in hand, Paris is your place. Any of the windy streets will do, but a walk along **the Seine** is assured to create romantic memories—especially if you pick a bridge for a sunset kiss. For a straight-from-the-movies moment, pretend you're Audrey Hepburn and Cary Grant in *Charade* and take a nighttime boat tour, making sure to time it so that you see the Eiffel Tower sparkle at the top of the hour.

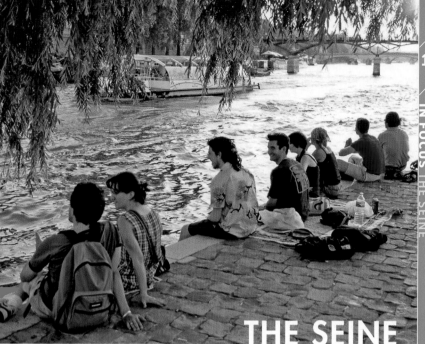

# THE SEINE

No matter how you approach Paris—historically, geographically, or emotionally—the Seine flows through its heart, dividing the City of Light into two banks, the *Rive Droite* (Right Bank) and the *Rive Gauche* (Left Bank).

The Seine has long been used as a means for transportation and commerce and although there are no longer any factories along its banks, all manner of boats still ply the water. You'll see tugboats, fire and police boats, the occasional bobbing houseboat, and many kinds of tour boats; it might sound hokey, but there's really no better introduction to the City of Light than a boat cruise, and there are several options, depending on whether you want commentary on the sights or not. Many of the city's most famous attractions can be seen from the river, and are especially spectacular at dusk, as those celebrated lights of Paris glint against the sky.

# FROM ILE DES CYGNES TO THE LOUVRE

Musée d'Orsay clock

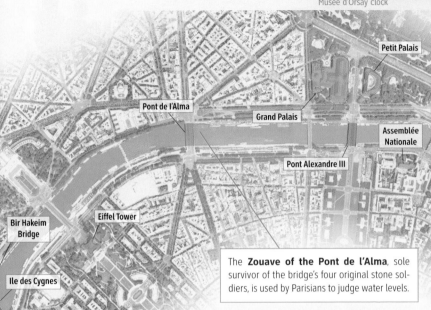

Petit Palais

Pont de l'Alma

Grand Palais

Assemblée Nationale

Pont Alexandre III

Bir Hakeim Bridge

Eiffel Tower

Ile des Cygnes

The **Zouave of the Pont de l'Alma**, sole survivor of the bridge's four original stone soldiers, is used by Parisians to judge water levels.

Whether you hop on a boat cruise or stroll the quays at your own pace, the Seine comes alive when you get off the busy streets of Paris. At the western edge of the city on the **Ile des Cygnes** (literally the Isle of Swans), a small version of the Statue of Liberty stands guard. Auguste Bartholdi designed the original statue, given as a gift from France to America in 1886, and in 1889 a group of Americans living in Paris installed this ¼ scale bronze replica—it's 37 feet, 8 inches tall.

You can get to the Ile des Cygnes via the **Bir Hakeim** bridge—named for the 1942 Free French battle in Libya—whose lacy architecture horizontally echoes the nearby **Eiffel Tower**. You might recognize the view of the bridge from the movie *Last Tango in Paris.*

As you make your way downstream you can drool in envy at the houseboats docked near the bronze lamp–lined Pont Alexandre III. No other bridge over the Seine epitomizes the fin-de-siècle frivolity of the Belle Epoque: It seems as much created of cake frosting and sugar sculptures as of stone and iron, and makes quite the backdrop for fashion shoots and weddings. The elaborate decorations include Art Nouveau lamps, cherubs, nymphs, and winged horses at either end. The bridge was built, like the Grand Palais and Petit Palais nearby, for the 1900 World's Fair.

Along the banks of the Seine     *Bouquinistes* (book sellers) near the Seine

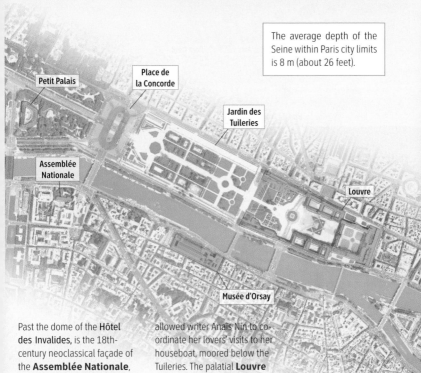

The average depth of the Seine within Paris city limits is 8 m (about 26 feet).

Petit Palais

Place de la Concorde

Jardin des Tuileries

Assemblée Nationale

Louvre

Musée d'Orsay

Past the dome of the **Hôtel des Invalides,** is the 18th-century neoclassical façade of the **Assemblée Nationale**, the palace that houses the French Parliament. Across the river stands the **Place de la Concorde.** Also look for the great railway station clocks of the Musée d'Orsay that once allowed writer Anaïs Nin to co-ordinate her lovers' visits to her houseboat, moored below the Tuileries. The palatial **Louvre** museum, on the Right Bank, seems to go on and on as you continue up the Seine.

## PERFECT PICNIC PLACES

Paris abounds with romantic spots to pause for a picnic or a bottle of wine, but the Seine has some of the best.

Try scouting out a place on the point of Ile St-Louis; at sunset you can watch the sun slip beneath receding arches of stone bridges.

The long, low quays of the Left Bank, with its public sculpture work, are perfect for an alfresco lunch.

# FROM PONT DES ARTS TO JARDIN DES PLANTES

At the water's edge.

Pont des Arts

Pont Neuf

Châtelet Theatres

Hotel de Ville

Institut de France

Ile de la Cité

Conciergerie

Notre-Dame

The Institut de France

Parisians love to linger on the elegant **Pont des Arts** footbridge that streches between the palatial Louvre museum and the Institut de France. Napoléon commissioned the original cast-iron bridge with nine arches; it was rebuilt in 1984 with seven arches.

Five carved stone arches of the **Pont Neuf**—the name means "new bridge" but it actually dates from 1605 and is the oldest bridge in Paris—connect the Left Bank to the Ile de la Cité. Another seven arches connect the Ile and the Right Bank. The pale gray curving balustrades include a row of stone heads; some say they're caricatures of King Henry IV's ministers, glaring down at the river.

On the Right Bank at the end of the Ile de la Cité is the **Hôtel de Ville (City Hall)**—this area was once the main port of Paris, crowded with boats delivering everything from wood and produce to visitors and slaves.

Medieval turrets rise up from **Ile de la Cité,** part of the original royal palace; the section facing the Right Bank includes the **Conciergerie**, where Marie Antoinette was imprisoned in 1793 before her execution.

## PARIS PLAGE

**Paris Plage,** literally Paris Beach, is Mayor Bertrand Delanoë's summer gift to Parisians and visitors. In August the roads along the Seine are closed, tons of sand are brought in and decorated with palm trees, and a slew of activities are organized, from free early-morning yoga classes to evening samba and swimming (not in the Seine, but in the fabulous Josephine Baker swimming pool). Going topless is discouraged, but hammocks, kids' playgrounds, rock-climbing, and cafés keep everyone entertained.

View of the Seine and the Pont des Arts

As you pass the end of the island, you'll notice a small grated window: this is the evocative Deportation Memorial.

Next to the Ile de la Cite is the lovely residential **Ile St-Louis**; keep an eye out for the "proper" depth measuring stick on Ile St-Louis, near the Tour d'Argent restaurant.

Notre-Dame

Also on the Ile de la Cité is the cathedral of **Notre-Dame,** a stunning sight from the water. From the side it looks almost like a great boat sailing down the Seine.

Sightseeing boats turn near the public sculpture garden at the **Jardin des Plantes**, where you'll get a view of the huge national library, **Bibliothèque François Mitterrand**—the four towers look like opened books. Moored in the Seine near the bibliothèque is the Josephine Baker swimming pool with its retractable roof. Paris used to have several floating pools, including the elaborate Piscine Deligny, which was used in the Paris Olympics in 1924; it inexplicably sank in 1993.

Ile St-Louis

Jardin des Plantes

Bibliothéque Francois Mitterand

# PLANNING A BOAT TOUR ON THE SEINE

■ Most boat tours last about an hour; in the winter, even the interior of the boats can be cool, so take an extra scarf or sweater.

■ It never hurts to book ahead since schedules vary with the season and the (unpredictable) height and mood of the Seine.

■ As you float along, consider that Parisians used similar boats as a form of public transportation until the 1930s. Not really like Venice; more like the Staten Island ferry.

■ For optimal Seine enjoyment, combine a boat tour with a stroll—walk around Ile St-Louis, stroll along the Left Bank quays near the Pont Neuf, or start at the quay below the Louvre and walk to the Eiffel Tower, past the fabulous private houseboats.

## WHICH BOAT IS FOR YOU?

| If you want... lots of information | ☎ 01–42–25–96–10 ⊕ www.bateaux-mouches.fr ✉ €10 Ⓜ Alma-Marceau | |
|---|---|---|
| | The massive, double-decker **Bateaux Mouches,** literally "fly boats," offer prerecorded commentary in seven languages. | Departs from the Pont de l'Alma (Right Bank) daily April to September: every 20, 30, or 45 min., from 10:15 AM to 11 PM; daily: October through March approximately every hour from 11 AM to 9 PM. |
| If you want... to do your own thing | ☎ 08–25–05–01–01 ⊕ www.batobus.com ✉ €13, €17 *for 2 consecutive days* | |
| | The commentary-free **Batobus** boat-bus service allows you to hop on and off at any of the eight stops along the river. (Note: there's no service early January through early February.) | Departs from 8 locations: Eiffel Tower, Champs Elysées, Musée d'Orsay, Louvre, St. Germain-des-Pres, Notre-Dame, Hotel de Ville, and Jardin des Plantes. |
| If you want... to impress a date or client | ☎ 01–44–54–14–70 ⊕ www.yachtsdeparis.fr ✉ €198–249 *for dinner cruise* Ⓜ Bastille | |
| | The **Yachts de Paris** specialize in gorgeous boats—expensive, yes, but glamorous as all get-out, with surprisingly good meals. | Departs from Quai de Javel (west of the Eiffel Tower); dinner cruises leave from Port Henri IV (near Bastille). |
| If you want... the Seine, with music | ☎ 01–43–54–50–04 ⊕ www.calife.com ✉ €49 *and up for dinner cruise* Ⓜ Louvre-Rivoli | |
| | **Le Calife** is the Aladdin's lamp of the Seine, moored across from the Louvre. Jazz, piano music, and evenings devoted to French song makes this a quirky and charming choice. | Departs from the Quai Malaquais, opposite the Louvre and just west of the Pont des Arts footbridge. |

# Ile de la Cité and Ile St-Louis

**WORD OF MOUTH**

"I loved strolling around Ile St. Louis, although really strolling around any part of Paris was lovely."

—tcreath

# GETTING ORIENTED

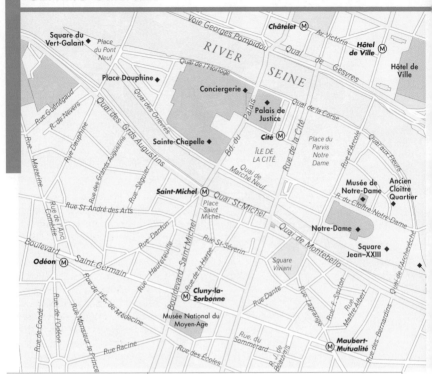

## BEST CAFÉS

**La Charlotte de l'Isle.** The witch from *Hansel and Gretel* might take a fancy to this spot, set with fairy lights, teapots, and puppets. Hot chocolate and delicious cakes satisfy all sorts of cravings.

✉ *24 rue St-Louis-en-l'Ile, Ile St-Louis* ☎ *01–43–54–25–83* ⊙ *2–8 PM, Thurs.–Sun.* Ⓜ *Pont Marie.*

**Le Saint Régis.** This is the most low-key of the cafés huddled on this touristy corner, and attracts more locals than the others. ✉ *6 rue Jean de Bellay* ☎ *01–43–54–59–41* Ⓜ *Pont Marie.*

## TOP REASONS TO GO

**Notre-Dame.** This Gothic cathedral has always been the spiritual heart of Paris. Go inside to gaze at its famed rose windows, climb the towers to talk with the gargoyles, or wander around back to contemplate the stunning architecture from the quiet Square Jean-XXIII. At the end of the square in front of Notre-Dame, is the fascinating Crypte Archéologique, a dig exposing the remains of the Roman community that once occupied the island.

**Sainte-Chapelle.** Visit on a sunny day to best appreciate the exquisite stained glass in this 13th-century chapel built for King Louis IX (St-Louis) and now often used for choral concerts.

**Strolling the islands.** Start with the oldest bridge in Paris, the Pont Neuf, incongruously called "the new bridge," and give a nod to the statue of Henry IV, who once proudly said, "I make love, I make war, and I build." From here, walk to Place Dauphine and stroll wherever whim takes you—every inch of these two islands begs for a photo.

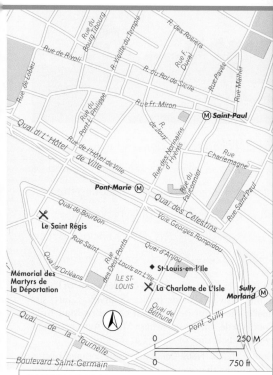

**2**

Pont-Marie ⓜ

Le Saint Régis

Mémorial des Martyrs de la Déportation

St-Louis-en-l'Île

La Charlotte de L'Isle

Sully Morland ⓜ

Pont Sully

0    250 M

0    750 ft

## MAKING THE MOST OF YOUR TIME

This little area of Paris is easily walkable and packed with sites and stunning views, so give yourself as much time as possible to explore. With Notre-Dame, the Conciergerie, and Sainte-Chapelle, you could spend a day wandering, but the islands are easily combined with St-Germain. The Rue de Buci is a perfect place to pick up a picnic lunch to enjoy at the leafy Square du Vert-Galant at the tip of Ile de la Cité. If you have limited time in the area, just make sure you see Notre-Dame and go for a stroll.

## GETTING HERE

Ile de la Cité and Ile St-Louis are in the 1$^{er}$ and 4$^e$ arrondissements (the Boulevard du Palais is the dividing line between the 1$^{er}$ and 4$^e$ arrondissements on Ile de la Cité). If you're too far away to get here on foot, take the métro to St-Michel station or La Cité.

## ICE CREAM VS. GELATO

Cafés all over sell this haute couture brand of ice cream, but the headquarters of **Berthillon** (✉ 31 rue St-Louis-en-l'Île, Ile St-Louis ☎ 01-43-54-31-61) is *the* place to come for this amazing treat. It features more than 30 flavors that change with the seasons, including scrumptious *chocolat au nougat* and mouth-puckering *cassis* (black currant). Expect to wait in line. The shop and adjacent tea salon is open Wednesday to Sunday 10–8 but closed during the peak summer season, from July 20 to September 1.

Also popping up all over Paris—there were 28 outlets at this writing, including the popular spot on Ile St-Louis (✉ 47 rue St-Louis-en-l'Île, Ile St-Louis ☎ 01-44-07-48-08)—and winning converts faster than you can finish a double scoop, is the **Amorino** chain of gelaterias. Popular flavors include rich *Bacio* (dark chocolate and hazelnuts) and *spécialités* such as amaretto laced with crunchy biscuits and almonds. The shop is open every day, noon to midnight.

Sightseeing
★★★★
Dining
★★
Lodging
★★★
Shopping
★★
Nightlife
★

At the heart of Paris, linked to the banks of the Seine by a series of bridges, are two small islands: Ile de la Cité and Ile St-Louis. They're the perfect place to start exploring the city. The Ile de la Cité is anchored by mighty Notre-Dame; farther east lies the exclusive Ile St-Louis, a tiny enclave dotted with charming hotels, cozy restaurants, and small shops.

At the western tip of Ile de la Cité is regal **Place Dauphine,** one of Paris's oldest squares. The impressive Palais de Justice (Supreme Court) sits between **Sainte-Chapelle,** the exquisite medieval chapel of Mad King Louis IX, and the **Conciergerie,** the prison where Marie-Antoinette and other bluebloods awaited their slice of history at the guillotine.

The Gothic powerhouse that is **Notre-Dame** originally loomed over a medieval huddle of buildings that were later ordered razed by Baron Haussmann, the 19th-century civic planner who transformed Paris into the city we see today. In front of the cathedral is now the Place du Parvis, also known as *kilomètre zéro,* the point from which all roads in France are measured. On the north side of the square is the **Hôtel-Dieu** (translated nonliterally as "general hospital"), immortalized by Balzac as the squalid last stop for the city's most unfortunate, but which today houses a modern hospital. Just behind the cathedral lies Rue du Cloître-Notre-Dame, which cuts through the **Ancien Cloître Quartier,** on whose narrow streets you can imagine the medieval quarter as it once was, densely packed and teeming with activity. At 10 rue Chanoinesse, a plaque commemorates the tragic, 12th-century love affair between the philosopher Peter Abélard and his young conquest, Héloïse.

At the farthest eastern tip of Ile de la Cité is the **Mémorial des Martyrs de la Déportation,** all but hidden in a pocket-size park. A set of stairs leads down to the impressive and moving memorial to the 200,000 French citizens who died in Nazi concentration camps.

The nearby Pont St-Louis, which seems to be always occupied by an accordion player or group of musicians, leads to the Ile St-Louis, one of the city's best places to wander. There are no cultural hot spots, just a few streets that may make you think you've stumbled into a village, albeit an unusually tony one. Small hotels, restaurants, art galleries, and shops selling everything from cheese to pâté to silk scarves line the main drag, Rue St-Louis-en-L'Ile. There were once two islands here, the Ile Notre-Dame and the Ile aux Vaches ("Cow Island," a former grazing pasture), both owned by the church. Speculators bought the islands, joined them, and sold the plots to builders who created what is today some of the city's most elegant and expensive real

### MONSIEUR GUILLOTIN

Beheading was a popular means of punishment long before the French Revolution, but it was Dr. Joseph-Ignace Guillotin who suggested that there was a more humane way of effecting decapitation than by use of a sword or ax. Not surprisingly, Dr. Guillotin's descendants changed their surname.

estate. Baroque architect Louis Le Vau (who later worked on Versailles) designed fabulous private homes for aristocrats, including the majestic mansions, the Hôtel Lambert and the Hôtel de Lauzun on the lovely quai d'Anjou.

## TOP ATTRACTIONS

Updated by
Linda Hervieux

**Conciergerie.** Much of Ile de la Cité's medieval buildings fell victim to wunderkind planner Baron Georges-Eugène Haussmann's ambitious rebuilding program of the 1860s. Among the rare survivors are the jewel-like Sainte-Chapelle, a vision of shimmering stained glass, and the Conciergerie, the former city prison where Marie-Antoinette and other victims of the French Revolution spent their last days.

Built by Philip IV in the 13th and 14th centuries, the Conciergerie was part of the original palace of the kings of France, before the royals moved into the Louvre, in 1358; in 1391, this palace was turned into a prison. During the French Revolution, the Conciergerie famously imprisoned Queen Marie-Antoinette as she awaited her fatal trip to the guillotine. You can visit a re-creation of Marie-Antoinette's cell, see lifelike wax figures sadly await their fate behind bars, and read letters penned by some of Paris's famous revolutionaries. The chapel's stained glass is emblazoned with the initials M. A.; it was commissioned after the queen's death by her daughter. Outside, in the courtyard, victims of the Terror spent their final days playing piquet, writing letters to loved ones, washing clothes, and waiting for the dreaded climb up the staircase to the Chamber of the Revolutionary Council to hear its final verdict. The building takes its name from the palace's *concierge,* or high-level keeper of the palace. Free guided tours in English are offered most days at 11 and 3. Call to confirm. ⊠ *2 bd. du Palais, Ile de la Cité* ☎ *01–53–40–60–80* ⊕ *conciergerie.monuments-nationaux.fr* 🎟 *€7, joint ticket with Sainte-Chapelle €11* ⊗ *Mar.–Oct., daily 9:30–6; Nov.–Feb., daily 9–5* Ⓜ *Cité.*

**Mémorial des Martyrs de la Déportation** *(Memorial of the Deportation).* On the eastern tip of the Ile de la Cité lies this extraordinary monument to the 200,000 men, women, and children who died in Nazi concentration camps during World War II. The evocative memorial was intentionally designed to be claustrophobic; a light at the end of the long, narrow tunnel that is the main part of the installation symbolizes hope. The walls are studded with 200,000 pieces of quartz crystal. ⊠ *Ile de la Cité* 🎫 *Free* 🕙 *Mar.–Oct., daily 10–noon and 2–7; Nov.–Feb., daily 10–noon and 2–5* Ⓜ *Maubert Mutualité.*

Fodor's Choice   **Notre-Dame**
★   *See the highlighted listing in this chapter.*

Fodor's Choice   **Sainte-Chapelle**
★   *See the highlighted listing in this chapter.*

## WORTH NOTING

Fodor's Choice   **Ancien Cloître Quartier.** Hidden in the shadows of Notre-Dame is this
★   magical, often-overlooked tangle of medieval streets. Through the years lucky folk, including Ludwig Bemelmans (who created the beloved *Madeleine* books) and the Aga Khan have called this area home, but back in the Middle Ages this was the domain of cathedral seminary students. One of them was the celebrated Peter Abélard (1079–1142)—philosopher, questioner of the faith, and renowned declaimer of love poems. Abélard boarded with Notre-Dame's clergyman, Fulbert, whose 17-year-old niece, Héloïse, was seduced by the compelling Abélard, 39 years her senior. She became pregnant and the vengeful clergyman had Abélard castrated; amazingly, he survived and fled to a monastery, while Héloïse took refuge in a nunnery. The poetic, passionate letters between the two cemented their fame as thwarted lovers, and their story inspired a devoted following during the romantic 19th century. They still draw admirers to the Père Lachaise Cemetery, where they're interred *ensemble*. The clergyman's house at 10 rue Chanoinesse was redone in the 1800s, but a plaque commemorates the lovers; the Ancien Cloître just might have you reciting love poems. ⊠ *Rue du Cloître-Notre-Dame north to quai des Fleurs, Ile de la Cité* Ⓜ *Cité.*

**Palais de Justice.** The city's law courts were built by Baron Haussmann in his characteristically weighty neoclassical style in about 1860, on the site of the former royal palace of St-Louis that later housed Parliament until the French Revolution. ⊠ *4 bd. du Palais, Ile de la Cité* Ⓜ *Cité.*

**Place Dauphine.** The Surrealists loved Place Dauphine, which they called "le sexe de Paris" because of its suggestive V shape. Its origins were much more proper: it was built by Henry IV, who named the square in homage to his successor, called the dauphin, who became Louis XIII when Henry was assassinated. ■ TIP→ Snag a table at one of the restaurant terraces here to enjoy one of the best places in Paris to dine en plein air. ⊠ *Ile de la Cité* Ⓜ *Cité.*

# SAINTE-CHAPELLE

⊠ *4 bd. du Palais, Ile de la Cité* ☎ *01–53–40–60–80* ⊕ *sainte-chapelle.monuments-nationaux.fr* 🎟 *€8, joint ticket with Conciergerie €11* ⊘ *Mar.–Oct., daily 9:30–6; Nov.–Feb., daily 9–5* Ⓜ *Cité.*

## TIPS

■ To avoid waiting in killer lines, plan your visit for a weekday morning, the earlier the better, though be aware that sunset is the best time to see the rose window.

■ Come on a sunny day to appreciate the full effect of the light streaming in through all that beautiful stained glass.

■ You can buy a joint ticket with the Conciergerie; buy the ticket there, though, where the lines are shorter, though you'll still have to go through a longish metal detector line to get into to Sainte-Chapelle.

■ The chapel is especially magical during the regular concerts held here; call for the schedule.

■ Free guided tours in English are offered most days at 11 and 3. Call ahead to confirm.

Built by the obsessively pious Louis IX (1226–70), this Gothic jewel is home to the oldest stained-glass windows in Paris. The chapel was constructed over three years, at phenomenal expense, to house the king's collection of relics acquired from the impoverished emperor of Constantinople. These included Christ's Crown of Thorns, fragments of the Cross, and drops of Christ's blood—though even in Louis's time these were considered of questionable authenticity. Some of the relics have survived and can be seen in the treasury of Notre-Dame, but most were lost during the Revolution.

### HIGHLIGHTS

The upper chapel is where the famed beauty of Sainte-Chapelle comes alive: 6,458 square feet of stained glass is delicately supported by painted stonework that seems to disappear in the colorful light streaming through the windows. The lowest section of the windows was restored in the mid-1800s, but otherwise this chapel presents intact, incredibly rare stained glass. Deep reds and blues dominate the background glass, noticeably different from later, lighter medieval styles such as those in Notre-Dame's rose windows. This chapel is essentially an enormous magic lantern illuminating the 1,130 figures from the Bible, to create—as one writer poetically put it—"the most marvelous colored and moving air ever held within four walls." You'll no doubt be transfixed by the stained glass in the upper chapel, but don't miss the detailed carvings on the columns and the statues of the apostles.

The lower chapel is a bit gloomy and plain, but notice the low vaulted ceiling decorated with fleurs-de-lis and cleverly arranged *L*s for Louis. The dark spiral staircase near the entrance takes you upstairs.

**Square du Vert-Galant.** The equestrian statue of the Vert Galant himself—amorous adventurer Henry IV—keeps a vigilant watch over this leafy square at the western end of the Ile de la Cité. The dashing but ruthless Henry, king of France from 1589 until his assassination in 1610, was a stern upholder of the absolute rights of monarchy, and a notorious womanizer. He is probably best remembered for his cynical remark that "*Paris vaut bien une messe*" ("Paris is worth a mass"), a reference to his readiness to renounce Protestantism to gain the throne of predominantly Catholic France. To ease his conscience, he issued the Edict of Nantes in 1598, according French Protestants (almost) equal rights with their Catholic countrymen. The square is a great place to picnic—you can almost dangle your feet in the Seine. ■TIP→ It's also the departure point for the Vedette tour boats on the Seine (at the bottom of the steps to the right). ⊠ *Ile de la Cité* Ⓜ *Pont Neuf.*

**St-Louis-en-L'Ile.** You can't miss the unusual lacy spire of this church as you approach the Ile St-Louis; it's the only church on the island and there are no other steeples to compete with it. It was built from 1652 to 1765 to the Baroque designs of architect François Le Vau, brother of the more famous Louis, who designed several mansions nearby—as well as the Palace of Versailles. St-Louis's interior was essentially stripped during the Revolution, as were so many French churches, but look for the bizarre outdoor iron clock, which dates from 1741. ⊠ *Rue St-Louis-en-L'Ile, Ile St-Louis* Ⓜ *Pont Marie.*

## DINING AT A GLANCE

For full reviews ⇨ Chapter 17

Moderate Dining

**Mon Vieil Ami,** *Modern French,* 69 rue St-Louis-en-l'Isle

# NOTRE-DAME

Notre-Dame is the symbolic heart of Paris and, for many, of France itself. Napoléon was crowned here, and kings and queens exchanged marriage vows before its altar. There are a few things worth seeing inside the Gothic cathedral, but the real highlights are the exterior architectural details and the unforgettable view of Paris, framed by stone gargoyles, from the top of the south tower.

### THE STONE GARGOYLES

Notre-Dame's gargoyles were designed by Eugène Viollet-le-Duc, the architect who oversaw the cathedral's 19th-century renovations. Technically they're chimeras, not gargoyles, as they're purely ornamental; a true "gargoyle" is a carved sculpture that functions as a waterspout.

## OUTSIDE NOTRE-DAME

Begun in 1163, completed in 1345, badly damaged during the Revolution, and restored by the architect Eugène Viollet-le-Duc in the 19th century, Notre-Dame may not be France's oldest or largest cathedral, but in beauty and architectural harmony it has few peers. The front entranceways seem like hands joined in prayer, the sculpted kings on the facade form a noble procession, and the west (front) rose window gleams with what seems like divine light.

The most dramatic approach to Notre-Dame is from the Rive Gauche, crossing at the Pont au Double from quai de Montebello, at the St-Michel métro or RER stop. This bridge will take you to the open square, place du Parvis, in front of the cathedral. (The more direct metro stop is Cité.)

### THE WEST (FRONT) FACADE

The three front entrances are, left to right: the Portal of the Virgin, the Portal of the Last Judgment (above), and the Portal of St. Anne, the oldest of the three. Above the three front entrances are the 28 restored statues of the kings of Israel, the Galerie des Rois.

## INSIDE THE CATHEDRAL

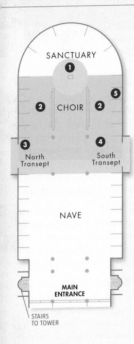

SANCTUARY

❶

CHOIR

❷        ❷        ❺

❸                ❹
North          South
Transept      Transept

NAVE

MAIN
ENTRANCE

STAIRS
TO TOWER

❶ **The Pietà**, behind the choir, represents the Virgin Mary mourning over the dead body of Christ.

❷ **The biblical scenes** on the north and south screens of the choir represent the life of Christ and the apparitions of Christ after the Resurrection.

❸ **The north rose window** is one of the cathedral's original stained-glass panels; at the center is an image of Mary holding a young Jesus.

❹ At the south (right) entrance to the choir, you'll glimpse the haunting 12th-century statue of **Notre-Dame de Paris**, "Our Lady of Paris," the Virgin, for whom the cathedral is named.

❺ **The treasury**, on the south side of the choir, holds a small collection of religious garments, reliquaries, and silver- and gold-plate.

**MAKING THE CLIMB** A separate entrance, to the left of the front facade if you're facing it, leads to the 387 stone steps of the south tower. These steps take you to the bell of Notre-Dame (as tolled by the fictional Quasimodo). Looking out from the tower, you can see how Paris—like the trunk of a tree developing new rings—has grown outward from the Ile de la Cité. To the north is Montmartre; to the west is the Arc de Triomphe, at the top of the Champs-Elysées; and to the south are the towers of St-Sulpice.

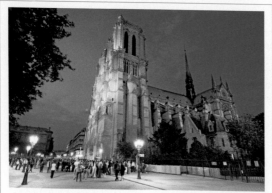

Place du Parvis

Detail of the Gallery of Kings, over the front entrance.

Notre-Dame was one of the first Gothic cathedrals in Europe and one of the first buildings to make use of **flying buttresses**—exterior supports that spread out the weight of the building and roof. At first people thought they looked like scaffolding that the builders forgot to remove. ■TIP→ The most tranquil place to appreciate the architecture of Notre-Dame is from the lovely garden behind the cathedral, Square Jean-XXIII. By night, take a boat ride on the Seine for the best view—the lights at night are magnificent.

**Place du Parvis** is *kilomètre zéro*, the spot from which all distances to and from the city are officially measured. A polished brass circle set in the ground, about 20 yards from the cathedral's main entrance, marks the exact spot.

**The Crypt Archéologique** (entrance down the stairs in front of the cathedral) is a quick visit but very interesting, especially for kids and archaeology buffs. It gives an "under the city" view of the area, with remains from previous churches that were built on this site, scale models charting the district's development, and artifacts dating from 2,000 years ago.

☎ 01-42-34-56-10
🌐 www.notredame deparis.fr
✉ Cathedral free. Towers: €8. Crypt €4. Treasury €2.50.
🕐 Cathedral daily 8–6:45. Towers Apr.–June and Sept., daily 10 AM–6:30; July and Aug., weekdays 10 AM–6:30, weekends 10 AM–11 PM; Oct.–Mar., daily 10–5:30. Note: towers close early when overcrowded. Treasury Mon.–Fri. 9:30–6 PM, Sat. 9:30–6:30, Sun. 1:30–6:30. Crypt Tues.–Sun. 10–6. Museum Wed. and weekends 2:30–6.

## SOMETHING TO PONDER

Do Notre-Dame's hunchback and its gargoyles have anything in common other than bad posture? Quasimodo was created by Victor Hugo in the novel *Notre-Dame de Paris*, published in 1831. The incredible popularity of the book made Parisians finally take notice of the cathedral's state of disrepair and spurred Viollet-le-Duc's renovations. These included the addition of the gargoyles, among other things, and resulted in the structure we see today. and the Panthéon.

■TIP→ The best time to visit Notre-Dame is early in the morning, when the cathedral is at its brightest and least crowded.

■TIP→ There are free guided tours in English on Wed. and Thurs. at 2 PM, and Sat. at 2:30 PM.

# La Tour Eiffel and Les Invalides

## WORD OF MOUTH

"Paris illuminated at night is quite spectacular, the buildings take on an ethereal quality in their yellow glow. The night breeze whispered around our ears and of course the Eiffel Tower stole the show."

—aussie_10

# GETTING ORIENTED

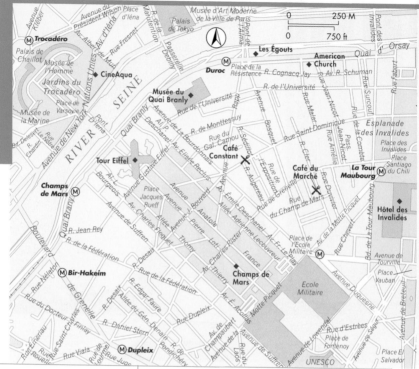

## GETTING HERE

*This neighborhood covers the 7ᵉ arrondissement.* The most romantic way to get to the Tour Eiffel is by boat—see the Seine In-Focus section for details. Otherwise, you can head for RER C, station Champs de Mars/Tour Eiffel. For the best view, get off at the Trocadéro station (métro Line 9 or 6) and make the short walk over the Pont (bridge) d'Iéna to the tower. For the Musée Rodin, get off at Varenne (Line 13). Use this stop, or La Tour Maubourg (Line 8), for Napoléon's Tomb and Hôtel des Invalides.

## TOP REASONS TO GO

**La Tour Eiffel.** No question: the ultimate symbol of France is worth a visit at least once in your life.

**Musée Rodin.** This regal 18th-century *hôtel particulier* (private mansion), once Rodin's workshop, is a must for fans of the master sculptor. The garden makes a perfect setting for Rodin's raw physical sculptures.

**Napoléon's tomb.** The golden-domed Hôtel des Invalides is a strikingly fitting place for Napoléon's remains. Military history buffs will appreciate a visit to the adjoining Musée de l'Armée.

**A boat ride.** Whether you choose a guided tour on the Bateaux Mouches, or the unguided Batobus (a water taxi), a ride along the Seine is a relaxing way to see the city's highlights without traffic or crowds. Go after dark to appreciate the lights.

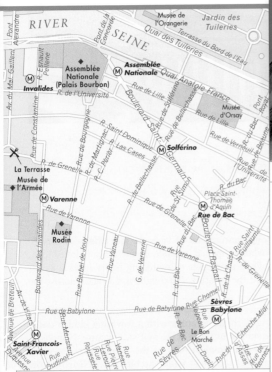

**3**

## BEST CAFÉS

**Café Constant.** This casual café by star chef Christian Constant, who has a veritable empire of restaurants along this street, is a good choice for lunch or dinner. And, at €16 for two courses (at lunch), it's a bargain in this high-end neighborhood. It's closed Monday. ✉ *139 rue St-Dominique, Tour Eiffel/Invalides* ☎ *01-47-53-73-34* Ⓜ *La Tour-Maubourg, Invalides.*

**Café du Marché.** On the quaint Rue Cler, this cramped café, popular with locals, serves French classics at good prices. Prepare to wait, as service is slow—you'll have to ask repeatedly for bread and water—but it's all part of the scene. ✉ *38 rue Cler, Tour Eiffel/Invalides* ☎ *01-47-05-51-27* Ⓜ *La Tour-Maubourg, École Militaire.*

**La Terrasse.** Of the three well-positioned cafés at busy Place des Invalides, this one is the best choice, with good salads, sandwiches, and French classics like steak tartare. The staff is friendly, too. ✉ *2 pl. des Invalides, Tour Eiffel/Invalides* ☎ *01-45-55-00-02* Ⓜ *La Tour-Maubourg.*

## MAKING THE MOST OF YOUR TIME

This neighborhood is home to one of the world's great sites, the Eiffel Tower. Depending on the time of year, you can wait a long time to ascend the tower (lines are shorter at night), but even if you stay firmly on the ground, it's worth a trip to see this landmark up close. Afterward, explore Rue St-Dominique's shops, bakeries, and restaurants.

If you're up for a picnic, grab fixings on rue Cler (between rue de Grenelle and Avenue de La Motte Piquet), a pedestrian-only market street, and double back to the Champ de Mars, the grassy park at the foot of the tower.

If you have a day to spare, visit the Musée Rodin. If you're pressed for time, do a quick tour of the garden (€1 entry) where many of the best-known sculptures can be seen. From here, it's a short walk to Napoléon's over-the-top Tomb at the Hôtel des Invalides, which also houses the Musée de l'Armée, devoted to military history. Alternately, if you're keen on art from Asia, Africa, or the Americas, devote an hour to the Musée du Quai Branly.

Sightseeing
★★★★★
Dining
★★★
Lodging
★★★★★
Shopping
★★★★
Nightlife
★★★

One of Paris's most upscale neighborhoods, the posh 7ᵉ *arrondissement* is home to the French *bourgeoisie* and well-heeled expats, where nearly every elegant block affords a view of the ultimate symbol of France—the Eiffel Tower.

Lording over the southwestern end of Paris, **La Tour Eiffel** was considered a monstrosity when it opened in 1889. Today it is a beloved icon, especially at night when thousands of twinkling lights sparkle at the top of every hour and the rotating searchlight is a beacon across the Paris night sky.

There are other larger-than-life sights here, too, notably **Hôtel des Invalides,** a sprawling Baroque complex with a towering golden dome under which lies the enormous tomb of the pint-size dictator, Napoléon. Along the river, the **Palais Bourbon,** seat of the French Parliament, is an 18th-century homage to ancient Greek architecture. Nearby is the modern, rectangular **Musée du Quai Branly** built by star architect Jean Nouvel. Don't miss the **Musée Rodin,** where the master's outsize sculptures, oozing sensuality, dot the garden and the interior of the Hôtel Biron, the artist's onetime home and workshop.

From the Tour Eiffel east, the walkway along the Seine will take you past one of Paris's most unusual museums, **Les Egouts** (the Sewers—and they are indeed working sewers), and the **American Church.** Cross the **Pont Alexandre III,** the city's most ornate bridge spanning the Seine from Invalides to the Grand Palais. Built between 1896 and 1900, it is bedecked with gilded sculptures, cherubs, and Art Nouveau lamps. It was named for a Russian czar to celebrate Franco-Russian friendship.

## TOP ATTRACTIONS

**Fodor's Choice**
★

Updated by
Linda Hervieux

**Hôtel des Invalides.** Les Invalides (pronounced *lehz-ahn-vah-leed*), as this Baroque complex is known, is the eternal home of Napoléon Bonaparte (1769–1821), or more specifically, the little dictator's tomb, which lies under the towering golden dome. There are two churches here: **St-Louis des Invalides Church,** built between 1677 and 1706, later subdivided into the **Eglise du Dome** and the **Eglise des Soldats** (Soldiers' Church).

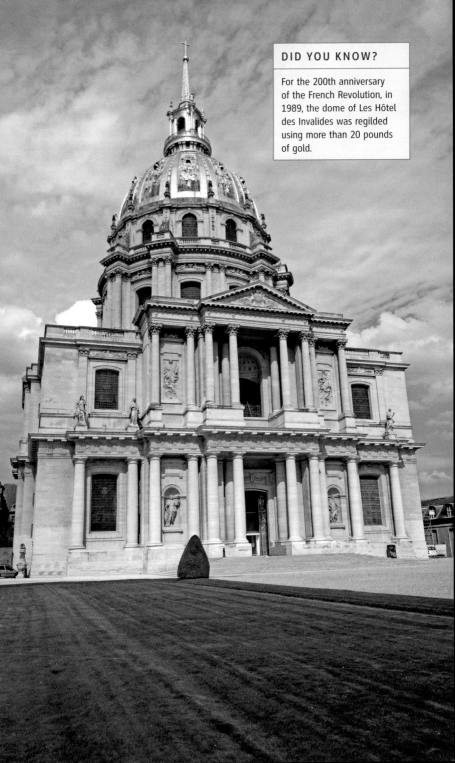

Louis XIV ordered this complex built in 1670 to house-disabled soldiers, and at one time 4,000 military men lived here. Today, a portion of it remains a veterans' residence and hospital. There's also the **Musée de l'Armée,** an exhaustive collection of military artifacts from antique armor to weapons. The World Wars Department, also housed here, chronicles the great wars that ravaged Europe.

If you see only one sight here, make it the **Eglise du Dome** at the back of the complex. Napoléon's tomb was moved here in 1840 from the island of Saint Helena, where the emperor died in forced exile. Napoléon's body is protected by a series of no fewer than six coffins, one inside the next (sort of like a Russian nesting doll), which is then encased in a sarcophagus of red quartzite. The bombastic tribute is ringed by statues symbolizing Napoléon's campaigns of conquest. To see more Napoléoniana, check out the collection in the Musée de l'Armée featuring the emperor's trademark gray frock coat and huge bicorne hat. Look for the figurines reenacting the famous coronation scene when Napoléon crowns his empress, Josephine. (Notice the heavily rouged cheeks; Napoléon hated pale skin.) You can see a grander version of this scene hanging in the Louvre by the painter David.

For the 200th anniversary of the French Revolution, in 1989, the dome was regilded using more than half a million gold leaves, or more than 20 pounds of gold. Renovations of the church and the museum are ongoing, so parts of it may be closed. The **Esplanade des Invalides,** the great lawns in front of the building, are favorite spots for pickup soccer and Frisbee games, sunbathing, and dog walking—despite signs asking you to stay off the grass. ■TIP→ The best entrance to use is at the southern end, on Place Vauban (Avenue de Tourville). The ticket office is here, as is Napoléon's Tomb. There are automatic ticket machines at the main entrance on the Place des Invalides. ⊠ *Pl. des Invalides, Tour Eiffel* ☎ *01–44–42–38–77* ⊕ *www.invalides.org* ⊠ *€9* ⊙ *Eglise du Dôme and museums Apr.–Sept., daily 10–6; Oct.–Mar., daily 10–5. Closed 1st Mon. of every month* Ⓜ *La Tour-Maubourg/Invalides.*

Fodor's Choice   **Musée Rodin.** *See the highlighted listing in this chapter.*
★

**Musée du Quai Branly.** Paris's newest museum was built by top architect Jean Nouvel to house the state-owned collection of "non-Western" art, culled from several other museums. Despite the interminable queues after the opening in 2006, the museum drew criticism for a seemingly incoherent assemblage of artifacts, from antiquity to the modern age. Critics questioned the connection between funeral masks from Melanesia, Siberian shaman drums, Indonesian textiles, and African statuary. A corkscrew ramp leads from the lobby to a cavernous exhibition space, color-coded to designate sections from Asia, Africa, Oceania, and the Americas. The lighting is dim, sometimes too dim to read the information panels (which makes the €5 audioguide a good idea). Renowned for his bold modern edifices, Nouvel has said he wanted the museum to follow no rules. The exterior resembles a massive rust-color rectangle suspended on stilts. There are boxy shapes stuck to the facade facing the Seine, and louvered panels on the opposite side. The colors (dark reds, oranges, and yellows) are meant to evoke the tribal art within. A "living wall" of some 150 species of exotic plants grows on the exterior, which is surrounded by a wild jungle garden with swampy patches—an impressive sight after dark when scores of cylindrical colored lights are illuminated; think numerous mini-light sabers poking out of the ground. The name, strangely taken from the street address, is thought by many to be temporary until, after a respectable waiting period, it can be rechristened in honor of its chief backer, former President Jacques Chirac. ■TIP➔ Feel like splurging? Les Ombres restaurant on the museum's fifth floor (separate entrance) boasts one of the best views of the Tour Eiffel—and prices to match. The budget-conscious can enjoy the garden at Le Café Branly on the ground floor. ⊠ 37 Quai Branly, Trocadéro/Tour Eiffel ☎ 01–56–61–70–00 ⊕ www.quaibranly.fr ⊠ €8.50 ☉ Tues., Wed., and Sun. 11–7, Thurs.–Sat. 11–9 Ⓜ Iéna, Alma-Marceau.

**Fodor'sChoice**
★

**Tour Eiffel.** See the highlighted listing in this chapter.

**OFF THE BEATEN PATH**

Paris's most ornate front door can be found at **29 av. Rapp**, a few minutes' walk from the Pont de l'Alma. The six-story hôtel particulier to which it's attached is an Art Nouveau gem, built in 1901 by Jules Lavirotte, who used brick, stone, and ceramics—the first time ceramics were used to this extent in Paris—to create his whimsical motifs inspired by nature. The historical plaque in front of the building notes that the architect's rebellious style added a "breath of youth and fantasy." Notice the expressions of the pair of nude sculptures: she with a smirk and a jaunty hand on hip; he with a hand cupped to his mouth, calling out to someone. The house was owned by ceramics expert Alexandre Bigot, who frequently teamed up with Lavirotte. The door is the most intriguing feature: carved wood with large oval windows resembling an owl's eyes. The metal handle takes the shape of a curled lizard, its head arching back. Twisting leaves and vines curl around the stone door frame; a woman's head (possibly the architect's wife) is centered at the top, a furry critter crawling down her neck, its pointed nose suspended just above the door. Walk around the corner to 3 Square Rapp to see the house Lavirotte later built for himself.

## WORTH NOTING

**American Church.** Not to be confused with the American Cathedral, across the river at 23 avenue George V, the staff of this neo-Gothic church welcomes English-speaking foreigners. Built in 1927–31, the church hosts free classical music concerts on Sunday from September to June at 5 PM. ⊠ 65 quai d'Orsay, Trocadéro/Tour Eiffel ☎ 01–40–62–05–00 ⊕ www.acparis.org ☉ Mon.–Sat. 9–noon and 1–10:30, Sun. 3–7:30 Ⓜ Alma-Marceau; RER: Pont de l'Alma.

**Champ de Mars.** This long span of grass, flanked by tree-lined paths, lies between the Eiffel Tower and École Militaire. It was previously used as a parade ground and was the site of the world exhibitions of 1867, 1889 (when the tower was built), and 1900. Today the park, landscaped at the start of the 20th century, is a great spot for picnics, pickup soccer, outdoor concerts, or just hanging out. You can sprawl out on the center span of grass—unusual for Paris. There's also a playground where kids can let off steam. Ⓜ École Militaire; RER: Champ de Mars.

There are more than 20,000 Vélib bicycles in use as part of Paris's self-service rental-bike program.

☺ **Les Egouts** *(the Sewers)*. Leave it to Paris to make even the sewers romantic. Part exhibit but mostly, well, sewer, this 1,650-foot stretch of tunnels is a fascinating—and surprisingly non-smelly—look at the underbelly of Paris. Complete with street signs mirroring those above ground, visitors can walk the so-called galleries of this city beneath the city. Walkways flank tunnels of whooshing drain water (wastewater is channeled separately in pipes) that are wide enough to allow narrow barges to dredge sand and sediment. Lighted panels, photos, and explanations in English detail the workings of the 1,300 mi of sewers. Immortalized as the escape routes of the Phantom of the Opera and Jean Valjean in *Les Misérables*, in real life the 19th-century sewers have a florid history. Since Napoléon ordered the underground network built to clean up the squalid streets, the sewers have played a role in every war, secreting revolutionaries and spies and their stockpiles of weapons. Grenades from World War II were recovered not far from where the gift shop now sits. The display cases of stuffed rat toys and "Eau de Paris" glass carafes fold into the walls when the water rises after heavy rains. Buy your ticket at the kiosk on the Left Bank side of the Pont de l'Alma and allow 30 minutes for your visit. Guided tours by friendly *égoutiers* (sewer workers) are available on request, but in French only. ⊠ *Opposite 93 quai d'Orsay, Trocadéro/Tour Eiffel* ☎ *01–53–68–27–81* ⊕ *www.paris.fr* 🎫 *€4.30* ☉ *May–Sept., Sat.–Wed. 11–5; Oct.–Apr., Sat.–Wed. 11–4; closed last 3 wks of Jan.* Ⓜ *Alma-Marceau; RER: Pont de l'Alma.*

**Palais Bourbon.** The most prominent feature of the Palais Bourbon— home of the **Assemblée Nationale,** the French Parliament since 1798—is its colonnaded facade, commissioned by Napoléon to match that of

## Bicycling in Paris

You've seen those 1930s photographs of Paris—men in berets bicycling the streets, a baguette tucked under one arm; elegant women in billowing skirts gliding past the Eiffel Tower on two wheels. Until recently though, it was difficult for visitors to cycle in Paris without signing up for a bike tour. That changed in the summer of 2007, when the City of Paris introduced **Vélib**—a bike rental program.

**Vélib** (⊕ www.velib.paris.fr/), an amalgam of *vélo* (bike) and *liberté* (liberty), has been a resounding success. You can't miss the silver-and-purple bikes at more than 1,450 docking stations—and growing—all over the city. The environment-friendly intent of the scheme is to complement the public transport system, encouraging people to use the bikes for short trips around town. With more than 60 million trips, the bikes are showing some wear and tear, so check yours over thoroughly before taking it out.

There are several stands near the Eiffel Tower—one on Quai Branly at Avenue de la Bourdonnaise, another on Bourdonnaise at the corner of Avenue Rapp, and a third at Rue de Grenelle. This neighborhood is ideal for cycling: the roads are wide, there are several bicycle lanes, and most important, the terrain is gloriously flat. Try a relaxing ride across the Champs de Mars, along Rue St-Dominique, and around Invalides, for starters.

You'll pay €1 a day, or €5 for a seven-day pass, to use Vélib. If you ride for less than 30 minutes at a time, there's no additional fee (you get a code to use through the day, which allows you to take out a bike whenever you want one). If you keep a bike for more than 30 minutes, you pay an additional €1, then €2 for the next 30 minutes, and then €4 for each half hour on top of that. If you're spending a lot of time in Paris, opt for the €29 annual pass, which has no daily fee. (There is also a combination métro/bike pass available.) The system accepts debit or credit cards that contain an electronic chip that can be read by the French system; not all cards work, but American Express does. If your card is rejected, don't despair: **Fat Tire Bike Tours** (⊕ www. fattirebiketoursparis.com ☏ 01–56–58–10–54) offers inexpensive rentals (rates start at €2.50 per hour).

Regardless of how you get around, here are some rules to remember: Stop at red lights (or risk a fine), and watch for vehicles turning right, which may not see you. Cyclists are allowed in most, but not all, bus lanes (watch for no-cycling signs).

The French cycle in high-heeled boots and miniskirts, business suits and loafers—so don't worry if didn't pack the right biking clothes. Helmets are almost never worn (except by kids) and Vélib rentals don't include them.

the Madeleine, across the Seine. Jean-Pierre Cortot's sculpted pediment portrays France holding the tablets of Law, flanked by Force and Justice. There are sometimes outdoor photo exhibitions here, on the Assemblée's railings, and there are always fine views across the Seine to Place de la Concorde and the church of the Madeleine. ⊠ *Pl. du Palais-Bourbon, St-Germain-des-Prés* ⊙ *During temporary exhibits only* Ⓜ *Assemblée Nationale.*

# MUSÉE RODIN

✉ *79 rue de Varenne, Trocadéro/Tour Eiffel* ☎ *01–44–18–61–10* ⊕ *www.musee-rodin.fr* 💶 *€6; gardens only, €1; free 1st Sun. of month* ⊙ *Tues.–Sun. 10–5:45* Ⓜ *Varenne.*

Auguste Rodin (1840–1917) briefly made his home and studio in the Hôtel Biron, a grand 18th-century *hôtel particulier* (private mansion) that now houses the museum dedicated to his work. He died rich and famous, but many of the sculptures that earned him his place in history were originally greeted with contempt by the public, which was unprepared for his powerful brand of sexuality and raw physicality. A major renovation will close parts of the Hôtel Biron throughout 2011.

**HIGHLIGHTS**

Most of Rodin's well-known sculptures are in the gardens. The front garden is dominated by *The Gates of Hell* (circa 1880). Inspired by the monumental bronze doors of Italian Renaissance churches, Rodin set out to illustrate stories from Dante's *Divine Comedy*. He worked on the sculpture for more than 30 years, and it serves as a "sketch pad" for many of his later works. Look carefully and you can see miniature versions of *The Kiss* (bottom right), *The Thinker* (top center), and *The Three Shades* (top center).

The museum's interior, though showing its age, still serves as an elegantly creaky setting for two floors of Rodin's work including *The Bronze Age*, inspired by a pilgrimage to Italy and the sculptures of Michelangelo; the work was so realistic, critics accused Rodin of having cast a real body in plaster.

There's also a room of impressive works by Camille Claudel (1864–1943), Rodin's student and longtime mistress. A remarkable sculptor in her own right, her torturous relationship with Rodin eventually drove her out of his studio—and out of her mind. In 1913 she was packed off to an asylum, where she remained until her death.

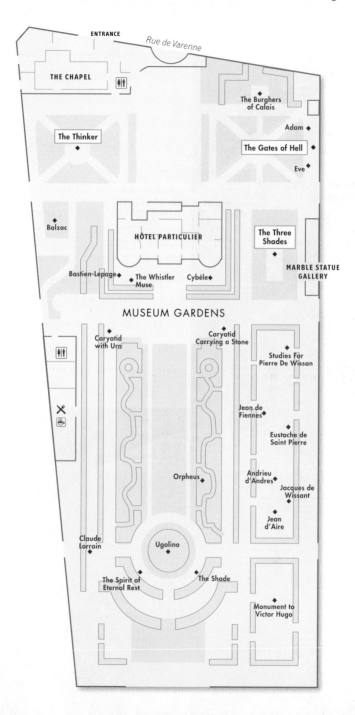

ENTRANCE

*Rue de Varenne*

THE CHAPEL

The Burghers of Calais

Adam

The Thinker

The Gates of Hell

Eve

3

Balzac

HÔTEL PARTICULIER

The Three Shades

Bastien-Lepage

The Whistler Muse

Cybéle

MARBLE STATUE GALLERY

MUSEUM GARDENS

Caryatid with Urn

Caryatid Carrying a Stone

Studies For Pierre De Wissan

Jean de Fiennes

Eustache de Saint Pierre

Orpheus

Andrieu d'Andres

Jacques de Wissant

Jean d'Aire

Claude Lorrain

Ugolino

The Spirit of Eternal Rest

The Shade

Monument to Victor Hugo

New York has the Statue of Liberty, London has Big Ben—and Paris has the Eiffel Tower. This symbol of Paris, recognized the world over, did not, however, begin life as the beloved icon it is today. Engineer Gustave Eiffel's iron creation for the 1889 World's Fair was greeted with disgust by Parisians, who dubbed it the Giant Asparagus. French author Guy de Maupassant supposedly hated the tower so much that he often ate lunch there, explaining that it was the only place in the city where he could avoid seeing it. Parisians eventually warmed to the tower, an inescapable part of the landscape that has captured the minds and hearts of generations.

Total height: 1,063 feet

■ The 200 millionth visitor went to the top of the Eiffel Tower in 2002.

■ To get to the first viewing platform, Gustave Eiffel originally used avant-garde

■ Every 7 years the tower is repainted. Thejob takes 15 months and uses 60 tons of "Tour Eiffel Brown" paint in three shades—lightest on top, darkest at the bottom

# LA TOUR EIFFEL

hydraulic cable elevators designed by American Elisha Otis for two of the curved base legs of the tower. French elevators with a chain-drive system were used in the other two legs. During the 1989 renovation, all the elevators were rebuilt by the Otis company.

■ An expensive way to beat the queue  is to reserve a table at **Le Jules Verne**, the restaurant on the 2nd level, which has a private elevator. Taken over by star chef Alain Ducasse, count on a dinner bill of €450 for 2 with wine, though there's an €85 prix-fine menu at lunch (without wine). ⊕ www.lejulesverne-paris.com ☏ 01–45-55-61-44.

■ If you're in good shape, you can take the stairs to the 2nd level. If you want to go to the top you have to take the elevator.

■ The tower nearly became a giant heap of scrap in 1909, when its concession expired, but its use as a radio antenna saved the day.

■ The tower is most breathtaking at night, when the girders are illuminated. The light show, conceived to celebrate the turn of the millennium, was so popular that the 20,000 lights were reinstalled for permanent use in 2003. It does its electric shimmy for 5 minutes every hour on the hour (cut from 10 to save energy) until 1 am.

## NEED A BITE?

**58 Tour Eiffel**, the restaurant on the first level, serves a good-value, self-service lunch. There is table service at dinner.

**Le Café Branly**, in the nearby Musée du Quai Branly, 27 Quai Branley, Trocadéro/Tour Eiffel, 01-47-53-68-01 is a good choice for lunch or a late-afternoon snack.

The base formed by the tower's feet is 410 by 410 feet.

☏ 01-44-11-23-23

⊕ www.tour-eiffel.fr

🎫 By elevator: 1st and 2nd levels €8, top €13; By stairs: 1st and 2nd levels only, €4.50

🕙 June 13-Aug. 29, daily 9AM-midnight* (11PM for summit); Aug. 30-Dec. 31, 9:30AM-11PM* (10:30PM for summit); Jan. 1-June 12, 9:30-11PM* (10:30 for summit); Stairs: June 13-Aug. 29, 9 AM-midnight; Aug.30-Dec.31, 9:30AM-6:30PM
*LAST TICKET SOLD

Ⓜ Bir-Hakeim, Trocadéro, Ecole Militaire; RER Champ de Mars

■ TIP→ Beat the crush by reserving your tickets online.

AT A GLANCE

# Dining at a Glance

For full reviews ⇨ Chapter 17.

**INEXPENSIVE DINING**
**Le Café Constant,** *Bistro,* 139 rue St-Dominique

**Les Cocottes de Christian Constant,** *French,* 135 rue St-Dominique

**Thoumieux,** *Bistro,* 79 rue St-Dominique

**MODERATE DINING**
**D'Chez Eux,** *Basque,* 2 av. de Lowendal

**L'Agassin,** *Bistro,* 8 rue Malar

**L'Ami Jean,** *Basque,* 27 rue Malar

**L'Os à Moelle,** *Bistro,* 3 rue Vasco-de-Gama

**Le 153 Grenelle,** *Bistro,* 153 rue Grenelle

**EXPENSIVE DINING**
**Au Bon Accueil,** *Bistro,* 14 rue de Monttessuy

**Chez les Anges,** *Bistro,* 54 bd. de la Tour-Maubourg

**Il Vino,** *French Fusion,* 13 bd. de La Tour-Maubourg

**Jules Verne,** *Haute French,* Tour Eiffel

**L'Arpège,** *Haute French,* 84 rue de Varenne

**Le Troquet,** *Haute French,* 21 rue François-Bonvin

**Le Violon d'Ingres,** *Haute French,* 135 rue St-Dominique

# The Champs-Élysées

**WORD OF MOUTH**

"First stop: Arc de Triomphe. We decide to go to the top. We mistakenly enter the long, winding staircase instead of the elevator and walk 284 painful steps to the stop along a narrow, winding staircase. Enjoyed the views especially the streets that look like the spokes of a wheel. Got near dizzy going down those steps again!"

—ramekin4

# GETTING ORIENTED

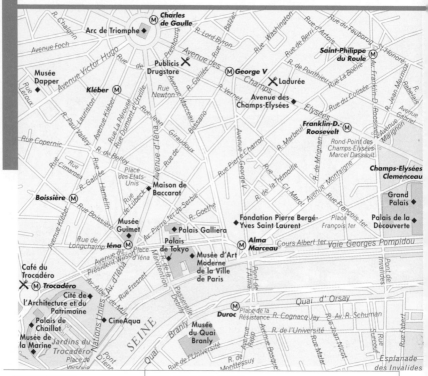

## GETTING HERE

*This neighborhood includes the 8ᵉ and 16ᵉ arrondissements.* For the top of the Champs-Élysées/ Arc de Triomphe, take métro Line 1, 2, or 6, or the RER A, to    Charles-de-Gaulle–Étoile. For the bottom of the avenue, near the Grand Palais, go to the Champs-Élysées–Clemenceau métro station (line 1). For the Palais de Chaillot, use the Trocadéro métro station on lines 6 and 9.

## TOP REASONS TO GO

**The Champs-Élysées.** One of the best times to stroll the wide sidewalks of this famous avenue is at dusk as the famous lights are coming on. Great if you can splurge in the upscale boutiques on and around the avenue but many will, instead, practice the fine Parisian art of lèche-vitrines, or window shopping (literally, "window licking").

**Palais de Chaillot.** A favorite of fashion photographers, this statue-lined plaza-terrace at the Place du Trocadéro boasts the city's best view of the Eiffel Tower.

**Musée Guimet.** One of the city's finest smaller museums with a world-class collection of art from all over Asia. Don't miss the rare Khmer sculptures from Cambodia.

**A *macaron* from Ladurée.** Is it worth lining up for 30 minutes for a little taste of heaven? The answer is yours to make, but rest assured that the *macarons* (meringue cookies) made by this famous *pâtissier* since 1862 are as good as ever. They come in more than two dozen flavors.

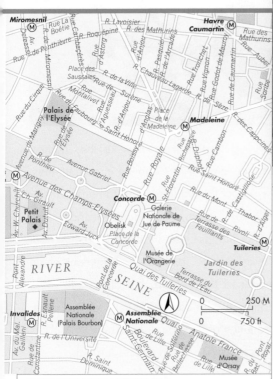

**4**

## BEST CAFÉS

**Café du Trocadéro.** Of the cafés that ring this square, this is the only one with a view of the Eiffel Tower. The friendly staff and good food make it a solid choice. ⊠ *8 pl. du Trocadéro, Trocadéro* ☎ *01–44–05–37–00* Ⓜ *Trocadéro.*

**Publicis Drugstore.** At the top of the Champs, this funky spot is part restaurant, part mini-department store stocked with high-end items like Dior baby clothes. Fine wine and cigars (and public toilets) are in the basement. Prices are moderate if you order the prix-fixe menu and the food is good. ⊠ *133 av. des Champs-Élysées, Champs-Élysées* ☎ *01–44–43–77–64* Ⓜ *Charles-de-Gaulle-Étoile.*

**Ladurée.** This jewel-box tea salon—the most opulent branch of the Ladurée empire—is worth the splurge for lunch (reserve a table), or come for afternoon tea and dessert. ⊠ *75 av. des Champs-Élysées, Champs-Élysées* ☎ *01–40–75–08–75* Ⓜ *George V.*

## MAKING THE MOST OF YOUR TIME

This neighborhood is an essential stop for every first-time visitor to Paris, and returning travelers will find plenty to do, too. Try to leave yourself a long day to tour some museums around Place du Trocadéro before heading to the Champs-Élysées, worth a walk from end to end. Stop for lunch or dessert at one of the cafés or tea salons. And try to detour down the Avenue Montaigne, Paris's answer to Rodeo Drive. If your time is limited, you can just come for a stroll at night, when the Champs is alight: there are bars and nightclubs for all tastes, or you can keep it low key and head to one of the big movie houses with cushy seats showing English-language films (look for v.o. for *version originale*).

Sightseeing
★★★★★

Dining
★★★

Lodging
★★★★★

Shopping
★★★★

Nightlife
★★★★★

Welcome to bling-bling Paris. Make no mistake, the Champs-Élysées, while ceding some of its elegance in recent times, remains the city's—if not the world's—most famous avenue. Like New York's Times Square, or London's Piccadilly Circus, the Avenue des Champs-Élysées inspires boldness. Parisians complain that fast-food joints and anonymous chain stores have cheapened the avenue, but others are more philosophical, noting there is something here for everyone: if you can't afford lunch at Ladurée, there's always McDonald's (and the view from the second floor is terrific).

Anchoring the Champs is the mighty **Arc de Triomphe**, Napoléon's monument to himself. At the other end, the exquisitely restored **Grand Palais** plays host to some of the city's grandest art exhibitions. Across the street, the permanent art collection is free at the **Petit Palais**, and there's also a quiet garden café. Between here and **Place du Trocadéro**, a busy traffic circle, you can find several museums housed in some of the city's most impressive buildings: at the **Palais de Chaillot** complex is the **Cité de l'Architecture et du Patrimoine**, a must for architecture buffs, and across the plaza is the charming **Musée de la Marine.** Farther on, the Asian art collection is tops at the **Musée Guimet.** For 20th-century art, the **Musée d'Art Moderne de la Ville de Paris**, on Avenue du Président-Wilson, has an impressive free permanent collection. Contemporary-art lovers should also check out what's showing next door at the trendy **Palais de Tokyo.** These twin buildings were built for the 1937 World's Fair, and are impressive simply for their monumental facades. Across the street is the **Palais Galliera**, a museum showing fashion-themed special exhibitions.

## TOP ATTRACTIONS

Updated by
Linda Hervieux

**Arc de Triomphe**

*See the highlighted listing in this chapter.*

**Avenue des Champs-Élysées.** Marcel Proust lovingly described the genteel elegance of this storied avenue, the Champs-Élysées (pronounced chahnz-eleezay, with an "n" sound instead of "m" and no "p"), during its Belle Époque heyday, when its cobblestones resounded with the clatter of horses and carriages. Today, despite unrelenting traffic and the intrusion of chain stores and fast-food restaurants, the avenue still sparkles. There's always something happening here: the stores are open late—and many are

> ### DID YOU KNOW?
>
> The monument at the Place de l'Alma, at the bottom of the Champs-Élysées, has become Princess Diana's unofficial shrine, where bouquets and messages are still placed by her admirers—city workers regularly clean up flowers, graffiti, and photographs. The replica of the Statue of Liberty's flame predates Diana's car accident though: it was donated by Paris-based American companies in 1989 in honor of the bicentennial of the French Revolution.

open on Sunday (a rarity in Paris), the nightclubs remain top destinations, and the cafés offer prime people-watching—though you'll pay for the privilege: after all, this is Europe's most expensive stretch of real estate. Along the 2-km (1¼-mi) stretch, you can find the marquee names in French luxury, including Cartier, the perfumier Guerlain, and Louis Vuitton. Newer arrivals, like the cavernous Sephora are fun to check out because, in the bigger-is-better spirit of the Champs, there are often events and giveaways. Car manufacturers try to out-bling each other with space-age showrooms. Old stalwarts are still going strong, if a bit faded, like the Lido cabaret and Fouquet's, whose celebrity clientele extends from James Joyce to President Nicolas Sarkozy, who celebrated his election night victory at this restaurant in May 2007. The avenue is also the setting for the last leg of the Tour de France bicycle race (the third or fourth Sunday in July), and ceremonies on Bastille Day (July 14) and Armistice Day (November 11). The Champs-Élysées, which translates as "Elysian Fields" (the resting place of the blessed in Greek mythology), began life as a cow pasture and in 1666 was transformed into a park by the royal landscape architect André Le Nôtre. Traces of its green origins are visible near Concorde, where elegant 19th-century park pavilions house the historic restaurants Ledoyen, Laurent, and Le Pavillon Élysées Lenôtre. Ⓜ *Champs-Élysées–Clemenceau, Franklin-D.-Roosevelt, George V, Étoile.*

★ **Cité de l'Architecture et du Patrimoine.** It took 10 years and $114 million to transform the City of Architecture and Heritage into one of the world's great architectural museums. Reopened in September 2007 to much fanfare, the former French Monuments Museum's three cavernous galleries (86,000 square feet) contain some 350 plaster-cast reproductions of the greatest gems of French architecture. Copies include partial facades of the most important gothic churches, massive carved doors, and the curved 16th-century staircase to the organ loft at St-Maclou church in

# ARC DE TRIOMPHE

✉ *Pl. Charles-de-Gaulle,
Champs-Élysées* ☎ *01–
55–37–73–77* ⊕ *www.
arc-de-triomphe.monuments-
nationaux.fr/* 🎟 *€9, free
under 18* ⊙ *Apr.–Sept., daily
10 AM–11 PM; Oct.–Mar., daily
10 AM–10:30 PM* Ⓜ *Métro or
RER: Étoile.*

## TIPS

■ France's Unknown Soldier is buried beneath the arch; the flame is rekindled every evening at 6:30, which is the most atmospheric time to visit. To beat the crowds, though, come early in the morning or buy your ticket online (€1.60 service fee).

■ Be wary of the traffic circle that surrounds the arch. It's infamous for accidents—including one several years ago that involved the French transport minister. Use the underground passage from the northeast corner of the Avenue des Champs-Élysées.

Inspired by Rome's Arch of Titus, this colossal, 164-foot triumphal arch was ordered by Napoléon—who liked to consider himself the heir to the Roman emperors—to celebrate his military successes. Unfortunately, Napoléon's strategic and architectural visions were not entirely on the same plane, and the Arc de Triomphe proved something of an embarrassment: although the emperor wanted the monument completed in time for an 1810 parade in honor of his new bride, Marie-Louise, the arch was still only a few feet high, and a dummy arch of painted canvas was strung up to save face. Empires come and go, but Napoléon's had been gone for more than 20 years before the Arc de Triomphe was finally finished, in 1836.

### Highlights

The Arc de Triomphe is known for its magnificent sculptures by François Rude, including *The Departure of the Volunteers in 1792*, better known as *La Marseillaise*, to the right of the arch when viewed from the Champs-Élysées. Names of Napoléon's generals are inscribed on the stone facades—the underlined names identify the hallowed figures who fell in battle.

The traffic circle around the Arc is named for Charles de Gaulle, but it's known to Parisians as "L'Étoile," or the Star—a reference to the streets that fan out from it.

Climb the stairs to the top of the arch and you can see the star effect of the 12 radiating avenues and the vista down the Champs-Élysées toward Place de la Concorde and the distant Musée du Louvre.

There is a small museum halfway up the arch, devoted to its history.

# Hemingway's Paris

There is a saying: "Everyone has two countries, his or her own—and France." For the Lost Generation after World War I, these words rang particularly true. Lured by favorable exchange rates, free-flowing alcohol, and a booming arts scene, many American writers, composers, and painters moved to Paris in the 1920s and 1930s, Ernest Hemingway among them. He arrived in Paris with his first wife, Hadley, in December 1921 and made for the Rive Gauche—the Hôtel Jacob et d'Angleterre, to be exact (still operating at 44 rue Jacob). To celebrate their arrival the couple went to the Café de la Paix for a meal they nearly couldn't afford.

Hemingway worked as a journalist and quickly made friends with expat writers such as Gertrude Stein and Ezra Pound. In 1922 the Hemingways moved to 74 rue du Cardinal Lemoine, a bare-bones apartment with no running water (his writing studio was around the corner, on the top floor of 39 rue Descartes). Then, in 1924, the couple and their baby son settled at 113 rue Notre-Dame des Champs. Much of *The Sun Also Rises,* Hemingway's first serious novel, was written at nearby café La Closerie des Lilas. These were the years in which he forged his writing style, paring his sentences down to the pith. As he noted in *A Moveable Feast,* "hunger was good discipline." There were some especially hungry months when Hemingway gave up journalism for short-story writing, and the family was "very poor and very happy."

They weren't happy for long: in 1926, as *The Sun Also Rises* made him famous, Hemingway left Hadley and the next year wed his mistress, Pauline Pfeiffer, then moved to 6 rue Férou, near the Musée du Luxembourg, whose collection of Cézanne landscapes (now in the Musée d'Orsay) he revered.

For gossip and books, and to pick up his mail, Papa would visit Shakespeare & Co., then at 12 rue de l'Odéon, owned by Sylvia Beach, who became a trusted friend. For cash and cocktails Hemingway usually headed to the upscale Rive Droite. He collected the former at the Guaranty Trust Company, at 1 rue des Italiens. He found the latter, when he was flush, at the bar of the Hôtel Crillon, or, when poor, at the Caves Mura, at 19 rue d'Antin, or Harry's Bar, still in brisk business at 5 rue Daunou. Hemingway's legendary association with the Hôtel Ritz was sealed during the Liberation in 1944, when he strode in at the head of his platoon and "liberated" the joint by ordering martinis all around. Here Hemingway asked Mary Welsh to become his fourth wife, and here also, the story goes, a trunk full of notes on his first years in Paris turned up in the 1950s, giving him the raw material to write *A Moveable Feast.*

Rouen. The famous stained-glass windows of the Chartres cathedral are represented, along with an assembly of gargoyles practically leaping off the back wall of the soaring first-floor gallery. Just below it is the door to an interactive room for children. The video-game set will love the video monitors, with joysticks, that allow a 360-degree view of some of the most impressive cathedrals. The upper-floor gallery is devoted to modern architecture, with models and video explainers of myriad building projects, as well as a life-size replica of a postwar apartment in Marseille designed by the urban-planning pioneer Le Corbusier. Don't miss the gallery of murals with stellar reproductions of frescoes and windows of medieval chapels and other buildings through the ages. Some critics have griped that reproductions are not so impressive in a country with plenty of the real thing, but this museum has nevertheless succeeded in amassing a fine "best of" collection under one roof. ■TIP→ Leave between 1½ and 3 hours for a visit and spring for the €5 English "visioguide," an excellent audiovisual guide to the collection. ⊠ *1 pl. du Trocadéro, Trocadéro/Tour Eiffel* ☎ *01–58–51–52–00* ⊕ *www.citechaillot.fr* ⊠ *€8; €10 with temporary exhibits* ⊗ *Fri.–Mon. and Wed. 11–7, Thurs. 11–9* Ⓜ *Trocadéro.*

**Grand Palais.** With its curved-glass roof and gorgeous restored Belle Époque ornamentation, you can't miss the Grand Palais whether you're approaching from the Seine or the Champs-Élysées. It forms an elegant duo with the Petit Palais across Avenue Winston-Churchill: both stone buildings, adorned with mosaics and sculpted friezes, were built for the 1900 World's Fair, and, like the Eiffel Tower, were not supposed to be permanent. The art shows staged here are often the hottest ticket in town. Previous popular shows include "Marie Antoinette" and "Picasso and the Masters." To skip the long lines, it pays to book an advance ticket online, which will cost you an extra euro. ⊠ *Av. Winston-Churchill, Champs-Élysées* ☎ *01–44–13–17–17* ⊕ *www.grandpalais.fr, www.rmn.fr for reservations* ⊠ *€12* ⊗ *Wed.–Mon. 10–10, Thurs. 10–8* Ⓜ *Champs-Élysées–Clemenceau.*

**Musée d'Art Moderne de la Ville de Paris** *(Paris Museum of Modern Art).* Although the city's modern-art museum hasn't generated a buzz comparable to that of the Centre Georges Pompidou, it can be a more pleasant experience because, like many smaller museums, there are often no crowds. The building reopened after a long renovation in February 2006, and its vast, white-walled galleries make an ideal backdrop for the museum's temporary exhibitions of 20th-century art. The permanent collection on the lower floor takes over where the Musée d'Orsay leaves off, chronologically speaking: among the earliest works are Fauvist paintings by Maurice Vlaminck and André Derain, followed by Pablo Picasso's early experiments in Cubism. Other highlights include works by Robert and Sonia Delaunay, Chagall, Matisse, Rothko, and Modigliani. ⊠ *11 av. du Président-Wilson, Trocadéro/Tour Eiffel* ☎ *01–53–67–40–00* ⊕ *www.mam.paris.fr* ⊠ *Permanent collection free, temporary exhibitions €5–€12, depending on exhibition* ⊗ *Tues.–Sun. 10–6, Thurs. until 10 for temporary exhibits* Ⓜ *Alma Marceau, Iéna.*

★ **Musée Dapper.** A well-curated museum dedicated to African art, the Dapper is famous for its stunning temporary mask exhibitions. Created by Christiane Falgayrettes-Leveau and her husband, Michel Leveau, in 1986, it's a calm place to visit, and makes a good pairing with a stop at the nearby Musée Guimet. Most of the visitor information is in French, but see the Web site for English descriptions of current exhibitions (there is no permanent collection). ⊠ *35 rue Paul Valéry, Champs-Élysées* ☎ *01–45–00–91–75* ⊕ *www.dapper.com.fr* ⊠ *€6* ⊗ *Wed.–Mon. 11–7; usually closed mid-July–Sept.* Ⓜ *Charles-de-Gaulle–Étoile.*

**Fodor's** Choice
★
**Musée Guimet.** One of the best smaller museums in Paris, the Guimet National Museum of Asian Arts has a world-class collection that traces its roots to the Lyonnais industrialist Émile Guimet. His extensive travels in the late 19th century resulted in a priceless collection of Indo-Chinese and Far Eastern treasures. The collection, enriched by the state's vast holdings, is laid out geographically in airy, light-filled rooms, thanks to a top-end renovation (1998–2000). Just past the entry, you can find the largest collection of Khmer sculpture outside of Cambodia, including astonishing 12th-century statues of female divinities. The second floor has statuary and masks from Nepal, ritual funeral objects from Tibet and jewelry, and fabrics from India. Peek into the old library rotunda, with wood-paneled walls and ionic columns topped with carytids: this is where Monsieur Guimet used to entertain the city's notables; and Mata Hari danced here in 1905. The China collection is comprehensive, spanning the dynasties. On the third floor, is an 18th-century model of a Chinese pavilion in delicately sculpted ivory, with tiny figurines. Up the stairs is the China Laquer Rotunda with two large screens from the Qing dynasty with flora and fauna motifs. (There's also a nice view of Paris.) Pick up a free English-language audioguide and brochure at the entrance. If you need a pick-me-up, stop at the basement café, Salon des Porcelaines, for a ginger milk shake. ■TIP→ Don't miss the Guimet's impressive Buddhist Pantheon, with two floors of Buddhas from China and Japan, and a Japanese garden. Admission is free and it's just up the street at 19 av. d'Iéna. ⊠ 6 pl. d'Iéna, Trocadéro/Tour Eiffel ☎ 01–56–52–53–00 ⊕ www.museeguimet.fr ⊠ €6.50, €9.50 with temporary exhibition ⊗ Wed.–Mon. 10–6 Ⓜ Iéna, Boissiére.

**Palais de Chaillot.** This honey-color Art Deco cultural center on Place du Trocadéro was built in the 1930s to replace a Moorish-style building constructed for the World's Fair of 1878. The plaza-terrace is a top draw for camera-toting visitors intent on snapping the perfect shot of the Eiffel Tower. In the building to the left is the **Cité de l'Architecture et du Patrimoine**—an excellent architecture museum—and the **Théâtre National de Chaillot,** which occasionally stages plays in English. Also here is the Institut Français d'Architecture, an organization and school. The twin building to the right contains the **Musée de la Marine,** an excellent small museum with a nautical theme; and the **Musée de l'Homme,** which is closed for renovation and set to reopen, as the Musée de l'Humanité, in 2012 or beyond. Also here is the cozy Café de l'Homme, which has a fantastic view of the tower, but a pricey menu that is not nearly as stellar. The garden leading to the Seine has sculptures and dramatic fountains and is a dramatic staging ground for fireworks on July 14, Bastille Day. ⊠ Pl. du Trocadéro, Trocadéro/Tour Eiffel Ⓜ Trocadéro.

**Palais de Tokyo.** In a space that was derelict for more than a decade, this Art Nouveau twin of the Musée d'Art Moderne reopened in 2002 as a trendy, stripped-down space for contemporary arts with unorthodox, ambitious programming. There is no permanent collection; instead, dynamic temporary exhibits spread over a large, open area reminiscent of a construction site, with a trailer for a ticket booth. Instead of traditional museum guards, young art students—most of whom speak at least some English—are on hand to help explain the installations. The

The Musée Guimet features Asian art and an auditorium for concerts and other events.

cultural programming extends to debates, concerts, readings, and fashion shows. There's also a cafeteria, a funky restaurant, an offbeat gift shop, and a bookstore. ✉ *13 av. du Président-Wilson, Trocadéro/Tour Eiffel* ☎ *01–47–23–54–01* ⊕ *www.palaisdetokyo.com* 💰 *€6* ⊙ *Tues.– Sun. noon–midnight* Ⓜ *Iéna*.

**NEED A BREAK?** For an inexpensive bite, check out the Palais de Tokyo restaurant, Tokyo Eat (✉ *13 av. du Président-Wilson, Trocadéro/Tour Eiffel* ☎ *01–47–20– 00–29*), the only museum café in town with tables filled with hip locals, especially at lunch.

## WORTH NOTING

☺ **Aquarium de Paris Cinéaqua.** An aquarium and a cinema might seem like a strange combination, but there's a good story behind this extremely cool space. Empty for years, this underground extension of the Palais Chaillot was historically designated as an aquarium, which forced the new owner, a Japanese investor who wanted to open an animation studio, to include fish in his floor plan. The animation studio is no more, but there are two cinemas, which share space with some 9,000 fish. There are scores of workshops for kids (in French but the staff speaks English) in animation, art, and dance, There may be a puppet or magic show. To keep adults busy, there are full-length films playing on one big screen (check the Web site for times); the second screen shows sea-related films. A huge tank full of small sharks serves the same purpose, with lounge chairs positioned in front for little and big kids, both of whom seem to love the set-up. There is also an upscale restaurant,

Ozu, serving—yes—sushi and other Japanese specialties. ⊠ *5 av. Albert De Mun, Champs-Élysées* ☎ *01–40–69–23–23* ⊕ *www.cineaqua. com* ⊠ *€19.50, €15.50 ages 13–17, €12.50 ages 3–12* ☉ *Daily 10–8* Ⓜ *Trocadéro.*

**Fondation Pierre Bergé–Yves Saint Laurent.** With his business partner, Pierre Bergé, the iconic late fashion designer Yves Saint Laurent reopened his former atelier in 2004 as a gallery and archive of his work. Unfortunately, YSL's private collection of dresses can be viewed only on private group tours booked in advance. What you can

see here are temporary exhibits that change every few months, most with themes related to the fashion house, such as retrospectives on fashionista doyenne Nan Kempner, and another on YSL photographer David Seidner. ⊠ *3 rue Léonce Reynaud, Trocadéro/Tour Eiffel* ☎ *01–44–31–64–31* ⊕ *www.fondation-pb-ysl.net* ⊠ *€5* ☉ *Tues.–Sun. 11–6* Ⓜ *Alma-Marceau.*

**Maison de Baccarat.** Designer Philippe Starck brought an irreverent *Alice in Wonderland* approach to the HQ and museum of the venerable Baccarat crystal firm. Relocated to the 16ᵉ arrondissement in 2003, Starck played on the building's surrealist legacy: Cocteau, Dalí, Buñuel, and Man Ray were all frequent guests of the mansion's onetime owner, Countess Marie-Laure de Noailles. At the entrance, talking heads are projected onto giant crystal urns, and a lighted chandelier is submerged in an aquarium. Upstairs, the museum, which is a generous term for the splendid but rather small collection, features masterworks created by Baccarat since 1764, including soaring candlesticks made for Czar Nicholas II and the perfume flacon Dalí designed for Schiaparelli. ⊠ *11 pl. des États-Unis, Trocadéro/Tour Eiffel* ☎ *01–40–22–11–00* ⊕ *www. baccarat.fr* ⊠ *€5* ☉ *Mon. and Wed.–Sat. 10–6:30* Ⓜ *Iena.*

☾ ★ **Musée de la Marine** *(Maritime Museum).* Inside this charming, little-known museum you can find a treasure trove of sculpture and art with a nautical theme. There are impressive models of vessels from 17th-century flagships to modern warships. Kids can climb a step to get a closer look at a model aircraft carrier, cut in half, with its decks exposed. The main gallery features several figureheads recovered from sunken ships, including a giant Henri IV, with hand on heart, miraculously saved from a shipwreck in 1854 during the Crimean War. Another enormous representation of Napoléon, in his favored guise as a Roman emperor, was taken from the prow of the frigate *Iéna* in 1846. There is also a metal diving suit from 1882, and the menu from a 1935 voyage of the SS *Normandie* cruise ship (halibut and fresh peas were served). There are usually two temporary exhibitions, one focusing on artwork taken from the museum's collection, as well as borrowed works, including some lovely Impressionist paintings. ✉ *17 pl. du Trocadéro, Trocadéro/Tour Eiffel* ☎ *01–53–65–69–69* ⊕ *www.musee-marine.fr* ✉ *€7, free 18 and under; €9 with temporary exhibition* ☉ *Wed.–Mon. 10–6* Ⓜ *Trocadéro.*

↻ **Palais de la Découverte** *(Palace of Discovery).* This science museum and planetarium behind the Grand Palais has a wide variety of exhibits on subjects from electricity to climate change to nuclear physics. After a merger with Cité des Sciences in 2009, the Palais's days were said to be numbered but, as of this writing, the museum is still open. Built for the 1937 World's Fair, the museum bills itself as the first interactive museum. There's also a planetarium with several shows daily. ✉ *Av. Franklin-D.-Roosevelt, Champs-Élysées* ☎ *01–56–43–20–20* ⊕ *www.palais-decouverte.fr* ✉ *€7, €4.50 under 18; planetarium additional €3.50* ☉ *Tues.–Sat. 9:30–6, Sun. 10–7* Ⓜ *Champs-Élysées–Clemenceau.*

**Palais Galliera.** This regal mansion, built from 1878 to 1894, is closed for renovation until mid-2011. It is home to the Musée Galliera, also called the Musée de la Mode (Fashion Museum), though it opens only for temporary exhibitions on costume and clothing design. Past shows have featured the city-owned museum's vast collection of dresses organized under various themes, such as the "high-tech" crinoline styles of the Second Empire (1852–70). The 2003 Marlene Dietrich show was credited with influencing designers, who incorporated the looks in their runway collections. The lovely garden along Avenue du Président Wilson, restored in 2005 to its 19th-century style, is open during the renovation. ✉ *10 av. Pierre-1er-de-Serbie, Trocadéro/Tour Eiffel* ☎ *01–56–52–86–00* ⊕ *www.paris.fr/musees/* ✉ *€7, admission varies* ☉ *Tues.–Sun. 10–6 during temporary exhibits only* Ⓜ *Iéna.*

**Petit Palais.** The little cousin of the Grand Palais across the street has a free permanent collection of French painting and furniture, with canvases by Courbet and Bouguereau. The temporary exhibitions are often excellent, and the building itself—a 1902 cream puff of marble and gilt, with huge windows overlooking the Seine—is worth a look. Outside, keep an eye out for two excellent sculptures: French World War I hero Georges Clemenceau, facing the Champs-Élysées; and Jean Cardot's resolute image of Winston Churchill, facing the Seine. ■TIP➜ **Tucked in the courtyard is a quiet garden with palm trees and a café—an ideal spot to rest weary feet.** ✉ *Av. Winston-Churchill, Champs-Élysées* ☎ *01–53–43–40–00* ⊕ *www.petitpalais.paris.fr* ✉ *Permanent collection free; temporary exhibit entry fees vary* ☉ *Tues.–Sun. 10–6, Thurs. until 8 for temporary exhibits* Ⓜ *Champs-Élysées–Clemenceau.*

4

## Dining at a Glance

For full reviews ⇨ Chapter 17.

**INEXPENSIVE DINING**

**Chez Savy,** *Bistro,* 23 rue Bayard

**Le Hide,** *Haute French,* 10 rue du Général Lanzerac

**Le Petit Rétro,** *Bistro,* 5 rue Mesnil

**MODERATE DINING**

**Au Petit Verdot du 17$^e$,** *Bistro,* 9 rue Fourcroy

**Goupil le Bistro,** *Bistro,* 4 rue Claude Debussy

**Kifuné,** *Japanese,* 44 rue St-Ferdinand

**L'Huîterie,** *Seafood,* 16 rue Saussier-Leroy

**La Fermette Marbeuf 1900,** *Brasserie,* 5 rue Marbeuf

**La Table de Joël Robuchon,** *Modern French,* 16 av. Bugeaud

**La Table de Lauriston,** *Bistro,* 129 rue de Lauriston

**Rech,** *Seafood,* 62 av. Des Ternes

**EXPENSIVE DINING**

**Alain Ducasse au Plaza Athénée,** *Haute French,* Hôtel Plaza Athénée, 25 av. Montaigne

**L'Arôme,** *Modern French,* 3 rue St-Philippe du Roule

**L'Astrance,** *Haute French,* 4 rue Beethoven

**Le Bristol,** *Haute French,* Hôtel Bristol, 112 rue du Faubourg St-Honoré

**Le Cinq,** *Haute French,* Hôtel Four Seasons George V, 31 av. George V

**Le Cristal Room,** *Haute French,* 11 pl. des États-Unis

**Dominique Bouchet,** *Bistro,* 11 rue Treilhard

**Guy Savoy,** *Haute French,* 18 rue Troyon

**Hiramatsu,** *French Fusion,* 52 rue de Longchamp

**Ledoyen,** *Haute French,* 1 av. Dutuit, on Carré des Champs-Élysées

**Pierre Gagnaire,** *Haute French,* 6 rue de Balzac

**Les Saveurs de Flora,** *Haute French,* 36 av. George V

**Spoon, Food & Wine,** *Modern French,* 14 rue de Marignan

**Stella Maris,** *French Fusion,* 4 rue Arsène-Houssaye

**La Table du Lancaster,** *Haute French,* Hotel Lancaster, 7 rue de Berri

**Taillevent,** *Haute French,* 15 rue Lamennais

# The Faubourg St-Honoré and Les Halles

## WITH THE LOUVRE

**WORD OF MOUTH**

"The real secret of the Louvre: use a Museum Pass and get there at 9:00 AM . . . We waltzed in from the Palais-Royal/Musée du Louvre métro station, through the Passage Richelieu, checked our coats, and flashed our Museum Passes—no line! We made a beeline for the *Mona Lisa* . . . We were practically alone . . . She smiled, we smiled, it was magic."

—bardo

# GETTING ORIENTED

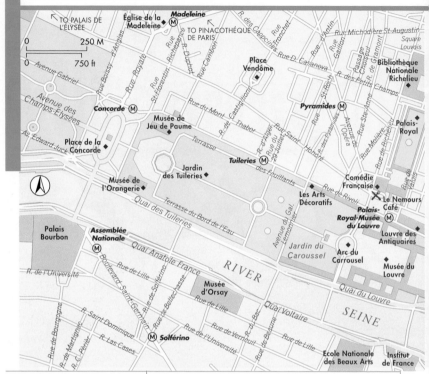

| GETTING HERE | TOP REASONS TO GO |
|---|---|
| *The Faubourg St-Honoré and Les Halles includes the 1er and 2e arrondissements.* If you're heading to the Louvre, take the 1 métro line to the Louvre/Rivoli or Palais-Royal/Musée du Louvre stop. For the Tuileries, use the Tuileries stop on the same line. For Place de la Concorde, use the Concorde stop on Line 1, 8, or 12. This is a good starting point for a walk on Rue St-Honoré. If you're going to Les Halles, take the 4 line to Les Halles or the 1 line to Châtelet. | **Musée du Louvre.** The world's first great art museum is worth a long visit to see some of the most-renowned works of art, from the serenely smirking *Mona Lisa* to the statuesque *Venus de Milo*.<br><br>**Tuileries to Place de la Concorde.** For centuries, Parisians and visitors alike have strolled the length of this magnificent garden to the gold-tipped obelisk at the Place de la Concorde.<br><br>**Galerie Vivienne.** The prettiest 19th-century glass-roofed shopping arcade left in Paris, this *passage* is worth a stop for shopping, lunch, or afternoon tea.<br><br>**Palais-Royal.** Visit these arcades and the romantic garden and understand why the French writer Colette called the view from her window "a little corner of the country."<br><br>**Rue St-Honoré.** Shop 'til you drop and maybe spot a star along this prestigious shopping street. |

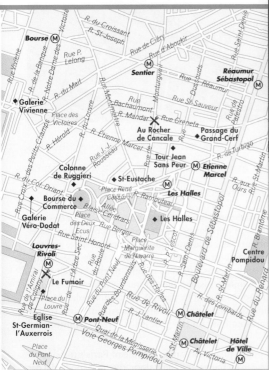

**BEST CAFÉS**

**Le Fumoir.** Once a *très* hip destination, Le Fumoir still draws crowds. Equal parts café, bar, and restaurant, it's a good place to sip coffee and read the paper, or enjoy a cocktail before settling into the back salon for dinner. Reservations are a good idea for dinner and Sunday brunch (€21). ⊠ *Pl. du Louvre, 6 rue de l'Amiral-Coligny, Louvre/Tuileries* ☎ *01–42–92–00–24* Ⓜ *Louvre.*

**Le Nemours.** Adjacent to the Palais-Royal and steps from the Musée du Louvre, this café with rows of tables on a lively plaza is a great place to map out your day over a croissant and *café crème.* ⊠ *2 pl. Colette, Beaubourg/Les Halles* ☎ *01–42–61–34–14.*

**Au Rocher de Cancale.** As its impressive old facade attests, this café dates to 1846, when rue Montorgueil was the place to buy oysters (Cancale is a famous oyster town in Brittany). Today the terrace is a perfect spot for lunch. Try one of the huge salads. ⊠ *78 rue Montorgueil, Beaubourg/Les Halles* ☎ *01–42–33–50–29.*

**MAKING THE MOST OF YOUR TIME**

Try to devote two days, or more—one alone for the Louvre— to these vastly different neighborhoods. The narrow sidewalks of the Faubourg St-Honoré are lined with some of the city's finest boutiques but if the crowds get too thick, it's easy to seek refuge down the many small side streets. Or head to the Place de la Concorde, gateway to the Tuileries garden. At the eastern end, the old market district, Les Halles, has enjoyed a renaissance in recent years with trendy shops and restaurants popping up around cobbled Rue Montorgueil, where traffic is mercifully restricted.

If you're headed to the mammoth Musée du Louvre, it's best to have a game plan in mind. First step: avoid the lines at the main entrance under the pyramid by using the underground entrance in the Carrousel Du Louvre, 99 rue de Rivoli, where there are ticket machines.

Sightseeing
★★★★
Dining
★★
Lodging
★★★★
Shopping
★★★★★
Nightlife
★★

The neighborhoods of the Faubourg St-Honoré and Les Halles are a study in contrasts, from très chic to more mercantile, with the Louvre in the midst of the bustle. ·

The impossibly posh **Faubourg St-Honoré** has been a fashionista destination for three centuries, as popular now as it was when royal mistresses shopped here. Just about every chic boutique has a branch here, and this is where you can find some of the city's best hotels. Once the stomping ground of kings and queens, today it's home to the French president and the American and British ambassadors. To the east, **Les Halles** has risen from its roots as the city's vermin-infested wholesale food market to a booming quarter with expensive apartments and trendy shops, cafés, and bars centered on the pedestrian streets Montorgueil and Montmartre.

In between these opposite poles you can find some of Paris's top draws, namely the mighty **Musée du Louvre** and, next door, the majestic **Jardin des Tuileries**. The garden is home to the **Musée de l'Orangerie**, with its curved galleries showcasing Monet's *Water Lilies*, while the nearby **Musée des Art Décoratifs** is a must for design buffs. In the Place Colette, the stately theater, the **Comédie Française**, is still going strong after 400 years, and at the edge of the square is the psychedelic sculpture—doubling as a métro entrance—of the *kiosque des noctambules* (kiosk of the night-crawlers), designed by artist Jean-Michel Othoniel.

Hidden just off Place Colette is the **Palais-Royal**, a romantic garden ringed by arcades with boutiques selling everything from antique war medals to the latest frock by Stella McCartney. A stone's throw away is the **Galerie Vivienne**, the exquisitely restored 19th-century shopping arcade.

Recalling the area's history as a food hub, there's a small cluster of shops stocking everything a well-dressed kitchen needs (during her years in Paris, American chef Julia Child was a regular at the legendary E. Dehillerin, at 18–20 rue Coquillière). This is the gateway to **Les Halles** (pronounced leh-*ahl*), which was until 1969 the city's wholesale food market, but has since flailed for an identity. It's currently a plaza and garden with a cavernous shopping mall lurking beneath, but plans are underway—once again—to renovate.

## TOP ATTRACTIONS

Updated by
Linda Hervieux

★ **Les Arts Décoratifs.** Sharing a wing of the Musée du Louvre, but with a separate entrance and admission charge, the **Musée des Arts Décoratifs** is home to a stellar collection of decorative arts. Spread across nine floors, the vast holdings include altarpieces from the Middle Ages and furnishings from the Italian Renaissance to the present day. There are period rooms reflecting the ages, such as the early 1820s salon of the Duchesse de Berry, who actually lived in the building, and several rooms reproduced from designer Jeanne Lanvin's 1920s apartment. Don't miss the gilt-and-green velvet bed of the Parisian courtesan who inspired the boudoir in Émile Zola's novel *Nana*. You can hear Zola's description of it on the free English audioguide, which is highly recommended. Don't miss the impressive jewelry gallery on the second floor.

The arts center comprises two other museums—more aptly called departments—which play host to temporary exhibitions. The **Musée de la Mode et du Textiles** (Museum of Fashion and Textiles), for instance, spotlights designers such as Sonia Rykiel. The other department, the **Musée de la Publicité**, is dedicated to advertising and publicity. There is also a quiet restaurant, **Le Saut du Loup**, with an outdoor terrace that serves lunch even on Monday when the museum is closed. A joint ticket is available with the Musée Nissim de Camondo (€10.50). ■TIP→ If you're combining a visit here with the Musée du Louvre, note that the museums close on different days, so don't come on Monday or Tuesday. ⊠ *107 rue de Rivoli, Louvre/Tuileries* ☎ *01–44–55–57–50* ⊕ *www.lesartsdecoratifs.fr* 🎟 *€8–€16.50, depending on which museums you wish to visit* ⊙ *Tues., Wed., and Fri. 11–6, Thurs. 11–9, weekends 10–6* Ⓜ *Palais-Royal.*

★ **Galerie Véro-Dodat.** This is another lovely 19th-century passage, with a dozen artsy boutiques selling art, furniture, and accessories. The headliner tenants are Christian Louboutin, at Rue Jean-Jacques Rousseau, whose red-soled stilettos are favorites of Angelina and Madonna and other members of the red-carpet set. On the opposite end, at the Rue du Bouloi entrance, star cosmetics maker Terry De Gunzburg has a boutique, By Terry. ⊠ *19 rue Jean-Jacques Rousseau, Louvre/Tuileries* Ⓜ *Palais-Royal.*

★ **Galerie Vivienne.** The grand dame of Paris's 19th-century *passages couverts*, or covered arcades, a walk through this beautifully restored gallery, with its tiled floor, will send you back to a time of gaslights and horse-drawn carriages. Parisians came to passages like this one to escape the muddy streets, and show amid the boutiques under the glass-and-iron roofs—the world's first shopping malls. Today, the Galerie Vivienne still attracts top-flight shops such as **Jean-Paul Gaultier** (6 rue Vivienne), as well as some more affordable ones. ■TIP→ The Place des Victoires, a few steps away, is one of Paris's most picturesque squares. In the center is a statue of an outsized Louis XIV (1643–1715), the Sun King, who appears almost as large as his horse. ⊠ *Main entrance at 4 rue des Petits-Champs, Louvre/Tuileries* Ⓜ *Palais-Royal/Bourse.*

**NEED A BREAK?**

**A Priori Thé** (⊠ **35 Galerie Vivienne, Louvre/Tuileries** ☎ **01–42–97–48–75**) has been comforting travelers for nearly 30 years with its teas, sweets,

### DID YOU KNOW?

La Fontaine des Mers (the Fountain of the Seas) is one of two fountains flanking the towering stone obelisk on the Place de la Concorde.

and popular Sunday brunch (€30). The reassuringly familiar menu includes brownies and cheesecake created by American owner Peggy Hancock. Or enjoy a glass of wine with some *saucisson* or *pâté* at the bar of the exclusive wine shop **Legrand Filles et Fils** (⌧ *7/11 Galerie Vivienne, Louvre/ Tuileries* ☎ *01–42–60–07–12* ⊕ *www.caves-legrand.com*), in business since 1880. High-end wine tastings (€100 and up, about two hours, with food; some in English) are held Tuesdays at 8 PM. Reservations are essential.

**Les Halles.** For 801 years, this is the district that fed Paris, with acres of food halls overflowing with meats, fish, and vegetables. Sensuously described in Émile Zola's novel *The Belly of Paris*, Les Halles was teeming with life—though not all of it good: hucksters and homeless shared these streets with prostitutes (who still ply their trade on nearby Rue St-Denis). And the plague of cat-size rats didn't cease until the market moved to the suburbs in 1969. Today, you can still see stuffed pests hanging by their tails in the windows of the circa-1872 shop Julien Aurouze (8 rue des Halles) whose sign, *Destruction des Animaux Nuisibles* (in other words, vermin extermination), says it all.

All that remains of the 19th-century steel-and-glass markets is a portion of the superstructure in the **Jardins des Halles,** an ill-conceived plaza and garden with a magnificent backdrop: the church of **St-Eustache,** a Gothic gem. Below ground is a sprawling, much-maligned mall, the **Forum des Halles,** worth a stop only if you're looking for easy access to a plethora of chain stores. Also here, at the entrance called Porte St-Eustache, is the **Forum des Images,** which offers some 6,500 films available for viewing on individual screens. The mayor's office has promised a renovation by 2012, though work is yet to begin.

The streets surrounding Les Halles have become some of the city's trendiest with boutiques, bars, and restaurants galore that have sent rents skyrocketing. The street that once supplied Paris with its oysters, Rue **Montorgueil** (which translates to Mount Pride), is lined with small shops selling everything from meat to cheese to bread. Running parallel, Rue **Montmartre** is a good place to buy foie gras at one of the small specialty shops clustered near St-Eustache, although you may prefer a skirt or handbag at one of the hip shops that have replaced the butchers and bakers. Still, Les Halles has not totally outlived its seedy reputation and the plaza is best avoided late at night. ⌧ *For plaza/garden, entrance on Rue Berger or Rue du Jour. For mall, main entrance on Rue Pierre Lescot Beaubourg/Les Halles* ⊕ *www.forum-des-halles.com* ⊙ *Mall, Mon.–Sat. 10–8* Ⓜ *Les Halles; RER: Châtelet Les Halles.*

Fodor's Choice ★ **Jardin des Tuileries.** *See the highlighted listing in this chapter.*

Fodor's Choice ★ **Musée de Louvre.** *See the highlighted listing in this chapter.*

★ **Musée de l'Orangerie.** People line up for hours for a glimpse of Claude Monet's huge, meditative *Water Lilies* (*Nymphéas*), displayed in galleries designed in 1914 by the master himself. The museum, once a winter greenhouse for the Tuileries' citrus trees, was renovated in 2006. The small, excellent collection includes early-20th-century paintings by Renoir,

# JARDIN DES TUILERIES

✉ *Bordered by Quai des Tuileries, Pl. de la Concorde, Rue de Rivoli, and the Louvre* ☎ *01–40–20–90–43* Ⓜ *Tuileries or Concorde* ◷ *June, July, and Aug., daily 7–11; Apr., May, and Sept., daily 7:30–9; Oct.–Mar., daily 7:30–7:30* ⛶ *Free.*

## TIPS

■ Garden buffs will enjoy the small bookstore at the entrance to the Tuileries on the Place de la Concorde. Besides books on gardening and plants (including some titles in English), there are also gift items, knickknacks, and toys for the junior gardener. Open from 10 am to 7 pm.

■ The Tuileries is one of the best places in Paris to take your kids if they're itching to run around. There's a carrousel (€2) and in summer, an amusement park.

■ If you're hungry, there are two open-air cafés, both moderately priced, not far from the Place de la Concorde entrance. Café Renard (01–42–96–50–56) serves typical French fare. Across the way,

■ (01–42–96–63–03), has an Italian menu.

The Tuileries was once *the* place to see and be seen in Paris. This most French of French gardens, with verdant lawns, manicured rows of trees, and gravel paths, was designed by André Le Nôtre for Louis XIV. After the king moved his court to Versailles, in 1682, the gardens became a popular place for stylish Parisians to stroll. The name is derived from the factories once dotting this area that produced *tuiles*, or roof tiles, fired in kilns called *tuileries*. Monet and Renoir captured the Tuileries with paint and brush, and it's no wonder the Impressionists loved it—the gray, austere light of Paris's famously overcast days make the green trees appear even greener.

### HIGHLIGHTS

The garden still serves as a setting for one of Paris's most lovely walks. Laid out before you is a vista of Paris's must-see monuments, with the Louvre at one end and the Place de la Concorde at the other. The Tour Eiffel is on the Seine side, along with the Musée d'Orsay, reachable across a footbridge in the center of the garden. A good place to begin is at the Louvre end, at the **Arc du Carrousel**, a stone-and-marble arch ordered by Napoléon to showcase the bronze horses he stole from St. Mark's Cathedral in Venice. The horses were eventually returned, and replaced here with a statue of a *quadriga*, a four-horse chariot. On the Place de la Concorde end, twin buildings bookend the garden. On the Seine side, the former royal greenhouse is now the exceptional **Musée de l'Orangerie,** home to the largest display of Monet's lovely *Water Lilies* series, as well as a sizable collection of early-20th-century paintings. On the opposite end is the **Musée du Jeu de Paume,** which has temporary photography exhibits.

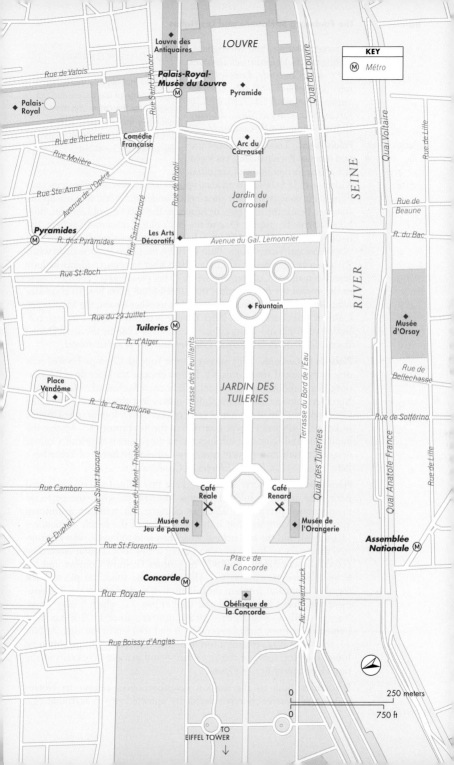

Cézanne, Matisse, and Modigliani, among others. ✉ *Jardin des Tuileries at Pl. de la Concorde, Louvre/Tuileries* ☎ *01–44–77–80–07* ⊕ *www.musee-orangerie.fr* 🎫 *€7.50, €13.50 for same-day entry to Musée d'Orsay* ☉ *Wed.–Mon. 9–6* Ⓜ *Concorde.*

Fodor's Choice ★ **Palais-Royal.** This most romantic and quiet of Paris gardens, enclosed within the former home of Cardinal Richelieu (1585–1642), is an ideal spot to while away an afternoon, cuddling with your sweetheart on a bench under the trees, soaking up the sunshine beside the fountain, or browsing the 400-year-old arcades, now home to chic boutiques. One of the city's oldest restaurants is here, the haute-cuisine Le Grand Véfour, where brass plaques recall regulars like Napoléon and Victor Hugo. Built in 1629, the *palais* became royal when Richelieu bequeathed it to Louis XIII. Other famous residents include Jean Cocteau and Colette, who wrote of her pleasurable "country" view of the *province à Paris*. Today, the garden often plays host to giant-size temporary art installations sponsored by another tenant, the Ministry of Culture. The courtyard off Place Colette is outfitted with a strange collection of black-and-white columns created in 1986 by the artist Daniel Buren. ✉ *Pl. du Palais-Royal, Louvre/Tuileries* Ⓜ *Palais-Royal.*

**Place de la Concorde.** This square at the foot of Champs-Élysées was originally named after Louis XV. It later became the Place de la Révolution, aka guillotine headquarters, where crowds cheered as Louis XVI, Marie-Antoinette, and some 2,500 others lost their heads. Renamed Concorde in 1836, it got a new centerpiece: the 75-foot granite Obelisk of Luxor, a gift from Egypt quarried in the 8th century BC. Among the handsome 18th-century buildings facing the square is the Hôtel Crillon, originally built as a private home by Gabriel, architect of Versailles's Petit Trianon. ✉ *Champs-Élysées* Ⓜ *Concorde.*

**Place Vendôme.** Property laws have kept this refined square spare and pure. The architect Jules-Hardouin Mansart designed the perfectly proportioned plaza in 1702 as an octagon. To maintain a uniform appearance, Mansart built only the facades of the *hôtels particuliers* (mansions), and the lots behind were then sold to buyers who customized their palaces. In the square's center, a 144-foot column erected by Napoléon was toppled in 1871 by painter Gustave Courbet and his band of Revolutionaries. The Third Republic stuck the pieces back together again and sent him the bill, though he died before the first payment was due. Chopin lived and died at No. 12, which is also where Napoléon III enjoyed trysts with his mistress; since 1902 it has been home to Chaumet, one of several high-end jewelers in the area. At No. 15, the Hotel Ritz remains a top destination where celebs can often be found quaffing some of the city's best—and priciest—cocktails in the tiny Hemingway Bar. Ⓜ *Opéra.*

**St-Eustache.** Built as the market neighborhood's answer to Notre-Dame, this massive church is decidedly squeezed into its surroundings.

Constructed between 1532 and 1640, with foundations dating to 1200, the church mixes a Gothic exterior, complete with impressive flying buttresses, and a Renaissance interior. On the east end, Dutch master Rubens' *Pilgrims of Emmaus* (1611) hangs in a small chapel. Two chapels to the left you will find Keith Haring's *The Life of Christ*, a triptych in bronze and white-gold patina. It was given to the church after the American artist's death in 1990, in recognition of the crusading parish's efforts to help victims of AIDS. Outside is the gigantic stone head with a hand cupped to its ear: *L'Écoute* by Henri de Miller. On the Rue Montmartre side of the church, look for the small door to Saint Agnes's crypt, topped with a stone plaque noting the date, 1213, below a curled fish, an indication the patron made his fortune in fish. ⊠ *2 impasse St-Eustache, Beaubourg/Les Halles* ⊕ *www.saint-eustache.org for concert info* ⊙ *Daily 9:30–7* Ⓜ *Les Halles; RER: Châtelet Les Halles.*

## WORTH NOTING

**Bibliothèque Nationale Richelieu.** Superceded by the Bibliothèque Nationale François-Mitterand, France's longtime national library now hosts temporary photography exhibits, some featuring prints culled from its collection of legends such as Cartier-Bresson and Man Ray, others by contemporary photographers. The library is open during a five-year renovation set to end in 2015. ⊠ *58 rue de Richelieu, Opéra/Grands Boulevards* ☎ *01–53–79–59–59* ⊕ *www.bnf.fr* 🎫 *Free–€7, depending on show* ⊙ *Tues.–Sat. 10–7, Sun. noon–7* Ⓜ *Bourse.*

**Bourse du Commerce.** Best approached from the rear, the old Commerce Exchange looks like a giant spaceship about to lift off. Now home to the Paris Chamber of Commerce, it's worth a stop inside to see the beautifully restored iron-and-glass dome, which Victor Hugo dismissively likened to a jockey's cap. Still, it was the first iron structure built in France, in 1809, atop the wheat market. Behind it, the 100-foot-tall **Colonne de Ruggieri** is a remnant of the Hôtel de la Reine, a mansion built here in 1572 for Catherine de' Medici. The column, which miraculously escaped destruction through the ages, was used as a platform for stargazing by her powerful astrologer, Cosimo Ruggieri. Legend has it that on stormy nights, a silhouetted figure can be seen in the metal cage at the top. ■TIP➔ If you want to learn more about the building of the dome, check out the short video simulation of its construction in the Musée des Arts and Métiers. ⊠ *2 rue de Viarmes, Halles* Ⓜ *Métro or RER: Les Halles.*

**Comédie Française.** Mannered productions of Molière, Racine, and Corneille appear regularly on the bill here, but only in French. Founded in 1680 by Louis XIV, the theater finally opened its doors to the public in 1799. It nearly burned to the ground a hundred years later; what you're looking at dates from 1900. The comedienne Sarah Bernhardt began her career here. ⊠ *1 pl. Colette, Louvre/Tuileries* ☎ *08–25–10–16–80* ⊕ *www.comedie-francaise.fr* Ⓜ *Palais-Royal.*

**Église de la Madeleine.** With its rows of uncompromising columns, this enormous neoclassical edifice in the center of the Place de la Madeleine was consecrated as a church in 1842, nearly 78 years after construction

*Continued on page 102*

# Musée du Louvre

Try to wrap your mind around this: The Louvre has about 35,000 pieces of art in its collection, with representations from nearly every civilization on earth, and more than 645,000 square feet of exhibition space. It's gone through countless cycles of construction and demolition, expansion and renovation, starting as a medieval fortress, then becoming a royal residence before opening its doors as the Museum Central des Arts at the end of the 18th century.

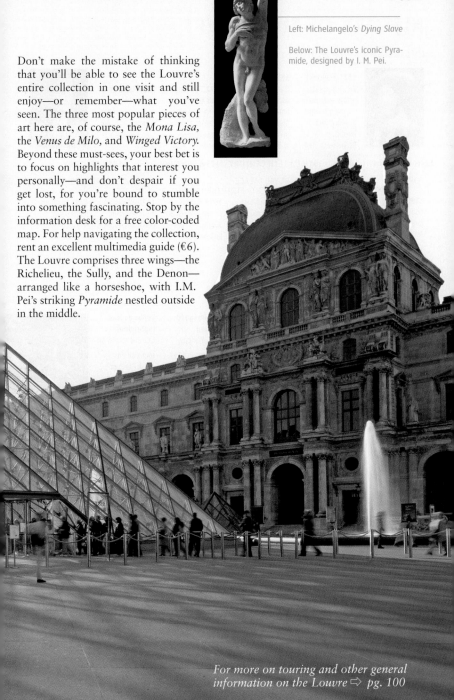

Don't make the mistake of thinking that you'll be able to see the Louvre's entire collection in one visit and still enjoy—or remember—what you've seen. The three most popular pieces of art here are, of course, the *Mona Lisa*, the *Venus de Milo*, and *Winged Victory*. Beyond these must-sees, your best bet is to focus on highlights that interest you personally—and don't despair if you get lost, for you're bound to stumble into something fascinating. Stop by the information desk for a free color-coded map. For help navigating the collection, rent an excellent multimedia guide (€6). The Louvre comprises three wings—the Richelieu, the Sully, and the Denon—arranged like a horseshoe, with I.M. Pei's striking *Pyramide* nestled outside in the middle.

*For more on touring and other general information on the Louvre ⇨ pg. 100*

# HISTORY OF THE LOUVRE

## Evolution of the Building

**1527. François I** (left) expands the palace, demolishing many original buildings and re-building in the new Renaissance style.

**1655-58.** The Queen Mother, Anne of Austria, orders up private apartments and imports Italian artists to decorate it.

**1672. Sun King Louis XIV** moves the royal court to Versailles and the Louvre is abandoned.

**1756. Louis XV** (right) resumes construction. After a century, the Cour Carrée finally gets a roof.

| 12TH C. | 13TH C. | 14TH C. | 15TH C. | 16TH CENTURY | 17TH CENTURY | 18TH CENTURY |
|---------|---------|---------|---------|--------------|--------------|--------------|

**FORTRESS**  ▲            **ROYAL PALACE**            ▲  **ROYAL ARTS ACADEMY**  ▲

**1190. Philippe Auguste** builds a fortress to protect Paris.

**1364. Charles V** converts it into a royal palace.

Henry IV adds the Grand Gallery and begins the passage to the adjacent Tuileries Palace. Work halts upon his death in 1610.

**1660.** Architect Louis LeVau is hired to finish the Louvre. Erasing all medieval traces, he adds pavilions, rebuilds facades, and doubles the palace's width.

**1699.** Royal Academy of Painting and Sculpture stages first exhibition.

**1791.** Revolutionary government declares the Louvre a national museum.

**1793.** Doors open to the public. Admission is free.

## Acquisition of Art

*17TH CENTURY*
*18TH CENTURY*

**Mona Lisa**
Leonardo da Vinci, 1503-06.

Purchased by Francois I under unknown circumstances. It later adorned Napoléon I's bedroom wall.

**The Slaves**
Michelangelo 1513-1515.

From François I's collection. **Entered the Louvre in 1794.**

**Pilgrimage to Cythera**
1717, Watteau.

**Acquired in 1793.**

**Coronation of Napoléon**
1806-07, Jacques Louis David.

**Commissioned by Napoléon,** whose collection fell into state hands after his defeat in 1815.

**Venus de Milo (Aphrodite)**
Late 2nd century BC.

Found on the Greek island of Milos in 1820 and purchased by the French ambassador to Turkey, who presented it to Louis XVIII. **Placed in the Louvre in 1821.**

**The Raft of the Medusa**
1819, Géricault.

Purchased after the artist's death, 1824.

*18TH CENTURY*
*19TH CENTURY*

**1803.** Renamed Musée Napoléon and stocked with booty from the emperor's many conquests.

**1852. Napoléon III** (right) lays the cornerstone of the New Louvre.

**1939.** Artwork is hidden as World War II erupts.
**1940.** Near-empty museum reopens.

**1989.** I.M. Pei's controversial glass *Pyramide* rises over the new entrance in the Cour Napoléon.
**1993.** Renovated Richelieu Wing reopens.

| 19TH CENTURY | 20TH CENTURY | 21ST CENTURY |
| --- | --- | --- |

**NATIONAL MUSEUM**

**1815.** Artworks plundered by **Napoléon**, returned to their native countries after his defeat.

**1852-1861.** Collection expands with works acquired from Egypt, Spain and Mexico. Cour Napoléon completed.

**1871.** Mob sets fire to Tuileries Palace. Louvre is damaged.

**1945.** Asian collection sent to the new Musée Guimet.

**1981. President François Mitterrand** (above) kicks off Grand Louvre project to expand and modernize the museum.

**2000.** Non-French works destined for the future Musée de Quai Branly shown at Louvre.

**2010.** New Islamic art wing is projected to open.

**Winged Victory of Samothrace**
Around 190 BC.

Discovered on the Greek island of Samothrace in 1863 by a French archaeologist who sent the pieces to be reassembled at the Louvre. Her right hand (in nearby glass case) was discovered in 1950.

**Louis XV's Coronation Crown**
1793. Apollo Gallery

**Acquired in 1852.** Original stones replaced with paste in 1729.

**Seated Scribe**
Around 2500 BC.

Discovered in Saqqara, Egypt in 1850. **Given to France by the Egyptian government in 1854.**

**The Lacemaker**
Vermeer, 1669-70.

**Purchased at auction in Paris, 1870.**

**The Turkish Bath**
Ingres, 1862.

**Gift to the Louvre, 1911.** Commissioned by Napoleon but deemed too shocking to display. Revealed to the public in 1905.

**Gabrielle d'Estrées and One of Her Sisters**
Unknown artist, 1594.

**Purchased in 1937.** This (nipple-pinching) scene could represent sisterly teasing related to the pregnancy of Gabrielle, the favorite mistress of Henri IV.

19TH CENTURY
20TH CENTURY

21ST CENTURY
20TH CENTURY

# RICHELIEU WING

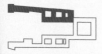

### COLLECTIONS

Near East Antiquities
Islamic Arts
French Painting
French Sculpture
Northern Schools
Decorative Arts

**Below Ground & Ground Floor.** Entering from the Pyramide, head upstairs to the sculpture courtyards, Cour Marly and Cour Puget. In Cour Marly you'll find the **Marley Horses** (see right). Salle 2 has fragments from Cluny, the powerful Romanesque abbey in Burgundy that dominated 11th-century French Catholicism. Salles 4–6 follows the evolution of French sculpture, and in Salles 7–10 you'll find funerary art. In Cour Puget, products from the Académie Royale, the art school of 18th-century France, fill Salles 25–33. Behind this is the Near East Antiquities Collection. Salle 3's centerpiece is the Codex of Hammurabi, an 18th-century BC black-diorite stela containing the world's oldest written code of laws. In Salle 4, you'll find **Lamassu** (see right).

**First Floor.** Head straight through Decorative Arts to see the magnificently restored **Royal Apartments of Napoléon III** (see right).

**Second Floor.** Much of this floor is dedicated to French and Northern School paintings. At the entrance is a 14th-century painting of John the Good—the oldest-known individual portrait from the north of Italy. In Salle 4 hangs *The Madonna of Chancellor Rolin*, by the 15th-century Early Netherlandish master Jan van Eyck (late 14th century–1441). Peter Paul Rubens's (1577–1640) the *Disembarkation of Maria de' Medici at the Port of Marseille* is in Salle 18. In Salle 31 are several paintings by Rembrandt van Rijn (1606–69). The masterpiece of the Dutch collection is Vermeer's *The Lacemaker* (see right).

Also worth noting are three private collections displayed in Salles 20–23. The terms of the legacies prevent these collections from being broken up, and they cover a stunning range of work, from Canaletto to Degas.

### TIPS

■ The Passage Richelieu entrance, reserved for ticket holders, is an easy way into the museum—or out for a lunch break. (Hold onto your ticket!)

■ Enjoy a different perspective on I.M. Pei's pyramid from the terrace of Café Richelieu on the first floor.

■ The 25 paintings by Rubens commisioned by Marie de Medici for the Luxembourg Palace hang in Salle 18 on the second floor. (You can see the aging queen in her finery in Salle 15).

■ To see what's on the minds of the museum staff, check out the Painting of the Month in Salle 17, French section, on the 2nd floor.

# DON'T MISS

### LAMASSU, 8TH CENTURY         SALLE 4

With their fierce beards and gentle eyes, these massive winged beasts are benevolent guardians straight from the dreamworld. Magical for children and adults, the strangely lifelike sculptures are located in the Near Eastern antiquities collection. The winged bull demigods are part of the Cour Khorsabad, a re-creation of the temple erected by Assyrian king Sargon II. ✚ *Sully, ground floor*

Lamassu

### THE LACEMAKER, 1669–1671        SALLE 38

This is a small but justifiably famous gem of Dutch optical accuracy (and a must-see for fans of the movie and book, *Girl With a Pearl Earring*, to see how his style evolved over a 5-year period.) Here, Jan Vermeer (1632–75) painted the red thread in the foreground as a slightly blurred jumble, just as one would actually see it if focusing on the girl. The lacemaker's industriousness represents domestic virtue, but the personal focus of the painting is far more engaging than a simple morality tale. ✚ *Richelieu, second floor*

The Lacemaker

### MARLY HORSES, 1699–1740        COUR MARLY

During the dramatic 1989 reorganization of the Louvre, two courtyards were elegantly glassed over to match the entrance pyramid. The dramatic glass-roofed Marly sculpture court houses several sculptures from Louis XIV's garden at Marly, including two magnificent winged horses by Antoine Coysevox. Later, the artist's nephew Guillaume Coustou created two accompanying earthbound horse sculptures for Louis XV; their fame was such that, during the Revolution, these sculptures were moved to the Tuileries gardens for public viewing. Now the four original horses greet visitors to the Richelieu Wing, ready to gallop off into the museum; replicas stand guard in the Tuileries. ✚ *Richelieu, lower ground floor*

The Marly Horses

### ROYAL APARTMENTS
### OF NAPOLÉON III, 1860s        SALLE 87

These dozen reception rooms, hung with crystal chandeliers, elaborate mirrors, and imperial velour, are a gilt-covered reminder that the Louvre was a palace for centuries, regally designed to impress. En route, you'll pass decorative items like the solid-crystal Restoration dressing table (Salle 77) that prepare you for the eye-popping luxury of the Second Empire. ✚ *Richelieu, first floor*

Royal Apartments of Napoléon

# SULLY WING

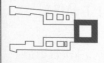

**Below Ground & Ground Floor.** The entrance into the Sully Wing is more impressive than the entrances to the others—you get to walk around and through the 13th-century foundations and the **Medieval Moat** (see right). In Salle 12 you'll find **Ramses II** (see right). Salles 14 and 15 will delight mummy enthusiasts, and there are rare examples of Egyptian funerary art.

Upstairs, the northern galleries of the Sully continue the ancient Iranian collection begun in the Richelieu Wing. To the right is the Greek collection home to the famous 2nd-century BC **Venus de Milo** (see right).

**First Floor.** The northern galleries of the first floor continue with the Decorative Arts collection including works from all over Europe, and connect with the Napoléon III apartments.

**Second Floor.** Sully picks up French painting in the 17th century where the Richelieu leaves off. The Académiciens are best exemplified by Nicolas Poussin (1594–1665), Salle 19), who was the first international painting star to come from France. The antithesis of this style was the candlelighted modest work by outsider Georges de La Tour (Salle 28) such as in his Magdalene of Night Light.

The Académie Royale defined the standards of painting through revolution, republic, and empire. Exoticism wafted in during the Napoleonic empire, as seen in **Turkish Bath** (see right) paintings of Jean-Auguste-Dominique Ingres (1780–1867). Fresh energy crackled into French painting in the 18th century. Antoine Watteau (1684–1721), was known for his theatrical scenes and fêtes galantes, portrayals of well-dressed figures in bucolic settings. In Pilgrimage to the Island of Cythera (Salle 36), he used delicate brushstrokes and soft tones to convey the court set, here depicted arriving on (or departing from) Cythera, the mythical isle of love.

**TIPS**

■ Don't miss the Sleeping Hermaphrodite at the entrance to Salle 17 on the ground floor.

■ Be sure to look up as you make your way up Escalier Henri II. It took four years to complete this 16th-century vaulted ceiling.

■ Need a bathroom? There are some tucked between Salles 22 and 23 on the 1st floor. (And admire the colorful, 4,000-year-old Seated Scribe in Salle 22.)

■ For a breather, duck into this nook off Salle 49 on the 2nd floor, between the two Vernets. Sit on the bench and enjoy a view of the Cour Carrée, one of the oldest parts of the Louvre.

# DON'T MISS

### RAMSES II APPROX. 1200 BC          SALLE 12

The sphinx-guarded Egyptian Wing is the biggest display of Egyptian antiquities in the world after the Cairo museum—not surprising, considering that Egyptology as a Western concept was invented by a Frenchman, Champollion, founder of the Louvre's Egypt collection and translator of the hieroglyphics on the Rosetta Stone. This statue from the site of Tanis, presumed to be Ramses II, never fails to stop visitors' breath with its gleaming stone, beatific expression, and perfect proportions. ⚜ *Sully, ground floor*

Ramses II

### VENUS DE MILO, APPROX. 120 BC          SALLE 12

After countless photographs and bad reproductions, the original Aphrodite continues to fascinate those who gaze upon her. The armless statue, one of the most reproduced and recognizable works of art in the world, is actually as beautiful as they say—and worth the trouble to push past the lecturing curators and tourist groups to get a closer look at the incredible skill with which the Greeks turned cold marble into something vibrant and graceful. She was unearthed on the Greek island of Milos in the 19th century and sold for 6,000 francs to the French ambassador in Constantinople, who presented her to King Louis XVIII. ⚜ *Denon, ground floor*

Venus de Milo

### MEDIEVAL MOAT, 13TH BC          MEDIEVAL LOUVRE

Wander around the perimeter of the solidly-built original moat (no longer filled with water) to reach the remarkable Salle Saint-Louis with its elegant columns and medieval artifacts. Keep an eye out for the parade helmet of Charles VI, which was dug up in 169 fragments and astonishingly reassembled. ⚜ *Sully, lower ground floor*

Medieval Moat

### THE TURKISH BATH, 1862          SALLE 60

Though Jean-August-Dominique Ingres' (1780–1867) long-limbed women hardly look Turkish, they are singularly elegant and his polished immaculate style was imitated by an entire generation of French painters. This painting is a prime example of Orientalism, where Western artists played out fantasies of the Orient in their work. Popular as a society portrait painter, Ingres returned repeatedly to langorous nudes—compare the women of the *Turkish Bath* with the slinky figure in his *La Grande Odalisque,* in the Denon Wing. ⚜ *Sully, second floor*

The Turkish Bath

# THE DENON WING

**Below Ground & Ground Floor.** To the south and east of the *Pyramide* entrance are galleries displaying early Renaissance Italian sculpture, including a 15th-century Madonna and Child by the Florentine Donatello (1386–1466). Before going upstairs, it's worth walking through the galleries of Etruscan and Roman works. In Salle 18 you'll find the 6th-century Etruscan Sarcophagus from Cerveteri, showing a married couple pieced together from thousands of clay fragments.

Drift upstairs to Italian sculpture on the ground level, concluding with Salle 4, where you'll find Michelangelo's Slaves (1513–15).

**First Floor.** Walk up the marble Escalier Daru to discover the sublime **Winged Victory of Samothrace** (see right). Then head to the Gallerie d'Apollon, reopened in 2004 after a stunning renovation. Built in 1661 but not finished until 1851, the hall was a model for Versaille's Hall of Mirrors.

Back out and into Paintings, you'll find four by Leonardo da Vinci (1452–1519). His enigmatic, androgynous St-John the Baptist hangs here, along with more overtly religious works such as the 1483 Virgin of the Rocks. Take a close look at the pretty portrait of La Belle Ferronnière, which Leonardo painted a decade before the **Mona Lisa** (see right); it will give you something to compare with Mona when you finally get to meet her in the Salle des Etats, near Salles 5 and 6. Head across to Salle 75 for an artistic 180°: the gleaming pomp and circumstance of a new empire with the **Coronation of Napoléon** (see right) by French classicist Jacques-Louis David (1748–1825).

In Salle 77 is the gruesome 1819 **The Raft of the Medusa**, (see right) by Théodore Géricault (1791–1824).

## TIPS

■ Don't skip the coat check on the ground floor tucked behind the stairs. Much of the museum is hot and stuffy.

■ For a peek at history in the making, see the new Islamic Arts department taking shape from the windows in Salles 1 and 2 on the first floor. (Projected opening, late 2010).

■ For an easy escape, duck out the Porte de Lions at the end of the wing. On your way out, check out the Goyas in Salle 32 on the first floor. (But don't forget your coat!)

■ Don't miss the glass case near Winged Victory of Samothrace on the first floor. It contains her two-fingered hand.

# DON'T MISS

**MONA LISA, 1503**                    **SALLE 7**

The most famous painting in the world, La Gioconda (*La Joconde* in French) is tougher than she looks: the canvas was stolen from the Louvre by an Italian nationalist in 1911, recovered from a Florentine hotel, and survived an acid attack in 1956. She is believed to be the wife of Francesco del Giocondo, a Florentine millionaire, and was probably 24 when she sat for this painting; some historians believe the portrait was actually painted after her death. Either way, she has become immortal through da Vinci's ingenious "sfumato" technique, which combines glowing detail with soft, depth-filled brushwork. ✛ *Denon, first floor*

Mona Lisa

**5**

**THE RAFT OF THE MEDUSA, 1819**       **SALLE 77**

Théodore Géricault was inspired by the grim news report that survivors of a wrecked French merchant ship were left adrift on a raft without supplies. Géricault interviewed survivors, visited the morgue to draw corpses, and turned his painting of the disaster into a strong indictment of authority, the first time an epic historical painting had taken on current events in this way. Note the desperate energy from the pyramid construction of bodies on the raft and the manipulation of greenish light. ✛ *Denon, first floor*

The Raft of the Medusa

**WINGED VICTORY OF SAMOTHRACE,305 BC   STAIRS**

Poised for flight at the top of the Escalier Daru, this exhilarating statue was found on a tiny Greek island in the northern Aegean. Depicted in the act of descending from Olympus, Winged Victory, or Nike, to the Ancient Greeks, was carved to commemorate the naval victory of Demetrius Poliorcetes over the Turks. ✛ *Denon, first floor*

Winged Victory of Samothrace

**CORONATION OF NAPOLÉON, 1805**       **SALLE 75**

Classicist Jacques-Louis David (1748–1825) was the ultimate painter-survivor: he began his career under the protection of the King, became official designer of the Revolutionary government, endured two rounds of exile, and became one of the greatest of Napoléon's painters. Here, David avoided the politically fraught moment of December 2, 1804—when Napoléon snatched the crown from the hands of Pope Pius VII to place it upon his own head—choosing instead the romantic moment when the new emperor turned to crown Joséphine. ✛ *Denon, first floor*

Detail from the Coronation of Napoléon

# PLANNING YOUR VISIT

## TOURS

Pick up a slick multimedia guide at the entrance to each wing; €6 buys you information on 250 artworks, four self-guided tours, and a "Where Am I?" function you can click to get your bearings.

Formal Louvre guided tours are available from the front desk, which also has thematic leaflets to self-guide through a particular trail—some designed especially for kids. The Louvre has a phenomenal program of courses and workshops (mostly in French); see Web site for details.

## ACCESSIBILITY

Wheelchair visitors can skip the long entry line and use the marvelous cylinder lift inside the entrance pyramid.

## WITH KIDS

Begin your tour in the Sully Wing at the Medieval Moat, which leads enticingly to the sphinx-guarded entrance of the Egyptian Wing, a must for mummy enthusiasts.

For a more in-depth visit, you can reserve private kid-centric family tours such as the Paris Muse Clues (www.parismuse. com) Don't forget the Tuileries is right next door (with carnival rides in summer).

## ENTRY TIPS

Those in the know head straight for the entrance in the underground mall, Carrousel du Louvre (99 rue de Rivoli), which has automatic ticket machines. Another time-saving option is to book tickets online and have them mailed to you before you even leave home. Be sure to hold onto your ticket. You can come and go as often as you like during one day. The shortest entry lines tend to be around 1 PM Prices drop after 6 PM for the late-night Wednesday and Friday openings; crowds thin out in the evening. Remember that the Louvre is closed on Tuesday!

## A WHIRLWIND TOUR

If you've come to Paris and feel you must go to the Louvre to see the Big Three—**Venus de Milo, Winged Victory**, and **Mona Lisa**—even though you'd rather be strolling along the Champs-Elysees, it can be done in an hour or less if you plan well. Start in Denon and head upstairs through Estruscan and Greek antiquities, walking down the long hall of sculptures until you see the Winged Victory in front of you. Take a right and head up the staircase through French painting to the Mona Lisa. Then go back down under the Pyramid to Richelieu to see the Venus de Milo.

✉ Palais du Louvre, Louvre/Tuileries

☎ 01–40–20–53–17 (information)

🌐 www.louvre.fr

💶 €9, €6 after 6 PM Wed. and Fri. Free 1st Sun. of month, under 18 (anytime); €11 for Napoléon Hall exhibitions

🕐 Mon., Thurs., and weekends 9–6; Wed. and Fri. 9 AM–10 PM

Ⓜ Palais-Royal / Musée du Louvre

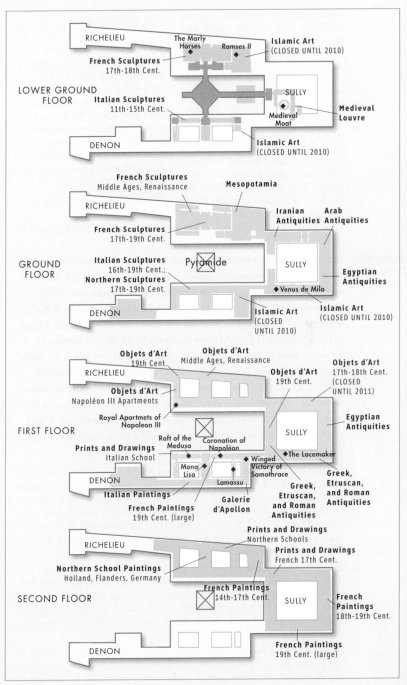

**LOWER GROUND FLOOR**

RICHELIEU

The Marly Horses ◆

**French Sculptures** 17th-18th Cent.

Ramses II ◆

**Islamic Art** (CLOSED UNTIL 2010)

**Italian Sculptures** 11th-15th Cent.

SULLY

Medieval Moat ◆

**Medieval Louvre**

DENON

**Islamic Art** (CLOSED UNTIL 2010)

**GROUND FLOOR**

**French Sculptures** Middle Ages, Renaissance

**Mesopotamia**

RICHELIEU

**French Sculptures** 17th-19th Cent.

**Iranian Antiquities**

**Arab Antiquities**

**Italian Sculptures** 16th-19th Cent.; **Northern Sculptures** 17th-19th Cent.

Pyramide

SULLY

◆ Venus de Milo

**Egyptian Antiquities**

DENON

**Islamic Art** (CLOSED UNTIL 2010)

**Islamic Art** (CLOSED UNTIL 2010)

**FIRST FLOOR**

**Objets d'Art** 19th Cent.

**Objets d'Art** Middle Ages, Renaissance

**Objets d'Art** 19th Cent.

**Objets d'Art** 17th-18th Cent. (CLOSED UNTIL 2011)

RICHELIEU

**Objets d'Art** Napoléon III Apartments ◆

Royal Apartmets of Napoleon III

**Egyptian Antiquities**

**Prints and Drawings** Italian School

Raft of the Medusa ◆

Coronation of Napoléon

SULLY

◆ The Lacemaker

Mona Lisa ◆

◆ Winged Victory of Samothrace

DENON

Lamassu ◆

**Greek, Etruscan, and Roman Antiquities**

**Italian Paintings**

**French Paintings** 19th Cent. (large)

Galerie d'Apollon

**Greek, Etruscan, and Roman Antiquities**

**SECOND FLOOR**

**Prints and Drawings** Northern Schools

**Prints and Drawings** French 17th Cent.

RICHELIEU

**Northern School Paintings** Holland, Flanders, Germany

**French Paintings** 14th-17th Cent.

SULLY

**French Paintings** 18th-19th Cent.

DENON

**French Paintings** 19th Cent. (large)

began. Initially planned as a Baroque building, it was later razed and begun anew by an architect who had the Roman Pantheon in mind. Interrupted by the Revolution, the site was razed yet again when Napoléon decided to make it into a Greek temple dedicated to the glory of his army. Those plans changed when the army was defeated and the emperor deposed. Other ideas for the building included making it into a train station, a market, and a library. Finally, Louis XVIII decided to make it a church, which it still is today. There are also concerts here. ⊠ *Pl. de la Madeleine, Faubourg* ⊕ *www.eglise-lamadeleine.com* ☉ *Daily 9–7* Ⓜ *Madeleine.*

> **DID YOU KNOW?**
>
> The Place de la Madeleine has what may be Paris's nicest public toilet. Opened in 1905, the Art Nouveau loo features colorful tiles and cubicle doors of stained glass and carved wood. There's an old shoe-shine chair and an attentive attendant. Look for the underground entrance on the corner near the flower market on Rue du Surène. Free. It's open 10–noon and 1–6:15.

**NEED A BREAK?**

Cheap eats in the Madeleine? Even most Parisians don't know it's possible, but there are two reasonable options in this posh *place*. One is in the basement of the Église: if you're standing in front of the steps to the church, walk to the right, turn the corner, and find a door to the Foyer de la Madeleine (⊠ *14 rue de Surène, Madeleine* ☎ *01–47–42–39–84*), where a team of friendly church ladies will serve you lunch for €9. There's a choice of two main courses, plus a simple starter and a dessert. The fare, if not fancy, is solid, and the wine is a great deal at €4 for a generous carafe. Served 11:45–2, it's best to come on the early side because the food is not made to order. The other option is to cross the *place* and scout out the Marché de la Madeleine (⊠ *Best entrance at 7 rue de Castellane, Madeleine*), a food court hidden inside an office building with half a dozen small restaurants. Try the inexpensive *pho*, Vietnamese soup, at La Tonkinoise.

**Église St-Germain-l'Auxerrois.** Across from the Louvre's Cour Carée, this church, founded in 500 AD, is one of the city's oldest. The current building dates from the 13th century, and the bell, from 1529, still tolls weekly masses. Actress Eva Longoria and NBA star Tony Parker were married here in 2007. In the courtyard there's a menagerie of creepy animals carved in stone. ⊠ *Rue St-Germain-l'Auxerrois, Louvre/Tuileries* ⊕ *www.saintgermainauxerrois.cef.fr* ☉ *Daily 8–7* Ⓜ *Louvre/Rivoli.*

**Louvre des Antiquaires.** As the many vacant shops attest, this three-level mall of antiques dealers opposite the Louvre has seen happier days. Still, it's a sort of minimuseum, with exquisite vintage jewelry and pretty bibelots, vying for space alongside vases by Art Deco master Lalique. ⊠ *Main entrance: 2 pl. du Palais-Royal, Louvre/Tuileries* ☉ *Tues.–Sun. 11–7* Ⓜ *Palais-Royal.*

**Musée du Jeu de Paume.** This 19th-century building at the entrance to the Jardin des Tuileries, on the Rue de Rivoli side, was once used for *jeu de paume* (or "palm game," a forerunner of tennis). It later served as a transfer point for art looted by the Germans in World War II. Today it's been given another lease on life as an ultramodern, white-walled showcase for temporary photography exhibits displaying icons such as Richard Avedon and Lee Miller as well as up-and-comers. ⊠ *1 pl. de la Concorde, Louvre/Tuileries* ☎ *01–47–03–12–50* ⊕ *www. jeudepaume.org* 🎫 *€7* ⊙ *Tues. noon–9, Wed.–Fri. noon–7, weekends 10–7* Ⓜ *Concorde.*

**Palais de l'Elysée.** Madame de Pompadour, Napoléon, Joséphine, the Duke of Wellington, and Queen Victoria all stayed at this palace, today the home of the French president. Originally built as a private mansion in 1718, it has housed presidents only since 1873. Unfortunately, you can only visit the building and its gardens during *Patrimony Days,* the third weekend in September; at all other times it's closed to the public. ⊠ *55 rue du Faubourg St-Honoré, Champs-Élysées* Ⓜ *Miromesnil.*

**Passage du Grand-Cerf.** This pretty glass-roofed *passage,* or arcade, was built in 1825 and expertly renovated in 1988. Today it's home to about 20 shops, many of them small designers selling original jewelry or house-wares. ⊠ *8 rue Dussoubs, Beaubourg/Les Halles* Ⓜ *Étienne Marcel.*

**NEED A BREAK?**

Founded in 1903 and patronized by literary lights like Marcel Proust and Gertrude Stein, Angélina (⊠ *226 rue de Rivoli, Louvre/Tuileries* ☎ *01–42–60–82–00*) is famous for its (€6.90) *chocolat l'Africain,* hot chocolate topped with whipped cream. The frescoes and mirrors are showing the tea-room's age, so finicky Proust might now reserve his affections for a *maca-ron* at Ladurée (⊠ *16 rue Royal* ☎ *01–42–60–21–79*), the elegant bakery and tea salon a short walk away.

**Pinacothèque de Paris.** It was considered folly when this privately funded museum, which has only temporary exhibitions, opened in 2003, as skeptics questioned whether Paris needed another art museum. The Pinacothèque has proved critics wrong, though, mounting well-regarded shows of Roy Lichtenstein and Jackson Pollack, and Old Masters such as Rembrandt and Vermeer. ⊠ *28 pl. de la Madeleine, Opéra* ☎ *01–42–68–02–01* ⊕ *www.pinacotheque.com* 🎫 *€10* ⊙ *Daily 10:30–6* Ⓜ *Madeleine.*

**OFF THE BEATEN PATH**

**Tour Jean Sans Peur.** This unimposing little tower is all that remains of a sprawling mansion on the edge of the city walls built in 1369 by Jean Sans Peur (John the Fearless), the Duke of Burgundy. He ordered the tower built in 1409 as an extension of the house—his bedroom was here—and then the defensive turret after he arranged the assassina-tion of the king's brother during the Hundred Years' War. The second-floor vaulted ceiling resembles a leafy tree, a masterwork of medieval architecture. Kids will enjoy the climb up to see the restored red velvet latrine, considered state-of-the-art in its time. Don't forget to pick up the brochure in English at the front desk. ⊠ *20 rue Étienne Marcel, Beaubourg/Les Halles* ☎ *01–40–26–20–28* ⊕ *www.tourjeansanspeur. com* 🎫 *€5* ⊙ *Nov.–Apr., Wed. and weekends 1:30–6; May–Sept., Wed.–Sun. 1:30–6* Ⓜ *Étienne Marcel.*

# Dining at a Glance

For full reviews ⇨ Chapter 17

**INEXPENSIVE DINING**
**Higuma,** *Japanese,* 32 and 32 bis, rue Ste-Anne

**La Bourse ou la Vie,** *Bistro,* 12 rue Vivienne

**La Ferme Opéra,** *Café,* 55–57 rue St-Roch

**Zen,** *Japanese,* 8 rue de l'Echelle

**MODERATE DINING**
**Au Gourmand,** *Bistro,* 17 rue Molière

**Au Pied de Cochon,** *Brasserie,* 6 rue Coquillière

**Café Marly,** *Café,* Cour Napoléon du Louvre, enter from Louvre courtyard, 93 rue de Rivoli

**Chez Georges,** *Bistro,* 1 rue du Mail

**L'Ardoise,** *Bistro,* 28 rue du Mont Thabor

**La Robe et le Palais,** *Wine Bar,* 13 rue des Lavandières-Ste-Opportuneen

**Le Grand Colbert,** *Brasserie,* 2–4 rue Vivienne

**Les Fines Gueules,** *Bistro,* 28 rue du Mont Thabor

**Macéo,** *Modern French,* 43 rue Crois des Petits Champs

**Pinxo,** *Modern French,* Hôtel Plaza Paris Vendôme, 4 rue du Mont Thabor

**Restaurant du Palais-Royal,** *Bistro,* Jardins du Palais-Royal, 110 Galerie Valois

**Willi's Wine Bar,** *Modern French,* 13 rue des Petits-Champs

**Yam'Tcha,** *French Fusion,* 4 rue Sauval

**EXPENSIVE DINING**
**Le Grand Véfour,** *Haute French,* 17 rue Beaujolais

# Les Grands Boulevards

**WORD OF MOUTH**

"The Paris Opera (Opéra Garnier) tour was well worth the price and the guide was fantastic."

—dolciani

# GETTING ORIENTED

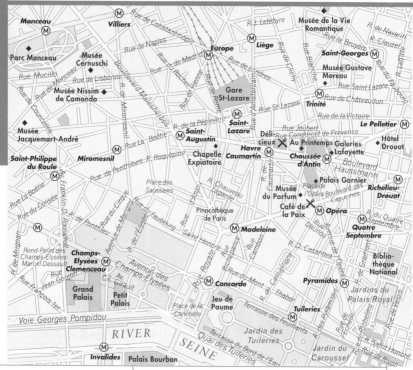

| GETTING HERE | TOP REASONS TO GO |
|---|---|
| *This neighborhood covers parts of the 2ᵉ, 3ᵉ, 8ᵉ, and 9ᵉ arrondissements.* Take the métro to the Opéra station, named for the elegant opera house. Just behind it, you can find the department stores Galeries Lafayette and Au Printemps, which each have three buildings (women's, men's, home), along Baron Haussmann's wide avenues known as the Grands Boulevards. If you're planning to visit the numerous small museums, take the métro to Parc Monceau. | **Les Grands Magasins.** Sample a new perfume under the magnificent dome at Galeries Lafayette, pick out a new outfit, wander the sumptuous food halls, or gaze at Parisian rooftops from the outdoor café at Au Printemps.<br><br>**Palais Garnier.** It may not be haunted by the Phantom, but this 19th-century opera house still dazzles. Enjoy a ballet or an opera, take the guided tour, or simply wander the opulent halls bedecked in marble and gold leaf.<br><br>**Musée Jacquemart-André.** Peruse the private collection of Italian Renaissance masterpieces and admire the elegant furnishings in one of the city's grandest mansions.<br><br>**Parc Monceau.** Join the well-dressed children of well-heeled Parisians and frolic on some of the prettiest lawns in the city.<br><br>**Les Passages.** Stroll the Passages Jouffroy and Verdeau and imagine what the original shopping malls were like 200 years ago. |

## MAKING THE MOST OF YOUR TIME

If you're a serious shopper, plan on a daylong visit to this neighborhood, beginning with the department stores near the Opéra métro stop. Nearly every French chain has a shop dotting the boulevard, which changes name several times (Boulevard Haussmann, des Capucines, Monceau, Temple, etc.) as it plods its way from west to east. If shopping isn't your bag, plan on a long afternoon's visit: tour the Palais Garnier or one or two museums, or bring a picnic lunch to lovely Parc Monceau on the western edge.

## BEST CAFÉS

Few cafés are as grand as the **Café de la Paix**. Once described as the "center of the civilized world," it was a meeting place for the glitterati of the Belle Époque. It's still an elegant place to enjoy a coffee or a late-afternoon apéritif overlooking the Palais Garnier. ⊠ *5 pl. de l'Opéra, Opéra/Grands Boulevards* ☎ *01-40-07-36-36* Ⓜ *Havre Caumartin, Opéra.*

Edgy and cool, Café de la Ville is a favorite with locals. Open until 2 AM, it's best for an evening aperitif and snack. A DJ spins tunes on weekend nights. ⊠ *34 bd. de Bonne Nouvelle* ☎ *01-48-24-48-09* Ⓜ *Poissonière.*

How about a view with your lunch? Perched on the top floor of Printemps Beauté/Maison store, Déli-Cieux serves cafeteria-style breakfast, lunch, and snacks. It's not too expensive, and the view from the outdoor terrace is priceless. It's open until 10 PM on Thursday. ⊠ *Corner of bd. Haussmann and Rue du Havre, 9th fl., Opéra/Grands Boulevards* ☎ *01-42-82-62-76* Ⓜ *Havre-Caumatin, Opéra.*

**6**

Sightseeing
★★★

Dining
★★★

Lodging
★★★★★

Shopping
★★★★★

Nightlife
★★★★★

In Belle Époque Paris, the Grand Boulevards were the place to see and be seen: in the cafés, at the opera, or in the ornate passages, the glass-covered arcades that were the world's first shopping malls. If you close your eyes, you can almost imagine the Grands Boulevards immortalized on canvas by the Impressionists: well-dressed Parisians strolling wide avenues dotted with shops, cafés, and horse-drawn carriages—all set against a backdrop of stately Haussmannian buildings. Today, despite the chain stores, sidewalk vendors, and fast-food joints, the Grands Boulevards remain the city's shopping epicenter, home to the most popular department stores, Galeries Lafayette and Au Printemps, near Place de l'Opéra at the heart of the long chain of avenues.

Camille Pissarro painted these streets in summer and winter but to modern-day shopaholics, the change in seasons signals something else entirely: the biannual sales (*soldes*). In early January, and again in late June, Paris writhes in a veritable frenzy of commerce that lasts four weeks, with markdowns increasing as the end of the period, regulated by the state, nears.

Shopping aside, the Grands Boulevards are a cultural destination anchored by the **Palais Garnier**, the magnificent opera house commissioned by Napoléon III. The neighborhood is also home to some of the city's best small museums, all former private collections housed in 19th-century *maisons particuliers* (or mansions) that alone are worth the trip. The exquisite **Musée Jacquemart-André** plays host to an impressive collection of Italian Renaissance art, while the jewel box **Musée Nissim de Camondo** remembers one family's tragic end. The **Musée Cernuschi** has an impressive collection of Asian art, and the **Musée Gustave Moreau** is a quirky tribute to the Symbolist master.

## TOP ATTRACTIONS

Updated by
Linda Hervieux

**Au Printemps.** More upscale than rival Galeries Lafayette, this vast department store, spread across three buildings, has been luring shoppers since 1865. Admire the Belle Époque green-and-gold dome now home to Brasserie Printemps on the sixth floor of the main store. The ninth-floor cafeteria-style restaurant at Printemps Beauté/Maison (the beauty and home store) has a large outdoor terrace with a great view. ✉ *64 bd. Haussmann, Opéra/Grands Boulevards* ☎ *01–42–82–57–87* ⊕ *www.printemps.com* ⏱ *Mon.–Wed., Fri., and Sat. 9:35–8, Thurs. 9:35* AM*–10* PM Ⓜ *Havre Caumartin, Opéra.*

> ### SUPER SHOPPING TIP
>
> Galeries Lafayette and Au Printemps each offer 10% off discount cards to foreign visitors. Some items, usually designer clothing and sale items, are excluded. To get one, go to the welcome desk on the main floor of either store. Remember to bring a passport or driver's license.

**Galeries Lafayette.** The stunning Byzantine glass *coupole*, or dome, is not to be missed—just wander to the center of the perfume and cosmetics department on the main floor and look up. Next door, the excellent Lafayette Gourmet food hall, on the second floor of the men's store, has one of the city's best selections of delicacies. Try the apricot-pistachio bread at Eric Kayser or a green tea éclair from Japanese-French baker Sadaharu Aoki. ✉ *40 bd. Haussmann, Opéra/Grands Boulevards* ☎ *01–42–82–34–56* ⊕ *www.galerieslafayette.com* ⏱ *Mon.–Wed., Fri., and Sat. 9:30–8, Thurs. 9:30–9* Ⓜ *Chaussée d'Antin, Opéra; RER: Auber.*

OFF THE
BEATEN
PATH

**Musée Gustave Moreau.** A visit to the town house and studio of painter Gustave Moreau (1826–98), a high priest of the Symbolist movement, is one of the most unique experiences in Paris. Moreau had always planned to have his home made into a museum after his death, so he created a light-flooded gallery on the two top floors to best show off his dark paintings. Some of the works appear unfinished, such as the *Unicorns*, inspired by the medieval tapestries in the Musée Cluny: Moreau refused to work on it further, spurning the wishes of a wealthy would-be patron. His interpretation of Biblical scenes and Greek mythology combine flights of fantasy with a keen use of color, shadow, and tracings influenced by Persian and Indian miniatures. The Symbolists loved objects, and Moreau was no different. His cramped private apartment on the first floor is jam-packed with bric-a-brac, and artworks cover every inch of the walls. From Galeries Lafayette (or the Chaussée D'Antin métro stop), follow Rue de la Chaussée d'Antin up to the Trinité church, turn right on Rue St-Lazare, and left on Rue de la Rochefoucauld. The museum is a block up on the right. ✉ *14 rue de la Rochefoucauld, Opéra/Grands Boulevards* ☎ *01–48–74–38–50* ⊕ *www.musee-moreau. fr* €5 ⏱ *Wed.–Mon. 10–12:45 and 2–5:15* Ⓜ *Trinité.*

Fodor'sChoice
★

**Musée Cernuschi.** Italian banker Enrico Cernuschi came to Paris for his Republican democratic ideals, only to be arrested during the 1871 Paris Commune; he subsequently decided to wait out the unrest by traveling the world—and collecting Asian art. On his return, he had a special

*Continued on page 115*

6

# C'EST *SUPER* CHIC:
## HOW NOT TO LOOK LIKE AN AMERICAN IN PARIS

It's hard to imagine a trip to Paris that doesn't include, at the very least, an afternoon of shopping. But the question is what to wear *while* you're shopping—and sightseeing, and eating at a café—since fashion will always reign supreme in the City of Light.

No matter where you live or what your style, from the moment you step off the plane you'll obsess over how to achieve the relaxed, elegant way Parisian women dress. You'll marvel at how they casually toss a scarf around their neck and have it look amazing, or how they can make a 15-year-old cashmere cardigan look fresh with a skinny belt. Suddenly, virtually all the clothes in your suitcase may feel outdated, frumpy, and wrong.

But fret not, *ma chère amie.* You're not destined to walk around Paris feeling less-than. We've given you a fail-safe guide that promises to keep you looking fabulous as you stroll down the Champs-Elysées or around the Marais. But we can't promise that once you hit the streets of this fashion-obsessed city, that your credit card won't max out faster than you can say *oh la la.*

## LA JEUNE FEMME

She's that young wisp of a thing standing on rue Oberkampf, chatting with her friends, cigarette in hand, looking as if she's had less than her eight hours—and whatever she has on, she wears it well.

Denim mini

Antoine & Lili

Vanessa Bruno tote

Repetto ballet flats

Converse high top

L'Autre Cafe, Oberkampf

**INSPIRATION:** Audrey Tautou

**BEST ACCESSORY:** The huge, costume cocktail ring you found at the bar last night.

**FAVORITE PARTS OF TOWN:** Canal St-Martin, Oberkampf, the Bastille.

**BIGGEST SPLURGE:** Are those 200 euro jeans from Colette really considered a splurge when you wear them every day?

**CHIC BOUTIQUE:** Thank goodness the designers have secondary lines! Now you'll only spend one paycheck at Antoine & Lili.

**CHAIN STORE KNOCKOFF:** Never underestimate the genius that is H&M.

**FAVORITE PICK—ME—UP:** A croque madame and side of *frites*.

**MODE OF TRANSPORT:** Get thee a boyfriend with a Vespa! Otherwise, it's the métro for you.

**WON'T LEAVE THE HOUSE WITHOUT:** Your trendy new cell phone.

**MUST-HAVE ITEM:** Nearly-destroyed high-top Converse. Hands down.

## LA DAME ELEGANTE

How's she so stunning at the Sunday market, children in tow, no make-up, hair up in a knot? Easy—she's meticulous about skincare, has in-laws with a house in the south, and is carrying the latest bag from Longchamps.

Cartier necklace

agnès b.

Longines watch

Lamarthe bag

Café L'Etoile Manquante

Cacharel perfume

**INSPIRATION:** Juliette Binoche

**BEST ACCESSORY:** The 400 euro cashmere Chanel sweater you just scored from that fabulous consignment shop on rue St-Honoré. It retailed for more than double the price!

**FAVORITE PARTS OF TOWN:** The Marais, Rive Gauche.

**BIGGEST SPLURGE:** It's hard to resist those new platform sandals from Dior.

**CHIC BOUTIQUE:** You can't get enough of Chloé, but you'll settle for anything from Vanessa Bruno.

**CHAIN STORE KNOCKOFF:** How is it that you ever survived without agnès b.?

**FAVORITE PICK—ME—UP:** Lentil and poached egg salad and sparkling water.

**MODE OF TRANSPORT:** You take the métro, but chances are you have an Audi that'll get you and the kids out of town.

**WON'T LEAVE THE HOUSE WITHOUT:** The scarf your grandmother bought you for Christmas.

**MUST-HAVE ITEM:** Every elegant woman needs a trench coat.

## LA GRANDE DAME

You can't miss her walking down the Champs-Elysées—she's still turning heads, with her Chanel suit, Hermès scarf, and her near-perfect posture. Something to aspire to...

Cartier earrings

Les Ambassadeurs, Place de la Concorde

Roger Vivier flats

Place Vendome Square

Cartier tank watch

**INSPIRATION:** Catherine Deneuve

**BEST ACCESSORY:** Your favorite companions: your two French poodles.

**FAVORITE PARTS OF TOWN:** The Faubourg St-Honoré and the Grand Boulevards to name a few...but definitely not the Rive Gauche.

**BIGGEST SPLURGE:** Does it really have to be just one? If so, a private jet will do.

**CHIC BOUTIQUE:** Only the standards—that's Chanel and Hermès, darling...

**CHAIN STORE KNOCKOFF:** What's a knockoff?

**FAVORITE PICK—ME—UP:** Foie gras or steak tartare...plus champagne.

**MODE OF TRANSPORT:** Having a driver is really the only way to get around with all those shopping bags.

**WON'T LEAVE THE HOUSE WITHOUT:** Your Chanel No. 5.

**MUST-HAVE ITEM:** A Kelly bag, of course!

IN FOCUS 6

C'EST SUPER CHIC: HOW NOT TO LOOK LIKE AN AMERICAN IN PARIS

## SCARF–TYING 101

**THE FRENCH KNOT**
Wrap around once so both ends are behind your neck; bring ends forward and tie double-knot to the side, under chin.

**THE NECK WRAP**
With a square scarf, make a triangle. Bring to neck with point facing downward; wrap long ends around back and bring forward; tie loose double-knot, just off-center.

**THE SQUARE KNOT**
Tie around neck with ends in front. Alternate wrapping ends up and through neck loop until they reach the back. Tie end tips and tuck in knot.

## DO'S & DON'TS OF DRESSING IN PARIS

■ When in doubt, DO wear black.

■ DON'T overdo jewelry. A minimalist look is better.

■ For those on the smaller side, DO go braless—they're decidedly optional.

■ DON'T get a french manicure (the French don't!). Your best bet is to keep nails short with clear polish.

■ DO wear your glasses if they're funky and colorful. Bonus for not having to schlep solution on the plane!

■ If you visit in summer, DON'T dress like you're going to camp.

■ DO bring a scarf or two. You'll look instantly chic with one wrapped loosely around your neck.

■ DON'T match your shoes to your bag—or spend time worrying about matching too much at all.

■ DO carry a backpack— but only if it's small, sleek, and doesn't say college student.

■ DO rock your best t-shirt and a pair of Chucks with just about anything—even a skirt!

# Paris's Covered Arcades

Before there were the *grands maga-sins,* there were the *passages couverts,* covered arcades that offered the early-19th-century Parisian shopper a little bit of heaven: a hodgepodge of shops under one roof, and a respite from the mud and grit of streets that did not have sidewalks. They would later be called the world's first shopping malls and for several decades, until the rise of the department stores in the latter part of the century, they would rule as the top places to wander, as well as shop. Technical and architectural wonders of the time, the vaulting iron and frosted glass structures inspired artists and writers such as Émile Zola.

Of the 150 arcades built around Paris in the early 1800s, only about a dozen are still in business today, if just barely, and mostly in the 2ᵉ and 9ᵉ arrondissements. Two arcades still going strong are the fabulously restored Galerie Vivienne (⊠ *4 rue Petits Champs, 2ᵉ*) and the Galerie Véro-Dodat (⊠ *19 rue Jean-Jacques Rousseau, 1ᵉʳ*), both lined with glamorous boutiques such as Jean-Paul Gaultier and shoe-maker-to-the-stars Christian Louboutin *(see Chapter 5: The Faubourg St-Honoré).*

Three other modest passages that still charm, though their looks have faded, can be found end-to-end off the Grands Boulevards, east of Place de l'Opéra. Begin with the most refined, the **Passage Jouffroy** (⊠ *10 bd. Montmartre, 9ᵉ*), which contains the Musée Grevin and a selection of shops and bistros, as well as the well-regarded budget Hotel Chopin at No. 46. Pop out at the northern end of Passage Jouffroy and cross the Rue de la Grange-Batelière into the **Passage Verdeau** (*9ᵉ*), where you can browse old glamour shots of Paris and New York at Photo Verdeau at No. 16, or pick up some antique candlesticks—or a cow skull—at the quirky red-walled Valence gallery at No. 22. On the southern end of the Passage Jouffroy, across Boulevard Montmartre, is the **Passage des Panoramas** (*2ᵉ*). The granddaddy of the arcades, built in 1800, it was the first public space in Paris equipped with gaslights in 1817. Though the vacant storefronts betray a sad modern history, the old-fashioned window displays of the few philatelist shops that remain offer a glimpse of what aristocratic life was like back when a weekend stroll through the passages was *de rigueur.*

mansion built on the edge of Parc Monceau to house his treasures, which include a two-story bronze Buddha from Japan. Cernuschi loved bronze, but he also had a stunning eye for everything from Neolithic pottery (3rd millennium BC) to funeral statuary, painted 8th-century silks, and contemporary paintings. ⊠ *7 av. Velasquez, Parc Monceau* 📞 *01-53-96-21-50* ⊕ *www.paris.fr/musees* 💳 *Free* ⊙ *Tues.–Sun. 10–6* Ⓜ *Monceau.*

**Fodor'sChoice** ★ **Musée Jacquemart-André.** Perhaps the city's best small museum, the opulent Musée Jacquemart-André is home to a vast collection of art and furnishings lovingly assembled in the late 19th century by banking heir Edouard André and his artist wife, Nélie Jacquemart. Their midlife marriage in 1881 raised eyebrows—he was a dashing bachelor and a Protestant, and she, no great beauty, hailed from a modest Catholic family. Still, theirs was a happy union fused by a common passion for art. For six months a year, the couple traveled, most often to Italy, where they cherry-picked works from the Renaissance, their preferred period. Their collection also includes French painters Fragonard, Jacques-Louis David, and François Boucher, and Dutch masters Van Dyke and Rembrandt. The mansion itself is a star attraction, sweeping the visitor back to the Belle Époque. The elegant ballroom, equipped with collapsible walls operated by state-of-the-art hydraulics, could

hold 1,000 guests. The winter garden was a wonder of its day, spilling into the *fumoir,* where the dashing André would share cigars with the *grands hommes* (important men) of the day. You can tour the separate bedrooms—his in dusty pink, hers in pale yellow. The former dining room, now an elegant café with an outdoor terrace, has one of the mansion's several stunning ceilings by Tiepolo. Don't forget the free audioguide in English. ■ TIP→ Plan on a Sunday visit and enjoy the popular brunch (€26) in the café from 11 to 3. Reservations are not accepted, so come early or later to avoid waiting in line. ✉ *158 bd. Haussmann, Parc Monceau* ☎ *01–45–62–11–59* ⊕ *www.musee-jacquemart-andre.com/* ⬚ *€10* ⊙ *Daily 10–6; Mon. until 9:30 during exhibitions* Ⓜ *St-Philippe-du-Roule, Miromesnil.*

**Fodor's**Choice
★ **Palais Garnier.** Haunt of the Phantom of the Opera and the real-life inspiration for Edgar Degas's dancer paintings, the opulent Palais Garnier, also called the Opéra Garnier, is one of two homes of the National Opera of Paris. The building was begun in 1860 by then-unknown architect Charles Garnier, who finished his masterwork 15 long years later, way over budget. Festooned with (real) gold leaf, colored marble, paintings, and sculpture from the top artists of the day, the opera house was about as subtle as Versailles and sparked controversy in post-Revolutionary France. The sweeping marble staircase, in particular, drew criticism from a public skeptical of its extravagance. But Garnier, determined to make a landmark that would last forever, spared no expense. The magnificent grand foyer, restored in 2004, is one of the most exquisite salons in France. In its heyday, the cream of Paris society strolled all 59 yards of the vast hall at intermission, admiring themselves in the towering mirrors. To see the opera house, buy a ticket for an unguided visit, which allows access to most parts of the building, though notably not the auditorium. There is also a small ballet museum with a few works by Degas and the tutu worn by prima ballerina Anna Pavlova when she danced her epic Dying Swan in 1905. To get to it, pass through the unfinished entrance built for Napoléon III and his carriage (construction was abruptly halted when the emperor abdicated in 1873). On the upper level of the opera house, you can also see a sample of the auditorium's

original classical ceiling, which was later replaced with a modern version by an eightysomething Mark Chagall. His trademark willowy figures encircling the dazzling crystal chandelier—today the world's third largest—shocked an unappreciative public upon its debut in 1964. Critics who fret that Chagall's masterpiece clashes with the fussy crimson-and-gilt decor can take some comfort in knowing that the original ceiling is preserved underneath, encased in a plastic dome.

The Palais Garnier plays host to the Paris Ballet as well as a few operas each season (most are performed at the Opéra Bastille). If you're planning to see a performance, reserve two months in advance, when tickets go on sale (€5–€172), though sometimes you can get lucky last minute at the box office. ■TIP→ To learn about the building's history, and get a taste of aristocratic life during the Second Empire, take the entertaining guided tour (€12) in English. The ticket also allows entry to the auditorium. ⊠ *Pl. de l'Opéra, Opéra/ Grands Boulevards* ☎ *08–92–89–90–90; 01–41–10–08–10 for tours* ⊕ *www.operadeparis.fr* 🎫 *€12 for guided visit; €8 for solo visit* ⊗ *Daily 10–5* Ⓜ *Opéra.*

> ### DID YOU KNOW?
>
> The inspiration for the mysterious lake underneath the Palais Garnier in *The Phantom of the Opera* occurred when construction of the building was delayed while the marshy site was drained. Rumors of an underground river began to circulate, and from there it was a small leap for Gaston Leroux to invent the Phantom sailing on an underground waterway. In the movie version, a vengeful Phantom sent the opera's chandelier crashing into the audience, an idea also inspired by real life: in 1896 one of the counterweights of the 8-ton crystal chandelier fell, crushing a woman in her red velvet seat.

☺ ★ **Parc Monceau.** This exquisitely landscaped park began in 1778 as the Duc de Chartres's private garden. Though some of the parkland was sold off under the Second Empire (creating the exclusive real estate that now borders the park), the refined atmosphere and some of the fanciful faux-ruins have survived. Immaculately dressed children play, watched by their nannies, while lovers picnic on the grassy lawns. In 1797 André Garnerin, the world's first-recorded parachutist, staged a landing in the park. The rotunda—known as the Chartres Pavilion—is surely the city's grandest public restroom; it started life as a tollhouse. ⊠ *Entrances on Bd. de Courcelles, Av. Velasquez, Av. Ruysdaël, Av. van Dyck, Parc Monceau* Ⓜ *Monceau.*

## WORTH NOTING

**Chapelle Expiatoire.** Built in 1815, this neoclassical temple marks the original burial site of Louis XVI and Marie-Antoinette. After the deposed monarchs took their turns at the guillotine on Place de la Concorde, their bodies were taken to a nearby mass grave. A loyalist marked their place, and their remains were eventually retrieved by the dead king's brother, Louis XVIII, who moved them to the Basilica of St. Denis. He then ordered the monument (which translates to Expiatory, or Atonement, Chapel) built on this spot, in what is now the leafy Square Louis XVI off Boulevard Haussmann. Two stone tablets are inscribed with the last missives of the doomed royals, including pleas to God to forgive their Revolutionary enemies. The subtle tribute is in sharp contrast to Napoléon's splashy memorial at Les Invalides. ⊠ *29 rue Pasquier, Opéra/Grands Boulevards* ☎ *01–44–32–18–00* 🖅 *€5* ⊙ *Thurs.–Sat. 1–5* Ⓜ *St-Augustin.*

**Hôtel Drouot.** Hidden away in a small antiques district not far from the opera house is Paris's central auction house, selling everything from bric-a-brac to old clothes to rare Chinese lacquered boxes to Renoirs. You can walk in off the street and browse through the open sales-rooms, which can be tons of fun depending on what's on the selling block. Mingle with a mix of art dealers, ladies who lunch, and art amateurs hoping to unearth an unidentified masterpiece. Anyone can attend the sales and viewings. ■ TIP➔ Don't miss the small galleries and antiques dealers in the Quartier Drouot, a warren of small streets around the auction house, notably on rues Rossini and de la Grange-Batelière. ⊠ *9 rue Drouot, Opéra/Grands Boulevards* ☎ *01–48–00–20–00* ⊕ *www. drouot.com* ⊙ *Viewings of merchandise Mon.–Sat. 11–6. Auctions begin at 2* Ⓜ *Richelieu Drouot.*

**NEED A BREAK?**

**Just steps from the Drouot auction house, J'go** (⊠ *4 rue Drouot, Grands Boulevards* ☎ *01–40–22–09–09*), one of two Paris outposts of the Toulouse wine bar and restaurant, is a perfect spot for an evening apéritif or a light dinner. The cozy bar serves an impressive menu of *grignotages* (tapas) from France's southwest, such as peppery foie gras on toast or Basque cheese with jam, either of which is nicely paired with a glass of *madiran,* a hearty red from the Pyrénées. The restaurant upstairs serves rib-sticking special-ties such as lamb stuffed with foie gras. The name is a play on the French "J'y vais," or "I go there."

**Musée Grévin.** If you like wax museums, this one founded in 1882 ranks with the best of them. Pay the steep entry price and begin by ascending a grand Phantom-of-the-Opera–like staircase that leads into the Palais des Mirages, a mirrored salon from the 1900 Paris Exposition that trans-forms into a hokey light-and-sound show the kids will love (it was a childhood favorite of designer Jean-Paul Gaultier). From there, get set for a cavalcade of nearly 300 statues, from Elvis to Ernest Hemingway, Picasso to NBA star (and Frenchman) Tony Parker. Every king of France is here, along with Michael Jackson and newcomer Barack Obama, plus scores of more-obscure French singers and celebrities. ⊠ *10 bd. Montmar-tre, Opéra/Grands Boulevards* ☎ *01–47–70–85–05* ⊕ *www.grevin.com* 🖅 *€20* ⊙ *Weekdays 10–6:30, weekends until 7* Ⓜ *Grands Boulevards.*

**Musée Nissim de Camondo.** The story of the Camondo family is steeped in tragedy, and it's all recorded within the walls of this superb museum. Patriarch Moïse de Camondo, born in Istanbul to a successful banking family, built this showpiece mansion in 1911 in the style of the Petit Trianon at Versailles, and stocked it with some of the most exquisite furniture, *boiseries* (wainscoting), and bibelots of the mid- to late 18th

# Spas for Paris Pampering

After a long day of shopping, nothing beats a retreat to a Parisian spa. They're easy to find, with one or two in the department stores and an *institut de beauté* on practically every corner. The French consider a *soin* (treatment) and a spell in a *hammam* (steam room) essential to ensuring *bien-être* (well-being), and Parisiennes have been waxing and plucking since Marie-Antoinette soaked in tubs of milk. Make like a local and treat yourself to an hour (or more) of pampering. Reserve about a month in advance, two months for a weekend appointment. Tax and service charges are included in the prices, but a tip (€5–€10) is customary for good service. These are some top-rated spas:

The Zen **Cinq Mondes** (✉ *6 sq. de l'Opera Louis Jouvet, 9e, Opéra/Grands Boulevards* ☎ *01–42–66–00–60* ⊕ *www.cinqmondes.com* Ⓜ *Opéra*), in the shadow of the opera house, offers a wide range of treatments starting at €49. The two-hour "reviving tropical ritual" includes a Japanese bath of flowers and essential oils, and a steam bath, followed by a scrub and a vigorous massage for €182.

**Spa Nuxe** (✉ *32 rue Montorgueil, 1er, Beaubourg/Les Halles* ☎ *01–55–80–71–40* ⊕ *www.nuxe.com* Ⓜ *Les Halles*) is a hip spa by the creators of Nuxe skin-care products. The ancient cellar with arched corridors has cozy treatment rooms. The specialty is the *rêve*

*de miel* (honey dream), a 1½-hour scrub, wrap, and massage for €145. There's a branch in Au Printemps.

**Harnn & Thann** (✉ *11 rue Molière, 1er, Opéra/Grands Boulevards* ☎ *01–40–15–02–20* ⊕ *www.harnn.fr* Ⓜ *Pyramides*) specializes in Thai treatments. If time is limited, try the "express Paris-Bangkok," a 30-minute all-body massage for €40.

At **La Bulle Kenzo** (✉ *1 rue du Pont Neuf, 1er, Louvre/Tuileries* ☎ *01–42–36–56–73* ⊕ *www.labullekenzo.com* Ⓜ *Pont-Neuf*) choose from a series of New Age-meets-space-age massages aimed at stimulating the senses by mixing textures, pressures, and temperatures in an ultra-cool setting in the Kenzo store. €110 for one hour.

At **Joïya** (✉ *6 rue de la Renaissance, 8e, Champs Elysées* ☎ *01–40–70–16–49* ⊕ *www.joiya.fr* Ⓜ *Alma Marceau, Franklin D. Roosevelt*) rejuvenate head-to-toe, literally, with the Russie Blanche (White Russia) treatment for €130.

**Nickel** (✉ *48 rue des Francs-Bourgeois, 4e, Le Marais* ☎ *01–42–77–41–10* ⊕ *www.nickel.fr* Ⓜ *St-Paul*) is the place for men. Specializing in men's products and body treatments, the spa offers a manicure-pedicure for €25, or try a "super clean corps" body scrub plus one-hour massage for €69.

6

century. Despite his vast wealth and purported charm, his wife left him five years after their marriage. Then his son, Nissim, was killed in World War I. Upon Moïse's death in 1935, the house and its contents were left to the state as a museum, and named for his lost son. A few years later, daughter Irène, her husband, and two children were murdered at Auschwitz. No heirs remained and the Camondo name died out. Today, the house remains an impeccable tribute to Moïse's life, from the gleaming salons to the refined private rooms, including the state-of-the-

## Dining at a Glance

For full reviews ⇨ Chapter 17.

**INEXPENSIVE DINING**
**Chartier**, *Bistro*, 7 rue du Faubourg-Montmartre

**Julien**, *Brasserie*, 16 rue du Faubourg St-Denis

**MODERATE DINING**
**Aux Lyonnais**, *Bistro*, 32 rue St-Marc

**Drouant**, *Modern French*, 16–18 pl. Gaillon

**Frenchie**, *Bistro*, 5 rue de Nil

**Le Vaudeville**, *Brasserie*, 29 rue Vivienne

**Racine**, *Wine Bar*, 8 passage des Panoramas

**EXPENSIVE DINING**
**Senderens**, *Haute French*, 9 pl. de la Madeleine

art kitchen. You can even see the condolence letter written by Marcel Proust, a family friend, after Nissim's death. There are background materials and an excellent free audioguide in English. ⊠ *63 rue de Monceau, Parc Monceau* ☎ *01–53–89–06–50* ⊕ *www.lesartsdecoratifs.fr* 🎟 *€6, €10.50 joint ticket with Musée des Arts Décoratifs* ⊙ *Wed.–Sun. 10–5:30* Ⓜ *Villiers.*

**Musée de la Vie Romantique.** A visit to the charming Museum of the Romantic Life, dedicated to novelist George Sand (1804–76), will transport you to the countryside. In a pretty 1830s mansion at the end of a tree-lined courtyard, the small permanent collection includes drawings by Delacroix and Ingrès, among others, though Sand is the star. There are glass cases stuffed with her jewelry and snuff boxes, and even a mold of the hand of composer Frederic Chopin, one of her many lovers. The museum, about a five-minute walk from the Musée Gustave Moreau, is in the picturesque neighborhood once called New Athens, a reflection of the architectural tastes of the writers and artists who lived there. There is usually an interesting temporary exhibit. ■TIP→ The garden café is a nice place to have lunch or afternoon tea; it's open from Easter to late October. ⊠ *16 rue Chaptal, Opéra/Grands Boulevards* ☎ *01–55–31–95–67* ⊕ *www.vie-romantique.paris.fr* 🎟 *Free (€7 temporary exhibits)* ⊙ *Tues.–Sun. 10–6* Ⓜ *Blanche, Pigalle, St-Georges.*

**Musée du Parfum.** More of a showroom than a museum, the small exhibit run by *parfumier* Fragonard above its boutique on Rue Scribe is heavy on decorative objects associated with perfume, including crystal bottles, gloves, and assorted bibelots. The shop is a good place to find gifts to take home, like the €12 honey body lotion, myriad soaps, and, of course, perfume. ⊠ *9 rue Scribe, Opéra* ☎ *01–47–42–04–56* ⊕ *www.fragonard.com* 🎟 *Free* ⊙ *Mon.–Sat. 9–6, Sun. 9–5* Ⓜ *Opéra.*

# Montmartre

**WORD OF MOUTH**

"[One of my favorite free things to do was] climbing to the top of the hill to Sacré Coeur on a cold winter morning and watching the sunrise. I loved the quiet peacefulness of the sleepy city just waking up. Plus, no (or very small) crowds."

—lmf

# GETTING ORIENTED

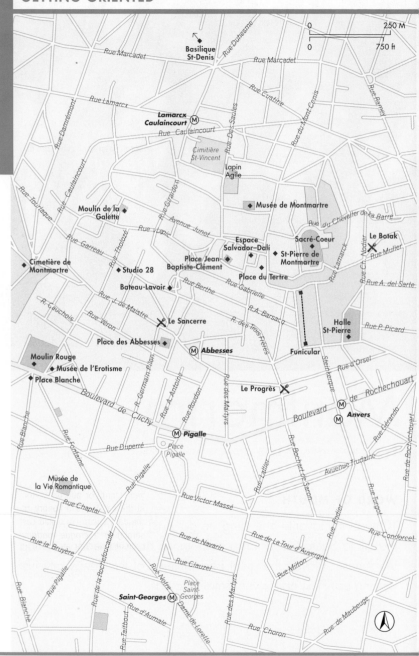

Rue Marcadet

Basilique
St-Denis

Rue Duhesme

Rue Marcadet

Rue Custine

Rue Ramey

Rue Lamarcx

Rue du Mont-Cenis

Lamarcx
Caulaincourt Ⓜ

Rue  Caulaincourt

Rue  Des  Saules

Cimitière
St-Vincent

Lapin
Agile

Rue Dammemont

Rue Caulaincourt

♦ Musée de Montmartre

Rue du Chevalier de la Barre

Rue Tourlaque

Rue  Caulaincourt

Moulin de la ♦
Galette

Avenue Junot

Rue VLoric

Espace
Salvador–Dalí ♦

Sacré-Coeur
♦

Le Botak
♦

Rue Ch. Nodier

Rue Mutler

Rue  Garreau

Rue  d'Tholozé

Rue des Grandes

Place Jean- ♦
Baptiste-Clément

♦ St-Pierre de
Montmartre

Rue Lamarck

Rue A. del Sarte

Cimetière de ♦
Montmartre

♦ Studio 28

Place du Tertre

Bateau-Lavoir ♦

Rue Berthe

Rue Gabrielle

R.A. Barsacq

R. Gauchois

R.-J. de Maistre

✕ Le Sancerre

R. des Trois-Frères

Halle
St-Pierre ♦

Rue P. Picard

Rue Véran

Place des Abbesses ♦

Ⓜ *Abbesses*

Moulin Rouge
♦

♦ Musée de l'Erotisme

♦ Place Blanche

Boulevard  de  Clichy

R.-Germain-pilon

Rue-A.-Antoine

Rue Poulbot

Rue des Martyrs

Funicular

Stenkerque

Rue d'Orsel

de  Rochechouart

R. Blanche

Rue Fontaine

Le Progrès ✕

Boulevard

Rue Géranda

Ⓜ
Ⓜ  *Anvers*

Ⓜ *Pigalle*

Rue Duperré

Place
Pigalle

Rue Pigalle

Rue Lallier

Rue Bochart de Saron

Rue de Rochechouart

Musée de
la Vie Romantique

Rue Chaptal

Avenue Trudaine

Rue Turgot

Rue la Bruyère

Rue Victor Massé

Rue Pigalle

Rue de Navarin

Rue de La Tour d'Auvergne

Rue Milton

Rue Rodier

Rue Conforcet

Rue Blanche

Rue Pigalle

Rue de la Rochefoucauld

Rue Clauzel

Saint-Georges Ⓜ

Rue Notre  Dame-de-Lorette

Place
Saint-
Georges

Rue Taitbout

Rue d'Aumale

Rue des Martyrs

Rue Choron

Rue de Maubeuge

| 0 | | 250 M |
|---|---|---|
| 0 | | 750 ft |

## TOP REASONS TO GO

**Sacré-Coeur.** The best view of Paris is worth the climb—or the funicular ride—especially at twilight when the city lights spread out in a magnificent panorama below the hill of Montmartre.

**Place des Abbesses.** Capturing the classic Montmartre village feel, this square is a perfect starting point for a walking tour of the tiny streets that spread out from here in all directions.

**Carré Roland Dorgelès.** One of Paris's best photo ops can be snapped from this tiny square that overlooks the historic Montmartre vineyard, and the famous pink-and-green cabaret Lapin Agile.

**Bateau-Lavoir.** The evolution of modern art owes much to this modest building where Cubism was born.

## MAKING THE MOST OF YOUR TIME

Devote a day to this neighborhood if you want to see more than the obligatory Sacré-Coeur basilica. If possible, avoid weekends when the narrow—and extremely hilly—streets are jam-packed. Start your visit at the métro station Abbesses and from here, explore the cobbled streets and staircases that make up the "real" Montmartre. If you're pressed for time, follow the signs from Abbesses to the funicular and take it straight up to Sacré-Coeur.

## GETTING HERE

*Montmartre is in the 18ᵉ arrondissement.* Take Line 2 to Anvers métro station, and then take the funicular (costs one métro ticket) up to Sacré-Coeur. Or, take Line 12 to Abbesses station and take your time wandering up to the basilica. For a scenic tour for the cost of a métro ticket, hop the public bus, Monmartrobus, near métro station Jules-Joffrin (Line 12): the bus winds through the hilly streets of Montmartre, with a convenient stop at Sacré-Coeur.

## BEST CAFÉS

**Le Botak.** On the eastern side of Sacré-Coeur, at the bottom of the stairs, you'll find the leafy Square Louise Marie and this café, which serves a small, ever-changing menu of French home cooking like *saumon au pistou* (salmon in pesto) and *poulet botak,* roasted chicken with garlic and mashed potatoes (about €18 for two courses). Or come for a late-afternoon apéritif. ⊠ *1 rue Paul Albert, Montmartre* ☎ *01–46–06–98–30* Ⓜ *Anvers.*

**Le Progrès.** This picturesque corner café draws a quirky mix, from retirees sipping espresso at the counter to hipsters, artists, and discriminating tourists. The food is good, with classics like steak tartare and roasted lamb (€13.60 for two courses). If you're craving the tastes of home, the excellent cheeseburger (€14) comes with a heap of crispy fries. ⊠ *7 rue Trois Frères, Montmartre* ☎ *01–42–64–07–37* Ⓜ *Abbesses.*

**Le Sancerre.** There's a cool vibe at this café-bar near the Abbesses métro stop. Enjoy a coffee or a happy-hour cocktail on the terrace (well-heated year-round) or pull up a stool at the bar. If you're hungry, try the daily *cocotte* (a baked casserole) or a *croque madame* (grilled ham and cheese with a fried egg, salad on the side). ⊠ *35 rue des Abbesses, Montmartre* ☎ *01–42–58–08–20* Ⓜ *Abbesses.*

7

Sightseeing
★★★★

Dining
★★★

Lodging
★★

Shopping
★★★

Nightlife
★

Montmartre has become almost too charming for its own good. Yes, it feels like a village (if you can see through the crowds); yes, there are working artists here (though far fewer than there used to be); and yes, the best view of Paris is yours for free from the top of the hill (if there's no haze). That's why on any weekend day, year-round, you can find hordes of visitors crowding these cobbled alleys, scaling the staircases that pass for streets, and queuing to see Sacré-Coeur, the "sculpted cloud," at the summit.

If you're lucky enough to have a little corner of Montmartre to yourself, you'll understand why locals love it so. Come on a weekday, or in the morning or later in the evening. Stroll around **Place des Abbesses,** where the rustic houses and narrow streets escaped the heavy hand of urban planner Baron Haussmann. Until 1860, the area was in fact a separate village, dotted with windmills. Today, there are only two windmills left as well as one quaint vineyard (unfortunately, the vineyard is not open to visitors).

Always a draw for bohemians and artists, many of whom had studios at **Bateau-Lavoir** and **Musée de Montmartre,** resident painters have included Géricault, Renoir, Suzanne Valadon and her son Maurice Utrillo, Picasso, van Gogh, and of course Henri Toulouse-Lautrec, whose iconic paintings of the cancan dancers at the **Moulin Rouge** are now souvenir-shop fixtures from **Place du Tertre** to the Eiffel Tower. You can still see shows at the Moulin Rouge and the pocket-size cabaret **Lapin Agile** (*see the Nightlife chapter*), though much of the entertainment here is on the seedier side—the area around Pigalle is the city's largest red-light district. The *quartier* is a favorite of filmmakers, and visitors still seek out Café des Deux Moulins (15 rue Lepic), the real-life café where Audrey Tautou worked in 2001's *Amélie.* Movie biz roots run deep here—the blockbuster *Moulin Rouge* took its inspiration from here. In 1928, **Studio 28** opened as the world's first cinema for experimental films.

**DID YOU KNOW?**

Like many of the "streets" in Montmartre, the Rue du Calvaire, off the Place du Terte, is actually a staircase rather than a traditional thoroughfare.

## TOP ATTRACTIONS

Updated by
Linda Hervieux

**Bateau-Lavoir** *(Wash-barge)*. The birthplace of Cubism isn't open to the public, but a display in the front window details this unimposing building's rich history. Montmartre poet Max Jacob coined the name for the original building here, which reminded him of the laundry boats that used to float in the Seine, and he joked that the warren of paint-splattered artists' studios needed a good hosing down (wishful thinking, since the building had only one water tap). It was in the original Bateau-Lavoir that, early in the 20th century, Pablo Picasso, Georges Braque, and Juan Gris made their first bold stabs at Cubism, and Picasso painted the groundbreaking *Les Demoiselles d'Avignon* here in 1906–07. The experimental works of the artists weren't met with open arms, even in liberal Montmartre. Writer Roland Dorgèles, in a teasing protest, once tied a loaded paintbrush to the tail of a donkey belonging to the Lapin Agile cabaret and sold the resulting work for 400 francs. All but the facade was rebuilt after a fire in 1970. Like the original building, the Bateau houses artists and their studios. ⊠ *13 pl. Émile-Goudeau, Montmartre* Ⓜ *Abbesses.*

**Halle St-Pierre.** This elegant iron-and-glass 19th-century market hall at the foot of Sacré-Coeur stages dynamic exhibitions of *art brut* (raw art), or outsider and folk art. The artists featured are contemporary and out of the mainstream. There are usually one or two shows on at any time. There's also a good bookstore and a café serving light food such as savory tarts, salads, and desserts. ⊠ *2 rue Ronsard, Montmartre* ☎ *01–42–58–72–89* ⊕ *www.hallesaintpierre.org* ⊠ *Museum €7.50* ⊙ *Daily 10–6. Closed weekends in Aug.* Ⓜ *Anvers.*

**Moulin de la Galette.** Of the 14 windmills (*moulins*) that used to sit atop this hill, only two remain. Known collectively as Moulin de la Galette—the name comes from the fact that the owners once sold rye bread—the more storied is known as Le Blute-fin: it's on a leafy hillock across from 88 rue Lepic. In the late 1800s there was a dance hall on the site, famously painted by Renoir (you can see the painting in the Musée d'Orsay). Unfortunately, the windmill is on private land and can't be visited. Just down the street is the other moulin, Le Radet, perched atop a well-regarded restaurant (called Le Moulin de la Galette) at 83 rue Lepic. ⊠ *Le Blute-fin, corner of Rue Lepic and Rue Tholozé, Montmartre* Ⓜ *Abbesses.*

**Place des Abbesses.** This triangular square is typical of the countrified style that has made Montmartre famous. Now a hub for shopping and people-watching, the *place* is surrounded by hip boutiques, sidewalk cafés, and shabby-chic restaurants—a prime habitat for the young, neobohemian crowd and a sprinkling of expats. Trendy streets like Rue Houdon and Rue des Martyrs have attracted small designers and some shops are open on Sunday afternoons. The entrance to the Abbesses métro station, designed by the great Hector Guimard as a curving, sensuous mass of delicate iron, is one of only two original Art Nouveau métro canopies left in Paris. Ⓜ *Abbesses.*

**Fodor's** Choice
★

**Sacré-Coeur.** *See the highlighted listing in this chapter.*

# A Scenic Walk in Montmartre

One of the prettiest walks in Paris begins at the Lamarck-Caulaincourt (Line 12) métro station. Climb the stairs, cross Rue Caulaincourt and look for a second set of stairs at Rue Girardon. At the top is Place Dalida, with a voluptuous bust of the beloved French torch singer (1933–87). The stone house on the right is the 18th-century Château des Brouillards (Castle of the Mist). Turn down the romantic alley of the same name, where the painter Renoir used to live in a small house. Then, from Place Dalida, head down the winding Rue Abreuvoir, one of the most-photographed streets in Paris, which leads past the Maison Rose (famously painted by resident artist Maurice Utrillo). Turn left on Rue des Saules where you can find Paris's only vineyard across from the cabaret **Lapin Agile**, famously committed to canvas by Picasso and still going strong today. The vineyard produces 125 gallons of Clos Montmartre wine per year (which is aged in the *mairie,* or "town hall," of the 18ᵉ arrondissement and sold for charity)—it's hardly *grand cru,* but the harvest celebration and parade in early October is great fun.

Backtrack up Rue des Saules and turn left on Rue Cortot, where you can find the **Musée de Montmartre**. Composer Eric Satie, who played piano at the Chat Noir nightclub, lived a few doors down at No. 6, in a closet-apartment 6 feet by 4 feet (with a 9-foot ceiling and skylight). Turn right onto Rue Mont Cenis to the **Place du Tertre**, a lovely square now nearly ruined by hordes of artists peddling cheap wares and busloads of tourists crowding the mediocre cafés. Easily overlooked is the understated **St-Pierre de Montmartre**, one of the city's oldest churches. End your walk at **Sacré-Coeur** basilica, a white confection with Byzantine-style domes.

## WORTH NOTING

**Basilique de St-Denis.** Built between 1136 and 1286, the St-Denis basilica is perhaps the most important Gothic church in the Paris region. It was here, under dynamic prelate Abbé Suger, that Gothic architecture (typified by pointed arches and rib vaults) was said to have made its first appearance. The kings of France soon chose St-Denis as their final resting place, and their richly sculpted tombs—along with what remains of Suger's church—can be seen in the choir area at the east end of the church. The basilica was battered during the Revolution; afterward, Louis XVIII reestablished it as the royal burial site by moving the remains of Louis XVI and Marie-Antoinette here to join centuries' worth of monarchial bones. The vast 13th-century nave is a brilliant example of structural logic; its columns, capitals, and vault are a model of architectural harmony. The facade, retaining the rounded arches of the Romanesque that preceded the Gothic style, is set off by a small rose window, reputedly the earliest in France. You can also check out the extensive archaeological finds, such as a Merovingian queen's grave goods; there's information in English. ⊠ *1 rue de la Légion d'Honneur, St-Denis* ☎ *01-48-09-83-54* 🎫 *Choir and tombs €7* ☉ *Apr.–Sept., Mon.–Sat. 10–6:15, Sun. noon–6:15; Oct.–Mar., Mon.–Sat. 10–5,*

# SACRÉ-COEUR

✉ *Pl. du Parvis-du-Sacré-Coeur, Montmartre* ☎ *01–53–41–89–00* ◷ *Basilica daily 6 am–11 pm; dome and crypt Oct.–Mar., daily 9–6; Apr.–Sept., daily 9–7* 💳 *Free; dome €5* ⊕ *www.sacre-coeur-montmartre.com* Ⓜ *Anvers, plus funicular.*

TIPS

■ The best time to visit Sacré-Coeur is early morning or early evening, and preferably not on a Sunday, when the crowds are thick. If you're coming to worship, there are daily masses.

■ Photographers angling for the perfect shot of the church should aim for a clear blue-sky day or come at dusk, when the pink sky plays nicely with the lights of the basilica.

■ The funicular, recommended for those short on time and energy, costs one métro ticket each way.

It's hard to not feel as though you're climbing up to heaven when you visit Sacré-Coeur, the white castle in the sky, perched atop Montmartre. The French government built this church in 1873 as a symbol of the return of self-confidence after the devastating years of the Commune and Franco-Prussian War. It was designed by architect Paul Abadie, using elements from Romanesque and Byzantine architectural styles—a mélange many critics dismissed as gaudy. Construction lasted until World War I, and the church was consecrated in 1919.

**HIGHLIGHTS**

Many people come to Sacré-Coeur to admire the superlative view from the top of the 271-foot-high dome, the second-highest point in Paris after the Eiffel Tower. If you opt to skip the climb up the spiral staircase, the view from the front steps is still well worth the trip.

Don't miss spending some time inside the basilica gazing at the massive golden mosaic set high above the choir. Created in 1922 by Luc-Olivier Merson, *Christ in Majesty* depicts Christ with a golden heart and outstretched arms, surrounded by various figures, including the Virgin Mary and Joan of Arc. It remains one of the largest mosaics of its kind and is meant to represent France's devotion to the Sacred Heart. There are also the seemingly endless vaulted arches in the basilica's crypt, the portico's bronze doors—decorated with biblical scenes, including the Last Supper—and the stained-glass windows, which were installed in 1922, destroyed by a bombing during World War II (there were miraculously no deaths), and later rebuilt in 1946. In the basilica's 262 foot-high campanile hangs La Savoyarde, one of the world's heaviest bells, weighing about 19 tons.

7

*Sun. noon–5:15. Guided tours in English by reservation ⊕ saint-denis. monuments-nationaux.fr* Ⓜ *St-Denis Basilique.*

**Cimetière de Montmartre.** Overshadowed by better-known Père-Lachaise, this cemetery is just as picturesque. It's the final resting place of a host of luminaries, including painters Degas and Fragonard; Adolphe Sax, inventor of the saxophone; dancer Vaslav Nijinsky; composers Hector Berlioz and Jacques Offenbach. The Art Nouveau tomb of novelist Émile Zola (1840–1902) lords over a lawn near the entrance—though Zola's remains were removed to the Panthéon in 1908. ⊠ *20 av. Rachel, Montmartre* ⊗ *Mar. 16–Nov. 5, weekdays 8–6, Sat. 8:30–6, Sun. 9–6; Nov. 6–Mar. 15, weekdays 8–5:30, Sat. 8:30–5:30, Sun. 9–5:30* Ⓜ *Blanche.*

**Espace Salvador-Dalí** *(Dalí Center).* One of several museums dedicated to the Surrealist master, the collection in this black-walled exhibition space includes about 300 works, mostly etchings and lithographs (some for sale). The two dozen sculptures include several versions of Dalí's melting bronze clock and variations on the Venus de Milo. A multimedia pioneer ahead of his time, there are videos with Dalí's voice, and temporary exhibits have included the mustached man's foray into holograms. There's plenty of information in English, including an audioguide. ⊠ *11 rue Poulbot, Montmartre* ☎ *01–42–64–40–10* ⊠ *€10* ⊕ *www.daliparis. com* ⊗ *Daily 10–6* Ⓜ *Abbesses.*

**OFF THE BEATEN PATH**

**Le 104.** This exciting new art space, called Le Cent Quatre, is worth the trek to the 19e arrondissement for fans of offbeat art-in-the-making. Opened in fall 2008 on the former site of the city morgue, this three-story complex is a work in progress, with various components, such as a restaurant, library, and children's area set to open throughout 2009 under one cavernous glass roof. The final outcome is uncertain, but certain to change. Sound mysterious? That's the idea. Artists compete for one of seven ateliers (studio spaces), which they can occupy for up to a year. What they create—there are no limits—is on view throughout the process; the ateliers take turns opening throughout the day to give you a peek. There are many other things going on, including exhibitions, performances, concerts, and lectures. If you come at night, be aware of your surroundings; the 10-minute walk from the Stalingrad métro station can be a bit dodgy. ■ TIP→ Check the schedule on the Web site before you go. The best times are weekend afternoons or weekdays between 4 and 6 PM. ⊠ *104 rue d'Aubervilliers or 5 rue Curial, Stalingrad* ☎ *01–53–35–50–01* ⊕ *www.104.fr* ⊠ *Free entry and atelier visits; some events require a ticket, prices vary* ⊗ *Tues.–Thurs. 11–9, Fri. and Sat. 11–11, Sun. 11–9* Ⓜ *Stalingrad.*

**Moulin Rouge.** When the world-famous cabaret opened in 1889, aristocrats, professionals, and the working classes all flocked to see the scandalous performers. The cancan was considerably more kinky in Toulouse-Lautrec's day—girls used to kick off their knickers—than it is today. *(See the Nightlife section.)* There's not much to see from the outside, but a decent gift shop around the corner (11 rue Lepic) sells official merchandise, from jewelry to sculpture, by reputable French makers. ⊠ *82 bd. de Clichy, Montmartre* ☎ *01–53–09–82–82* ⊕ *www. moulin-rouge.fr* Ⓜ *Blanche.*

**Musée de l'Érotisme.** What better place for the Museum of Erotic Art than smack in the heart of the city's red-light district? Though the subject matter is a bit limited, the collection is a respectable mix of world art, such as carvings from Africa, Indonesia, and Peru; Chinese ivories; and Japanese prints. There are racy cartoons by Robert Crumb and photographs of Pigalle prostitutes and bordellos, some quite chic, from the 1930s and '40s. Three floors are dedicated to temporary exhibitions by contemporary artists and photographers. There's a "forbidden film" section of old-time pornography and scenes cut from films from the 1950s, '60s, and '70s (it's mostly a tease to get you to buy the DVD that's available for sale in the gift shop). ⊠ *72 bd. de Clichy, Montmartre* ☎ *01–42–58–28–73* ⊠ *€8* ☉ *Daily 10 AM–2 AM* Ⓜ *Blanche.*

**Musée de Montmartre.** In its turn-of-the-20th-century heyday, the building—now home to Montmartre's historical museum—was a studio block for painters, writers, and cabaret artists. Foremost among them was Renoir—he painted the *Moulin de la Galette,* an archetypal scene of sun-drenched revelers, while he lived here—and Maurice Utrillo, Montmartre painter par excellence. The museum recaps the area's history; the strong points are the many Toulouse-Lautrec posters and original Eric Satie scores. Temporary exhibitions focus on local art and history, and famous residents like Jean Marais, the late, dashing actor who dabbled in painting and sculpture. Check out the view from the second floor of the tiny vineyard—the only one in Paris—on Rue des Saules. There's some basic info available in English. ⊠ *12 rue Cortot, Montmartre* ☎ *01–49–25–89–37* ⊕ *www.museedemontmartre.fr* ⊠ *€8* ☉ *Wed.–Sun. 11–6* Ⓜ *Lamarck Caulaincourt.*

**Place Blanche.** Today this boulevard is crammed with tourist buses and sex shops, but the side streets are worth exploring for their cafés, nightclubs, boutiques, and antiques shops. The name—White Square—comes from the clouds of chalky dust that used to be churned up by carts carrying plaster of Paris down from quarries. Crushed wheat and flour from the nearby windmills added to the powdery atmosphere. The Boulevard de Clichy, which intersects the square, was virtually an artists' highway at the turn of the 20th century; Degas lived and died at No. 6, Picasso lived at No. 11, and art supply stores and dealers lined the street. Ⓜ *Blanche.*

**Place du Tertre.** This once-charming square now generally teems with crowds of tourists and hordes of street artists clamoring to do your portrait. The ubiquitous souvenir shops were once home to artists who for decades called this tumbling square (*tertre* means "hillock") home. For an easy descent from the top of the hill, walk to the back of the square and find Rue du Calvaire, which is actually a picturesque staircase. Ⓜ *Abbesses.*

> ## PICASSO LIVED HERE
>
> Picasso lived at three different addresses in Montmartre: on Rue Gabrielle when he first arrived; at Bateau-Lavoir; and at No. 11 boulevard de Clichy. The area is virtually littered with "Picasso Lived Here" plaques.

**Place Jean-Baptiste-Clément.** Clément, a singer, was "Mayor of Montmartre" during the heady 70 days of the 1871 Commune, when this area actually seceded from Paris. Painter Amedeo Modigliani (1884–1920) had a studio here at No. 7, and Picasso lived around the corner at 49 rue Gabrielle. Look for the octagonal tower at the north end of the square; it's all that's left of Montmartre's first water tower, built around 1840 to boost the area's feeble water supply. ■ TIP➔ On weekends, the tower plays host to tastings of the local wine. Recognized more for its kitsch factor than for its quality, Clos du Montmartre (red or white) will run you €60 a bottle; most of the profits go to charity. A tasting will set you back only €5 (glass included). ⊠ *Pl. Jean-Baptiste-Clément, Montmartre* Ⓜ *Abbesses.*

**St-Pierre de Montmartre.** Tucked in the shadow of mighty Sacré-Coeur is one of the oldest churches in Paris. Built in the 12th century as part of a substantial Benedictine monastery, this small church has undergone numerous renovations; thus the 18th-century facade built under Louis XIV clashes with the mostly medieval interior, decorated with impressive 20th-century stained-glass windows. ⊠ *Off Pl. du Tertre, Montmartre* Ⓜ *Anvers.*

**Studio 28.** This little movie house has a distinguished history: when it opened in 1928, it was the first theater in the world purposely built for *art et essai,* or experimental film. Through the years artists and writers flocked here to see the "seventh art" creations by directors such as Jean Cocteau, Luis Bruñel, François Truffaut, and Orson Welles. Today it's a repertory cinema, showing first-runs, just-runs, and previews, usually in their original language. There's a cute bar and café in the back that opens at 3 PM each day. ⊠ *10 rue Tholozé, Montmartre* ☎ *01–46–06–36–07* ⊕ *www.cinemastudio28.com* Ⓜ *Abbesses.*

# Le Marais

**WORD OF MOUTH**

"There are frequently very entertaining street performers in the plaza outside the Pompidou Center. Also, next to the Pompidou Center is the colorful and whimsical Stravinsky fountain."

—Nikki

# GETTING ORIENTED

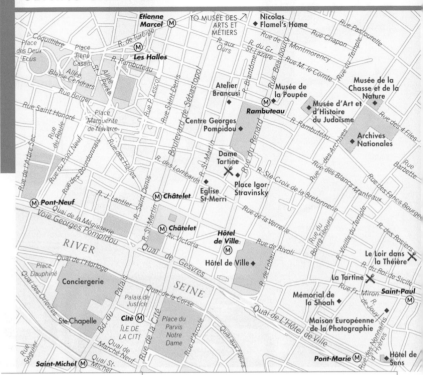

TO MUSÉE DES
ARTS ET
MÉTIERS

## GETTING HERE

*Le Marais includes the 3ᵉ and 4ᵉ arrondissements.* It's a pleasant walk from the Beaubourg—the area around Centre Pompidou—into Le Marais. Rue Rambuteau turns into Rue de Francs Bourgeois, which runs right past the Place des Vosges. If you're going by métro and plan to wander around the streets of Le Marais, the closest stop is St-Paul on the 1 line. If you're going to the Pompidou, take the 11 line to Rambuteau. For the Musée Picasso, the closest stop is St-Sébastien Froissart on the 8 line. For the 3ᵉ arrondissement, get off at Arts et Métiers on the 3 or 11 line.

## TOP REASONS TO GO

**Centre Pompidou.** This striking building is the city's leading modern art museum; it also presents films, theater, and dance performances.

**Place des Vosges.** Paris's prettiest square surrounds a manicured park whose inviting patches of grass are—unusual for Paris—accessible to those needing a siesta.

**Musée Picasso.** This is a must-stop for fans of the master, but note that it's closed through February 2012 for renovations.

**Jewish history tour.** The historic Jewish quarter has two world-class sites: Mémorial de la Shoah (the Holocaust Memorial) and the Musée d'Art et d'Histoire du Judaïsme, with fascinating artwork and cultural artifacts.

**No reason at all.** Lose yourself in this neighborhood. Explore the tiny streets near the Centre Pompidou, grab a falafel sandwich on the Rue des Rosiers, or people-watch in a café on the Rue Vieille du Temple.

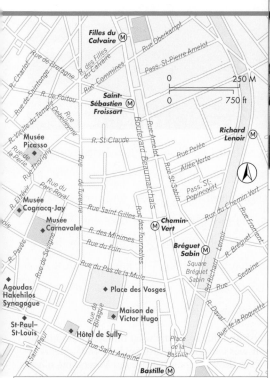

## MAKING THE MOST OF YOUR TIME

Le Marais has something for everyone and how much time you spend here depends on how much time you have in Paris. One day seems painfully short, but it would afford you a walking tour. Leave at least two days if your itinerary includes the Centre Pompidou and the Musée Picasso. In three days, you could cover some of the smaller museums, well worth the time as many of them are housed in exquisite mansions. If time permits, wander to the 3$^e$ arrondissement to see the charming streets, away from the crowds, or visit the science-centric Musée des Arts et Métiers. Leave time to peek into private courtyards, and picnic in the Place des Vosges. Sunday afternoon is a lively time to come when many shops, notably on the Rue Francs-Bourgeois, open for a few hours. Nightlife is tops as well with an incomparable café and bar scene, particularly those aimed at the gay community.

## BEST CAFÉS

**Dame Tartine.** There are many cafés around the Centre Pompidou, but this one overlooking the Stravinsky fountain, with its colorful sculptures, is a good choice. You won't go wrong with a homemade quiche, salad, or a classic *cassoulet*. ⊠ *2 rue Brisemiche, Le Marais* ☎ *01–42–77–32–22* Ⓜ *Rambuteau.*

**La Tartine.** This calm café on busy Rue de Rivoli is a local favorite with an impressive wine list. Try the €8 French onion soup or a hearty *tartine* (toasted bread) topped with ham, cheese, paté, or dry sausage. ⊠ *24 rue de Rivoli, Le Marais* ☎ *01–42–72–76–85* Ⓜ *St-Paul.*

**Le Loir dans la Théière.** Sink into one of the comfortable shabby armchairs at this popular tearoom, whose name translates to the Dormouse in the Teapot (from Alice in Wonderland). The sweet and savory tarts are stellar, but the real stars are desserts like the decadent chocolate crumble tart. ⊠ *3 rue des Rosiers, Le Marais* ☎ *01–42–72–90–61* Ⓜ *St-Paul.*

**8**

**Sightseeing**
★★★★★
**Dining**
★★★★
**Lodging**
★★★★
**Shopping**
★★★★★
**Nightlife**
★★★★

From swampy to swanky, Le Marais has a fascinating history that continues to evolve. Like an aging pop star, the *quartier* has remade itself many times, and today retains several identities: the city's epicenter of cool with hip boutiques, designer hotels, and art galleries galore; the hub of Paris's gay community; and, though fading, the nucleus of Jewish life. You could easily spend your entire visit to Paris in this neighborhood, there is that much to do.

"Marais" means marsh and that is exactly what this area was until the 12th century when it was converted to farmland. In 1605, Henri IV began building the Place Royale (today's Place des Vosges, the oldest square in Paris), which touched off a building boom, and the wealthy and fabulous moved in. Despite the odors—the area was one of the city's smelliest—it remained the chic quarter until Louis XIV moved his court to Versailles, trailed by dispirited aristocrats unhappy to decamp to the country. Merchants moved into their exquisite *hôtels particuliers* (private mansions), which are some of the city's best surviving examples of Baroque architecture. Here you can see the hodgepodge of narrow streets that so vexed Louis Napoléon and his sidekick, Baron Haussmann, who feared a redux of the famous *barricades* that revolutionaries threw up to thwart the monarchy. Haussmann leveled scores of blocks like these, creating the wide arrow-straight avenues that are a hallmark of modern Paris. Miraculously, the Marais escaped destruction, though much of it fell victim to neglect and ruin. Thanks to restoration efforts over the past half century, the district is enjoying its latest era of greatness and the apartments here—among the city's oldest—are also the most in demand, with *beaucoup* charm, exposed beams, and steep crooked staircases barely wide enough to fit a supermodel. (Should you be lucky enough to find an elevator, don't expect it to fit your suitcase.) Notice the impressive *portes cochères*, the huge doors built to accommodate aristocratic carriages that today open into many sublime courtyards and hidden gardens.

The 4*e* arrondissement, the Marais's glitzier half, is sandwiched between two opposite poles—the regal **Place des Vosges** in the east and the eye-teasing modern masterpiece **Centre Pompidou** in the west. Between these points you'll find most of the main sites, including the **Musée Picasso**, the **Maison Européenne de la Photographie,** and the **Musée Carnavalet,** which is the best place to see how the city evolved through the ages. To tour an exquisitely restored 17th-century hôtel particulier, visit the excellent **Musée Cognacq-Jay** (like the Carnavalet, admission is free) or wander into the manicured back garden of the magnificent **Hôtel de Sully.** To the north, the quieter 3*e* arrondissement is a lovely neighborhood to explore. Techies will appreciate a stop at the **Musée des Arts and Métiers,** Europe's oldest science museum.

**FREE IN LE MARAIS**

The **Maison Européenne de la Photographie** is free on Wednesday after 5; the **Mémorial de la Shoah** and the **Maison de Victor Hugo** are always free, as are the extensive permanent collections of the **Musée Carnavalet** and the **Musée Cognacq-Jay**. The Atelier Brancusi, a small exhibition space at the **Centre Pompidou**, is always free while the museum itself, along with the **Musée Picasso** and the Musée de la Chasse et de la Nature, is free the first Sunday of the month (like all national museums). The **Église St-Merri** has free, weekend classical music concerts.

Paris's **Jewish quarter** has existed here in some form since the 13th century and still thrives around the Rue des Rosiers, even as hip boutiques encroach on the traditional bakeries, delis, and falafel shops. Not far away is the beating heart of the gay Marais, radiating out from Rue Vieille du Temple, along the Rue St-Croix de la Bretonnerie to Rue du Temple, where you can find trendy cafés and shops, and cool nightspots aimed at gays and welcoming to all.

The 3*e* arrondissement half of Le Marais, north of Rue des 4-Fils, has evolved into one of the most interesting areas to explore. Here you can find art galleries, trendy boutiques, many by small designers, and funky cafés and bars off the tourist track. This is one of Paris's most in-demand areas to live, and finding an apartment to rent—most of them small walk-ups—is a rarity. Wander up Rue de Bretagne, the main drag, with its newly widened sidewalks, and stop for lunch at the Marché des Enfants Rouges (No. 39)—the oldest covered market in Paris (open Tuesday through Sunday). Pop into one of the art galleries occupying former industrial spaces and mansions around the Rue Charlot. Across the street is the 19th-century iron-and-glass Le Carreau du Temple, a former clothes market slated to open in 2012 as a performing arts and sports center. This is the site of the former Templar Tower, where Louis XIV and Marie Antoinette were imprisoned before their date with the guillotine (Napoléon later razed it).

## TOP ATTRACTIONS

**Fodor's** Choice ★ **Centre Pompidou**

*See highlighted listing in this chapter.*

Updated by
Linda Hervieux

**Église St-Merry.** This impressive Gothic church, in the shadow of the Centre Pompidou, was completed in 1550 and has a turret containing the oldest bell in Paris (cast in 1331) and an 18th-century pulpit supported on carved palm trees. There are free concerts Saturday at 8 PM and Sunday at 4 PM. ⊠ *76 rue de la Verrerie, Beaubourg/Les Halles* ☎ *01–42–71–93–93* ⊕ *www.accueilmusical.com* Ⓜ *Hôtel de Ville.*

**Hôtel de Sully.** This early Baroque gem, built in 1624, is one of the city's loveliest hôtels particuliers; among the back courtyard's sculpted rows of hedges you can find a door that opens into the Place des Vosges. Like much of the area, it fell into ruin until the 1950s, when it was rescued by the administration of French historic monuments, **Caisse Nationale des Monuments Historiques,** which has its headquarters here. This is also one of two homes of the Jeu de Paume (the other is in the Tuileries), which stages regular photography exhibitions. Near the entrance on the Rue de Rivoli, the bookstore, which stocks many unusual guides on Paris (some in English), is worth a stop to admire the 17th-century ceiling of painted beams. The recently renovated private apartment of the Duchess de Sully—four rooms furnished with period pieces—is open for visits by reservation, for a small charge. ⊠ *62 rue St-Antoine, Le Marais* ☎ *01–44–61–20–00 Hotel de Sully; 01–42–74–47–75 Jeu de Paume* ☽ *Tues.–Sun. 10–7 Hotel de Sully, Tues.–Fri. noon–7, weekends 10–7 Jeu de Paume* Ⓜ *St-Paul.*

**Hôtel de Ville.** Overlooking the Seine, City Hall is the residence and offices of the popular Mayor Bertrand Delanoë. The building, rebuilt after an attack by rioting crowds in 1873, is one of the city's most stunning, made all the more dramatic by elaborate nighttime lighting. There are frequent free photography exhibits celebrating famous photographers like Doisneau or notable subjects like Grace Kelly—to find the entrance, look for the lines on the Rue de Rivoli. Occasionally the building opens its reception halls for public events and the grand public square in front of the building often plays host to temporary exhibits. In August there's a beach volleyball court here; in winter it's an open-air ice rink with inexpensive skate rental. ⊠ *Pl. de l'Hôtel-de-Ville, Le Marais* Ⓜ *Hôtel de Ville.*

★ **Maison Européenne de la Photographie** *(European Photography Center).* Much of the credit for photography's current perch in the city's cultural scene can be given to MEP (whose director, Jean-Luc Monterosso, also founded Paris's hugely successful Mois de la Photographie festival held in November in even-numbered years). This terrific center hosts up to four well-curated exhibitions every three months, featuring the work of photographers from around the world. A show on American superstar Annie Leibovitz could overlap with a retrospective of Irish photography in the 19th century. Programs and guided tours are available in English. ⊠ *5 rue de Fourcy, Le Marais* ☎ *01–44–78–75–00* ⊕ *www.mep-fr.org* ☑ *€6.50, free Wed. after 5 PM* ☽ *Wed.–Sun. 11–8* Ⓜ *St-Paul.*

**Maison de Victor Hugo.** France's most famous scribe lived in the northeast corner of Place des Vosges between 1832 and 1848. The house's first floor is dedicated to temporary exhibits that often have modern ties to Hugo's work. In Hugo's apartment on the second floor, you can see the tall desk, next to the short bed, where he began writing his master-work *Les Misérables* (as always, standing up). There are manuscripts and early editions of that famous work on display, as well as others such as *The Hunchback of Notre Dame.* You can see illustrations of Hugo's writings by other artists, including Bayard's rendition of the impish Cosette holding her giant broom (which has graced countless *Les Miz* T-shirts). The collection includes many of Hugo's own, some-times macabre, ink drawings (he was a fine artist) and furniture from several of his homes. Particularly impressive is the room of carved and painted Chinese-style wooden panels that Hugo designed for the house of his mistress, Juliet Drouet, on the island of Guernsey, during the writer's exile there. Try to spot the intertwined Vs and Js. (Hint: Look for the angel's trumpet in the left corner.) ✉ *6 pl. des Vosges, Le Marais* ☎ *01–42–72–10–16* ⊕ *www.musee-hugo.paris.fr* ⊉ *Free; temporary exhibitions, €7* ☉ *Tues.–Sun. 10–6* Ⓜ *St-Paul.*

**Mémorial de la Shoah** *(Memorial to the Holocaust).* The first installation of this stunning memorial and museum is the deeply moving Wall of Names, tall plinths honoring the 76,000 French Jews deported from France to the Nazi concentration camps; only 2,500 survived. Opened in 2005, the center has an archive on the victims, a library, and a gal-lery hosting temporary exhibitions. The permanent collection includes riveting artifacts and photographs from the camps, along with video testimony from survivors. The children's memorial is particularly poi-gnant and not for the faint of heart—scores of back-lighted photographs show the faces of many of the 11,000 murdered French children. The crypt, a giant black marble Star of David, contains ashes recovered from the camps and the Warsaw ghetto. You can see the orderly drawers containing small files on Jews kept by the French police. (France only officially acknowledged the Vichy government's role in 1995.) The his-tory of anti-Semitic persecution in the world is revisited as well as the rebounding state of Jewry today. There is a free guided tour in English the second Sunday of every month at 3 PM. ✉ *17 rue Geoffroy-l'Asnier, Le Marais* ☎ *01–42–77–44–72* ⊕ *www.memorialdelashoah.org* ⊉ *Free* ☉ *Sun.–Wed. 10–6, Thurs. 10–10, Fri. 10–6* Ⓜ *Pont Marie.*

Fodor'sChoice ★ **Musée Carnavalet.** If it has to do with Paris history, it's here. This collec-tion is a fascinating hodgepodge of Parisian artifacts and art, from the prehistoric canoes used by Parisii tribes to the furniture of the cork-lined bedroom where Marcel Proust labored over his evocative novels. You can get a great feel for the evolvement of the city through the ages thanks to scores of paintings. The museum fills two adjacent mansions, the Hôtel Le Peletier de St-Fargeau and the Hôtel Carnavalet. The latter is a Renaissance jewel that in the mid-1600s became the home of writer Madame de Sévigné. The long-lived Sévigné wrote hundreds of frank and funny letters to her daughter, giving an incomparable view of both public and private life during the time of Louis XIV. The museum offers a glimpse into her world, but the collection covers far more than just the 17th century. The exhibits on the Revolution are especially inter-esting, with scale models of guillotines, a replica of the Bastille prison carved from one of its stones, even a cast-iron stove in the shape of the Bastille. There is an amazing assortment of reconstructed interiors from

8

# CENTRE POMPIDOU

✉ *Pl. Georges-Pompidou, Beaubourg/Les Halles* Ⓜ *Rambuteau* ☎ *01–44–78–12–33* ⊕ *www.centrepompidou.fr* 🎫 *€12 May–Aug.; €10 Sept.–Apr.; €8–€9 temporary exhibits* ⊗ *Wed.–Mon. 11–9, temporary exhibitions 11–10, Atelier Brancusi 2–6.*

## TIPS

■ The Pompidou's permanent collection takes up a relatively small amount of the space when you consider this massive building's other features: temporary exhibition galleries, with a special wing for design and architecture; a highly regarded free reference library (there's often a queue of university students on Rue Renard waiting to get in); and the basement, which includes two cinemas, a theater, a dance space, and a small, free exhibition space.

■ On your way up the escalator, you'll have spectacular views of Paris, ranging from the Tour Montparnasse, to the left, around to the hilltop Sacré-Coeur on the right.

■ The trendy rooftop restaurant, Georges (P01–44–78–47–99), is a romantic spot for dinner. Be sure to reserve a table near the window.

■ There are public toilets in the basement that don't have the long lines of those on the ground floor.

Love it or hate it, the Pompidou is certainly the city's most unique-looking building. Most Parisians have warmed to the industrial, Lego-like exterior that caused a scandal when it opened in 1977. Named after French president Georges Pompidou (1911–74), it was designed by then-unknowns Renzo Piano and Richard Rogers. The architects' claim to fame was putting the building's guts on the outside and color-coding them: water pipes are green, air ducts are blue, electrics are yellow, and things like elevators and escalators are red. Art from the 20th century to the present day is what you can find inside. ■TIP➡ If you want to sound like a Parisian, ask directions to "Beaubourg" (pronounced Boh-boorh), which is what the locals call the Pompidou, using the old name of the plaza.

### HIGHLIGHTS

The **Musée National d'Art Moderne** (*Modern Art Museum*, entrance on Level 4) occupies the top two levels. Level 5 is devoted to modern art, 1905–60 including major works by Matisse, Modigliani, Marcel Duchamp, and Picasso; Level 4 is dedicated to contemporary art from the '60s on, including video installations. Outside, next to the museum's sloping plaza—where throngs of teenagers hang out (and there's free Wi-Fi)—is the **Atelier Brancusi** (*Brancusi Studio*). This small, airy museum contains four rooms reconstituting Brancusi's Montparnasse studios with works from all periods of his career. On the opposite side, in the **Place Igor-Stravinsky,** is the Stravinsky fountain, which has 16 gyrating mechanical figures in primary colors, including a giant pair of ruby red lips. On the opposite side of Rue Rambuteau, on the wall at the corner of Rue Clairvaux and Passage Brantôme, is the appealingly bizarre mechanical brass-and-steel clock, **Le Défenseur de Temps.**

alcove with a doorway. Here used to sit an elegant fountain, built in 1710, that was the source of this neighborhood's drinking water. Try to make out the nearly invisible Latin inscription in gold lettering thanking the prince de Soubise for donating the land. ⊠ *60 rue des Francs-Bourgeois, Le Marais* ☎ *01–40–27–60–96* ⊕ *www.archivesnationales.culture. gouv.fr* 🎫 *Free; €3 temporary exhibitions* ⊘ *Mon. and Wed.–Fri. 10–12:20 and 2–5:30, weekends 2–5:30* Ⓜ *Rambuteau.*

**Hôtel de Sens.** Though much-restored, this small medieval castle still shows its Gothic lines. Built for the Archbishop of Sens in 1475, the building developed a decidedly more secular side while Henri IV's first wife lived here after her marriage was annulled. Marguerite—aka La Reine Margot—was renowned for her lovers (she supposedly collected locks of their hair to make wigs for herself) and launched the style for heavy powdering to conceal her terrible smallpox scars. She named this street after the fig tree she had cut down, as it was inconveniencing her carriages. (Notice the fig tree defiantly planted in the lovely back garden, which is worth a visit alone.) Today the building houses occasional exhibits and a fine-arts library, the **Bibliothèque Forney.** ⊠ *1 rue du Figuier, Le Marais* ☎ *01–42–78–14–60* 🎫 *Exhibitions €3* ⊘ *Tues.–Sat. 1–7* Ⓜ *Pont Marie.*

**8**

☺ **Musée de la Chasse et de la Nature.** Mark this down as one of Paris's most bizarre—and fascinating—collections. The museum, which opened in 2007 in the gorgeous 17th-century Hôtel de Guénégaud, features lavishly appointed rooms stocked with hunt-theme art, antique weaponry, and taxidermy animals. In a tribute to Art Nouveau, the decor includes chandeliers curled like antlers and matching railings. Older kids will appreciate the jaw-dropping Trophy Room with an impressive menagerie of beasts, not to mention the huge polar bear stationed outside. There is a lovely multimedia exhibit on the myth of the unicorn; as well as an interactive display of bird calls. Temporary exhibits and silent auctions take place on the first floor. It's worth a quick visit for the elegant rooms alone. ⊠ *62 rue des Archives, Le Marais* ☎ *01–53–01–92–40* ⊕ *www.chassenature.org* 🎫 *€6* ⊘ *Weekdays 11–6* Ⓜ *Rambuteau.*

**Musée Cognacq-Jay.** One of the loveliest museums in Paris, this 16th-century rococo-style mansion contains an outstanding collection of mostly 18th-century artwork in its *boiserie* (intricately carved wood paneling) rooms. A tour through these rooms allows a rare glimpse into how wealthy 19th-century Parisians lived. Ernest Cognacq, founder of the (now closed) department store La Samaritaine, and his wife, Louise Jay, amassed furniture, porcelain, and paintings—notably by Fragonard, Watteau, François Boucher, and Tiepolo—to create one of the world's finest private collections of this period. Some of the best displays are also the smallest, like the tiny enamel portraits showcased on the third floor, or, up in the attic, the glass cases filled with exquisite inlaid snuff boxes, sewing cases, pocket watches, perfume bottles, and cigar cutters. There are no exhibit descriptions in English, but pamphlets and museum guides are sold in English. ⊠ *8 rue Elzévir, Le Marais* ☏ *01–40–27–07–21* ⊕ *www.cognacq-jay.paris.fr* ⊠ *Free for permanent collection, €5 for exhibits* ⊙ *Tues.–Sun. 10–6* Ⓜ *St-Paul.*

☺ **Musée de la Poupée** (*Doll Museum*). This charming museum is home to an impressive collection of dolls from antique Bisque-head models to Barbies. Arranged in glass cases with sometimes elaborate clothing and accessories, the dolls offer a window in the playtime habits of children through the ages. There are detailed explanations in English. Don't miss the well-preserved *mignonettes* (19th-century porcelain-faced miniatures) or their elegant wicker *trousseaux* of clothes. Read the story about two of their owners, little French sisters Charlotte and Suzanne, who each received one for her 11th birthday. Too vast to display at one time, the collection changes regularly. There's usually a temporary exhibition, as well as frequent programs for kids (in French only), a gift shop, and doll hospital. ■TIP→ If you're hungry, stop by the inviting Le Hangar restaurant right next door. This neighborhood favorite serves up Lyonnaise and other classic French specialties, such as sautéed foie gras with creamy mashed potatoes. ⊠ *Impasse Berthaud, Le Marais* ☏ *01–42–72–73–11* ⊕ *www.museedelapoupeeparis.com* ⊠ *€8* ⊙ *Tues.–Sun. 10–6* Ⓜ *Rambuteau or Hôtel de Ville.*

OFF THE
BEATEN
PATH

**Nicolas Flamel's Home.** Built in 1407 and reputed to be the oldest house in Paris, this abode has a mystical history. Harry Potter fans should take note: This was the real-life home of Nicolas Flamel, the alchemist whose sorcerer's stone is the source of immortality in the popular book series, really existed. A wealthy scribe, merchant, and dabbler in the mystical arts, Flamel willed his home to the city as a dormitory for the poor, on the condition that boarders pray daily for his soul. Today, the building, undergoing much-needed renovations, is home to apartments and a restaurant. ⊠ *51 rue Montmorency, Le Marais* Ⓜ *Rambuteau.*

**St-Paul–St-Louis.** The leading Baroque church in Le Marais, its dome rising 180 feet above the crossing, was begun in 1627 by the Jesuits, who modeled it after their Gesù church in Rome. Dark and brooding, the church contains Delacroix's *Christ on the Mount of Olives* in the transept and a shell-shaped holy water font at the entrance, which was donated by Victor Hugo, who lived in nearby Place des Vosges. Hugo's beloved daughter, Léopoldine, was married here in 1843—though only to meet a tragic end nine months later, when she fell into the Seine and drowned, along with her husband Charles, who tried to save her. ■TIP→ Compare the church's soot-stained exterior with the squeaky clean Hôtel de Sully (No. 62) to see what Paris's buildings would look like without regular cleanings. ⊠ *99 rue St-Antoine, Le Marais* Ⓜ *St-Paul.*

# PLACE DES VOSGES

✉ *Off Rue des Francs Bour-*
*geois, near Rue de Turenne*
Ⓜ *Bastille or St-Paul* 🎟 *Free*
🕓 *Open year-round.*

### TIPS

■ Unlike so many parks in Paris, one of the best things about the Place des Vosges is that you're allowed to sit—or snooze or snack—on the grass.

■ There is no better spot in Le Marais for a picnic. Drop by the street market on nearby Boulevard Richard Lenoir on Thursday and Saturday mornings to pick up lunch fixings. (It's on bd. Richard Lenoir between rues Amelot and St-Sabin.)

■ The most likely approach to the Place des Vosges is from Rue des Francs Bourgeois, the main shopping street. However, for a grander entrance walk along Rue St-Antoine until you get to Rue de Birague, which leads directly into the square.

The oldest square in Paris and—dare we say it?—the most beautiful, the Place des Vosges is one of Europe's oldest stabs at urban planning. The precise proportions offer a placid symmetry, but things weren't always so calm. Four centuries ago this was the site of the Palais des Tournelles, home to King Henri II and Queen Catherine de' Medici. The couple staged regular jousting tournaments, and during one of them, in 1559, Henry was fatally lanced in the eye. Catherine fled for the Louvre, abandoning her palace and ordering it destroyed. Years later Henry IV commissioned the Place Royal, opened in 1612. Napoléon renamed it Place des Vosges to honor the French regional *départment* Vosges, the first in the country to cough up taxes for the Revolutionary government.

### HIGHLIGHTS

At the base of the 36 redbrick-and-stone houses—nine on each side of the square—is an arcaded, covered walkway lined with art galleries, shops, and cafés. There's also an elementary school, a synagogue (whose barrel roof was designed by Gustav Eiffel), and several chic hotels. The formal, gated garden's perimeter is lined with chestnut trees; inside are a children's play area and a fountain.

Aside from hanging out in the park, people come here to see the house of the man who once lived at No. 6—Victor Hugo, the author of *Les Misérables* and *Notre-Dame de Paris (The Hunchback of Notre-Dame)*.

**8**

# Dining at a Glance

For full reviews ⇨ Chapter 17

**INEXPENSIVE DINING**

**Au Bourguignon du Marais**, *Bistro*, 52 rue François-Miron

**Breizh Café**, *French*, 109 rue Vieille du Temple

**Cantine Merci**, *Café*, 111 blvd. Beaumarchais

**Chez Marianne**, *Middle Eastern*, 2 rue des Hospitalières-St-Gervais

**L'As du Falafel**, *Israeli*, 34 rue des Rosiers

**MODERATE DINING**

**Bu Bar**, *Wine Bar*, 3 rue des Tournelles

**Chez Julien**, *Bistro*, 1 rue du Pont Louis-Philippe

**Cru**, *Modern French*, 7 rue Charlemagne

**Derrière**, *Bistro*, 69 rue de Gravilliers

**L'Ambassade d'Auvergne**, *Bistro*, 22 rue du Grenier St-Lazare

**Le Georges**, *Modern French*, Centre Pompidou, 6th fl.

**Le Rouge Gorge**, *Bistro*, 12 rue Pecquay

**Restaurant le Gaigne**, *Wine Bar*, 8 rue St-Paul

**EXPENSIVE DINING**

**Benoît**, *Bistro*, 20 rue St-Martin

**Le Dôme du Marais**, *Bistro*, 53 bis, rue des Francs-Bourgeois

**Le Murano**, *Modern French*, 13 bd. du Temple

# Canal St-Martin, Bastille, and Oberkampf

**WORD OF MOUTH**

"Friday morning we headed to the Paris Canal boats near the Musée d'Orsay for a Canal Saint-Martin cruise. We all REALLY enjoyed this cruise and I highly recommend it. Then we strolled around the Parc de la Villette."

—K2DangerGirl

# GETTING ORIENTED

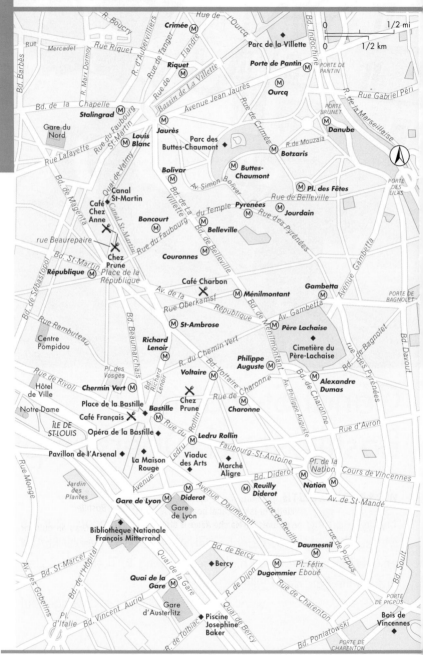

## TOP REASONS TO GO

**Canal St-Martin.** The scenic canal has evolved into one of the city's top hangouts—it's great for strolling and galleries, shops, and cafés abound.

**Place de la Bastille.** The flashpoint of the French Revolution still draws modern-day agitators and their frequent noisy demonstrations. It's also a nightlife destination for all ages and home to the Opéra Bastille.

**Cimetière du Père Lachaise.** The final address of dozens of celebrities, from Chopin to Oscar Wilde to Jim Morrison, whose elaborate tombs are laid out along twisting, tree-shaded paths.

**Parc de la Villette.** Home to the city's well-regarded science museum and planetarium, this is a good place to take the kids, or grown-up science buffs.

**Viaduc des Arts/Promenade Plantée.** An abandoned rail line serves as the setting for this lovely garden and 2.7-mi walkway perched atop the **Viaduc des Arts,** a collection of artisan shops focused on design.

## MAKING THE MOST OF YOUR TIME

The Canal St-Martin is one of the city's most popular destinations, particularly on Sunday afternoon, when the streets are closed to cars. Have lunch in one of the cafés, grab a Velib' rental bike *(see "Bicycling in Paris" Close-Up, Chapter 3)* and head to Parc de la Villette, or take a canal boat tour. A Sunday morning stop at the picturesque Marché Aligre is also recommended; even if you're not buying. The heaps of fresh produce and colorful flowers hawked by excited vendors are worth seeing. On any day the Place de la Bastille is a lively place to stop for drinks or lunch; if time is limited, reserve this neighborhood for after dark, when the streets around Place de la Bastille and Oberkampf really come to life.

## GETTING HERE

*Canal St-Martin, Bastille, and Oberkampf include the 10e, 11e, 12e, 19e, and 20e arrondissements. The Bastille métro stop, on the 1, 5, and 8 lines, is a good place to start. For Canal St-Martin, use the Place de la République stop (lines 3, 5, 8, 9, 11) and walk along Rue Faubourg du Temple, or go to Gare de l'Est stop (lines 4, 5, 7) and walk along Rue des Récollets to the canal. For Oberkampf, go to the Parmentier stop on the 3 or the Oberkampf stop on the 9. For the Cimetière Pere Lachaise, take the 3 to the eponymous stop.*

## BEST CAFÉS

**Café Charbon.** This ultracool café, with a restored zinc bar, mirrored walls, and mismatched chandeliers is a neighborhood institution. ✉ *109 rue Oberkampf, Oberkampf* ☎ *01–43–57–55–13* Ⓜ *Parmentier.*

**Café Français.** A sidewalk perch for people-watching is *de rigeur* on the Place de la Bastille, and this café on the corner of Rue St-Antoine seems a bit more special. ✉ *3 pl. de la Bastille, Bastille* ☎ *01–40–29–04–02* Ⓜ *Bastille.*

**Chez Prune.** Grab an outdoor table at this neighborhood hot spot on the Canal St-Martin and watch the world go by. ✉ *36 rue Beaurepaire,* ☎ *01–42–41–30–47* Ⓜ *Jacques Beaurepaire, République.*

**9**

Sightseeing
★★
Dining
★★★★
Lodging
★★
Shopping
★★★★
Nightlife
★★★★★

The Bastille used to be the star of this area and a stop here—home turf of the French Revolution—was a must. The small streets forking off the Place de la Bastille still buzz at night, with bars and music clubs and the top-flight Opéra Bastille, but today the neighborhoods farther afield are the real draw, having evolved into some of Paris's hottest and hippest destinations. The Canal St-Martin, once the down-and-out cousin on the northeastern border, is now trend-spotting central, brimming with funky bars, cafés, art galleries, and boutiques. The scene is similar to the south, on rues Oberkampf, St-Maur, and Jean-Pierre-Timbaud, where artists and small designers have set up shop, and where a substantial slice of the city's *bobo* (bourgeois-bohemian) set is buying up the (momentarily) still-affordable apartments.

The areas to the north and east of the canal are also flourishing, around the rougher streets near **Ménilmontant** and **Belleville**, home to a small Chinatown (watch your purse and avoid wearing attention-getting jewelry). The city's largest cemetery, **Père Lachaise**, is here, with a roster of famous tenants including Proust, Oscar Wilde, and Jim Morrison. Not far away is the impressively wild **Parc Buttes-Chaumont**, with grassy fields, a small Greek-style temple, and sweeping hilltop views of Paris. It's a perfect place for a picnic lunch and to let museum-weary kids work off some steam. There are two other notable parks to the east: **Parc de la Villette**, which is also home to the city's well-regarded science museum, and the **Bois de Vincennes**.

Not far from the Bastille opera house, the **Viaduc des Arts** is a much-admired urban renewal project that turned an old elevated rail line into arcaded design-focused studios and shops. Along the top, the **Promenade**

**Plantée** makes for a lovely stroll through the 12e arrondissement, a nice middle-class neighborhood with stately apartment buildings and the pretty **Square Trousseau,** gateway to the **Marché d'Aligre,** one of the city's best covered markets. Come on Sunday morning with a shopping basket—or just your camera—when the vendors spill over into neighboring streets.

To the south of **Bastille,** the old wine warehouses at **Bercy** have been transformed into a veritable village of shops and restaurants bordering Park de Bercy. Directly across the Seine, is the **Bibliothéque National François Mitterand,** the National Library of France, a sprawling complex of modern glass towers heralded as the world's most modern library when it opened in 1998.

## TOP ATTRACTIONS

Updated by
Linda Hervieux

**Bercy.** Tucked away south of the Gare de Lyon in the 12$^e$ arrondissement, these blocks of stone warehouses once stored wine imported from the provinces (you can still see the old train tracks on which they were brought in). Today, the buildings in what is now called **Bercy Village** have been transformed into shops and restaurants (most are open on Sunday). Adjacent to the village, the **Parc de Bercy,** with its lawns crisscrossed by gravel paths, is a favorite destination for residents: it includes the **Jardin Yitzhak Rabin,** a contemporary garden named for the late Nobel peace prizewinner. On the western edge of the park, near the Bercy métro stop, is the **Palais Omnisports,** a venue for concerts as well as sports. Nearby, at 51 rue de Bercy, is a quirky Cubist Frank Gehry building now home to the **Cinémathèque Française,** a film-buff's paradise showing classic films, many in English. There are frequent homages to directors and actors, as well as a cinema library and museum *(see the listing in Ch. 15 Performing Arts).* ⊠ *Bercy Village, 28 rue François Truffaut, Bercy/Tolbiac* ☎ *08–25–16–60–75* ⊕ *www.bercyvillage.com* ☉ *Daily 11–9* Ⓜ *Cour St-Emilion, Bercy.*

**Bibliothéque National François Mitterand.** The National Library of France, across the sleek Simone de Beauvoir footbridge from **Bercy Park,** is a modern complex of four 24-story L-shaped buildings representing open books. Commissioned by President Mitterrand before his death, the library was said to be the world's most modern when it opened in 1998, but it was quickly mired in controversy when it was discovered that despite a $1.5 billion price tag, measures weren't taken to protect the books and rare documents, which were baking in the sun within the glass towers (moveable shutters were eventually added). There is a sunken center courtyard with pine trees and basement reading rooms (it's free, and anyone can enter). Frequent temporary exhibitions are often presented, though usually not as racy as 2008's adults-only show on erotica (which featured a giant X lighted up on one of the towers). ⊠ *Quai François Mauriac, Bibliothèque* ☎ *01–53–79–59–59* ⊕ *www. bnf.fr* ☉ *Tues.–Sat. 10–7, Sun. 1–7* 🖾 *Free; exhibitions €7* Ⓜ *Bibliothèque, Quai de la Gare.*

**9**

**DID YOU KNOW?**

The Canal St-Martin has become one of Paris's most atmospheric places to stroll. The streets are lined with boutiques, galleries, and cafés.

**NEED A BREAK?** **Pink Flamingo** (✉ *67 rue Bichat, Canal St-Martin* ☎ *01-42-02-31-70*) is an American-owned pizzeria that will deliver your pie directly to the banks of the canal—they spot you thanks to the pink balloon you're holding.

Fodor's Choice  **Canal St-Martin.** The once-forgotten canal has morphed into one of the
★    city's hippest places to wander by day—and party by night. A good time to come is Sunday afternoon, when the Quai de Valmy is closed to cars and some of the shops are open. Rent a bike at one of the many Velib stations, stroll along the banks, or go native and cuddle quai-side in the sunshine with someone special.

The 2.7-mi canal began life as a source of clean drinking water for Paris, so ordered by Napoléon to improve sanitation and health standards. It opened in 1825 between the Seine at the southern end at Place de la Bastille, and the Canal de l'Ourcq to the north near La Villette. Baron Haussmann later ordered a mile-long stretch of it to be covered—this is today's Boulevard Richard Lenoir—from Rue Faubourg du Temple to the Bastille. These days you can take a boat tour from end to end through the canal's nine locks: along the way, the bridges swing or lift open. An amusing one is the drawbridge with four giant pulleys at Rue de Crimée, near La Villette.

In recent years, gentrification has swept the canal, with artists taking over formerly industrial spaces, and creating studios and galleries. The bar and restaurant scene is flourishing, and small designers have set up shop, fleeing expensive rents in Le Marais. Young families have flocked here as well, undeterred by the area's still-rough edges: the canal is a frequent staging ground for housing advocates protesting on behalf of the many homeless who live along these banks. To explore this evolving quartier in depth, set out on foot: start on the Quai de Valmy at Rue Faubourg du Temple (use the République métro stop). Here, at Square Frédéric Lemaître, there is a good view of one of the locks (behind you the canal disappears underground). A good place to pick up a sandwich or crepe to go is Quai Gourmand at No. 79. As you head north, detour onto side streets like Rue de Lancry, with bars, restaurants, and small shops. A swing bridge across the canal connects Lancry to the Rue de la Grange aux Belles. Cross the bridge and take the second right onto Rue Bichat. Midway down the block is the entrance to the courtyard of the massive Hôpital Saint-Louis, built in 1607 to house plague victims and still a working hospital today. The grounds, flanked by grand brick-and-stone buildings with steeply sloping roofs, are worth a look.

Back on Quai Valmy, just before the Rue des Récollets, fashionistas should check out two trendy boutiques: Sandro at No. 93 and, next door, one of the larger shops of the Antoine & Lili chain *(see Chapter 16, Shopping, for details)*. Just beyond, Jardin Villemin, on the former site of another hospital, is now the 10$^e$ arrondissement's largest park (4.5 acres).

If you're in the Canal St-Martin area at night, you can catch a live music show and a bite to eat at the mostly-soul Bizz'Art club-restaurant at No. 167 Quai Valmy *(see Chapter 14, Nightlife, for more details)*. Point Ephémère, at No. 200, is another happening spot with an art gallery, café, club, and DJ scene. Just past the Place Stalingrad is the Rotonde de la Villette, a lively square with restaurants and twin MK2 cinemas on either side of the canal, with a boat to ferry ticket-holders across. On the approach to Parc de la Villette, there are antiques shops along the quai and a few floating restaurants and theaters. **Canauxrama** offers 2½-hour boat cruises through the locks (€15 adults). Check the Web site for times (⊕ *www.canauxrama.com*). Embarkation is at each end of canal: at Bassin de la Villette (*13 quai de la Loire, La Villette*) or Marina Arsenal (*50 bd. de la Bastille, Bastille*). Ⓜ *Jaurès (northern end) or Bastille (southern end).*

**NEED A BREAK?** With an unassuming white facade and a classically French interior, the **Hôtel du Nord** (✉ *102 quai de Jemmapes, République* ☎ *01-40-40-78-78* Ⓜ *Jacques Bonsergent*) looks like a movie set, and, in fact, it was famously used by Marcel Carné in his 1938 namesake movie. The film's star, actress-icon Arletty, claimed to be unmoved by the romantic canal-side setting, uttering the memorable line "Atmosphere, atmosphere, I've had it with atmosphere!" Today the restaurant, beautifully restored, is a hipster favorite.

★ Cimetière du Père Lachaise

*See highlighted listing in this chapter.*

**Marché Aligre.** Place d'Aligre is home to two of Paris's best markets: the lively outdoor Marché Aligre and the covered Marché Beauvau. Open at 8 AM every day but Monday, both are great places to pick up the essentials for a picnic lunch, which you can enjoy in the small park nearby at Square Trousseau. The picturesque outdoor market has dozens of excitable vendors, their stands spilling over with fresh fruits and vegetables, bouquets of flowers, and regional products such as jams and honey. The best bargains are had just before the closing time at 1:30 PM, and many vendors will give you a taste of their goods if you're looking to buy. The covered market, which closes in the afternoon and reopens 4–7:30 PM, is more expensive, but stocks everything from cheese to dried sausage to Belgian beer. Sunday morning is a fun time to visit, when the markets are at their most boisterous and what seems like at least half the 12$^e$ arrondissement comes to shop. Don't forget your camera. ✉ *Pl. d'Aligre, Bastille* Ⓜ *Ledru-Rollin/Bastille.*

**Opéra de la Bastille.** Paris's main opera house opened its doors on July 14, 1989, to mark the bicentennial of the French Revolution. The fabulous acoustics of the steeply sloping, stylish auditorium have earned more plaudits than the modern facade designed by Uruguay-born architect Carlos Ott. If you want to see a show, reserve your seat well in advance, or take your chances on the same day, when any unclaimed seats (at all price levels) are released shortly before showtime. There are also 62 standing room-only tickets available before each show for €5. Be sure to line up at least two hours before the curtain. ✉ *Pl. de la Bastille, Bastille/Nation* ☎ *08-92-89-90-90 tickets; 0033-1-72-29-35-35 from outside of France* ⊕ *www.operadeparis.fwwarningr* Ⓜ *Bastille.*

# CIMITÈRE DU PÈRE LACHAISE

✉ Entrances on Rue des Ron-
deaux, Bd. de Ménilmontant,
and Rue de la Réunion, Père
Lachaise ☎ 01–55–25–82–10
⊕ www.pere-lachaise.com
☉ Easter–Sept., daily 8–6;
Oct.–Easter, daily 8–dusk
Ⓜ Gambetta, Philippe-
Auguste, Père-Lachaise.

## TIPS

■ Pinpoint grave sites on the Web site before you come, but buy a map anyway outside the entrances—you'll still get lost, but that's part of the fun. Don't be surprised to see locals hanging out on benches, feeding the feral cats.

■ Note that the two biggest draws are Jim Morrison's grave (with its own guard to keep Doors fans under control) and the life-size bronze figure of French journalist Victor Noir, whose alleged fertility-enhancing power accounts for the patches rubbed smooth by hopeful hands.

■ One of the best days to visit Père-Lachaise is on All Saints' Day (November 1), when Parisians en masse bring flowers to adorn the graves of favorite dead celebrities.

Press a lipsticked kiss to Oscar Wilde's tombstone or bring a red rose for "the little sparrow" Edith Piaf—the cobblestone avenues and immense trees make the 118-acre cemetery a worthwhile trip. Named for Pére Fran-çois de la Chaise, Louis XIV's confessor, Père-Lachaise has some political history attached to it—it was the site of the Paris Commune's final battle on May 28, 1871, when 147 rebels were lined up and shot against the Mur des Fédérés (*Federalists' Wall*) in the southeast corner.

### HIGHLIGHTS

Aside from the sheer aesthetic beauty of the cemetery, the main attraction is what (or who, more accurately) is belowground. Here's a list of grave sites you won't want to miss:

**1. Pierre Abélard** (1079–1142), French philosopher, lover of Heloïse

**2. Honoré de Balzac** (1799–1850), French writer

**3. Sarah Bernhardt** (1844–1923), French actress

**4. Georges Bizet** (1838–75), French composer

**5. Maria Callas** (1923–77), Greek-American opera singer

**6. Frédéric Chopin** (1810–49), Franco-Polish composer

**7. Sidonie-Gabrielle Colette** (1873–1954), French writer

**8. Jacques-Louis David** (1748–1825), French painter

**9. Eugène Delacroix** (1798–1863), French painter

**10. Max Ernst** (1891–1976), German painter

**11. Théodore Géricault** (1791–1824), French painter

**12. Stéphane Grappelli** (1908–97), French jazz violinist

**13. Baron Haussmann** (1809–91), French civic planner

**14. Sedegh Hedayat** (1903–51), Iranian writer

**15. Heloïse** (1101–62), scholar, lover of Pierre Abélard

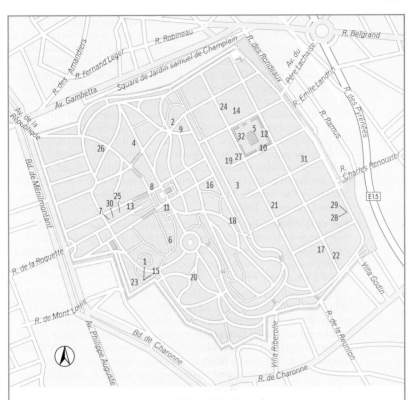

16. **Jean Auguste Dominique Ingres** (1780–1867), French painter
17. **Amedeo Clemente Modigliani** (1884–1920), Italian painter
18. **Molière (Jean-Baptiste Poquelina)** (1622–73), French playwright and actor
19. **Yves Montand** (1921–91), French/Italian actor and singer
20. **Jim Morrison** (1943–71), American musician
21. **Victor Noir** (1848–70), French journalist
22. **Edith Piaf** (1915–63), French singer
23. **Camille Pissarro** (1830–1903), French painter
24. **Marcel Proust** (1871–1922), French intellectual and writer
25. **Giaocchino Rossini** (1792–1868), Italian composer
26. **Georges-Pierre Seurat** (1859–91), French painter
27. **Simone Signoret** (1921–85), French actress
28. **Gertrude Stein** (1874–1946), American writer
29. **Alice B. Toklas** (1877–1967), American writer
30. **Louis Visconti** (1791–1853), French architect
31. **Oscar Wilde** (1854–1900), Irish writer
32. **Richard Wright** (1908–60), American writer

9

⟳ **Parc des Buttes-Chaumont.** If you're tired of perfectly manicured Parisian parks with lawns that are off-limits to your weary feet, this is the place for you. This lovely 61-acre hilltop park in the untouristy 19$^e$ arrondissement has grassy fields, leafy walkways, waterfalls, and commanding views of Paris. Swans glide around the lake at the base of a rocky cliff topped with a mini Greek-style temple. Built in 1863 on abandoned gypsum quarries and a former gallows, this was northern Paris's first park, part of Napoléon III's planned greening of Paris (the emperor had spent years in exile in London, where he fell in love with the public parks). It's a good place to take the kids, with pony rides and an open-air puppet theater, Guignol de Paris(€2.50 charge; shows at 3:30 PM Wednesday and weekends; weather permitting, closed in winter), not far from the entrance at Buttes-Chaumont métro stop. ✉ *Entrances on Rue Botzaris or Rue Manin, Buttes-Chaumont* Ⓜ *Laumière, Buttes-Chaumont, Botzaris.*

⟳ **Parc de la Villette.** This 130-acre ultramodern park was once an abattoir, but don't let its history put you off: today it's the perfect place to entertain sightseeing-weary kids, with futuristic gardens, an excellent science museum, a music complex, and a cinema. You could easily spend a whole day here.

The park itself was designed in the 1980s by postmodern architecture star Bernard Tschumi, who successfully incorporated industrial elements, children's games (don't miss the dragon slide), lots of green space, and dreamlike light sculptures along the canal into one vast yet unified playground. A great place for a picnic, the lawns of La Villette attract rehearsing samba bands and pickup soccer games. In summer there's a free outdoor cinema festival—people gather at dusk to picnic and watch movies on a huge inflatable screen.

In cold weather, you can visit the museums, the submarine, the Espace Chapiteaux (a circus tent featuring superb contemporary acrobatic theater performances), and **La Géode**—it looks like a huge silver golf ball but is actually an Omnimax cinema made of polished steel, with an enormous hemispherical screen. The ambitious **Cité des Sciences et de l'Industrie** (✉ *30 av. Corentin-Cariou, La Villette* ☎ *01–40–05–70–00* ⊕ *www.cite-sciences.fr* Ⓜ *Porte de la Villette*) tries to do for science and industry what the Pompidou does for modern art. There are 60 or so colorful interactive contraptions, and the multilingual children's workshops are perfect ways to while away rainy afternoons. The museum is open Tuesday through Saturday 10–6 and Sunday until 7; admission ranges from €3 for the submarine, to €15.50, depending on whether you visit the planetarium, take a workshop, or see an exhibition. Young kids will like the fish-tank wall in the basement. The postmodern **Cité de la Musique** is a music academy designed by geometry-obsessed Christian de Portzamparc. It has a state-of-the-art concert hall and the spectacular **Musée de la Musique** (✉ *221 av. Jean-Jaurès, La Villette* ☎ *01–44–84–44–84* ⊕ *www.cite-musique.fr* Ⓜ *Porte de Pantin*). The music museum contains some 900 instruments; their sounds and story are evoked through wireless headphones (ask for English commentary). The museum is open Tuesday through Thursday noon–6, Friday and Saturday noon–10, and Sunday 10–6; admission is €8.

All that's left of the slaughter-house is **La Grande Halle**, a magnificent iron-and-glass building now used for exhibitions, performances, and trade shows. Across the plaza, the outdoor terrace at **Café de la Musique** (✉ *213 av. Jean-Jaurès, La Villette* ☎ *01–48–03–15–91* Ⓜ *Porte de Pantin*) is an inviting place to have a drink on a sunny day.

**Place de la Bastille.** Nothing remains of the infamous Bastille prison, destroyed more than 200 years ago, though tourists still ask bemused Parisians where to find it. Until the late 1980s, there was little more to see here than a busy traffic circle ringing the **Colonne de Juillet** *(July Column)*, a memorial to the victims of later uprisings in 1830 and 1848. The opening of the Opéra Bastille in 1989 rejuvenated the area, however, drawing art galleries, bars, and restaurants to the narrow streets, notably along Rue de Lappe—once a haunt of Edith Piaf—and Rue de la Roquette.

Before it became a prison, the Bastille St-Antoine was a defensive fortress with eight immense towers and a wide moat. It was built by Charles V in the late 14th century and transformed into a prison during the reign of Louis XIII (1610–43). Famous occupants included Voltaire, the Marquis de Sade, and the Man in the Iron Mask. On July 14, 1789, it was stormed by an angry mob that dramatically freed all of the remaining prisoners (there were only seven, including one lunatic), launching the French Revolution. The roots of the revolt ran deep. Resentment toward Louis XVI and Marie-Antoinette had been building amid a severe financial crisis. There was a crippling bread shortage, and the free-spending monarch was blamed. When the king dismissed the popular finance minister, Jacques Necker, enraged Parisians took to the streets. They marched to Les Invalides, helping themselves to stocks of arms, then continued on to the Bastille. A few months later, what was left of the prison was razed—and 83 of its stones were carved into miniature Bastilles and sent to the provinces as a memento (you can see one of them in the Musée Carnavalet). The key to the prison was given to George Washington by Lafayette, and has remained at Mount Vernon ever since. Today, nearly every major street demonstration in Paris—and there are many—passes through this square. Ⓜ *Bastille.*

Ⓒ **Pavillon de l'Arsenal.** If your knowledge of Paris history is *nul* (negligible), stop here for an easy and entertaining explainer. Built in 1879 as a private museum, this restored glass-and-iron building today showcases the city's urban development through the ages. The first floor features a giant floor model of Paris today. Along the walls, a snappy timeline tracks the development of the growing city under each ruler, with text in French and English, accompanied by maps from various periods, photographs, and video displays. The second floor is dedicated to temporary architecture-themed exhibits. ⊠ *21 bd. Morland, Bastille* ☎ *01–42–76–33–97* ⊕ *www.pavillon-arsenal.com* ✉ *Free* ⊙ *Tues.–Sat. 10:30–6:30, Sun. 11–9* Ⓜ *Sully-Morland, Bastille.*

★ **Viaduc des Arts/Promenade Plantée.** This redbrick viaduct was once a train line to the Bastille. Today, the arcades beneath the elevated tracks have been transformed into stylish boutiques—many focused on decor and design—and artisans' workshops. Above, the Promenade Plantée, a 2.8-mi walkway lined with flowers and trees, offers a bird's-eye view along Avenue Daumesnil in the heart of the 12$^e$ arrondissement. It served as a setting for the 2004 film *Before Sunset* starring Ethan Hawke and Julie Delpy. The promenade ends at the Jardin de Reuilly. From here, you can continue your walk to the Bois de Vincennes. ⊠ *Av. Daumesnil, Bastille* Ⓜ *Bastille, Gare de Lyon.*

## WORTH NOTING

☽ **Bois de Vincennes.** Like the Bois de Boulogne to the west, the lovely Vincennes Woods was landscaped by Napoléon III, and it is a much-loved retreat on the city's eastern border. The bois traces its roots back to the 13th century when Philippe Auguste created a hunting preserve here in the shadow of the royal **Château de Vincennes**. In 1731, Louis XV created a park and opened it to the public. Today, the bois features lush lawns, a flower garden, and summertime jazz concerts. Rowboats are for hire at the two lakes, **Lac Daumesnil**, which has two islands, and **Lac des Minimes**, which has three. There's also a zoo and a racetrack, the **Hippodrome de Vincennes**, a small farm, several cafés, and an amusement park in the spring. You can rent a bike at the Château de Vincennes métro stop. To reach the park, use the Château de Vincennes stop (Line 1) or Porte Dorée (Line 8). **The impressive Château de Vincennes** (⊠ *Av. de Paris, Bois de Vincennes* ☎ *01–48–08–31–20* ⊕ *www.chateau-vincennes.fr* ✉ *€8* ⊙ *May–Aug., daily 10–6; Sept.–Apr., daily 10–5* Ⓜ *Château de Vincennes*) was once the largest château in Europe. On the northern edge of the Bois, it was built and expanded by various kings between the 12th and 14th centuries.

The imposing high-walled castle was France's medieval Versailles, surrounded by a dry moat and dominated by a 170-foot keep. The royal residence eventually became a state prison, holding illustrious convicts such as philosopher Diderot. The château has undergone a spectacular renovation, and work continues in some parts. **The Parc Floral de Paris** (⊠ *Rte. de la Pyramide, Bois de Vincennes* ✉ *€5* ⊙ *Apr.–Sept., daily 9:30–8; Oct.–Mar., daily 9:30–5* Ⓜ *Château de Vincennes*) is the Bois de Vincennes's 70-acre park and flower garden. It has a lake and water garden and is renowned for its seasonal displays of blooms. It also contains a miniature train, a game area, and an "exo-tarium" with tropical fish and reptiles; in summer, an outdoor jazz festival makes this the most popular weekend picnic site in the city. The 35-acre Parc Zoologique, the largest zoo in France, is closed for renovations until

## CLOSE UP

## Bastille at Night

From Place de la Bastille, take Rue de la Roquette and turn right onto Rue de Lappe, Paris's answer to Bourbon Street, once a haunt of artists and writers like Henry Miller. Today it draws a mostly young crowd to its many bars and restaurants, though there's something for everyone. Detour down the tiny passage Louis Philippe to find Café de la Danse, one of the city's best venues to see all sorts of live music. In the early 1900s, Auvergne immigrants brought *bal musette*—accordion-driven popular music—with them, and many later collaborated with gypsy jazzman Django Reinhardt. One of its anchors is the Balajo dance club at No. 9 rue de Lappe (*see Chapter 14, Nightlife*), established in 1930 and still going strong. In recent years, these tangled streets have added shops, theaters, and galleries to the constantly evolving bar lineup.

2014. ✉ *53 av. de St-Maurice, Bois de Vincennes* ☎ *01–44–75–20–00* Ⓜ *Porte Dorée.*

An exceptional Art Deco building that once held an African art museum now teems with fish instead of artifacts. The **Palais de la Porte Dorée Tropical Aquarium** (✉ *293 av. Daumesnil, Bois de Vincennes* ☎ *01–53–59–58–60* 💶 *€4.50, €5.70 during exhibitions* ☉ *Tues.–Sun. 10–5:30* Ⓜ *Porte Dorée*) has a basement full of tanks of colorful tropical fish, crocodiles, and turtles, but the building itself is even more captivating; built for the Colonial Exhibition in 1931, it has an ornate facade depicting France's erstwhile overseas empire. Sharing the building is the **Cité Nationale de l'Historie de l'Immigration** (✉ *293 av. Daumesnil, Bois de Vincennes* ☎ *01–53–59–58–60* 💶 *€5* ☉ *Tues.–Fri. 10–5:30, weekends 10–7* Ⓜ *Porte Dorée*), which focuses on the history of immigration in France through permanent and temporary exhibits.

☾ **La Maison Rouge.** Former gallery owner Antoine de Galbert established this art foundation, where temporary exhibitions with a real flair for contemporary trends—a rarity for Paris galleries—are mounted several times a year. Check the Web site to see what's on. The building itself is a treat, too: it's an industrial space cleverly redone and anchored by the original courtyard building, now painted bright red (hence the foundation's name). ✉ *10 bd. de la Bastille, Bastille* ☎ *01–40–01–08–81* ⊕ *www.lamaisonrouge.org* 💶 *€7* ☉ *Wed.–Sun. 11–7, Thurs. 11–9* Ⓜ *Quai de la Rapée/Bastille.*

OFF THE BEATEN PATH

**Musée Edith Piaf.** True fans will appreciate the tiny two-room apartment where the "little sparrow" lived for a year, when she was 28 years old and sang in the working-class cafés on Rue Oberkampf. The flat was obtained by Les Amis d'Edith Piaf in 1978 and is now a shrine to the pint-sized crooner, whose life-size photo (she was 4 feet, 9 inches) greets visitors at the door. The red walls are covered with portraits of Piaf done by her many artist friends. Her books and handbags are here, as well as a few dresses and her size 4 shoes. Her personal letters are framed. ✉ *5 rue Crespin du Gast, Oberkampf* ☎ *01–43–55–52–72*

9

## Dining at a Glance

For full reviews ⇨ Chapter 17.

**INEXPENSIVE DINING**
**Dong Huong**, *Vietnamese*, 14 rue Louis-Bonnet

**La Table de Claire**, *Bistro*, 30 rue Emile Lepeu

**Le Baron Bouge**, *Wine Bar*, 1 rue Théophile Roussel

**Le Martel**, *North African*, 3 rue Martel

**Unico**, *Latin American*, 15 rue Paul-Bert

**MODERATE DINING**
**Astier**, *Bistro*, 44 rue Jean-Pierre Timbaud

**Au Trou Gascon**, *Bistro*, 40 rue Taine

**Bofinger**, *Brasserie*, 5–7 rue de la Bastille

**Chez Omar**, *North African*, 47 rue de Bretagne

**Jacques Mélac**, *Wine Bar*, 42 rue Léon-Frot

**La Boulangerie**, *Bistro*, 15 rue des Panoyaux

**Le Baratin**, *Bistro*, 3 rue Jouye Rouve

**Le Bistro Paul Bert**, *Bistro*, 18 rue Paul Bertc

**Le Chateaubriand**, *Bistro*, 44 rue du Bac

**Le Repaire de Cartouche**, *Bistro*, 8 bd. des Filles du Calvaire

**Sardegna a Tavola**, *Italian*, 1 rue de Cotte

**EXPENSIVE DINING**
**Au Boeuf Couronné**, *Brasserie*, 188 av. Jean-Jaurès

---

✆ *Free, donations encouraged* ⊙ *By reservation only; no English spoken; Mon.–Wed. 1–6* PM Ⓜ *Ménilmontant.*

☾ **Piscine Josephine Baker.** This stunning floating aquatic center, named after the much-beloved American entertainer, features a pool with a retractable glass roof, two solariums, a steam room, Jacuzzis, and a gym. Entry is a bargain €6 (or €3 for the pool only). Check the opening hours and schedule of classes online. ⊠ *21 Quai François Mauriac, Bibliothèque* ☎ *01–56–61–96–50* ⊕ *www.paris.fr/portail/Sport/Portal.lut?page_id=6085* ⊙ *Weekdays 7–10, Sat. 7–8, Sun. 7–9* Ⓜ *Quai de la Gare, Bibilothèque François Mitterrand.*

# The Quartier Latin

**WORD OF MOUTH**

"Our next stop was the Museum of the Middle Ages (Musée National du Moyen-Age), formally called Musée Cluny . . . The museum had many gorgeous things but it is most famous for its tapestries . . . They were stunning! I am so happy to have gotten to see them."

—bardo1

# GETTING ORIENTED

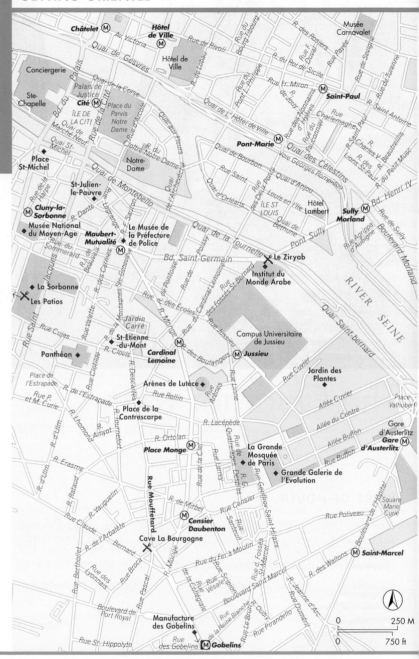

## TOP REASONS TO GO

**Musée National du Moyen-Age.** On the site of an ancient Roman bath, this former abbey is home to the famous Lady and the Unicorn tapestries; the building, tranquil garden, and extensive collection have the hush of a medieval monastery.

**Shakespeare & Company.** This legendary English-language bookstore is more than a shopping destination; it's a meeting place for young expats and curious travelers alike.

**Rue Mouffetard.** Stroll down this winding market street to construct a picnic à la française with fresh breads, deliciously smelly cheeses, and briny fresh oysters.

**Jardin des Plantes.** This is a great spot to picnic or to rest your tired feet on one of the many shaded benches.

**La Grande Mosquée de Paris.** Enjoy a mint tea in the leafy courtyard of Paris's most beautiful mosque.

## MAKING THE MOST OF YOUR TIME

The Quartier Latin is the perfect place to wander sans itinerary, though there is no shortage of sites worth seeing. Shopping here is generally more affordable, though less original, than in other neighborhoods, and there are lots of new- and used-book stores, many of which stock English-language titles. Pick up a picnic at the many food shops along Rue Mouffetard (closed Monday), or head to the open-air market at Place Monge (Wednesday, Friday, and Sunday mornings), then savor your booty on a bench at the Jardin des Plantes. Sip mint tea either in the courtyard café at the lovely Grande Mosquée (Mosque) de Paris or take in a terrific view on the roof of the Institut du Monde Arabe (closed Monday). Stroll the hilly streets around the Panthéon on your way to see the treasures at the Musée National du Moyen-Age (closed Tuesday). Finish with a sunset apéritif on one of the barge cafés (open spring to fall) along the Seine, across from Notre-Dame.

## GETTING HERE

*The Quartier Latin is the 5$^e$ arrondissement.* Take Line 4 to métro St-Michel to start exploring at the Lucifer-slaying fountain near Shakespeare & Co., across the Seine from Notre-Dame. Go to the Cluny stop on Line 10 if you're heading to the Musée Cluny. The Place Monge stop on Line 7 puts you near the Panthéon and Rue Mouffetard, the Mosquée de Paris, and the Jardin des Plantes.

Les Gobelins neighborhood straddles the 5$^e$, 13$^e$, and 14$^e$ arrondissements, but is considered part of the 5e because of the Manufacture des Gobelins.

## BEST CAFÉS

**Cave La Bourgogne.** Settle in at this old-school bistro for coffee, or take a seat at the zinc bar for a glass of wine. ⊠ *144 rue Mouffetard, Quartier Latin* ☎ *01–47–07–82–80.*

**Les Patios.** Near the Sorbonne, all you need to fit in at this brasserie is a newspaper or a fat novel. The outdoor terrace is perfect for people-watching. ⊠ *5 pl. de la Sorbonne, Quartier Latin* ☎ *01–43–54–34–43.*

**Le Ziryab.** This café/outdoor terrace on the top floor of the Institut du Monde Arabe is a great place for an affordable Lebanese lunch or dinner, with fantastic views. It's closed Monday. ⊠ *Institut du Monde Arabe, 1 rue des Fossés-St-Bernard, Quartier Latin* ☎ *01–55–42–55–42.*

**10**

Sightseeing
★★★★
Dining
★★★
Lodging
★★★★
Shopping
★★★
Nightlife
★★★

The Quartier Latin is the heart of student Paris—and has been for more than 800 years. France's oldest university, *La Sorbonne,* was founded here in 1257, and the neighborhood takes its name from the fact that Latin was the common language of the students, who came from all over Europe. Today the area is full of cheap and cheerful cafés, bars, and shops.

The main drag, **Boulevard St-Michel,** is a bustling street where bookshops have given way to chain clothing stores and fast-food joints—but don't let that stop you! There are (almost) as many French people wandering the streets here as there are tourists. At **Place St-Michel,** the symbolic gateway to the quartier, notice the 19th-century fountain depicting St. Michael slaying the "great dragon," Satan, a symbolic warning to rebellious locals from Napoléon III. Today the fountain serves as a meeting spot and makes a rather fine metaphor for the boulevard it anchors: a bit grimy but extremely popular.

When you've had enough of the crowds, turn off the boulevard and explore the side streets, where you can find quirky boutiques and intimate bistros. Or stop for a demi (a half pint of draft beer) at one of the many cafés on the **Place de la Sorbonne,** ground zero for students (and their many noisy demonstrations). Around the winding streets behind the **Panthéon,** where French luminaries are laid to rest, you can still find plenty of academics arguing philosophy while sipping espresso, but today the 5e arrondissement is also one of Paris's most charming and sought-after (read: expensive) places to live.

Shop along **Rue Mouffetard** as Parisians do—all the while complaining about the high prices—for one of the best selections of runny cheeses, fresh breads, and charcuterie. Grab a seat in a bustling café—or do as the locals do and stand at the bar, where drinks are always cheaper. Film buffs won't have to look far to find one of the small cinema revival houses showing old American films in English (look for v.o. for version originale). Not far from *"le Mouffe"* is the gorgeous white La Grande

**Mosquée de Paris** with its impressive minaret. Just beyond the mosque is the **Jardin des Plantes**—a large, if somewhat bland, botanical garden that is home to three natural-history museums, most notably the **Grande Galerie de l'Evolution.** Inside, kids can marvel at enormous whale skeletons, along with all sorts of taxidermy. Some of Paris's most intriguing sites are in this neighborhood, including the **Musée National du Moyen-Age** and the innovative **Institut du Monde Arabe.** See ancient history mingle with modern life at the **Arènes de Lutèce,** a Roman amphitheater and favorite soccer pitch for neighborhood kids.

## TOP ATTRACTIONS

Updated by
Linda Hervieux

Ⓒ **Grande Galerie de l'Evolution** *(Great Hall of Evolution).* With a parade of taxidermied animals ranging from the tiniest dung beetle to the tallest giraffe, this museum in the Jardin des Plantes is an excellent break for kids who have been reluctantly trudging through the Louvre. The flagship of the three natural-history museums in the Jardin des Plantes, it is easily the most impressive. The original 1889 building was renovated in 1994, and has a ceiling that changes color to suggest storms, twilight, or the hot savanna sun. Don't miss the gigantic skeleton of a blue whale, and the stuffed royal rhino—he came from the menagerie at Versailles, where he was a pet of Louis XV. Some English-language information boards are available, but not many. ■TIP➔ Hang on to your ticket; it'll get you a discount at the other museums within the Jardin des Plantes. ⊠ 36 *rue Geoffroy-St-Hilaire, Quartier Latin* ☎ 01–40–79–54–79 ⊕ *www. mnhn.fr* ⊠ €9 ⊗ *Wed.–Mon. 10–6* Ⓜ *Pl. Monge or Jussieu.*

★ **Institut du Monde Arabe.** Architect Jean Nouvel is a master of glass construction; here, at the Institute of the Arab World, he tempers transparency with a mesmerizing facade of variable, irislike apertures that control the light entering the building, evoking a Moorish-style screen. The institute's layout reinterprets the traditional enclosed Arab courtyard. Inside, items largely on loan from Syria and Tunisia present Arab culture from prehistory to the present day, with an emphasis on painting and medicine, but the temporary exhibitions tend to be a bigger draw than the permanent collection. The museum also includes performance spaces, a sound-and-image center, a vast library, and a permanent collection of Arab-Islamic art, textiles, and ceramics. Information in English is limited, but temporary exhibitions usually have English audioguides. ■TIP➔ Glass elevators whisk you to the ninth floor, where you can sip mint tea in the rooftop café, Le Ziryab, while feasting on one of the best views in Paris. ⊠ *1 rue des Fossés-St-Bernard, Quartier Latin* ☎ 01–40–51–38– 38 ⊕ *www.imarabe.org* ⊠ *Exhibitions €12.30, museum €6.60* ⊗ *Tues.– Sun. 10–6* Ⓜ *Cardinal Lemoine.*

Ⓒ **Jardin des Plantes** *(Botanical Gardens).* Bordered by the Seine, Gare d'Austerlitz, and the ugly, utilitarian Jussieu University campus, this swath of greenery is much loved by residents but hardly the most impressive of Parisian gardens. Come to picnic, or, if you have kids, take them to the excellent **Grande Galerie de l'Evolution** *(above)* or one of the other two other natural-history museums here: the **Galerie de Paléontologie,** which exhibits some dinosaurs, and the **Galerie de Minéralogie**

## Shakespeare & Company

In the shadow of Notre-Dame across the Seine, this English-language bookstore is one of Paris's most eccentric and lovable literary institutions. Founded by George Whitman, this maze of new and used books has offered a sense of community (and often a bed) to wandering writers since the 1950s. The store takes its name from Sylvia Beach's original Shakespeare & Company, which opened in 1919 at 12 rue d'Odeon, welcoming the likes of Ernest Hemingway, James Baldwin, and James Joyce. Beach famously bucked the system when she published Joyce's *Ulysses* in 1922, but her original store closed in 1941. After the war Whitman picked up the gauntlet, naming his own bookstore after its famous predecessor.

Today, Shakespeare & Company welcomes a new generation of Paris dreamers. Walk up the almost impossibly narrow stairs to the second floor and you'll see laptop computers and sleeping bags tucked between the aging volumes and under dusty daybeds; it's sort of like a hippie commune. A revolving cast of characters helps out in the shop or cooks meals for fellow residents. They're in good company; Henry Miller, Samuel Beckett, and William Burroughs are among the famous writers to benefit from Whitman's hospitality.

**Shakespeare & Company** (✉ *37 rue de la Bûcherie* ☎ *01–43–25–40–93*) is open daily 10 AM to 11 PM (Sunday 11 AM to 11 PM) and has readings most Monday evenings. Check the Web site (⊕ *www.shakespeareandcompany. com*) for a schedule of events.

with rocks and minerals. Plant lovers will enjoy the botanical garden, the rose garden, and the several greenhouses from the 1930s that are filled with tropical and desert plants. The garden is also home to the Ménagerie, one of the world's oldest zoos, founded by Napoléon. It's a small, rather sad zoo by North American standards, and is utterly forgettable, but if your kids are bored, take them to see the two notable inhabitants: Kiki, an ancient Seychelles tortoise, and Nanette, a 40-something orangutan. ■TIP→ Keep your ticket: entrance to any of these sites will get you a discount to other museums within the gardens. ✉ *Entrances on Rue Geoffroy-St-Hilaire, Rue Cuvier, Rue de Buffon, and Quai St-Bernard, Quartier Latin* ☎ *01–40–79–54–79* ⊕ *www. mnhn.fr* ✉ *Museums and zoo €4–€8 (free, 4 and under), greenhouses €2.50* ☉ *Museums Wed.–Mon. 10–5 or 6. Zoo daily 9–5. Garden daily 7:30–5:30* Ⓜ *Gare d'Austerlitz, Jussieu.*

**Fodor's Choice** **Musée National du Moyen-Age** *(National Museum of the Middle Ages, ★ also called the Musée Cluny).* Built on the ruins of Lutecia's Roman Baths, the **Hôtel de Cluny** has been a museum since medievalist Alexandre Du Sommerard established his collection here in 1844. The over-the-top mansion was a choice location for such a collection; the 15th-century building was created for the abbot of Cluny, leader of the most powerful monastery in France. Symbols of the abbot's power literally surround the building, from the crenellated walls that proclaimed his independence from the king, to the carved Burgundian grapes, symbolizing

10

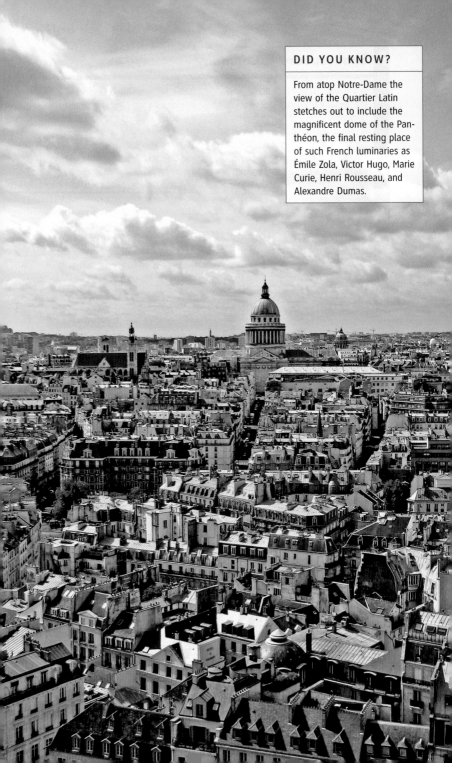

his valuable vineyards, twining up the entrance. The scallop shells *Coquilles-Saint-Jacques* covering the facade are a symbol of religious pilgrimage, another important source of income for the abbot; the well-traveled pilgrimage route to Spain, Rue St-Jacques, once ran just around the corner. The highlight of the collection is the world-famous *Dame à la Licorne* (*Lady and the Unicorn*) tapestry series, woven in the 15th or 16th century, probably in Belgium. The tapestries are an allegorical representation of the five senses. In each, a unicorn and a lion surround an elegant young woman against an elaborate millefleur (literally, 1,000 flowers) background. The enigmatic sixth tapestry, *Mon seul désir,* is thought to symbolize love or understanding. The collection also includes the original sculpted heads of the *Kings of Israel and Judah* from Notre-Dame, discovered in 1977: the statues were decapitated when they adorned the western facade of the cathedral during the Revolution, but the heads were saved and hidden by a nobleman near today's Galeries Lafayette. You can also visit the remnants of the city's Roman baths—hot (*caldarium*) and cold (*frigidarium*), the latter containing the *Boatmen's Pillar,* Paris's oldest sculpture. A charming garden is laid out in the medieval style, using the flora depicted in the unicorn tapestries. ✉ *6 pl. Paul-Painlevé, Quartier Latin* ☎ *01–53–73–78–00* ⊕ *www.musee-moyenage.fr* ✂ *€8 (includes English audio guide), free 1st Sun. of month* ⊙ *Wed.–Mon. 9:15–5:45* Ⓜ *Cluny–La Sorbonne.*

**WORD OF MOUTH**

"The Musée Cluny (Musée National du Moyen-Age) would be my recommendation for those who love either medieval tapestries or Roman architecture (it was built on the site of old Roman baths)."
—Kate_W

**NEED A BREAK?**

**Place de la Contrescarpe.** This popular square behind the Panthéon doesn't start to really swing until dusk, when its cafés and bars fill up. **Café Delmas** (✉ *2 pl. de la Contrescarpe* ☎ *01–43–26–51–26*), has a large terrace and serves food every day until 2 AM. During the day the Place de la Contrescarpe has something of an intimate, small-town feel to it as people haggle over produce at the daily market at the bottom of Rue Mouffetard. ✉ *Quartier Latin* Ⓜ *Monge.*

**Panthéon.** Rome has St. Peter's, London has St. Paul's, and Paris has the Panthéon, whose enormous dome dominates the Left Bank. Built as a church, it has long been the resting place of a virtual who's who of France's cultural and political elite, including Voltaire, Zola, Dumas, Victor Hugo, Rousseau, and Marie Curie. Begun in 1764, the building was almost complete when the French Revolution erupted. By then, architect Jacques-German Soufflot had died, supposedly from worrying that the dome would collapse. He needn't have fretted: the dome is so perfect that Foucault used this space to test his famous pendulum to prove the rotation of the earth. The best view is had from outside, however, as the vast neoclassical interior looks more like an abandoned wine cellar than a hallowed burial ground. It's entirely empty except for the 19th-century murals lining the walls and a model of Foucault's pendulum hanging

**10**

from the center of the dome. The famous residents are in the crypt. There is little info in English—and none on the people buried here, so if you're a history buff, do your homework before you come. ✉ *Pl. du Panthéon, Quartier Latin* ☎ *01–44–32–18–00* ⊕ *pantheon. monuments-nationaux.fr/en/* ⊠ *€8* ☉ *Apr.–Sept., daily 10–6:30; Oct.–Mar., daily 10–6* Ⓜ *Cardinal Lemoine; RER: Luxembourg.*

Fodor'sChoice **Rue Mouffetard.** This winding cob-
★ blestone street is one of Paris's oldest—it was once a Roman road leading south from Lutecia (the Roman name for Paris) to Italy. The upper half of the street is dotted with restaurants that can get rather touristy; the lower half is home to a lively market, open Tuesday through Sunday, when couples

are inspired to dance in the street to old Paris accordion tunes. The highlight of *le Mouffe* is the stretch in between, where, as your nose will tell you, the shops are literally spilling into the street with luscious offerings such as roasting chickens and potatoes, rustic saucisson, pâtés, and pungent cheeses, especially at Androuët (No. 134). You can find everything you'll need for a picnic as well as gifts to bring home to your favorite foodie. If you're here in the morning, Le Mouffetard Café (No. 116) is a good place to stop for breakfast (for about €8). For one of the best baguettes in Paris detour to the nearby Boulanger de Monge, which includes a scrumptious selection of organic offerings, at 123 rue Monge. Note that most of the shops are closed Monday.

## WORTH NOTING

🕭 **Arènes de Lutèce** *(Lutetia Amphitheater).* This Roman amphitheater, designed as a theater and circus, was almost completely destroyed by barbarians in AD 280. The site was rediscovered in 1869, and you can still see part of the stage and tiered seating. Along with the remains of the baths at Cluny, the arena constitutes rare evidence of the powerful Roman city of Lutetia that flourished on the Rive Gauche in the 3rd century. Today it's a favorite spot for picnicking, or a pickup game of soccer or *boules*. ✉ *Entrance at 47 rue Monge or Rue de Navarre, Quartier Latin* ⊠ *Free* ☉ *Daily 8–dusk* Ⓜ *Pl. Monge.*

★ **La Grande Mosquée de Paris.** This awe-inspiring white mosque was built between 1922 and 1925 and has tranquil arcades and a minaret decorated in the style of Moorish Spain. Enjoy a sweet mint tea and an exotic pastry in the charming courtyard tea salon or tuck into some couscous in the restaurant. Prayer rooms are not open to the public. There are inexpensive—and quite rustic—hammams, or Turkish steam baths, with scrubs and massages on offer (check Web site for prices). ☒ *2 pl. du Puits de l'Ermite; entrance to tea salon and restaurant at 39 rue Geoffroy Saint-Hillaire, Quartier Latin* ☎ *01–43–31–38–20* ⊕ *www. la-mosque.com* ☒ *Guided tour €3* ⊗ *Guided tours in French, daily 9–noon and 2–8* Ⓜ *Pl. Monge.*

**Manufacture des Gobelins.** Tapestries have been woven on this spot in southeastern Paris, on the banks of the long-covered Bièvre River, since 1662. Guided tours combine historical explanation with the chance to admire both old tapestries and today's weavers at work in their airy workshops. To get here from the Place de la Contrescarpe, go south on Rue Mouffetard and continue down Rue de Bazeilles, which becomes Avenue des Gobelins (about a 15-minute walk). Entry is by guided tour only. Call ahead to check that the guide on duty speaks English. ☒ *42 av. des Gobelins, Les Gobelins* ☎ *01–44–08–52–00* ☒ *€8* ⊗ *Tues.–Thurs., guided tours at 2 and 2:45* Ⓜ *Gobelins.*

**Place St-Michel.** This square was named for Gabriel Davioud's grandiose 1860 fountain sculpture of St. Michael vanquishing Satan—a loaded political gesture from Napoléon III's go-to guy, Baron Haussmann, who hoped St-Michael would quell the Revolutionary fervor of the neighborhood. Today the fountain is a good starting point for a walking tour. ☒ *Quartier Latin* Ⓜ *Métro or RER: St-Michel.*

**St-Étienne-du-Mont.** This beautiful church has been visited by several popes, owing to the fact that Ste-Geneviève, the patron saint of Paris, is buried here. The chaotic combination of the building's Gothic, Renaissance, and early Baroque styles contrasts with the cold and pure classicism of the Panthéon. St-Étienne contains the only rood screen in Paris—a masterwork of carved knot work dating from 1525—and the church's organ is the oldest in the city, from 1631. An archbishop of Paris was stabbed to death here in 1857 by a defrocked priest angry over church celibacy laws. Look for the marker in the floor near the entrance. ☒ *30 rue Descartes, Quartier Latin* Ⓜ *Cardinal Lemoine.*

**St-Julien-le-Pauvre.** This tiny shrine in the shadow of Notre-Dame is one of the three oldest churches in Paris, and now serves as a Greek Catholic parish church. Founded in 1045, it became a meeting place for university students in the 12th century. This was Dante's church when he was in Paris writing his *Divine Comedy* in 1300. Today's structure dates mostly from the 1600s, but keep an eye out for older pillars, which crawl with carvings of demons. The church holds classical and gospel concerts, or you can simply perch on a bench in the garden to enjoy the view of Notre-Dame. ☒ *1 rue St-Julien-le-Pauvre, Quartier Latin* Ⓜ *St-Michel.*

**OFF THE BEATEN PATH**

**Le Musée de la Préfecture de Police.** Crime buffs will enjoy this museum hidden on the second floor of the $5^e$ arrondissement's police station. Although the exhibits are in French only, the photographs, letters, drawings, and memorabilia of some of the city's most sensational crimes are easy enough to follow. Relics include a guillotine, old uniforms, and remnants of the World War II occupation, including what's left of a firing post, German machine guns, and the star insignias worn by Jews.

AT A GLANCE

## Dining at a Glance

For full reviews ⇨ Chapter 17

**INEXPENSIVE DINING**
**L'Avant-Goût,** *Bistro,* 26 rue Bobillot

**L'Ourcine,** *Bistro,* 92 rue Broca

**La Chine Massena,** *Chinese,* Centre Commercial Massena, 13 pl. de Venetie

**Le Bambou,** *Vietnamese,* 70 rue Baudincourt

**Le Pré Verre,** *Modern French,* 8 rue Thénard

**Ribouldingue,** *Bistro,* 10 rue St-Julien-le-Pauvre

**MODERATE DINING**
**Chez René,** *Bistro,* 14 bd. St-Germain

**Itinéraires,** *Bistro,* 5 rue de Pontoise

**Le Buisson Ardent,** *Bistro,* 25 rue Jussieu

**Les Papilles,** *Wine Bar,* 30 rue Gay-Lussac

**EXPENSIVE DINING**
**La Tour d'Argent,** *Haute French,* 15 quai de la Tournelle

✉ *4 rue de la Montagne Ste-Geneviève, Quartier Latin* ☎ *01–44–41–52–50* ✉ *Free* ⊙ *Weekdays 9–5, Sat. 10–5* Ⓜ *Maubert-Mutualité.*

**La Sorbonne.** You can't get into Paris's most famous university without a student ID, although you can try to talk your way past a friendly guard. If you succeed, enter on Rue Victor Cousin, cross the cobbled courtyard where students have gathered for nine centuries, and peek into the muraled lecture halls. Today, La Sorbonne remains the heart and soul of the Quartier Latin, though it is also known as Paris IV, one of several campuses that make up the public Université de Paris. ✉ *1 rue Victor Cousin, Quartier Latin* Ⓜ *Cluny-La Sorbonne.*

# St-Germain

**WORD OF MOUTH**

"Stroll the side streets in St-Germain ($6^e$ arr) and window gaze at the fantastic and out-of-this-world artworks. Most windows are lit in the evenings, so this can be done at any time."

—di2315

# GETTING ORIENTED

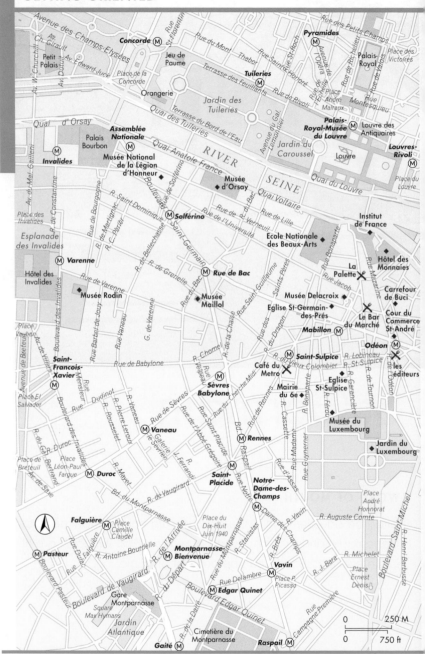

## TOP REASONS TO GO

**Musée d'Orsay.** The graceful vaulted ceiling and abundance of natural light in this train-station-turned-museum is a reminder of why the Impressionist painters thought that train stations were the cathedrals of the 19th century.

**Jardin du Luxembourg.** Take in a puppet show, wander the tree-lined gravel paths, enjoy an art exhibition at the museum, or just laze by the fountain at this most elegant of Parisian gardens.

**Boulevard St-Germain.** The main artery of this chic neighborhood is lined with shops, art galleries, and cafés. The top boutiques are clustered around Rue de Rennes, off the main stretch; for more art galleries, head north to Rue de Seine.

**Cafés, cafés, cafés.** This is excellent people-watching territory. Take a seat at one of the many cafés, hang out, and watch the world go by.

## MAKING THE MOST OF YOUR TIME

Aim for an early start—have a *café crème* at a café along the river and get to the Musée d'Orsay early, when crowds are thinner. Leave some time for window-shopping around the Boulevard St-Germain and Rue de Rennes on your way to the Jardin du Luxembourg. You might want to plan your visit on a day other than Monday, when Orsay, many of the art galleries, and even some shops are closed. The Delacroix and Maillol museums are closed on Tuesday.

## GETTING HERE

*The St-Germain neighborhood is the 6ᵉ arrondissement and a bit of 7ᵉ.* To get to the heart of this area, take the Line 4 métro to St-Germain-des-Près. For shopping, use this station or St-Sulpice. It's a short walk to the Jardin du Luxembourg, or take the RER B line to the Luxembourg station. For the Musée d'Orsay, take the Line 10 métro to Solferino or the RER C line to the Musée d'Orsay.

## BEST CAFÉS

**Le Bar du Marché.** Grab a sidewalk table—if you're lucky—or stand at the bar, skip the food, and order an apéritif at this constantly packed little bar. The feel is classic French with a splash of kitsch, right down to the waiters in overalls and berets. ⊠ *75 rue de Seine, St-Germain-des-Prés* ☎ *01–43–26–55–15.*

**La Palette.** The terrace of this corner café, opened in 1902, is a favorite haunt of local gallery owners and Beaux Arts students. Meals are served at lunch, and sandwiches and lighter fare are available at other times of day. Come at sunset—or later—when the scene gets lively. ⊠ *43 rue de Seine, St-Germain-des-Prés* ☎ *01–43–26–68–15.*

**les éditeurs.** This trendy café favored by the Parisian publishing set is a perfect place to sip a kir (white wine with black currant syrup) from a perch on the skinny sidewalk or at an inside table shadowed by book-lined walls. ⊠ *4 carrefour de l'Odéon, St-Germain-des-Prés* ☎ *01–43–26–67–76* ⊕ *www. leslediteurs.fr.*

**Café du Métro.** Settle in at this friendly café-brasserie for hot chocolate or French onion soup after an exhausting round of shoe shopping around the Rue de Rennes. Closed Sunday. ⊠ *67 rue de Rennes, St-Germain-des-Prés* ☎ *01–45–48–58–56.*

Sightseeing
★★★★★
Dining
★★★
Lodging
★★★★★
Shopping
★★★★★
Nightlife
★★

If you had to choose the most classically parisien neighborhood in Paris, this would be it. St-Germain-des-Prés has it all: genteel blocks lined with upscale art galleries, storied cafés, designer boutiques, and a fine selection of museums. Cast your eyes upward after dark and you may spy a frescoed ceiling in a tony apartment. These historic streets can get quite crowded, so mind your elbows and plunge in.

This *quartier* is named for the oldest church in Paris, **St-Germain-des-Prés**, and it's become a prized address for Parisians and expats alike. Despite its pristine facade, though, this wasn't always silver-spoon territory. Claude Monet and Auguste Renoir shared a cramped studio at 20 rue Visconti, and the young Picasso barely eked out an existence in a room on the Rue de Seine. By the 1950s St-Germain bars bopped with jazz, and the likes of Albert Camus, Jean-Paul Sartre, and Simone de Beauvoir puffed away on Gaulois while discussing the meaninglessness of existence at Café Flore. Nearby in the 7$^e$ arrondissement, the star attraction is the **Musée d'Orsay,** home to a world-class collection of Impressionist paintings in a converted Belle Époque rail station on the Seine. It's famous for having some of Paris's longest lines, so a visit to d'Orsay should be planned with care. There are also several smaller museums worth a stop, including the impressive **Musée Maillol,** a private collection in an elegant mansion dedicated to the work of sculptor Aristide Maillol, and the **Musée du Luxembourg,** which stages excellent temporary exhibitions on the edge of the gardens. The **Musée Delacroix,** in lovely Place Furstenburg, is home to a small collection of the Romantic master's works. Not far away is the stately **Église St-Sulpice,** where you can see two impressive Delacroix frescoes.

Paris is a city for walking, and St-Germain is one of the most enjoyable places to practice the art of the *flâneur,* or stroller. Make your way to the busy crossroads of **Carrefour de Buci,** dotted with cafés, flower markets, and shops. Rue de l'Ancienne is so named because it was the first home of the legendary Comédie Française; it cuts through to busy Place de l'Odéon and Rue St-André des Arts. Along the latter you can find

The cafés in St-Germain-des-Prés are perfect for people-watching along with coffee, dinner, or a cocktail.

the historic **Cour du Commerce St-André** (opposite No. 66), a charming cobbled passageway lined with cafés, including, halfway down on the left, Paris's oldest, Le Procope.

Make sure you save some energy for the exquisite **Jardin du Luxembourg**, a classic French garden, whose tree-lined paths have attracted fashionable wanderers through the ages, though the swish of crinolines has given way to the crunch of designer tracksuits sported by Parisians on their morning constitutional. Fortunately, there are lots of chairs for resting those weary feet.

## TOP ATTRACTIONS

Updated by Linda Hervieux

Fodor'sChoice ★

**Carrefour de Buci.** This colorful crossroads (carrefour is French for "intersection") was once a notorious Rive Gauche landmark: during the 18th century it contained a gallows, and during the French Revolution the army used the site to enroll its first volunteers. Many royalists and priests lost their heads here during the bloody course of the Terror. There's certainly nothing sinister about the carrefour today; brightly colored flowers are for sale alongside take-out ice-cream and snack kiosks. Devotees of the superb, traditional bakery Carton (at No. 6) line up for pastries (try their *tuiles* cookies). ■TIP➔ Rue de Buci has several good épiceries and boulangeries stocked with the fixings for a perfect picnic. Ⓜ *Mabillon.*

**Église St-Germain-des-Prés.** Paris's oldest church was built to shelter a simple shard of wood, said to be a relic of Jesus's cross brought back from Spain in AD 542. Vikings came down the Seine and sacked the church, and Revolutionaries used it to store gunpowder, yet the elegant building has defied history's abuses: its 11th-century Romanesque tower continues to be the central symbol of the neighborhood. The colorful 19th-century frescoes in the nave are by Hippolyte Flandrin, a pupil of the classical master Ingres. The church stages superb organ concerts and recitals. Step inside for spiritual nourishment, or pause in the square to people-watch—there's usually a street musician tucked against the church wall, out of the wind. ☒ *Pl. St-Germain-des-Prés, St-Germain-des-Prés* ☼ *Daily 8–7:30* Ⓜ *St-Germain-des-Prés.*

**Fodor's**Choice ★ **Église St-Sulpice.** Dubbed the Cathedral of the Rive Gauche, this enormous 17th-century Baroque church has entertained some unlikely christenings—among them the Marquis de Sade and Charles Baudelaire—as well as the nuptials of novelist Victor Hugo. The church's most recent appearance was a supporting role in the best-selling novel *The Da Vinci Code,* and it now draws scores of tourists to its obelisk, a sundial built in the 1730s. The 18th-century facade was never finished, and its unequal towers add a playful touch to an otherwise sober design. There are two magnificent Delacroix frescoes in a chapel to the right of the entrance. ■ TIP→ The congregation makes for good people-watching when there are confirmations and weddings.

**QUICK BITES**

The slightly shabby **Café de la Mairie** on the square, once the haunt of existentialist author Albert Camus, is a good place to spy celebrities like actress Catherine Deneuve, who lives nearby, and other St-Germain celebrities are occasionally spotted in the square's Café de la Mairie, once the haunt of existentialist author Albert Camus. ☒ *Pl. St-Sulpice, St-Germain-des-Prés* ☼ *Weekdays 7:30–7:30* Ⓜ *St-Sulpice.*

**Fodor's**Choice ★ **Jardin du Luxembourg**

*See the highlighted listing in this chapter.*

**Fodor's**Choice ★ **Musée d'Orsay**

*See the highlighted listing in this chapter.*

**NEED A BREAK?**

Secreted away in the Maison de la Chine (China House), **Shanghai Café** is a little-known oasis of calm in this bustling 'hood. Come for lunch (best to reserve) or a lovely afternoon tea, and try a green-tea éclair or another of the exotic pastries. To find it, head to the back of the Maison de la Chine and pass through a small outpost of the upscale Hong Kong boutique Shanghai Tang. Closed Sunday. ☒ *76 rue Bonaparte, St-Germain-des-Prés* ☎ *01–40–51–95–17* ⊕ *www.maisondelachine.fr.*

# 11

**CLOSE UP**

# Dueling Cafés

**Les Deux Magots** (✉ 6 pl. St-Germain-des-Prés) and the neighboring **Café de Flore**, at (✉ 172 b. St-Germain) have been duking it out on this bustling corner in St-Germain for more than a century. Les Deux Magots, the snootier of the two, is named for the two Chinese figurines, or *magots*, inside, and has hosted the likes of Oscar Wilde, Hemingway, James Joyce, and Richard Wright. Jean-Paul Sartre and Simone du Beauvoir frequented both establishments, though they are claimed by the Flore.

The two cafés remain packed, though these days you're more likely to rub shoulders with tourists than with philosophers. Still, if you're in search of that certain *je ne sais quoi* of the Rive Gauche, you can do no better than to station yourself at one of the sidewalk tables—or at a window table on a wintry day—to watch the passing parade. Stick to a croissant and an overpriced coffee or an early-evening apéritif; the food is expensive and nothing special.

★ **Musée du Luxembourg**. Marie de Medici's gracious palace, built in 1615, is now home to the French Senate and this small museum, which stages prestigious (and crowded) temporary exhibitions. The curators are free spirits; there may be a show on old Italian masters, or a tribute to a forgotten French fauvist, or a double-bill featuring Miró and Warhol. There's information in English as well as audioguides. The extended hours are convenient and advance tickets (available online for a €1 surcharge) allow you to cut the line. ✉ *19 rue de Vaugirard, St-Germain-des-Prés* ☎ *01–42–34–25–95* ⊕ *www.museeduluxembourg.fr* 💳 *€11* ⏱ *Mon. and Fri. 10:30–10, Tues.–Thurs. 10:30–7, weekends 9:30–8* Ⓜ *St-Sulpice, Rennes.*

## WORTH NOTING

Fodor's Choice
★ **Cour du Commerce St-André**. Like an 18th-century engraving come to life, this charming street arcade is a remnant of *ancien* Paris with its enormous uneven cobblestones. Famed for its rabble-rousing inhabitants—journalist Jean-Paul Marat ran the Revolutionary newspaper *L'Ami du Peuple*, at No. 8, and the agitator Georges Danton lived at No. 20—it's also home to Le Procope, Paris's oldest café. This passageway also contains a turret from the 12th-century wall of Philippe-Auguste (visible through the windows of the Catalogne tourist office). ✉ *Linking Bd. St-Germain and Rue St-André-des-Arts, St-Germain-des-Prés* Ⓜ *Odéon.*

**Ecole Nationale des Beaux-Arts**. Occupying three large mansions near the Seine, the national fine-arts school—today the breeding ground for painters, sculptors, and architects—was once the site of a convent founded in 1608 by Marguerite de Valois, the first wife of Henri IV. After the Revolution the convent was turned into a museum for works of art salvaged from buildings attacked by the rampaging French mobs. In 1816 the museum was turned into a school. Today its peaceful

# JARDIN DU LUXEMBOURG

✉ *Bordered by Bd. St-Michel and rues de Vaugirard, de Medicis, Guynemer, and Auguste-Comte, St-Germain-des-Prés* 🎟 *Free* ☉ *Daily 7:30 or 8:15–dusk (hrs vary depending on the season)* Ⓜ *Odéon; RER: B Luxembourg.*

### TIPS

■ So you can't sit in the grass—feel free to move the green chairs around to create an ideal picnic spot or people-watching perch.

■ If you're eager to burn off that breakfast pain au chocolat, the Jardin du Luxembourg has a well-maintained trail around the perimeter frequented by a surprising (for France) number of joggers—mostly groups of buff cops. It is one of the few public places where you can spy the French clad in (perfectly matching) athletic wear.

■ If you're looking for a familiar face, one of the original (miniature) casts of the Statue of Liberty was installed in the gardens in 1906.

The Luxembourg Gardens has all that is charming, unique, and befuddling about Parisian parks: cookie-cutter trees, ironed-and-pressed walkways, sculpted flower beds, and immaculate emerald lawns meant for admiring, not for lounging. The tree- and bench-lined paths are, however, a marvelous reprieve from the bustle of the two neighborhoods it borders: the Quartier Latin and St-Germain-des-Près. Beautifully austere during the winter months, the garden grows intoxicating as spring brings blooming beds of daffodils, tulips, and hyacinths, and the circular pools teem with boats nudged along by children. The park's northern boundary is dominated by the Palais du Luxembourg, home of the Musée du Luxembourg and the Sénat (Senate), which is one of two chambers that make up the Parliament.

### HIGHLIGHTS

The original inspiration for the gardens came from Marie de Medici, nostalgic for the Boboli gardens of her native Florence. She is commemorated by the **Fontaine de Medicis**.

A sweet attraction is the **Théâtre des Marionnettes** where, on weekends at 11 and 3:15 and on Wednesday at 3:15 (hours may vary), you can catch a classic *guignols* (marionette shows) for a small charge. The wide-eyed kids might be the real attraction; their expressions of utter surprise, despair, and glee have fascinated the likes of Henri Cartier-Bresson and François Truffaut. The park also has a merry-go-round, swings, and pony rides; the bandstand hosts free concerts on summer afternoons.

Check out the rotating photography exhibits hanging on the perimeter fence near the entrance on the Boulevard St-Michel and rue Vaugirard.

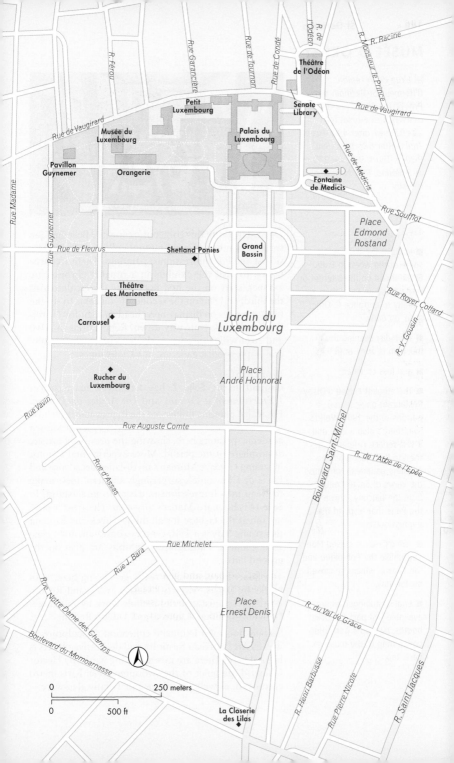

# MUSÉE D'ORSAY

✉ *1 rue de la Légion d'Honneur, St-Germain-des-Prés* ☎ *01–40–49–48–14*
⊕ *www.musee-orsay.fr*
💳 *€9.50; €7 after 4:15 except Thurs. after 6* ⊙ *Tues.–Sun. 9:30–6, Thurs. 9:30 AM–9:45 PM*
Ⓜ *Solférino; RER: Musée d'Orsay.*

TIPS

■ Lines at the d'Orsay are some of the worst in Paris. Book ahead on the Internet or buy a Museum Pass; then go directly to entrance C. Otherwise, go early.

■ Thursday evening the museum is open until 9:45

■ and less crowded.

■ The elegant Musée d'Orsay Restaurant once served patrons of the 1900 World's Fair; there's also a café and a self-service cafeteria on the top floor just after the Cézanne galleries. Don't miss the views of Sacré-Coeur from the balcony—this is the Paris that inspired the Impressionists.

■ The d'Orsay is closed Monday, unlike the Pompidou and the Louvre, which are closed on Tuesday.

■ English audioguides are available just past the ticket booths; pick up a free color-coded map of the museum here, too.

Opened in 1986, this gorgeous, renovated Belle Époque train station has a world-famous collection of Impressionist and Postimpressionist paintings. There are three floors; to visit the exhibits in a roughly chronologic manner, start on the first floor, take the escalators to the third, and end on the second. If you came to see the biggest names on display here, head straight for the top floor and work your way down. Renovations in 2010 and 2011 will close parts of the museum, including several Impressionist galleries, at various times.

### HIGHLIGHTS

Ground floor: **Salle 7** has Courbet's masterpieces *L'Enterrement à Ornans* and *Un Atelier du Peintre.* His realist painting influenced the Impressionists, whose work is upstairs. There are also works by lesser-known academic painters here, showing the prevailing artistic atmosphere of the period. More experimental visions, including Gustave Moreau's myth-laden decadence and Puvis de Chavanne's surprisingly modern lines, make the leap into Impressionism easier to understand. In **Salle 14** is Édouard Manet's *Olympia.* The artist is poking fun at the fashion for all things Greek and Roman; this young lady is a 19th-century courtesan, not a classical goddess. Photography exhibits are also on the ground floor.

Top floor: Impressionism really gets going here, with works by Degas, Monet, Pissarro, Sisley, and Renoir. Postimpressionist galleries include work by van Gogh, Gauguin, Toulouse-Lautrec, and Odilon Redon.

Second floor: An exquisite collection of sculpture as well as Art Nouveau furniture and decorative objects is housed here. There are rare surviving works by Hector Guimard (designer of the swooping green Paris métro entrances), as well as Lalique and Tiffany glassware.

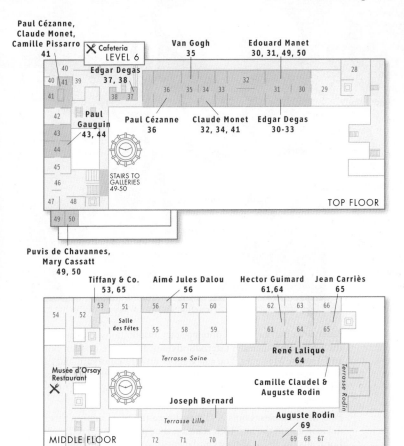

**Paul Cézanne,**
**Claude Monet,**
**Camille Pissarro**
**41**

⊁ Cafeteria
LEVEL 6

**Van Gogh**
**35**

**Edouard Manet**
**30, 31, 49, 50**

**Edgar Degas**
**37, 38**

**Paul**
**Gauguin**
**43, 44**

**Paul Cézanne**
**36**

**Claude Monet**
**32, 34, 41**

**Edgar Degas**
**30-33**

STAIRS TO
GALLERIES
49-50

TOP FLOOR

**Puvis de Chavannes,**
**Mary Cassatt**
**49, 50**

**Tiffany & Co.**
**53, 65**

**Aimé Jules Dalou**
**56**

**Hector Guimard**
**61,64**

**Jean Carriès**
**65**

Salle
des Fétes

Terrasse Seine

**René Lalique**
**64**

Musée d'Orsay
Restaurant
⊁

**Camille Claudel &**
**Auguste Rodin**

**Joseph Bernard**

**Auguste Rodin**
**69**

Terrasse Lille

Terrasse Rodin

MIDDLE FLOOR

**Temporary**
**Exhibitions**

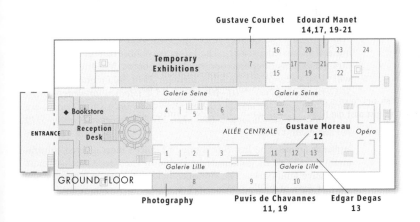

**Gustave Courbet**
**7**

**Edouard Manet**
**14,17, 19-21**

**Temporary**
**Exhibitions**

Galerie Seine

Galerie Seine

◆ Bookstore

ENTRANCE

Reception
Desk

ALLÉE CENTRALE

**Gustave Moreau**
**12**

Opéra

Galerie Lille

Galerie Lille

GROUND FLOOR

**Photography**

**Puvis de Chavannes**
**11, 19**

**Edgar Degas**
**13**

The Musée d'Orsay features mesmerizing late-19th-century art, including Paul Cézanne's *Apples and Oranges.*

courtyards harbor some contemporary installations and exhibits, and the school staff includes international art stars like Christian Boltanski and Annette Messager. You can wander into the courtyard and galleries of the school to see the casts and copies of the statues stored here for safekeeping during the Revolution. ⊠ *14 rue Bonaparte, St-Germain-des-Prés* ☉ *Daily 1–7* Ⓜ *St-Germain-des-Prés.*

**Hôtel des Monnaies.** Louis XVI transferred the royal mint to this imposing mansion in the late 18th century; then it was moved to Pessac, near Bordeaux, in 1973. Weights and measures, medals, and limited-edition coins are still made here, though, and the **Musée de la Monnaie** has an extensive collection of coins, documents, engravings, and paintings. If those offerings don't thrill, you can watch the coin-metal craftspeople at work in their ateliers overlooking the Seine, each Wednesday and Friday at 2:15 PM; advance reservations are necessary (you can e-mail musee@monnaiedeparis.fr). The Hôtel plays host to excellent temporary exhibitions of contemporary art and photos. Major construction will close parts of the building through 2012. ⊠ *11 quai de Conti, St-Germain-des-Prés* ☎ *01–40–46–55–35* ⊕ *www.monnaiedeparis.fr/musee* ▨ *€5, €3 for atelier visit by reservation only, entry prices vary for temporary exhibitions* ☉ *Tues.–Fri. 11–5:30, weekends noon–5:30* Ⓜ *Pont Neuf, Odéon.*

**Institut de France.** The *Institute* is one of France's most revered cultural institutions, and its golden dome is one of the Rive Gauche's most impressive landmarks. The site once held the Tour de Nesle, which formed part of Philippe-Auguste's medieval fortification wall along the Seine; the tower had many royal occupants, including Henry V of England. In 1661 the wealthy Cardinal Mazarin willed 2 million French *livres* (pounds) for the construction of a college. It's also home to the Académie Française: protectors of the French language. The edicts issued by this fusty group of 40 "perpétual" (lifelong) members are happily ignored by the French public, who prefer to send an e-mail rather than the Académie-approved *courriel*. The Institute is off-limits to visitors except for tours arranged by private guides. Check for guided visits in the weekly listings in *Pariscope* and *L'Officiel des Spectacles* magazines. ⊠ *Pl. de l'Institut, St-Germain-des-Prés* Ⓜ *Pont Neuf.*

**Mairie du 6ᵉ.** The "town hall" of the 6ᵉ arrondissement (as "mairie" is roughly translated) often plays host to impressive free art exhibitions and other cultural offerings. Stop by the *accueil* (reception desk) on the ground floor to see what's on or to pick up information on other timely happenings around this artsy district. ⊠ *78 rue Bonaparte, St-Germain-des-Prés* ☎ *01–40–46–76–60* ⊕ *www.mairie6.paris.fr* ⌸ *Free* ⊙ *Weekdays 8:30–5, Thurs. until 7:30.*

**Musée Delacroix.** The final home of artist Eugène Delacroix (1798–1863) contains only a small collection of his sketches and drawings, but you can see the studio he had built in the large garden at the back to work on the frescoes he created for St-Sulpice Church, where they remain on display today. The museum also plays host to temporary exhibitions, such as Delacroix's experiments with photography. France's foremost Romantic painter had the good luck to live on **Place Furstenberg,** one of the smallest, most romantic squares in Paris, which is worth a visit in itself. ⊠ *6 rue Furstenberg, St-Germain-des-Prés* ☎ *01–44–41–86–50* ⊕ *www.musee-delacroix.fr* ⌸ *€5* ⊙ *Wed.–Mon. 9:30–5* Ⓜ *St-Germain-des-Prés.*

★ **Musée Maillol.** Bronzes by Art Deco sculptor Aristide Maillol (1861– 1944), whose voluptuous, stylized nudes adorn the Tuileries gardens, can be admired at this handsome mansion lovingly restored by his former model and muse, Dina Vierny. The museum is particularly moving because it's Vierny's personal collection. She met Maillol when she was a teenager and he was already an old man. The stunning life-size drawings upstairs are both erotic and tender—age gazing on youth with fondness and longing. The museum often stages popular temporary exhibits of 20th-century painters such as Jean-Michel Basquiat and Francis Bacon—they're worth the wait. ⊠ *61 rue de Grenelle, St-Germain-des-Prés* ☎ *01–42–22–59–58* ⊕ *www.museemaillol.com* ⌸ *€8* ⊙ *Wed.–Mon. 11–6* Ⓜ *Rue du Bac.*

**Musée National de la Légion d'Honneur.** A must for military-history buffs only, the National Museum of the Legion of Honor is dedicated to homegrown and foreign military leaders. Housed in an elegant neoclassical mansion just across from the Musée d'Orsay, the museum features a vast collection of military decorations and paintings and video tributes to various luminaries, including U.S. general Dwight Eisenhower, a Légion member who led the Allied liberation of France in 1944. Entrance is free, and there are free English audioguides. ⊠ *2 rue de Bellechasse, St-Germain-des-Prés* ☎ *01–40–62–84–25* ⊕ *www. musee-legiondhonneur.fr* ⌸ *Free* ⊙ *Wed.–Sun. 1–6* Ⓜ *Solférino; RER: Musée d'Orsay.*

# Dining at a Glance

*For full reviews ⇨ Chapter 17.*

**INEXPENSIVE**

**Au Sauvignon,** *Wine Bar,* 80 rue des St-Péres

**Boucherie Roulière,** *Bistro,* 24 rue des Canettes

**Chez Maître Paul,** *Bistro,* 12 rue Monsieur-le-Prince

**CoCo & Co.,** *Bistro,* 11 rue Bernard Palissy

**L'Epigramme,** *Bistro,* 9 rue de l'Éperon

**La Ferrandaise,** *Bistro,* 8 rue de Vaugirard

**Le Bouillon Racine,** *Brasserie,* 3 rue Racine

**Ze Kitchen Galerie,** *Modern French,* 4 rue des Grands-Augustins

**MODERATE DINING**

**Alcazar,** *Brasserie,* 62 rue Mazarine

**Fògon St-Julien,** *Spanish,* 45 quai des Grands-Augustins

**Huîtrerie Régis,** *Seafood,* 3 rue de Montfaucon

**Josephine Chez Dumonet,** *Bistro,* 117 rue du Cherche-Midi

**La Bastide Odéon,** *Bistro,* 7 rue Corneille

**Le 21,** *Modern French,* 21 rue Mazarine

**Le Comptoir du Relais Saint-Germain,** *Bistro,* 9 carrefour de l'Odéon

**Yen,** *Japanese,* 22 rue St-Benoît

**EXPENSIVE DINING**

**Gaya Rive Gauche,** *Modern French,* 44 rue du Bac

**Hélène Darroze,** *Haute French,* 4 rue d'Assas

**Lapérouse,** *Bistro,* 51 quai des Grands Augustins

**L'Atelier de Joël Robuchon,** *Modern French,* 5 rue Montalembert

**Les Bouquinistes,** *Bistro,* 53 quai des Grands-Augustins

# Montparnasse

**WORD OF MOUTH**

"The neat thing about Montparnasse is that it doesn't feel like just another Paris neighborhood. It has an ambience more like a village."

—Robespierre

# GETTING ORIENTED

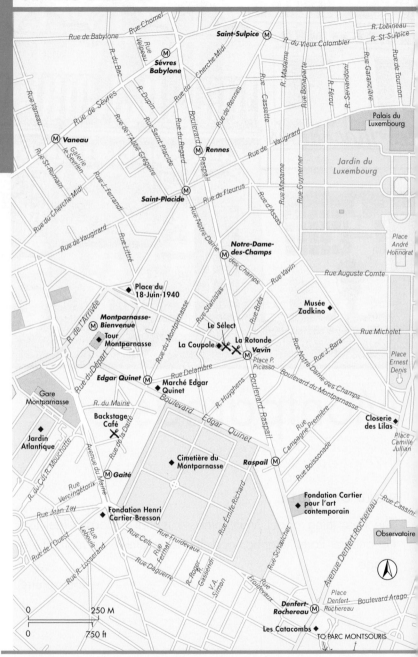

## TOP REASONS TO GO

**Catacombs.** It's not a great place to visit if you're claustrophobic or uncomfortable about the macabre, but if you're into the history of Paris, you won't want to miss this underground mecca of bones.

**Fondation Cartier pour l'art contemporain.** If cutting-edge art is what you're after, don't miss what's on view at this exhibition space. The building was designed by internationally acclaimed Jean Nouvel, the darling of Paris architecture.

**Fondation Henri Cartier-Bresson.** No photography fan should pass up the chance to see Cartier-Bresson's restored atelier, which features a small collection of his work as well as photographs from young, contemporary artists.

**The Tour Montparnasse.** Even though this 680-foot black behemoth of a skyscraper is one of the most hated buildings in Paris, the view from the open-air roof terrace is one of the best spots to see the City of Light.

## MAKING THE MOST OF YOUR TIME

If you can get to the top of the Tour Montparnasse on a clear day, you'll be rewarded with the best view in all of Paris. The viewing deck is open until 10:30 PM, so you can watch the lights sparkle on the Eiffel Tower at the top of the hour. The Catacombs and the Fondation Henri Cartier-Bresson are closed on Monday. The Cimetière du Montparnasse is open daily. La Coupole is perfect for a celebratory evening, but make reservations for this famous brasserie well in advance.

## GETTING HERE

*Montparnasse includes the 14ᵉ and 15ᵉ arrondissements.* Take line 4 to Montparnasse-Bienvenue for the Tour Montparnasse; walk along the Boulevard du Montparnasse to hit the cafés. Or take Line 4 to the Raspail métro stop for the Cimetière du Montparnasse or the Fondation Henri Cartier-Bresson. To visit the Catacombs, take the 4 to Denfert-Rochereau. Other nearby métro stops include the Edgar Quinet stop on the 6 line and the Gaîté stop on the 13 line.

## BEST CAFÉS

**Backstage Café.** Settle into a comfy chair and order a creation from the extensive cocktail list; this hot spot is on one of Montparnasse's most lively streets, aptly named Rue de la Gaîté (or "Cheerful Street"). ✉ *31 bis, rue de la Gaîté, Montparnasse* ☎ *01-43-20-68-59* Ⓜ *Edgar Quinet.*

**La Rotonde.** This café, a second home to foreign artists and political exiles in the 1920s and '30s, has a less exotic clientele today, but it's still very pleasant to have coffee on the sunny terrace. ✉ *105 bd. Montparnasse, Montparnasse* ☎ *01-43-26-48-26* Ⓜ *Vavin.*

**Le Sélect.** Isadora Duncan and Hart Crane used to hang out here; now it's a popular spot for a post-cinema beer or a well-made cocktail. ✉ *99 bd. Montparnasse, Montparnasse* ☎ *01-45-48-38-24* Ⓜ *Vavin.*

Sightseeing
★★★

Dining
★★★

Lodging
★★

Shopping
★

Nightlife
★★

Once a warren of artist studios and swinging cafés, much of Montparnasse was leveled in the 1960s to make way for a gritty train station and Paris's only—and much maligned— skyscraper, Tour Montparnasse. Over the years, this neighborhood has evolved into a place where Parisians can find more reasonable rents, well-priced cafés, and the kind of real-life vibe lost in some of the trendier parts of the city.

Despite the soulless architecture, the modernity of **Tour Montparnasse** has its advantage: the rooftop terrace has the best panoramic view of Paris. It's okay to feel smug during your ascent, as you consider yourself savvy for avoiding long lines at Tour Eiffel. And you can reward yourself with a fancy cocktail at Le Bar Américain on the 56th floor.

The other star attraction of Montparnasse is belowground. The maze-like tunnels of the Paris **Catacombs** contain the bones of centuries' worth of Parisians, moved here when disease, spread by rotting corpses, threatened the city center.

The café society that flourished in the early 20th century—Picasso, Modigliani, Hemingway (where *didn't* he drink?), Man Ray, and even Trotsky raised a glass here—is still evident along the Boulevard du Montparnasse. The Art Deco interior of **La Coupole** attracts diners seeking piles of golden *choucroute*.

Along the Boulevard Raspail you can see today's cutting-edge art stars at the **Fondation Henri Cartier-Bresson** or the **Fondation Cartier pour l'art contemporain**, or pay your respects to Baudelaire, Alfred Dreyfus, or Simone de Beauvoir in the **Cimetière du Montparnasse**.

## TOP ATTRACTIONS

Updated by
Linda Hervieux

★ **Les Catacombes.** This is just the thing for anyone with morbid interests: what you'll see after a descent through dark, clammy passages is Paris's principal ossuary, which also once served as a hideout maze for the French Resistance. Bones from the defunct Cimetière des Innocents were the first to arrive in 1786, when decomposing bodies started seeping into the cellars of the market at Les Halles, drawing swarms of ravenous rats. The legions of bones dumped here are stacked not by owner but by type—rows of skulls, packs of tibias, and piles of spinal disks, often rather artfully arranged. Be prepared for stairs and

**12**

a long underground walk; the floor can be damp, so wear appropriate shoes. Note that you won't be shrouded in tomblike darkness: the tunnels are well lighted. Among the nameless 6 million or so are the bones of Madame de Pompadour (1721–64), laid to rest with the riffraff after a lifetime spent as the mistress of Louis XV. Unfortunately, one of the most interesting aspects of the catacombs is one you probably won't see: *cataphiles*, mostly art students, have found alternate entrances into the 300 km (186 mi) of tunnels and here they make art, party, and raise hell. The site was closed for several months in 2009 after vandals caused serious damage. ⊠ *1 pl. Denfert-Rochereau, Montparnasse* ☎ *01–43–22–47–63* ⊕ *www.catacombes-de-paris.fr* ⊠ *€7* ◷ *Tues.–Sun. 10–5* Ⓜ *Métro or RER: Denfert-Rochereau.*

**Cimetière du Montparnasse.** Many of the neighborhood's most illustrious residents are buried here, a stone's throw from where they lived and loved: Charles Baudelaire, Frédéric Bartholdi (who designed the Statue of Liberty), Alfred Dreyfus, Guy de Maupassant, and, more recently, photographer Man Ray, playwright Samuel Beckett, writers Marguerite Duras, Jean-Paul Sartre, and Simone de Beauvoir, actress Jean Seberg, and singer-songwriter Serge Gainsbourg. ⊠ *Entrances on Rue Froidevaux, Bd. Edgar Quinet, Montparnasse* ◷ *Mar. 16–Nov. 5, weekdays 8–6, Sat. 8:30–6, Sun. 9–6; Nov. 6–Mar. 15, weekdays 8–5:30, Sat. 8:30–5:30, Sun. 9–5:30* Ⓜ *Raspail, Gaîté.*

★ **Fondation Cartier pour l'art contemporain.** There's no shortage of museums in Paris, but this eye-catching contemporary-art gallery may be the city's best place to view cutting-edge art. Funded by luxury giant Cartier, the foundation is at once an architectural landmark, a corporate collection, and an exhibition space. Architect Jean Nouvel's 1993 building is a glass house of cards layered seamlessly between the boulevard and the garden. Along with high-quality exhibitions of contemporary art, the foundation hosts performance nights (contemporary dance, music, film, fashion) on Thursday evenings, some in English. These "Nuits Nomades" start at 8:30. ⊠ *261 bd. Raspail, Montparnasse* ☎ *01–42–18–56–50* ⊕ *fondation. cartier.com* ⊠ *€6.50* ◷ *Tues. 11–10, Wed.–Sun. 11–8* Ⓜ *Raspail.*

★ **Fondation Henri Cartier-Bresson.** Photography has deep roots in Montparnasse, as great experimenters like Louis Daguerre and Man Ray lived and worked here. In keeping with this spirit of innovation, Henri Cartier-Bresson, legendary photographer and creator of the Magnum photo agency, opened this foundation supporting contemporary photography in 2003. The restored 1913 artists' atelier holds three temporary exhibitions each year. Be sure to go up to the top floor to see a small gallery of Cartier-Bresson's own work. ✉ *2 impasse Lebouis, Montparnasse* ☎ *01–56–80–27–00* ⊕ *www.henricartierbresson.org* 🎟 *€6, free on Wed. 6:30 PM–8:30 PM* ☺ *Tues.–Sun. 1–6:30, Wed. 1–8:30, Sat. 11–6:45* Ⓜ *Gaîté, Edgar Quinet.*

**WORD OF MOUTH**

"On our last trip to Paris we visited the Montparnasse tower the day we arrived. It was great to look down over Paris and get our bearings. The view was better than any map!" —highflyer

★ **Musée Zadkine.** The sculptor Ossip Zadkine spent nearly four decades living in this bucolic retreat near the Jardin du Luxembourg, creating graceful, elongated figures known for their clean lines and simplified features. Zadkine, a Russian-Jewish émigré, moved to Paris in 1910 and fell into a circle of avant-garde artists. His early works, influenced by African and Greek and Roman art, later took a Cubist turn, no doubt under the influence of his friend, the founder of the Cubist movement: Pablo Picasso. The one-level museum displays a substantial portion of the 400 sculptures and 300 drawings bequeathed to the city by his wife, the artist Valentine Prax. There are busts in bronze and stone reflecting the range of Zadkine's style, and an airy back room filled with lithe female nudes in polished wood. The leafy garden is worth the trip alone, containing a dozen statues nestled in the trees, including "The Destroyed City," a memorial to the Dutch city of Rotterdam, destroyed by the Germans in 1940. ✉ *100 bis, rue d'Assas, Montparnasse* ☎ *01–55–42–77–20* ⊕ *www.zadkine.paris.fr* 🎟 *Free; fee (varies) for temporary exhibitions only* ☺ *Tues.–Sun. 10–6* Ⓜ *Vavin, Notre-Dame-des-Champs.*

**Tour Montparnasse.** Continental Europe's tallest skyscraper offers visitors a stupendous view of Paris from its 56th-floor observation desk, renovated in 2005, or you can climb another three flights to the open-air roof terrace. Completed in 1973, the 680-foot building attracts 800,000 gawkers each year; on a clear day you can see for 40 km (25 mi). A glossy brochure, "Paris Vu d'en Haut" ("Paris from on High"), explains what to look for. Have a cocktail with your view at **Le Bar Américain** on the 56th floor, which also serves light food, or splurge on dinner in **Le Ciel de Paris** restaurant. ✉ *Rue de l'Arrivée, Montparnasse* ☎ *01–45–38–52–56; 01–40–64–77–64 Le Ciel de Paris* ⊕ *www.tourmontparnasse56.com* 🎟 *€10.50* ☺ *Apr.–Sept., daily 9:30 AM–11:30 PM; Oct.–Mar., Sun.–Thurs. 9:30 AM–10:30 PM, Fri. and Sat. 9:30 AM–11 PM; last elevator 30 mins before closing* Ⓜ *Montparnasse Bienvenüe.*

## WORTH NOTING

**Closerie des Lilas.** Now a pricey bar-restaurant, the Closerie remains a staple of all literary tours of Paris. Commemorative plaques are bolted to the bar like so many name tags—as if they were still saving seats for their former clientele—an impressive list of literati including Zola, Baudelaire, Rimbaud, Apollinaire, Beckett, and, of course, Hemingway. (Hemingway wrote pages of *The Sun Also Rises* here; he lived around the corner at 115 rue Notre-Dame-des-Champs.) Although the lilacs that graced the garden are gone—they once shaded such habitués as

## CLOSE UP

# Artists, Writers, and Exiles

**12**

Paris became a magnet for the international avant-garde in the mid-1800s and remained Europe's creative capital until the 1950s. It all began south of **Montmartre** when Romantics, including writers Charles Baudelaire and George Sand (with her lover, Polish composer Frédéric Chopin), moved into the streets below Boulevard de Clichy. Impressionist painters Claude Monet, Edouard Manet, and Mary Cassatt had studios here, near Gare St-Lazare, so they could commute to the countryside. In the 1880s the neighborhood dance halls had a new attraction: the cancan, and in 1889 the **Moulin Rouge** cabaret was opened. Toulouse-Lautrec designed posters advertising the neighborhood stars, and sketched prostitutes in his spare time.

The artistic maelstrom continued through the Belle Époque and beyond. In the early 1900s Picasso and Braque launched Cubism from a ramshackle hillside studio, the **Bateau-Lavoir**, and a similar beehive of activity was established at the south end of the city in a curious studio building called La Ruche (the beehive, at the Convention métro stop). Artists from different disciplines worked together on experimental productions. In 1917 the modernist ballet *Parade* hit the stage, danced by impresario Sergei Diaghilev's Ballet Russes, with music by Erik Satie and costumes by Picasso—and everyone involved

was hauled off to court, accused of being cultural anarchists.

World War I shattered this creative frenzy, and when peace returned, the artists had moved. The narrow streets of **Montparnasse** had old buildings suitable for studios, and the area hummed with a wide, new, café-filled boulevard. At No. 27 rue Fleurus, Gertrude Stein held court with her partner, Alice B. Toklas. Picasso drew admirers to **La Rotonde**, and F. Scott Fitzgerald drank at the now-defunct Dingo. In the '30s **La Coupole** became a favorite brasserie of Henry Miller, Anaïs Nin, and Lawrence Durrell.

The Spanish Civil War and World War II brought an end to carefree Montparnasse. But the literati reconvened in **St-Germain-des-Prés**. **Café de Flore** and **Deux Magots** had long been popular with an alternative crowd. Expat writers Samuel Beckett and Richard Wright joined existentialists Jean-Paul Sartre, Simone de Beauvoir, and Albert Camus in the neighborhood, drawn into the orbit of literary magazines and publishing houses.

Although Paris can no longer claim to be the epicenter of Western artistic innovation, pockets of outrageous creativity still bubble up. The galleries on Rue Louise Weiss in **Tolbiac** and open-studio weekends in **Belleville** and **Oberkampf** reveal the city's continuing artistic spirit.

---

Ingres, Whistler, and Cézanne—the terrace still opens onto a garden wall of luxuriant evergreen foliage. There is live music each evening in the piano bar. ✉ *171 bd. du Montparnasse, Montparnasse* ☎ *01–40–51–34–50* Ⓜ *Vavin; RER: Port Royal.*

**La Coupole.** One of Montparnasse's most famous brasseries, La Coupole opened in 1927 and soon became a home-away-from-home for Apollinaire, Cocteau, Satie, Stravinsky, and (again) Hemingway. In the 1980s the brasserie was bought by the Flo chain, which preserved the superb Art Deco interior, including pillars by Chagall and Brancusi. The place retains its hustle and bustle—with scurrying waiters and the overwhelming noise of clinking glasses and clattering silverware. ✉ *102 bd. du Montparnasse, Montparnasse* ☎ *01–43–20–14–20* ⊙ *Daily 8:30 AM–1 AM* Ⓜ *Vavin.*

**Jardin Atlantique** *(Atlantic Garden).* Built above the tracks of Gare Montparnasse, this park nestled among tall modern buildings is named for its assortment of trees and plants found in coastal regions near the Atlantic Ocean. At the far end of the garden, you'll find twin small museums devoted to World War II: the **Mémorial du Maréchal-Leclerc,** named for the liberator of Paris, and the adjacent **Musée Jean-Moulin,** devoted to the leader of the French Resistance. Both feature memorabilia and share a common second floor showing photo and video footage (with English subtitles) of the final days of the war and the liberation of Paris. Entrance is free; temporary exhibitions cost a few euros. In the center of the park, what looks like a quirky piece of metallic sculpture is actually a meteorological center, with a battery of flickering lights reflecting temperature, wind speed, and monthly rainfall. ✉ *1 pl. des Cinq-Martyrs-du-Lycée-Buffon, Montparnasse* ☎ *01–40–64–39–44* ⊕ *www.ml-leclerc-moulin.paris.fr* ⊙ *Jardin 8–dusk; musée Tues.–Sun. 10–6* Ⓜ *Montparnasse Bienvenüe.*

**Marché Edgar Quinet.** This excellent street market sells everything from fresh fruit to hot crêpes to wool shawls on Wednesday and Saturday. This is a good place to pick up lunch to go before strolling through Cimetière du Montparnasse just across the street. ✉ *Bd. du Edgar Quinet at métro Edgar Quinet.*

**Place du 18-Juin-1940.** Next to Tour Montparnasse, this square commemorates Charles de Gaulle's famous radio broadcast from London urging the French to resist the Germans after the Nazi invasion of May 1940. It was in this square that German military governor Dietrich von Choltitz surrendered to the Allies in August 1944, ignoring Hitler's orders to destroy the city as he withdrew. Ⓜ *Montparnasse Bienvenüe.*

# Western Paris

**WORD OF MOUTH**

"The pedestrian Rue de l'Annonciation is very near the Balzac House museum. That has free entry now. You could get out at Passy métro stop, see the Musée du Vin and Balzac's House and then go shopping on Rue de l'Annonciation and meander up to Rue de Passy and the Muette métro stop."

—Christina

# GETTING ORIENTED

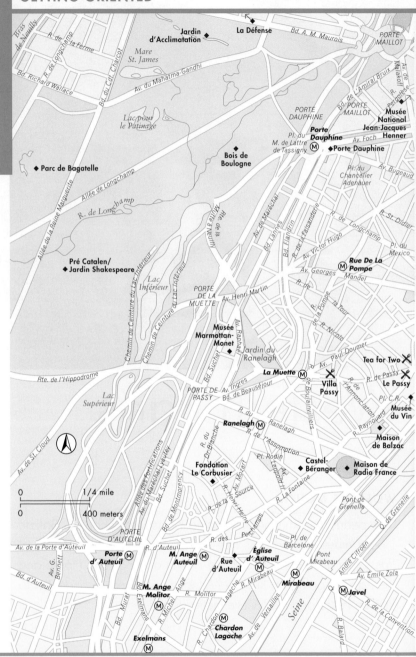

PORTE MAILLOT

Bras de Neuilly

R. de Longchamp

R. de la Ferme

Bd. Richard Wallace

Bd. du Cdt. Charcot

Mare St. James

Jardin d'Acclimatation ◆

La Défense ◆

Bd. A. M. Maurois

Av. du Mahatma-Gandhi

Lac pour le Patinage

Av. de Malakoff

Av. de l'Amiral Bruix

PORTE DAUPHINE

PORTE MAILLOT

Pl. de la Porte Maillot

Musée National Jean-Jacques Henner

◆ Parc de Bagatelle

Bois de Boulogne ◆

Allée de Longchamp

Av. Foch

Pl. du M. de Lattre de Tassigny

Porte Dauphine Ⓜ

◆Porte Dauphine

Pl. du Chancelier Adenauer

Av. Bugeaud

Allée de la Reine Marguerite

R. de Longchamp

Bd. Flandrin

Bd. Lannes

R. de la Faisanderie

R. de Longchamp

R. St.-Didier

Pl. du Mexico

Av. de Maréchal

Rte. de la Muette à Neuilly

Av. Victor Hugo

Pré Catelan/ ◆ Jardin Shakespeare

Lac Inférieur

Chemin de Ceinture du Lac Intérieur

Chemin de Ceinture du Lac Inférieur

PORTE DE LA MUETTE

Av. Henri Martin

Av. Georges Mandel

R. de la Pompe

Rue De La Pompe Ⓜ

R. de la Tour

R. Nicolo

Rte. de l'Hippodrome

Musée Marmottan-Monet ✕

Av. Raphaël

Bd. Suchet

Jardin du Ranelagh

La Muette Ⓜ

Av. Ingres

Bd. de Beauséjour

Av. Paul-Doumer

Tea for Two ✕

R. de Passy

Le Passy ✕

R. de l'Annonciation

Pl. C.R.

Musée du Vin ◆

R. Raynouard

Villa Passy

R. de Boulainvilliers

Lac Supérieur

PORTE DE PASSY

Av. Ingres

R. du Ranelagh

R. de l'Assomption

Ranelagh Ⓜ

Q. de Grenelle

Maison de Balzac ◆

Av. des fortifications

Av. du Maréchal Lyautey

Bd. Suchet

R. du Dr.-Blanche

Pl. Rodin

Castel-Béranger ◆

Av. Th. Gautier

R. La Fontaine

◆ Maison de Radio France

Av. de St.-Cloud

Bd. de Montmorency

Fondation Le Corbusier ◆

R. du Docteur Blanche

R. Mozart

R. Henri Heine

La Source

Pont de Grenelle

PORTE D'AUTEUIL

R. des Perchamps

Pl. de Barcelone

Av. Émile Zola

André Citroën

Av. de la Porte d'Auteuil

R. d'Auteuil

Porte d'Auteuil Ⓜ

M. Ange Auteuil Ⓜ

Rue d'Auteuil

Église d'Auteuil ◆

Pont Mirabeau

Av. G. Bennett

Bd. d'Auteuil

R. Molitor

M. Ange Molitor Ⓜ

R. Michel Ange

R. Mirabeau

Mirabeau Ⓜ

Av. de Versailles

Javel Ⓜ

R. de la Convention

Bd. Exelmans

Bd. Murat

R. Chardon Lagache

Chardon Lagache Ⓜ

Exelmans Ⓜ

R. Balard

Seine

Lagache

0 ____ 1/4 mile

0 ____ 400 meters

**13**

## TOP REASONS TO GO

**Musée Marmottan Monet.** If you're a fan of Monet, don't miss this gem of a museum tucked away deep in the 16ᵉ.

**Bois de Boulogne.** Whether you spend your afternoon in a rowboat or wandering gardens filled with foliage, the Bois is the perfect escape from the city.

**Jardin d'Acclimatation.** There's not a child under the age of 5 who won't love this amusement park on the northern edge of the Bois de Boulogne.

**Fondation Le Corbusier.** The iconic Modernist designs of Swiss-born pioneering architect Le Corbusier fill this compelling museum, which was built as a private house—one of the first Corbusier was commissioned to do in Paris.

## MAKING THE MOST OF YOUR TIME

If this isn't your first time in Paris, or even if it is and you've had enough of the touristy central part of the city, this neighborhood is a great choice and can be treated like a day trip. Spend the morning admiring the Monets at the uncrowded Musée Marmottan Monet (closed Monday), then take in the Art Nouveau architecture on Rue la Fontaine. If your goal is to leave the city lights behind altogether, pack a picnic, and spend the day in the Bois de Boulogne.

## GETTING HERE

*Western Paris includes the 16ᵉ and 17ᵉ arrondissements.* Take Line 9 to La Muette métro stop for the Musée Marmottan Monet, or to the Jasmin stop (also Line 9) to explore Rue la Fontaine. Take Line 6 to the Passy stop for the Musée du Vin or to reach the main drag, Rue de Passy. For the Bois de Boulogne, take Line 2 to the Porte Dauphin stop or RER C to Avenue Foch. For the Jardin d'Acclimatation enter the park from the Les Sablons or Port Maillot métro stops on Line 1. If you're heading out to La Défense, it's the end of Line 1.

## BEST CAFÉS

**Le Passy.** The plush chestnut-and-cream decor of this café is the work of one of Givenchy's nephews. Cocktails are classy, the food—such as grilled lamb with tarragon—is yummy, and candlelight makes everyone look that much more glamorous. Closed Sunday. ⊠ *2 rue de Passy, Trocadéro–Tour Eiffel* ☎ *01–42–88–31–02* Ⓜ *Passy.*

**Tea for Two.** Despite the name, this thoroughly French café is a must for an inexpensive lunch. Try a savory brick (pronounced breek), a flaky pastry stuffed with luscious fillings such as seasoned chicken or salmon. Or enjoy afternoon tea with a slice of homemade tarte du citron. Closed evenings and Sunday. ⊠ *4 rue de la Tour, Trocadéro–Tour Eiffel* ☎ *01–40–50–90–46* Ⓜ *Passy.*

**Villa Passy.** The leafy, tucked-away courtyard of this café just off Rue de Passy may make you think you've stumbled into a small village. Sit outside on a cushioned banquette shaded by ivy and order the plat du jour, prepared with fresh market ingredients. Try the €23 Sunday brunch. ⊠ *4 impasse des Carrières, Trocadéro–Tour Eiffel* ☎ *01–45–27–68–76* Ⓜ *Passy.*

Sightseeing
★★
Dining
★
Lodging
★
Shopping
★

Welcome to Paris at its most prim and proper—but hardly stodgy. This genteel area is a study in smart urban planning, with classical architecture and newer construction commingling as easily as the haute bourgeoisie inhabitants mix with their American expat neighbors. There's no shortage of celebrities seeking some peace and quiet here, but you're just as likely to find well-heeled families who decamped from the center of the city in search of a spacious apartment.

A walk along the main avenues gives you a sense of Paris's finest Art Nouveau and Modernist buildings, including **Castel-Béranger**, by Hector Guimard, and the **Fondation Le Corbusier** museum, a prime example of the Swiss architect's Modernist style. This neighborhood is also home to one of the city's best and most overlooked museums—the **Musée Marmottan Monet**—which has an astonishing collection of Impressionist art. Enjoy a dégustation (tasting) at the **Musée du Vin** or simply find a café on Rue de Passy and savor a moment in one of the city's most exclusive enclaves. If it's a leafy landscape you're after, spend an afternoon at the **Bois de Boulogne,** especially if you have kids. At *Le Bois,* you can explore the Pré Catelan and Bagatelle gardens, both meticulously landscaped and surrounded by woods. Head to the old-fashioned amusement park at the Jardin d'Acclimatation or take a rowboat out on one of the park's two bucolic lakes. You can also rent a bike and hit the 14 km (9 mi) of marked trails.

## TOP ATTRACTIONS

Updated by
Linda Hervieux

**Bois de Boulogne**

*See highlighted listing in this chapter.*

Fodor's Choice
★

**Castel-Béranger.** It's a shame you can't go inside this house, considered the city's first Art Nouveau structure, dreamed up in 1898 by Hector Guimard. The wild combination of materials and the grimacing grillwork led neighbors to call this the Castle Dérangé (Deranged), but

13

this private commission catapulted the 27-year-old Guimard into the public eye, leading to his famous métro commission. After admiring the sea-inspired front entrance, go partway down the alley to admire the inventive treatment of the traditional Parisian courtyard, complete with a melting water fountain. Just up the road at No. 60 is the **Hotel Mezzara**, designed by Guimard in 1911 for textile designer Paul Mezzara. You can trace Guimard's evolution by walking to the subtler Agar complex at the end of the block (at the corner of Rue la Fontaine and Rue Gros). Tucked beside the stone entrance at the corner of Rue Gros is a tiny café-bar with an Art Nouveau glass front and furnishings. ✉ *14 rue la Fontaine, Passy-Auteuil* Ⓜ *Ranelagh; RER: Maison de Radio France.*

**WORD OF MOUTH**

"The Musée Marmottan in the 16th is not as well-known as many museums, but it's well worth a visit. It has the largest collection of Monets in the world, a beautiful collection of illuminated manuscripts and it's located in a beautiful mansion with park views on the western edge of the 16th arrondissement." —Kate W

**QUICK BITES** It seats just 15, but charming **Café Antoine** (✉ *17 rue la Fontaine, Passy-Auteuil* ☎ *01-40-50-14-30*) warrants a visit for its Art Nouveau facade, floor tiles, and carved wooden bar. Count on €35 for a meal, or share a charcuterie plate (about €17) and wine.

**Fondation Le Corbusier** *(Le Corbusier Foundation)*. Fresh from a major renovation, the 1923 Maison La Roche is a stellar example of Swiss architect Le Corbusier's innovative construction techniques based on geometric forms, recherché color schemes, and an unblushing use of iron and concrete. The sloping ramp that replaces the traditional staircase is one of the most eye-catching features. ✉ *10 sq. du Docteur Blanche, Passy-Auteuil* ☎ *01-42-88-41-53* ⊕ *www.fondationlecorbusier.asso. fr* ✆ *€5* ⊙ *Tues.–Fri. 10–12:30 and 1:30–6 (only until 5 Fri.), Mon. 1:30–6* Ⓜ *Jasmin; Michel Ange Auteuil.*

**Fodor's Choice** ★ **Musée Marmottan Monet.** A few years ago the underrated Marmottan tacked MONET onto its official name—and justly so, as this is the largest collection of the artist's works anywhere. Monet's works, donated by his son Michel, occupy a specially built basement gallery in this elegant 19th-century mansion, once the hunting lodge of the Duke de Valmy, where you can find such captivating works as the *Cathédrale de Rouen* series (1892–96) and *Impression: Soleil Levant* (*Impression: Sunrise,* 1872), the work that helped give the Impressionist movement its name. Other exhibits include letters exchanged by Impressionist painters Berthe Morisot and Mary Cassatt. Upstairs, the mansion still feels like a graciously decorated private home. Empire furnishings fill the salons overlooking the Jardin de Ranelagh on one side and the hotel's private yard on the other. There's also a captivating room of illuminated medieval manuscripts. To best understand the collection's context, buy an English-language catalog in the museum shop on your way in. ✉ *2 rue Louis-Boilly, Passy-Auteuil* ☎ *01-44-96-50-33* ⊕ *www.marmottan. com* ✆ *€9* ⊙ *Tues. 11–9, Wed.–Sun. 11–6* Ⓜ *La Muette.*

# BOIS DE BOULOGNE

✉ *Porte Dauphine for the main entrance; Porte Maillot or Les Sablons for northern end; Porte d'Auteuil for southern end* ☎ *01–40–71–75–60 Parc de Bagatelle; 01–40–67–90–82 Jardin d'Acclimatation* ⊕ *www.jardinacclimation.fr* ⊙ *Daily; hrs vary according to time of yr but are generally around 9:30 AM to dusk* 🎟 *Parc de Bagatelle free except during exhibitions; otherwise: adults €5, children €2.50, under 7 free; Jardin Shakespeare: €1; Jardin d'Acclimatation: €2.90, does not include individual ride tickets.*

When Parisians need a day in the great outdoors close to home, they head to the Bois de Boulogne. The Bois is not a park in the traditional sense—more like a tamed forest, as it was once a royal hunting ground. On nice days the park is filled with cyclists, rowers, joggers, *pétanque* players, and picnickers enjoying the formal gardens, romantic lakes, and wooded paths.

### HIGHLIGHTS

The **Parc de Bagatelle** is a floral garden of irises, roses, tulips, and water lilies, at its most colorful between April and June. **Pré Catelan** contains one of Paris's largest trees: a copper beech more than 200 years old. The romantic Le Pré Catelan restaurant, where *le tout Paris* of the Belle Époque used to dine on the elegant terrace, still lures diners and wedding parties, especially on weekends. The **Jardin Shakespeare** inside the Pré Catelan has a sampling of the flowers, herbs, and trees mentioned in Shakespeare's plays, and becomes an open-air theater for the Bard's works in spring. The **Jardin d'Acclimatation,** on the northern edge of the park, is a fabulous amusement park where it seems every child under the age of 5 in Paris spends his or her summer Sunday afternoons. Highlights include boat trips along an "enchanted river," and an aviary. A miniature railway shuttle runs from Porte Maillot on Wednesday and weekends beginning at 1:30; tickets cost €2.70 (round-trip). Rent boats or bikes for a few euros at **Lac Inférieur.** You can row or take a quick ferry to the island restaurant **Chalet des Iles.** Two popular horse-racing tracks are in the park, the **Hippodrome de Longchamp** and the **Hippodrome d'Auteuil.** Fans of the French Open can visit its home base, **Stade Roland-Garros** (tours in English Wednesday to Sunday at 11 AM and 3 PM, €10), and true devotees can check out the **Tenniseum** (tennis museum, €15 with stadium entry).

## TIPS

■ The main entrance to the Bois de Boulogne is off Avenue Foch near the Porte Dauphine métro stop on the 2 line, best for accessing Pré Catelan and Jardin Shakespeare off Route de la Grande-Cascade. For Jardin d'Acclimatation, off Boulevard Des Sablons, take the 1 line to Les Sablons or Porte Maillot, where you can ride the petit train to the amusement park. The Parc de Bagatelle, off Route de Sèvres-à-Neuilly, can be accessed from either Porte Dauphine or Porte Maillot, though it's a bit of a hike.

■ You'll want to leave the park by dusk, as the Bois becomes a distinctly adult playground after dark.

★ **Musée National Jean-Jacques Henner.** French artist Jean-Jacques Henner (1829–1905) was a star in his day, though his luminous nudes and clear-eyed portraits are largely forgotten today. This elegant museum stocked with his works reopened in late 2009 after a two-year renovation that restored the *maison particulière* (private mansion) to its 19th-century glory. Henner's style is hard to categorize: he painted more than 400 portraits, including a substantial number sold in America, with a Realist's eye—red nose, mottled skin, and all. But there is much beauty as well, as in *Lady with Umbrella*, a portrait of a fur-clad artistocrat with glistening blue eyes. Yet many of his soft-featured nudes betray other influences. Don't miss them in the light-filled atelier on the museum's third floor, where they share space with a series of religious paintings, notably the haunting *Saint Sebastian,* and a stark portrayal of a lifeless Christ, whose luminescent white skin is offset by a shock of flaming red hair. Henner never lived here; his heirs bought the home from the family of painter Guillaume Dubufe, and it opened as a museum in 1924. There is some information in English. ✉ *43 av. de Villiers* ☎ *01–47–63–42–73* ⊕ *www.musee-henner.fr* 🎟 *€5* ⊙ *Wed.–Sun. 11–6; 1st Thurs. of month 11–9* Ⓜ *Métro: Malesherbes.*

## WORTH NOTING

**OFF THE BEATEN PATH**

**La Défense.** First conceived in 1958, this Modernist suburb just west of Paris was inspired by Le Corbusier's dream of high-rise buildings, pedestrian walkways, and sunken vehicle circulation. Built as an experiment to keep high-rises out of the historic downtown, the Parisian business hub has survived economic uncertainty to become a surprising success. Visiting La Défense gives you a crash course in contemporary skyscraper evolution, from the solid blocks of the 1960s and '70s to the curvy fins of the '90s and beyond. Today 20,000 people live in the suburb, but 150,000 people work here, and many more come to shop in its enormous mall. While riding the métro Line 1 here, you'll get a view of the Seine, then emerge at a pedestrian plaza studded with some great public art, including César's giant thumb and one of Calder's great red "stabiles." The **Grande Arche de La Défense** dominates the area; it was designed as a controversial closure to the historic axis of Paris (an imaginary line that runs through the Arc de Triomphe, the Arc du Carrousel, and the Louvre glass pyramid). Glass bubble elevators in a metal-frame tower whisk you a heart-jolting 360 feet to the viewing platform. ✉ *Parvis de La Défense, La Défense* ☎ *01–49–07–27–27* ⊕ *www.grandearche.com* 🎟 *Grande Arche €10* ⊙ *Apr.–Aug., daily 10–8; Sept.–Mar., daily 10–7* Ⓜ *Métro or RER: Grande Arche de La Défense.*

**Maison de Balzac.** The modest Paris home of the great French 19th-century novelist Honoré de Balzac (1799–1850) contains exhibits charting his tempestuous yet prolific career. Balzac penned the nearly 100 novels and stories known collectively as *The Human Comedy,* many of them set in Paris. You can still feel his presence in his study and pay homage to his favorite coffeepot—his working hours were fueled by his tremendous consumption of the "black ink." English-language information is available. ✉ *47 rue Raynouard, Passy-Auteuil* ☎ *01–55–74–41–80* ⊕ *www.*

13

*paris.fr/musees/ 🖃 Free, except rare during temporary exhibitions, then €5 🕙 Tues.–Sun. 10–6* Ⓜ *Passy; La Muette.*

**DINING AT A GLANCE**

*For full reviews ⇨ Chapter 17.*

**EXPENSIVE DINING**
Le Pré Catelan, *Haute French,* Rue de Surèsnes

**Maison de Radio France.** Headquarters to France's state radio, this imposing 1962 circular building is more than 500 yards in circumference. It's said to have more floor space than any other building in France and features a 200-foot tower that overlooks the Seine. Radio France sponsors more than 100 concerts a year, including performances by its own Orchestre Philharmonique de Radio France and the Orchestre National de France. Though many of these concerts take place at venues throughout the city, several are held here, and some are free. 🖂 *116 av. du Président-Kennedy, Passy-Auteuil* ☎ *01–56–40–15–16* ⊕ *www. radiofrance.fr* Ⓜ *Ranelagh; RER: Maison de Radio France.*

**Musée du Vin.** Fans of wine making will enjoy this quirky museum housed in a 15th-century abbey, a reminder of Passy's roots as a pastoral village. Though hardly exhaustive, the collection includes old wine bottles, glassware, and ancient wine-related pottery excavated in Paris. Wine making paraphernalia shares the grottolike space with hokey figures retired from the city's wax museum, including Napoléon appraising a glass of Burgundy, but you can partake in a thoroughly nonhokey wine tasting, or bring home one of the 200-plus bottles for sale in the tiny gift shop. Pick up a free audio guide in English. If you call ahead, the staff will arrange a guided tour in English. You can book ahead for lunch, too. 🖂 *Rue des Eaux/5 sq. Charles Dickens, Passy-Auteil* ☎ *01–45–25–63–26* ⊕ *www.museeduvinparis.com* 🖃 *€11.90 with glass of wine; wine tastings €17–€27, includes admission* 🕙 *Tues.–Sun. 10–6* Ⓜ *Passy.*

**Porte Dauphine métro entrance.** Visitors come here to snap pictures of the queen of subway entrances, one of the city's two remaining Art Nouveau canopied originals designed by Hector Guimard (the other is at the Abbesses stop on Line 12). The flamboyant "crown" of amber-painted panels and runaway metal struts adorns this whimsical 1900 creation. The entrance is on the Bois de Boulogne side of Avenue Foch, so make certain to take the Boulevard de l'Amiral Bruix exit from the Line 2 station if you're traveling by métro.

**Rue d'Auteuil.** This narrow, crooked shopping street escaped Haussmann's urban renovations and today still retains the country feel of old Auteuil. Molière once lived on the site of No. 2; Racine was on nearby Rue du Buis; the pair met up to clink glasses and exchange drama notes at the Mouton Blanc Inn, now a brasserie, at No. 40. Numbers 19–25 and 29 are an interesting combination of 17th- and 18th-century buildings, which have evolved into a mixture of private housing and shop fronts. At the foot of the street, the scaly dome of the **Église d'Auteuil** (built in the 1880s) is an unmistakable small-time cousin of the Sacré-Coeur. Rue d'Auteuil is at its liveliest on Wednesday and Saturday mornings, when a much-loved street market crams onto Place Jean-Barraud. Ⓜ *MichelAnge Auteuil, Eglise d'Auteuil.*

# Nightlife

**WORD OF MOUTH**

"The Ice Kube Bar at the Kube Hotel is still considered trendy. Parkas are provided in the 38€ rate."

—kerouac

# NIGHTLIFE PLANNER

## Hours

Bars tend to stay open until between midnight and 2 AM, with no specific last call. Clubs often stay open until 4 AM, and many until dawn.

If you want to hit bars at a relatively quiet hour, go for an *apéritif* around 6 PM. Many places offer drink specials at this time, and it's also when Parisians congregate to make late-night plans. Many bars charge slightly higher prices after 10.

## Wine Bars

Wine bars are different from regular bars in that they serve simple meals and snacks (charcuterie, cheese) as well as wine; they usually close earlier than full-fledged bars—somewhere between 10 and midnight.
⇨ For reviews of bars à vins, see the Wine Bars section in the Where to Eat chapter.

## Table Service, or Non?

Some bars have table service; at others (designated by SERVICE AU BAR signs), you must fetch your own drinks.

## Getting Past the Bouncer

It shouldn't surprise any nightlife lover that the more *branché* (literally, "plugged-in" or trendy) the spot, the knottier the door-entry problem will be. Most bars aren't a problem, but when it comes to clubbing, don't assume you're going to get in just because you show up. This is particularly true at the hot spots near the Champs-Élysées. A limo at your disposal and global fame aren't essential to pass muster, but you absolutely must have a cocky yet somehow simultaneously polite attitude and look fabulous. Having a high female quotient in your party definitely helps (fashion models are a particular plus). Solo men—or, worse, groups of men—are going to have a tougher time, unless they are high rollers and have reserved a table (bottle purchase *obligatoire*).

## Late-Night Transportation

The last métro runs between 12:30 AM and 1 AM Monday through Sunday, but there is new late-night service on Friday and Saturday until 2 AM. After that, you can take a cab, but it can be extremely difficult to find one in the wee hours. Taxi stands boast long lines for few cabs, and calling Taxi Bleu (☎08–91–70–10–10) or Taxi G-7 (☎01–47–39–47–39) is unpredictable on weekends. Another option is the Noctilien, the sometimes rowdy night-bus system (⇨ see By Bus in Paris Travel Smart). A new option is the Velib, if you stay within biking distance of chosen destinations, though after a few champagnes it may be better to do like the Parisians and just stay out until the métro starts running again at 5:45 AM.

## What to Wear

Parisians are chic, so if you want to blend in (and get into clubs), dress up. Men, you can wear your jeans—designer jeans, that is—but leave the sneakers at your hotel and try adding a blazer. Ladies, dressing up doesn't necessarily mean a dress and heels—Parisian girls manage to look like a million bucks in jeans and a chic top.

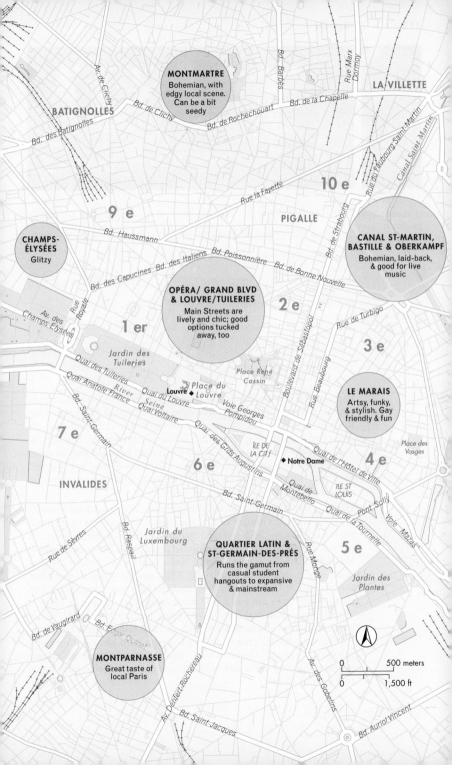

**MONTMARTRE**
Bohemian, with edgy local scene. Can be a bit seedy

BATIGNOLLES

Bd. des Batignolles

Av. de Clichy

Bd. de Clichy

Bd. de Rochechouart

Bd. Barbès

Bd. de la Chapelle

Rue Marx Dormoy

LA VILLETTE

Rue du Faubourg Saint-Martin

Canal Saint-Martin

Rue la Fayette

**9 e**

Bd. Haussmann

**10 e**

PIGALLE

Bd. de Strasbourg

**CHAMPS-ÉLYSÉES**
Glitzy

Bd. des Capucines    Bd. des Italiens    Bd. Poissonnière    Bd. de Bonne Nouvelle

**CANAL ST-MARTIN, BASTILLE & OBERKAMPF**
Bohemian, laid-back, & good for live music

Av. des Champs-Élysées

Rue Royale

**OPÉRA/ GRAND BLVD & LOUVRE/TUILERIES**
Main Streets are lively and chic; good options tucked away, too

**2 e**

Rue de Turbigo

**3 e**

**1 er**

Jardin des Tuileries

Quai des Tuileries

River

Quai du Louvre

Quai Anatole France

Seine

Quai Voltaire

Place René Cassin

**Louvre** ◆ Place du Louvre

Voie Georges Pompidou

Boulevard de Sébastopol

Rue Beaubourg

**LE MARAIS**
Artsy, funky, & stylish. Gay friendly & fun

Place des Vosges

**7 e**

Bd. Saint-Germain

Quai des Grands Augustins

ÎLE DE LA CITÉ

◆ Notre Dame

Quai de l'Hôtel de Ville

**4 e**

**6 e**

INVALIDES

Bd. Saint-Germain

Quai de Montebello

ÎLE ST LOUIS

Quai de la Tournelle

Pont Sully

Voie Mazas

Rue de Sèvres

Bd. Raspail

Jardin du Luxembourg

**QUARTIER LATIN & ST-GERMAIN-DES-PRÉS**
Runs the gamut from casual student hangouts to expansive & mainstream

Rue Monge

**5 e**

Jardin des Plantes

Bd. de Vaugirard

Bd. Edgar Quinet

**MONTPARNASSE**
Great taste of local Paris

Av. Denfert-Rochereau

Bd. Saint-Jacques

Av. des Gobelins

Bd. Auriol Vincent

0    500 meters
0    1,500 ft

Updated
by Mary
Papenfuss

You haven't seen Paris until you've seen the city at night. Throngs fill popular streets and the air fills with the melody of French conversation and the clinking of glasses. This is when Parisians let down their hair and reveal their true bonhomie, laughing and dancing, flirting and talking. Parisians love to savor life together: they dine out, drink endless espressos, offer innumerable toasts, and are often so reluctant to separate that they party all night.

Parisians go out weekends and weeknights, late and early. And they tend to frequent the same places once they've found spots they like: it could be a wine bar, corner café, or hip music club, and you can often find a welcoming "the-gang's-all-here" atmosphere. A wise way to spend an evening is to pick an area in a neighborhood that interests you, then give yourself time to browse. Parisians love to bar hop and the energy shifts throughout the evening, so be prepared to follow the crowds all night.

Nightlife hot spots are scattered throughout the city, with each neighborhood offering a unique vibe. If you prefer clinking drinks with models and celebrities, check out the Champs-Élysées area, but be prepared to shell out *beaucoup* bucks and stare down surly bouncers. Easygoing, bohemian-chic revelers can be found in the northeastern districts like Canal St-Martin and Belleville, while students tend to pour into the Bastille, St-Germain-des-Prés, and the Quartier Latin. Gays and party-hearty types can nail a wild time nearly every night in Le Marais. Grands Boulevards and Rue Montorgueil, just north of Les Halles, is party central for young professionals and the fashion crowd, and the Pigalle/Montmartre area is always hopping with plenty of theaters, cabarets, bars, and concert venues. Warmer months draw the adventurous to floating clubs and bars, moored along the Seine from Bercy to the Eiffel Tower.

An evening at Au Lapin Agile, one of Paris's original cabarets (founded in 1860), usually consists of live music and singing, unlike some of the racier cabaret shows.

## BARS

★ **Alcazar** (✉ 62 *rue Mazarine, 6ᵉ, St-Germain-des-Prés* ☎ 01–53–10–19–99 Ⓜ *Odéon*) is Sir Terence Conran's makeover of a 17th-century Parisian *jeu de paume* court that features a stylish mezzanine-level bar under a greenhouse-glass roof. The vibe changes from Wednesday to Saturday as spicy DJs spin mixes into the wee hours.

★ **American Bar at La Closerie des Lilas** (✉ 171 *bd. du Montparnasse, 6ᵉ, Montparnasse* ☎ 01–40–51–34–50 Ⓜ *Montparnasse*) lets you drink in the swirling action of the adjacent restaurant and brasserie at a piano bar hallowed by plaques honoring such former habitués as Man Ray, Jean-Paul Sartre, Samuel Beckett, and Ernest Hemingway, who talks of "the Lilas" in *A Moveable Feast*.

**Andy Wahloo** (✉ 69 *rue des Gravilliers, 3ᵉ, Le Marais* ☎ 01–42–71–20–38 Ⓜ *Arts et Métiers*) has a hip crowd and an Andy Warhol-meets-*Casablanca* decor. Fans of the ginger-rum Wahloo *spéciales* relax on oversize paint-can stools beneath high-kitsch silk-screened Moroccan coffee ads, and listen to funky Arabic Raï remixes.

★ **Apicius** (✉ 20 *rue d'Artois, 8ᵉ, Champs-Élysées* ☎ 01–43–80–19–66 Ⓜ *George V*) offers sublime elegance mere steps from the Champs-Élysées. Wander through the luxe front garden and chateau restaurant to the sleekly modern black bar where couture cocktails are concocted to suit any cultured taste. Closed weekends.

**Bar Fleur's** (✉ 3 *rue des Tournelles, 4ᵉ, Le Marais* ☎ 01–42–71–04–51 Ⓜ *Bastille*) offers an incomparable pistil-packin' experience for bloom lovers who savor top-shelf champagne and vodka: it's a combination bar and exotic florist.

**Bar du Marché** (✉ *16 rue de Buci, 6ᵉ, St-Germain/Buci* ☎ *01–43–26–55–15* Ⓜ *Mabillon/Odeon*) is a local legend where waiters wearing red overalls and revolutionary "Gavroche" hats serve drinks every day of the week, with particular zeal around happy hour. With bottles of wine at about €25, it draws a quintessential Left Bank mix of expat locals, fashion-house interns, and even some professional rugby players. Sit outside on the terrace and enjoy the prime corner location.

**Barramundi** (✉ *3 rue Taitbout, 9ᵉ, Opéra/Grands Boulevards* ☎ *01–47–70–21–21* Ⓜ *Richelieu Drouot*) lures the city's nouveau-riche chic, who chill to electro-lounge tunes and world music in the cool gold ambience, and sip tropical drinks like piña coladas and the exotically dubbed "sex on the beach" cocktail at the long copper bar.

**Barrio Latino** (✉ *46–48 rue du Faubourg St-Antoine, 12ᵉ, Bastille* ☎ *01–55–78–84–75* Ⓜ *Bastille*) rocks the rafters for adventurers who love to indulge in Latin cultures from Brazilian to Cuban in the middle of Paris. The quirky four-story hacienda-resto, two dance bars, and top-floor nightclub fuel the devoted who shake to salsa and samba beats all night. The pricey €20 weekend entrance fee includes a drink.

**Bar Sans Nom** (✉ *49 rue de Lappe, 12ᵉ, Bastille* ☎ *01–48–05–59–36* Ⓜ *Bastille*) is a cozy getaway in the increasing hubbub of the Bastille. The warm, red decor exudes a sultry glow, and hip lounge music adds to the charm. The flaming Kucaracha shot will turn up the heat.

**Bound Bar** (✉ *49–51 av. George V, 8e, Champs-Élysées* ☎ *01–53–67–84–60* Ⓜ *George V*) is the decadently techno-glam former home of Barfly, featuring black chandeliers, a gleaming bar that seems to go on forever, and glowing purple light. It buzzes with a classy mix of tourists and after-work professionals chilling to lounge music. The location, off the Champs-Élysées, makes it the perfect stop for an evening apéritif.

**Buddha Bar** (✉ *8 rue Boissy d'Anglas, 8ᵉ, Champs-Élysées* ☎ *01–53–05–90–00* Ⓜ *Concorde*) is past its prime with Parisians, but visitors can't seem to get enough of the high-camp towering gold Buddha that holds court over giant palm fronds, red satin walls, colorful chinoiserie, and a spacious mezzanine bar that, in turn, overlooks a dining room serving pan-Asian fare.

★ **Café Charbon** (✉ *109 rue Oberkampf, 11ᵉ, Oberkampf* ☎ *01–43–57–55–13* Ⓜ *St-Maur, Parmentier*) seduces neighborhood bohos with its warm wooden Belle Époque charm and floor-to-soaring-ceiling mirrors. The attached Nouveau Casino offers cutting-edge live performances.

**Café la Fourmi** (✉ *74 rue des Martyrs, 18ᵉ, Montmartre* ☎ *01–42–64–70–35* Ⓜ *Pigalle*) is one of Pigalle's trendiest addresses, with a funky spacious bar-café where cool locals party.

★ **Chao Ba** (✉ *22 bd. de Clichy, 18ᵉ, Montmartre* ☎ *01–46–06–72–90* Ⓜ *Pigalle*) transports colonial French Indochine to the foot of Montmartre with a glam gold interior, comfy bamboo chairs on two floors, and exotic drinks like the popular Kamikaze. DJs mix it up with techno and lounge music weekends.

exquisite manga-inspired decor, the top-shelf DJs for weekend dancing, and its kooky, disco-ball-and-kid-sumo-adorned bathrooms. It was featured as a chic eatery in *Sex and the City*; need we say more?

**L'Éclaireur** (✉ *8–10 rue Boissy d'Anglas, 10ᵉ, Louvre/Tuileries* ☎ *01–53–43–09–99* Ⓜ *Concorde*) is a spacious venue, boasting a lavish decor and intriguing mix of cocktails—next door to a hip boutique of the same name.

**La Belle Hortense** (✉ *31 rue Vielle-du-Temple, 4ᵉ, Le Marais* ☎ *01–48–04–74–60* Ⓜ *St-Paul*) is heaven for anyone who ever wished they had a book in a bar (or a drink in a bookstore). The *bar litteraire* is the infamous spot where gal-about-town Catherine M. launched her *vie sexuelle* that became a baudy bestseller.

14

### APÉRITIFS

For *apéritifs* French style, try a *pastis*—anise-flavored liquor such as Pernod or Ricard that turns cloudy when water is added. Ask for "*un petit jaune, s'il vous plait.*" A *pineau* is cognac and fruity grape juice. The *kir* (white wine with a dash of black-currant syrup) is a popular drink, too; a *kir royale* is made with champagne. For the adventurous, try absinthe, the vivid green, once-outlawed liquor that's making a comeback around town—check out **La Fée Verte** (✉ *108 rue de la Roquette* ☎ *01–43–72–31–24*) in the Bastille area; the food is good, too.

**La Chaise au Plafond** (✉ *10 rue du Trésor, 4ᵉ, Le Marais* ☎ *01–42–76–03–22* Ⓜ *St-Paul*) offers the feel of a traditional bistro with offbeat touches like the swirling black cowhide splotches suspended from the ceiling. It's an excellent spot for wine sipping and people-watching in the bustling Marais.

★ **La Favela Chic** (✉ *18 rue du Faubourg du Temple, 11ᵉ, République* ☎ *01–40–21–38–14* Ⓜ *République*) took the scene early, forging Oberkampf's hip reputation. Back behind courtyard gates, this popular Latin cocktail bar offers caipirinhas and mojitos, guest DJs presenting an eclectic mix of samba, soul and hip-hop, and a nonstop dance scene.

★ **La Perle** (✉ *78 rue Vielle-du-Temple, 3ᵉ, Le Marais* ☎ *01–42–72–69–93* Ⓜ *Chemin-Vert*) is a bustling, buzzy Marais masterpiece, where straights, gays, and lesbians of all types come to mingle. The crowd makes this place interesting, not the neon lights, diner-style seats, or stripped-down decor. Its status as a fashionista hot spot bounced even higher when Galliano stopped by, and it continues to pack in some of the city's fashion movers and shakers, from midafternoon on.

**Le Café Noir** (✉ *65 rue Montmartre, 2ᵉ, Les Halles* ☎ *01–40–39–07–36* Ⓜ *Étienne Marcel*) lures Parisians from Bobos to *pompiers* (fire fighters) to its elegantly worn digs that feature a pipe-smoking papier-mâché fish, a leopard-print-covered old motorbike, cool *alcool,* and friendly staff. (The restaurant with the same name is unrelated.)

★ **Le Fumoir** (✉ *6 rue Amiral-de-Coligny, 1ᵉʳ, Louvre/Tuileries* ☎ *01–42–92–00–24* Ⓜ *Louvre*) is an oh-so-reliably ultrachic charmer across from the Louvre where fashionable neighborhood gallery owners and professionals meet for late-afternoon wine, early-evening cocktails, or dinner. It features a super-stocked bar in the front, an ample multilingual library in the back, and chess boards for the clientele to use while sipping martinis.

**Le Refuge des Fondus** (✉ *17 rue des 3 Frères, 18ᵉ, Montmartre* ☎ *01–42–55–22–65* Ⓜ *Anvers*) appeals to the kid in us all by serving wine in baby bottles to packs of giggling, happy campers seated shoulder-to-shoulder at long wooden tables. The 30-year-old bar-resto thus dodges taxes imposed on alcohol served in stemmed glasses. Goo-Goo!

**Le Rendez-Vous Des Amis** (✉ *23 rue Gabrielle, 18ᵉ, Montmartre* ☎ *01–46–06–01–60* Ⓜ *Abbesses*) is an intriguing midway breather if you climb the hill of Montmartre by foot. There's a jovial staff, eclectic music, and a century's worth of previous patrons immortalized in photos.

Step into **Le Rosebud** (✉ *11 bis, rue Delambre, 14ᵉ, Montparnasse* ☎ *01–43–35–38–54* Ⓜ *Vavin*) through the Art Nouveau front door of this one-time haunt of Jean-Paul Sartre and you're instantly immersed in the dark, moody, fourth dimension of Old Montparnasse, where white-jacketed servers and red-lacquered tables transport you into the past.

**Le Sancerre** (✉ *35 rue des Abbesses, 18ᵉ, Montmartre* ☎ *01–42–58–08–20* Ⓜ *Abbesses*), a café by day, turns into an essential watering hole for Montmartrois and artists at night, with Belgian beers on tap and an impressive list of cocktails. It was spruced up in 2007 but still maintains its traditional old-school vibe.

**Le Trésor** (✉ *7 rue du Trésor, 4ᵉ, Le Marais* ☎ *01–42–71–35–17* Ⓜ *St-Paul*) is lively and sophisticated, with mismatched Baroque furnishings in a large space, and a chill vibe on a tiny street a tad separate from the sometimes madding crowd of Le Marais.

**Qui Êtes-Vous, Polly Maggoo?** (✉ *3–5 rue du Petit Pont, 5ᵉ, Latin Quarter* ☎ *01–46–33–33–64* Ⓜ *St-Michel*) is a convivial hangout legendary as the student rioters' unofficial HQ during the May '68 uprising and named after the satirical French art-house movie about a supermodel. Weekends are wild, with drinks at the wacky tile bar and live Latino music that keeps the party thumping until morning.

**Sanz Sans** (✉ *49 rue du Faubourg St-Antoine, 11ᵉ, Bastille/Nation* ☎ *01–44–75–78–78* Ⓜ *Bastille*) glows in red velvet and gilt with lamp shades fashioned from cymbals, which the staff clang mischievously. Arrive early on weekends, when it's heaving with cosmopolitan twentysomethings juicing up for a night of dancing until dawn.

## HOTEL BARS

Some of Paris's best hotel bars mix historic pedigrees with hushed elegance; others go for a modern, edgy luxe. They offer an opportunity to experience the atmosphere of some of the chicest spots in Paris. But high prices and the fickle Parisian fashion pack ensure that only the latest, highly hyped bars draw in locals regularly.

Fodor's Choice ★ **The Hemingway Bar & the Ritz Bar** (⊠ *15 pl. Vendôme, 1er, Louvre/Tuileries* ☎ *01–43–16–30–30* Ⓜ *Opéra*) are steps from each other at the super-luxe Ritz hotel; both serve the cocktails of world-famous bartender Colin Field. The Hemingway bar stays true to the old guard, and is decorated with photos taken by the great writer himself. The reopened Ritz Bar (formerly the Cambon) woos a trendy clientele with muted lighting, luxurious seating, and above-average lounge music.

**Hôtel Le Bristol** (⊠ *112 rue du Faubourg St-Honoré, 8e, Champs-Élysées* ☎ *01–53–43–43–00* Ⓜ *Miromesnil*) attracts the rich and powerful. Cocktails are stellar, and the music is an ultrachic blend of jazz–lounge. For a precocktail treat, check out the occasional mini-runway shows at teatime. ■ TIP→ **Try the famous Crazy Horse cocktail.**

Fodor's Choice ★ **Hôtel Costes** (⊠ *239 rue St-Honoré, 1er, Louvre/Tuileries* ☎ *01–42–44–50–25*) draws the big names, and not just during fashion week. Despite years on the scene, this place has lost none of its flair, or star clientele. Expect to cross paths with anyone from Kylie Minogue to Bruce Willis, as long as you make it past the chilly greeting of the statuesque hostess. Dressing to kill is strongly advised, especially for newcomers; otherwise expect all the tables to be suddenly reserved.

**Hôtel Meurice** (⊠ *228 rue de Rivoli, 1er, Louvre/Tuileries* ☎ *01–44–58–10–66* Ⓜ *Tuileries*) converted its ground-floor Fontainebleau library into an intimate bar with wood paneling and huge murals depicting the royal hunting forests of Fontainebleau. Its loyal fashion crowd is continually wooed by Philippe Starck decor updates and lubricated with the bar's famous Bellinis. ■ TIP→ **Try the Meurice Millenium cocktail, made with champagne, rose liqueur, and Cointreau.**

**Hôtel Plaza Athénée** (⊠ *25 av. Montaigne, 8e, Champs-Élysées* ☎ *01–53–67–66–00* Ⓜ *Champs-Élysées–Clemenceau*) is Paris's perfectly chic chill-out spot, with a sexy, glowing bar designed by Philippe Starck protégé Patrick Jouin. Gather here for an apéritif to stoke your energy before hitting the nearby club scene. ■ TIP→ **You'll find one of the most inventive cocktail lists in town here: try the acclaimed Rose Royale, with champagne and freshly crushed raspberries.**

★ **L'Hôtel** (⊠ *13 rue des Beaux-Arts, 6e, St-Germain-des-Prés* ☎ *01–44–41–99–00* Ⓜ *St-Germain-des-Prés*) offers an exquisite, hushed Baroque hideaway bar that makes for the perfect discreet rendezvous. Designed in typically jaw-dropping Jacques Garcia style, it boasts a photo of a louche Keanu Reeves on the wall and evokes the decadent spirit of one-time resident Oscar Wilde.

**Le Bar at George V** (⊠ *31 av. George V, 8e, Champs-Élysées* ☎ *01–49–52–70–00* Ⓜ *George V*) is an ultraluxe, clubby hideaway in the Four Seasons Hotel, perfect for star gazing from the plush wine-red armchairs, cognac in hand. The charm still lures the glitterati, especially during fashion weeks.

★ **Murano Urban Resort** (⊠ *13 bd. du Temple, 3e, République* ☎ *01–42–71–20–00* Ⓜ *Filles du Calvaire, République*) is Paris's epitome of space-age-bachelor-pad-hipness *du jour* with a black-stone bar, candy-color walls, and a friendly staff. It overflows nightly with beautiful Marais culture vultures, and is grabbing the late-night buzz with its theme soirées.

**14**

★ **Pershing Hall** (✉ *49 rue Pierre Charron, 8ᵉ, Champs-Élysées* ☎ *01–58–36–58–36* Ⓜ *George V*) has an überstylish lounge in muted colors and minimalist lines, and an enormous "vertical garden" in the simply stunning courtyard. The chic ambience and hip lounge music make this a neighborhood jewel.

**Regina's Bar Anglais** (✉ *2 pl. des Pyramides, 2ᵉ, Louvre* ☎ *01–42–60–31–10* Ⓜ *Louvre Rivoli*) offers an oasis of Englishness in the sea of trendy French bars, with comfy leather armchairs and a tasteful Belle Époque decor. The verdant terrace is a magnet in the warmer months.

## CABARETS

Paris's cabarets range from boîtes once haunted by Picasso and Piaf to those sinful showplaces where *tableaux vivants* offer acres of bare female flesh. Some of these places, like the Lido, are more Vegas than the petticoat vision re-created by Hollywood in Baz Luhrmann's *Moulin Rouge*—but the rebirth of burlesque is making some of the old-school venues more popular. You can dine at many cabarets, but the food isn't the attraction. Prices range from about €24 (admission plus one drink) to more than €130 (dinner plus show).

Fodor'sChoice **Au Lapin Agile** (✉ *22 rue des Saules, 18ᵉ, Montmartre* ☎ *01–46–06–85–87* Ⓜ *Lamarck Caulaincourt*) is an authentic survivor from the 19th century, and considers itself the doyen of cabarets. Founded in 1860, it still inhabits a modest house, once a favorite subject of painter Maurice Utrillo. It became the home-away-from-home for Braque, Modigliani, Apollinaire, and Picasso—who once paid for a meal with one of his paintings, then promptly exited and painted another that he named after this place. There are no topless dancers—this is a genuine French cabaret with songs, poetry, and humor in a publike setting.

**Bobino** (✉ *20 rue Gaîté, 14ᵉ, Montparnasse* ☎ *01–43–27–24–24* Ⓜ *Edgar Quinet Gaîté*) reopened in 2007, and what a buzz it started. The wow renovation turned this onetime concert hall into a glitzy, electrifying restaurant-cabaret-lounge-club, where the party starts when the cabaret ends at 11:30. It's a feast for eyes and appetite.

★ **Crazy Horse** (✉ *12 av. George V, 8ᵉ, Champs-Élysées* ☎ *01–47–23–32–32* Ⓜ *Alma-Marceau*) has honed striptease to an elegant art. Founded in 1951 and renovated in 2007, it's renowned for gorgeous dancers and raunchy routines characterized by lots of humor and few clothes. Burlesque artist extraordinaire and fashion show regular Dita von Teese has been known to perform here, elevating the reputation of this haunt.

**Le Belle Villoise** (✉ *19, 21 rue Boyer, 20ᵉ, Eastern Paris* ☎ *01–46–36–07–07* Ⓜ *Gambetta, Ménilmontant*) is a multi-use exhibition space that functions as a bar, dance club, restaurant, and performance venue, with concerts, and burlesque shows.

★ **Le Limonaire** (✉ *18 cité Bergère, 9ᵉ, Opéra/Grands Boulevards* ☎ *01–45–23–33–33* Ⓜ *Grands Boulevards*) oozes Parisian charm and serves food until 10 PM Tuesday–Sunday before giving way to the singing of traditional French songs of "expression," with musical accompaniment *bien sûr*. There's no entrance fee; musicians pass the hat.

The Paradis Latin cabaret is one of the liveliest spots on the Left Bank.

**Lido** (✉ *116 bis, av. des Champs-Élysées, 8ᵉ, Champs-Élysées* ☎ *01–40–76–56–10* Ⓜ *George V*) stars the supercalifragilisticexpialidelicious Blubell Girls, in feathers, spangles, boas, and lots of skin. The owners claim that no show this side of Vegas rivals it for special effects.

**Michou** (✉ *80 rue des Martyrs, 18ᵉ, Montmartre* ☎ *01–46–06–16–04* Ⓜ *Pigalle*) presents an over-the-top show by the always-decked-out-in-blue owner Michou. The show features "tranformiste" men on stage in extravagant drag, performing with high camp for a radically different cabaret experience. Dinner shows are €105 and €135, or you can watch from the bar for €35, which includes a drink.

**Moulin Rouge** (✉ *82 bd. de Clichy, 18ᵉ, Montmartre* ☎ *01–53–09–82–82* Ⓜ *Blanche*) offered a circuslike atmosphere when it opened in 1889, and lured Parisians of all social stripes. Think elephants, donkey rides for the ladies, and the incomparable cancan revue. Today, the cancan is still a popular highlight of what is now more a Vegas-y show, starring 100 dancers, acrobats, ventriloquists, and contortionists, and more than 1,000 costumes. Dinner starts at 7, revues at 9 and 11 (arrive 30 minutes early). Men are expected to wear a jacket and tie. Prices range from €80 for just a revue to €180 for luxe dinner and a show.

★ **Paradis Latin** (✉ *28 rue du Cardinal Lemoine, 5ᵉ, Quartier Latin* ☎ *01–55–26–10–10* Ⓜ *Cardinal Lemoine*) peppers its quirky show with acrobatics and eye-popping lighting effects, in a building by Gustav Eiffel, making it the liveliest and trendiest cabaret on the Left Bank. It's closed Tuesday.

## CLUBS

Paris's hyped *boîtes de nuit*—more often referred to as simply *boîtes* (nightclubs)—tend to be expensive and exclusive. If you're friends with a regular or you've modeled in *Vogue*, you'll have an easier time getting through the door. Cover charges at some spots push the €20 range, with drinks at the bar starting at €10 for a beer. Others are free to enter, but getting past the doorman can still be an issue. Locals looking to dance tend to stick to the smaller clubs, where the cover ranges from free (usually on slower weekdays) to €15 and the focus is on the music and upbeat atmosphere. Club popularity depends on the night or event, as Parisians are more loyal to certain DJs than venues and often hit two or three spots before ending up at one of the many after-parties, which can last until noon the next day.

**Black Calvados** (⊠ *40 av. Pierre, 1er, de Serbie 8ᵉ, Champs-Élysées* ☎ *01–47–20–77–77* Ⓜ *Saint-Philippe-du-Roule*), known as "BC" to its trend-setting devotees, is a sleek bar where the party starts late (don't bother coming before 1 AM) and lasts until morning. Ring the buzzer out front for the doorman to assess your worth—this is a celebrity hangout. Inside, try the Black Kiss, a shot of black vodka served on ice with sugar-cube lips. ■ TIP➔ If all else fails, head upstairs to the smaller but equally sexy bar-restaurant and order a midnight snack of Kobe miniburgers.

**Cab** (⊠ *2 pl. du Palais-Royal, 1er, Louvre/Tuileries* ☎ *01–58–62–56–25* Ⓜ *Palais-Royal*) is a popular fashion-centric club across from the Louvre, where models, photographers, and stylists bypass the lesser beings at the velvet rope. If you make it inside, you'll appreciate the chic Space Odyssey atmosphere. Depending on the night, you'll hear funk, hip-hop, electro, or house.

**Chez Castel** (⊠ *15 rue Princesse, 6ᵉ, St-Germain-des-Prés* ☎ *01–40–51–52–80* Ⓜ *St-Germain-des-Prés, Mabillon*) is the swankiest of private Paris clubs: a three-story gold-and-red-velvet mansion with vaulted ceilings where celebrities like Monica Bellucci and Vincent Cassel cavort far from the St-Germain tourists. Making reservations at the two dining rooms (one more formal than the other) will ease your entry.

**L'Élysée Montmartre** (⊠ *72 bd. de Rochechouart, 18ᵉ, Montmartre* ☎ *01–44–92–45–47* Ⓜ *Anvers*) rocks the rafters of an old concert hall with music that runs the gamut of hits from the 1940s to 1980s (emphasis on the latter); the DJ is backed by a 10-piece orchestra.

**La Coupole** (⊠ *100 bd. du Montparnasse, 14ᵉ, Montparnasse* ☎ *01–43–20–14–20* Ⓜ *Vavin*), the gorgeous dance hall beneath the famous brasserie, has "Latin Fever" nights on Friday from 7:45 PM (for beginners) until dawn. Saturday has the popular "Re-Definition" night of hip-hop, R&B, and afro-zouk from 11:30.

**La Java** (⊠ *105 rue du Faubourg du Temple, 10ᵉ, République* ☎ *01–42–02–20–52* Ⓜ *Belleville*), the spot where Piaf and Chevalier made their names, has reinvented itself as a dance club with rock–pop music and live performances by up-and-coming bands.

**La Scène Bastille** (⊠ *2 bis, rue des Taillandiers, 11ᵉ, Bastille/Nation* ☎ *01–48–06–50–70* Ⓜ *Bastille*) is one of the more refreshing venues in the Bastille club scene, with a laid-back, eclectic crowd and a cozy (if uncreatively decorated) lounge atmosphere. A variety of theme nights keep this place interesting, especially the "Techno Sweet Peak" and "In Funk We Trust." Gay nights also attract a lively crowd.

**Le Balajo** (⊠ *9 rue de Lappe, 11ᵉ, Bastille* ☎ *01–47–00–07–87* Ⓜ *Bastille*), a casual dance club in an old ballroom, has been around since 1936. Latin groove, funk, and R&B disco are the standards, with old-style musette Sunday afternoons, salsa on Tuesday and Thursday nights. Saturday is ladies' night with half-price entrance charge.

★ **Le Baron** (⊠ *6 av. Marceau, 8ᵉ, Champs-Élysées* ☎ *01–47–20–04–01* Ⓜ *Alma-Marceau*), formerly a seedy "hostesse" bar, didn't bother to update its decadent cabaret decor (red banquettes, mirror ball, and baronial top-hat sign) when it opened in 2004—and it didn't need to. Models, musicians, and Oscar winners party until morning while indulging in the bar's classic cocktail: a mix of red fruits, champagne, and vodka called the Baron Deluxe. It's notoriously difficult to get in.

★ **Le Batofar** (⊠ *11 quai François Mauriac, 13ᵉ, Bercy/Tolbiac* ☎ *09–71–25–50–61* Ⓜ *Bibliothèque*) is an old tugboat refitted as a hip bar and concert venue. Music at this trendy yet reasonably priced spot is eclectic, from live world-beat to electronic and techno. ■ TIP→ **(Stylish) sneakers are recommended on the slippery deck.**

**Le Djoon** (⊠ *22 bd. Auriol, 13ᵉ, Bibliothèque* ☎ *01–45–70–83–49* Ⓜ *Bibliothèque*) attracts a devoted dance crowd—it's not the place to stand around. With inspiration from the '80s New York house scene, the DJ mixes afro, disco, and funk. It's a taxi ride away from everywhere, but a fun diversion from the normally cramped clubs. Club open Friday-Saturday from 11:30 to 5am, and Sunday from 6 to 1 AM.

**Le Duplex** (⊠ *2 bis, av. Foch, 16ᵉ, Champs-Élysées* ☎ *01–45–00–45–00* Ⓜ *Charles de Gaulle–Étoile*) offers three rockin' rooms, all underground, each with its own character and music, from techno to vintage disco. The hot spot draws a mixed-aged group of friendly locals.

**Le Gibus** (⊠ *18 rue du Faubourg du Temple, 11ᵉ, République* ☎ *01–47–00–78–88* Ⓜ *République*) is one of Paris's most famous music venues. More than 6,500 concerts (including the Police, Deep Purple, and Billy Idol) have packed in fans for 30 years. Today the Gibus's cellars are *the* place for trance, techno, hip-hop, and hard-core.

★ **Le Nouveau Casino** (⊠ *109 rue Oberkampf, 11ᵉ, République* ☎ *01–43–57–57–40* Ⓜ *Parmentier*) is a concert hall and club tucked behind the Café Charbon. Pop and rock concerts prevail during the week, with clubbing on Friday and Saturday from midnight until dawn. Electronic, house, disco, and techno DJs are the standard.

**Le Red Light** (⊠ *34 rue du Départ, 15ᵉ, Montparnasse* ☎ *01–42–79–94–94* Ⓜ *Montparnasse Bienvenüe*) has two giant dance floors playing mainly house and electronic music by big-name international DJs every Friday and Saturday from midnight until dawn. It draws a casual, mixed crowd.

★ **Le Rex** (⊠ *5 bd. Poissonnière, 2ᵉ, Opéra/Grands Boulevards* ☎ *01–42–36–10–96* Ⓜ *Grands Boulevards*) is a temple of techno and house, popular

**14**

**CLOSE UP**

# After-Hours Restaurants

Craving steak au poivre after a post-midnight party? Most late-night brasseries and 'round-the-clock restaurants don't need reservations. Here are some of the best.

**Á la Cloche d'Or** (⊠ *3 rue Mansart, 9ᵉ, Montmartre* ☎ *01–48–74–48–88* Ⓜ *Place de Clichy*) is a Paris classic, whose traditional French dishes satisfied the likes of the late president François Mitterrand and Moulin Rouge dancers (though not together). It's open until 4 AM every day but Sunday. It also shuts down in August.

**Au Chien Qui Fume** (⊠ *33 rue du Pont-Neuf, 1ᵉʳ, Louvre/Tuileries* ☎ *01–42–36–07–42* Ⓜ *Les Halles*), open until 2 AM, is a picturesque spot founded in 1740 and decorated with drôle, old master–style paintings of smoking dogs. Traditional French cuisine and seafood platters are served until 1 AM.

**Au Pied de Cochon** (⊠ *6 rue Coquillière, 1ᵉʳ, Beaubourg/Les Halles* ☎ *01–40–13–77–00* Ⓜ *Les Halles*) once catered to the all-night workers at the adjacent Les Halles food market. Its Second Empire carvings have been restored, and traditional dishes like pig's trotters and chitterling sausage still grace the menu. And you haven't tasted pig's trotters until you've tasted them at 6 AM. This place is nothing less than an institution, and it's open 24 hours daily.

**Grand Café Capucines** (⊠ *4 bd. des Capucines, 9ᵉ, Opéra/Grands Boulevards* ☎ *01–43–12–19–00* Ⓜ *Opéra*) has an exuberant pseudo–Belle Époque dining room that matches the bustling mood of the neighboring Opéra; it serves excellent oysters, fish, and meat dishes at hefty prices, and is open around the clock.

**Le Bienvenu** (⊠ *42 rue d'Argout, 2ᵉ, Louvre/Tuileries* ☎ *01–42–33–31–08* Ⓜ *Louvre*) doesn't look like much (notice the kitsch mural on the back wall), but it serves simple French food and couscous in the wee hours of the morning until 6 AM.

**Le Lup** (⊠ *2–4 rue du Sabot, 6ᵉ, St-Germain-des-Prés* ☎ *01–45–48–86–47*) offers a sultry boudoir-style ambience of red velvet and soft lights that lures thirtysomething clubbers, the post-opera set, and hungry night owls, who duck in for a bite to eat from the upscale menu. The two-story rococo salon is perfect for drinks or dessert, and a spin along the small dance floor. It's open 10 PM to 5 AM Thursday to Saturday.

**Le Tambour** (⊠ *41 rue Montmartre, 2ᵉ, Beaubourg/Les Halles* ☎ *01–42–33–06–90* Ⓜ *Étienne Marcel, Les Halles*) wins hands-down for wackiness and flea-market charm. The eye-catching decor includes everything but the proverbial kitchen sink. The food's especially fine here—think onion soup, foie gras, steak tartare, and confit de canard. Open 6 PM–6 AM; last dinner service at 3:30 AM.

**Les Coulisses** (⊠ *1 rue St-Rustique, 18ᵉ, Montmartre* ☎ *01–42–62–89–99* Ⓜ *Abbesses*), near picturesque Place du Tertre, has more character than most late-night restaurants, with red banquettes and 18th-century Venetian mirrors that make it look like an Italian theater. The food—traditional French—is served until 2 AM. There's a club in the basement, open Thursday to Saturday, where dancers work up a late-night appetite.

with students and open Wednesday through Sunday. One of France's most famous DJs, Laurent Garnier, is sometimes at the turntables.

**Les Folie's Pigalle** (✉ *11 pl. Pigalle, 9ᵉ, Montmartre* ☎ *01–48–78–55–25* Ⓜ *Pigalle*) is a former cabaret decorated like a '30s-era bordello. It cultivates a decadent ambience, with music that ranges from house and techno to R&B and electro. After-parties hop on Sunday morning.

★ **Mathi's Bar** (✉ *3 rue Ponthieu, 8ᵉ, Champs-Élysées* ☎ *01–53–76–01–62* Ⓜ *Saint-Philippe-du-Roule*) is one of the best-kept secrets on the Paris bar-lounge scene. If you can talk your way past the stern door-people, you can mingle with the oligarchs, artists, and visiting American movie stars in the poshly decadent atmosphere. It gets cozier on weekends.

**Mix Club** (✉ *24 rue de l'Arrivee, 14ᵉ, Montparnasse* ☎ *01–56–80–37–37* Ⓜ *Montparnasse-Bienvenue*), a massive, self-described "temple of house music" has enough sound-system wattage, blinding lights, and dancing bodies to land you in the ninth circle of Disco Inferno.

**Neo** (✉ *23 rue de Ponthieu, 8ᵉ, Champs-Élysées* ☎ *01–42–25–57–14* Ⓜ *Franklin-D.-Roosevelt*) is a disco with rock-and-roll trimmings, a sleek dance floor.

**Paris Paris** (✉ *5 av. de l'Opéra, 2ᵉ, Opéra* ☎ *01–42–60–64–45* Ⓜ *Pyramides*) proves that you don't need much in the way of decor to be a success. Fans, dancing to top-shelf DJs, are having too much fun to care that there's not much more than black walls and neon.

**Pop-In** (✉ *105 rue Amelot, 4ᵉ, République* ☎ *01–48–05–56–11* Ⓜ *Saint-Sebastien-Froissart*), on a back street just off the Boulevard Beaumarchais (which links the Bastille to République), is a dark, hard-partying boho playhouse with a pronounced English-rocker feel.

**Queen** (✉ *102 av. des Champs-Élysées, 8ᵉ, Champs-Élysées* ☎ *08–92–70–73–30* Ⓜ *George V*), the mythic gay club of the '90s, is not quite as monumental as it once was, but it still packs 'em in and the doors are still difficult to get through, especially—inevitably—on weekends. Proudly hosting a fantastic roster of top DJs, it's known for its campy soirées. These days it attracts a gay-straight mix of international partygoers eager to dance on podiums.

**Sens** (✉ *23 rue de Ponthieu, 8ᵉ, Concorde* ☎ *01–42–25–95–00*) is all about the music, with a superb sound system and meticulous house DJs who spin a mix of techno and disco. Saved by its always slightly off-peak popularity, it nurtures a kind of retro superiority that continues to attract models and trendies.

**Showcase** (✉ *Pont Alexandre III, 8ᵉ, Concorde* ☎ *01–45–61–25–43*) takes the gold medal for best location: under the golden Pont Alexandre bridge. Inside, a long bar, two VIP sections, and a stage that hosts a diverse range of talented groups and DJs makes this a mandatory stop on any night of clubbing.

**WAGG** (✉ *62 rue Mazarine, 6ᵉ, St-Germain-des-Prés* ☎ *01–55–42–22–01* Ⓜ *Odéon*) is tucked beneath the popular bar-resto Alcazar, in a vaulted stone cellar that was Jim Morrison's hangout back in its '70s incarnation as the Whiskey-a-Go-Go. It's now a welcoming dance club featuring vintage disco, funk, groove, and salsa (the latter on Sunday

**14**

nights, with classes that start at 3:30 PM, with state-of-the-art sound, lighting, and guest DJs.

The **White Room** (⊠ *At Maison Blanche restaurant, 15 av. Montaigne, 8ᵉ, Champs-Élysées* ☎ *01–47–23–55–99* Ⓜ *Charles de Gaulle–Étoile*) is a very-of-the-moment Saturday-only hip-hop and disco party in a—you guessed it—white room. It boasts a stellar view from its top-floor vantage, and attracts the St. Tropez set and other VIPs, who buy bottles because the bar is way too small.

## GAY AND LESBIAN BARS AND CLUBS

Gay and lesbian bars and clubs are mostly concentrated in Le Marais and include some of the hippest addresses in the city. Keep in mind, however, that many of these sites fall in and out of favor at lightning speed. The best way to find out what's hot is by picking up a copy of *Têtu* or *2X*, the free "agendas" (listings for hot spots and events) that can be found in any of the bars listed below.

### FOR MEN AND WOMEN

**Banana Café** (⊠ *13 rue de la Ferronnerie, 1ᵉʳ, Beaubourg/Les Halles* ☎ *01–42–33–35–31* Ⓜ *Châtelet Les Halles*) draws a trendy and scantily clad mixed crowd, and offers show tunes in the cellar, where dancing on tables is the norm. Monday night is the "soirée sans interdit" (where nothing is forbidden)—ooh la la!

★  **L'Open Café** (⊠ *17 rue des Archives, 4ᵉ, Le Marais* ☎ *01–42–72–26–18* Ⓜ *Hôtel de Ville*) is a relaxed, packed Marais favorite with a disco-café vibe that draws suits to punks, and is less of a gay meat market than neighboring Café Cox.

**Madame Arthur** (⊠ *75 bis, rue des Martyrs, 18ᵉ, Montmartre* ☎ *01–42–54–49–14* Ⓜ *Pigalle*) stages a wacky burlesque drag show—men dressed as famous French female vocalists—for a completely different cabaret experience. Boys, as they say, will be girls.

**Tango** (⊠ *11 rue au Maire, 3ᵉ, Le Marais* ☎ *01–42–72–17–78* Ⓜ *Arts et Métiers*) has carefully safeguarded its dance-hall origins and lures a friendly mixed crowd of gays, lesbians, and "open minded" heteros. Before midnight, the DJ plays classic chansons (French torch songs), so arrive early to waltz and swing!

### MOSTLY MEN

★  **Bar d'Art/Le Duplex** (⊠ *25 rue Michel-Le-Comte, 3ᵉ, Beaubourg/Les Halles* ☎ *01–42–72–80–86* Ⓜ *Rambuteau*) throbs with young tortured-artist types who enjoy the frequent art exhibitions, alternative music, and mood-inspiring ambient lighting.

**Café Cox** (⊠ *15 rue des Archives, 4ᵉ, Le Marais* ☎ *01–42–72–08–00* Ⓜ *Hôtel de Ville*) is a prime gay pickup joint. Behind the frosted glass windows of the fire-engine red hot spot, men appraise the talent.

**Club 18** (⊠ *18 rue de Beaujolais, 3ᵉ, Louvre* ☎ *01–42–97–52–13* Ⓜ *Palais Royale*) takes gay pride to the heart of the Louvre district on the weekends. This elegant spot is the oldest gay club in Paris and boasts a well-earned reputation as a "friendly party scene."

**Le Dépôt** (✉ *10 rue aux Ours, 3ᵉ, Beaubourg/Les Halles* ☎ *01–44–54–96–96* Ⓜ *Étienne Marcel*) is a cruising bar, club, and back room. The ever-popular Gay Tea Dance spices up Sunday afternoons.

**Les Bains-Douches** (✉ *7 rue du Bourg-l'Abbé, 3ᵉ, Le Marais* ☎ *01–53–01–40–60* Ⓜ *Étienne Marcel*) is an institution that has evolved into one of the hottest gay clubs in the city on Friday through Sunday nights—think Studio 54 à la gay français. There are theme nights and guest DJs; be prepared for a wild time.

**Raiddbar** (✉ *23 rue du Temple, 3ᵉ, Le Marais* ☎ *01–47–27–80–25* Ⓜ *Hôtel de Ville, St-Paul*) is popular and friendly, with a darker downstairs bar and potent drinks. The men are hot, and so is the steamy shower show presented after 11 PM—not for timid voyeurs.

## MOSTLY WOMEN

**Chez Moune** (✉ *54 rue Pigalle, 9ᵉ, Pigalle* ☎ *01–45–26–64–64* Ⓜ *Pigalle*) boasts a claim to fame as the first lesbian cabaret in the city, and showcases singers, transformistes, striptease acts, and DJs that keep the devoted dancing until dawn.

**So What!** (✉ *30 rue du Roi de Sicile, 4ᵉ, Le Marais* Ⓜ *St-Paul*) is a happening lesbian bar that welcomes all comers (including small groups of men) to this popular spot in the heart of the gay district. The DJ in the tiny basement cooks on Friday and Saturday nights.

**3W** (✉ *8 rue des Ecouffes, 4ᵉ, Le Marais* ☎ *01–48–87–39–26* Ⓜ *St-Paul*), as in "Women With Women," is a pillar of the lesbian scene.

# JAZZ CLUBS

**Bar le Houdon** (✉ *5 rue des Abbesses, 18ᵉ, Montmartre* ☎ *01–42–62–21–34* Ⓜ *Abbesses*) transforms from humdrum café to warm jazz venue Friday and Saturday. The musicians are top-notch and the price is right.

**Caveau de la Huchette** (✉ *5 rue de la Huchette, 5ᵉ, Quartier Latin* ☎ *01–43–26–65–05* Ⓜ *St-Michel*) is one of the few surviving cellar clubs from the 1940s. It boasts the "best boppers" in the city, and packs 'em in for swing dancing and Dixieland tunes. It's killer for everyone but claustrophobics.

**Le Petit Journal** (✉ *71 bd. St-Michel, 5ᵉ, Quartier Latin* ☎ *01–43–26–28–59* Ⓜ *Luxembourg* ✉ *13 rue du Commandant-Mouchotte, 14ᵉ, Montparnasse* ☎ *01–43–21–56–70* Ⓜ *Montparnasse Bienvenüe*), with two locations, has long attracted great French and international jazz names. It specializes in big band (Montparnasse) and Dixieland (St-Michel) jazz, with dinner served from 8:30 to midnight.

**Le Sunset** (✉ *60 rue des Lombards, 1ᵉʳ, Beaubourg/Les Halles* ☎ *01–40–26–46–60* Ⓜ *Châtelet Les Halles*) hosts French and American musicians, with an accent on electronic jazz fusion and groove.

**Le Sunside** (✉ *60 rue des Lombards, 1ᵉʳ, Beaubourg/Les Halles* ☎ *01–40–26–46–60* Ⓜ *Châtelet Les Halles*), connected to Le Sunset, specializes in classic jazz and swing.

**Lionel Hampton Jazz Club** (✉ *Méridien Hotel, 81 bd. Gouvion–St-Cyr, 17ᵉ, Champs-Élysées* ☎ *01–40–68–30–42* Ⓜ *Porte Maillot*), named for

14

# Jazz Clubs

The French fell hard for jazz nearly a century ago, during World War I, but the real coup de foudre—literally "lightning bolt" or figuratively "love at first sight"—came after the war when Yank sax man Sidney Bechet and 19-year-old song-and-dance vamp Josephine Baker of St. Louis joined a European tour of the Revue Nègre musical. Baker, or the "Black Venus that haunted Baudelaire," as she was known by French critics, instantly became the sweetheart of Paris. Note: a larger-than-life picture of Baker wearing only a smile, a string of pearls, and a thigh-high skirt today adorns a wall of historic photographs along the platform of the Tuileries métro.

By 1934 France had created its own impressive claim to jazz fame, the all-string Quintette du Hot Club de France, which featured Gypsy guitarist Django Reinhardt and his partner, violinist Stéphane Grappelli. They, in turn, influenced string players from country musicians to Carlos Santana. Reinhardt performed throughout much of World War II in the underground French jazz scene. In the 1950s, Paris grew to become a major destination of the bebop diaspora, and expat jazz musicians including Bechet, Bud Powell, and Dexter Gordon played the venues along with such jazz greats as Dizzy Gillespie, Charlie Parker, and Miles Davis. France embraced the evolving jazz sound that many Americans were still struggling to accept and provided a worshipful welcome to musicians battling discrimination at home. In Paris, Davis said, he was "treated like a human being."

Want to experience a night of jazz yourself?

The French obsession with jazz continues to this day, and travelers seeking a quintessential Parisian experience have the opportunity to hear jazz artists from all over the world nearly any night of the week. Aficionados can choose from traditional jazz to the latest experimental efforts, in clubs ranging from casual to chichi, sedate to hopping. Many venues present a wide range of music: a good option is the double club on Rue des Lombards near Les Halles: Le Sunside specializes in more traditional jazz, and its downstairs sister, Le Sunset, features edgier options.

Music generally begins after 9 PM, so plan accordingly. You can dine at some of the clubs, including Le Petit Journal Montparnasse, or in the Hotel Méridien on the Champs-Élysées, which houses the classy Lionel Hampton Jazz Club.

As everywhere else in the city, the French folks at the clubs tend to dress more stylishly than the average traveler with a limited wardrobe, but they're generally a tolerant bunch, particularly in venues frequented by students and in the heart of tourist areas like Caveau de la Huchette, a hot cellar dance club across the river from Notre-Dame. Keep in mind, though, that the French are serious about their jazz: with a few exceptions, the audience is generally focused and quiet during performances.

14

Recognizable names to watch for include expat Yank flute and sax man Bobby Rangell and singer Sara Lazarus, and much-loved French musicians like the pianists Alain Jean-Marie and Pierre de Bethman, sax man Didier Malherbe, and Olivier Ker Ourio on the harmonica. You might want to check out a jazz style you're less likely to find at home, though, like the latest iteration of Gypsy musette—a distinctive, swing-infused interpretation of old Paris dance music—presented by virtuosos like accordionist Richard Galliano, violinist Didier Lockwood, and the guitar-picking Ferre brothers, Boulou and Elios. Look for them at Duc Des Lombards.

The best place to find out what's playing and even purchase tickets is at ⊕ *www.infoconcert.com* or on club Web sites, some of which offer English versions. *Pariscope, Jazz Magazine,* and *Jazz Hot,* available at newsstands, also have listings in French. Reservations can be critical, especially for leading U.S. jazz musicians.

Entrance charges are rarely more than €20 and often less. Some venues have free jam sessions, depending on the night, so check listings. Drink prices can be sky-high, but most table staff won't harass budget-conscious customers nursing a single drink.

Another way to experience a variety of top-quality jazz is by attending world-renowned Paris festivals that run from early spring through September, including the **Banlieues Bleues** (☎ *01–49–22–10–10* ⊕ *www.banlieuesbleues.org*), the **Paris Jazz Festival** (☎ *01–46–21–08–37* ⊕ *www.parisjazzfestival2008.com*), and the **Villette Jazz Festival** (☎ *01–44–84–44–84* ⊕ *www.cite-delamusique.fr*).

*Word of Mouth*

*"OK, if I were hip . . . and wanted jazz . . . I'd stay in the 10th and find my way to New Morning jazz club."*
—SuzieC

the American vibraphonist adored by Parisians, hosts a roster of international jazz musicians in a classy set of rooms.

Fodor'sChoice    **New Morning** (✉ *7 rue des Petites-Ecuries, 10ᵉ, Opéra/Grands Boule-*
★    *vards* ☎ *01–45–23–51–41* Ⓜ *Château d'Eau*) is the premier spot for serious fans of avant-garde jazz, folk, and world music. The look is spartan, the mood reverential.

## PUBS

Pubs wooing English-speaking clients with selections of British and Irish beers are becoming increasingly popular with Parisians. They're also good places to find reasonably priced food at off hours.

**Auld Alliance** (✉ *80 rue François Miron, 4ᵉ, Le Marais* ☎ *01–48–04–30–40* Ⓜ *St-Paul*) has Scottish shields on the walls and the bar staff dresses in kilts for special events. There are more than 120 whiskeys, Scottish beer, soccer, and rugby on TV, and sometimes live music.

**Café Oz** (✉ *8 bd. Montmartre, 9ᵉ, Grands Boulevards* ☎ *01–47–70–18–52* Ⓜ *Grands Boulevards*) zips you Down Under to big-screen soccer and rugby games amid Aussie expats.

★    **Corcoran's Irish Pub** (✉ *23 bd. Poissonière, 2e, 1ᵉʳ, Grands Boulevards* ☎ *01–40–39–00–16* Ⓜ *Grands Boulevards*) is a great find: it's roomy (great for conversations) and has an ample menu, a gorgeous bar, and old-timey photos and quotations on the walls—such as "He who opens his mouth most is the one who opens his purse least."

The **Frog pubs** (✉ *25 cour St-Emilion, 12ᵉ, Bercy/Tolbiac* ☎ *01–43–40–70–71* Ⓜ *Cour St-Emilion* ✉ *116 rue St-Denis, 2ᵉ, Beaubourg/Les Halles* ☎ *01–42–36–34–73* Ⓜ *Etienne Marcel* ✉ *9 rue Princesse, 6ᵉ, St-Germain* ☎ *01–40–51–77–38* Ⓜ *Mabillon* ✉ *114 av. de France, 13ᵉ, Bibliotheque* ☎ *01–45–84–34–26* Ⓜ *Bibliothèque François*) are four fun British-style pubs in Paris.

**Kitty O'Shea's** (✉ *10 rue des Capucines, 2ᵉ, Opéra* ☎ *01–40–15–00–30* Ⓜ *Opéra*) is an ever-popular Irish pub near the Place Vendôme that draws a posh after-work crowd as well as salt-of-the-earth punters. Authentic trimmings like stained glass and Gaelic street signs highlight the decor, and a hearty restaurant serves burgers and fish-and-chips.

**Le Truskel** (✉ *12 rue Feydeau, 2ᵉ, Les Halles* ☎ *01–40–26–59–97* Ⓜ *Étienne Marcel*) —what looks and sounds and feels like an English pub but kicks booty like a punk club? Le Trusk, whose basement showcases gigs by the globe's hottest new alternative acts while a loud, happy Parisian rocker crowd staggers around the roomy bar.

# Performing Arts

**WORD OF MOUTH**

"You might consider getting tickets for a ballet performance at Opéra Garnier . . . We also went to an instrumental performance at Sainte-Chapelle, and that was a wonderful and restful way to see the chapel and enjoy the music."

—maryanntex

# PERFORMING ARTS PLANNER

## Festivals

The music and theater season generally runs from September to June, but summer is packed with all sorts of performing arts festivals.

The annual Chopin Festival is a highlight at the picturesque **Orangerie de Bagatelle** (✉ Parc de Bagatelle, Allée de Longchamp, 16ᵉ, Bois de Boulogne ☎ 01–45–00–22–19 Ⓜ Porte Maillot, then Bus 244) in late June and early July.

Free outdoor classical concerts lure fans to the **Parc Floral** (☎ 01–49–57–24–84 ⊕ www.parcfloraldeparis.com) of the Bois de Vincennes on August and September weekends at 4 (entrance to the park is €3). This is also the spot that hosts the **Paris Jazz Festival** each weekend in summer.

The annual **Villette Jazz Festival** (☎ 01–40–03–75–75 ⊕ www.villette.com) is held at the Parc de La Villette every fall.

The **Quartier d'Eté** (☎ 01–44–94–98–00 ⊕ www.quartierdete.com) festival in July and August, held throughout Paris, attracts international stars of dance, classical music, and jazz.

## Ticket Prices and Discounts

As anywhere in the world, it's best to buy tickets in advance, especially for popular events.

Events range in price from about €5 for standing room at the Opéra Bastille or €7 for a circus performance to upward of €180 for an elaborate National Opéra production. Most performances, however, are in the €15–€25 range. Discounts are often available for limited-visibility seats, students, and senior citizens. Movies cost about €6–€10.50, but many cinemas have reduced rates on Monday or Wednesday.

Half-price tickets for same-day theater performances are available at the **Kiosques Théâtre** (✉ Across from 15 pl. de la Madeleine, Opéra/Grands Boulevards Ⓜ Madeleine ✉ Outside Gare Montparnasse, Pl. Raoul Dautry, Montparnasse Ⓜ Montparnasse Bienvenüe ✉ Pl. des Ternes, Champs-Elysées Ⓜ Ternes), open Tuesday to Saturday 12:30 to 8 and Sunday 12:30 to 4.

Half-price tickets are also available at many theaters during the first week of each new show, and inexpensive tickets are often available at the last minute.

FNAC (⊕ www.fnacspectacles.com) and Virgin Megastores (⊕ www.virginmega.fr) sell tickets in stores and online. Both have locations on the Champs-Élysées and branches in other neighborhoods.

## Where to Get Info

Detailed entertainment listings in French can be found in the weekly magazines *Pariscope* and *L'Officiel des Spectacles*, available at newsstands and in bookstores; in the Wednesday entertainment insert *Figaroscope*, in the *Figaro* newspaper (⊕ scope.lefigaro.fr/theatres-spectacles); and in the weekly *À Nous Paris*, distributed free in the métro. The Webzine *Paris Voice* (⊕ www.parisvoice.com) offers superb highlights in English. Most performing arts venues also have their own Web sites, and many include listings and other helpful information in English.

The Web site of the Paris Tourist Office (⊕ www.parisinfo.com) has theater and music listings in English.

Updated
by Mary
Papenfuss

The performing-arts scene in Paris runs the gamut from high-brow to lowbrow, cheap (or free) to break-the-bank expensive. Venues are indoors and outdoors, opulent or spartan, and dress codes vary accordingly. Regardless of the performance you choose, it's unlikely to be like anything you've seen before. Parisians have an audacious sense of artistic adventure and a stunning eye for scene and staging. An added bonus in this city of classic beauty is that many of the venues themselves—from the opulent interior of the Opéra Garnier to the Art Deco splendor of the Théâtre des Champs-Élysées—are a feast for the eyes.

One thing that sets Paris apart in the arts world is the active participation of the Ministry of Culture, which sponsors numerous concert halls and theaters, like the Comédie Française, that tend to present less commercial, though artistically captivating, productions. Other theaters, like the Théâtre de Marigny and Palais de Chaillot, are known for sold-out shows and decade-long production runs.

Most performances are in French, although you can find English theater productions. English-language movies are often presented undubbed, with subtitles. Of course, you don't need to speak the language to enjoy opera, classical music, dance, or the circus.

## CIRCUS

Italian Antonio Franconi helped launch the first Cirque Olympique, considered the start of the modern circus, in Paris in 1783—and the French have been hooked ever since. Circus acts are cherished as high art in Paris—for all ages. The city boasts a 19th-century permanent circus theater and sprouts tents in every major park to present spectacles from the sublime to the quirky.

**Cirque de Paris** (⊠ *115 bd. Charles de Gaulle, Villeneuve-la Garenne* ☎ *01–47–99–40–40* Ⓜ *Porte de Clignancourt, then Bus 137*) offers a memorable suburban "Day at the Circus" on Wednesday and Sunday: a peek behind the scenes in the morning, lunch with the artists, and a performance in the afternoon. Reservations obligatoire.

**Cirque d'Hiver Bouglione** (⊠ *110 rue Amelot, 11ᵉ, République* ☎ *01–47–00–28–81* ⊕ *www.cirquedhiver.com* Ⓜ *Filles du Calvaire*) brings together two famous circus institutions: the beautiful Cirque d'Hiver hall, constructed in 1852, and the Bouglione troupe, known for its rousing spectacle of acrobats, jugglers, clowns, trapeze artists, tigers, and housecats that leap through rings of fire.

**CHURCH CONCERTS**

There's something majestic about listening to classical music under the airy roof of a medieval stained-glass church, where many free or almost-free lunchtime and evening concerts are performed. Check weekly listings and flyers posted at the churches for information.

**15**

**Cirque Diana Moreno Bormann** (⊠ *112 rue de la Haie Coq, 19ᵉ, Porte de La Chapelle* ☎ *06–10–71–83–50* ⊕ *www.cirque-diana-moreno.com* Ⓜ *Porte d'Auberviliers*) is a charming family circus fun for all ages; performances are presented at 3 on Saturday, Sunday, and Wednesday.

**Cirque National Alexis Gruss** (⊠ *Route de l'Hippodrome, 16ᵉ, Bois de Boulogne* ☎ *01–45–01–71–26* ⊕ *www.alexis-gruss.com* Ⓜ *Ranelagh*), founded in 1854, remains an avowedly old-fashioned production with showy horseback riders, trapeze artists, and clowns. It runs November through February, with performances Saturday (including a dinner show for €90), Sunday, and Wednesday.

**Parc de la Villette** (⊠ *211 av. Jean-Jaurès, La Villette* ☎ *01–40–03–75–75* Ⓜ *Porte de Pantin*) features an *Espace Chapiteaux*, a high-tech circus tent complex that hosts innovative circus performers including students from the National Circus Arts Center. It focuses on contemporary performance art—not to be missed by "new circus" fans.

## CLASSICAL MUSIC

**Cité de la Musique** (⊠ *In Parc de La Villette, 221 av. Jean-Jaurès, 19ᵉ, La Villette* ☎ *01–44–84–45–00* ⊕ *www.cite-musique.fr/anglais* Ⓜ *Porte de Pantin*) presents a varied program of classical, experimental, and world-music concerts in a postmodern setting.

**IRCAM** (⊠ *1 pl. Igor-Stravinsky, 4ᵉ, Beaubourg/Les Halles* ☎ *01–44–78–48–43* ⊕ *www.ircam.fr* Ⓜ *Châtelet, Les Halles, Hôtel de Ville*) organizes contemporary classical music concerts in its own theater and at the Centre Pompidou next door.

**Maison de Radio France** (⊠ *116 av. du Président-Kennedy, 16ᵉ, Passy-Auteuil* ☎ *01–56–40–15–16* ⊕ *www.radiofrance.fr* Ⓜ *Ranlagh, Mirabeau*) is home to France's many state-owned radio stations as well as the Orchestre National de France and Orchestre Philharmonique de Radio France. ■**TIP→** The public can attend orchestra concerts on-site, as well as live broadcasts and recordings for free, space permitting; show up an hour in advance at the Grand Hall for tickets.

Fodor's Choice ★ **Salle Cortot** (⊠ *78 rue Cardinet, 17ᵉ, Parc Monceau* ☎ *01–47–63–85–72* ⊕ *www.ecolenormalecortot. com* Ⓜ *Malesherbes*) is an acoustic gem built by Auguste Perret in 1918. At the time he promised to construct "a hall that sounds like a Stradivarious." Jazz and classical concerts are held here. ■TIP➔ Free student recitals are offered at 12:30 on Tuesday and Thursday.

**Salle Gaveau** (⊠ *45 rue la Boétie, 8ᵉ, Champs-Élysées* ☎ *01–49–53–05–07* ⊕ *www.sallegaveau.com* Ⓜ *Miromesnil*) is a small, perfectly appointed gold-and-white hall of 1,200 seats with a distinctly Parisian allure and remarkable acoustics. It hosts chamber music, piano, and vocal recitals.

**Salle Pleyel** (⊠ *252 rue du Faubourg-St-Honoré, 8ᵉ, Concorde* ☎ *01–42–56–13–13* ⊕ *www.sallepleyel.fr* Ⓜ *Ternes*), a beloved concert hall fresh from an acclaimed major renovation, features varied musical presentations from international stars like Lionel Hampton to repeat performances by the Orchestre de Paris.

**Théâtre des Champs-Élysées** (⊠ *15 av. Montaigne, 8ᵉ, Champs-Élysées* ☎ *01–49–52–50–50* Ⓜ *Alma-Marceau*) was the scene of the famous Battle of the Rite of Spring in 1913, when police had to be called in after the audience ripped up the seats in outrage at Stravinsky's *Le Sacre du Printemps* and Nijinsky's choreography. Today this elegantly restored and plush performance temple is worthy of a visit if only for one of the most striking examples of Art Deco architecture in Paris. It also hosts top-notch opera, dance performances, jazz, world music, and orchestra and chamber concerts.

> **MUSEUM CONCERTS**
>
> Museums also host classical concerts; tickets are usually sold separately from admission. The Auditorium du Louvre presents chamber music, string quartets, and a special series of promising new musicians on Thursday; the Musée du Moyen-Age stages medieval music concerts between October and July, including the free *l'Heure Musicale* on Friday at 12:30, and Saturday at 4; and the Musée d'Orsay often offers small-scale concerts in the lower-level auditorium.

## DANCE

Classical ballet takes the stage in Paris in places as varied as the old opera house and sports stadiums. More avant-garde or up-and-coming choreographers tend to show their works off in the smaller performance spaces of the Bastille and Le Marais, and in theaters in nearby suburbs.

**Centre National de la Danse** (⊠ *1 rue Victor Hugo, Pantin* ☎ *01–41–83–98–98* ⊕ *www.cnd.fr* Ⓜ *Hoche or RER: Pantin*), after being sidelined by politics and budget problems for a decade, opened in a former administrative center of the Pantin suburb of Paris. The space is dedicated to supporting professional dancers, with classes, rehearsal studios, and a multimedia dance library. A regular program of performances, expositions, and conferences is also open to the public.

**Maison des Arts de Créteil** (✉ *Pl. Salvador Allende, Creteil* ☎ *01–45–13–19–19* ⊕ *www.maccreteil.com* Ⓜ *Créteil-Préfecture*), just outside Paris, is a popular venue for dance; it often attracts top-flight international and French companies, such as Blanca Li, Bill T. Jones, and the cutting-edge annual EXIT Festival.

FodorśChoice
★

**Opéra Garnier** (✉ *Pl. de l'Opéra, 9ᵉ, Opéra/Grands Boulevards* ☎ *08–92–89–90–90* Ⓜ *Opéra*) is the sumptuous Napoléon III home of the prestigious Ballet de l'Opéra National de Paris, and rarely hosts other dance companies. Note that many of the cheaper seats have obstructed views, more of an obstacle in dance than in opera performances.

**Théâtre de la Bastille** (✉ *76 rue de la Roquette, 11ᵉ, Bastille/Nation* ☎ *01–43–57–42–14* Ⓜ *Bastille*) merits mention as an example of the innovative activity in the Bastille area; it has an enviable record as a launching pad for tomorrow's modern-dance stars.

**Théâtre de la Cité Internationale** (✉ *17 bd. Jourdan, 14ᵉ, Parc Montsouris* ☎ *01–43–13–50–50* Ⓜ *RER: Cité Universitaire*) is a complex of three theaters in the heart of the Cité Internationale Universitaire de Paris, an international student residence community and park. It hosts young avant-garde companies and is also the main venue for the Presqu'Iles de la Danse festival in February.

**Théâtre de la Ville and Théâtre des Abbesses** (✉ *2 pl. du Châtelet, 4ᵉ, Beaubourg/Les Halles* Ⓜ *Châtelet* ✉ *31 rue des Abbesses, 18e, Montmartre* ☎ *01–42–74–22–77 for both* Ⓜ *Abbesses*) are *the* top venues for contemporary dance. Troupes like Anne-Teresa de Keersmaeker's Rosas company are presented here. Both theaters also offer a variety of world music. Book early; shows sell out quickly.

## MOVIES

The French call films the *septième art* (seventh art) and discuss the latest releases with the same intensity as they do gallery openings or theatrical debuts. So you're as likely to see people lining up for a Hitchcock retrospective or a hard-hitting documentary as for a Hollywood cream puff. Paris has hundreds of cinemas showing contemporary and classic French and American movies, as well as a tempting menu packed with independent, international, and documentary films. The city offers many theaters in addition to the Cinémathèque Française that show classic and independent films, often found in the Quartier Latin. Film presentations are often organized around retrospectives.

### FIRST-RUN FILMS

First-run cinemas are clustered around the principal tourist areas, such as the Champs-Élysées, Boulevard des Italiens near the Opéra, Bastille, Châtelet, and Odéon. Films are almost always offered in their original language (look for VO or version originale) as well as dubbed in French. Check for listings online (⊕ *www.allocine.fr*). If you're looking for a memorable cinema, check out some of the following.

FodorśChoice
★

**La Pagode** (✉ *57 rue de Babylone, 7ᵉ, Invalides* ☎ *01–45–55–48–48* Ⓜ *St-François Xavier*) —where else but in Paris would you find movies screened in an antique pagoda? A Far Eastern fantasy, this structure was built in 1896 as a ballroom for the wife of the owner of Le Bon Marché department store. In the 1970s it was slated for demolition but saved by a grassroots wave of support spearheaded by director Louis Malle. Though the fare is standard, the surroundings are enchanting. Come early for tea in the garden (summer only).

**MK2 Bibliothèque** (⊠ *128–162 av. de France, 13ᵉ, Tolbiac* ☎ *08–92–69–84–84* Ⓜ *Quai de la Gare, Bibliothèque*) is a slick, 14-*salle* cineplex in the shadow of Mitterrand's National Library, with trademark scarlet-red two-person chairs—they fit two people without a divider; sort of like watching a movie at home on your couch—as well as four restaurants, music and DVD shops, and even a DJ bar, the Limelight.

> ### MOVIE-GOING TIPS
>
> Most theaters run English-language films undubbed, with subtitles. When checking movie listings, note that VO means *version originale*; films that are dubbed are VF (*version française*). Some theaters post two show times: the *séance*, when the commercials, previews, and, occasional short films begin; and the feature presentation, which usually starts 10–25 minutes later. It's worth noting that in France, commercials tend to be more inventive than North American ads, so the *séance* isn't quite the time-waster you'd expect.

**UGC Ciné-Cité Bercy** (⊠ *2 cour St-Emilion, 12ᵉ, Bercy* ☎ *08–92–70–00–00* Ⓜ *Cour St-Emilion*) is a mammoth 18-screen complex in the Bercy Village shopping area. For sound and seating, it's one of the best.

### REVIVAL FILMS AND ALTERNATIVE SPACES

**Accatone** (⊠ *20 rue Cujas, 5ᵉ, Quartier Latin* ☎ *01–46–33–86–86* Ⓜ *Cluny–La Sorbonne, Luxembourg*) features a steady stream of European art films.

**Action Écoles** (⊠ *23 rue des Écoles, 5ᵉ, Quartier Latin* ☎ *01–43–25–72–07* Ⓜ *Maubert Mutualité*) specializes in American classics and cult films.

**Cinéma des Cinéastes** (⊠ *7 av. de Clichy, 17ᵉ, Montmartre* ☎ *08–92–68–97–17* Ⓜ *Place de Clichy*) shows previews of feature films, as well as documentaries, short films, and rarely shown movies; it's in an old cabaret transformed into a movie theater and wine bar.

Fodor'sChoice
★
**Cinémathèque Française** (⊠ *51 rue de Bercy, 12ᵉ, Bercy* ☎ *01–71–19–33–33* ⊕ *www.cinematheque.fr* Ⓜ *Bercy*) is a mecca for cinephiles brought up on Frederico Fellini, Igmar Bergman, and Alain Resnais. Its spectacular home, in the former American Center designed by Frank Gehry, opened in October 2005 and includes elaborate museum exhibitions as well as four cinemas and a video library.

**La Géode** (⊠ *At Cité des Sciences et de l'Industrie, Parc de La Villette, 26 av. Corentin-Cariou, 19ᵉ, La Villette* ☎ *08–92–68–45–40* Ⓜ *Porte de La Villette*) screens wide-angle Omnimax films—usually documentaries—on a gigantic spherical surface.

The Frank Gehry–designed Cinémathèque Française presents an ever-changing range of films and exhibitions.

**Le Balzac** (✉ *1 rue Balzac, 8ᵉ, Champs-Élysées* ☎ *01–45–61–10–60* Ⓜ *George V*) often presents directors' talks before screenings and features concerts as well as live music for silent classics.

**Le Forum des Images** (✉ *Forum des Halles, Porte St-Eustache entrance, 1ᵉʳ, Beaubourg/Les Halles* ☎ *01–44–76–63–00* Ⓜ *Les Halles*), emerging from a massive state-of-the-art renovation, organizes thematic screenings, often presenting directors or a film expert for discussion beforehand, along with archival films and videos, workshops, and lectures.

**Parc de La Villette** (✉ *In Prairie du Triangle at Parc de La Villette, 221 av. Jean-Jaurès, 19ᵉ, La Villette* ☎ *01–40–03–75–75* Ⓜ *Porte de Pantin, Porte de La Villette*) shows €2 (and sometimes free) movies outdoors, July and August. Most people take along a picnic. You can rent deck chairs and blankets by the entrance.

**St-André-des-Arts** (✉ *30 rue St-André-des-Arts, 6ᵉ, Quartier Latin* ☎ *01–43–26–48–18* Ⓜ *St-Michel*), one of a number of popular cinemas near the Sorbonne, is also one of the best cinemas in Paris. It hosts an annual festival devoted to a single director, such as Bergman or Tarkovski.

## OPERA

**Opéra Comique** (✉ *5 rue Favart, 2ᵉ, Opéra/Grands Boulevards* ☎ *08–25–01–01–23* ⊕ *www.opera-comique.com* Ⓜ *Richelieu Drouot*) is a gem of an opera house whose reputation was forged by its former director, enfant terrible Jérôme Savary. As well as staging operettas, the hall hosts modern dance, classical concerts, and vocal recitals. Tickets usually range from €6 to €50 and can be purchased at the theater, by mail, online, or by phone.

**Opéra de la Bastille** (✉ *Pl. de la Bastille, 12ᵉ, Bastille/Nation* ☎ *08–92–89–90–90* ⊕ *www.opera-de-paris.fr* Ⓜ *Bastille*), the mammoth ultra-modern facility designed by architect Carlos Ott and built in 1989, long ago took over the role of Paris's main opera house from the Opéra Garnier. Like the building, performances tend to be on the avant-garde side—you're as likely to see a contemporary adaptation of *La Bohème* as you are to hear Kafka set to music. Tickets for Opéra de Paris productions range from €5 to €200 and generally go on sale at the box office a month before shows, earlier by phone and online. The opera season usually runs September through July, and the box office is open Monday–Saturday 11–6:30.

**Fodor'sChoice**
★

**Opéra Garnier** (✉ *Pl. de l'Opéra, 9ᵉ, Opéra/Grands Boulevards* ☎ *08–92–89–90–90* ⊕ *www.opera-de-paris.fr* Ⓜ *Opéra*), the magnificent and magical former haunt of the Phantom of the Opera, painter Edgar Degas, and any number of legendary opera stars, still hosts performances of the Opéra de Paris, along with a fuller calendar of dance performances, as the theater is the official home of the Ballet de l'Opéra National de Paris. The grandest opera productions are usually mounted at the Opéra de la Bastille, whereas the Garnier now presents smaller-scale operas such as Mozart's *La Clemenza di Tito* and *Così Fan Tutte*. Gorgeous and intimate though the Garnier is, its tiara-shaped theater means that many seats have limited visibility, so it's best to ask specifically what the sight lines are when booking (partial view in French is *visibilité partielle*. ■ TIP→ The cheaper seats are often those with partial views. Seats generally go on sale at the box office a month before any given show, earlier by phone and online; you must appear in person to buy the cheapest tickets. Last-minute discount tickets, if available, are offered 15 minutes before a performance for senior citizens and anyone under 28. The box office is open 11–6:30 daily.

**Théâtre Musical de Paris** (✉ *Pl. du Châtelet, 1ᵉʳ, Beaubourg/Les Halles* ☎ *01–40–28–28–40* ⊕ *www.chatelet-theatre.com* Ⓜ *Châtelet*), better known as the Théâtre du Châtelet, presents some of the finest opera productions in the city and regularly attracts international divas like Cecilia Bartoli and Anne-Sofie von Otter. It also hosts classical concerts, dance performances, and the occasional play.

## THEATER

A number of theaters line the Grands Boulevards between the Opéra and République, but no Paris equivalent of Broadway or the West End exists. Shows are mostly in French, with a few notable exceptions listed below. English-language theater groups playing in various venues throughout Paris and its suburbs include the **International Players** (⊕ *www.internationalplayers.info*). Broadway-scale singing-and-dancing musicals are generally staged at either the Palais des Sports or the Palais des Congrès.

**Café de la Gare** (✉ *41 rue du Temple, 4ᵉ, Le Marais* ☎ *01–42–78–52–51* Ⓜ *Hôtel de Ville*) offers a fun opportunity to experience a particularly

Parisian form of theater, the *café-théâtre*—part satire, part variety revue, jazzed up with slapstick humor, and performed in a café salon. ■TIP→ You'll need a good grasp of French slang and current events to keep up with the jokes.

**Casino de Paris** (✉ *16 rue de Clichy, 9ᵉ, Opéra/Grands Boulevards* ☎08-92-69-89-26⊕ *www.casinodeparis.fr* Ⓜ *Trinité*), once a favorite of the immortal Serge Gainsbourg, has a horseshoe balcony, a cramped, cozy music-hall feel, and performances by everyone from whirling dervishes to Young Turk singers.

**Comédie des Champs-Élysées** (✉ *15 av. Montaigne, 8ᵉ, Champs-Élysées* ☎*01-53-23-99-19* Ⓜ *Alma-Marceau*) offers intriguing productions in its small theater, next door to the larger Théâtre des Champs-Élysées.

Fodor'sChoice ★ **Comédie Française** (✉ *Salle Richelieu, 2 rue de Richelieu, 1ᵉʳ* ☎*08-25-10-16-80* Ⓜ *Palais-Royal–Musée du Louvre* ✉ *Studio Théâtre, Galerie du Carrousel du Louvre, 99 rue de Rivoli, 1ᵉʳ, Louvre/Tuileries* ☎*01-44-58-98-58* Ⓜ *Palais-Royal* ✉ *Théâtre du Vieux Colombier, 21 rue Vieux Colombier, 6ᵉ, St-Germain-des-Prés* ☎*01-44-39-87-00* Ⓜ *St-Sulpice*) dates from 1680 and is the most hallowed institution in French theater. It specializes in splendid classical French plays by the likes of Racine, Molière, and Marivaux. ■TIP→ Buy tickets at the box office, by telephone, or online. If the theatre is sold out, turn up an hour before the performance and wait in line for cancellations.

**La Cartoucherie** (✉ *In Bois de Vincennes* ☎*01-43-74-88-50 or 01-43-74-87-63* Ⓜ *Château de Vincennes, then shuttle bus or Bus 112*) a complex of five theaters (Théâtre du Soleil, Théâtre de l'Aquarium, Théâtre de la Tempête, Théâtre de l'Epée de Bois, and the Théâtre du Chaudron) in a former munitions factory, lures cast and spectators into an intimate theatrical world. The resident director is the revered Ariane Mnouchkine. Go early for a simple meal; actors often help serve "in character."

☾ **Le Lucernaire** (✉ *53 rue Notre-Dame-des-Champs, 6ᵉ, Montparnasse* ☎*01-42-22-26-50* Ⓜ *Notre-Dame-des-Champs*) wins a standing ovation as far as cultural centers are concerned. With two theaters (six performances a night), three movie screens, an art gallery, a bookstore, a lively bar, and the equally lively surrounding neighborhood of Vavin, it caters to young intellectuals—and, thanks to the puppet shows (Wednesday and Saturday), their children, too.

**Odéon–Théâtre de l'Europe** (✉ *Pl. de l'Odéon, 6ᵉ, St-Germain-des-Prés* ☎*01-44-85-40-00* Ⓜ *Odéon*) was once home to the Comédie Française. Today, this always exciting venue focuses on pan-European theater, offering a variety of European-language productions in Paris.

**15**

**Sudden Theatre** (✉ *14 bis, rue Ste-Isaure, 18ᵉ, Montmartre* ☎ *01–42–62–35–00* Ⓜ *Jules Joffrin*) is a tiny, contemporary theater and acting academy offering regular English-language productions.

**Théâtre Darius Milhaud** (✉ *80 allée Darius Milhaud, 19ᵉ, La Villette* ☎ *01–42–01–92–26* Ⓜ *Porte de Pantin*) presents classics by Camus and Baudelaire, as well as occasional productions in English.

**Théâtre de la Huchette** (✉ *23 rue de la Huchette, 5ᵉ, Quartier Latin* ☎ *01–43–26–38–99* Ⓜ *St-Michel*) is a tiny Rive Gauche theater that has been staging the titanic Romanian-French writer Ionesco's *The Bald Soprano* and *The Lesson* since 1957, and also stages other productions. (The box office is open Monday–Saturday 5 PM–9 PM.)

**Théâtre de la Renaissance** (✉ *20 bd. St-Martin, 10ᵉ, Opéra/Grands Boulevards* ☎ *01–42–02–47–35* Ⓜ *Strasbourg St-Denis*) was put on the map by Belle Époque superstar Sarah Bernhardt (she was the manager from 1893 to 1899). Big French stars often perform here.

**Théâtre des Bouffes du Nord** (✉ *37 bis, bd. de la Chapelle, 10ᵉ, Stalingrad/La Chapelle* ☎ *01–46–07–34–50* Ⓜ *La Chapelle*) is the wonderfully atmospheric, slightly decrepit home of English director Peter Brook, who regularly delights with his quirky experimental productions in French and, sometimes, English, too.

**Théâtre du Palais-Royal** (✉ *38 rue Montpensier, 1ᵉʳ, Louvre/Tuileries* ☎ *01–42–97–40–00* ⊕ *www.theatrepalaisroyal.com* Ⓜ *Palais-Royal*) is a sumptuous 750-seat Italian theater bedecked in gold and purple in the former residence of Cardinal Richelieu.

**Théâtre Marigny** (✉ *Carré Marigny, 8ᵉ, Champs-Élysées* ☎ *01–53–96–70–30* Ⓜ *Champs-Élysées–Clemenceau*) offers top-flight theater, often with a big-name French star topping the bill.

**Théâtre Mogador** (✉ *25 rue de Mogador, 9ᵉ, Opéra/Grands Boulevards* ☎ *08–20–88–87–86* Ⓜ *Trinité*), one of Paris's most sumptuous theaters, features musicals and other productions with a pronounced popular appeal.

**Théâtre National de Chaillot** (✉ *1 pl. du Trocadéro, 16ᵉ, Trocadéro/Tour Eiffel* ☎ *01–53–65–30–00* Ⓜ *Trocadéro*) is a cavernous place in the shadow of the Eiffel Tower, with two theaters dedicated to drama and dance. Major dance companies like the Ballet Royal de Suède and William Forsythe's company also visit regularly.

# Shopping

**WORD OF MOUTH**

"I have a list of items that are 'must buys' for me and for gifts At Galeries Lafayette Gourmet. I will share my gift guide: chocolates, various cooking spice mixtures, and salts, too many flavors to choose from! This time it was violet infused salt and also violet infused mustard as well as some fleur de sel."

—lauriew1234

# SHOPPING PLANNER

## In this Chapter

## Top Paris Shopping Experiences

**Visiting Le Bon Marché.** The city's chicest and oldest department store is a great first stop for an overview of the current season's pieces from all the top designers.

**Shopping at the Food Markets.** Year-round and in any weather, the city's open-air food markets are an integral part of daily Paris life.

**Le Marais.** This is one of Paris's most charming places to stroll and shop, with tons of local boutiques and French-owned chains, along cobblestone streets.

## Opening Hours

Store hours can be tricky in Paris. Aside from department stores, which keep slightly longer hours and are usually open late one weeknight, shops tend to open around 10 or 11 AM and close around 7 PM. It's not unusual to find a "back at 3" sign taped on the doors of smaller boutiques at lunchtime. Plan to do most of your foraging between Tuesday and Saturday, as the majority of shops, including department stores, are closed Sunday and some on Monday as well. You can find areas—particularly Le Marais—where stores are open on Sunday. However, if you're making a special trip somewhere, always call ahead to check hours.

## How to Do Duty-Free

A value-added tax (V.A.T.; T.V.A. in French) of approximately 19.6% is imposed on most consumer goods. Non–EU residents can reclaim part of this tax. To qualify for a refund, you must purchase €175 of goods in the same shop on the same day, you must have stayed three months or less in the EU at the time of purchase, and you must have your passport validated by customs within three months after the date of purchase. Ask for a *détaxe* form at the time of purchase; smaller stores will fill it out for you, department stores have special *détaxe* desks.

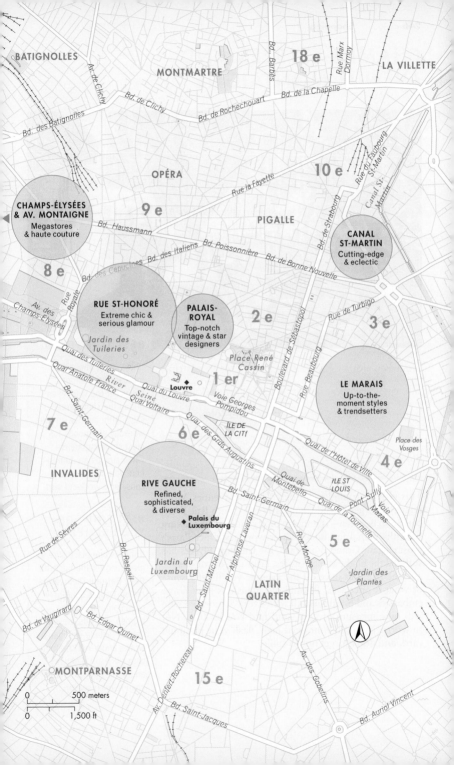

# CHAMPS-ÉLYSÉES AND AVENUE MONTAIGNE

Step into your Chanel suit, gird your loins, and plunge into Paris's most elegant and daunting hunting grounds, where royals, jet-setters, starlets, and other glitterati converge in pursuit of the luxurious life.

This elegant triangle—bordered by the avenues Montaigne, Georges V, and Champs-Élysées, with Rue François 1$^{er}$ in between—is home to pretty much all the luxury Goliaths with a few added lesser worthies. Once Paris's most elegant Grand Boulevard, the Champs-Élysées has suffered the blight of megastores, fast food, movie chains, and the like, but once off the avenue, you'll get a sense of what it once was. Palatial old mansions now house embassies and boutiques, all with liveried doormen who will take measure of you—and find you lacking. Not to worry, just hold your head high, flash your platinum card, and don't forget not to smile.

## BEST TIME TO GO

Unlike other shopping meccas, these streets never get too wild, even during the semiannual sales. Although we advise weekday afternoons for most shopping areas—when crowds are tame—here you might want to consider a weekend visit.

## BEST FIND FOR YOUR SISTER

If there's one place sure to give bang for the buck, it's **Petit Bateau**. Their comfy cotton T-shirts are highly prized among Parisian women and kids. Wardrobe staples include cardigans, wraps, and V-necks, along with silky-soft nighties and undies in colors that change each season.

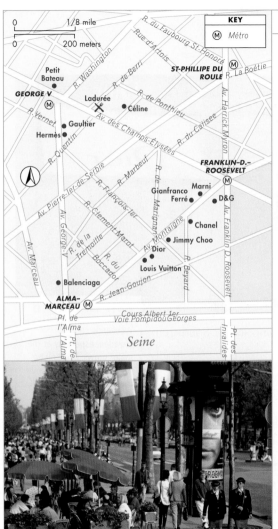

## REFUELING

Not only is **Ladurée** one of the world's legendary *pâtis-series*, but the Champs-ÉlyséesÉlysées location also keeps great hours: from early breakfast (doors open at 7:30 AM) to a post-theater snack, just amble over whenever the urge strikes. Whether you desire a cup of their famously rich hot choco-late; a refreshing raspberry, litchee, and rose-petal ice-cream sundae; a melt-in-your-mouth mille-feuille; or a hearty club sandwich, you'll find plenty to choose from at fairly reason-able prices (it's still Paris, dahling), all perfectly scrumptious.

## WHAT YOU'LL WANT

### CLASSY COUTURE

**Chanel.** Elegant, classic looks, with sex appeal and lasting value.

**Gaultier.** Only his spec-tacular garments could outshine this fantasyland boutique.

### IN-YOUR-FACE OPULENCE

**Balenciaga.** Fashion's dar-ling, Nicolas Ghesquière, does futurism in nylon and patent leather.

**Celine.** Feminine dress-for-success and sporty styles that are sensual and smart.

**Dior.** Don't be fooled by the prim lavender exterior. Inside is pure vixen.

**Dolce & Gabbana.** Liber-ate your inner sex god-dess: everything here is meant to entice.

**Marni.** Dares to be dif-ferent. Sort of an "upper crust slumming it" effect.

### SHOES AND ACCES-SORIES

**Hermès.** The go-to for those who prefer their logo discrete yet still want instant recognition.

**Jimmy Choo.** Starlets adore his glitzy stilettos and fabulous flats.

**Louis Vuitton.** The Champs-ÉlyséesÉlysées megastore houses this ever-morphing line in a gorgeous space.

16

# RUE ST-HONORÉ

You're just as likely to bump into a Saudi princess as a Japanese DJ on what is unarguably one of the world's great shopping streets. All the big names in luxury rub elbows here, along with scores of independents with loads of attitude and fashion cachet.

What really makes this street special, though, is the plenitude of its attractions. Turn the corner and there's the sweeping Place Vendôme, an ex-palace and haven for world-class jewelers. Enter the breathtaking Palais Royal gardens, whose noble mien has been invigorated by the arrival of American bad-boy designers Marc Jacobs and Rick Owens, eco-chic diva Stella McCartney, and other gems. With Place de la Concorde and the Tuileries flanking its borders, you'll know you're strolling Paris's most splendid shopping promenade.

## BEST TIME TO GO

Weekends can get crowded, especially at the major draws, like Colette. But maybe that's the point: the fabulous seek to mull with their own kind, and aspirants can catch a few of their rays.

## BEST FIND FOR THE BABYSITTER

If you can't drop a cool thousand at the oh-so-fabulous **Colette**, head straight for the checkout counter for the adorable tongue-in-chic items in every price range. Cartoon-character key chains and delicate silk-string bracelets (some with tiny diamonds) elate fashionistas—and it's all wrapped up in a Colette bag. *Sigh.*

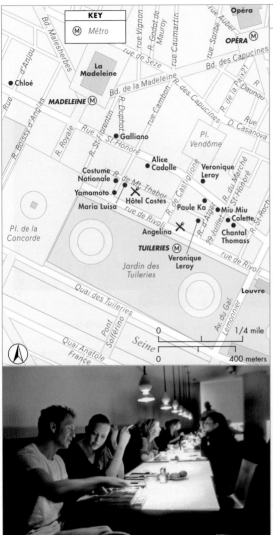

KEY
Ⓜ Métro

## WHAT YOU'LL WANT

**GLAMOUR AND GLITZ**
**Chloé.** Always fresh and original.

**Costume Nationale.** You are the rock star and his girlfriend: expensive looks, unbridled sex appeal.

**Galliano.** Ushered in a new era with his revival of the bias-cut gown—a bona fide fashion legend.

**Miu Miu.** Shoes and accessories scream opulence; the clothes favor sleek refinement.

**Paule Ka.** Movie-star icons are her inspiration. Think Audrey—Hepburn and Tautou, that is.

**Veronique Leroy.** Bewitching colors and sexy peekaboo detailing have garnered serious clout among fashion mavens.

**FASHION FORECASTERS**
**Maria Luisa.** Edgy designs provide the litmus test for what's to come.

**Yamamoto.** New to the neighborhood, this stark white boutique offsets the exquisite designs for men and women.

**LUXE DOWN UNDER**
**Alice Cadolle.** Movie stars and society brides flock to Rue St-Honoré for bespoke perfection; there's ready-to-wear on Rue Cambon.

**Chantal Thomass.** From dominatrix to dewy ingénue—whatever your pleasure, you can find it here.

16

## REFUELING

A cocktail at the **Hotel Costes** reassures that you, too, are one of the anointed. Beware: drop-dead-gorgeous waitresses tend to fluster the faint of heart. Chanel-suited dowagers know where to go for a luscious and restorative cup of hot chocolate. **Angelina**, like its quintessentially Parisian clientele, may be a bit frayed at the edges, but that only adds to its charm. Go at teatime for a truly sinful experience.

# CANAL ST-MARTIN

"Off the beaten track" aptly describes this up-and-coming neighborhood, dotted with galleries, vintage shops, and iconoclastic boutiques.

Although you're not likely to forget you're in Paris, the pace here is noticeably slower. The canal's cobblestones, plane trees, and arched bridges provide the atmosphere, and its stone embankments make an excellent spot to take in the scene. Or, as Parisians do on temperate evenings, share a bite and a bottle of wine with friends. And the shopping: low-key cool reigns here, none of the high-wattage, high-profile designers that vie for the big bucks in Paris's tony neighborhoods. The area's hipster equivalent of mom-and-pop shops ensure a few choice finds that will be seen on you and only you. Walk along Avenue Beaurepaire, the area's shopping epicenter, toward the canal. From here, you'll want to check out some of the smaller streets, especially Rue de Marseille and Rue de Lancry, and meander along the canal—a great way to discover a *quartier* that's still one of Paris's best-kept secrets.

## BEST TIME TO GO

If you want to experience the neighborhood at its most tranquil, go on a weekday. If it's the scene you're after, plan on a Saturday afternoon visit.

## BEST FIND FOR A PICKY HIPSTER

Cool, colorful bracelets and intricate Gothic-inspired chokers are all in rubber at **Idé Co**. Or, for the best-cut velour jeans this side of the Atlantic, go to **Boutique Renhsen**.

**Rouge Kaki.** Design-savvy accessories at Rouge Kaki, on Rue de Lancryn are so appealing you'll want one of everything.

16

## WHAT YOU'LL WANT

### UNDERGROUND CHIC

**Antoine & Lili.** The whole exuberant universe, with women's, kids', and housewares all on the same block. Everything bursts with color, imagination, and charm.

**Boutique Renhsen.** Fashionistas swear by the jeans and comfy sportswear and accessories.

**Dupleks.** "Ethical designers" but no lack of design daring. Sexy micro-blazers and form-flattering tunics can be worn in perfectly good conscience.

**Liza Korn.** Charmingly eccentric and original clothing, shoes, jewelry, and stylish kids' clothes.

**Stella Cadente.** Ultrafeminine separates and sought-after bags are the rage for bright young things.

### MUST-HAVES

**Alter Mundi.** This department store for equitable commerce champions sleek-and-chic designs in everything from tableware to original artworks. Clever clothes, accessories, and jewelry, too.

**Idé Co.** Witty items for the home and updates on all the French staples.

### BRILLIANT BIJOUX

**Médecine Douce.** Whimsical, wearable baubles perfectly in tune with an avant-garde canal-side crowd.

## REFUELING

To really immerse yourself in the scene, join the young designers and artists at **Chez Prune**. On warm days, its canal-side spot makes it the place to be. Or drop in to **Le Verre Volé** for regional wine, biodynamic authentic charcuterie, and excellent company. For atmosphere and a little history to boot, lunch at the **Hotel du Nord** (movie buffs will know it from the eponymous 1938 Marcel Carné film).

# LE MARAIS

Le Marais has just about stolen the show as the city's hottest shopping spot—for sheer volume it can't be beat. Not to mention atmosphere: from the elegant Place des Vosges to the stately Musée Picasso, its irregular streets and ancient *hôtels particuliers* give it the air of Old Paris.

Rue Francs Bourgeois is the shopping-central spine from which the upper and lower Marais branch out. As Le Marais's popularity grows, so, too, does the variety of its attractions. The neighborhood's newest frontier is its northeastern edge—the haut Marais—where ultrastylish boutiques and design ateliers are found amid tiny centuries-old millinery shops. Between Rue de Bretagne and Boulevard du Temple to the east you can find à la mode boutiques too numerous to list (and still relatively undertouristed). Rue Charlot is one of the area's primary draws, along with upper Rue Vieille du Temple and Rue de Poitou in between. But this is by no means an exhaustive selection. The best idea is to get out there and wander, because in this lovely quartier, everywhere the eye rests, it rests happily.

## BEST TIME TO GO

If being jostled by tourists and cranky Parisians isn't your thing, head over between Tuesday and Friday after 11 AM. Remember, Le Marais is one of the few places in Paris where shops open up on Sunday. If you're short on time or need a last-minute shopping fix, Le Marais is your best bet.

## BEST FIND FOR YOUR COWORKER

For those challenged in the gift-finding department, you'll think you've landed in heaven at **Muji**. This store has a flurry of fun, unusual items for the office, home, and bath; many are purse-size, so stuff your suitcase full and *finally* please everyone.

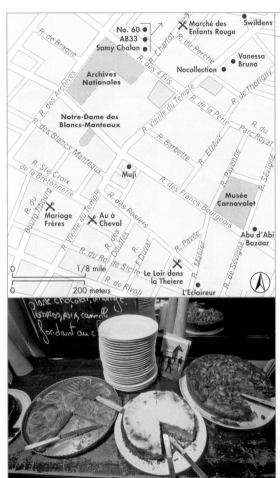

## WHAT YOU'LL WANT

**SHOWSTOPPING CHIC**

**Abu d'Abi Bazaar.** This is your one-stop outfitter with color-coded racks of the season's standouts.

**Antik Batik.** Diaphanous silks, vivid colors, and sparkling beadwork add up to thrilling pieces that look great day and night.

**L'Éclaireur.** High-concept fashion for the impossibly hip crowd.

**No. 60.** Slinky tops, avant-garde leather, and bottle-leg jeans add up to flattering rocker chic.

**Nocollection.** Oh-so-pretty silk dresses and separates in soft fabrics and romantic colors.

**Samy Chalon.** This designer works magic with handmade knitwear—refreshingly original and wondrously sexy.

**Swildens.** Timeless casuals with plenty of broken-in leather, chunky knits, and hip accessories.

**Vanessa Bruno.** Paris's "it" girl combines high style and wearability in her ultrapopular separates and accessories.

**TEATIME**

**Mariage Frères.** Elbow your way in for any and every kind of tea, as well as tea-scented jams, chocolates, and gorgeous teaware.

**16**

### REFUELING

Lines are out the door for brunch at **Le Loir dans la Theiere**, so go at teatime instead. It's really what this place is all about—with its comfy, overstuffed chairs, large selection of teas, and glorious pastries, it provides the perfect late-afternoon pick-me-up. Join the Parisians in their favorite activity and grab an outdoor table at **Au Fer à Cheval**— a prime people-watching spot (and the coffee's not so bad either). Nary a tourist lands here at Paris's oldest covered market, **Marché des Enfants Rouge**, where on warm (and not-so-warm) days you can sit in the semi-outdoors under a translucent roof for a satisfying Italian or Japanese lunch or just an espresso.

# RIVE GAUCHE

Ever since the '60s, when Yves Saint Laurent cashed in on the neighborhood's bohemian-artistic allure, the Rive Gauche has been synonymous with iconoclastic style.

All the major names in French fashion have since taken his lead, transforming the Rive Gauche into a bastion of Parisian chic. Trendsetters line the jumble of streets in the 6$^e$ arrondissement, around Rue Bonaparte, Rue du Four, Rue du Dragon, and Boulevard St-Germain, and tons of exciting boutiques border the charming streets near St. Sulpice. In the 7$^e$ arrondissement there is the Rue de Grenelle, the venerable, treasure-lined Rue des Saints Pères, Rue du Bac, and that jewel of a department store, Le Bon Marché. To see it all would take weeks; with a well-drawn-out plan, however, you can see quite a lot in an afternoon or two. There's always the option of doing what Parisians do best: stroll, observe, discover.

## BEST TIME TO GO

Although Tuesday through Friday afternoons are recommended, this area covers enough ground never to seem too overcrowded, even on weekends.

## BEST FIND FOR A SWEET TOOTH

**Ladurée's** stylish boxes alone are worth the purchase; filled with their legendary lighter-than-air *macarons*—in flavors like salted caramel, rose, or cassis-violet—they make a celestial offering.

You can take it with you! **Pierre Hermé**, Paris's star *pâtissier*, offers a scrumptious, zesty lemon cake preboxed and dense enough to survive the trip home. Maybe.

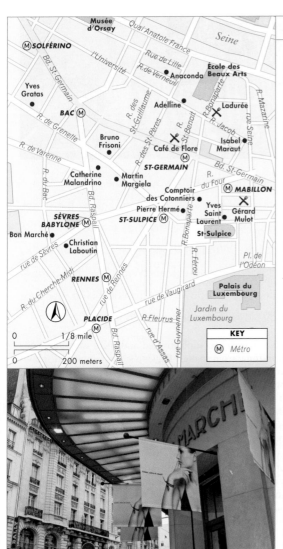

Musée d'Orsay
Quai Anatole France
*Seine*
(M) SOLFÉRINO
l'Université
Rue de Lille
Bd. St-Germain
Rue de Verneuil
Anaconda
École des Beaux Arts
Yves Gratas
R. de Grenelle
BAC (M)
R. des St-Guillaume
Adelline
R. des St-Pères
R. St-Benoît
R. Bonaparte
Ladurée
R. Jacob
R. Mazarine
R. de Varenne
Bruno Frisoni
Café de Flore
Isabel Marant
R. de Seine
ST-GERMAIN
Bd. St-Germain
Catherine Malandrino
Martin Margiela
R. du Four
(M) MABILLON
R. du Bac
Bd. Raspail
Comptoir des Cotonniers
Yves Saint Laurent
Gérard Mulot
SÈVRES BABYLONE (M)
Pierre Hermé
ST-SULPICE (M)
R. Bonaparte
St-Sulpice
Bon Marché
rue de Sèvres
Christian Laboutin
R. Férou
Pl. de l'Odéon
R. du Cherche-Midi
RENNES (M)
rue de Rennes
rue de Vaugirard
Palais du Luxembourg
PLACIDE (M)
R.Fleurus
Jardin du Luxembourg
Bd. Raspail
rue Guynemer
rue d'Assas
0    1/8 mile
0    200 meters

KEY
(M) Métro

**16**

### REFUELING

With the Luxembourg Gardens nearby, pick up picnic savories and sweets from the excellent pâtisserie-traiteur-chocolatier **Gérard Mulot**. Try a yummy shrimp-salad sandwich or *paté en croute* topped off with a few delectable *macarons*.

If you prefer to be served (however haughtily), the illustrious **Café de Flore** offers better-than-average café fare with excellent opportunities for people-watching—inside and out.

## WHAT YOU'LL WANT

### CLOTHES À LA MODE
**Catherine Malandrino.** Feminine dresses, jackets, and skirts go seamlessly from office to evening.

**Comptoir des Cotonniers.** Comfortable, affordable, and superchic clothes make this chain popular.

**Isabel Marant.** Bobo (bourgeois Bohemian) chic with supple leathers, fur, and floral silks.

**Maison Martin Margiela.** You'll love wearing the soft jersey tops over slouchy tailored pants, or some of the edgier designs.

**Yves St Laurent.** Impeccable styling and consummate glamour—ever at fashion's vanguard.

### EXCEPTIONAL GEMS
**Adelline.** A veritable treasure trove of modern, streamlined designs.

### WELL-SHOD CHIC
**Bruno Frisoni.** Alluring with more than a hint of naughtiness, each shoe is a work of art.

**Christian Louboutin.** Sensational, vertiginous styles take glamour (and you) to new heights.

**Le Bon Marché.** A one-stop shop for all the top names in footwear.

**Robert Clergerie.** These shoes are hailed for excellent craftsmanship and enduring style.

Updated by
Jennifer Ditsler-
Ladonne

Nothing, but nothing, can push you into the current of Paris life faster than a few hours of shopping. Follow the example of Parisians, who slow to a crawl as their eyes lock on a tempting display. Window-shopping is one of this city's greatest spectator sports; the French call it *lèche-vitrine*— literally, "licking the windows"—which is fitting because many of the displays look good enough to eat.

Store owners in Paris play to sophisticated audiences with voracious appetites for everything from spangly flagship stores to minimalist boutiques to under-the-radar spots in 19th-century glass-roofed passages. Parisians know that shopping isn't about the kill, it's about the chase: walking down cobblestone streets looking for items they didn't know they wanted, they're casual yet quick to pounce. They like being seduced by a clever display and relish the performance elements of browsing. Watching them shop can be almost as much fun as shopping yourself.

And nowhere is the infamous Parisian "attitude" more palpable than in the realm of fine shopping—and the more *haute* the more hauteur. Parisians are a proud bunch, and they value decorum. Look good; dress to make an impression. You must say *bonjour* upon entering a shop and *merci, au revoir* when leaving, even if it's to no one in particular. Think of it more as announcing your coming and going. Beyond this, protocol becomes less prescribed and more a matter of good judgment. If a salesperson is hovering, there's a reason; let him or her help you. To avoid icy stares once and for all, confidence and politeness go a long way.

As for what to buy, the sky's the limit in terms of choices. If your funds aren't limitless, however, take comfort in knowing that treasures can be found on a budget. And if you do decide to indulge, what better place to make that once-in-a-blue-moon splurge? When you get home and friends ask where you got those to-die-for shoes, with a shrug you'll casually say, "These? Oh . . . I bought them in Paris."

Pierre Hardy makes some of the most sought-after shoes and purses in Paris.

# ACCESSORIES: BAGS, SCARVES, GLOVES, AND MORE

**Alexandra Sojfer** (✉ *218 bd. St-Germain, 7ᵉ, St-Germain-des-Prés* ☎ *01–42–22–17–02* Ⓜ *Rue du Bac*), the proprietress, is the queen of walking sticks. The late president François Mitterrand bought his at this tiny shop, which also has an amazing range of umbrellas.

**Causse** (✉ *12 rue de Castiglione, 1ᵉʳ, Louvre/Tuileries* ☎ *01–49–26–91–43* Ⓜ *Tuileries*) dates back to a time when the quality of the gloves said it all. Supple python or cherry-lacquered lambskin may not have been the rage in 1897 when this eminent glove maker was founded, but its 100-plus years in the business add up to unparalleled style and fit.

**Goyard** (✉ *233 rue St-Honoré, 1ᵉʳ, Louvre/Tuileries* ☎ *01–42–60–57–04* Ⓜ *Tuileries*) is the choice of royals, blue bloods, and the like (clients have included Sir Arthur Conan Doyle, Gregory Peck, and the Duke and Duchess of Windsor). Parisians swear by the colorful totes because of their durability and longevity; they're copious enough for a mile-long baguette, and durable enough for a magnum of champagne. What's more, they easily transition into ultrachic beach or diaper bags.

★ **Hermès** (✉ *24 rue du Faubourg, St-Honoré, 8ᵉ, Louvre/Tuileries* ☎ *01–40–17–47–17* Ⓜ *Concorde* ✉ *42 av. Georges V, 8ᵉ, Champs-Élysées* ☎ *01–47–20–48–51* Ⓜ *George V*) was established as a saddlery in 1837 and went on to create the eternally chic Kelly (named for Grace Kelly) and Birkin (named for Jane Birkin) handbags. The silk scarves are legendary for their rich colors and intricate designs, which change yearly. Other accessories are also extremely covetable: enamel bracelets, dashing silk-twill ties, and small leather goods. During semiannual sales, in January and July, prices are slashed up to 50%, and the crowds line up for blocks.

★ **Jamin Puech** (✉ *43 rue Madame, 6ᵉ, St-Germain-des-Prés* ☎ *01–45–48–14–85* Ⓜ *St-Sulpice* ✉ *68 rue Vieille-du-Temple, 3ᵉ, Le Marais* ☎ *01–48–87–84–87* Ⓜ *St-Paul* ✉ *26 rue Cambon, 1ᵉʳ, Louvre/Tuileries* ☎ *01–40–20–40–28* Ⓜ *Concord*) thinks of its bags not just as a necessity, but as jewelry. Nothing's plain Jane here; beaded bags swing from thin link chains, fringes flutter from dark embossed-leather totes, small evening purses are covered with shells, oversize sequins, or hand-dyed crochet. The collections fluctuate with the seasons but never fail to be whimsical, imaginative, and highly coveted.

Fodor'sChoice **Louis Vuitton** (✉ *101 av. des Champs-Élysées, 8ᵉ, Champs-Élysées* ☎ *08–10–81–00–10* Ⓜ *George V* ✉ *6 pl. St-Germain-des-Prés, 6ᵉ, St-Germain-des-Prés* ☎ *08–10–81–00–10* Ⓜ *St-Germain-des-Prés* ✉ *22 av. Montaigne, 8ᵉ, Champs-ÉlyséesÉlysées* ☎ *08–10–81–00–10* Ⓜ *Franklin-D.-Roosevelt*) has spawned a voracious fan base from Texas to Tokyo with its mix of classic leather goods and the saucy revamped versions orchestrated by Marc Jacobs. Jacobs's collaborations, such as with Japanese artist Takashi Murakami, have become instant collectibles (and knockoffables). This soaring cathedral-esque paean to luxury (and consumption) is unsurpassed.

**Loulou de la Falaise** (✉ *21 rue Cambon, 1ᵉʳ, Louvre/Tuileries* ☎ *01–42–60–02–66* Ⓜ *Concorde*) was Yves Saint Laurent's original muse: she was at his side for more than 30 years of collections and designed his accessories line, and this paragon of the fashion aristocracy has her own boutique where you can find her much-sought-after clothing, accessories, jewelry, cashmere sweaters, mink cardigans, and more.

**Maison Fabre** (✉ *128–129 Galerie de Valois, 1ᵉʳ, Louvre/Tuileries* ☎ *01–42–60–75–88* Ⓜ *Palais Royal Musée du Louvre*), founded in 1924, is home to one of the historic gantiers. Until you've eased into an exquisite pair of gloves handcrafted by Fabre, you probably haven't experienced the sensation of having a second skin far superior to your own. Styles range from classic to haute: that is, elbow-length croc leather, coyote-fur mittens, peccary driving gloves.

**Marie Mercié** (✉ *23 rue St-Sulpice, 6ᵉ, St-Germain-des-Prés* ☎ *01–43–26–45–83* Ⓜ *Mabillon, St-Sulpice*) is one of Paris's most fashionable hat makers. Her husband, Anthony Peto, makes men's hats and has a store at 56 rue Tiquetonne.

**Miguel Lobato** (✉ *6 rue Malher, 4ᵉ, Le Marais* ☎ *01–48–87–68–14* Ⓜ *St-Paul*) is a sweet little boutique with accessories for the woman who wants it all: beautiful high heels by Balenciaga, Chloé, and Pierre Hardy and fabulous bags by Martin Margiela, Alexander McQueen, and Costume National are just the start.

**Peggy Huynh Kinh** (✉ *9 rue Coëtlogon, 6ᵉ, Quartier Latin* ☎ *01–42–84–83–82* Ⓜ *St-Sulpice*) is a former architect who's now behind the structural line of bags at Cartier. She shows her own line of accessories at this eponymous boutique—understated totes, shoulder bags, wallets, and belts in high-quality leather, as well as a line of office accessories.

**DISCOUNT**

**Jamin Puech Inventaire** (✉ *61 rue d'Hauteville, 10ᵉ, Canal St-Martin* ☎ *01–40–22–08–32* Ⓜ *Poissonnière*) has last season's models, but no one will guess; savings are 30% to 60%.

# ANTIQUES

There are really two major antiques neighborhoods in Paris: Carré Rive Gauche and Village St-Paul; both are in lovely, historic districts. From charming French kitchen wares to *ancien régime*–era artifacts, there's plenty here for everyone. Antiques go through a rigorous evaluation for historical value before they're put on sale, so if you see something in a shop, it's permissible to take it out of the country. Dealers handle all customs forms.

Fodor's Choice ★    **Carré Rive Gauche** (✉ *Between St-Germain-des-Prés and Musée d'Orsay, 6ᵉ, St-Germain-des-Prés* Ⓜ *St-Germain-des-Prés, Rue du Bac*) is where you'll find museum-quality pieces. Head to the streets between Rue du Bac, Rue de l'Université, Rue de Lille, and Rue des Sts-Pères to find more than 100 associated shops, marked with a small, blue square banner on their storefronts.

**Drouot auction house** (✉ *9 rue Drouot, 9ᵉ, Opéra/Grands Boulevards* ☎ *01–48–00–20–20* Ⓜ *Richelieu Drouot*) is the world-famous auction house that draws all the top dealers as well as savvy novices and those who just love the chase. It's near the Opéra.

**Village St-Paul** (✉ *Enter from Rue St-Paul, 4ᵉ, Le Marais* Ⓜ *St-Paul*) is a clutch of streets with many antiques shops, in the beautiful historic netherworld tucked between the fringes of Le Marais and the banks of the Seine.

# BEAUTY

When it comes to *maquillage* (makeup), many Parisian women head directly to **Monoprix**, an urban supermarket–dime store that's a gold mine for reasonable, good-quality cosmetics. Brand names to look for are Bourjois, whose products are made in the Chanel factories, and Arcancil. For a great bargain on the best French products, check out the host of "parapharmacies" that have sprung up throughout the city: the French flock here to stock up on pharmaceutical skin-care lines, hair-care basics, and great baby-care necessities normally sold in the more expensive pharmacies. Look for the Roc line of skin products, hair care by Réné Furterer or Phytologie, the popular Caudalíe line of skin care made with grape extracts, or the Nuxe line of body oils and creams infused with a slight gold hue that French actresses swear by, all of which are more expensive back home, if you can find them.

**Anne Sémonin** (✉ *2 rue des Petits-Champs, 2ᵉ, Beaubourg/Les Halles* ☎ *01–42–60–94–66* Ⓜ *Palais-Royal* ✉ *108 rue du Faubourg St-Honoré, 8ᵉ, Champs-Élysées* ☎ *01–42–66–24–22* Ⓜ *Champs-Élysées–Clemenceau*) sells skin-care products made out of seaweed and trace elements, as well as essential oils that are popular with fashion models.

16

**By Terry** (⊠ *36 Galerie Véro-Dodat, 1ᵉʳ, Louvre/Tuileries* ☎ *01–44–76–00–76* Ⓜ *Louvre, Palais-Royal*) is the brainchild of Terry de Gunzburg, Yves Saint Laurent's former director of makeup. This small, refined store sells her own brand of ready-to-wear makeup that's a favorite of French actresses and socialites. Upstairs, specialists create what de Gunzburg calls *haute couleur*, exclusive made-to-measure makeup tailored for each client (very expensive; book far in advance).

**Codina** (⊠ *24 rue Violet, 15ᵉ, Trocadéro/Tour Eiffel* ☎ *01–78–09–56–30* Ⓜ *Dupleix*) extracts its organic oils using the oldest oil press in Paris. The more than 60 varieties—many exotic—include argan to combat wrinkles, wheat germ and apricot for supple skin, borage and cassis for a detoxified glow, and cherry seed for regeneration. Parisian sylphs adore their exclusive bar shampoos, shea-butter-infused creams, and heavenly soaps. There are also dozens of the purest French-extracted essential oils for less than you'll pay stateside.

**Make Up for Ever** (⊠ *5 rue la Boétie, 8ᵉ, Champs-Élysées* ☎ *01–53–05–93–30* Ⓜ *St-Augustin*), at the back of a courtyard, is a must-stop for makeup artists, models, and actresses. The ultrahip selection has hundreds of hues for foundation, eye shadow, powder, and lipstick.

**Mon Soin du Visage** (⊠ *3 rue Maître-Albert, 5ᵉ, Sorbonne* ☎ *01–46–33–33–20* Ⓜ *Maubert Mutualité*) joins age-old Japanese beauty tonics—like sake and wasabi, for their anti-aging and restorative properties—with botanical and floral essences, to create unique blends that hydrate, purify, and rejuvenate the skin. All-organic products include botanical essences to clarify, cleansers, and a range of skin-specific moisturizers to promote suppleness, balance, and regeneration.

**Sephora** (⊠ *70 av. des Champs-Élysées, 8ᵉ, Champs-Élysées* ☎ *01–53–93–22–50* Ⓜ *Franklin-D.-Roosevelt* ⊠ *11 rue de l'Arc en Ciel, in Forum des Halles, 1ᵉʳ, Beaubourg/Les Halles* ☎ *01–40–13–72–25* Ⓜ *Châtelet Les Halles*), the leading chain of perfume and cosmetics megastores in the world, sells its own makeup as well as many of the big brands.

**Shu Uemura** (⊠ *176 bd. St-Germain, 6ᵉ, St-Germain-des-Prés* ☎ *01–45–48–02–55* Ⓜ *St-Germain-des-Prés*) has enhanced those whose faces are their fortune for decades. Models swear by the cleansing oil; free samples are proffered. A huge range of colors, every makeup brush imaginable, and a no-pinch eyelash curler keep fans coming back.

# BOOKS

The scenic open-air *bouquinistes* bookstalls along the Seine are stacked with secondhand books (mostly in French), prints, and souvenirs. French-language bookshops—specializing in art, film, literature, and philosophy—can be found in the scholarly Quartier Latin and the publishing district, St-Germain-des-Prés. For English-language books and magazines, try the following.

**Abbey Bookstore** (⊠ *29 rue de la Parcheminerie, 5ᵉ, Quartier Latin* ☎ *01–46–33–16–24* Ⓜ *Cluny–La Sorbonne*) is Paris's Canadian bookstore, with books on Canadian history and new and secondhand Québécois and English-language novels. The Canadian Club of Paris also organizes regular poetry readings and literary conferences here.

**Comptoir de l'Image** (⊠ *44 rue de Sévigné, 3ᵉ, Le Marais* ☎ *01–42–72–03–92* Ⓜ *St-Paul*) is where designers John Galliano, Marc Jacobs, and Emanuel Ungaro stock up on old copies of *Vogue, Harper's Bazaar,* and *The Face.* It also sells trendy magazines like *Dutch, Purple,* and *Spoon;* designer catalogs from the past; and rare photo books.

★  **La Hune** (⊠ *170 bd. St-Germain, 6ᵉ, St-Germain-des-Prés* ☎ *01–45–48–35–85* Ⓜ *St-Germain-des-Prés*), sandwiched between the Café de Flore and Les Deux Magots, is a landmark for intellectuals. French literature is downstairs, but the main attraction is the comprehensive collection of international books on art and architecture upstairs. You can hang out until midnight with all the other genius-insomniacs.

**Les Editions Ofr** (⊠ *20 rue Dupetit Thouars, 3ᵉ, Temple* ☎ *01–42–45–72–88* Ⓜ *Marais*) gets magazines from the most fashionable spots in the world before anyone else. The store is messy, but you can rub shoulders with photo and press agents and check out the latest in underground, art, and alternative monthlies.

★  The **Red Wheelbarrow** (⊠ *22 rue St-Paul, 4ᵉ, Le Marais* ☎ *01–48–04–75–08* Ⓜ *St-Paul*) is *the* Anglophone bookstore: if it was written in English, you can get it here. The store also has a collection of special-edition historical reads, and a great selection of children's books. Check out its flyers for info on English-language readings, given at least once a month; local artists and visiting authors pitch in on events.

**Shakespeare & Company** (⊠ *37 rue de la Bûcherie, 5ᵉ, Quartier Latin* ☎ *01–43–25–40–93* Ⓜ *St-Michel*), the sentimental Rive Gauche favorite, is named after the bookstore whose American owner, Sylvia Beach, first published James Joyce's *Ulysses.* Nowadays it specializes in expat literature. You can count on a couple of eccentric characters somewhere in the stacks, a sometimes-spacey staff, the latest titles from British presses, and hidden secondhand treasures in the odd corners and crannies. Poets give readings upstairs on Monday at 8 PM; there are also tea-party talks on Sunday at 4 PM.

**Taschen** (⊠ *2 rue de Buci, 6ᵉ, St-Germain-des-Prés* ☎ *01–40–51–79–22* Ⓜ *Mabillon*) is perfect for night owls, as it's open until midnight on Friday and Saturday. The Starck-designed shelves and desks hold glam titles on photography, fine art, design, fashion, and fetishes.

**Tea & Tattered Pages** (⊠ *24 rue Mayet, 6ᵉ, St-Germain-des-Prés* ☎ *01–40–65–94–35* Ⓜ *Duroc*) is the place for bargains: cheap secondhand paperbacks plus new books (publishers' overstock) at low prices. Tea and brownies are served, and browsing is encouraged.

Fodor's Choice  **Village Voice** (⊠ *6 rue Princesse, 6ᵉ, St-Germain-des-Prés* ☎ *01–46–*
★  *33–36–47* Ⓜ *Mabillon*) is a heavy hitter in Paris's ever-thriving expat literary scene. It's known for its excellent current and classic book selections, frequent book signings, and readings by authors of legendary stature along with up-and-comers, all run by a knowledgeable and friendly staff. There's always a fresh stash of English-language periodicals and magazines.

16

## Museum Stores

**CLOSE UP**

These days it seems contemporary museum stores hawk their stock-in-trade images on everything from playing cards to neckties. The boutiques below are an antidote to these "mug-and-tote" chains and—dare we say it—are worth the trip, whether you visit the museum or not.

**107Rivoli** (✉ *107 rue de Rivoli, 1ᵉʳ, Louvre/Tuileries* ☎ *01–42–60–64–94* Ⓜ *Louvre Rivoli, Châtelet*) is the consummate museum store, inside the Musée des Arts Décoratifs. The boutique carries books, jewelry, fashion accessories, paper products, toys, tableware, and objects inspired by the past but with an up-to-date design. Some of the contemporary pieces are limited editions.

**Black Block** (✉ *13 av. du président Wilson, 16ᵉ, Trocadéro/Tour Eiffel* ☎ *01–47–23–37–04* Ⓜ *Iéna/Alma Marceau*), inside the Palais de Tokyo, has merchandise by contemporary artists and designers as edgy and subversive as the museum's exhibits.

There's everything from ultrahip T-shirts, jewelry, bags, and watches to CDs, limited-edition art, and exuberantly colored sex toys. And, if you have a late-night hankering to shop, it's open until midnight.

**La Chalcographie du Louvre** (✉ *Louvre museum store, 1ᵉʳ, Louvre/Tuileries* ☎ *01–40–20–59–35* Ⓜ *Palais-Royal/ Musée du Louvre*) is an extraordinary find. More than 13,000 prints from the Louvre's collection can be sent to the museum's own print shop for a relatively minor investment. The most popular images are in stock, easy to view, and can walk right out with you.

**Musée Baccarat** (✉ *11 pl. des États-Unis, 16ᵉ, Trocadéro/Tour Eiffel* ☎ *01–40–22–11–00* Ⓜ *Iéna/Boissière*) has a gorgeous gallery filled with contemporary crystal by top-name designers, as well as stemware, vases, tableware, jewelry, chandeliers, and even furniture. It's all here, it's all for sale, and it's all breathtaking.

**W. H. Smith** (✉ *248 rue de Rivoli, 1er, Louvre/Tuileries* ☎ *01–44–77–88–99* Ⓜ *Concorde*) carries a multitude of travel and language books, cookbooks, and fiction for adults and children. It also has the best selection of foreign magazines and newspapers in Paris (which you're allowed to peruse without interruption—many magazine dealers in France aren't so kind).

# CLOTHING: CHILDREN'S

Most top designers make minicouture, which usually costs unearthly prices. The following are stores for true children's clothing, as opposed to shrunken versions of adult designer outfits.

**Alice à Paris** (✉ *9 rue de l'Odeon, 6ᵉ, St-Germain-des-Prés* ☎ *01–42–22–53–89* Ⓜ *St-Placide* ✉ *64 rue Condorcet, 9ᵉ, Montmartre/Pigalle* ☎ *01–48–78–17–31* Ⓜ *Pigalle*) stocks inventive, stylish, affordable and, above all, kid-proof clothing. These adorable outfits, for children from birth to 10 years old, are functional takes on classic styles in durable cottons and woolens.

★ **Baghère** (✉ *17 rue de Tournon, 6ᵉ, St-Germain-des-Prés* ☎ *01–43–29–37–21* Ⓜ *Odéon*) is a favorite of movie-star moms. Designer Sylvie Loussiers's meticulous care with fabrics and cuts ensures supremely elegant clothing for kids from birth to age 8. Whether a charming pair of top-stitched overalls with dainty shell buttons, a tiny cashmere cardigan, or a winsome dress in a Liberty print, each piece is of heirloom quality.

Fodor'sChoice **Bonpoint** (✉ *64 av. Raymond Poincaré, 16ᵉ, Trocadéro/Tour Eiffel*
★ ☎ *01–47–27–60–81* Ⓜ *Trocadéro* ✉ *15 rue Royale, 8ᵉ, Louvre/Tuileries* ☎ *01–47–42–52–63* Ⓜ *Madeleine*) is for the prince or princess in your life (royalty *does* shop here). Yes, prices are high, but the quality is exceptional. Styles range from sturdy play clothes to the perfect emerald-green hand-smocked silk dress, a mini leopard-print jacket, or a midnight-blue velvet suit for Little Lord Fauntleroy.

**Bonton** (✉ *5 bd. des Filles du Calvaire, 3ᵉ, Le Marais* ☎ *01–53–63–14–41* Ⓜ *Filles du Calvaire* ✉ *82 rue de Grenelle, 7ᵉ, St-Germain-des-Prés* ☎ *01–44–39–09–20* Ⓜ *Rue du Bac*) takes the prize for most-coveted duds among those who like to think of the child as fashion accessory. (Moms may find some useful wardrobe pointers, too.) Sassy separates in saturated colors layer beautifully, look amazing and manage to be perfectly kid-friendly. Bonton sells toys and furniture, too.

★ **Petit Bateau** (✉ *116 av. des Champs-Élysées, 8ᵉ, Champs-Élysées* ☎ *01–40–74–02–03* Ⓜ *George V* ✉ *53 bis, rue de Sèvres, 6ᵉ, St-Germain-des-Prés* ☎ *01–45–49–48–38* Ⓜ *Sèvres-Babylone*) provides a fundamental part of the classic French wardrobe from cradle to teen and beyond: the T-shirt, cut close to the body, with smallish shoulders (they work equally well with school uniforms or vintage Chanel). The high-grade cotton clothes follow designs that haven't changed in decades—onesies and pajamas for newborns, T-shirts that change color for every season, underwear sets, and dresses with tiny straps for summer. Stock up—if you can find this brand back home, the prices are sure to be higher.

**Pom d'Api** (✉ *28 rue du Four, 6ᵉ, St-Germain-des-Prés* ☎ *01–45–48–39–31* Ⓜ *St-Germain-des-Prés*) lines up footwear for babies and preteens in quality leathers and vivid colors. Expect well-made, eye-catching fashion—bright gold sneakers and fringed suede boots, as well as classic Mary Janes in shades of silver, pink, and gold. There are also utility boots for boys and sturdy rain gear.

**Wowo** (✉ *11 rue de Marseille, 10ᵉ, République* ☎ *01–53–40–84–80* Ⓜ *République*) is an original line of well-made clothes for children from three months to preteen. Designer Elizabeth Relin blends her fashion sensibility and love of color with her respect for the world of childhood—no pop tarts here.

# CLOTHING: DISCOUNT

**A.P.C.** (✉ *20 rue André del Sarte, 18ᵉ, Montmartre* ☎ *01–42–62–10–88* Ⓜ *Château Rouge*) opened its surplus store steps away from Sacré-Coeur. No need to wait for the sales; their funky classics can be found here for a whopping 50% off.

16

**Et Vous** (⊠ *17 rue Turbigo, 2ᵉ, Les Halles* ☎ *01–40–13–04–12* Ⓜ *Étienne Marcel*) is a great alternative to the regular boutiques because the clothes are still very much in style and are 50% off. You'd never know you were in a stock store if you walked in off the street. There are accessories, too.

**Le Dépôt Vente de Passy** (⊠ *14 rue de la Tour, 16ᵉ, Trocadéro/Tour Eiffel* ☎ *01–45–20–95–21* Ⓜ *Passy* ⊠ *109 rue de Courcelles, 17e, Champs-Élysées* ☎ *01–40–53–80–82* Ⓜ *Wagram*) specializes in barely worn designer ready-to-wear from big names, including Chanel, Dior, Hermès, Gucci, and Prada. Few can pass up one of last season's outfits at one-third the price, or forgo browsing the vast selection of accessories: bags, belts, scarves, shoes, and costume jewelry.

**L'Habilleur** (⊠ *44 rue de Poitou, 3ᵉ, Le Marais* ☎ *01–48–87–77–12* Ⓜ *St-Sébastien Froissart*) is a favorite with the fashion press and anyone looking for a deal. For women there's a great selection from designers like Issey Miyake, Stefano Mortari, Paul & Joe, and Giorgio Brato. Men can find suits from Roberto Collina and Paul & Joe at slashed prices.

**Rue d'Alésia** (Ⓜ *Alésia*), in the 14ᵉ arrondissement, is the main place to find shops selling last season's fashions at a discount. Be forewarned: most of these shops are much more downscale than their elegant sister shops; dressing rooms are not always provided.

**Zadig et Voltaire** (⊠ *22 rue Bourg Tibourg, 4ᵉ, Le Marais* ☎ *01–44–59–39–62* Ⓜ *Hôtel de Ville*) has new unsold stock from last season. You'll find a great selection of beautiful cashmere sweaters, silk slip dresses, rocker jeans, and leather jackets, all in their signature luscious colors for at least 40% off.

# CLOTHING: MEN'S AND WOMEN'S

**Agnès b** (⊠ *2, 3, and 6 rue du Jour, 1ᵉʳ, Beaubourg/Les Halles* ☎ *01–42–33–04–13* Ⓜ *Châtelet Les Halles* ⊠ *6 rue Vieux Columbier, 6ᵉ, Germain-des-Prés* ☎ *01–44–39–02–60* Ⓜ *St-Sulpice* ⊠ *38 av. George V, 8ᵉ, Champs-Élysées* ☎ *01–40–73–81–10* Ⓜ *George V*) embodies the quintessential French approach to easy but stylish dressing. There are many branches, and the clothes are also sold in department stores, but for the fullest range go to Rue du Jour, where Agnès takes up most of the street (women's wear at No. 6, children at No. 2, menswear at No. 3, or the newest store at Avenue George V. For women, classics include sleek black-leather jackets, flattering black jersey separates, and trademark wide-stripe T-shirts. Children love the two-tone T-shirts proclaiming their age. And the stormy-gray velour or corduroy suits you see on those slouchy, scarf-clad men? Agnès b.

**A.P.C.** (⊠ *38 rue Madame, 6ᵉ, St-Germain-des-Prés* ☎ *01–42–22–12–77* Ⓜ *St-Sulpice* ⊠ *112 rue Vieille du Temple, 3ᵉ, Le Marais* ☎ *01–42–78–18–02* Ⓜ *Filles du Calvaire*) may be antiflash, but a knowing eye can always pick out their jeans in a crowd. The clothes are rigorously well-made; prime wardrobe pieces include dark indigo and black denim, zip-up cardigans, and peacoats.

**Balenciaga** (✉ *10 av. George V, 8ᵉ, Champs-Élysées* ☎ *01–47–20–21–11* Ⓜ *Alma-Marceau*) is now in the hands of Nicolas Ghesquière—guess what inspired him when he designed this boutique? Notice the tile, the wavy line of the store, that slice of turquoise blue, the aloe plants. The clothes are interesting, sometimes beautiful, as Ghesquière plays with volume (bubbling skirts, superskinny pants) and references (robot, futuristic). The accessories and menswear are often more approachable, like the perfectly tooled leather bags and narrow suits. (You got it, a swimming pool.)

**Boutique Renhsen** (✉ *22 rue Beaurepaire, 10ᵉ, République* ☎ *01–48–04–01–01* Ⓜ *République*) is popular for its jeans: slender, supple, and ultraflattering—but those in the know come for the stylish separates in natural fibers and the range of must-have accessories.

**Charvet** (✉ *28 pl. Vendôme, 1ᵉʳ, Opéra/Grands Boulevards* ☎ *01–42–60–30–70* Ⓜ *Opéra*) is the Parisian equivalent of a Savile Row tailor: a conservative, aristocratic institution famed for made-to-measure shirts, exquisite ties, and accessories; for garbing John F. Kennedy, Charles de Gaulle, and the Duke of Windsor; and for its regal address. Although the exquisite silk ties, in hundreds of colors and patterns, and custom-made shirts for men are the biggest draw, refined pieces for women and girls, as well as adorable miniatures for boys, round out the collection.

**Costume Nationale** (✉ *5 rue Cambon, 1ᵉʳ, Louvre/Tuileries* ☎ *01–40–15–04–36* Ⓜ *Tuileries*) is all about sharp styling and unerring sophistication. Ennio Capasa's flawlessly cut suits confer high-powered status, and teensy dresses with plunging necklines shoot for unabashed allure. Shoes and accessories are surprisingly versatile.

**Dolce & Gabbana** (✉ *54 av. Montaigne, 8ᵉ, Champs-Élysées* ☎ *01–42–25–68–78* Ⓜ *Alma-Marceau* ✉ *3 rue Faubourg St-Honoré, 8ᵉ, Louvre/Tuileries* ☎ *01–44–94–95–95* Ⓜ *Concorde*) offers a sexy, young-Italian-widow vibe with a side of moody boyfriend. Svelte silk dresses, sharply tailored suits, and plunging necklines are made for drama. Women's clothes are at Avenue Montaigne; men's are at Rue St-Honoré.

**D&G** (✉ *244 rue de Rivoli, 1ᵉʳ, Louvre/Tuileries* ☎ *01–42–86–00–44* Ⓜ *Concorde*), the Dolce & Gabbana sportswear line, rocks the concept of day wear with leather, denim, and splashy florals spiked with lingerie details. There are clothes for men, women, and even kids.

**Eric Bompard** (✉ *75 bd. Haussmann, 8ᵉ, Opéra/Grands Boulevards* ☎ *01–42–68–00–73* Ⓜ *Miromesnil* ✉ *46 rue du Bac, 7ᵉ, Germain-des-Prés* ☎ *01–42–84–04–36* Ⓜ *Rue du Bac* ✉ *91 av. des Champs-Élysées, 8ᵉ, Champs-Élysées* ☎ *01–53–57–89–60* Ⓜ *George V*) provides stylish Parisians an excellent service, with luxury cashmeres in every color, style, and weight; yarns range from light as a feather to a hefty 50-ply for the jaunty caps. The store caters to men and woman (there are some kids' models, too. Styles are updated seasonally, yet tend toward the classic.

**G-Star Store** (✉ *46 rue Étienne Marcel, 2ᵉ, Beaubourg/Les Halles* ☎ *01–42–21–44–33* Ⓜ *Étienne Marcel*) is a haven for fans of raw denim. It, uniquely, stocks the designs of the Dutch-based label G-Star, whose

16

# Jardin du Palais Royal

Paris's secret oasis no more. With the arrival of Marc Jacobs, Rick Owens, and Stella McCartney, the palace and gardens of the Jardin du Palais Royal officially joins the ranks of fashion hot spots. Not that it ever lacked allure; those in the know have come here for fabulous shoes, artisanal perfumes, and vintage haute couture for years. Shopping in Paris is no common experience, but shopping at the Palais Royal—under its neat rows of lime and chestnut trees and vaulted arcades—is almost worship.

Entering the gardens from the Rue St-Honoré, you'll encounter the Colonnes de Buren, a series of sculpted columns, covering the first inner courtyard. Galerie de Montpensier is the long arcade to your left; Galerie de Valois flanks the the gardens to your right.

### GALERIE DE VALOIS

No. 156: **Pierre Hardy:** head-turning heels that tantalize while they flatter, with some of Paris's best bags to match (☎ *01–42–60–59–75*).

No. 142: **Les Salons du Palais-Royal Shiseido:** Serge Lutens, nose par excellence, offers his renowned scents in this jewel of a boutique, along with some signature perfumes (☎ *01–49–27–09–09*).

No. 138–139: **Jérôme l'Huillier:** color-saturated silks in sexy, mod styles, with sleek new takes on the wrap dress (☎ *01–49–26–07–07*).

No. 130–133: **Rick Owens:** over-the-top rock-star glamour with an avant-garde edge, he's making serious fashion waves worldwide (☎ *01–40–20–42–52*).

No. 128–129: **Maison Fabre:** has made some of the most beautiful gloves in

the world since 1924. Styles in python, peccary, and crocodile fit like a second skin (☎ *01–42–60–75–88*).

No. 124: **Acne Studio:** Swedish design for men and women who demand it all: style, fit, comfort, and plenty of cool (☎ *01–42–60–16–62*).

No. 114–121: **Stella McCartney:** This warm, feminine boutique reflects her A-list creds, achieved over years of steady success. The wearable-yet-sexy separates are a must in any well-appointed wardrobe.

### GALERIE DE MONTPENSIER

No. 63–64: **Maison de Vacances:** quilts, pillows, and other decor items in silk, marabou, cashmere, and washed leather, plus cheeky handbags and slippers (☎ *01–47–03–99–74*).

No. 56–62: **Marc Jacobs:** from flapper to prom queen to motorcycle moll—iconic American style updated (☎ *01–55–35–02–60*).

No. 31: **Gabrielle Geppert:** think Belle de Jour and Krystle Carrington—why buy a knockoff when you can have the original? Bags, jewelry, and sunglasses, too (☎ *01–42–61–53–52*).

No. 26: **Qeelin:** the premier Chinese jeweler offers gem-encrusted styles from its signature teddy bear to the elegant lotus, designed specially for the launch of this boutique (☎ *01–49–26–96–90*).

No. 20–24: **Didier Ludot:** this legend in vintage couture covers the greats in French fashion from the '20s to the '80s; his personal take on the little black dress can be found across the gardens at 125 Galerie de Valois (☎ *01–42–96–06–56*).

highly desirable jeans have replaced Levi's as the ones to be seen in. There are also military-inspired clothing, bags, and T-shirts.

**Kokon To Zaï** (✉ *48 rue Tiquetonne, 2ᵉ, Beaubourg/Les Halles* ☎ *01–42–36–92–41* Ⓜ *Étienne Marcel*) is a Japanese expression to sum up opposing extremes (such as hot and cold, young and old). It's also a hip boutique selling the work of more than 20 young designers, and now their own label, KTZ, as well as jewelry, shoes, and accessories.

**L'Éclaireur** (✉ *40 rue de Sevigné, 3ᵉ, Le Marais* ☎ *01–48–87–10–22* Ⓜ *St-Paul* ✉ *12 rue Mahler, 4ᵉ, Le Marais* ☎ *01–44–54–22–11* Ⓜ *St-Paul*) is split with women's wear in one shop, and men's around the corner. It maintains an avant-garde aesthetic, with tastes for designers such as Martin Margiela, Paul Harnden, and Ann Demeulemeester, plus labels such as Tramando and Lanvin.

**Lucien Pellat-Finet** (✉ *1 rue Montalembert, 7ᵉ, St-Germain-des-Prés* ☎ *01–42–22–22–77* Ⓜ *Rue du Bac*) does cashmere that shakes up the traditional world of cable knits—here, sweaters for men, women, and children come in punchy colors and cheeky motifs. A psychedelic mushroom may bounce across a sky-blue crewneck; a crystal-outlined skull could grin from a sleeveless top. The cashmere's wonderfully soft—and the prices are accordingly high.

★ **Maison Martin Margiela** (✉ *25 bis, rue de Montpensier, 1ᵉʳ, Louvre/Tuileries* ☎ *01–40–15–07–55* Ⓜ *Palais-Royal* ✉ *23 passage Potier, 1ᵉʳ, Louvre/Tuileries* ☎ *01–40–15–06–44* Ⓜ *Palais-Royal* ✉ *13 rue de Grenelle, 7ᵉ, St-Germain-des-Prés* ☎ *01–45–49–06–68* Ⓜ *St-Sulpice*), the famously elusive Belgian designer, has a devoted following for his cut—sometimes oversize but never bulky—and for his innovative technique, from spiraling seams to deconstructed shirts. Be sure to look for Ligne 6, his secondary line of more casual (and less expensive) clothes for women. The Passage Potier location carries men's clothing only.

**Marc Jacobs** (✉ *56–62 Galerie de Montpensier, 1ᵉ, Louvre/Tuileries* ☎ *01–55–35–02–60* Ⓜ *Palais Royal Musée du Louvre* ✉ *19 place du Marché St-Honoré, 1ᵉʳ, Louvre/Tuileries* Ⓜ *Tuileries*) remains the darling of American style with his singular take on 20th-century American classics—from flapper-style (big flowers, unstructured lines, drop waists, flounces) to '60s prom (empire waists, copious tulle) with a bit of motorcycle chic thrown in. Metallics appear in most every collection, as do breezy, feminine fabrics and lots of layers. Ready-to-wear is at Palais Royal. The secondary line Marc by Marc Jacobs is at Marché St-Honoré. Mens and accessories are at both.

**Maria Luisa** (✉ *7 rue Rouget de l'Isle, 1er, Louvre/Tuileries* ☎ *01–47–03–96–15* Ⓜ *Concorde*) is one of the most important names in town for cutting-edge fashion. The store at No. 7 is considered a "style laboratory" for young designers, along with established designers (like Balenciaga and Demeulemeester), and carries top-name accessories and shoes, including Paris's exclusive on Manolo Blahnik.

**Prada** (✉ *10 av. Montaigne, 8ᵉ, Trocadéro/Tour Eiffel* ☎ *01–53–23–99–40* Ⓜ *Alma-Marceau* ✉ *6 rue du Faubourg St-Honoré, 8ᵉ, Louvre/Tuileries* ☎ *01–58–18–63–30* Ⓜ *Concorde* ✉ *5 rue de Grenelle, 6ᵉ, St-Germain-des-Prés* ☎ *01–45–48–53–14* Ⓜ *St-Sulpice*) spins gold out of fashion straw. Knee-length skirts, peacock colors, cardigan sweaters, geometric prints; the waiting lists cross continents. Shoes, bags, and other accessories for men and women perennially become cult items.

**Rick Owens** (✉ *130–133 Galerie de Valois, 1er, Louvre/Tuileries* ☎ *01–40–20–42–52* Ⓜ *Palais Royal–Musée du Louvre*) expertly finessed the jump from L.A. rock-star chic to Paris offbeat elegance. Lately defined more by glamour than grunge, his lush fabrics and asymmetrical designs have evolved to a new level of artistry—and wearability. Owens still loves a paradox (shrouding while revealing), and mixes high luxury with a bit of the tooth and the claw. You'll find shoes, furs, and even furniture here.

**Sonia Rykiel** (✉ *175 bd. St-Germain, 6e, St-Germain-des-Prés* ☎ *01–49–54–60–60* Ⓜ *St-Germain-des-Prés* ✉ *70 rue du Faubourg St-Honoré, 8e, Louvre/Tuileries* ☎ *01–42–65–20–81* Ⓜ *Concorde*) has been designing insouciant knitwear since the '60s. The women's boutiques (No. 175 and St-Honoré) tempt with sexy keyhole sweaters, opulent furs, accessories dotted with rhinestones, and soft leather bags.

**Surface to Air** (✉ *68 rue Charlot, 3e, Le Marais* ☎ *01–44–61–76–27* Ⓜ *Filles du Calvaire*) has an air of counterculture chic and promotes itself as a style lab: cool and understated, the focus is on design. Women's separates range from metallic jeans to asymmetrical minidresses, along with some gorgeous shoes and accessories; menswear includes enigmatic T-shirts, streamlined jeans, and cropped leather jackets.

**Yohji Yamamoto** (✉ *25 rue du Louvre, 47 rue Étienne Marcel, 1er, Beaubourg/Les Halles* ☎ *01–42–21–42–93* Ⓜ *Étienne Marcel* ✉ *4 rue Cambon, 1er, Louvre/Tuileries* ☎ *01–40–20–00–71* Ⓜ *Concord*) brings couture and the ready-to-wear Y's line for men and women together under one roof, with Y-3 sportswear around the corner at 47 rue Étienne Marcel. A master of the drape, fold, and twist, Yamamoto favors predominantly black clothes that are both functional and edgy. Pleats, florals, and brilliant colors now punctuate each collection.

# CLOTHING: VINTAGE

**Anouschka** (✉ *6 av. du Coq, 9e, Opéra/Grands Boulevards* ☎ *01–48–74–37–00* Ⓜ *St-Lazare, Trinité*) has set up shop in her apartment (by appointment only, Monday to Saturday) and has rack upon rack of vintage clothing dating from the '30s to the '80s. It's the perfect place to find a '50s cocktail dress in mint condition or a mod jacket for him. A former model herself, she calls this a "designer laboratory," and teams from top fashion houses often pop by looking for inspiration.

★ **Didier Ludot** (✉ *Jardins du Palais-Royal, 20 Galerie Montpensier, 1er, Louvre/Tuileries* ✉ *24 Galerie Montpensier, 1er, Louvre/Tuileries* ✉ *125 Galerie de Valois, 1er, Louvre/Tuileries* ☎ *01–42–96–06–56* Ⓜ *Palais-Royal*) is one of the world's most famous vintage clothing dealers and an incredibly charming man to boot. (A tip: be nice to the dogs.) Riffle through French couture from the '20s to the '80s on the racks: wonderful Chanel suits, Balenciaga dresses, and Hermès scarves. He has three boutiques: No. 20 houses his amazing collection of vintage couture; No.

24 the vintage ready-to-wear; and across the way at No. 125 you can find his own vintage-inspired black dresses and his coffee-table book aptly titled *The Little Black Dress*.

**Gabrielle Geppert** (⊠ *31 Galerie de Montpensier, 1ᵉʳ, Louvre/Tuileries* ☎ *01–42–61–53–52* Ⓜ *Palais Royal Musée du Louvre*) carries Cardin, Pucci, a little Chanel, and plenty of classy no-names—what's here is exactly what Gabrielle likes: from a '50s-era fully sequined cape and '60s jet-beaded minidress to an '80s number right at home under the disco ball. Fabulous designer shades, handbags, and jewelry, too.

**Réciproque** (⊠ *89, 92, 93, 95, and 101 rue de la Pompe, 16ᵉ, Trocadéro/ Tour Eiffel* ☎ *01–47–04–30–28* Ⓜ *Rue de la Pompe*) is Paris's largest and most exclusive swap shop. Savings on designer wear—Hermès, Dior, Chanel, and Louis Vuitton—are significant, but prices aren't as cheap as you might expect, and there's not much in the way of service or space. The shop at No. 101 specializes in leather goods. Both locations are closed Sunday and Monday.

**Scarlett** (⊠ *10 rue Clément-Marot, 8ᵉ, Trocadéro/Tour Eiffel* ☎ *01–56– 89–03–00* Ⓜ *Alma-Marceau*) offers exceptional vintage couture by the likes of Chanel, Hermès, and Louis Vuitton.

16

# CLOTHING: WOMEN ONLY

## CLASSIC CHIC

**AB33** (⊠ *33 rue Charlot, 3ᵉ, Le Marais* ☎ *01–42–71–02–82* Ⓜ *Filles du Calvaire*) is like a sleek boudoir—complete with comfy chair and scented candles—and the clothes here are unabashedly feminine: separates in luxury fabrics from top designers, irresistible silk lingerie, dainty jewelry, and a selection of accessories celebrate that certain French *je ne sais quoi*.

**Alberta Ferretti** (⊠ *418 rue St-Honoré, 8ᵉ, Louvre/Tuileries* ☎ *01–42– 60–14–97* Ⓜ *Madeleine/Concorde*) puts out come-hither designs. Sheer, cutout, and structured by turns, these super-feminine creations seek to enchant—and succeed. Lacquered silk dresses in opulent hues resemble molten candies.

**Celine** (⊠ *36 av. Montaigne, 8ᵉ, Champs-Élysées* ☎ *01–56–89–07–91* Ⓜ *Franklin-D.-Roosevelt*) was venerable and dusty before designer Michael Kors showed up in the late '90s with his version of Jackie O, "the Greek magnate years" and put Celine back on the map. Phoebe Philo gave the brand a jolt in 2009, drawing raves from critics for her focused, streamlined, and ultra-flattering styles.

**Claudie Pierlot** (⊠ *1 rue Montmartre, 1ᵉʳ, Louvre/Tuileries* ☎ *01–42–21– 38–38* Ⓜ *Étienne Marcel* ⊠ *23 rue du Vieux Colombier, 6ᵉ, St-Germain- des-Prés* ☎ *01–45–48–11–96* Ⓜ *St-Sulpice*) is deservedly lauded for its smart, urban clothes that unite youthful chic with solid designs; they also successfully transition over several seasons. The irresistible combination of classic looks, good tailoring, and affordability keeps loyal fans coming back year after year.

**Comptoir des Cotonniers** (✉ *33 rue des Francs-Bourgeois, 4ᵉ, Le Marais* ☎ *01–42–76–95–33* Ⓜ *St-Paul* ✉ *59 rue Bonaparte, 6ᵉ, St-Germain-des-Prés* ☎ *01–43–26–07–56* Ⓜ *St-Sulpice* ✉ *342 rue St-Honoré, 1ᵉʳ, Louvre/Tuileries* ☎ *01–42–60–10–75* Ⓜ *Tuileries*) is a star for its smart, wearable styles that stress ease and comfort over fussiness. Separates in natural fibers—cotton, silk, and cashmere blends—can be light and breezy or cozy and warm, but are always soft, flattering, and in a range of beautiful colors. Styles for moms and daughters age four and up.

**Cotélac** (✉ *284 rue St-Honoré, 1ᵉʳ, Louvre/Tuileries* ☎ *01–47–03–21–14* Ⓜ *Tuileries* ✉ *30 rue Montmartre, 1ᵉʳ, Beaubourg/Les Halles* ☎ *01–40–28–13–84* Ⓜ *Les Halles* ✉ *17 rue du Cherche Midi, 6ᵉ, St-Germain-des-Prés* ☎ *01–42–84–10–25* Ⓜ *Sèvres-Babylone*) gives feminine shapes an edge in earthy tones from azure to deep aubergine. The figure-skimming and frillier separates beg to be layered.

**Et Vous** (✉ *6 rue des Francs-Bourgeois, 3ᵉ, Le Marais* ☎ *01–42–71–75–11* Ⓜ *St-Paul* ✉ *271 rue St-Honoré, 1ᵉʳ, Louvre/Tuileries* ☎ *01–47–03–00–31* Ⓜ *Tuileries*) takes its cue from the catwalk, turning out affordable, extremely well-cut clothing: pants (low waist/slim hip), knee-skimming skirts, chunky sweaters, and classic work wear with individual details.

**Jérôme L'Huillier** (✉ *138–139 Galerie de Valois, 1ᵉʳ, Louvre/Tuileries* ☎ *01–49–26–07–07* Ⓜ *Palais Royal Musée du Louvre*) cut his teeth at the ateliers of Balman and Givenchy, and it shows. A wizard with silk in all its iterations (the joyously colored prints are L'Huillier's own designs), you can find lively, sexy new takes on the wrap dress, along with rainbow-hue blouses, sexy empire-waist dresses, and velvet trench coats in jewel colors.

**Nocollection** (✉ *96 rue Vieille du Temple, 3e, Le Marais* ☎ *01–40–26–57–80* Ⓜ *Filles du Calvaire*) incorporates ravishing colors with flattering styles and soft fabrics to create a collection friendly to women of every size and shape. Up-to-the-moment styles make a statement while still allowing for plenty of sensuality, and, best of all, comfort.

**Paul & Joe** (✉ *46 rue Étienne Marcel, 2ᵉ, Beaubourg/Les Halles* ☎ *01–40–28–03–34* Ⓜ *Étienne Marcel* ✉ *2 av. Montaigne, 8ᵉ, Champs-Élysées* ☎ *01–47–20–57–50* Ⓜ *George V* ✉ *66 rue des Saints Péres, 7ᵉ, St-Germain-des-Prés* ☎ *01–42–22–47–01* Ⓜ *St-Germain-des-Prés*) is designer Sophie Albou's eclectic, girlish blend of modern trends. There's a retro feel to the diaphanous blouses, A-line jackets with matching short shorts, and swingy felt coats. In summer she'll mix in a little hippie chic. The secondary line, Paul & Joe Sister—with a decidedly younger clientele—brings a slouchy, casual edge to the line: from hipster overalls to minidresses.

**Paule Ka** (✉ *20 rue Malher, 4ᵉ, Le Marais* ☎ *01–40–29–96–03* Ⓜ *St-Paul* ✉ *192 bd. St-Germain, 7ᵉ, St-Germain-des-Prés* ☎ *01–45–44–92–60* Ⓜ *St-Germain-des-Prés* ✉ *223 rue St-Honoré, 1ᵉʳ, Louvre/Tuileries* ☎ *01–42–97–57–06* Ⓜ *Tuileries*) has that movie-star glamour down pat. For daytime, perfectly cut silk belted shirtdresses with matching coats, for evening, gemstone-studded gowns and furs. Both Audrey and Katherine would have made this their second home.

It's free to window-shop at Christian LaCroix's St-Germain boutique but it's hard to not fall in love with his designs.

**Tara Jarmon** (✉ *400 rue St-Honoré, 1ᵉʳ, Louvre/Tuileries* ☎ *01–40–15–02–134* Ⓜ *Concord* ✉ *75 rue des Saints-Péres, 6ᵉ, St-Germain-des-Prés* ☎ *01–45–44–36–14* Ⓜ *St-Germain-des-Prés* ✉ *73 av. des Champs-Élysées, 8ᵉ, Champs-Élysées* ☎ *01–45–63–45–41* Ⓜ *George V*) has her bases covered when it comes to that coveted French élan: sleek designs, excellent quality, luxe fabrics, and prices well within the stratosphere. With styles that vie with the high-profile designers, and accessories to match, this label is fast becoming the chic Parisian's wardrobe essential.

**Ventilo** (✉ *27 bis, rue du Louvre, 2ᵉ, Louvre/Tuileries* ☎ *01–44–76–83–00* Ⓜ *Louvre* ✉ *13–15 bd. de la Madeleine, 1ᵉʳ, Louvre/Tuileries* ☎ *01–42–60–46–40* Ⓜ *Madeleine*) brings cool ethnic style to the city. Where else can you find a bright-orange silk-shantung ball skirt with mirror appliqué or a modern Mongol leather coat lined in fur? There's also room for classics to mix and match, such as handmade wool turtlenecks and zippered riding pants that fit perfectly.

**Veronique Leroy** (✉ *10 rue d'Alger, 1ᵉʳ, Louvre/Tuileries* ☎ *01–49–26–93–59* Ⓜ *Tuileries*) highlights a woman's silhouette while paying close attention to details like open seam work and perfect draping. Slinky silk-jersey dresses, form-flattering sweaters in dusky hues, and lacy dresses with come-hither necklines help explain her current darling-of-the-fashion-world status.

## COUTURE HOUSES

No matter, say the French, that fewer and fewer of their top couture houses are still headed by compatriots. It's the creativity, the workmanship, the *je ne sais quoi* that remains undeniably Gallic. Haute couture, defined by inimitable handwork, is increasingly buoyed by ancillary lines—ready-to-wear, perfume, sunglasses, you name it—that fill the windows of the boutiques. The successes of some houses have spurred the resuscitation of a few more, such as Nina Ricci, now helmed by the young Belgian designer Olivier Theyskens, and Lanvin, with women's wear by Moroccan-born designer Alber Elbaz. Most of the high-fashion shops are on Avenue Montaigne, Avenue George V, and Rue du Faubourg St-Honoré on the Rive Droite, though St-Germain-des-Prés has also become a stomping ground. The following are a few of Paris's haute-couture highlights. Exchange rates being what they are, couture is not in the realm of most of us—but Paris is for dreaming, after all.

★ **Chanel** (⊠ *42 av. Montaigne, 8ᵉ, Champs-Élysées* ☎ *01–47–23–74–12* Ⓜ *Franklin-D.-Roosevelt* ⊠ *31 rue Cambon, 1ᵉʳ, Louvre/Tuileries* ☎ *01–42–86–26–00* Ⓜ *Tuileries*) is helmed by Karl Lagerfeld, whose collections are steadily vibrant. The historic center is at the Rue Cambon boutique, where Chanel once perched high up on the mirrored staircase watching audience reactions to her collection debuts. Great investments include all of Coco's favorites: the perfectly tailored tweed suit, a lean, soigné black dress, a quilted bag with a gold chain, or a camellia brooch.

**Christian Dior** (⊠ *30 av. Montaigne, 8ᵉ, Champs-Élysées* ☎ *01–40–73–54–44* Ⓜ *Franklin-D.-Roosevelt* ⊠ *16 rue de l'Abbé, 6ᵉ, St-Germain-des-Prés* ☎ *01–56–24–90–53* Ⓜ *St-Germain-des-Prés*) installed flamboyant John Galliano and embarked on a wild ride. Galliano's catwalks are always the most talked-about *evénéments* of the fashion season: they're opulent, crazy shows with strutting Amazons in extreme ensembles, iced champagne, and some of the most beautiful women in the world in attendance (not to mention the men). Despite the theatrical staging and surreal high jinks, his full-length body-skimming evening dresses cut on the bias are gorgeous in whatever fabric he chooses. So what if he pairs them with high-tops and a Davy Crockett raccoon hat? It's fashion, darling.

**Emanuel Ungaro** (⊠ *2 av. Montaigne, 8ᵉ, Champs-Élysées* ☎ *01–53–57–84–95* Ⓜ *Alma-Marceau*) has recently been a revolving door for young design talent. With lots of slinky hot pink, sequins, micro minis, and bared shoulders, her first collection seemed a tad impractical (unless perhaps you're a pole dancer, since pasties were a featured item). Critics may not get the last laugh, however, as the boutique is teeming with newfound fans.

Fodor's Choice **Galliano** (⊠ *384 rue St-Honoré, 1ᵉʳ, Louvre/Tuileries* ☎ *01–55–35–40–★ 40* Ⓜ *Concorde*), fittingly enough, landed an address with Revolutionary history for his first namesake store. What more can be said about John Galliano, a living hyperbole? Well, the boutique pairs glass and stone, a high-tech plasma screen grabs your eye, and a Diptyque candle *(see the Diptyque shop listed under Home Decor, below)* scents the air. Clothes ricochet between debauchery, humor, and refinement, but look past the wackier distractions to find what he does best: flattering long dresses, structured jackets, and heels that give the best leg.

**Jean-Paul Gaultier** (✉ *44 av. George V, 8ᵉ, Champs-Élysées* ☎ *01–44–43–00–44* Ⓜ *George V* ✉ *6 rue Vivienne, 2ᵉ, Opéra/Grands Boulevards* ☎ *01–42–86–05–05* Ⓜ *Bourse*) first made headlines with his celebrated corset with the ironic iconic breasts for Madonna but now sends fashion editors into ecstasy with his sumptuous haute-couture creations. Designer Philippe Starck spun an *Alice in Wonderland* fantasy for the boutiques, with quilted cream walls and Murano mirrors. Make no mistake, though, it's all about the clothes.

**Loris Azzaro** (✉ *65 rue de Faubourg St-Honoré, 8ᵉ, Louvre/Tuileries* ☎ *01–42–66–92–98* Ⓜ *Concorde*) is a master of the dramatic dress: floor-length columns with jeweled collars and sheer gowns with strategically placed sequins. When he saw his 1970s designs, now collector's items, worn by stars like Nicole Kidman and Liz Hurley, he decided to update his best sellers.

**Nina Ricci** (✉ *39 av Montaigne, 8ᵉ, Champs-Élysées* ☎ *01–40–88–67–60* Ⓜ *Franklin-D.-Roosevelt*) appeals to the leather-and-lace sensibility, in surprising ways; that is, the lace might be in leather. After fashion-favorite Olivier Theyskins's departure in 2009, Peter Copping (lately of Marc Jacobs–Louis Vuitton) grabbed the wheel, outdoing past Ricci designers in archly feminine touches: bows, ruffles, perforated leather, pastel silks, delicate florals, and frothy colors, along with sensuous lingerie touches. The airy white-on-white boutique remains one of Paris's dreamiest.

**Yves Saint Laurent** (✉ *38 and 32 rue du Faubourg St- Honoré, 8ᵉ, Louvre/Tuileries* ☎ *01–42–65–74–59* Ⓜ *Concorde* ✉ *6 pl. St-Sulpice, 6ᵉ, St-Germain-des-Prés* ☎ *01–43–29–43–00* Ⓜ *St-Sulpice*) revolutionized women's wear in the 1970s, putting pants in couture shows for the first time. His safari jackets, "le smoking" suits, Russian-boho collections, and tailored *Belle de Jour* suits are considered fashion landmarks—and these are big shoes to fill. Stefano Pilati, successor to the ingenious Tom Ford, started his tenure with a mellow hand in color and cut. The menswear collection, at No. 32 rue du Faubourg St-Honoré, can be relied on for Saint Laurent's classic pinstripes and satin-lapel tuxes.

### TRENDSETTERS

**Abou d'Abi Bazar** (✉ *125 rue Vieille du Temple, 3ᵉ, Le Marais* ☎ *01–42–71–13–26* Ⓜ *Filles du Calvaire* ✉ *15 rue Soufflot, 5ᵉ, Latin Quarter* ☎ *01–42–77–96–98* Ⓜ *Cluny la Sorbonne*) organizes its collection of up-to-the-moment designers on color-coordinated racks that highlight the asymmetrical design of this opulent boutique. Artsy and bohemian all at once, there is plenty to covet here, from frothy Isabel Marant silk-organza blouses to sumptuous cashmere-blend tunics and satin shirtwaist dresses. Reasonably priced picks make it a very desirable destination.

**Antik Batik** (✉ *26 rue St-Sulpice, 6ᵉ, St-Germain-des-Prés* ☎ *01–44–07–68–53* Ⓜ *Odéon* ✉ *113 Vielle du Temple, 3ᵉ, Le Marais* ☎ *01–48–87–39–46* Ⓜ *St-Paul* ✉ *18 rue de Turenne, 4ᵉ, Le Marais* ☎ *01–44–78–02–00* Ⓜ *St-Paul* ✉ *20 rue de Vaugirard, 6ᵉ, St-Germain-des-Prés* ☎ *01–43–25–30–22* Ⓜ *Odéon*) has a wonderful line of ethnically inspired clothes. There are row upon row of beaded and sequined dresses, Chinese silk tunics, short fur jackets, flowing organza separates,

16

and some of Paris's most popular handbags. Stores feature maxi and mini versions for mothers-to-be and kids from 2 to 12, too.

**Antoine & Lili** (✉ *95 quai de Valmy, 10ᵉ, République* ☎ *01–40–37–41–55* Ⓜ *Jacques-Bonsergent* ✉ *90 rue des Martyrs, 18e, Montmartre* ☎ *01–42–58–10–22* Ⓜ *Abbesses*) is a bright fuchsia-color store packed with eclectic objects from the East and its own line of clothing. The fantasy seems to work for the French, because these boutiques are always hopping. There's an ethnic rummage-sale feel, with old Asian posters, small lanterns, and basket upon basket of cheap little doodads, baubles, and trinkets for sale. The clothing itself has simple lines, and there are always plenty of picks in raw silk.

**Azzedine Alaïa** (✉ *7 rue de Moussy, 4ᵉ, Le Marais* ☎ *01–42–72–19–19* Ⓜ *Hôtel de Ville*) is one of the darlings of the fashion set with his perfectly proportioned "king of cling" dresses. And you don't have to be under 20 to look good in one of his dresses; Tina Turner wears his clothes well, as does every other beautiful woman with the courage and the curves. His boutique/workshop/apartment is covered with artwork by Julian Schnabel and is not the kind of place you casually wander into out of curiosity: the sales staff immediately make you feel awkward in that distinctive Parisian way.

**Catherine Malandrino** (✉ *10 rue de Grenelle, 6ᵉ, St-Germain-des-Prés* ☎ *01–42–22–26–95* Ⓜ *Sèvres-Babylone*) designs for the urban sophisticate, expertly combining glamour, smarts, and allure in her office-to-soirée styles. Dresses caress the body without clinging and incorporate ingenious details—cutout seams, a flattering wide bodice, transparent sleeves—for an ultrastylish look.

**Chloé** (✉ *54–56 rue du Faubourg St-Honoré, 8ᵉ, Louvre/Tuileries* ☎ *01–44–94–33–00* Ⓜ *Concorde* ✉ *44 av Montaigne, 8ᵉ, Champs-Élysées* ☎ *01–47–23–00–08* Ⓜ *Franklin-D.-Roosevelt*) is revising its image yet again with Hannah McGibbon at the helm; less romantic and feminine than days of yore, the line still features flowing layered dresses but with an asymmetric edge. Bold colors and patterns on lovely diaphanous fabrics made a big splash recently.

★ **Colette** (✉ *213 rue St-Honoré, 1ᵉʳ, Louvre/Tuileries* ☎ *01–55–35–33–90* Ⓜ *Tuileries*) is the place for ridiculously cool fashion par excellence. So the staff barely deigns to make eye contact—who cares! There are ultramodern trinkets and trifles of all kinds: perfumes; an exclusive handful of cosmetics, including Aesop and Kiehls; and loads of superchic jewelry . . . and that's just the ground floor. The first floor has wares (clothes, shoes, and accessories) from every internationally known and unknown designer with trendy street cred, a small library, the latest out-there CDs, and an art display space. The basement has a water bar (because that's what models eat) and a small restaurant that's good for a quick bite.

**Dupleks** (✉ *83 quai de Valmy, 10ᵉ, République* ☎ *01–42–06–15–08* Ⓜ *République*) calls itself a boutique for "*créateurs éthiques*"—and ethical they may be, but they've also got plenty of fashion savvy. Youthful designs range from the whimsical to überchic. The upbeat, friendly atmosphere makes browsing extra enjoyable.

CLOSE UP

# Notable Neighborhoods, Select Streets

Paris's legendary shopping destinations draw people the world over, but perhaps a deeper allure lies in the lesser-known attractions: the city harbors scores of hidden neighborhoods and shopping streets—some well traveled, others just emerging—that brim with treasure. Each carries its own distinct style that reflects the character of the particular *quartier*. Here are a few of Paris's most satisfying and *très branché* (very trendy) enclaves.

*Rue Keller, Rue Charonne (11e).* These streets are a haven for young clothing designers with panache. Stylish housewares, kids' clothes, jewelry, and art galleries augment the appeal. Start at the end of Rue Keller where it intersects with Rue de la Roquette: walk the length of this short street, then make a right onto Rue Charonne and meander all the way to Rue du Faubourg St-Antoine to discover a trove of great boutiques.

*Rue Oberkampf (11e).* At the outer edge of Le Marais, this street is well-known among young fashionistas for its eclectic atmosphere and bohemian flavor. High-end jewelry and of-the-minute boutiques are clustered amid stylish wine bars and comfy cafés.

*Rue des Abbesses, Rue des Martyrs (18e and 9e).* In the shadow of lofty Sacré-Coeur, the Rue des Abbesses is studded with shops—from vintage jewelry and unique clothing to antiques and upscale gardening. Turn onto the Rue des Martyrs and discover one of Paris's hottest emerging scenes, with trendy boutiques scattered among inviting cafés and pâtisseries.

*Rues Étienne Marcel, du Jour, Tiquetonne, and Montmartre (2e).* Just around the corner from teeming Les Halles, this area is jam-packed with big names (Yamamoto, Agnès b), but it also boasts multitudes of smaller boutiques (Madame à Paris, Shine) popular with hip young Parisians. It's worth at least an afternoon's wander.

*Rue du Bac (7e).* After browsing at Le Bon Marché turn the corner at the Grand Epicerie and stroll down this most bountiful of shopping streets. Old and well established, this is where the Paris beau monde finds everything from elegant linens and home furnishings to any item of apparel a grownup or child could possibly want.

*Rue Vavin (6e).* One of Paris's epicenters for outfitting those hopelessly chic Parisian children, this street is lined with boutique after boutique for tots. If you have the kids in tow, follow up with a pony ride at the Luxembourg gardens (weekends only). Jewelry, clothing, Savon de Marseille, and J.P. Hevin, one of Paris's top chocolatiers, give adults plenty to love, too.

*Rue Pont Louis Philippe (4e).* Long enjoyed for its multitude of elegant paper and stationery shops, here you can also find antiques, musical instruments, and classy clothing. A great spot for window-shopping en route from the Marais to the Ile St-Louis.

*Rue Francois Miron (from St-Paul métro to Place St-Gervais, 4e).* Many shoppers overlook this lovely street at Le Marais's Seine-side fringes, but there's plenty here to make a wander worthwhile. Parisians in the know head here for spices, top-notch designs for the home, antiques, jewelry, pretty cafés, and much more. Bonus: two of the oldest houses in Paris are here; they're the medieval half-timbered ones.

16

**E2** (✉ *40 rue Coquillière, 1ᵉʳ, Louvre/Tuileries* ☎ *01–47–70–17–20* Ⓜ *Louvre Rivoli*), by appointment only, houses a line by designers Michèle and Olivier Chatenet. You'll find their own label of ethnic-influenced fashion inspired by the '30s through the '70s; impeccable vintage couture finds like Chanel, Pucci, Lanvin, and Hermès; plus clothing remade with their own special customizing method. They take tired fashion and transform it—for example, sewing emerald-green sequins into the pleats of an ordinary gray kilt. With one of these creations, you'll definitely be dressed like no one else.

★ **Isabel Marant** (✉ *16 rue de Charonne, 11ᵉ, Bastille/Nation* ☎ *01–49–29–71–55* Ⓜ *Ledru-Rollin* ✉ *1 rue Jacob, 6ᵉ, St-Germain-des-Prés* ☎ *01–43–26–04–12* Ⓜ *St-Germain-des-Prés* ✉ *47 rue Saintonge, 3ᵉ, Le Marais* ☎ *01–42–78–19–24* Ⓜ *Filles du Calvaire*), a young designer, is a honeypot of bohemian rock-star style. Her separates skim the body without constricting: silk jersey dresses, loose sweaters ready to slip from a shoulder, tight little knitwear sets in cool colors. Look for the secondary line, Étoile, for a less-expensive take.

**Le66** (✉ *66 av. des Champs-Élysées, 8ᵉ, Champs-Élysées* ☎ *01–53–53–33–80* Ⓜ *Franklin-D.-Roosevelt*) makes shopping for just the right totally chic, totally black anything a breeze. This impossibly hip concept store, comprised of three boutiques on two levels (including shoes, jewelry, accessories, vintage, and men's), lines up all the top names that you know, along with those that you may not but should. Diffusion lines of the major labels, like DRKK Rick Owens, M Missoni, and See by Chloé, mingle with Tsumri Chisato, Helmut Lang, Ilaria Mistri, Carin Wester, and nearly 200 others, all hand-picked to ensure fabulousness. If pressed for time, it's a good bet for all-around satisfaction.

**Liza Korn** (✉ *19 rue Beaurepaire, 10ᵉ, République* ☎ *01–42–01–36–02* Ⓜ *République*) has charming vintage-inspired designs—say, a '60s-style lipstick-pink cashmere coat or a scarf of crimson cock feathers—that blend well with the designer's versatile separates. Bonus: a limited but perfectly adorable line for kids ages 1–10.

**Maje** (✉ *267 rue St-Honore, 2ᵉ, Louvre/Palais-Royal* ☎ *01–42–96–84–93* Ⓜ *Palais-Royal-Musée du Louvre* ✉ *49 rue Vielle du Temple, 3ᵉ, Le Marais* ☎ *01–42–74–63–77* Ⓜ *St. Paule* ✉ *42 rue du Four, 6ᵉ, St-Germain-des-Prés* ☎ *01–42–22–43–69* Ⓜ *St-Germain-des-Prés*) brings a certain ease to looking great. So comfortable you could sleep in them, these clothes are designed with real women in mind, not stick figures. Wildly popular dresses feature sensuous draping offset by a bodice, belt, or plunging neckline (or back). Seasonal collections include flirty updates on the shirtwaist, microminis, and lean, peg-leg trousers.

★ **Marni** (✉ *57 av. Montaigne, 8ᵉ, Champs-Élysées* ☎ *01–56–88–08–08* Ⓜ *Franklin-D.-Roosevelt*) is an Italian label with a fantastic take on boho chic—retro-ish prints and colors (citron yellow, seaweed green), funky fabrics (striped ticking, canvas), and accessories that suggest wanderlust (hobo bags).

**Miu Miu** (✉ *219 rue St-Honoré, 1ᵉʳ, Louvre/Tuileries* ☎ *01–58–62–53–20* Ⓜ *Tuileries*) is a St-Honoré boutique that dispenses with the designer's Modernist ethos in favor of a neo-baroque sensibility—and it influences everything from the velvet wallpaper to, perhaps, a lavish pair of ruby slippers. Although the shoes and accessories scream glitz, the clothes still favor sleek refinement, with the designer's notorious tension between minimalism and opulence.

**No60** (⊠ *60 rue Charlot, 3ᵉ, Le Marais* ☎ *01–44–78–91–90* Ⓜ *Filles du Calvaire*) aims for rock-star glamour. Not the tarted-up kind, though: think sophisticated, sexy, and up to the moment. You can find hot-ticket lines by the likes of Zucca, Collection Privé, Anne-Valéry Hash, and a bevy of handpicked designers.

**Samy Chalon** (⊠ *24 rue Charlot, 3ᵉ, Le Marais* ☎ *01–44–59–39–16* Ⓜ *Filles du Calvaire*) brings hand knits into the 21st century with inspired shapes. Updates on the classics are never bulky and ever flattering. Form-fitting crocheted skirt-and-sweater sets, long mohair wrap coats in deep crimson or indigo, light-as-air scarf-print skirts, and jaunty shrugs with leather insets are a few perennial favorites.

**Shine** (⊠ *15 rue de Poitou, 3ᵉ, Le Marais* ☎ *01–48–05–80–10* Ⓜ *Filles du Calvaire* ⊠ *65 rue Montmartre, 2ᵉ, Les Halles* ☎ *01–42–33–65–68* Ⓜ *Les Halles* ⊠ *8 rue du Vieux Colombier, 6ᵉ, St-Germain-des-Press* ☎ *01–42–22–20–24* Ⓜ *St-Sulpice*) outshines many of the boutiques even in its hip Marais location. Retro and übermodern, you can find only the sharper edge of chic (with a clientele to match): Marc by Marc Jacobs, See by Chloé, K by Karl Lagerfeld, and Helmut Lang.

**Stella Cadente** (⊠ *93 quai de Valmy, 10ᵉ, République* ☎ *01–42–09–27–00* Ⓜ *République*) is a touch of schoolgirl, a dash of Wonder Woman, et voilà! Cadente's whimsicality encompasses a graceful chiffon shift as easily as a cropped leather jacket in metallic lavender. Her signature shooting star is emblazoned on the sought-after bags, and her sparkly jewelry is ultrapopular.

**Stella McCartney** (⊠ *114-121 Galerie de Valois, 1ᵉʳ, Palais Royal* ☎ *01–47–03–03–80* Ⓜ *Palais Royal/ Musée du Louvre*) has an uncanny knack for knowing what women want. After resuscitating the house of Chloé and then starting her own label in 2001, McCartney has steadily built on her success. Season after season, she channels the prevailing mood into innovative takes on classics like the boyfriend blazer, the silk sheath, and the cigarette jean. The clothes flatter real women, and the steep prices can be justified by their staying power (and the fact that nothing was killed in the making).

**Swilden's** (⊠ *22 rue de Poitou, 3ᵉ, Le Marais* ☎ *01–42–71–19–12* Ⓜ *St-Sebastien Froissart* ⊠ *38 rue Madame, 6ᵉ, St-Germain-des-Prés* ☎ *01–45–44–66–20* Ⓜ *St-Sulpice*) pioneered the trendy haut Marais and has since gained an ardent following of street-smart twenty- and thirty-somethings who insist as much on comfort as they do on cool. Slouchy separates in natural fibers and fetching colors are punctuated by pieces in leather and shearling, along with belted cardigans and long, drapey sweaters that can be worn almost year-round. The clothes accomplish that rare feat of being both of-the-moment and timeless.

★ **Vanessa Bruno** (⊠ *12 rue de Castiglione, 1ᵉʳ, Louvre/Tuileries* ☎ *01–42–61–44–60* Ⓜ *Pyramides* ⊠ *25 rue St-Sulpice, 6ᵉ, Quartier Latin* ☎ *01–43–54–41–04* Ⓜ *Odéon* ⊠ *100 rue Vieille du Temple, 3ᵉ, Le Marais*

16

☎ *01–42–77–19–41* Ⓜ *St-Sébastien-Froissart*) stirs up a new brew of feminine dressing: some androgynous pieces (skinny pants) plus delicacy (filmy tops) with a dash of whimsy (lace insets). Separates are coveted for their sleek styling, gorgeous colors, and unerring sexiness. Wardrobe staples include perfectly proportioned cotton tops and sophisticated dresses. Athé, the secondary or "diffusion" line, flies off the racks, so if you see something you love, grab it. Bruno's shoes and accessories are the cherry on the cake: her ultrapopular sequin-striped totes inspired an army of knockoffs.

**Zadig & Voltaire** (✉ *42 rue des Francs Bourgeois, 3ᵉ, Le Marais* ☎ *01–44–54–00–60* Ⓜ *St-Paul* ✉ *1–3 rue du Vieux Colombier, 6ᵉ, St-Germain-des-Prés* ☎ *01–43–29–18–29* Ⓜ *St-Sulpice*) is the A-list destination for young fashionistas, offering street wear at its funkiest: racy camisoles, cashmere sweaters in gorgeous colors, cropped leather jackets, and form-fitting pants to cosset those tiny French derrieres.

# DEPARTMENT STORES

For an overview of Paris *mode* (style), visit *les grands magasins*, Paris's monolithic department stores. Size up the sometimes ornate architecture, compare prices, and marvel at the historical value of it all—some of these stores have been around since 1860. Most are open Monday through Saturday from about 9:30 to 7, and some are open until 10 PM one weekday evening.

**Au Printemps** (✉ *64 bd. Haussmann, 9ᵉ, Opéra/Grands Boulevards* ☎ *01–42–82–50–00* Ⓜ *Havre Caumartin, Opéra, and RER: Auber*) is actually three major stores: Printemps de la Maison (home furnishings), Printemps de l'Homme (menswear—six floors of it), and the brilliant Printemps de la Mode (fashion, fashion, fashion), which has everything from cutting-edge to the teeny bopper. Be sure to check out the beauty area, with the Nuxe spa, hairdressers, and seemingly every beauty product known to woman under one roof. Fashion shows are held on Tuesday (all year) and Friday (April–October) at 10 AM under the cupola on the seventh floor of La Mode and are free. (Reservations can be made in advance by calling 01–42–82–63–17; tickets can also be obtained on the day of the show at the service desk on the first floor.)

**BHV** (✉ *52–64 rue de Rivoli, 4ᵉ, Beaubourg/Les Halles* ☎ *01–42–74–90–00* Ⓜ *Hôtel de Ville*), short for **Bazar de l'Hôtel de Ville**, houses an enormous basement hardware store that sells everything from doorknobs to cement mixers and has to be seen to be believed. There's even a hardware-theme café, where how-to demos are held. The fashion offerings are limited, but BHV is noteworthy for its huge selection of high-quality household goods, home-decor material, electronics, and office supplies. If you're looking for typically French household items (those heavy, gold-rimmed café sets, gorgeous French linen, or Savon de Marseille), this is your ticket.

**FNAC** (⊠ *Forum des Halles, 1ᵉʳ, Beaubourg/Les Halles* ☎ *01–40–41–40–00* Ⓜ *Les Halles* ⊠ *74 av. des Champs-Élysées, 8ᵉ, Champs-Élysées* ☎ *01–53–53–64–64* Ⓜ *Franklin-D.-Roosevelt* ⊠ *136 rue de Rennes, 6ᵉ, Montparnasse* ☎ *01–49–54–30–00* Ⓜ *St-Placide*) is a high-profile French "cultural" department store. Parisians flock here for the huge selection

of music and books, as well as photo, TV, and audio equipment.

★ **Galeries Lafayette** (⊠ *35–40 bd. Haussmann, 9ᵉ, Opéra/Grands Boulevards* ☎ *01–42–82–34–56* Ⓜ *Chaussée d'Antin, Opéra, Havre Caumartin* ⊠ *Centre Commercial Montparnasse, 14ᵉ, Montparnasse* ☎ *01–45–38–52–87* Ⓜ *Montparnasse Bienvenüe*) is one of those places that you wander into unawares, leaving hours later a poorer and humbler person. At the flagship store at 40 boulevard Haussmann, a Belle Époque stained-glass dome caps the world's largest perfumery. The store bulges with thousands of designers; free fashion shows are held Friday at 3 PM in the upstairs café (advance reservations are a must: call 01–42–82–36–40). A big draw is the delectable comestibles department, stocked with the best of everything from herbed goat cheese to Iranian caviar. Just across the street at 35 boulevard Haussmann is Galeries Lafayette Maison. The Montparnasse branch is a pale shadow of the Boulevard Haussmann behemoths.

Fodor's Choice ★ **Le Bon Marché** (⊠ *24 rue de Sèvres, 7ᵉ, St-Germain-des-Prés* ☎ *01–44–39–80–00* Ⓜ *Sèvres-Babylone*), founded in 1852, has emerged as the city's chicest department store. Long a hunting ground for linens and other home items, the store got a face-lift that brought fashion to the fore. The ground floor sets out makeup, perfume, and accessories; this is where celebs duck in for essentials while everyone pretends not to recognize them. Upstairs, do laps through labels chichi (Burberry, Sonia Rykiel) and überhip (Martin Margiela, Comme des Garçons). Menswear, under the moniker Balthazar, keeps pace with designers like Yves Saint Laurent, and Paul Smith. Zip across the second floor walkway to the mode section (above the next-door *épicerie*), home to streetwise designers and edgy secondary lines (and a funky café). French favorites include Athé by Vanessa Bruno, Zadig & Voltaire, Manoush, Isabel Marant's Étoile line, and Madame à Paris. Best of all, this department store isn't nearly as crowded as those near the Opéra. Don't miss **La Grande Épicerie** next door; it's the haute couture of grocery stores. Artisanal jams, olive oils, and much more make great gifts, and the luscious pastries and fruit beg to be chosen for a snack.

**BUDGET**

**Monoprix** (✉ *21 av. de l'Opéra, 1ᵉʳ, Opéra/Grands Boulevards* ☎ *01–42–61–78–08* Ⓜ *Opéra* ✉ *20 bd. de Charonne, 20e, Bastille/Nation* ☎ *01–43–73–17–59* Ⓜ *Nation* ✉ *50 rue de Rennes, 6ᵉ, St-Germain-des-Prés* ☎ *01–45–48–18–08* Ⓜ *St-Germain-des-Prés*), with branches throughout the city, is *the* French dime store par excellence, stocking everyday items like toothpaste, groceries, toys, typing paper, and bath mats—a little of everything. It also has a line of relatively inexpensive basic wearables for the whole family and isn't a bad place to stock up on French liqueurs at reasonable prices.

# FOOD AND WINE

In addition to the establishments listed below, don't overlook La Grande Épicerie next to Le Bon Marché department store.

**À la Mère de Famille** (✉ *35 rue du Faubourg-Montmartre, 9ᵉ, Opéra/Grands Boulevards* ☎ *01–47–70–83–69* Ⓜ *Cadet*) is an enchanting shop well versed in French regional specialties and old-fashioned bonbons, sugar candy, and more.

**Á l'Étoile d'Or** (✉ *30 rue Pierre Fontaine, 9ᵉ, Opéra* ☎ *01–48–74–59–55* Ⓜ *Pigalle*) is the quintessential dream of a candy shop. This whimsical confectionary will delight children of all ages, not to mention chocoholics, as it stocks some of the best-pedigreed chocolates in town (like Bernachon, from Lyon). Dedicated to the candies of France, it's a walk back in time, with classic sweets from every Gallic region. Although a tad out of the way, it's well worth the trip.

**Debauve & Gallais** (✉ *30 rue des Sts-Pères, 7ᵉ, St-Germain-des-Prés* ☎ *01–45–48–54–67* Ⓜ *St-Germain-des-Prés*) was founded in 1800. The two former chemists who ran it became the royal chocolate purveyors and were famed for their "health chocolates," made with almond milk. Test the benefits yourself with ganache, truffles, or *pistols* (flavored dark-chocolate disks).

**Fauchon** (✉ *26 pl. de la Madeleine, 8ᵉ, Opéra/Grands Boulevards* ☎ *01–70–39–38–00* Ⓜ *Madeleine*) remains the most iconic of Parisian food stores. It's expanding globally, but the flagship is still behind the Madeleine church. Established in 1886, it sells renowned pâté, honey, jelly, tea, and private-label champagne. Expats come for hard-to-find foreign foods (U.S. pancake mix, British lemon curd); those with a sweet tooth make a beeline for the *macarons* (airy, ganache-filled cookies) in the pâtisserie. There's a café for a quick bite. Prices can be eye-popping—marzipan fruit for €95 a pound?

**Hédiard** (✉ *21 pl. de la Madeleine, 8ᵉ, Opéra/Grands Boulevards* ☎ *01–43–12–88–88* Ⓜ *Madeleine*), established in 1854, was famous in the 19th century for its high-quality imported spices. These—along with rare teas and beautifully packaged house brands of jam, mustard, and cookies—continue to be a draw.

**Huilerie Artisanale J. Leblanc et Fils** (✉ *6 rue Jacob, 6ᵉ, St-Germain-des-Prés* ☎ *01–46–34–61–55* Ⓜ *Mabillon*) corrals everything you need for the perfect salad dressing into its small space: aged vinegars, *fleur de*

**CLOSE UP**

# The Best Chocolate in Paris

The French take chocolate seriously. There are dozens of chocolatiers to choose from, but the purveyors listed below are unusually distinguished for excellence and originality.

**Christian Constant** (✉ 37 rue d'Assas, 6ᵉ, Luxembourg ☎ 01–53–63–15–15 Ⓜ St-Placide) is deservedly praised for his delicate ganaches, perfumed with jasmine, ylang-ylang, or vervain. His famously rich hot chocolate is served by the pitcher at this café (one of Christian Constant's several restaurants), along with his excellent pastries.

**Jacques Genin** (✉ 133 rue de Turenne, 3ᵉ, Le Marais ☎ 01–45–77–29–01 Ⓜ Oberkampf) has made a serious pitch for perfection in every detail of this elegant boutique-café. Pared down to the essentials, Genin offers the very essence of great chocolate. Not too sweet, with hand-picked seasonal ingredients for the velvety ganaches. The pastries—refinements of French classics, like the mille feuille (voted best in Paris) and Paris Brest—and chocolates are all made on the premises. Stop in for a sublime hot chocolate, chocolate sampler, or simply the very best pastries anywhere. Everything is made on the premises.

**Jean-Paul Hévin** (✉ 231 rue Saint-Honoré, 1ᵉʳ, Louvre/Tuileries ☎ 01–55–35–35–96 Ⓜ Louvre/Tuileries ✉ 3 rue Vavin, 6ᵉ, Luxembourg ☎ 01–43–54–09–85 Ⓜ Vavin) has a formal tearoom at his Rue St-Honoré boutique, and there are "exhibits" of chocolates and pastries at Rue Vavin—Mr. Hévin hasn't earned his world-class chocolatier status because of his interiors, though: the 40 different varieties of chocolate each seem more delectable than the last.

**La Maison du Chocolat** (✉ 19 rue de Sèvre, 6ᵉ, St-Germain-des-Prés ☎ 01–45–44–20–40 Ⓜ Sèvres-Babylone ✉ 8 bd. de la Madeleine, 9ᵉ, Louvre/Tuileries ☎ 01–47–42–86–52 Ⓜ Madeleine ✉ 225 rue du Faubourg St-Honoré, 8ᵉ, Louvre/Tuileries ☎ 01–42–27–39–44 Ⓜ Ternes) is chocolate's gold standard. The silky ganaches are unparalleled in subtlety and flavor; the pastries—notably the *macarons*, are icing on the cake.

**Michel Chaudun** (✉ 149 rue de l'Université, 7ᵉ, Invalides ☎ 01–47–53–74–40 Ⓜ Invalides) is known for putting granules of cocoa beans into the chocolates to enhance intensity. His delicate *pavés*—squares of dark-chocolate truffle ganache topped with a dusting of cocoa—are fabulous.

**Pierre Hermé** (✉ 72 rue Bonaparte, 6ᵉ, Quartier Latin ☎ 01–43–54–47–77 Ⓜ Odéon ✉ 4 rue Cambon, 1ᵉʳ, Louvre/Tuileries ☎ 01–58–62–43–17 Ⓜ Concorde ✉ 185 rue de Vaugirard, 15ᵉ, Montparnasse ☎ 01–47–83–29–72 Ⓜ Pasteur) hardly needs an introduction. As Paris's (the world's?) most renowned pâtissier, Hermé's seasonal collections have titles such as "Fetish" or "Emotion." In his tireless quest for the new, the pastries can flounder—but the chocolate never wavers.

**Pierre Marcolini** (✉ 89 rue de Seine, 6ᵉ, St-Germain-des-Prés ☎ 01–44–07–39–07 Ⓜ Mabillon) proves it's all in the bean with his specialty *saveurs du monde* chocolates, made with a single kind of cacao from a single location such as Madagascar or Ecuador. Belly up to the wooden bar of this Belgian chocolatier for a selection of chocolates filled with ganache, caramel, or nuts.

16

*sel* (unprocessed sea salt), and more than 15 varieties of oils pressed the old-fashioned way, with a big stone wheel, from olives, hazelnuts, pistachios, or grape seed.

★ **La Dernière Goutte** (✉ *6 rue de Bourbon le Château, 6ᵉ, St-Germain-des-Prés* ☎ *01–46–29–11–62* Ⓜ *Odéon*), an inviting *cave* (literally wine store or wine cellar), focuses on wines by small French producers. Each is handpicked by the owner, along with a choice selection of estate champagnes, Armagnac, and the classic Vieille Prune (plum brandy). The friendly English-speaking staff makes browsing a pleasure. Don't miss the Saturday afternoon tastings.

★ **Ladurée** (✉ *16 rue Royale, 8ᵉ, Louvre/Tuileries* ☎ *01–42–60–21–79* Ⓜ *Madeleine* ✉ *75 av. des Champs-Élysées, 8ᵉ, Champs-Élysées* ☎ *01–40–75–08–75* Ⓜ *George V* ✉ *21 rue Bonaparte, 6ᵉ, Quartier Latin* ☎ *01–44–07–64–87* Ⓜ *Odéon*), founded in 1862, oozes period atmosphere—even at the new, large Champs-Élysées branch—but nothing beats the original tearoom on Rue Royale, with its pint-size tables and frescoed ceiling. Ladurée claims a familial link to the invention of the *macaron*, and appropriately there's a fabulous selection of these cookies: classics like pistachio, salted caramel, and coffee, and, seasonally, violet–black currant, chestnut, and lime-basil.

★ **Lavinia** (✉ *3–5 bd. de la Madeleine, 1ᵉʳ, Opéra/Grands Boulevards* ☎ *01–42–97–20–20* Ⓜ *St-Augustin*) has the largest selection of wine in one spot in Europe—more than 6,000 wines and spirits from all over the world, ranging from the simple to the sublime. On-site there are expert sommeliers to help you sort it all out, as well as a wine-tasting bar, a bookshop, and a restaurant.

**Le Palais des Thés** (✉ *64 rue Vieille du Temple, 3ᵉ, Le Marais* ☎ *01–48–87–80–60* Ⓜ *St-Paul*) is a comprehensive experience—white tea, green tea, black tea, tea from China, Japan, Indonesia, South America, and more. Try one of the flavored teas such as Hammam, a traditional Turkish recipe with date pulp, orange flower, rose, and red berries.

**L'Épicerie** (✉ *51 rue St-Louis-en-L'Ile, 4ᵉ, Ile St-Louis* ☎ *01–43–25–20–14* Ⓜ *Pont Marie*) sells 90 types of jam (try fig with almonds and cinnamon), 70 kinds of mustard (including one with chocolate and honey), numerous olive oils, caviar, and foie gras.

**Les Caves Augé** (✉ *116 bd. Haussmann, 8ᵉ, Opéra/Grands Boulevards* ☎ *01–45–22–16–97* Ⓜ *St-Augustin*), one of the best wineshops in Paris since 1850, is just the ticket, whether you're looking for a rare vintage or a seductive Bordeaux for a tête-à-tête. English-speaking Marc Sibard is a knowledgeable and affable adviser.

**Mariage Frères** (✉ *30 rue du Bourg-Tibourg, 4ᵉ, Le Marais* ☎ *01–42–72–28–11* Ⓜ *Hôtel de Ville* ✉ *13 rue des Grands-Augustins, 6ᵉ, St-Germain-des-Prés* ☎ *01–40–51–82–50* Ⓜ *Mabillon, St-Michel*), with its colonial *charme* and wooden counters, has 100-plus years of tea purveying behind it. Choose from more than 450 blends from 32 countries, not to mention teapots, teacups, books, and tea-flavor biscuits and candies. The tearoom serves high tea and a light lunch.

**Ryst-Dupeyron** (✉ *79 rue du Bac, 7ᵉ, St-Germain-des-Prés* ☎ *01–45–48– 80–93* Ⓜ *Rue du Bac*) specializes in fine wines and liquors, with port, calvados, and Armagnacs that date from 1878. A great gift idea: find a bottle from the year of a friend's birth and have it labeled with your friend's name. Personalized bottles can be ordered and delivered on the same day.

# HOME DECOR

**Agatha Ruiz de la Prada** (✉ *9 rue Guénégaud, 6ᵉ, Quartier Latin* ☎ *01– 43–25–86–88* Ⓜ *Odéon*) is nothing if not prolific. She designs clothing and accessories for the Spanish department store El Corte Inglés, watches for Swatch, and furniture for Amat. In this small store she also sells her own items, from bags and children's fashions to MP4s and digital picture frames.

**Alexandre Biaggi** (✉ *14 rue de Seine, 6ᵉ, St-Germain-des-Prés* ☎ *01–44– 07–34–73* Ⓜ *St-Germain-des-Prés*) specializes in 20th-century Art Deco and also commissions designs from such talented designers as Patrick Naggar and Hervé van der Straeten.

**Alter Mundi** (✉ *25 rue Beaurepaire, 10ᵉ, République* ☎ *01–42–00–15–73* Ⓜ *République* ✉ *9 rue de Rivoli, 4ᵉ, Le Marais* ☎ *01–44–07–22–28* Ⓜ *St-Paul*) may be the first "department store" for ethical commerce, but that doesn't mean they can't have fun. They carry great contemporary designs in everything from kitchenware and original artwork to leather-alternative bags and deconstructed scarves. Women's, kids', and decor at Beaurepaire, fashion only at Rivoli.

**A. Simon** (✉ *48 rue Montmartre, 2ᵉ, Beaubourg/Les Halles* ☎ *01–42–33– 71–65* Ⓜ *Étienne Marcel*) is where Parisian chefs come for their kitchen needs—from plates and glasses to pans, dishes, and wooden spoons. The quality is excellent and the prices are reasonable.

**Astier de Villatte** (✉ *173 rue St-Honoré, 1ᵉʳ, Louvre/Tuileries* ☎ *01–42– 60–74–13* Ⓜ *Tuileries*) offers high-style interpretations of 18th-century table settings; live out your Baroque or Empire fancies with milk-white china sets.

**Avant-Scène** (✉ *4 pl. de l'Odéon, 6ᵉ, Quartier Latin* ☎ *01–46–33–12–40* Ⓜ *Odéon*) is good for original, poetic furniture. Owner Elisabeth Delacarte commissions limited-edition pieces from artists like Mark Brazier-Jones, Franck Evennou, and Hubert Le Gall.

**Catherine Memmi** (✉ *11 rue St-Sulpice, 6ᵉ, St-Germain-des-Prés* ☎ *01– 44–07–02–02* Ⓜ *St-Sulpice*), a trendsetter in pared-down housewares, also sells bath products, lamps, furniture, and home accessories.

**Christofle** (✉ *24 rue de la Paix, 2ᵉ, Opéra/Grands Boulevards* ☎ *01–42– 65–62–43* Ⓜ *Opéra* ✉ *9 rue Royale, 8ᵉ, Louvre/Tuileries* ☎ *01–55– 27–99–13* Ⓜ *Concorde, Madeleine*), founded in 1830, has fulfilled all kinds of silver wishes, from a silver service for the *Orient Express* to a gigantic silver bed. Come for timeless table settings, vases, jewelry boxes, and more.

**16**

The **Conran Shop** (✉ *117 rue du Bac, 7ᵉ, St-Germain-des-Prés* ☎ *01–42–84–10–01* Ⓜ *Sèvres-Babylone*) is the brainchild of British entrepreneur Terence Conran. The shop carries expensive contemporary furniture, beautiful bed linens, and items for every other room in the house—all marked by a balance of utility with not-too-sober style. Conran makes even shower curtains fun.

**Diptyque** (✉ *34 bd. St-Germain, 5ᵉ, St-Germain-des-Prés* ☎ *01–43–26–77–44* Ⓜ *Maubert Mutualité*) is famous for its candles and eaux de toilette and now body care in sophisticated scents like myrrh, fig tree, and quince. They're delightful but not cheap; the candles, for instance, cost nearly $1 per hour of burn time.

★ **E. Dehillerin** (✉ *18–20 rue Coquillière, 1ᵉʳ, Louvre/Tuileries* ☎ *01–42–36–53–13* Ⓜ *Les Halles*) has been around since 1820. Never mind the creaky stairs; their huge range of professional cookware in enamel, stainless steel, or fiery copper is gorgeous. Julia Child was a regular.

**Gien** (✉ *18 rue de l'Arcade, 8ᵉ, Louvre/Tuileries* ☎ *01–42–66–52–32* Ⓜ *Madeleine*) has been making fine china since 1821. The faience spans traditional designs, such as those inspired by Italian majolica or blue-and-white delftware, as well as contemporary looks.

**Idé Co.** (✉ *19 rue Beaurepaire, 10ᵉ, République* ☎ *01–42–01–00–11* Ⓜ *République*) offers small items for the home in a riot of color. You'll find kitchen staples, cappuccino bowls, and fabulous rubber jewelry and funky stuff for kids big and small.

**Kitchen Bazaar** (✉ *Galerie des 3 Quartiers, 23 bd. de la Madeleine, 1ᵉʳ, Opéra/Grands Boulevards* ☎ *01–42–60–50–30* Ⓜ *Madeleine* ✉ *50 rue Croix des Petits-Champs, 1ᵉʳ, Louvre/Tuileries* ☎ *01–40–15–03–11* Ⓜ *Palais-Royal/Musée du Louvre*) gleams with an astonishing array of culinary essentials. Don't be surprised at the urge to replace every utensil in your kitchen with these up-to-the-minute designs.

**Laguiole** (✉ *29 rue Boissy d'Anglas, 8ᵉ, Champs-Élysées* ☎ *01–40–06–09–75* Ⓜ *Concorde*) is the name of the country's most famous brand of knives. Today designers like Philippe Starck and Sonia Rykiel have created special models for the company.

★ **Le Monde Sauvage** (✉ *11 rue de l'Odéon, 6ᵉ, Quartier Latin* ☎ *01–43–25–60–34* Ⓜ *Odéon*) is a must-visit for home accessories—reversible silk bedspreads in rich colors, velvet throws, hand-quilted bed linens, silk floor cushions, Venetian mirrors, and the best selection of hand-embroidered curtains in silk, cotton, linen, or velvet.

★ **Maison de Baccarat** (✉ *11 pl. des États-Unis, 16ᵉ, Trocadéro/Tour Eiffel* ☎ *01–40–22–11–00* Ⓜ *Trocadéro*) was once the home of Marie-Laure de Noailles, known as the Countess of Bizarre. Now it's a museum and crystal store. Philippe Starck revamped the space with his signature cleverness—yes, that's a chandelier floating in an aquarium and, yes, that crystal arm sprouting from the wall alludes to Jean Cocteau (a friend of Noailles). Follow the red carpet to the jewelry room, where crystal baubles hang from bronze figurines, and to the immense table stacked with crystal items for the home.

★ **Muji** (✉ *47 rue des Francs Bourgeois, 4ᵉ, Le Marais* ☎ *01–49–96–41–41* Ⓜ *St-Paul* ✉ *27 and 30 rue St-Sulpice, 6ᵉ, St-Germain-des-Prés* ☎ *01–46–34–01–10* Ⓜ *Odéon*) runs on the concept of *kanketsu*, or simplicity, and the resulting streamlined designs are all the rage in Europe. Must-haves include a collection of mininecessities—travel essentials, wee office gizmos, purse-size accoutrements—so useful and adorable you'll want them all.

**R & Y Augousti** (✉ *103 rue du Bac, 7ᵉ, St-Germain-des-Prés* ☎ *01–42–22–22–21* Ⓜ *Sèvres-Babylone*) are two Paris-based designers who make furniture and objects for the home from nacre, ostrich, palm wood, and parchment. Also for sale are their hand-tooled leather bags and belts.

★ **Sentou** (✉ *29 rue Francois Miron, 4ᵉ, Le Marais* ☎ *01–42–78–50–60* Ⓜ *Tuileries* ✉ *26 bd. Raspail, 7ᵉ, St-Germain-des-Prés* ☎ *01–45–49–00–05* Ⓜ *Rue du Bac*) knocked the Parisian world over the head with its fresh designs. Avant-garde furniture, rugs, and a variety of home accessories line the cool showroom. Look for the April Vase, old test tubes linked together to form different shapes, or the oblong suspended crystal vases and arty tableware.

**Van der Straeten** (✉ *11 rue Ferdinand Duval, 4ᵉ, Le Marais* ☎ *01–42–78–99–99* Ⓜ *St-Paul*) is the lofty gallery-cum-showroom of Paris designer Hervé van der Straeten. He started out creating jewelry for Saint Laurent and Lacroix, designed a perfume bottle for Christian Dior, and moved on to making rather baroque and often wacky furniture. On show are furniture, jewelry, and startling mirrors.

**16**

# JEWELRY

Most of the big names are on or near Place Vendôme. Designer semiprecious and costume jewelry can generally be found in boutiques on Avenue Montaigne and Rue du Faubourg St-Honoré and in St-Germain-des-Prés.

**Adelline** (✉ *54 rue Jacob, 6ᵉ, St-Germain-des-Prés* ☎ *01–47–03–07–18* Ⓜ *St-Germain-des-Prés*), creates the effect of having landed in Ali Baba's cave: each is more gorgeous than the next, and the bounty of beautiful shapes and styles satisfies a large range of tastes. Huge cabochon rings, jeweled cuffs in a web of gold, and simple cord-and-gem bracelets cannot fail to make a statement.

**Agatha** (✉ *45 rue Bonaparte, 6ᵉ, St-Germain-des-Prés* ☎ *01–46–33–20–00* Ⓜ *St-Germain-des-Prés*) is the perfect place to buy a moderately priced piece of fun jewelry. Agatha's line of earrings, rings, hair accessories, bracelets, necklaces, watches, brooches, and pendants is ever popular with Parisians. Styles change quickly, but classics include charm bracelets and fine gold necklaces with whimsical pendants.

**Alexandre Reza** (✉ *21 pl. Vendôme, 1ᵉʳ, Opéra/Grands Boulevards* ☎ *01–42–61–51–21* Ⓜ *Opéra*), one of Paris's most exclusive jewelers, is first and foremost a gemologist. He travels the world looking for the finest stones and then works them into stunning pieces, many of which are replicas of jewels of historical importance.

**Arthus-Bertrand** (✉ 6 pl. St-Germain-des-Prés, 6ᵉ, St-Germain-des-Prés ☎ 01–49–54–72–10 Ⓜ St-Germain-des-Prés), which dates back to 1803, has glass showcases full of designer jewelry and numerous objects to celebrate births.

**Cartier** (✉ 23 pl. Vendôme, 1ᵉʳ, Louvre/Tuileries ☎ 01–44–55–32–20 Ⓜ Tuileries, Concorde ✉ 154 av. des Champs-Élysées, 8ᵉ, Champs-Élysées ☎ 01–58–18–17–78 Ⓜ George V) flashes its jewels at more than half a dozen boutiques in the city. Longtime favorites such as the Trinity rings and Tank watches compete for attention with the newer Asian-inspired Baiser du Dragon jewelry and the colorful Délices de Goa collection.

**Chanel Jewelry** (✉ 18 pl. Vendôme, 1ᵉʳ, Opéra/Grands Boulevards ☎ 01–55–35–50–00 Ⓜ Tuileries, Opéra) feeds off the iconic design elements of the pearl-draped designer: quilting (reimagined for gold rings), camellias (now brooches), and shooting stars (used for her first jewelry collection in 1932, now appearing as diamond rings).

Fodor'sChoice **Dary's** (✉ 362 rue St-Honoré, 1ᵉʳ, Louvre/Tuileries ☎ 01–42–60–95–23
★ Ⓜ Tuileries) brings to realization the best of a Paris shopping experience—a wonderful, family-run, Ali Baba–ish cavern teeming with artists, actors, models, and jewelry lovers. You'll need to take your time though, because the walls are filled with row upon row of antique jewels from every era, more modern secondhand jewelry, and drawer upon drawer of vintage one-of-a-kinds.

**Dinh Van** (✉ 16 rue de la Paix, 2ᵉ, Opéra/Grands Boulevards ☎ 01–42–61–74–49 Ⓜ Opéra ✉ 22 rue François 1ᵉʳ, 8ᵉ, Champs-Élysées ☎ 01–56–64–09–91 Ⓜ Franklin-D.-Roosevelt ✉ 58 rue Bonaparte, 6ᵉ, St-Germain-des-Prés ☎ 01–56–24–10–00 Ⓜ St-Germain-des-Prés), just around the corner from Place Vendôme's titan jewelers, thumbs its nose at in-your-face opulence. The look here is refreshingly spare. Best sellers include a hammered gold orb necklace and leather-cord bracelets joined with geometric shapes in white or yellow gold, some with pavé diamonds.

**Dior Joaillerie** (✉ 28 av. Montaigne, 8ᵉ, Champs-Élysées ☎ 01–47–23–52–39 Ⓜ Franklin-D.-Roosevelt ✉ 8 pl. Vendôme, 1ᵉʳ, Opéra/Grands Boulevards ☎ 01–42–96–30–84 Ⓜ Opéra) got a big dollop of wit and panache when it signed on young designer Victoire de Castellane to create Dior's first line of fine jewelry. She does oversize rings, hoop earrings, and bracelets swinging with diamonds, and—lest you forget the amped-up spirit at Dior house—white-gold death's-head cufflinks.

**Médecine Douce** (✉ 10 rue de Marseile, 10ᵉ, Canal St-Martin ☎ 01–48–03–57–28 Ⓜ République) proffers sculptural pieces that combine leather, suede, rhinestones, sheered agate, or resin with whimsical themes: orbs, owls, pom poms, and a saucy monkey. The wildly popular lariat necklace can be looped and dangled according to the mood du jour.

**Viveka Bergström** (✉ 23 rue de la Grange, 10ᵉ, Canal St-Martin ☎ 01–40–03–04–92 Ⓜ République) leads the ranks of designers who thumb their noses at the pretensions of traditional costume jewelry—these baubles just want to have fun! Whether it's a bracelet of oversize rhinestones, a ring of fluorescent pink resin, or a necklace of her signature angel wings, each piece proffers an acute sense of style while not taking itself too seriously.

**Yves Gratas** (✉ *9 rue Oberkampf, 11ᵉ, Le Marais* ☎ *01–49–29–00–53* Ⓜ *Oberkampf*) has a knack for pairing gems of varying sizes, brilliance, and texture, allowing each stone to influence the design. Whether it's a spectacular necklace of sapphire beads to be worn long or doubled, or a simple agate sphere tipped in gold and dangling like a tiny planet, the pieces feel like one organic whole.

# LINGERIE

**Alice Cadolle** (✉ *4 rue Cambon, 1ᵉʳ, Louvre/Tuileries* ☎ *01–42–60–94–22* Ⓜ *Concorde* ✉ *255 rue St-Honoré, 1ᵉʳ, Louvre/Tuileries* ☎ *01–42–60–94–94* Ⓜ *Concorde*) has been selling lingerie to Parisians since 1889. Ready-to-wear bras, corsets, and sleepwear fill the Rue Cambon boutique; on Rue St-Honoré, Madame Cadolle offers made-to-measure service.

Fodor'sChoice **Chantal Thomass** (✉ *211 rue St-Honoré, 1ᵉʳ, Louvre/Tuileries* ☎ *01–42–60–40–56* Ⓜ *Tuileries*), a legendary lingerie diva, is back with this *Pillow Talk*–meets–Louis XV–inspired boutique. This is French naughtiness at its best, striking the perfect balance between playful and seductive. Sheer silk negligees edged in Chantilly lace and lascivious bra-and-corset sets punctuate the signature line.

**Erès** (✉ *2 rue Tronchet, 8ᵉ, Opéra/Grands Boulevards* ☎ *01–47–42–28–82* Ⓜ *Madeleine* ✉ *40 av. Montaigne, 8ᵉ, Louvre/Tuileries* ☎ *01–47–23–07–26* Ⓜ *Franklin-D.-Roosevelt*) has the most modern line of swimwear and lingerie in town: streamlined shapes in classic colors uncluttered by lace. This lingerie masters the art of soft sheer tones and is comfortable, flattering, and subtly sexy.

**Fifi Chachnil** (✉ *231 rue St-Honoré, 1ᵉʳ, Louvre/Tuileries* ☎ *01–42–61–21–83* Ⓜ *Tuileries* ✉ *68 rue Jean-Jacques Rousseau, 1ᵉʳ, Beaubourg/Les Halles* ☎ *01–42–21–19–93* Ⓜ *Étienne Marcel*) girls are real boudoir babes, with a fondness for quilted-satin bed jackets and lingerie in candy-land colors. The look is cheerfully sexy, with checkered push-up bras, frilled white knickers, and peach-satin corsets.

★ **Les Folies d'Elodie** (✉ *56 av. Paul Doumer, 16ᵉ, Trocadéro/Tour Eiffel* ☎ *01–45–04–93–57* Ⓜ *Trocadéro*), a large, lush boutique, can trick you out in anything from a 1950s-style cotton bra and panties à la Bardot to a risqué sheer-silk nightgown. Everything is handmade, with an emphasis on the grown-up rather than the little-girlish.

**Princesse Tam Tam** (✉ *5 rue Montmartre, 1ᵉʳ, Les Halles* ☎ *01–45–08–50–69* Ⓜ *Les Halles* ✉ *53 rue Bonaparte, 6ᵉ, St-Germain-des-Prés* ☎ *01–43–29–01–91* Ⓜ *St-Germain-des-Prés* ✉ *20 rue St-Antoine, 4ᵉ, Le Marais* ☎ *01–42–77–27–38* Ⓜ *Bastille*) is the go-to for affordable and beguiling bra-and-panty sets that combine sex appeal and playfulness.

16

Designed for mileage as much as allure, the softer-than-soft cotton wrap tops and nighties, lace-edged silk tap pants, camisoles, slips, and adorable separates for the boudoir are comfortable *and* comely.

**Sabbia Rosa** (⊠ *71–73 rue des Sts-Pères, 6ᵉ, St-Germain-des-Prés* ☎ *01–45–48–88–37* Ⓜ *St-Germain-des-Prés*) is a discreet, boudoirlike boutique you could easily walk straight past. It is, however, one of the world's finest lingerie stores and the place where actresses Catherine Deneuve and Isabelle Adjani (and others who might not want to reveal their errand) buy superb French silks.

# MARKETS

### FLEA MARKETS

Fodor's Choice ★

**Marché aux Puces St-Ouen** (Ⓜ *Porte de Clignancourt* ⊕ *www.parispuces. com*), also referred to as **Clignancourt**, on Paris's northern boundary, still attracts the crowds when it's open—Saturday to Monday, from 9 to 6—but its once-unbeatable prices are now a relic of the past. This century-old labyrinth of alleyways packed with antiques dealers' booths and *brocante* stalls sprawls for more than a square mile. Old Vuitton trunks, ormolu clocks, 1930s jet jewelry, and vintage garden furniture sit cheek by jowl. Arrive early to pick up the most worthwhile loot (like old prints). Be warned—if there's one place in Paris where you need to know how to bargain, this is it! If you're arriving by métro, walk under the overpass and take the first left at the Rue de Rosiers to reach the epicenter of the market. Around the overpass huddle stands selling dodgy odds-and-ends (think pleather, knockoff shoes, and questionable gadgets). These blocks are crowded and gritty; be careful with your valuables. If you need a breather from the hundreds of market vendors, stop for a bite in one of the rough-and-ready cafés. A good pick is **Le Soleil** (⊠ *109 av. Michelet* ☎ *01–40–10–08–08*).

**Porte de Vanves & Porte de Montreuil** (Ⓜ *Porte de Vanves/Porte de Montreuil*), on the southern and eastern sides of the city, are smaller flea markets. Vanves is a hit with the fashion set and specializes in smaller objects—mirrors, textiles, handbags, clothing, and glass—as well as books, posters, and postcards. It's open on weekends only from 8 to 5, but arrive early if you want to find a bargain: the good stuff goes fast, and stalls are liable to be packed up before noon. In Montreuil, plow through the cheap housewares, leather goods, and hardware to the bric-a-brac stalls toward the markets' western edge and don't be put off by its tatty look. Patient seekers are often amply rewarded.

### FOOD MARKETS

Year-round and in any weather, the city's open-air food markets play an integral part of daily life, attracting the entire spectrum of Paris society, from the splendid matron, her minuscule dog in tow, to the mustachioed regular picking up his daily baguette. Although some markets are busier than others, there's not a market in Paris that doesn't captivate the senses. Each season has its delicacies: *fraises des bois* (wild strawberries) and tender asparagus in spring, squash blossoms and fragrant herbs in summer, saffron-tinted chanterelles in autumn, bergamot oranges in late winter. Year-round you can find pungent *lait cru* (unpasteurized) cheeses, charcuterie, and unfarmed game and fish. Many of the better-known open-air markets are in areas you'd visit for sightseeing. To get a list of market days in your area, ask your concierge or check the markets section on the Web site ⊕ *www.paris.fr/EN*.

If you're unused to the metric system, it may be helpful to know that *une livre* is French for a pound; *une demi-livre* is a half pound. For cheese or meats, *un morceau* will get you a piece, *une tranche* a slice.

Most markets are open from 8 AM to 1 PM three days a week year-round (usually the weekend and one weekday, but never Monday) on a rotating basis. The following are a few of the best.

**Boulevard Raspail** (✉ *6ᵉ, St-Germain-des-Prés* Ⓜ *Rennes*), between Rue du Cherche-Midi and Rue de Rennes, is the city's major *marché biologique*, or organic market, bursting with produce, fish, and eco-friendly products. It's open Tuesday and Friday.

**Marché d'Aligre** (✉ *Rue d'Aligre, 12ᵉ, Bastille/Nation* Ⓜ *Ledru-Rollin*), open until 1 every day except Monday, is arguably the most locally authentic market. Don't miss the covered hall on the Place d'Aligre, where you can stop by a unique olive oil boutique for prebottled oils from top producers.

**16**

**Rue de Buci** (✉ *6ᵉ, St-Germain-des-Prés* Ⓜ *Odéon*) is where vendors often have tastes of their wares to tempt you: slices of sausage, slivers of peaches. It's closed Sunday afternoon and Monday.

**Rue Lévis** (✉ *17ᵉ, Parc Monceau* Ⓜ *Villiers*), near Parc Monceau, has Alsatian specialties and a terrific cheese shop. It's closed Sunday afternoon and Monday.

**Rue Montorgueil** (✉ *1ᵉʳ, Beaubourg/Les Halles* Ⓜ *Châtelet Les Halles*) has evolved from an old-fashioned market street into a chic *"bobo"* (bourgeois bohemian) zone; its stalls now thrive amid stylish cafés and the oldest oyster counter in Paris.

**Rue Mouffetard** (✉ *5ᵉ, Quartier Latin* Ⓜ *Monge*), near the Jardin des Plantes, reflects its multicultural neighborhood; it's a vibrant market with a laid-back feel that still smacks of old Paris. It's best on weekends.

# PERFUME

**Annick Goutal** (✉ *14 rue de Castiglione, 1ᵉʳ, Louvre/Tuileries* ☎ *01–42–60–52–82* Ⓜ *Concorde*) sells its own line of signature scents, which come packaged in gilded gauze purses. Gardenia, Passion, Petit Chêne, and l'Eau d'Hadrien are ones to look for.

**Comme des Garçons Perfume Shop** (✉ *23 pl. du Marché St-Honoré, 1ᵉʳ, Louvre/Tuileries* ☎ *01–47–03–15–03* Ⓜ *Tuileries*) is devoted to the ultraconceptual Japanese label's perfumes, scented candles, and incense. The shop is worth a visit simply to admire the whiter-than-white store design with pink-tinted lighting.

★ **Editions de Parfums Frédéric Malle** (✉ *37 rue de Grenelle, 7ᵉ, St-Germain-des-Prés* ☎ *01–42–22–76–40* Ⓜ *Rue du Bac* ✉ *140 av. Victor Hugo, 16ᵉ, Trocadéro/Tour Eiffel* ☎ *01–45–05–39–02* Ⓜ *Victor Hugo* ✉ *21* *rue du Mont Thabor, 1ᵉʳ, Louvre/Tuileries* ☎ *01–42–22–77–22* Ⓜ *Tuileries*) is based on a simple concept: take the nine most famous noses in France and have them edit singular perfumes. The result? Exceptional, highly concentrated fragrances. Le Parfum de Thérèse, for example, was created by famous Dior nose Edmond Roudnitska for his wife. Monsieur Malle has devised high-tech ways to keep each smelling session unadulterated. At the Rue de Grenelle store, individual scents are released in glass columns; stick your head in and sniff. The Avenue Victor Hugo boutique has a glass-fronted "wall of scents"; at the push of a button a selected fragrance mists the air.

**Guerlain** (✉ *68 av. des Champs-Élysées, 8ᵉ, Champs-Élysées* ☎ *01–45–62–52–57* Ⓜ *Franklin-D.-Roosevelt*) reopened its historic address in 2005 after a spectacularly opulent renovation befitting the world-class perfumer. Still the only Paris outlet for legendary perfumes like Shalimar and L'Heure Blue, they've added several new signature scents (Rose Barbare, Cuir Beluga), and the perfume "fountain" allows for personalized bottles in several sizes to be filled on demand. Or, for a mere €30,000, a customized scent can be blended just for you. Also here are makeup, scented candles, and a spa featuring their much-adored skin-care line.

**L'Artisan Parfumeur** (✉ *32 rue du Bourg Tibourg, 4ᵉ, Le Marais* ☎ *01–48–04–55–66* Ⓜ *Hôtel de Ville*) is known for its own brand of scents for the home and perfumes with names like Méchant Loup (Big Bad Wolf).

FodorśChoice **Les Salons du Palais-Royal Shiseido** (✉ *Jardins du Palais-Royal, 142 Gal-*
★ *erie de Valois, 1ᵉʳ, Louvre/Tuileries* ☎ *01–49–27–09–09* Ⓜ *Palais-Royal*) douses its old-new *pharmacie* decor in shades of lilac. Every year Shiseido's creative genius, Serge Lutens, dreams up two new scents, which are then sold exclusively in this boutique. Each is compellingly original, from the strong *somptueux* scents, often with musk and amber notes, to intense florals (Rose de Nuit).

**Parfums de Nicolaï** (✉ *69 av. Raymond Poincaré, 16ᵉ, Trocadéro/Tour Eiffel* ☎ *01–47–55–90–44* Ⓜ *Victor-Hugo* ✉ *80 rue de Grenelle, 7ᵉ, Trocadéro/Tour Eiffel* ☎ *01–45–44–59–59* Ⓜ *Dupleix* ✉ *28 rue de Richelieu, 1ᵉʳ, Louvre/Tuileries* ☎ *01–44–55–02–02* Ⓜ *Palais-Royal*) is run by a member of the Guerlain family: Patricia de Nicolaï. Children's, women's, and men's perfumes are on offer (including some unisex), as well as sprays for the home and scented candles.

# SHOES

**Berluti** (✉ *26 rue Marbeuf, 8ᵉ, Champs-Élysées* ☎ *01–53–93–97–97* Ⓜ *Franklin-D.-Roosevelt*) has been making exquisite and expensive men's shoes for more than a century. "Nothing is too beautiful for feet" is Olga Berluti's motto; she even exposes her creations to the moonlight to give them an extra-special patina. One model is named after Andy Warhol; other famous clients of the past include the Duke of Windsor, Fred Astaire, and James Joyce.

FodorśChoice **Bruno Frisoni** (✉ *34 rue de Grenelle, 7ᵉ, St-Germain-des-Prés* ☎ *01–42–*
★ *84–12–30* Ⓜ *St-Germain-des-Prés*) has an impressive pedigree, most lately as art director for Roger Vivier. His first boutique for women is

# Worth a Look

There are some stores that are worth visiting, whether or not you're going to make a purchase; check these out for a priceless slice of Parisian life.

**Deyrolle** (✉ *46 rue du Bac, 7ᵉ, St-Germain-des-Prés* ☎ *01–42–22–30–07* Ⓜ *Rue du Bac*), the fascinating 19th-century taxidermist, has long been a stop for curiosity seekers. A fire in early 2008 destroyed much of the shop, though one room is still open and there are plans to rebuild.

**Merci** (✉ *111 bd. Beaumarchais, 3ᵉ, Le Marais* ☎ *01–42–77–00–33* Ⓜ *St-Sebastien Froissart*) is the world's most gorgeous charity shop, put together by Marie-France and Bernard Cohen of the luxury kid's line, Bonpoint. Everything here—designer and vintage clothes, furniture, antiques, jewelry, and housewares—has been plucked straight from many top-tier designers and are offered at a discount. Five percent of the proceeds are earmarked to aid disadvantaged children in Madagascar.

Have you always wanted to decorate your home like the grand homes of Paris? **Zuber** (✉ *3 rue des Saints-Pères, 6ᵉ, St-Germain-des-Prés* ☎ *01–42–77–95–91* Ⓜ *St-Germain-des-Prés*)

has operated nonstop for more than two centuries as the world's oldest producer of prestige hand-printed wallpapers, renowned for their magnificent panoramic scenes. Warning: with only one scene produced per year, the wait can be nearly 10 years long. They appear at Sotheby's, too, from time to time. Opulent Restoration-era wallpapers (including metallics, silks, velvets, and pressed leather) make modern statements and can be purchased in 32-foot rolls for slightly less than a king's ransom.

For elegant decorating on a smaller scale, **Hervé Gambs** (✉ *9 bis, rue des Blancs-Manteaux, 4ᵉ, Louvre/ Tuileries* ☎ *01–44–59–88–88* Ⓜ *Hôtel de Ville* ✉ *21 rue St-Sulpice, 6ᵉ, St-Germain-des-Prés* ☎ *01–70–08–09–08* Ⓜ *Odéon*) has the chutzpah to vie with Mother Nature. Take home one of his all-silk floral creations—think a no-care stem of orchids or a pristine bouquet of calla lilies—and dazzle your houseguests. Seasonal and holiday-appropriate displays change every few months. Gambs's own pedestal candles and sculptural vases styled from natural forms make great gifts.

**16**

lined with ultrasexy, ultrasophisticated shoes and bags in vivid colors. The vertiginous tapered heels, lean platforms, and delicately conceived flats mix glamour with a hint of S&M.

★ **Christian Louboutin** (✉ *19 rue Jean-Jacques Rousseau, 1ᵉʳ, Beaubourg/Les Halles* ☎ *01–42–36–53–66* Ⓜ *Palais-Royal* ✉ *38–40 rue de Grenelle, 7ᵉ, St-Germain-des-Prés* ☎ *01–42–22–33–07* Ⓜ *Sèvres-Babylone*) shoes carry their own red carpet with them, in their trademark crimson soles. Whether tasseled, embroidered, or strappy, in Charvet silk or shiny patent leather, these heels are always perfectly balanced. No wonder they set off such legendary legs as Tina Turner's and Gwyneth Paltrow's.

**Giuseppe Zanotti Design** (✉ *12 av. Montaigne, 8ᵉ, Champs-Élysées* ☎ *01–47–20–07–85* Ⓜ *Franklin-D.-Roosevelt* ✉ *233 rue St-Honoré, 1ᵉʳ, Louvre/Tuileries* ☎ *01–47–03–02–60* Ⓜ *Tuileries* ✉ *22 rue de Grenelle, 7ᵉ,*

*St-Germain-des-Prés* ☎ *01–42–22–04–18* Ⓜ *Rue du Bac*) makes every pair of shoes a fetish, if not downright dangerous. Dagger-like metal spike heels, shiny croc stilettos, slinky python booties, and jewel-encrusted black-satin pumps beg to be noticed. More toned-down models, like pony-fur flats in a leopard print, can be had, too.

**Jimmy Choo** (✉ *34 av. Montaigne, 8ᵉ, Champs-Élysées* ☎ *01–47–23–03–39* Ⓜ *Franklin-D.-Roosevelt* ✉ *376 rue St-Honoré, 1ᵉʳ, Louvre/Tuileries* ☎ *01–58–62–50–40* Ⓜ *Concord*) is the place for mile-high heels and strappy flats. Bags, evening clutches, and small leather items in metallics, reptile, and colorful canvas with leather accents are seasonal favorites. What more can be said that *Sex and the City* didn't?

**K. Jacques** (✉ *16 rue Pavée, 4ᵉ, Le Marais* ☎ *01–40–27–03–57* Ⓜ *St. Paul*) has shod everyone from Brigitte Bardot to Drew Barrymore. The St-Tropez–based maker of strappy flats has migrated to the big time while still keeping designs classic and comfortable. From gladiator-style to demure mules, metallics to neutrals, these are perennial favorites.

**Michel Perry** (✉ *243 rue St-Honoré, 1ᵉʳ, Louvre/Tuileries* ☎ *01–42–44–10–07* Ⓜ *Tuileries*) is known for his polished, slender, mile-high shoes. Napa leather and patent ankle boots in fire-engine red and supersexy python platforms with bags to match punctuate the collection.

★ **Pierre Hardy** (✉ *156 Galerie de Valois, Palais Royal gardens, 1ᵉʳ, Louvre/Tuileries* ☎ *01–42–60–59–75* Ⓜ *Palais Royal Musée du Louvre*) completes the triumvirate (with Frisoni and Louboutin) of anointed Paris shoe designers. Armed with a pedigree—Dior, Hermès, Balenciaga—Hardy opened his own boutique in 2003 and made serious waves. The shoes are unmistakable: sky-scraping platforms and wedges double as sculpture with their breathtaking details. His sensational bags, introduced in 2006, became instant classics.

**Robert Clergerie** (✉ *18 av. Victor Hugo, 16ᵉ, Champs Élysées* ☎ *01–45–01–81–30* Ⓜ *Charles de Gaulle–Étoile* ✉ *5 rue du Cherche-Midi, 6ᵉ, St-Germain-des-Prés* ☎ *01–45–48–75–47* Ⓜ *St-Sulpice*) knows that the shoes make the woman. Styles combine visionary design, first-rate craftsmanship, and wearability with legendary staying power. Plus, they're still a relative bargain on this side of the Atlantic.

**Rodolphe Ménudier** (✉ *14 rue de Castiglione, 1ᵉʳ, Louvre/Tuileries* ☎ *01–42–60–86–27* Ⓜ *Tuileries*) spins a hard-edge sexiness, from its interior design—think sleek black windows, metal cupboards, and a wall covered in white crocodile leather—to its pointy-toe high heels. Stilettos with ankle straps? *Mais oui.*

★ **Roger Vivier** (✉ *29 rue du Faubourg St-Honoré, 8ᵉ, Louvre/Tuileries* ☎ *01–53–43–00–85* Ⓜ *Concorde*) was known for decades for his Pilgrim-buckle shoes and inventive heels, and his name is being resurrected through the creativity of über-Parisienne Inès de la Fressange and the expertise of shoe designer Bruno Frisoni. The results are brilliant: leather boots that mold to the calf perfectly, satin evening sandals, and square-toe pumps in crocodile are some of what you might find.

**DISCOUNT**

In-the-know Parisians flock to the République *quartier* (near the République metro) to check out the luxury-shoe-lover-on-a-slender-budget boutiques on **Rue Meslay**. The discount stores are often jam-packed and the service is often rather dodgy, but for more than 50% off on last season's collections from the biggest names, it's well worth the visit.

**Michel Perry Collector** (✉ *42 rue de Grenelle, 7ᵉ, St-Germain-des-Prés* ☎ *01–42–84–12–45* Ⓜ *Rue du Bac*) is a mixed bag with reliably great finds: among those unsellable gladiator numbers you might turn up delicate silvery-pink pumps; you have to look to make the finds. Season-old collections of Michel Perry shoes are half off; during sales the store practically gives them away. The staff is helpful and fun.

**Mi-Prix** (✉ *27 bd. Victor, 15ᵉ, Montparnasse* ☎ *01–48–28–42–48* Ⓜ *Porte de Versailles*) is a jumble of end-of-series designer shoes and accessories from the likes of Alexandra Neel, Michel Perry, Valentino, and Rodolph Ménudier, priced at up to 70% below retail.

# SHOPPING ARCADES

**16**

Paris's 19th-century commercial arcades, or *passages,* are worth a visit for the architectural splendor of their glass roofs, decorative pillars, and mosaic floors. In 1828 there were 137, though only 24 are left.

★ **Galerie Véro-Dodat** (✉ *19 rue Jean-Jacques Rousseau, 1ᵉʳ, Louvre/Tuileries* Ⓜ *Louvre*) was built in 1826. At what is now the Café de l'Époque, the French writer Gérard de Nerval took his last drink before heading to Châtelet to hang himself. The gallery has painted ceilings and copper pillars and shops selling contemporary art and leather goods. It's best known, though, for its antiques stores.

Fodor's Choice ★ **Galerie Vivienne** (✉ *4 rue des Petits-Champs, 2ᵉ, Opéra/Grands Boulevards* Ⓜ *Bourse*), between the Bourse and the Palais-Royal, is home base for a range of interesting and luxurious shops as well as the lovely tearoom A Priori Thé and Cave Legrand, a terrific wineshop. Don't leave without checking out the Jean-Paul Gaultier boutique.

**Passage des Panoramas** (✉ *11 bd. Montmartre, 2ᵉ, Grands Boulevards* Ⓜ *Opéra/Grands Boulevards*), opened in 1800, is the oldest arcade extant; it's especially known for its stamp shops.

**Passage du Grand-Cerf** (✉ *145 rue St-Denis, 2ᵉ, Beaubourg/Les Halles* Ⓜ *Étienne Marcel*) has regained the interest of Parisians. La Parisette, a small boudoir-pink space at No. 1, sells fun accessories, and Marci Noum, at No. 4, riffs on street fashion. Silk bracelets, crystals, and charms can be nabbed at Eric & Lydie and Satellite.

**Passage Jouffroy** (✉ *12 bd. Montmartre, 9ᵉ, Grands Boulevards* Ⓜ *Grands Boulevards*) is full of shops selling toys, Oriental furnishings, and cinema books and posters. Pain D'épices, at No. 29, has dollhouse decor, and Au Bonheur des Dames, at No. 39, has all things embroidery.

**Passage Verdeau** (✉ *4–6 rue de la Grange Batelière, 9ᵉ, Opéra/Grands Boulevards* Ⓜ *Grands Boulevards*), across from Passage Jouffroy, has shops carrying antique cameras, comic books, and engravings.

# TOYS

**Au Nain Bleu** (⊠ *5 bd. Malesherbes, 8ᵉ, Louvre/Tuileries* ☎ *01–42–65–20–00* Ⓜ *Concorde*) is a high-priced wonderland of elaborate doll-houses, miniature sports cars, and hand-carved rocking horses.

**FNAC Toys** (⊠ *19 rue Vavin, 6ᵉ, St-Germain-des-Prés* ☎ *08–92–35–06–66* Ⓜ *Vavin*) may lack charm—it's a chain—but it makes up with variety. Some of the famous old names in French toys can be found here, including the much-loved wooden toys from Vilac, but the impressive collection is mostly contemporary (for kids from birth to age 12).

**Pain d'Epices** (⊠ *29 Passage Jouffroy, 9ᵉ, Grands Boulevards* ☎ *01–47–70–08–68* Ⓜ *Grands Boulevards*) has anything you can imagine for the French home (and garden) in miniature, including Lilliputian croissants, wine decanters, and minuscule instruments in their cases. Build-it-yourself dollhouses include a 17th-century town house and a *boulangerie* storefront. Upstairs are do-it-yourself teddy-bear kits and classic toys.

# Where to Eat

## WORD OF MOUTH

"Some typical/traditional French foods to look for in Paris are: crepes—sweet or savory, from street stands or as a main course from a restaurant specializing in crepes like Breizh Café which has outlets in Paris, Tokyo and Cancale—a tiny town in Brittany from which crepes come.

—JulieVikmanis

Updated by
Rosa Jackson

A new wave of culinary confidence is running through one of the world's great food cities and spilling over both banks of the Seine. Whether cooking up *grand-mère*'s roast chicken and *riz au lait* or placing a whimsical hat of cotton candy atop wild-strawberry-and-rose ice cream, Paris chefs are breaking free from the tyranny of tradition and following their passions.

Emblematic of this movement is the proliferation of haute cuisine—trained bistro chefs who have opened their own restaurants. Among the newcomers to the bistronomique scene are David Rathgeber, who has left Benoît to take over the chic Montparnasse bistro L'Assiette; Mickaël Gaignon, a veteran of Pierre Gagnaire and Le Pré Catelan who now runs the Marais bistro Le Gaigne; and Stéphane Marcouzzi, who was maître d'hôtel at Guy Savoy's Le Cap Vernet before opening L'Epigramme in St-Germain with chef Aymeric Kräml.

But self-expression is not the only driving force behind the current changes. A traditional high-end restaurant can be prohibitively expensive to operate. As a result, more casual bistros and cafés, which often have lower operational costs and higher profit margins, have become attractive businesses for even top chefs.

For tourists, this development can only be good news, since it makes the cooking of geniuses such as Joël Robuchon, Guy Savoy, Alain Senderens, and Pierre Gagnaire more accessible (even if these star chefs rarely cook in their lower-priced restaurants).

Like the chefs themselves, Paris diners are breaking away—albeit cautiously—from tradition. New restaurants and rapidly multiplying sandwich bars recognize that not everyone wants a three-course blow-out every time they dine out. And because Parisians are more widely traveled than in the past, many ethnic restaurants—notably the best North African, Vietnamese/Laotian, Chinese, Spanish, and Japanese spots—are making fewer concessions to French tastes, resulting in far better food.

**MONTMARTRE**
Mix of hip resto-lounges & quaint bistros

LA VILLETTE

BATIGNOLLES

Av. de Clichy

Bd. de Clichy

Bd. des Batignolles

Bd. de Rochechouart

Bd. de la Chapelle

Rue Marx Dormoy

Rue du Faubourg Saint-Martin

**8 e**

OPÉRA

**9 e**

Rue la Fayette

**10 e**

rue du Faubourg Saint-Martin

Canal Saint-Martin

**CHAMPS-ÉLYSÉES**
Luxe lane studded with star-chef eateries & celebrity clientele

Bd. Haussmann

PIGALLE

Bd. de Strasbourg

Bd. de Magenta

**CANAL ST-MARTIN**
Bobo bistros

Bd. des Capucines  Bd. des Italiens  Bd. Poissonnière  Bd. de Bonne Nouvelle

Rue Royale

**2 e**

Rue de Turbigo

**1 er**

**LOUVRE/ LES HALLES**
All-night eats

**3 e**

Av. des Champs-Élysées

Jardin des Tuileries

Quai des Tuileries

Place René Cassin

Boulevard de Sébastopol

Rue Beaubourg

**LE MARAIS**
Delis, teahouses and falafel shops

Quai Anatole France

River  Seine

Quai du Louvre

Place du Louvre

■ Louvre

Voie Georges Pompidou

Quai Voltaire

ÎLE DE LA CITÉ

Place des Vosges

Bd. Saint-Germain

Quai des Grds Augustins

**THE ISLANDS**
Few notable eateries

Quai de l'Hôtel de Ville

**4 e**

**7 e**

INVALIDES

**ST-GERMAIN**
Crème of the café crop

**6 e**

Bd. Saint-Germain

Quai de Montebello

ÎLE ST LOUIS

Pont Sully

Quai de la Tournelle

Voie Mazas

**BASTILLE**
Edgy eateries run by young chefs

Rue de Sèvres

Bd. Raspail

■ Palais du Luxembourg

Jardin du Luxembourg

Bd. Saint-Michel

Pt. Alphonse Laveran

**LATIN QUARTER**
Too many tourist traps; simple student cafés

**5 e**

Rue Monge

Jardin des Plantes

Av. des Gobelins

Bd. de Vaugirard

Bd. Edgar Quinet

**MONTPARNASSE**
Pricey brasseries & oysters on ice

Av. Denfert-Rochereau

Bd. Saint-Jacques

0    500 meters

0    1,500 ft

Bd. Auriol Vincent

# WHERE TO EAT PLANNER

## Dining Strategy

Where should we eat? With thousands of Paris eateries competing for your attention, it may seem like a daunting question. But fret not—our expert writers and editors have done the legwork. The 120-plus selections here represent the best this city has to offer. Search our "Best Bets" for top recommendations by price, cuisine, and experience; sample local flavor in the neighborhood features; or find a review quickly in the alphabetical listings. Delve in, and enjoy!

## Reservations

Restaurant staff will nearly always greet you with the phrase *"Avez-vous réservé?"* (Have you reserved?) and a confident *"Oui"* is the best answer, even in a neighborhood bistro. Most wine bars do not take reservations; reservations are also unnecessary for brasserie and café meals at odd hours.

## Children

Some restaurants provide booster seats, but don't count on them: be sure to ask when you confirm your reservation.

## Tipping and Taxes

According to French law, prices must include tax and tip (*service compris or prix nets*), but pocket change left on the table in cafés, or an additional 5% in better restaurants, is always appreciated. Beware of bills stamped SERVICE NOT INCLUDED in English or restaurants slyly using American-style credit-card slips, hoping that you'll be confused and add the habitual 15% tip.

## Hours

Paris restaurants generally serve food from noon to 2 PM and from 7:30 or 8 PM to about 11 PM. Brasseries have longer hours and often serve all day and late into the evening; some are open 24 hours. Surprisingly, many restaurants close on Saturday as well as Sunday, and Monday closings are also frequent. July and August are the most common months for annual closings but restaurants may also close for a week in February, around Easter, or at Christmas.

## Menus

All establishments must post menus outside so they're available to look over before you enter. Most have two basic types of menu: à la carte and fixed price (*prix fixe, le menu,* or *la formule*). Although it limits your choices, the prix fixe is usually the best value. If you feel like indulging, the *menu dégustation* (tasting menu), consisting of numerous small courses, let you sample the chef's offerings. ⇨ *See the Menu Guide at the back of this book for guidance with common French menu items.*

## What to Wear

Casual dress is acceptable at all but the fanciest restaurants—this usually means stylish sportswear, which might be a bit dressier than in the U.S. When in doubt, leave the T-shirts and sneakers behind. If an establishment requires jacket and tie, it's noted in the review.

# French Restaurant Types

**Bistro:** The broadest category, a bistro can be a simple, relaxed restaurant serving traditional fare or a chic hot spot where dinner costs more than €50 per person. The bistro menu, often written on a chalkboard, is fairly limited and usually changes with the season.

**Brasserie:** More informal than a bistro, the brasserie is large, lively, and almost always equipped with a bar. Ideal for relatively quick meals, it often specializes in Alsatian fare, like *choucroute garnie*, a mixed meat dish with sauerkraut and potatoes.

**Café:** Often an informal neighborhood hangout, the café may also be a showplace attracting a well-heeled crowd. A limited menu of sandwiches and simple dishes is usually available throughout the day. Beware of the prices: a half bottle of mineral water can cost €4 or more.

**French Fusion:** The French Fusion restaurant possesses discernable influences of both French cuisine and the cuisine of one other region or country.

**Haute French:** Ambitious and expensive, the Haute French restaurant is helmed by a pedigreed chef who prepares multicourse meals to be remembered.

**Modern French:** Although not necessarily superexpensive or pretentious, the Modern French restaurant boasts a creative menu that showcases a wide span of culinary influences.

# Prices

You'll be lucky to find a good bistro meal for €25 or less, even at lunch, so consider economizing on some meals to have more to spend on the others. Slurping inexpensive Japanese noodles on Rue Ste-Anne or having a picnic in a park at lunch will save euros for dinner. Some visitors rent apartments with kitchens, which allows them to shop at the city's wonderful markets.

## WHAT IT COSTS

|  | ¢ | $ | $$ | $$$ | $$$$ |
|---|---|---|---|---|---|
| AT DINNER | under €12 | €12–€17 | €18–€24 | €25–€32 | over €32 |

Price per person for a main course at dinner, including tax (19.6%) and service; note that if a restaurant offers only prix-fixe (set-price) meals, it has been given the price category that estimates the price of a main course at dinner.

# In this Chapter

# Smoking

**17**

Many Parisians are accustomed to smoking before, during, and after meals, but in January 2008, the national smoking ban was extended to restaurants, bars, and cafés. Many establishments have compensated by adding covered terraces for smokers, but inside, the air is much clearer.

# Wine

Most sommeliers are knowledgeable about their lists and will suggest what is appropriate after you've made your tastes and budget known. Simpler spots serve wine in carafes (*en carafe*, or *en pichet*). Many restaurants now sell wine by the glass, but beware of the price.

# BEST BETS FOR PARIS DINING

With thousands of restaurants to choose from, how will you decide where to eat? Fodor's writers and editors have selected their favorite restaurants by price, cuisine, and experience below. You can also search by neighborhood for excellent eating experiences—peruse the following pages for spotlights on specific neighborhoods.

## NORTH AFRICAN

Chez Omar, $$, p. 322
Le Martel, $-$$, p. 345

## SEAFOOD

Huîtrerie Régis, $$$, p. 330
L'Huîtrier, $$$, p. 355
Rech, $$$, p. 356

## SPANISH

Fogón St-Julien, $$$, p. 327

## VEGETARIAN

L'Arpège, $$$$, p. 337
L'As du Fallafel, $, p. 326
La Bastide Odéon, $$, p. 331
Macéo, $$$, p. 317
Rose Bakery, $, p. 344

## VIETNAMESE

Dong Huong, ¢, p. 345

# By Experience

## CHILD-FRIENDLY

Bofinger, $$$, p. 324
Cantine Merci, ¢, p. 322
L'As du Fallafel, $, p. 326
La Coupole, $$, p. 351
Le Troquet, $$$-$$$$, p. 352
Rose Bakery, $, p. 344

## DESSERT

Alain Ducasse au Plaza Athénée, $$$$, p. 339
Josephine Chez Dumonet, $$$, p. 331

Pierre Gagnaire, $$$$, p. 341
Taillevent, $$$$, p. 343

## DINNER PRIX FIXE

Bistrot des Deux Théâtres, $$, p. 343
Ribouldingue, $$, p. 329
Le Troquet, $$$-$$$$, p. 352
Le Vaudeville, $$$, p. 322
Villa Victoria, $$, p. 344

## EXPENSE ACCOUNT

Alain Ducasse au Plaza Athénée, $$$$, p. 339
La Fermette Marbeuf, $$$, p. 340
L'Arôme, $$$-$$$$, p. 339
Pierre Gagnaire, $$$$, p. 341

## GOOD FOR GROUPS

Bofinger, $$$, p. 324
La Chine Massena, $, p. 350
Les Saveurs de Flora, $$$$, p. 341

## GREAT VIEW

Lapérouse, $$$-$$$$, p. 332
La Tour d'Argent, $$$$, p. 327
Le Georges, $$-$$$, p. 323

## HOT SPOT

Derrière, $$$, p. 320
L'Atelier de Joël Robuchon, $$$$, p. 337

Le Murano, $$$-$$$$, p. 323
Thoumieux, $$-$$$, p. 338

## LATE-NIGHT

Au Pied de Cochon, $$, p. 316
Bofinger, $$$, p. 324
Julien, $$, p. 345
La Coupole, $$, p. 351
Le Vaudeville, $$$, p. 322

## LOTS OF LOCALS

Josephine Chez Dumonet, $$$, p. 331
La Ferrandaise, $$, p. 332
Le Petit Rétro, $$, p. 354
Unico, $$, p. 348

## LUNCH PRIX FIXE

La Boulangerie, $$, p. 358
Le Pré Verre, $, p. 328
Le Repaire de Cartouche, $$, p. 347
Taillevent, $$$$, p. 343
Willi's Wine Bar, $$, p. 318

## MOST ROMANTIC

Lapérouse, $$$-$$$$, p. 332

La Tour d'Argent, $$$$, p. 327
Le Pré Catelan, $$$$, p. 354
Restaurant du Palais-Royal, $$$, p. 318

## NEWCOMERS

Cantine Merci, ¢, p. 322
Cru, $$-$$$, p. 324
Derrière, $$$, p. 320
Frenchie, $$, p. 320
Guilo Guilo, $$$, p. 356
Jadis, $$-$$$, p. 352
L'Arôme, $$$$$$, p. 339
Yam'Tcha, $$$$$, p. 319
Josephine Chez Dumonet, $$$, p. 331

## OUTDOOR DINING

Au Bourguignon du Marais, $$, p. 323
Le Georges, $$-$$$, p. 323
Restaurant du Palais-Royal, $$$, p. 318

## WINE LIST

Cru, $$-$$$, p. 324
Josephine Chez Dumonet, $$$, p. 331
Le Pré Verre, $, p. 328
Le Repaire de Cartouche, $$, p. 347
Macéo, $$$, p. 317

## YOUNG CROWD

Derrière, $$$, p. 320
Le Murano, $$$-$$$$, p. 323
Unico, $$, p. 348

**17**

# ST-GERMAIN AND MONTPARNASSE
## 6E, 14E ARRONDISSEMENTS

Small bistros are moving into the spotlight in St-Germain, and crêpe stands, fish restaurants, and oyster bars attest to the Breton influence around Montparnasse.

Whether you're sipping rich hot chocolate at Les Deux Magots, diving into a platter of choucroute garnie at La Coupole or slurping *fines de claires* at the pristine oyster bar Régis, it's hard not to feel part of the café culture in St-Germain and Montparnasse. Along the broad boulevards you can find some of the city's classic brasseries. As much fun as these are for their storied settings and buzzy atmospheres, some of the area's best food is found at small bistros on narrow side streets. St-Germain is enjoying a revival as a foodie haunt, with Yves Camdeborde's Le Comptoir du Relais Saint-Germain the perfect example of the kind of market-inspired bistro that Parisians (and foreigners) adore. For a change of pace, try freshly made *galettes* (buckwheat crêpes) washed down with dry cider at one of Boulevard du Montparnasse's many crêperies.

## BRINY BLISS

Ever since the first trains from Brittany brought oyster-loving settlers to Montparnasse, the neighborhood has had a proud seafood tradition. The best oysters come from Normandy, Brittany, or Marennes-Oléron on the Atlantic coast. The knobbly shelled *creuses* are more common than the rounder *plates*, which are beloved by connoisseurs. Oysters can be dressed with vinegar and shallots, but a squeeze of lemon—or nothing at all—is probably the best accompaniment. Scoop the raw oyster from its shell with a small fork, slurp the juice, and chew a little before swallowing the taste of the sea.

# CLASSIC CAFÉ ITEMS

| THE ITEM | WHERE TO GET IT | WHY THERE? |
|---|---|---|
| Omelet | **Café de Flore** (✉172 bd. St-Germain, 6$^e$ ☎01-45-48-55-26), the last classic café that attracts genuine Left Bank intellectuals. | The omelet arrives pale on the outside and slightly runny within—i.e., perfect. Try ham and cheese or, for a splurge, crabmeat. |
| Chocolat chaud | **Les Deux Magots** (✉6 pl. St-Germain des Prés, 6$^e$ ☎01-45-49-31-29), which overlooks the ancient St-Germain des Prés church. | Made with milk and pure chocolate, this hot chocolate is served in a lovely white porcelain pitcher. |
| Choucroute garnie | **La Coupole** (✉102 bd. du Montparnasse, 14$^e$ ☎01-43-20-14-20), the Art Deco brasserie that never fails to entertain. | The choucroute garnie brings you heaps of sauerkraut topped with chunks of pork and sausages. |

## RESTAURANTS IN THIS AREA

**BISTRO**
Boucherie Roulière, $–$$
Chez Lulu–L'Assiette, $$
Chez Maître Paul, $$
Coco & Co., $
Josephine Chez Dumonet, $$$
La Bastide Odéon, $$
La Cerisaie, $
La Ferrandaise, $$
Le Comptoir du Relais Saint-Germain, $$
Les Bouquinistes, $$$
L'Epigramme, $
Le Timbre, $
**BRASSERIE**
Alcazar, $$$
La Coupole, $$
Le Bouillon Racine, $$
Le Dôme, $$$$
**CAFÉ**
Café de Flore, $$
**HAUTE FRENCH**
Hélène Darroze, $$$$
**JAPANESE**
Yen, $$$
**MODERN FRENCH**
Gaya Rive Gauche, $$$$
Le 21, $$$
**SEAFOOD**
Huîtrerie Régis, $$$

**17**

## PIQUE-NIQUE IN THE PARC

Everything you need for the perfect Luxembourg gardens picnic is just minutes away from the park. For cheese, **Fromagerie Quatrehomme** (✉ *62 rue de Sèvres* ☎ *01-47-34-33-45*). For cured meats and sparkling water, **Bon Marché's Grande Epicerie** (✉ *38 rue de Sèvres* ☎ *01-44-39-81-00*). For sourdough bread, **Boulangerie Poilâne** (✉ *8 rue du Cherche-Midi* ☎ *01-45-48-42-59*). For something sinfully sweet, **Pâtissier Pierre Hermé** (✉ *72 rue Bonaparte* ☎ *01-43-54-47-77*).

# QUARTIER LATIN, LES GOBELINS, AND THE ISLANDS

## 5E, 13E ARRONDISSEMENTS

### SECRET CELLAR

Few restaurants in Paris have a more storied history than the Seine-side **Tour d'Argent** (⊠ *15 quai de la Tournelle* ☎ *01–43–54–23–31*). It opened in 1780, only to be burned down nine years later by the same Revolutionaries who set the Bastille ablaze. When Paris was occupied by the Germans during World War II, La Tour became a popular dining destination for Nazi officers. Little did they know that the restaurant's laughably large stock of wine was safely hidden behind a brick wall. Today, the wine cellar contains almost 500,000 bottles of the world's finest wines.

Whether you're seeking a cheap Chinese eatery or a table for two at La Tour d'Argent, the Quartier Latin dishes up something for every taste and budget.

Thanks to its student population, the Quartier Latin caters to those on a budget with kebab shops, crêpe stands, Asian fast-food joints, and no-nonsense bistros. Look beyond the pedestrian streets such as Rue de la Huchette and Rue Mouffetard for less touristy eateries preferred by locals. As you might expect in an area known for its *gauche caviar* (wealthy intellectuals who vote Socialist), the Quartier Latin brims with atmospheric places to linger over a tiny cup of black coffee. Top-notch bistros lurk in the off-the-beaten-track 13$^e$ arrondissement, which is also home to the city's most authentic Chinese, Vietnamese, and Laotian restaurants along Avenue d'Ivry. Wander across the Seine to the Ile St-Louis for a meal in a long-established brasserie or classy bistro.

# UNCOVERING THE QUARTIER

## DODGING THE "FAUX BISTRO"

Is it a genuine bistro? It's often hard to tell. Tourist traps can seem thoroughly charming until the food arrives. The Quartier Latin is dangerous rip-off territory, but there are some sure bets: around Notre-Dame, try **Le Pré Verre** (⊠ *8 rue Thénard* ☎ *01–43–54–59–47*), where Philippe Delacourcelle tinkers successfully with Asian spices, and the Lyonnais-style bistro **Ribouldingue** (⊠ *10 rue St-Julien Le Pauvre* ☎ *01–46–33–98–80*), where the €27 prix fixe is one of the area's best bargains. You'll also find a few honest, old-fashioned bistros like **Au Moulin à Vent ("Chez Henri")** (⊠ *20 rue des Fossés St-Bernard* ☎ *01–43–54–99–37*) and **La Rôtisserie du Beaujolais** (⊠ *19 quai de la Tournelle* ☎ *01–43–54–17–47*), an annex of La Tour d'Argent. Tread carefully on the Ile St-Louis: star Alsatian chef Antoine Westermann's **Mon Vieil Ami** (⊠ *69 rue St-Louis en l'Ile* ☎ *01–40–46–01–35*) is the most reliable choice.

## THE ANATOMY OF A TABAC

In their primary function, selling cigarettes, *tabacs* play an essential role in the lives of most Parisians, but they're indispensable to those who don't smoke, too. At the small counter where customers pick up Gitanes or Marlboros, you also can buy métro or lottery tickets, phone cards, batteries, and chewing gum. Next to this counter is a bar perfect for a quick drink, like the one Audrey Tautou imbibed at the **Le Verre à Pied** (⊠ *118 bis, rue Mouffetard*) in the film *Amélie*. *Tabacs* often sell newspapers, which you can read while perched at the bar sipping an *express* (strong black coffee). Food is surprisingly palatable in *tabacs*—expect anything from a *jambon-beurre* (a ham sandwich) to hearty dishes such as boeuf Bourguignon. Many *tabacs*, like **Le Québec** (⊠ *45 rue Bonaparte* ☎ *01–43–26–00–11*), attract a variety of regulars, from moneyed businessmen to *les sans-abri* (the homeless),

## RESTAURANTS IN THIS AREA

**BISTRO**
Chez René, $$
Itinéraires, $$$
L'Avant Goût, $
L'Ourcine, $
Lapérouse, $$$–$$$$
Le Buisson Ardent, $
Ribouldingue, $$
**BRASSERIE**
Le Balzar, $$
**CHINESE**
La Chine Massena, $
**HAUTE FRENCH**
La Tour d'Argent, $$$$
**MODERN FRENCH**
Le Pré Verre, $–$$
Ze Kitchen Galerie, $$
**SPANISH**
Fogòn St-Julien, $$$
**VIETNAMESE**
Le Bambou,

**17**

# LE MARAIS, BASTILLE, NATION
## 3E, 4E, 11E, 12E, 20E ARROND.

### TARTE TATIN

For the perfect *tarte tatin*, which is like an upside-down apple pie, take a seat at the horseshoe-shaped bar of **Le Petit Fer à Cheval** (✉ *30 rue Vieille-du-Temple* ☎ *01–42–72–47–47*). The restaurant's recipe calls for juicy Gala apples, which produce a buttery, caramelized tarte that is served warm and pairs perfectly with a glass of hot wine. The *tarte* was first discovered by mistake in the 19th century at the Hôtel Tatin in Lamotte-Beuvron—the product of a botched apple pie recipe. It can be made with other fruit—like pineapple or pears—but nothing beats the classic, faithfully repro-duced at this Marais café.

The center of Jewish and gay life in Paris, Le Marais serves up the best falafel in town and some great bistro fare, too. Farther east, the Bastille area has attracted more than its share of gifted young chefs.

The once run-down Marais is now the epitome of chic, but you can still find reminders of its down-to-earth past along Rue des Rosiers, where falafel shops and Eastern European delis jostle with designer boutiques. For fantastic people-watching and food to match, pop into Le Petit Fer à Cheval or L'Étoile Manquante on Rue Vieille-du-Temple. Ambitious restaurants are few and far between in the Marais, but the new Breizh Café attracts many with its inexpensive and authentic galettes (buckwheat crêpes) made with quality ingredients. The bistro scene gets interesting east of the Bastille, where lower rents have encouraged young chefs to set up shop. Around Père Lachaise, the selection thins, but wander a little farther to multicultural Belleville to find an intriguing mix of Chinese and North African eateries.

# MARAIS NOSHES

| | THE OBVIOUS CHOICE | DON'T FORGET |
|---|---|---|
| **L'As du Fallafel** 34 rue de Rosiers | The falafel spécial, a packed pita with chickpea and herb balls, eggplant, harissa, hummus, and tahini. | Napkins and a glass of fresh-squeezed lemonade help tame this greasy feast. |
| **Chez Marianne** 2 rue Hospitalières St-Gervais | Chopped liver. Who'd have thought that chicken livers and onion fried in melted goose fat could ever taste this good? | A more genteel version of pastrami than the slabs of fatty meat you'll find back home, it'll satisfy any deli devotee. |
| **Korcarz** 29 rue de Rosiers | A loaf of shiny, sweet, and delicious challah. For best results, take the bread back to your hotel room and dip in salt and honey. | A pletzl, a small onion roll that—surprisingly—tastes great with jam for breakfast. |

**RESTAURANTS IN THIS AREA**

**BISTRO**
Astier, $$
Au Bourguignon du Marais, $$
Au Trou Gascon, $$$
Benoît, $$$
Derrière, $$
L'Ambassade d'Auvergne, $
La Boulangerie, $$
La Table de Claire, $–$$
Le Baratin, $$
Le Bistrot Paul Bert, $$
Le Chateaubriand, $$
Le Chez Julien, $$$
Le Repaire de Cartouche, $$
Restaurant le Gaigne, $$

**BRASSERIE**
Bofinger, $$$

**CAFÉ**
Cantine Merci, ¢

**ITALIAN**
Sardegna a Tavola, $$$

**LATIN AMERICAN**
Unico, $$

**MIDDLE EASTERN**
Chez Marianne, $$
L'As du Fallafel, $

**MODERN FRENCH**
Breizh Café, ¢
Cru, $$–$$$$
Le Georges, $$–$$$
Le Murano, $$$–$$$$
Mon Vieil Ami, $$

**NORTH AFRICAN**
Chez Omar, $$

**VIETNAMESE**
Dong Huong, ¢

17

## FANTASTIQUE THREE: THE RUE PAUL BERT

This side street between Bastille and Nation is home to three local favorites. **Bistrot Paul Bert** (⌧ 18 rue Paul Bert ☎ 01-43-72-24-01) boasts bistro classics, and its seafood annex, **L'Ecailler du Bistrot** (⌧ 22 rue Paul Bert ☎ 01-43-72-76-77), serves exemplary oysters. And the Argentinian **Unico** (⌧ 15 rue Paul Bert ☎ 01-43-67-68-08) draws hungry hordes for its charcoal-grilled steaks.

# MONTMARTRE, CANAL ST-MARTIN, NORTHEAST PARIS

## 10E, 18E, 19E ARRONDISSEMENTS

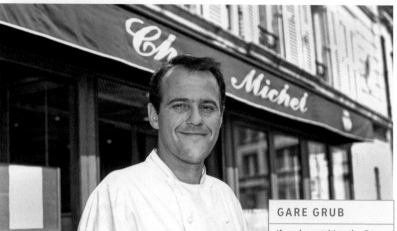

Perched above central Paris, Montmartre is buzzing with a hip vibe, and cutting-edge cafés are springing up along the banks of the Canal St-Martin.

Idyllic as the portrayal of Montmartre might seem in Jean-Pierre Jeunet's film *Amélie*, it's surprisingly close to reality. One of the most desirable areas in Paris, Montmartre seamlessly blends the trendy and the traditional. Less picturesque is the neighborhood around Gare du Nord and Gare de l'Est, but you can still find classic brasseries and tucked-away bistros, as well as the city's most authentic Indian restaurants. Head over to the up-and-coming Canal St-Martin to watch Parisian *bobos*, or bohemian bourgeois, in action. The area is home to fashion designers, artists, and media folk who make the most of the waterside cafés on sunny days. Restaurants are sparse in the undiscovered Buttes Chaumont area, but you won't have to worry about stumbling onto a tourist rip-off.

### GARE GRUB

If you're catching the Eurostar at Gare du Nord, it's worth planning ahead to fit in one last feast. Across the street from the train station, **Terminus Nord** (✉ *23 rue de Dunkerque* ☎ *01–42–85–05–15*) is a classic Art Deco brasserie where you can treat yourself to a seafood platter, bouillabaisse, or *sole meunière* before indulging in another house specialty, crêpes Suzette (flambéed in Grand Marnier). Just a few blocks farther, try the acclaimed **Chez Casimir** (✉ *6 rue Belzunce* ☎ *01–48–78–28–80*), run by the Breton chef Thierry Breton (*above*).

## CANAL-SIDE CAFÉS

More laid-back than the Seine with its vehicle-clogged *quais,* the Canal St-Martin attracts artsy young professionals who scorn the self-consciously elegant Rive Gauche. Its once-vibrant live music scene has been quelled somewhat in the last few years by the city's noise restrictions, but that hasn't made the cafés any less entertaining. At the scruffy, long-established **La Patache** (✉ *60 rue de Lancry* ☎ *01–42–08–14–35*), the owner provides scraps of paper at each table for note writing, in case customers feel too coy to speak to each other. Bohemian institution **Chez Adel** (✉ *10 rue de la Grange aux Belles* ☎ *01–42–08–24–61*) holds live concerts Tuesday to Saturday and avant-garde theater on Sunday. The café of choice on the water is **Chez Prune** (✉ *36 rue Beaurepaire, 10ᵉ* ☎ *01–42–41–30–47*), whose terrace is overrun with locals as soon as a ray of sunshine emerges.

### THE "NEW MONTMARTRE"

At the Montmartre restaurant **Guilo Guilo** (✉ *8 rue Garreau* ☎ *01–42–54–23–92*), a handful of diners perch around the counter while a Japanese chef who made his name in Kyoto turns out plate after perfect plate of inventive food (a signature dish is his foie gras sushi). Guilo Guilo is typical of the "new Montmartre," which stands in stark contrast to the area's ancient cobbled streets. The district's hip young population occupies the area, perfectly representing 21st-century Paris: nostalgic yet forward thinking. **Café Burq** (✉ *6 rue Burq* ☎ *01–42–52–81–27*) is a popular, slightly less ambitious Montmartre hangout. Owned by an architect and an actor, it buzzes with a fashionable crowd that comes for the 1970s decor but also for the satisfying bistro fare. On the other side of the *Butte Montmartre,* the friendly **Café Arrosé** (✉ *123 rue Caulaincourt* ☎ *01–42–57–14–30*) proves that even this once-sleepy part of Montmartre is coming to life.

### RESTAURANTS IN THIS AREA

**BISTRO**
Chez Casimir, $
Le Miroir, $
**BRASSERIE**
Au Bœuf Couronné, $$$
La Mascotte, $–$$
**HAUTE FRENCH**
Julien, $$
**JAPANESE**
Guilo Guilo, $$
**NORTH AFRICAN**
Le Martel, $–$$

17

# CHAMPS-ÉLYSÉES AND WESTERN PARIS

## 8E, 16E, 17E ARRONDISSEMENTS

Style often wins out over substance around the Champs-Élysées, but a handful of luxury restaurants continue to defy fashion.

Perma-tans and Botox are de rigueur at fashionable restaurants near the Champs-Élysées, where the St-Tropez set picks at dishes with names like "le tigre qui pleure," the weeping tiger, a Thai-style beef dish. Yet this part of Paris is also home to many of the city's most ambitious chefs, whose restaurants are surrounded by palatial hotels, bourgeois apartments, embassies, and luxury boutiques. Some, such as Eric Frechon at Le Bristol, offer sophisticated updates of French classics, whereas others, like Pierre Gagnaire, constantly push culinary boundaries in the manner of a mad scientist. A few solid bistros survive here, notably the Art Deco Savy. Unlike the uniformly chic 16$^e$, the 17$^e$ arrondissement has its bourgeois and its bohemian sides. Head over to Batignolles, where an organic market takes place on Saturday, to discover up-and-coming neighborhood bistros.

## SPOON-FED

Haute cuisine aside, the Champs-Élysées was something of a restaurant wasteland until Alain Ducasse opened his fusion bistro **Spoon** (⊠ *12 rue Marignan* ☎ *01–40–76– 34–44*). Ten years later, countless fashionable restaurants have come and gone—Nobu among the defunct—while Spoon has endured. In 2006 the restaurant received a makeover, but its acclaimed menu has not changed dramatically since the beginning. The secret to Spoon's success? Ducasse tacks on a few standards like steak tartare to his mix-and-match, continent-hopping formula. Bubble-gum ice cream, anyone?

# LUXE FOR LESS

## Hotel Dining Deals
### And what they're worth

What if you want to taste the good life on a more modest budget? A dinner for two at one of Paris's superexpensive hotel restaurants could easily cost as much your plane ticket. But high prices don't mean you can't catch a glimpse of the gilt. To experience haute hotel cuisine, try our tips for keeping your budget intact.

**Breakfast at Les Ambassadeurs, Hôtel de Crillon: €49**
**What you get:** An extravagant breakfast buffet (Mon.–Sat. 7:30–10 AM) amid the Italian marble and Baccarat crystal of an 18th-century ballroom. It's haute cuisine meets all-you-can-eat in an over-the-top setting.

**What you could've bought:** One ticket to the Disneyland Resort Paris (not including transportation to the park).

**Champagne at the Bar Vendôme, Le Ritz: €20**
**What you get:** A glass of Cuvée Ritz Brut in the lush garden of the Bar Vendôme, where a harpist plays in the afternoon and a pianist takes over later on.

**You could've bought:** Two sodas in a St-Germain café.

**Lunch at the Hôtel Bristol: €90**
**What you get:** A four-course meal at the famously

discreet Bristol, where the jet set saunters through the lobby bar. If this seems like a lot for a luxe lunch, consider that it's not difficult to spend more than €50 a head in a nearby bistro.

**You could've bought:** Lunch for two at the kitschy Nos Ancêtres Les Gauloises, a Gallic fantasyland on Ile St-Louis where tourists flock by the busload and foie gras is served in buckets.

**Nightcap at the Four Seasons' George V: €24**
**What you get:** A late-night cocktail (maybe a cognac?) at the George V's cozy bar. What would be an indefensible splurge at home is almost a must for rounding out a romantic evening.

**You could've bought:** A disposable camera at a kiosk by the Sacré-Coeur.

## RESTAURANTS IN THIS AREA

**BISTRO**
Au Petit Verdot du 17$^e$, $
Chez Savy, $$
Dominique Bouchet, $$$
Goupil le Bistro, $$
Le Petit Rétro, $$
La Table de Joël Robuchon, $$$$
La Table Lauriston, $$$
**BRASSERIE**
La Fermette Marbeuf 1900, $$$
**CARIBBEAN**
**FRENCH FUSION**
Hiramatsu, $$$$
Stella Maris, $$$–$$$$
**HAUTE FRENCH**
Alain Ducasse au Plaza Athénée, $$$$
Guy Savoy, $$$$
L'Astrance, $$$$
La Table du Lancaster, $$$$
Le Bristol, $$$$
Le Cinq, $$$$
Le Cristal Room, $$$$
Ledoyen, $$$$
Le Hide, $
Le Pré Catalan, $$$$
Pierre Gagnaire, $$$$
Senderens, $$$–$$$$
Taillevent, $$$$
**JAPANESE**
Kifune, $$$$
**MODERN FRENCH**
L'Arôme, $$$–$$$$
Spoon, Food & Wine, $$$$
**SEAFOOD**
L'Huîtrier, $$$
Rech, $$$

17

# TOUR EIFFEL AND LES INVALIDES
## 7E, 15E ARRONDISSEMENTS

Lively bistros and daring contemporary restaurants bring unexpected exuberance to the otherwise sedate streets around the Eiffel Tower and in the sprawling, residential 15$^e$.

Eerily quiet as it might sometimes seem, the 7$^e$ arrondissement has a food-loving population of locals and tourists who pack its best restaurants nightly. Since money is rarely an object in this area, you can find everything from top-notch contemporary restaurants—L'Arpège, 144 Petrossian, Gaya Rive Gauche, and L'Atelier de Joël Robuchon—to nostalgic bistros like Thoumieux and Le Café Constant, which appeal to aristocratic residents with comfort-food cravings. The 15$^e$ arrondissement is known for quaint eateries that provide great value for the money. Even its unlovely outer reaches are filled with warm bistros like L'Os à Moelle and Afaria. Explore the little-known area around Avenue Émile Zola to find the city's best Middle Eastern restaurants.

### JOYEUX JOËL

Tomato jelly topped with avocado purée? Thin-crusted mackerel tart? One of the best things about eating at **L'Atelier de Joël Robuchon** (✉ 5 rue Montalembert ☎ 01–42–22–56–56) is your position on the U-shaped bar, which encourages you to share opinions—or even a bite—of this cutting-edge fare with your neighbor. Creative small plates, like a flavor-packed little tower of roasted eggplant, zucchini, and tomato layered with buffalo mozzarella, or smoked foie gras and caramelized eel, make it clear that L'Atelier really is an artist's workshop.

## CULINARY TRENDSETTERS

### THE LEEK—C'EST CHIC

Vegetarianism was so uncommon in Paris that star chef Alain Passard caused a sensation when he declared a few years ago that he was bored with red meat and would be focusing on vegetables and fish. True to his word, Passard established a small farm outside Paris where he grows heirloom vegetables that are whizzed to his restaurant **L'Arpège** (✉ *84 rue Varenne* ☎ *01–45–51–47–33*) by high-speed train. Customers pay the price; a simple yet sensational beet dish costs €45. Though Paris is hardly a vegetarian paradise, Passard's initiative seems to have rubbed off on other chefs in the 7$^e$. **Le Violon d'Ingres** (✉ *135 rue St-Dominique* ☎ *01–45–55–15–05*) and **L'Atelier de Joël Robuchon** (✉ *5 rue Montalembert* ☎ *01–42–22–56–56*) both cater, with imagination, to vegetarians.

### A CONSTANT CONNECTION

During the 1980s Christian Constant trained a group of young chefs at the Hôtel Crillon who would go on to open their own trendsetting bistros, among them Yves Camdeborde (Le Comptoir), Christian Etchebest (Le Troquet), and Rodolphe Paquin (Le Repaire de Cartouche). Despite cherishing his mentor role, Constant still has a thriving career of his own. In 2006 he did away with the lobster dishes and wall-to-wall carpeting at his **Le Violon d'Ingres** (✉ *135 rue St-Dominique* ☎ *01–45–55–15–05*), transforming it into a happening bistro with a single €45 set menu that doesn't skimp on high-quality ingredients. He also runs three other successful restaurants in the same street: the no-reservations **Café Constant** (✉ *139 rue St-Dominique* ☎ *01–47–53–73–34*), specializing in fabulous, unfussy French food, the reliable fish restaurant **Les Fables de la Fontaine** (✉ *131 rue St-Dominique* ☎ *01–44–18–37–55*) with its desirable terrace, and **Les Cocottes** (✉ *135 rue St-Dominique [note this is the same building as Le Violon d'Ingres]* ☎ *01–45–50–10–31*), which serves nonstop all day, at a long counter.

## RESTAURANTS IN THIS AREA

**BASQUE**
L'Ami Jean, $$
**BISTRO**
Afaria, $
Au Bon Accueil, $$$
Chez les Anges, $$$$
D'Chez Eux, $$$
Jadis, $$–$$$
L'Agassin, $$
L'Os à Moelle, $$
Le 153 Grenelle, $$$
Le Café Constant, $
Thoumieux, $$–$$$
**BRASSERIE**
Thoumieux, $$–$$$
**HAUTE FRENCH**
Jules Verne, $$$$
L'Arpège, $$$$
Le Troquet, $$$–$$$$
Le Violon d'Ingres, $$$–$$$$
Les Saveurs de Flora, $$$$
**MODERN FRENCH**
L'Atelier de Joël Robuchon, $$$$
Les Cocottes de Christian Constant, $

17

# LOUVRE, LES HALLES, AND THE OPÉRA
## 1ER, 2E, 9E ARRONDISSEMENTS

All-night restaurants and hearty bistros continue to thrive around Paris's former wholesale market, creating a boisterous contrast with the elegant streets around the Louvre and Opéra.

Home to the city's wholesale food market until the 1960s, Les Halles is still the place to go for late-night onion soup or steak frites, washed back with gulps of cheap and tasty red wine. The streets grow more subdued around the Louvre and Palais Royal, where you can relax in elegant cafés, slurp oysters at a classic brasserie like Le Vaudeville or Gallopin, or treat yourself to a meal of a lifetime at Le Grand Véfour. Though Madeleine is a food hub, thanks to the gourmet emporiums Fauchon and Hédiard, good restaurants are scarce between here and Opéra. For a quick bite, wander over to Rue Ste-Anne for a cheap and satisfying bowl of Japanese noodles. Quick lunch options are plentiful in this area, since it's crawling with office workers who pack the organic café–juice bar Bioboa and the British-inspired sandwich shop Cojean.

### ESCAPE TO ASIA

If you can't face another slab of panfried foie gras, take a stroll down Rue Ste-Anne. The hub of the Japanese community in Paris is lined with noodle shops offering unparalleled value. At the ever-popular, cafeteria-style **Higuma** (⊠ *32 rue Ste-Anne* ☏ *01–47–03–38–59*), €10 will buy not just a sink-size bowl of ramen but a plate of six *gyoza* (pork-filled dumplings). For udon, squeeze into **Kunitoraya** (⊠ *39 rue Ste-Anne* ☏ *01–47–03–33–65*), where these thick wheat noodles are a specialty. Unique in Paris is **Zenzoo** (⊠ *2 rue Cherubini* ☏ *01–42–96–27–28*), which serves bubble tea made with tapioca, and dim sum–style Taiwanese food.

## INSIDE LES HALLES

Faced with the unsightly 1970s shopping mall known as the Forum des Halles, it's hard to conjure up the colors, sounds, and smells of the wholesale market that took place here until the late 1960s. Émile Zola dubbed Les Halles "the belly of Paris," and although the belly has shrunk significantly since the market moved to the suburb of Rungis in 1971, it's not completely empty. The cobblestone street market on Rue Montorgueil (open daily except Sunday afternoons and Monday) is still a feast for the senses. And some area restaurants continue to offer savory, market-inspired fare. Newcomers to Les Halles should tread carefully. A hub for 800,000 daily commuters, the area attracts chain restaurants and street hawkers. With all of the commotion, it's easy to overlook worthy shops and eateries.

### FOR SOMETHING SWEET
The scent of butter and almonds has been known to stop traffic outside the bakery and restaurant **Stohrer** (✉ *51 rue Montorgueil* ☎ *01–42–33–38–20*), founded in 1730. At the warehouse-style **Dehillerin** (✉ *18 rue Coquillière* ☎ *01–42–36–53–13*) nearby, cooks from around the world come searching for gleaming copper pots or silicone madeleine molds. Amateur and professional pastry chefs indulge their fantasies at **Detou** (✉ *58 rue Tiquetonne, 1er* ☎ *01–42–36–54–67*), which sells 3-kilogram hunks of Valrhona chocolate.

### FOR SOMETHING SAVORY
Hidden in an inconspicuous street, **Chez La Vieille** (✉ *1 rue Bailleul* ☎ *01–42–60–15–78*) serves uncompromising French country fare at lunchtime and on Thursday nights. If you're still not convinced that the spirit of Les Halles lives on, visit the brasserie **Au Pied de Cochon** (*see photo below,* ✉ *6 rue Coquillière* ☎ *01–40–13–77–00*) or the boisterous bistro **La Tour de Montlhéry-Chez Denise** (✉ *5 rue des Prouvaires, 1er* ☎ *01–42–36–21–82*) and enjoy restorative food in the wee hours, just like the market vendors used to do.

## RESTAURANTS IN THIS AREA

**BISTRO**
Au Gourmand, $$$
Aux Lyonnais, $$
Bistrot des Deux Théâtres, $$
Chartier, ¢–$
Chez Georges, $$$
Frenchie, $$
L'Ardoise, $$
La Bourse ou la Vie, $
Le Ch'ti Catalan, $
Les Fines Gueules, $$
Restaurant du Palais-Royal, $$$
Villa Victoria, $$
**BRASSERIE**
Au Pied de Cochon, $$
Le Grand Colbert, $$$
Le Vaudeville, $$$
**BRITISH**
Rose Bakery, $
**CAFE**
Café Marly, $$
La Ferme Opéra, ¢
**FRENCH FUSION**
Yam'Tcha, $$–$$$
**HAUTE FRENCH**
Le Grand Véfour, $$$$
**JAPANESE**
Higuma,
Zen, $
**MODERN FRENCH**
Drouant, $$$
Macéo, $$$
Pinxo, $$
Willi's Wine Bar, $–$$

17

# RESTAURANTS

*(In alphabetical order by arrondissement; use the coordinate (✛ 1:B2) at the end of each listing to locate a site on the corresponding map.)*

## 1 ER ARRONDISSEMENT

**$$$**    ✕ **Au Gourmand.** In a city where many restaurants seem to take custom-
BISTRO   ers for granted, it's always refreshing to come across someone who sounds delighted when you call to make a reservation. And the staff is just as eager to please once you're seated in the dining room, whose traditional theater-theme decor belies the kitchen's modern spirit. The cooking highlights vegetables from famed market gardener Joël Thié-bault: his multicolor tomatoes, for instance, might be displayed on a puff pastry base with the tiniest salad leaves, or a medley of sautéed spring vegetables accompany spoon-tender pork cheek. The best desserts are the least adventurous: try a variation on *pain perdu* (French toast), perhaps with figs, nuts, and almond ice cream. ⊠ *17 rue Molière, Louvre/Tuileries* ☎ *01–42–96–22–19* ⊕ *www.augourmand.fr* ▤ *MC, V* ◷ *Closed Sun., Mon., and 2 wks in mid-Aug. No lunch Sat.* Ⓜ *Palais Royal, Pyramides* ✛ *2:B6.*

**$$**    ✕ **Au Pied de Cochon.** One of the few remnants of Les Halles's rau-
BRASSERIE   cous all-night past is this brasserie, which has been open every day since 1946. Now run by the Frères Blanc group, it still draws both a French and a foreign crowd with round-the-clock hours and trademark traditional fare such as seafood platters, breaded pigs' trotters, beer-braised pork knuckle with sauerkraut, and cheese-crusted onion soup. It's perfect rib-sticking fare for a winter's day or to finish off a bar crawl. The dining room, with its white tablecloths and little piggy details, feels resolutely cheerful. ⊠ *6 rue Coquillière, Beaubourg/Les Halles* ☎ *01–40–13–77–00* ⊕ *www.pieddecochon.com* ▤ *AE, DC, MC, V* Ⓜ *Les Halles* ✛ *2:C6.*

**$$**    ✕ **Café Marly.** Run by the Costes brothers, this café overlooking the
CAFÉ   main courtyard of the Louvre and I.M. Pei's glass pyramid is one of the most stylish places in Paris to meet for a drink or a coffee, whether in the stunning jewel-toned dining rooms with their molded ceilings or on the long, sheltered terrace. Regular café service shuts down during meal hours, when fashion-conscious folks dig into Asian-inspired salads and pseudo-Italian pasta dishes. ⊠ *Cour Napoléon du Louvre, enter from Louvre courtyard, 93 rue de Rivoli, Louvre/Tuileries* ☎ *01–49–26–06– 60* ▤ *AE, DC, MC, V* Ⓜ *Palais-Royal* ✛ *4:B1.*

**¢**    ✕ **Higuma.** When it comes to steaming bowls of noodles, this no-frills
JAPANESE   dining room divided into three sections beats its many neighboring competitors. Behind the counter—an entertaining spot for solo diners—cooks toil over giant flames, tossing strips of meat and quick-fried vegetables, then ladling noodles and broth into giant bowls. A choice of *formules* (fixed price menu options) allows you to pair various soups and stir-fried noodle dishes with six delicious gyoza (Japanese dumplings), and the stir-fried dishes are excellent, too. Don't expect much in the way of service, but it's hard to find a more generous meal in Paris at this price. There is a more subdued annex (without the open kitchen) at

163 rue St-Honoré, near the Louvre. ⊠ *32 rue Ste-Anne, Opéra/Grands Boulevards* ☎ *01–47–03–38–59* ▭ *MC, V* Ⓜ *Pyramides* ✢ *2:B5.*

**$$** ✕ **L'Ardoise.** This minuscule storefront, decorated with enlargements of old sepia postcards of Paris, is a model of the kind of contemporary bistros making waves in Paris. Chef Pierre Jay's first-rate three-course dinner menu for €34 tempts with such original dishes as mushroom and foie gras ravioli with smoked duck; farmer's pork with porcini mushrooms; and red mullet with creole sauce (you can also order à la carte, but it's less of a bargain). Just as enticing are the desserts, such as a superb *feuillantine au citron*—caramelized pastry leaves filled with lemon cream and lemon slices—and a boozy baba au rhum. With friendly waiters and a small but well-chosen wine list, L'Ardoise would be perfect if it weren't often crowded and noisy. ⊠ *28 rue du Mont Thabor, Louvre/Tuileries* ☎ *01–42–96–28–18* ⊕ *www.lardoise-paris. com* ▭ *MC, V* ⊘ *Closed Mon., 1 wk in Jan. and late July–late Aug. No lunch Sun.* Ⓜ *Concorde* ✢ *1:H6.*

*BISTRO*
*Fodor's Choice*
★

**$$$$** ✕ **Le Grand Véfour.** Victor Hugo could stride in and still recognize this restaurant, which was in his day, as now, a contender for the title of most beautiful restaurant in Paris. Originally built in 1784, it has welcomed everyone from Napoléon to Colette to Jean Cocteau under its mirrored ceiling, and amid the early-19th-century glass paintings of goddesses and muses that create an air of restrained seduction. Foodies as well as the fashionable gather here to enjoy chef Guy Martin's unique blend of sophistication and rusticity, as seen in dishes such as frogs' legs with sorrel sauce, and oxtail *parmentier* (a kind of shepherd's pie) with truffles. There's an outstanding cheese trolley and for dessert, try the house specialty, *palet aux noisettes* (meringue cake with chocolate mousse, hazelnuts, and salted caramel ice cream). Prices are as extravagant as the decor, but there's an €88 lunch menu. ⊠ *17 rue de Beaujolais, Louvre/Tuileries* ☎ *01–42–96–56–27* ⊕ *www.grand-vefour. com* ♘ *Reservations essential* ▭ *AE, DC, MC, V* ⊘ *Closed weekends, Aug., and 1 wk in Apr. No dinner Fri.* Ⓜ *Palais-Royal* ✢ *2:B5.*

*HAUTE FRENCH*

**17**

**$$** ✕ **Les Fines Gueules.** Invest in good ingredients and most of the work is done: that's the principal of this wine bar/bistro that's developed a loyal following since opening in 2007. If you're not on first-name terms with food personalities like butcher Hugo Desnoyer, market gardener Joël Thiébault, and sausage-maker Thierry Daniel, you need only know that these are the crème de la crème of suppliers. Owner Arnaud Bradol wisely treats their products simply, often serving it raw alongside a salad or sautéed potatoes: the steak tartare with mesclun salad dressed in truffle oil is unparalleled. Beyond the tiny café-like area downstairs is a staircase leading to a cozy upstairs dining room, which is invariably lively. In keeping with the theme, wines are organic or natural and many are available by the glass. ⊠ *43 rue Croix des Petits Champs, Louvre/ Tuileries* ☎ *01–42–61–35–41* ♘ *Reservations essential* ▭ *AE, MC, V* Ⓜ *Palais Royal* ✢ *2:C6.*

*BISTRO*

**$$$** ✕ **Macéo.** Natural light streams through the restaurant, and a broad, curved staircase leads to a spacious upstairs salon. With reasonably priced set menus ranging from €32 (for the vegetarian menu) to €38 (for three courses at lunch or dinner), this is an ideal spot for a relaxed

*MODERN FRENCH*

meal after the Louvre. It's also a hit with vegetarians: chef Thierry Bourbonnais whips up a meatless set menu with two starter and two main course options—perhaps summer vegetables with mimolette cheese, followed by mini-pasta with wild mushrooms, herbs, and artichoke (though his efforts can be hit-or-miss). Meat lovers might sink their teeth into farmer's lamb with confit vegetables and mousseline potatoes. The wine list spotlights little-known producers alongside the big names—as befits this sister restaurant to Willi's Wine Bar. ☒ *15 rue des Petits-Champs, Louvre/Tuileries* ☎ *01–42–97–53–85* ⊕ *www. maceorestaurant.com* ▭ *MC, V* ☉ *Closed Sun. and 3 wks in Aug. No lunch Sat.* Ⓜ *Palais-Royal* ✛ *2:B5.*

**$$–$$$**
MODERN FRENCH
✕ **Pinxo.** The word *pinxo* (pronounced "peencho") means "to pinch" in Basque, and this is how the food in this fashionable hotel restaurant is meant to be eaten: often with your fingers, and off your dining companion's plate (each dish is served in three portions for sharing). Freed from the tyranny of the *entrée-plat-dessert* cycle, you can nibble your way through such minidishes as marinated herring with Granny Smith apple and horseradish, and squid cooked *à la plancha* (on a grill) with ginger and chili peppers. Alain Dutournier, who also runs the more formal Le Carré des Feuillants and the chic bistro Au Trou Gascon, drew on his southwestern roots to create this welcoming modern spot; granted, some dishes work better than others, but it's hard not to love a place that serves fried Camembert croquettes with celery sticks as a cheese course. ☒ *9 rue d'Alger, or through Hôtel Plaza Paris Vendôme, at 4 rue du Mont Thabor, Louvre/Tuileries* ☎ *01–40–20–72–00* ⊕ *www. pinxo.fr* ▭ *AE, MC, V* ☉ *Closed 2 wks in Aug.* ✛ *2:A6.*

**$$$**
BISTRO
✕ **Restaurant du Palais-Royal.** This stylish modern bistro decorated in jewel tones serves food to match its stunning location under the arcades of the Palais-Royal, facing its magnificent gardens. Sole, scallops, and risotto—including a dramatic black squid-ink and lobster version, or an all-green vegetarian one—are beautifully prepared, but juicy beef fillet with *pommes Pont Neuf* (thick-cut frites), and pedigreed chicken with potato puree are also popular with expense-account lunchers. Finish with an airy mille-feuille that changes with the seasons—berries in summer, chestnuts in winter—or a decadent *baba* doused with rum from Guadeloupe. Book in advance, especially in summer, when the terrace tables are hotly sought after. ☒ *Jardins du Palais-Royal, 110 Galerie Valois, Louvre/Tuileries* ☎ *01–40–20–00–27* ⊕ *www. restaurantdupalaisroyal.com* ◅ *Reservations essential* ▭ *AE, DC, MC, V* ☉ *Closed Sun.* Ⓜ *Palais-Royal* ✛ *2:B6.*

**¢–$$**
MODERN FRENCH
✕ **Willi's Wine Bar.** More a restaurant than a wine bar, this British-owned spot is a stylish haunt for Parisian and visiting gourmands who might stop in for a glass of wine at the oak bar or settle into the wood-beamed dining room. The selection of reinvented classic dishes changes daily and might include roast cod with artichokes and asparagus in spring, venison in wine sauce with roast pears and celery-root chips in fall, and mango candied with orange and served with vanilla cream in winter. Chef François Yon has been in the kitchen for 16 years, ensuring a consistency that isn't always reflected in the service. The restaurant is prix-fixe only but at the bar you order appetizers. The list of about

250 wines reflects co-owner Mark Williamson's passion for the Rhône Valley and Spanish sherries. ✉ *13 rue des Petits-Champs, Louvre/Tuileries* ☎ *01–42–61–05–09* ⊕ *www.williswinebar.com* ▭ *MC, V* ⊙ *Closed Sun. and 2 wks in Aug.* Ⓜ *Bourse* ⊹ *2:B5.*

$$–$$$

FRENCH FUSION

✕ **Yam'Tcha.** Adeline Grattard's little bistro has become so popular that tables are snapped up several weeks ahead, which is no surprise when you learn that she worked in the kitchens of L'Astrance before spending time in Hong Kong, where she picked up many of her techniques and ingredients. Inspired by Chinese cooking, many of her dishes rely on brilliant flavor combinations and very precise cooking. A signature dish is the roasted Challans duck (a cross between wild and domestic) with Sichuan-style eggplant: two elements that create magic together. Adeline's husband Chi Wa acts as a tea sommelier, introducing diners to earthy or grassy flavors that complement the food (Yam'Tcha means "to eat small steamed dishes while sipping tea"), though alcohol is also available. It's prix fixe only. ✉ *4 rue Sauval, Les Halles* ☎ *01–40–2–08–07* ⌷ *Reservations essential* ▭ *MC, V* ⊙ *Closed Mon. and Tues.* Ⓜ *Louvre-Rivoli or Les Halles* ⊹ *2:C6.*

$

JAPANESE

Fodor's Choice

★

✕ **Zen.** There's no shortage of Japanese restaurants in the area around the Louvre, but this one is a cut above much of the competition. The white-and-lime-green space feels refreshingly bright and modern, and you can perch at one of the curvy counters or settle in at a table. The menu has something for every taste, from warming ramen soups (part of a €9.90 lunch menu that includes five pork dumplings) to sushi and sashimi prepared with particular care. For a change, try the donburi, a bowl of rice topped with meat or fish, or Japanese curry with breaded pork or shrimp. A sign of the chef's pride in his food is that he offers cooking classes some Sundays (in French). ✉ *8 rue de l'Echelle, Louvre/Tuileries* ☎ *01–42–61–93–99* ⊕ *www.restaurant-zen.fr.cc* ▭ *MC, V* ⊙ *Closed 10 days in mid-Aug.* Ⓜ *Pyramides or Palais Royal* ⊹ *2:B6.*

17

# 2ᴱ ARRONDISSEMENT

$$

BISTRO

✕ **Aux Lyonnais.** With a passion for the old-fashioned bistro, Alain Ducasse resurrected this 1890s gem by appointing a terrific young chef to oversee the short, frequently changing, and reliably delicious menu of Lyonnais specialties. Dandelion salad with crisp potatoes, bacon, and a poached egg; watercress soup poured over parsleyed frogs' legs; and fluffy *quenelles de brochet* (pike-perch dumplings) show he is no bistro dilettante. The decor hews to tradition, too, with a zinc bar, an antique coffee machine, and original turn-of-the-20th-century woodwork. There's a limited-choice lunch menu for €26, but the temptation is strong to splurge on the more luxurious à la carte dishes. Tables turn relatively quickly, so despite the gorgeous setting this is not a spot for a romantic meal. ✉ *32 rue St-Marc, Opéra/Grands Boulevards* ☎ *01–42–96–65–04* ⊕ *www.auxlyonnais.com* ▭ *AE, MC, V* ⊙ *Closed Sun., Mon., and 2 wks in Aug. No lunch Sat.* Ⓜ *Bourse* ⊹ *2:B4.*

$$$

BISTRO

✕ **Chez Georges.** If you were to ask Parisian bankers, aristocrats, or antiques dealers to name their favorite bistro for a three-hour weekday lunch, many would choose Georges. The traditional fare, described in authentically indecipherable handwriting, is good—chicken-liver terrine, curly endive salad with bacon and a poached egg, steak with béarnaise—and the atmosphere is better, compensating for the steep prices. In the dining room, a white-clothed stretch of tables lines the mirrored walls and attentive waiters sweep efficiently up and down. Order one of the wines indicated in colored ink on the menu and you can drink as much or as little of it as you want (and be charged accordingly); there's also another wine list with grander bottles. ⊠ *1 rue du Mail, Louvre/ Tuileries* 🕾 *01–42–60–07–11* ⊟ *AE, MC, V* ☉ *Closed weekends, Aug., 1 wk at Christmas, and 1 wk in Feb.* Ⓜ *Sentier* ⊕ *2:C5.*

**$$$**
BISTRO
× **Derrière.** Mourad and Akim Mazouz, the pair behind the stylish Moroccan restaurant 404 and its neighboring bar Andy Wahloo (all three share the same address), have created another sensation with this apartment-restaurant in the back of a northern Marais courtyard. The door opens onto a living room with a Ping-Pong table, next to a long dining table surrounded by high-backed chairs. Nearby are the open kitchen and a room furnished with poufs and low sofas, where surreal videos (think naked circus) are projected onto the wall. A narrow stairway leads to more intimate rooms and, hidden at the end of the hallway behind a mirrored cupboard door, a fumoir. Furnished seemingly haphazardly with antiques and contemporary fixtures, Derrière surprises with the quality of its French comfort food: endive and celery root salad with apple and ham, beef cheeks bourguignon-style, and spit-roasted ham with wild mushrooms. The prices are not too shocking and the youthful crowd guarantees a good time, particularly if you book for the later sitting. ⊠ *69 rue de Gravilliers, Le Marais* 🕾 *01–44–61–91–95* ☙ *Reservations essential* ⊟ *AE, MC, V* ☉ *No lunch Mon.* Ⓜ *Arts et Métiers* ⊕ *2:E6.*

**$$$**
MODERN FRENCH
☾
× **Drouant.** Best known for the literary prizes awarded here since 1914, Drouant has shed its dusty image to become a forward-thinking restaurant. The man behind the transformation is Alsatian chef Antoine Westermann, who runs the hit bistro Mon Vieil Ami on Ile St-Louis. At Drouant the menu is more playful, revisiting the French hors d'oeuvres tradition with starters that come as a series of four plates. Diners can pick from themes such as French classics (like a deconstructed leek salad) or convincing minitakes on Thai and Moroccan dishes. Main courses similarly encourage grazing, with accompaniments in little cast-iron pots and white porcelain dishes. Even desserts take the form of several tasting plates. Pace yourself, since portions are generous and the cost of a meal quickly adds up. This is the place to bring adventurous young eaters, thanks to the €15 children's menu, and there's a special post-theater prix fixe (€40 for two courses, €52 for three) from 10:30 PM to midnight. The revamped dining room is bright and cheery, though the designer has gone slightly overboard with the custard-yellow paint and fabrics. ⊠ *16–18 pl. Gaillon, Opéra/Les Halles* 🕾 *01–42–65–15–16* ⊕ *www.drouant.com* ⊟ *AE, DC, MC, V* Ⓜ *Pyramides* ⊕ *2:B5.*

**$$**
BISTRO
Fodor's Choice
★
× **Frenchie.** Grégory Marchand worked in New York and with Jamie Oliver in London before opening this brick-and-stone-walled bistro on a pedestrian street near rue Montorgueil, which explains the tongue-in-cheek name. Though it hasn't had much press, word of mouth has quickly made it one of the most packed bistros in town. Marchand

owes a large part of his success to the great-value €35 three-course menu at dinner—boldly flavored dishes such as calamari gazpacho with squash blossoms, and melt-in-the-mouth braised lamb with roasted eggplant and spinach are excellent options. Desserts seem a tiny bit less stunning, but with good service and a laid-back atmosphere, this restaurant is headed for long-term success. It's prix fixe only. ⊠ *5 rue de Nil, Les Halles* ☎ *01–40–39–96–19* ⊕ *www.frenchie-restaurant.com* ⊟ *AE, MC, V* ⊘ *Closed Sun., Mon., 2 wks in Aug., 10 days at Christmas. No lunch Tues. or Sat.* Ⓜ *Sentier* ✛ *2:D5.*

$ ✕ **La Bourse ou La Vie.** If you've been dreaming of the perfect steak frites in Paris, head for this eccentric little place run by a former architect in BISTRO partnership with two loyal clients. The chairs in this cheery yellow-and-red dining room appear to have been salvaged from a theater, but they pair nicely with founder Patrice Tatard's theatrical streak. There's no questioning the threesome's enthusiasm for their new vocation when you taste the steak in its trademark creamy, peppercorn-studded sauce, accompanied by hand-cut french fries cooked to crisp perfection. Aside from steak dishes and a whole veal kidney with mustard sauce, there's little else on the menu. ⊠ *12 rue Vivienne, Louvre/Tuileries* ☎ *01–42–60–08–83* ⊟ *AE, MC, V* Ⓜ *Bourse* ✛ *2:C5.*

¢ ✕ **La Ferme Opéra.** If your arm aches from flagging down café waiters, CAFÉ take a break in this bright, friendly, self-service spot near the Louvre ⟳ that specializes in produce from the Ile-de-France region (around Paris). Inventive salads, sandwiches, and pastas are fresh and delicious, and for sweets there are wholesome fruit crumbles, tarts, and cheesecakes. Scones and freshly squeezed juices are served for breakfast every day, and there is brunch on Sunday from 11 AM to 4 PM. There's free Wi-Fi in the spacious, barnlike dining room. ⊠ *55 rue St-Roch, Opéra/Grands Boulevards* ☎ *01–40–20–12–12* ⊟ *MC, V* Ⓜ *Pyramides* ✛ *2:A5.*

$$$ ✕ **Le Grand Colbert.** One of the few independently owned brasseries left BRASSERIE in Paris, Le Grand Colbert, with its globe lamps and ceiling moldings, feels grand yet not overpolished. It attracts a wonderfully Parisian mix of elderly lone diners, business lunchers, tourists, and couples, all of whom come for the enormous seafood platters, duck foie gras with Sauternes jelly, and steak tartare, as well as a few southern-influenced dishes. Whet your appetite with one of the "unjustly forgotten" aperitifs, such as bitter Salers or sweet Lillet Blanc then expect neither a great bargain nor a life-changing meal: the kitchen does simple fare best. Finish with profiteroles (choux pastry filled with ice cream and smothered in hot chocolate sauce). Popular with a post-theater crowd since it's open until 3 AM (last orders before 1 AM), Le Grand Colbert is also

**17**

a pleasant destination between 3 and 6 PM for rich hot chocolate and cakes. ⊠ *4 rue Vivienne, Louvre/Tuileries* ☎ *01–42–86–87–88* ⊕ *www. legrandcolbert.fr* ⊟ *AE, DC, MC, V* Ⓜ *Bourse* ✛ *2:B5.*

**$$$**
BRASSERIE

✕ **Le Vaudeville.** Part of the Flo group of historic brasseries, Le Vaudeville tends to fill with journalists, bankers, and locals *d'un certain âge* who come for the good-value assortment of prix-fixe menus starting at €21, and highly professional service. Shellfish, house-smoked salmon, foie gras with raisins, slow-braised lamb, and desserts like the floating island topped with pralines are particularly enticing. Enjoy the graceful 1920s decor—almost the entire interior of this intimate dining room is done in real or faux marble—and lively dining until 1 AM daily. ⊠ *29 rue Vivienne, Opéra/Grands Boulevards* ☎ *01–40–20–04–62* ⊕ *www. vaudevilleparis.com* ⊟ *AE, DC, MC, V* Ⓜ *Bourse* ✛ *2:C5.*

## 3ᴱ ARRONDISSEMENT

¢
MODERN FRENCH

✕ **Breizh Café.** Eating a crêpe in Paris might seem a bit clichéd, until you venture into this modern offshoot of a crêperie in Cancale, Brittany. The pale-wood, almost Japanese-style decor is refreshing, but what really makes the difference are the ingredients—farmers' eggs, unpasteurized Gruyère, shiitake mushrooms, Valrhona chocolate, homemade caramel, and extraordinary butter from Breton dairy farmer Jean-Yves Bordier. You'll find all the classics among the galettes (buckwheat crêpes), but it's worth choosing something more adventurous like the *cancalaise* (traditionally smoked herring, potato, crème fraîche, and herring roe). You might also slurp a few Cancale oysters, a rarity in Paris, and try one of the 20 artisanal ciders on offer. The nonstop serving hours from noon to 11 PM can be a lifesaver if you're sightseeing in Le Marais. ⊠ *109 rue Vieille du Temple, Le Marais* ☎ *01–42–72–13–77* ⊕ *www. breizhcafe.com* ⌲ *Reservations essential* ⊟ *MC, V* ⊙ *Closed Mon., Tues., and Aug.* Ⓜ *St-Sébastien-Froissart* ✛ *4:F1.*

¢
CAFÉ

✕ **Cantine Merci.** Deep inside the city's latest concept store, whose proceeds go to charities for women in India and Madagascar, lurks the perfect spot for a quick and healthy lunch between bouts of shopping. The brief menu of soups, salads, risottos, and a daily hot dish is more than slightly reminiscent of Rose Bakery—salads such as fava beans with radish and lemon wedges or melon, cherry tomato, and arugula are bright, lively, and crunchy, and you can order a freshly squeezed juice or iced tea with fresh mint to wash it all down. Delicious homey desserts, might include cherry clafoutis or raspberry and pistachio crumble. ⊠ *111 bd. Beaumarchais, Le Marais* ☎ *01–42–77–78–92* ⊕ *www. merci-merci.com* ⊟ *MC, V* ⊙ *Closed Sun. No dinner* Ⓜ *St-Sébastien-Froissart* ✛ *2:G6.*

**$$**
NORTH AFRICAN
Fodor'sChoice
★

✕ **Chez Omar.** This is no longer the only trendy North African restaurant in town, but during fashion week you still might see top models with legs like gazelles touching up their lipstick in front of the vintage mirrors—though that doesn't stop them from digging into huge platters of couscous with grilled skewered lamb, spicy *merguez* sausage, lamb shank, or chicken, washed down with robust, fruity Algerian or Moroccan wine. Proprietor Omar Guerida speaks English and is famously friendly to all. The setting is that of a beautifully faded French bistro, complete with elbow-to-elbow seating, so be prepared to partake of your neighbors' conversations. ✉ *47 rue de Bretagne, République* ☎ *01–42–72–36–26* *Reservations not accepted* *No credit cards* *No lunch Sun.* Ⓜ *Temple, République* ✣ *2:F6.*

$ BISTRO ✕ **L'Ambassade d'Auvergne.** A rare Parisian bistro that refuses to change, the Ambassade claims one of the city's great restaurant characters: the maître d' Francis Panek, with his handlebar mustache and gravelly voice. Settle into the dining room in this ancient Marais house to try rich dishes from the Auvergne, a sparsely populated region in central France. Lighter dishes such as turbot with fennel are available, but it would be missing the point not to indulge in a heaping serving of lentils in goose fat with bacon or the Salers beef in red wine sauce with *aligot* (mashed potatoes with cheese). You might want to loosen your belt for the astonishingly dense chocolate mousse. The Auvergnat wines come with appetizing descriptions, but don't expect anything remarkable from this (justifiably) obscure wine region. ✉ *22 rue du Grenier St-Lazare, Le Marais* ☎ *01–42–72–31–22* *www.ambassade-auvergne.com* *AE, MC, V* Ⓜ *Rambuteau* ✣ *4:E1.*

$$–$$$ MODERN FRENCH ✕ **Le Georges.** One of those rooftop show-stopping venues so popular in Paris, Le Georges preens atop the Centre Georges Pompidou, accessed by its own entrance to the left of the main doors. The staff is as streamlined and angular as the furniture, and at night the terrace has distinct snob appeal. Come snappily dressed or you may be relegated to something resembling a dentist's waiting room. Part of the Costes brothers' empire, the establishment trots out fashionable dishes such as sesame-crusted tuna and coriander-spiced beef fillet flambéed with cognac. It's all considerably less dazzling than the view, except for the suitably decadent desserts (indulge in the Cracker's cheesecake with yogurt sorbet). ✉ *Centre Pompidou, 6th fl., 19 rue Rambuteau, Beaubourg/Les Halles* ☎ *01–44–78–47–99* *Reservations essential* *AE, DC, MC, V* *Closed Tues.* Ⓜ *Rambuteau* ✣ *4:E1.*

$$$–$$$$ MODERN FRENCH ✕ **Le Murano.** If you love Baccarat's Cristal Room, you'll simply adore the swank Murano Urban Resort's restaurant in the achingly chic northern Marais. There's nothing subtle about the dining room, whose ceiling drips with white tubes of various lengths, so dress to the nines and arrive with plenty of attitude (or brace yourself with three test tubes of alcohol at the bar). The chef puts the emphasis on the product with dishes like Breton sea bass with truffled asparagus ravioli. If you can survive the sneering once-over at the door, surprisingly good-humored dining-room staff add to the experience. ✉ *13 bd. du Temple, Le Marais* ☎ *01–42–71–20–00* *Reservations essential* *AE, DC, MC, V* Ⓜ *Filles du Calvaire* ✣ *2:G6.*

17

## 4E ARRONDISSEMENT

$$ BISTRO ✕ **Au Bourguignon du Marais.** The handsome, contemporary look of this Marais bistro and wine bar is the perfect backdrop for the good traditional fare and excellent Burgundies served by the glass and bottle. Unusual for Paris, food is served nonstop from noon to 11 PM, and you can drop by just for a glass of wine in the afternoon. Always on the

menu are Burgundian classics such as *jambon persillé* (ham in parsleyed aspic jelly), escargots, and *boeuf* b*ourguignon* (beef stewed in red wine). More up-to-date picks include a cèpe-mushroom velouté with poached oysters, though the fancier dishes are generally less successful. The terrace is hotly sought after in warmer months. ⌧ *52 rue François-Miron, Le Marais* ☏ *01–48–87–15–40* ▭ *AE, MC, V* ☽ *Closed Sun. and Mon., 3 wks in Aug., and 2 wks in Feb.* Ⓜ *St-Paul* ✛ *4:F2.*

**$$$–$$$$** ✕ **Benoît.** Without changing the vintage 1912 setting, superchef Alain
BISTRO   Ducasse and Thierry de la Brosse of L'Ami Louis have subtly improved
☙   the menu here, with dishes such as marinated salmon, frogs' legs in a morel-mushroom cream sauce, and an outstanding cassoulet served in a cast-iron pot. Alain Souliac, who previously worked for Ducasse in the French Basque country, keeps the kitchen running smoothly, and the waiters are charm incarnate. It's a splurge to be here, so go all the way and top off your meal with tarte tatin that's caramelized to the core or a rum-doused baba. ⌧ *20 rue St-Martin, Le Marais* ☏ *01–42–72–25–76* ⊕ *www.benoit-paris.com* ▭ *AE, MC, V* ☽ *Closed Aug. and 1 wk in Feb.* Ⓜ *Châtelet* ✛ *4:D1.*

**$$–$$$** ✕ **Cru.** It's hard to imagine a raw food restaurant in a city famous for
MODERN FRENCH   its slow-simmered dishes but, since opening in summer 2009, Cru has enjoyed instant success—the bucolic terrace in a cobbled Marais courtyard has something to do with this, as does the extensive menu's refusal to take the raw concept to extremes: a few cooked dishes are available, such as meat or fish prepared à la plancha and root vegetable "fries." If you decide to stick to the raw dishes, you won't be disappointed: the "green plate," variations on cucumber, displays the chef's well-judged creativity, while silky veal carpaccio with preserved lemon has a lively flavor. Most of the desserts depart from the raw theme, which is not necessarily a bad thing. The restaurant doubles as a wine bar, so there are plenty of interesting bottles to choose from. ⌧ *7 rue Charlemagne, Le Marais* ☏ *01–40–27–81–84* ⊕ *www.restaurantcru.fr* ▭ *MC, V* ☽ *Closed Mon. and 2 wks in Aug.* Ⓜ *St-Paul* ✛ *4:F3.*

**$$** ✕ **Bofinger.** One of the oldest, loveliest, and most popular brasseries in
BRASSERIE   Paris has generally improved in recent years, so stake out one of the
☙   tables dressed in crisp white linen under the glowing Art Nouveau glass cupola and enjoy classic brasserie fare (stick to trademark dishes such as the seafood choucroute, lamb fillet, or smoked haddock with spinach, as the seasonal specials can be hit-or-miss). Take advantage of the reduced French sales tax with prix-fixe menus for €22 (two courses) and €27.80 (three courses). ⌧ *5–7 rue de la Bastille, Bastille/Nation* ☏ *01–42–72–87–82* ▭ *AE, DC, MC, V* Ⓜ *Bastille* ✛ *4:H2.*

**$–$$** ✕ **Chez Julien.** This vintage bistro next to the Seine was easy to overlook
BISTRO   until the Costes Brothers—famous for stylish brasseries such as Café Marly and Georges—came along and worked their magic. With a terrace that now extends across the cobbled pedestrian street and a few modish touches in the turn-of-the-20th-century dining room that was once a boulangerie, Chez Julien is now one of Le Marais's hippest spots. The steep prices for rather ordinary food reflect this transformation, so you might like to skip the starters, linger over a thick steak with crisp shoestring fries or roast farmer's chicken with baby potatoes, and head

**CLOSE UP**

# Bars à Vins

*Bars à vins* (wine bars) are perfect for enjoying a glass (or bottle) of wine with a plate of cheese, charcuterie, or tasty hot meal—indeed, the food in many wine bars rivals that in very good bistros. Wine bar owners are often true wine enthusiasts, ready to dispense expert advice. With few exceptions, the focus is squarely on French wines, but there is plenty of terroir to explore. Hours vary, so check ahead if your heart is set on a particular place; many close around 10 PM.

**Au Sauvignon**. Edge your way in among the lively tipplers at this homey spot with a terrace. The simple menu makes ordering the right glass a breeze. ⊠ *80 rue des Sts-Pères, 7e, St-Germain-des-Prés* ☎ *01–45–48–49–02* Ⓜ *Sèvres-Babylone* ✛ *4:A3.*

**Bu Bar**. In summer look for the hip crowd spilling out the front of this signless wine bar in the Marais. It's named for Jean-Paul, the bartender (*bubar* or *barbu* is French slang for "bearded"). The wine menu—with many selections available by the glass—features French wines and small-batch vintages from South Africa, Chile, and Argentina. ⊠ *3 rue des Tournelles, 4e, Le Marais* ☎ *01–40–29–97–72* Ⓜ *Bastille* ✛ *4:G2.*

**Jacques Mélac**. This wine bar is named after the jolly owner who harvests grapes from the vine outside and bottles his own wines. Cheese is hacked from a giant hunk of Cantal, and the hot dish of the day is always tasty. ⊠ *42 rue Léon-Frot, 11e, Bastille/Nation* ☎ *01–43–70–59–27* Ⓜ *Charonne* ✛ *4:H2.*

**La Robe et le Palais**. Come here for the more than 120 French wines served *au compteur* (according to the amount consumed), and the selection of bistro-style food. ⊠ *13 rue des Lavandières-Ste-Opportune, 1er, Beaubourg/Les Halles* ☎ *01–45–08–07–41* Ⓜ *Châtelet Les Halles* ✛ *4:D1.*

**Le Baron Bouge**. Formerly Le Baron Rouge, this charming, unfancy wine bar near the Place d'Aligre market is a throwback to another era, with a few tables, and barrels along the walls. A fun time to come is Sunday morning (yes, morning) when it's packed with locas who have just been to the market. ⊠ *1 rue Théophile Roussel, 12e, Bastille/Nation* ☎ *01–43–43–14–32* Ⓜ *Ledru-Rollin* ✛ *4:H3.*

**Les Papilles**. Part wineshop and épicerie, part restaurant, Les Papilles has a winning formula—pick any bottle off the shelf and pay a €6 corkage fee to drink it with your meal. The southwestern-inspired bistro fare is delicious. ⊠ *30 rue Gay-Lussac, 5e, Quartier Latin* ☎ *01–43–25–20–79* Ⓜ *Cluny–La Sorbonne* ✛ *4:C5.*

**Racines**. The food is simple and hearty and the wines are all natural—sulfite-free, hand-harvested, and unfiltered—at this café in the atmospheric Passage des Panoramas. It's packed at mealtimes, so be sure to reserve. ⊠ *8 passage des Panoramas, 2e, Opéra/Grands Boulevards* ☎ *01–40–13–06–41* Ⓜ *Grands Boulevards, La Bourse* ✛ *2:C4.*

**Le Rouge Gorge**. This sophisticated Marais wine bar attracts discriminating locals who come for unusual wines by the glass and the hearty food with a Moroccan touch. ⊠ *8 rue St-Paul, 4e, Le Marais* ☎ *01–48–04–75–89* Ⓜ *La Bourse* ✛ *4:G3.*

**17**

into Le Marais for ice cream afterward. ⊠ *1 rue du Pont Louis-Philippe, Le Marais* ☎ *01–42–78–31–64* ⌕ *Reservations essential* ▤ *AE, MC, V* Ⓜ *Pont Marie* ✛ *4:E2.*

**$$**
MIDDLE EASTERN
✕**Chez Marianne.** You'll know you've found Marianne's when you see the line of people reading the bits of wisdom and poetry painted across the windows. This restaurant-deli serves excellent Middle Eastern and Jewish specialties like hummus, fried eggplant, and soul-warming chopped liver, which you can match with one of the affordable wines. The sampler platter lets you try four, five, or six items—even the smallest plate is a feast. Falafel sandwiches are served in the restaurant only on weekdays at lunch, though you can get them anytime at the takeout window. ⊠ *2 rue des Hospitalières-St-Gervais, Le Marais* ☎ *01–42–72–18–86* ▤ *MC, V* Ⓜ *St-Paul* ✛ *4:F2.*

**¢–$**
MIDDLE EASTERN
☺
✕**L'As du Fallafel.** Look no further than the fantastic falafel stands on the pedestrian Rue de Rosiers for some of the cheapest and tastiest meals in Paris. L'As (the Ace) is widely considered the best of the bunch, which accounts for the lunchtime line that extends into the street, despite the recent expansion of the dining room from 70 to 115 seats. A falafel sandwich costs €5 to go, €7 in the dining room, and comes heaped with grilled eggplant, cabbage, hummus, tahini, and hot sauce. The *shawarma* (grilled, skewered meat) sandwich, made with chicken or lamb, is also one of the finest in town. Though takeout is popular, it can be more fun (and not as messy) to eat off a plastic plate in one of the two frenzied dining rooms. Fresh lemonade is the falafel's best match. ⊠ *34 rue des Rosiers, Le Marais* ☎ *01–48–87–63–60* ▤ *MC, V* ☺ *Closed Sat. No dinner Fri.* Ⓜ *St-Paul* ✛ *4:F2.*

**$$**
MODERN FRENCH
Fodor'sChoice
★
✕**Mon Vieil Ami.** "Modern Alsatian" might sound like an oxymoron, but once you've tasted the food here, you'll understand. The updated medieval dining room—stone walls and dark-wood tables—provides a stylish milieu for the inventive cooking orchestrated by star Alsatian chef Antoine Westermann, which showcases heirloom vegetables (such as yellow carrots and pink-and-white beets) from star producer Joël Thiébault. Pâté *en croûte* (wrapped in pastry) with a knob of foie gras is hard to resist among the starters. Among the mains, red mullet might come in a bouillabaisse sauce with sautéed baby artichokes, and the shoulder of lamb with white beans, preserved lemon, and cilantro has become a classic. This is not necessarily the place for a romantic dinner since seating is a little tight, but the quality of the food never falters. Call during opening hours (11:30–2:30 and 7–11) to book, since they don't answer the phone the rest of the time. ⊠ *69 rue St-Louis-en-l'Ile, Ile St-Louis* ☎ *01–40–46–01–35* ⊕ *www.mon-vieill-ami.com* ▤ *AE, DC, MC, V* ☺ *Closed Mon., Tues., 3 wks in Jan., and 3 wks in Aug.* Ⓜ *Pont Marie* ✛ *4:E3.*

**$$**
BISTRO
✕**Restaurant le Gaigne.** Mickaël Gaignon worked with Pierre Gagnaire and Frédéric Anton before opening this pocket-size plum-and-ivory bistro in a quiet Marais street. His cooking shows the creativity of the first master chef and the attention to ingredients of the second: each dish highlights a single product, which is often organic. An example is *l'oeuf bio,* three soft-boiled organic eggs filled with creamed vegetables and served with toast fingers for dipping. Best value is the €39 tasting menu

(€54 with matching wines), which brings you five inventive courses; there's also a weekday lunch menu for €16 (two courses) or €22 (three courses). ✉ *12 rue Pecquay, Le Marais* ☎ *01–44–59–86–72* ⊕ *www. restaurantlegaigne.fr* ⌕ *Reservations essential* ▭ *AE, MC, V* ⊘ *Closed Sun., Mon., and Aug.* Ⓜ *Rambuteau* ✥ *4:F1.*

## 5ᴱ ARRONDISSEMENT

**\$\$–\$\$\$** ╳**Chez René.** After having been run by the same family for 50 years
BISTRO Chez René changed owners in 2007, though the new team has wisely preserved the bistro's traditional spirit, while brightening the decor with original vintage posters and adding chic touches such as valet parking and a heated terrace. The menu still consists mainly of Lyonnais classics, but you'll now find some of these grouped into color-theme menus such as "red" (beet salad, coq au vin, and Quincy wine) or "yellow" (Swiss chard gratin, pike-perch in beurre blanc sauce with steamed potatoes, and Mâcon wine). The best sign of the new regime's success is that the old regulars keep coming back, including the former owners, who live upstairs. ✉ *14 bd. St-Germain, Quartier Latin* ☎ *01–43–54–30–23* ▭ *AE, MC, V* ⊘ *Closed Sun., Mon., Christmas wk, and Aug. No lunch Sat.* Ⓜ *Maubert-Mutualité* ✥ *4:E4.*

**\$\$\$** ╳**Fogòn St-Julien.** The most ambitious Spanish restaurant in Paris occu-
SPANISH pies an airy Seine-side space, avoiding tapas-bar clichés. The seasonal all-tapas menu, at €49 per person, is the most creative choice, but that would mean missing out on the seven different takes on paella that are available daily: perhaps saffron with seafood (which could be a bit more generous), inky squid, vegetable, or Valencia-style with rabbit, chicken, and vegetables. Finish up with custardy crème Catalan and a glass of muscatel. ✉ *45 quai des Grands-Augustins, Quartier Latin* ☎ *01–43–54–31–33* ⊕ *www.fogon.fr* ⌕ *Reservations essential* ▭ *MC, V* ⊘ *Closed Mon., 2 wks in Aug./Sept., and 1 wk in Jan. No lunch Tues.–Fri.* Ⓜ *St-Michel* ✥ *4:C2.*

**\$\$** ╳**Itinéraires.** Having paid his dues in the tiny kitchen of Le Temps au
BISTRO Temps near the Bastille, young Lyonnais chef Sylvain Sendra is now happily ensconced in the spacious former premises of the noted Chez Toutoune. The once-faded surroundings have been revitalized and the taupe walls, a long *table d'hôtes* (shared table), and a bar for solo meals or tapas-style snacks are all new. Sendra's cooking, meanwhile, is as inspired as ever. Menu highlights include green asparagus with foie gras sauce and morsels of dried tuna, duck breast with beet and raspberry, and a deconstructed lemon tart with a touch of celery. Not everything works perfectly and there is the occasional glaring flaw, but €36 for three courses seems a reasonable price to pay for this level of creativity and comfort. ✉ *5 rue de Pontoise, Quartier Latin* ☎ *01–46–33–60–11* ⌕ *Reservations essential* ▭ *MC, V* ⊘ *Closed Sun., Mon., Aug., and 1 wk at Christmas* Ⓜ *Maubert-Mutualité* ✥ *4:E4.*

**\$\$\$\$** ╳**La Tour d'Argent.** La Tour d'Argent has had a rocky time in recent
HAUTE FRENCH years with the loss of a Michelin star, the death of owner Claude Ter-rail, but chef Stéphane Haissant has found his footing, and there's no denying the splendor of its setting overlooking the Seine. If you don't want to splash out on dinner, treat yourself to the three-course lunch

17

menu for a reduced price of €65; this entitles you to succulent slices of one of the restaurant's numbered ducks (the great duck slaughter began in 1919 and is now well past the millionth mallard, as your numbered certificate will attest). Don't be too daunted by the vast wine list—with the aid of the sommelier you can splurge a little (about €80) and perhaps taste a rare vintage Burgundy from the extraordinary cellars, which survived World War II. ⊠ *15–17 quai de la Tournelle, Quartier Latin* ☎ *01–43–54–23–31* ⊕ *www.latourdargent.com* ⌲ *Reservations essential. Jacket and tie* ⊟ *AE, DC, MC, V* ☉ *Closed Sun., Mon., and Aug.* Ⓜ *Cardinal Lemoine* ✛ *4:E4.*

**$$**
BRASSERIE
☺

✕ **Le Balzar.** Regulars grumble about the uneven cooking at Le Balzar, but they continue to come back because they can't resist the waiters' wry humor and the dining room's amazing people-watching possibilities (you can also drop in for a drink on the terrace). The restaurant attracts politicians, writers, tourists, and local eccentrics—and remains one of the city's classic brasseries: the perfect stop before or after a Woody Allen film in a local art-house cinema. Don't expect miracles from the kitchen, but stick to evergreens like snails in garlic butter, onion soup, panfried veal liver with sautéed potatoes, and baba au rhum for dessert. ⊠ *49 rue des Ecoles, Quartier Latin* ☎ *01–43–54–13–67* ⊕ *www.brasseriebalzar.com* ⌲ *Reservations essential* ⊟ *AE, DC, MC, V* Ⓜ *Cluny–La Sorbonne* ✛ *4:C4.*

**$–$$**
BISTRO

✕ **Le Buisson Ardent.** This charming Quartier Latin bistro with woodwork and murals dating from 1925 is always packed and boisterous. A glance at chef Stéphane Mauduit's €30 set menu—a bargain €18 at lunch for three courses—makes it easy to understand why. Dishes such as chestnut soup with spice bread, squid with chorizo and creamy quinoa, and quince Tatin (upside-down tart) with mascarpone and pink pralines put a fresh twist on French classics, and service is reliably courteous. Bread is made on the premises, and if you don't finish your bottle of wine, you can take it with you to savor the last drops. ⊠ *25 rue Jussieu, Quartier Latin* ☎ *01–43–54–93–02* ⊕ *www.lebuissonardent.fr* ⌲ *Reservations essential* ⊟ *MC, V* ☉ *Closed Sun. and Aug. No lunch Sat.* Ⓜ *Jussieu* ✛ *4:E4.*

**$–$$**
MODERN FRENCH

✕ **Le Pré Verre.** Chef Philippe Delacourcelle knows his cassia bark from his cinnamon thanks to a long stint in Asia. He opened this lively bistro with its purple-gray walls and photos of jazz musicians to showcase his unique culinary style, rejuvenating archetypal French dishes with Asian and Mediterranean spices. So popular has it proved, especially with Japanese visitors, that the restaurant opened a branch in Tokyo in late 2007. His bargain prix-fixe menus (€13.50 at lunch for a main dish, glass of wine, and coffee; €28.50 for three courses at dinner) change constantly, but his trademark spiced suckling pig with crisp cabbage is always a winner, as is his rhubarb compote with gingered white-chocolate mousse. Ask for advice in selecting wine from a list that highlights small producers. ⊠ *8 rue Thénard, Quartier Latin* ☏ *01–43–54–59–47* ⊕ *www.lepreverre.com* ⌕ *Reservations essential* ⊟ *MC, V* ☺ *Closed Sun. and Mon.* Ⓜ *Maubert-Mutualité* ✛ *4:D4.*

**$$** ✕ **Ribouldingue.** Find offal off-putting? Off-cuts take pride of place on

BISTRO the €27 prix fixe (there's no à la carte), but don't let that stop you from trying this bistro near the ancient St-Julien-le-Pauvre church. You can avoid odd animal bits completely, if you must, and still have an excellent meal—opt for dishes like marinated salmon or veal rib with fingerling potatoes—or go out on a limb with the *tétine de vache* (thin breaded and fried slices of cow's udder) and *groin de cochon* (the tip of a pig's snout). This adventurous menu is the brainchild of Nadège Varigny, daughter of a Lyonnais butcher (*quel surpise*). She runs the front of the house while chef Caroline Moncel turns out the impeccable food—veal kidney with potato gratin is a house classic and there are always three fish dishes. Don't miss the unusual desserts, like tangy ewe's-milk ice cream. ⊠ *10 rue St-Julien-le-Pauvre, Quartier Latin* ☏ *01–46–33–98–80* ⊟ *MC, V* ☺ *Closed Sun., Mon., 1 wk in spring, 3 wks in Aug., and 1 wk in winter* Ⓜ *St-Michel* ✛ *4:D3.*

## 6ᴱ ARRONDISSEMENT

**$$** ✕ **Alcazar.** When Sir Terence Conran opened this impressive 300-seat

BRASSERIE restaurant, he promised to reinvent the Parisian brasserie, and he's come close. Alcazar's mezzanine bar is famed for its DJ, and with its slick decor and skylight roof, it feels more like London than the Rive Gauche. The kitchen may have started out rather uncertain of what it wanted to accomplish, but the food is now resolutely French with the occasional Mediterranean touch, plus the house classic fish-and-chips. Prices are reasonable: a three-course lunch menu is €33 including a glass of wine and coffee; a dinner menu is €40. The chef seems to have found his groove with dishes such as salmon-and-ginger tataki and veal braised with morels. Lest you forget this is Conran land, there are also very good fish-and-chips and Irish coffee. For dessert, it's hard to pass up the profiteroles, mille-feuille, and baba au rhum. Sunday brunch is popular, and the restaurant has introduced "lyric nights" on Monday with a set menu. ⊠ *62 rue Mazarine* ☏ *01–53–10–19–99* ⊕ *www.alcazar.fr* ⊟ *AE, DC, MC, V* Ⓜ *Odéon* ✛ *4:B2.*

**$–$$** ✕ **Boucherie Roulière.** If it's steak you're craving, put your faith in Jean-

BISTRO Luc Roulière, a fifth-generation butcher who opened this long, narrow bistro near St-Sulpice church in 2006. Partner Franck Pinturier is from the Auvergne region, which is also known for its melt-in-the-mouth meat, so start with truffle-scented ravioli or a rich marrow bone before indulging in a generous slab of Limousin or Salers beef, excellent veal kidney, or, for the meat-shy, perhaps lobster or sea bass. The minimalist cream-and-brown dining room with checkerboard floor tiles and black-and-white photos on the walls keeps the focus on the food, and waiters are of the professional Parisian breed. ⊠ *24 rue des Canettes, St-Germain-des-Prés* ☏ *01–43–26–25–70* ⊟ *MC, V* ☺ *Closed Mon. and Aug.* Ⓜ *Mabillon* ✛ *4:B3.*

17

**$$** ✕**Café de Flore.** Picasso, Chagall, Sartre, and de Beauvoir, attracted by
CAFÉ  the luxury of a heated café, worked and wrote here in the early 20th
century. Today you'll find more tourists than intellectuals, and prices
are hardly aimed at struggling artists, but the outdoor terrace is popu-
lar with Parisians. The food is fine, but nothing special. ✉ *172 bd. St-
Germain, St-Germain-des-Prés* ☎ *01–45–48–55–26* ⊕ *www.cafedeflore.
com* ⊟ *AE, DC, MC, V* Ⓜ *St-Germain-des-Prés* ✛ *4:2A.*

**$$** ✕**Chez Maître Paul.** This calm and comfortable, if slightly shabby, spot
BISTRO  is a great place to discover the little-known cooking of the Jura and
Franche-Comté regions of eastern France. Though sturdy, this cuisine
appeals to modern palates, as you'll discover with the *montbéliard,* a
smoked sausage served with potato salad, or the veal sweetbreads with
morel mushrooms. The free-range chicken dishes are also good choices,
either in a sauce of *vin jaune*—a dry wine from the region that resembles
sherry—or baked in cream and cheese. The walnut meringue is sinfully wonderful, and there's a regional selection of Arbois wines. Best
value is the €37 prix fixe, which brings three courses plus a half-liter
of wine per person. ✉ *12 rue Monsieur-le-Prince, St-Germain-des-Prés*
☎ *01–43–54–74–59* ⊟ *AE, DC, MC, V* ☯ *Closed Sun. and 2 wks in
Aug.* Ⓜ *Odéon* ✛ *4:C3.*

**$** ✕**Coco & Co.** The name of this bistro just off Rue de Rennes is a play
BISTRO  on the words *cocorico* (the call of the rooster) and *cocotte* (a cast-iron
pot in which food is cooked and served). If this seems puzzling, you
need only enter the tiny wood-beamed dining room—there's more space
upstairs—to understand the theme: Coco & Co. is devoted to the egg in
all its forms, and whether you like yours baked with smoked salmon,
whisked into an omelet with truffle shavings, or beaten into fluffy pan-
cakes, there will be something for you on the blackboard menu. It's
perfect for a late breakfast or light lunch on weekdays (it opens at
11:30 AM), though rather mobbed for weekend brunch (noon–4:30 PM).
✉ *11 rue Bernard Palissy, St-Germain-des-Prés* ☎ *01–45–44–02–52*
⊕ *www.cocoandco.fr* ⊟ *MC, V* ☯ *Closed Mon. and Tues. No dinner
weekends* Ⓜ *St-Germain-des-Prés* ✛ *4:A3.*

**$$$$** ✕**Hélène Darroze.** The most celebrated female chef in Paris is now cook-
HAUTE FRENCH  ing at the Connaught in London, but her St-Germain dining room
was revamped in 2008 to create an even more exclusive setting for
her sophisticated take on southwestern French food. Darroze's intrigu-
ingly modern touch comes through in such dishes as a sublime duck
foie gras confit served with an exotic-fruit chutney or a blowout of
roast wild duck stuffed with foie gras and truffles. If the food, at its
best, lives up to the very high prices, the service sometimes struggles
to reach the same level. For a more affordable taste, try the relatively
casual Salon d'Hélène downstairs, which serves dishes starting at €6.50
a plate. ✉ *4 rue d'Assas, St-Germain-des-Prés* ☎ *01–42–22–00–11*
⊕ *www.helenedarroze.com* ✑ *Reservations essential* ⊟ *AE, DC, MC,
V* ☯ *Closed Sun. and Mon.* Ⓜ *Sèvres-Babylone* ✛ *4:A4.*

**$$–$$$** ✕**Huîtrerie Régis.** When the oysters are this fresh, who needs anything
SEAFOOD  else? That's the philosophy of this bright 14-seat restaurant with crisp
white tablecloths and convenient hours (11 AM–midnight), popular with
the area's glitterati. If you find yourself puzzling over the relative merits

of *fines de claires, spéciales,* and *pousses en claires,* you can always go with the €22.50 prix fixe that includes a glass of Muscadet, 12 No. 3 (medium) oysters, and coffee—or ask the knowledgeable waiters for their advice. You can supplement this simplest of meals with shrimp and perhaps a slice of freshly made fruit pie. Because of the lack of space, there's a minimum order of a dozen oysters per person. ✉ *3 rue de Montfaucon, St-Germain-des-Prés* ☎ *01–44–41–10–07* ⊕ *www. huitrerieregis.com* ⊟ *MC, V* ⊘ *Closed Mon. and mid-July to end of Sept.* Ⓜ *Mabillon* ✛ *4:B3.*

**$$$**
**BISTRO**
**Fodor's Choice**
★

✕**Josephine Chez Dumonet.** Theater types, politicos, and well-padded locals fill the moleskin banquettes of this venerable bistro, where the frosted-glass lamps and amber walls put everyone in a good light. Unlike most bistros, Josephine caters to the indecisive, since generous half portions allow you to graze your way through the temptingly retro menu. Try the excellent boeuf bourguignon, roasted saddle of lamb with artichokes, top-notch steak tartare prepared table-side, or anything with truffles in season; game is also a specialty in fall and winter. For dessert, choose between a mille-feuille big enough to serve three and a Grand Marnier soufflé that simply refuses to sink, even with prodding. The wine list, like the food, is outstanding if expensive. ✉ *117 rue du Cherche-Midi, St-Germain-des-Prés* ☎ *01–45–48–52–40* ⌲ *Reservations essential* ⊟ *AE, MC, V* ⊘ *Closed weekends* Ⓜ *Duroc* ✛ *3:G5.*

**$**
**BISTRO**
Ⓒ
**Fodor's Choice**
★

✕**L'Epigramme.** Great bistro food is not so hard to find in Paris, but only rarely does it come in a comfortable setting. At L'Epigramme, the striped orange-and-yellow chairs are softly padded, there's space between you and your neighbors, and a big glass pane lets in plenty of light from the courtyard. Service from Stéphane Marcouzzi's staff is also worthy of a much more expensive restaurant; he was maître d'hôtel at Le Cap Vernet before opening this bistro with Aymeric Kräml. The chef has an almost magical touch with meat: try his stuffed suckling pig with turnip choucroute, or seared slices of pink lamb with root vegetables in a glossy reduced sauce. In winter, the eleborate game dish *lièvre à la royale* (hare stuffed with goose or duck liver and cooked in wine) sometimes makes an appearance. Desserts are not quite as inspired, so try to take a peek at the plates coming out of the kitchen before making your choice. ✉ *9 rue de l'Eperon, St-Germain-des-Prés* ☎ *01–44–41–00–09* ⌲ *Reservations essential* ⊟ *AE, MC, V* ⊘ *Closed Sun., Mon., 3 wks in Aug., and 1 wk at Christmas* Ⓜ *Odéon* ✛ *4:C3.*

**$$**
**BISTRO**

✕**La Bastide Odéon.** The open kitchen of this popular Provençal bistro near the Jardin du Luxembourg allows you to watch the cooks at work. Chef Gilles Ajuelos demonstrates an expert, loving, and creative hand with Mediterranean cuisine—expect unusual dishes such as aged Spanish ham with a grilled pepper pipérade and artichokes; mushroom-and-pea risotto with arugula; and duck breast with orange sauce, date puree, polenta, and wild asparagus. To finish things off, try the pear poached with lemon and saffron, served with a fromage blanc sorbet. Unusual for Paris, an entire section of the menu is devoted to vegetarian dishes. (Ajuelos now also runs the traditional French bistro **La Marlotte** at [✉ *55 rue du Cherche-Midi* ☎ *01–45–48–86–79*].) ✉ *7 rue Corneille, St-Germain-des-Prés* ☎ *01–43–26–03–65* ⊕ *www.bastide-odeon.com*

**17**

◻ *AE, MC, V* ☺ *Closed Sun., Mon., and 3 wks in Aug.* Ⓜ *Odéon; RER: Luxembourg* ✛ *4:C4.*

**$$**
BISTRO
Fodor'sChoice
★

✕ **La Ferrandaise.** Portraits of cows adorn the stone walls of this bistro near the Luxembourg gardens, hinting at the kitchen's penchant for meaty cooking (Ferrandaise is a breed of cattle). Still, there's something for every taste on the market-inspired menu, which always lists three meat and three fish mains. Dill-marinated salmon with sweet mustard sauce is a typical starter, and a thick, milk-fed veal chop might come with a squash pancake and spinach. The dining room buzzes with locals who appreciate the good-value €32 prix fixe and the brilliant bento-box-style €15 lunch menu, in which three courses are served all at once. ◻ *8 rue de Vaugirard, St-Germain-des-Prés* ☎ *01–43–26–36–36* ⊕ *www.laferrandaise.com* ◻ *AE, MC, V* ☺ *Closed Sun. and 3 wks in Aug. No lunch Sat.* Ⓜ *Odéon, RER: Luxembourg* ✛ *4:C4.*

**$$$–$$$$**
BISTRO

✕ **Lapérouse.** Émile Zola, George Sand, and Victor Hugo were regulars here, and the restaurant's mirrors still bear diamond scratches from the days when mistresses didn't take jewels at face value. It's hard not to fall in love with this 17th-century Seine-side town house whose warren of intimate, woodwork-graced salons breathes history. A new chef, Jean-Sébastien Pouch, recently took over the kitchen; his cuisine seeks a balance between traditional and modern, often drawing on Mediterranean inspirations. For a truly intimate meal, reserve one of the legendary private *salons* where anything can happen (and probably has). You can also sample the restaurant's magic at lunch, when a bargain prix-fixe menu is served for €35–€45 in both the main dining room and the private salons. ◻ *51 quai des Grands Augustins, Quartier Latin* ☎ *01–43–26–68–04* ⊕ *www.laperouse.fr* ⌲ *Reservations essential* ◻ *AE, DC, MC, V* ☺ *Closed Sun. and Aug. No lunch Sat.* Ⓜ *St-Michel* ✛ *4:C2.*

**$$$–$$$$**
MODERN FRENCH

✕ **Le 21.** Paul Minchelli has always known that the best way to treat squeaky fresh seafood is to keep it as simple as possible. At his new, bistrolike space decorated in black and white, his cooking has become rather less austere, with dishes such as *gambas* (shrimp) with pasta and sweet tomato sauce (some might liken it to ketchup), or marinated herrings and mackerel. Popular with local gallery owners rather than tourists, this is a discreet spot for an intimate and rather expensive meal among the "gauche caviar" (well-off intellectuals) of St-Germain. Service is friendly and professional, though not always particularly quick. ◻ *21 rue Mazarine, St-Germain-des-Prés* ☎ *01–46–33–76–90* ◻ *MC, V* ☺ *Closed Sun., Mon., Aug., 2 wks at Christmas, and 1 wk at Easter* Ⓜ *Odéon* ✛ *4:B2.*

**$$**
BRASSERIE

✕ **Le Bouillon Racine.** Originally a *bouillon*—one of the Parisian soup kitchens popular at the turn of the 20th century—this two-story restaurant is now a lushly renovated Belle Époque haven with a casual setting downstairs and a lavish upstairs room. The menu changes seasonally: lamb knuckle with licorice, wild boar *parmentier* (like a shepherd's pie, with mashed potatoes on top and meat underneath), and roast suckling pig are warming winter dishes. For dessert, dig into crème brûlée with maple syrup or the *café liégois* (coffee-flavored custard topped with whipped cream), which comes in a jug. If you're on a budget, try the set menus ranging from €25 to €35. This is a good place to keep in mind for a late lunch or an early dinner, since it serves nonstop from noon until 11 PM, and you can also drop in for a Belgian waffle and hot chocolate in the afternoon ⊠ *3 rue Racine, St-Germain-des-Prés* ☎ *01–44–32–15–60* ⊕ *www.bouillon-racine.com* ▭ *AE, DC, MC, V* Ⓜ *Odéon* ✛ *4:C4.*

**$$** ✕ **Le Comptoir du Relais Saint-Germain.** Run by legendary bistro chef Yves
BISTRO Camdeborde, this tiny Art Deco hotel restaurant is booked up months in advance for the single dinner sitting that comprises a five-course, €48 set menu of haute-cuisine food. On weekends from noon to 9 PM and before 6 PM during the week a brasserie menu is served and reservations are not accepted, resulting in long lines and brisk service. Start with charcuterie or pâté, then choose from open-faced sandwiches like a smoked salmon–and–comté cheese croque monsieur, salads, and a handful of hot dishes such as braised beef cheek, roast tuna, and Camdeborde's famed deboned and breaded pig's trotter. Sidewalk tables make for prime people-watching in summer and Le Comptoir also runs a down-to-earth snack shop next door that serves crêpes and sandwiches. ⊠ *9 carrefour de l'Odéon, St-Germain-des-Prés* ☎ *01–44–27– 07–50* ▭ *MC, V* Ⓜ *Odéon* ✛ *4:B3.*

**$** ✕ **Le Timbre.** Working in a tiny open kitchen, Manchester native Chris
BISTRO Wright could teach many a French chef a thing or two about *la cuisine française.* He uses only the finest suppliers to produce a constantly changing seasonal menu that keeps the locals coming back: in fall you might sample the *cochon noir de Bigorre* (a pedigreed pig from southwest France) with marinated red cabbage, or blood sausage with french fries. The signature mille-feuille is spectacular, but try not to miss *le vrai et le faux fromage* (literally "the real and the fake cheese"): perhaps a two-year-old British cheddar juxtaposed with a farmer's goat cheese from the Ardèche. (The joke is that the English cheese is the real cheese and the French cheese is fake—although French people might read it the other way.) ⊠ *3 rue Ste-Beuve, Montparnasse* ☎ *01– 45–49–10–40* ⊕ *www.restaurantletimbre.com* ⬥ *Reservations essential* ▭ *MC, V* ⊙ *Closed Sun., Mon., Aug., and 10 days at Christmas* Ⓜ *Vavin* ✛ *4:A5.*

**$$$** ✕ **Les Bouquinistes.** Showcasing the talents of Guy Savoy protégé Williams
BISTRO Caussimon, this is the star chef Savoy's most popular "baby bistro," frequented by art dealers from the nearby galleries and the occasional *bouquiniste* (bookseller) from the quais across the street. Expect to hear more English than French in the cheery, contemporary dining room with its closely packed tables looking out onto the Seine, but the sophisticated seasonal cuisine—such as snails and mussels with gnocchi, followed by British Hereford beef with squash-stuffed rigatoni and a nougat crème brûlée—is as authentic as you could hope for. The €29 *retour du marché* (back from the market) lunch menu seems less imaginative than the pricier à la carte options—though it does include three courses, a glass of wine, and coffee. The wine list is extensive, with 180 wines and 12 champagnes. ⊠ *53 quai des Grands-Augustins, St-Germain-des-Prés* ☎ *01–43–25–45–94* ⊕ *www.lesbouquinistes.com* ▭ *AE, DC, MC, V* ⊙ *Closed Sun. and Aug. No lunch Sat.* Ⓜ *St-Michel* ✛ *4:C2.*

**17**

$$–$$$    ✕ **Yen.** If you're having what is known in French as a *crise de foie* (liver
JAPANESE    crisis), the result of overindulging in rich food, this chic Japanese noodle
house with a summer terrace and a VIP room upstairs is the perfect
antidote. The blond-wood walls soothe the senses, the staff is happy to
explain proper slurping technique, and the *soba* (buckwheat noodles),
served in soup or with a restorative broth for dipping, will give you
the courage to face another round of caramelized foie gras. The soba
noodles are made fresh on the premises every day, showing Parisians
that there is more to Japanese cuisine than sushi. Desserts come from
Sadaharu Aoki, who is famous for his green-tea éclairs. Prices are sober-
ing, but various set menus are available for €38 at lunch or €68 at
dinner. ⊠ *22 rue St-Benoît, St-Germain-des-Prés* 🕿 *01–45–44–11–18*
🖃 *AE, DC, MC, V* ☉ *Closed Sun. and 2 wks in Aug.* Ⓜ *St-Germain-
des-Prés* ✛ *4:A2.*

$$–$$$    ✕ **Ze Kitchen Galerie.** William Ledeuil made his name at the popular Les
MODERN FRENCH    Bouquinistes (a Guy Savoy baby bistro) before opening this contem-
Fodor's Choice    porary bistro in a loftlike space. The name might not be inspired, but
★    the cooking shows creativity and a sense of fun: from a deliberately
deconstructed menu featuring raw fish, soups, pastas, and *à la plancha*
(grilled) plates, consider the roast and confit duck with a tamarind-
and-sesame condiment and foie gras, or lobster with mussels, white
beans, and Thai herbs. A tireless experimenter, Ledeuil buys heirloom
vegetables direct from farmers and tracks down herbs and spices in
Asian supermarkets. The menu changes monthly and there are several
different prix-fixe options at lunch, starting at €29. ⊠ *4 rue des Grands-
Augustins, Quartier Latin* 🕿 *01–44–32–00–32* ⊕ *www.zekitchengalerie.
fr* ⚏ *Reservations essential* 🖃 *AE, DC, MC, V* ☉ *Closed Sun. No lunch
Sat.* Ⓜ *St-Michel* ✛ *4:C2.*

## 7ᴱ ARRONDISSEMENT

$$$    ✕ **Au Bon Accueil.** To see what well-heeled Parisians like to eat these days,
BISTRO    book a table at this chic little bistro run by Jacques Lacipière as soon as
you get to town. The contemporary dining room is unusually comfort-
able, and the sidewalk tables have an Eiffel Tower view; the excellent,
well-priced cuisine du marché has made this spot a hit. Typical of the
sophisticated fare from chef Naobuni Sasaki are veal rib with a fricas-
see of wild mushrooms and green asparagus, roast lobster with mush-
room risotto, and game in season. Homemade desserts could include
citrus terrine with passion-fruit sorbet or caramelized apple mille-feuille
with hazelnut ice cream. The €27 lunch menu, featuring dishes with a
distinct haute cuisine touch, must be one of the city's great bargains.
⊠ *14 rue de Monttessuy, Trocadéro/Tour Eiffel* 🕿 *01–47–05–46–11*
⊕ *www.aubonaccueilparis.com* ⚏ *Reservations essential* 🖃 *AE, MC,
V* ☉ *Closed weekends and 2 wks in Aug.* Ⓜ *Métro or RER: Pont de
l'Alma* ✛ *3:D1.*

$$$$    ✕ **Chez les Anges.** In the 1960s and '70s, Chez les Anges served celestial
BISTRO    Burgundian cooking. The restaurant has been through several incar-
nations since, but now, under Jacques and Catherine Lacipière, who
run the popular bistro Au Bon Accueil, it has recovered the original
name and spirit. The couple has made a few adjustments since opening,

renovating the dining room to better reflect the classy food and broadening the wine list. The €34, daily changing menu from chef Hidenori Kitaguchi is a notch above bistro fare. Lacipière goes further than most in his quest for quality products, bringing back ingredients such as line-caught sole and scallops every week from the town of St-Gilles-Croix-de-Vie on the Atlantic coast, and shopping daily at the Rungis market. Service is polished and thoughtful. ⊠ *54 bd. de la Tour-Maubourg, Trocadéro/Tour Eiffel* ☎ *01–47–05–89–86* ▭ *AE, DC, MC, V* ⊙ *Closed weekends* Ⓜ *Métro: La Tour-Maubourg* ✛ *3:E2.*

**$$$**
BISTRO
✕ **D'Chez Eux.** The red-checked tablecloths and jovial maître d'hôtel at this southwestern French bistro near the Ecole Militaire might seem like a tourist cliché—until you realize that the boisterous dining room is just as popular with food-loving locals and French politicians as it is with foreigners. The best way to start a meal here is with the "chariot" of starters, everything from lentil salad to ratatouille; just point to the ones you want. Classics among the main courses are duck confit with sautéed garlic potatoes, cassoulet, and game dishes in winter. Everything is hearty and delicious, if not especially refined—don't miss the gooey help-yourself chocolate mousse. Best value is the *tradition gourmande* set menu for €43, which brings you the hors d'oeuvres spread, a main course, three desserts (you can try them all), and coffee. ⊠ *2 av. de Lowendal, Trocadéro/Tour Eiffel* ☎ *01–47–05–52–55* ⊕ *www.chezeux. com* ▭ *AE, DC, MC, V* ⊙ *Closed Sun., Mon., and Aug.* Ⓜ *Varenne, Ecole Militaire* ✛ *3:E3.*

**$$$$**
MODERN FRENCH
✕ **Gaya Rive Gauche.** If you can't fathom paying €200 and up per person to taste the cooking of Pierre Gagnaire, the city's most avant-garde chef, at his eponymous restaurant, book a meal at this, his fashionable fish restaurant, instead. At Gaya Rive Gauche, Gagnaire uses seafood as a palette for his creative impulses: expect small portions of artfully presented food, as in a seafood gelée encircled by white beans and draped with Spanish ham, or cod "petals" in a martini glass with soba noodles, mango, and grapefruit. Don't miss the desserts, one of Gagnaire's great strengths. Aim for the main-floor room, with its fish-scale wall, natural lighting, and bar for solo diners. ⊠ *44 rue du Bac, St-Germain-des-Prés* ☎ *01–45–44–73–73* ⊕ *www.pierregagnaire.com* ⚲ *Reservations essential* ▭ *AE, MC, V* ⊙ *Closed Sun. No lunch in Aug.* Ⓜ *Rue du Bac* ✛ *3:H2.*

**¢–$$$$**
FRENCH FUSION
Fodor's Choice
★
✕ **Il Vino.** It might seem audacious to present hungry diners with nothing more than a wine list, but the gamble is paying off for Enrico Bernardo at his new restaurant with a branch in Courchevel, in the French Alps. Winner of the world's best sommelier award in 2005, this charismatic Italian left the George V to oversee a dining room where food plays second fiddle (in status, not quality). The hip decor—plum-color banquettes, body-hugging white chairs, a few high tables—attracts a mostly young clientele that's happy to play the game by ordering one of the blind, multicourse tasting menus. The €98 menu, with four dishes and four wines, is a good compromise that might bring you a white Mâcon with saffron risotto, crisp Malvasia with crabmeat and black radish, a full-bodied red from Puglia with Provençal-style lamb, sherrylike *vin jaune* d'Arbois with aged Comté cheese, and sweet Jurançon with berry crumble. You can also order individual wine-food combinations

17

à la carte or pick a bottle straight from the cellar and ask for a meal to match. ⊠ *13 bd. de la Tour-Maubourg* ☎ *01–44–11–72–00* ⊕ *www.ilvinobyenricobernardo. com* ⊟ *AE, DC, MC, V* Ⓜ *Invalides* ✛ *3:F2.*

$$$$
HAUTE FRENCH

✕ **Jules Verne.** Alain Ducasse doesn't set his sights low, so it was no real surprise when he took over this prestigious dining room on the second floor of the Eiffel Tower, and had designer Patrick Jouin give the room a neo-futuristic look in shades of brown. Sauces and pastries are prepared in a kitchen below the Champ de Mars before being whisked up the elevator to the kitchen, which is overseen by young chef Pascal Féraud. Most accessible is the €85 lunch menu (weekdays only), which brings you à la carte dishes in slightly smaller portions. Spend more (about €150–€200 per person without drinks) and you'll be entitled to more lavish dishes such as lobster with celery root and black truffle, and fricassee of Bresse chicken with crayfish. For dessert the kitchen reinterprets French classics, as in an unsinkable pink grapefruit soufflé with grapefruit sorbet. Book months ahead or try your luck at the last minute. ⊠ *Tour Eiffel, south pillar, Av. Gustave Eiffel* ☎ *01–45–55–61–44* ⊕ *www.lejulesverne-paris. com* ⌁ *Reservations essential. Jacket and tie* ⊟ *AE, DC, MC, V* Ⓜ *Bir-Hakeim* ✛ *3:C2.*

$$
BISTRO

✕ **L'Agassin.** André Le Letty, formerly of L'Anacréon, has transported his talent to a quiet side street with more than its share of great restaurants. Even if the bare walls and dark-wood tables and chairs make the dining room feel contemporary, there is something agreeably old-fashioned about a meal here, from the attentive and ever-polite service to the classic French dishes such as a whole duck *magret* with a fanned-out pear and side dish of white beans, or the popular veal kidney with mustard sauce. For dessert, the prune clafoutis with Armagnac ice cream is a must. Set menus are available starting at €23 at lunch and going up to €34. ⊠ *8 rue Malar, Invalides* ☎ *01–47–05–94–27* ⊕ *www. agassin-paris.fr* ⊟ *AE, MC, V* ☉ *Closed Sun., Mon., and Aug.* Ⓜ *La Tour-Maubourg* ✛ *3:E1.*

$$–$$$
BASQUE

✕ **L'Ami Jean.** If you love Yves Camdeborde's southwestern France–inflected cooking at Le Comptoir but can't get a table for dinner, head to this tavernlike Basque restaurant run by Camdeborde's longtime second-in-command, Stéphane Jégo. His style is remarkably similar to Camdeborde's, because he uses the same suppliers and shares his knack for injecting basic ingredients with sophistication reminiscent of haute cuisine. You can go hearty with Spanish *piquillo* peppers stuffed with salt cod paste or *poulet basquaise* (chicken stewed with peppers), or lighter with seasonal dishes that change weekly. The restaurant is popular with rugby fans (a sport beloved of Basques), who create a festive mood. Plan on reserving at least a week ahead for dinner. ☒ *27 rue Malar, Invalides* ☎ *01–47–05–86–89* ⊕ *www.amijean.eu* ⌂ *Reservations essential* ⊟ *MC, V* ☾ *Closed Sun., Mon., and Aug.* Ⓜ *Métro or RER: Invalides* ✛ *3:E1.*

**$$$$** ✕ **L'Arpège.** Breton-born Alain Passard, one of the most respected chefs
HAUTE FRENCH in Paris, famously shocked the French culinary world by declaring that he was bored with meat. Though his vegetarianism is more theoretical than practical—L'Arpège still caters to fish and poultry eaters—he does cultivate his own vegetables outside Paris, which are then zipped into the city by high-speed train. His dishes elevate the humblest vegetables to sublime heights: salt-roasted beets with aged balsamic vinegar, leeks with black truffles, black radishes, and cardoon with parmigiano-reggiano. Seafood dishes such as turbot cooked at a low temperature for three hours or lobster braised in vin jaune from the Jura are also extraordinary—as are the prices. The understated decor places the emphasis firmly on the food, but try to avoid the gloomy cellar room. ☒ *84 rue de Varenne, Invalides* ☎ *01–47–05–09–06* ⊕ *www.alain-passard.com* ⊟ *AE, DC, MC, V* ☾ *Closed weekends* Ⓜ *Varenne* ✛ *3:G2.*

**$$$$** ✕ **L'Atelier de Joël Robuchon.** Famed chef Joël Robuchon retired from
MODERN FRENCH the restaurant business for several years before opening this red-and-black-lacquer space with a bento-box-meets-tapas aesthetic. High seats surround two U-shaped bars, and this novel plan encourages neighbors to share recommendations and opinions. Robuchon's devoted kitchen staff whip up small plates for grazing (€10–€25) as well as full portions, which can turn out to be the better bargain. Highlights from the oft-changing menu have included an intense tomato jelly topped with avocado puree and thin-crusted mackerel tart, although his inauthentic (but who's complaining?) take on carbonara with cream and Alsatian bacon, and the *merlan* Colbert (fried herb butter) remain signature dishes. Bookings are taken for the first sittings only at lunch and dinner. ☒ *5 rue Montalembert, St-Germain-des-Prés* ☎ *01–42–22–56–56* ⊟ *MC, V* Ⓜ *Rue du Bac* ✛ *4:A2.*

**$$$** ✕ **Le 153 Grenelle.** Jean-Jacques Jouteux, a veteran of the French culinary
BISTRO scene (he most recently worked at Petrossian in Monaco), now presides over this bistro near the rue Cler street market. Here, in the sober gray dining room, the focus is on classic French cooking made with flawless ingredients: Think lemon sole with spinach or duck with turnips. Be sure to save room for one of the very classic desserts, such as *tarte fine aux pommes* or pears in wine. Befitting the chic area, service is polished and polite. ☒ *153 rue de Grenelle, Invalides* ☎ *01–45–51–54–12* ⊕ *www.153-grenelle.com* ⊟ *AE, MC, V* ☾ *Closed Sun., Mon., Aug., and 1 wk at Christmas* Ⓜ *École Militaire* ✛ *3:E2.*

**$** ✕ **Le Café Constant.** Middle-aged Parisians are a nostalgic bunch, which
BISTRO explains the popularity of this down-to-earth venue from esteemed chef Christian Constant. This is a relatively humble bistro with cream-color walls, red banquettes, and wooden tables, and you'll often see Constant himself perched at the bar at the end of the lunch service. The menu reads like a French cookbook from the 1970s—who cooks veal *cordon bleu* these days?—but with Constant overseeing the kitchen, the dishes taste even better than you remember. There's delicious and

**17**

creamy lentil soup with morsels of foie gras, and the artichoke salad comes with fresh—not bottled or frozen—hearts. A towering *vacherin* (meringue layered with ice cream) might bring this delightfully retro meal to a close. On weekdays there is a bargain lunch menu for €16 (two courses) or €23 (three courses). ✉ *139 rue St-Dominique, Invalides* ☎ *01–47–53–73–34* ⊕ *www.cafeconstant.com* ✍ *Reservations not accepted* ▭ *MC, V* ۞ *Closed Sun. No lunch Mon.* Ⓜ *Métro École Militaire, Métro or RER: Pont de l'Alma* ✚ *3:D2.*

**$$$** ╳ **Le Violon d'Ingres.** Following in the footsteps of Joël Robuchon and
HAUTE FRENCH  Alain Senderens, Christian Constant has given up the Michelin star chase in favor of more accessible prices and a packed dining room (book at least a week ahead). And with Stéphane Schmidt in charge of the kitchen here Constant can dash between his four restaurants on this street, making sure the hordes are happy. And why wouldn't they be? The food is sophisticated and the atmosphere is lively; you can even find signature dishes like the almond-crusted sea bass with rémoulade sauce (a buttery caper sauce), alongside game and scallops (in season), and comforting desserts like *pots de crème* and chocolate tart. The food is still heavy on the butter, but with wines starting at around €20 this is a wonderful place for a classic yet informal French meal. ✉ *135 rue St-Dominique, Invalides* ☎ *01–45–55–15–05* ⊕ *www.leviolondingres. com* ✍ *Reservations essential* ▭ *MC, V* Ⓜ *École Militaire* ✚ *3:D2.*

**$** ╳ **Les Cocottes de Christian Constant.** Chef Christian Constant has an
MODERN FRENCH  unfailing sense of how Parisians want to eat these days, as proved by the latest addition to his mini-restaurant empire near the Eiffel Tower. At Les Cocottes he's shifted the normally leisurely bistro experience into high gear, which allows him to keep prices moderate. Seated at a long counter on slightly uncomfortable stools that discourage lingering, diners can mix and match from a menu of soups, salads, *cocottes* (dishes served in cast-iron pots), *verrines* (starters presented in tapas-style glasses), and comforting desserts, all made from fresh, seasonal ingredients. ✉ *135 rue St-Dominique, Invalides* ☎ *01–45–50–10–31* ⊕ *www.leviolondingres.com* ▭ *MC, V* ۞ *Closed Sun.* Ⓜ *Métro École Militaire, Métro or RER: Pont de l'Alma* ✚ *3:D2.*

**$$–$$$** ╳ **Thoumieux.** Former Crillon chef Jean-François Piège and Thierry
BRASSERIE  Costes of the fashionable brasserie clan that created Café Marly and Le Georges are behind the revival of this old-world bistro. The space has been opened up to eliminate the private booths while thankfully preserving much of its vintage character with globe lights and etched mirrors. Despite its location in the sedate 7$^e$ arrondissement this has quickly become the place to be seen, with food that's a good notch above brasserie fare (a smaller and more ambitious "tasting laboratory" is scheduled to open upstairs in 2010). A juicy Angus beef hamburger comes with a superfluous shower of Parmesan and fries whose skinniness mirrors the waitresses' legs, while the more sophisticated slow-cooked salmon is accompanied by vegetables from star market gardener Joël Thiébault. For dessert, try the piping-hot churros with chocolate sauce. Reservations are taken exactly six days ahead. ✉ *79 rue St-Dominique, Trocadéro/Tour Eiffel* ☎ *01–47–05–49–75* ✍ *Reservations essential* ▭ *AE, MC, V m La Tour-Maubourg* ✚ *3:E1.*

# 8ᴱ ARRONDISSEMENT

**$$$$**
HAUTE FRENCH

✕**Alain Ducasse au Plaza Athénée.** The dining room at Alain Ducasse's flagship Paris restaurant gleams with 10,000 crystals, confirming that this is the flashiest place in town for a blowout meal. Clementine-color tablecloths and space-age cream-and-orange chairs with pullout plastic trays for business meetings provide an upbeat setting for the cooking of young Ducasse protégé chef Christophe Moret. Some dishes are subtle, whereas in others strong flavors overwhelm delicate ingredients; service is also a little inconsistent, with occasional long waits between courses. Even so, a meal here is delightfully luxe, starting with a heavenly *amuse-bouche* of langoustine with caviar and a tangy lemon cream. You can continue with a truffle-and-caviar fest, or opt for more down-to-earth dishes like lobster in spiced wine with quince or saddle of lamb with sautéed artichokes. ✉ *Hôtel Plaza Athénée, 25 av. Montaigne, Champs-Élysées* ☎ *01–53–67–65–00* ⊕ *www.alain-ducasse.com* ⌕ *Reservations essential. Jacket required* ▭ *AE, DC, MC, V* ⊗ *Closed weekends, 2 wks in late Dec., and mid-July–mid-Aug. No lunch Mon.–Wed.* Ⓜ *Alma-Marceau* ✛ *1:D6.*

**$$$**
BISTRO

✕**Chez Savy.** Just off the glitzy Avenue Montaigne, Chez Savy occupies its own circa-1930s dimension, oblivious to the area's fashionization. The Art Deco cream-and-burgundy interior is blissfully intact (avoid the back room unless you're in a large group), and the waiters show not a trace of attitude. Fill up on rib-sticking specialties from the Aveyron in central France—lentil salad with bacon, foie gras (prepared on the premises), perfectly charred lamb with feather-light shoestring frites, and pedigreed Charolais beef. Order a celebratory bottle of Mercury with your meal and feel smug that you've found this place. À la carte prices are high but there is a set menu for €30.50. ✉ *23 rue Bayard, Champs-Élysées* ☎ *01–47–23–46–98* ▭ *MC, V* ⊗ *Closed weekends and Aug.* Ⓜ *Franklin-D.-Roosevelt* ✛ *1:E5.*

**$$$–$$$$**
BISTRO

✕**Dominique Bouchet.** To taste the cooking of one of the city's great chefs, you no longer need to pay for the sumptuous backdrop once provided by the Hotel Crillon: Dominique Bouchet has left that world behind for an elegant bistro where contemporary art brightens cream-painted walls, and he seems all the happier for it. On the menu, refined French technique meets country-style cooking, as in leg of lamb braised in wine with roasted cocoa bean and potato puree, or a chocolate éclair with black cherries and ice cream. Sometimes the dishes can get a touch too complicated, but the warm and very professional service makes up for it. If you're feeling indecisive, you might treat yourself to the €98 tasting menu: a succession of six small plates followed by a dessert. ✉ *11 rue Treilhard, Champs-Élysées* ☎ *01–45–61–09–46* ⊕ *www.dominique-bouchet.com* ▭ *AE, MC, V* ⊗ *Closed weekends and 3 wks in Aug.* Ⓜ *Miromesnil* ✛ *1:F3.*

**$$$–$$$$**
MODERN FRENCH

✕**L'Arôme.** Eric Martins ran a popular bistro in the far reaches of the 15ᵉ arrondissement before opening this contemporary restaurant off the Champs-Élysées, and his background in haute cuisine—he worked at Ledoyen and Hélène Darroze, among others—makes the ambitious new restaurant an easy transition. And Chef Thomas Boullaut looks just as comfortable in the open kitchen, from where he turns out seasonal

**17**

dishes with a touch of finesse: foie gras confit with rosemary-poached quince and wild rose jam, scallops a la plancha with vanilla and spaghetti squash might be featured. The tasting menu for €89 (€129 with wine pairing) is a great way to get to know his cooking, and there are lunch menus for €32 and €39. Watch out for the pricey wines by the glass. ⊠ *3 rue St-Philippe du Roule, Champs-Élysées* ☎ *01–42–25–55–98* ⊕ *www.larome.fr* ⟋ *Reservations essential; Jacket required* ▭ *AE, MC, V* ⊘ *Closed Sat., Sun., 3 wks at Christmas.* Ⓜ *St-Philippe du Roule.* ✛ *1:E4.*

$$$   ✕ **La Fermette Marbeuf 1900.** Graced with one of the most mesmerizing
BRASSERIE   Belle Époque rooms in town—accidentally rediscovered during renovations in the 1970s—this is a favorite haunt of French celebrities, who adore the sunflowers, peacocks, and dragonflies of the Art Nouveau mosaic. The menu rolls out solid, updated classic cuisine: try the snails in puff pastry, beef fillet with pepper sauce, and the Grand Marnier soufflé—but ignore the limited-choice €32 prix fixe (€24.50 at lunch) unless you're on a budget: the options are a notch below what you get à la carte. Popular with tourists and businesspeople at lunch, La Fermette becomes truly animated around 9 PM. ⊠ *5 rue Marbeuf, Champs-Élysées* ☎ *01–53–23–08–00* ⊕ *www.fermettemarbeuf.com* ▭ *AE, DC, MC, V* Ⓜ *Franklin-D.-Roosevelt* ✛ *1:D5.*

$$$$   ✕ **La Table du Lancaster.** Operated by one of the most enduring families in
HAUTE FRENCH   French gastronomy (the Troisgros clan has run a world-famous restaurant in Roanne for three generations), this stylish boutique-hotel restaurant is the perfect setting for stellar cosmopolitan cuisine; try to sit in the stunning Asian-inspired courtyard with its red walls and bamboo. Often drawing on humble ingredients such as eel or pigs' ears, the food reveals fascinating flavor and texture contrasts, like silky sardines on crunchy melba toast or tangy frogs' legs in tamarind. Indeed, Michel Troisgros has a fondness for tart notes, as demonstrated in the classic Troisgros dish salmon with sorrel sauce or his "acidulated" seven-course menu for €145. Don't miss the desserts, such as not one but two slices of sugar tart, with grapefruit slices for contrast. On Sunday there's a special €65 lunch menu (€35 for kids). ⊠ *Hotel Lancaster, 7 rue de Berri, Champs-Élysées* ☎ *01–40–76–40–18* ⊕ *www.hotel-lancaster.fr* ⟋ *Reservations essential* ▭ *AE, DC, MC, V* ⊘ *No lunch Sat.* Ⓜ *George V* ✛ *1:D4.*

$$$$   ✕ **Le Bristol.** After a rapid ascent at his own new-wave bistro, which led
HAUTE FRENCH   to his renown as one of the more inventive young chefs in Paris, Eric
Fodor's Choice   Frechon became head chef at the Bristol, the home-away-from-home
★   for billionaires and power brokers. Frechon creates masterworks—say, farmer's pork cooked "from head to foot" with truffle-enhanced crushed potatoes—that rarely stray far from the comfort-food tastes of bistro cooking. The €85 lunch menu makes his cooking accessible not just to the palate but to many pocketbooks. No wonder his tables are so coveted. Though the two dining rooms are impeccable—an oval oak-panel one for fall and winter and a marble-floor pavilion overlooking the courtyard garden for spring and summer—they provide few clues to help the world-weary traveler determine which city this might be. ⊠ *Hôtel Bristol, 112 rue du Faubourg St-Honoré, Champs-Élysées* ☎ *01–53–43–43–00* ⊕ *www.hotel-bristol.com* ⟋ *Reservations essential. Jacket and tie* ▭ *AE, DC, MC, V* Ⓜ *Miromesnil* ✛ *1:F4.*

$$$$ ✗**Le Cinq.** Eric Briffard is not the most famous chef in Paris but he is one
HAUTE FRENCH of the best, as proved by his smooth transition into the role of head chef
Fodor'sChoice in the city's most deluxe dining room. You'll find all the luxury products
★ you might expect—lobster, truffles, game in season—but treated with
a light touch that often draws on Asian ingredients such as wasabi or
cassia bark. A perfect example is his abalone, a rare shellfish prized by
sushi chefs, prepared several ways: raw in a tartare, bathed in a creamy
chicken bouillon, meunière-style in watercress sauce, and perched atop
a bed of gingered kabocha squash. Desserts are ethereal and service is
unfailingly thoughtful: really, the only problem with a meal here is that
it has to end. Oh, and that it costs a small fortune—thankfully there
is an €85 prix fixe at lunch. ⊠ *Hôtel Four Seasons George V, 31 av.
George V, Champs-Élysées* ☎ *01–49–52–70–00* ⊕ *www.fourseasons.
com/paris* ⌲ *Reservations essential. Jacket and tie* ▭ *AE, DC, MC, V*
Ⓜ *George V* ✛ *1:D5.*

$$$$ ✗**Ledoyen.** Tucked away in the quiet gardens flanking the Champs-
HAUTE FRENCH Élysées, Ledoyen is a slightly faded study in the grandiose style of
Napoléon III. Young Breton chef Christian Le Squer's menu is a treat,
whether you opt for the lunchtime €88 prix fixe or the €198 tasting
extravaganza (€298 with matching wines). He uses flawless ingredients, as showcased in *les coquillages* (shellfish), a delicious dish of herb
risotto topped with lobster, langoustines, scallops, and grilled ham. The
turbot with truffled mashed potatoes is excellent, too, and don't skip the
superlative cheese trolley. ⊠ *1 av. Dutuit, on Carré des Champs-Élysées,
Champs-Élysées* ☎ *01–53–05–10–01* ⌲ *Reservations essential. Jacket
required* ▭ *AE, DC, MC, V* ☽ *Closed weekends and Aug. No lunch
Mon.* Ⓜ *Concorde, Champs-Élysées–Clemenceau* ✛ *1:F6.*

$$$$ ✗**Les Saveurs de Flora.** Alain Passard–trained Flora Mikula made her
HAUTE FRENCH name at Les Olivades, a Provençal bistro in the chic residential 7ᵉ,
before joining a gaggle of ambitious restaurateurs in this platinum-card
area. Moving away from the bistro register, she's turning out refined
food with southern twists in an unabashedly pink, boudoirlike setting.
Standout dishes on the changing seasonal menu are three soft-boiled
eggs with truffle, porcini, and foie gras, roasted scallops with herb
butter, and a spectacular Grand Marnier soufflé. To take advantage of
the superb cheese trolley, order from the pricier *carte* (*menu*); cheese
is not included in the €34 lunch menu. Service, like the food, is generally impeccable, with the occasional minor slip-up. ⊠ *36 av. George
V, Champs-Élysées* ☎ *01–40–70–10–49* ⊕ *www.lessaveursdeflora.com*
▭ *MC, V* ☽ *Closed Sun. and Aug. No lunch Sat. or Mon.* Ⓜ *Franklin-
D.-Roosevelt* ✛ *1:D5.*

$$$$ ✗**Pierre Gagnaire.** If you want to venture to the frontier of luxe cooking
HAUTE FRENCH today—and if money is no object—dinner here is a must. Chef Pierre
Gagnaire's work is at once intellectual and poetic, often blending three
or four unexpected tastes and textures in a single dish. Just taking in
the menu requires concentration (ask the waiters for help), so complex
are the multiline descriptions about the dishes' six or seven ingredients.
The Grand Dessert, a seven-dessert marathon, will leave you breathless,
though it's not as overwhelming as it sounds. The businesslike gray-
and-wood dining room feels refreshingly informal, especially at lunch,

**17**

but it also lacks the grandeur expected at this level. The uninspiring prix-fixe lunch (€105) and occasional ill-judged dishes (Gagnaire is a big risk taker, but also one of France's top chefs) linger as drawbacks, and prices keep shooting skyward, so Pierre Gagnaire is an experience best saved for the financial elite. ⊠ *6 rue de Balzac, Champs-Élysées* 🕾 *01–58–36–12–50* ⊕ *www.pierre-gagnaire.com* ⚑ *Reservations essential* ⊟ *AE, DC, MC, V* ☉ *Closed Sat., Aug., and 1 wk at Christmas. No lunch Sun.* Ⓜ *Charles-de-Gaulle–Étoile* ✛ *1:D4.*

$$$$
HAUTE FRENCH

✕ **Senderens.** Iconic chef Alain Senderens waited until retirement age to make a rebellious statement against the all-powerful Michelin inspectors, "giving back" the three stars he had held for 28 years and renaming his restaurant (it was Lucas Carton). He also updated the decor, juxtaposing curvy, white, new furnishings, and craterlike ceiling lights against the splendid Art Nouveau interior. The fusion menu spans the globe, though Senderens also, happily, reintroduces the occasional Lucas Carton signature dish such as polenta with truffles in winter. Some dishes work, as in warm semismoked salmon with Thai spices and cucumber, and some fall flat, as in a too-rich starter of roast foie gras with fig salad and licorice powder. Senderens takes his passion for food-and-drink matches to extremes, suggesting a glass of wine, whiskey, sherry, or even punch to accompany each dish. Upstairs, Le Passage Bar serves tapas-style dishes for less than €20 a plate, or €36 for four small courses. ⊠ *9 pl. de la Madeleine* *Opéra/Grands Boulevards* 🕾 *01–42–65–22–90* ⊕ *www.senderens.fr* ⊟ *AE, DC, MC, V* ☉ *Closed 3 wks in Aug.* Ⓜ *Madeleine* ✛ *1:H5.*

$$$$
MODERN FRENCH

✕ **Spoon.** Alain Ducasse's original fusion bistro has a silver screen lit with sculptures and a long central table where strangers share a unique dining experience. The mix-and-match menu hasn't changed significantly since the restaurant first opened, but you can now order the bento-style lunch for €33 or a more elaborate €80 tasting menu at dinner (€120 with matching wines). Fashion folk love this place for its many vegetable and pasta dishes and its irresistible desserts, such as the cheesecake or the chocolate pizza to share. If you've sampled the Spoon concept elsewhere in the world, don't expect the same here; each branch is tailored to a particular city's tastes, and what looks exotic in Paris (the Spoon Burger with a slice of bacon or foie gras) might seem humdrum in New York. ⊠ *12 rue de Marignan, Champs-Élysées* 🕾 *01–40–76–34–44* ⊕ *www.spoon-restaurants.com* ⚑ *Reservations essential* ⊟ *AE, DC, MC, V* ☉ *Closed weekends and Aug.* Ⓜ *Franklin-D.-Roosevelt* ✛ *1:E5.*

$$$$
FRENCH FUSION

✕ **Stella Maris.** A pretty Art Deco front window is the calling card for this pristine spot near the Arc de Triomphe. An expense-account crowd mixes with serious French gourmands here, to dine on the subtle cuisine of likable Japanese chef Tateru Yoshino, who trained with Joël Robuchon. Yoshino rewrites his menu four times a year but you can always find hints of Japan in dishes—made with organic ingredients—such as eel blanquette with grilled cucumber, salmon prepared four ways (in salt, marinated with dill, smoked, and panfried), and a unique take on the French classic *tête de veau*, with turtle jus. Put your trust in the chef by opting for the tasting menu (€99 or €130), or keep your budget in check with the €49 lunch menu or €70 seasonal menu. ✉ *4 rue Arsène-Houssaye, Champs-Élysées* ☎ *01–42–89–16–22* ⌕ *Reservations essential* ▭ *AE, DC, MC, V* ⊙ *Closed Sun. and 2 wks in Aug. No lunch Sat.* Ⓜ *Étoile* ✚ *1:C4.*

**$$$$**
HAUTE FRENCH

✕ **Taillevent.** Perhaps the most traditional—for many diners this is only high praise—of all Paris luxury restaurants, this grande dame basks in renewed freshness under brilliant chef Alain Solivérès, who draws inspiration from the Basque country, Bordeaux, and Languedoc for his daily-changing menu. Traditional dishes such as scallops meunière (with butter and lemon) are matched with contemporary choices such as a splendid spelt risotto with truffles and frogs' legs or panfried duck liver with caramelized fruits and vegetables. One of the 19th-century paneled salons has been turned into a winter garden, and contemporary paintings adorn the walls. The service is flawless, and the exceptional wine list is well priced. All in all, a meal here comes as close to the classic haute-cuisine experience as you can find in Paris. There's an €80 lunch menu, with wines by the glass starting at €10. ✉ *15 rue Lamennais, Champs-Élysées* ☎ *01–44–95–15–01* ⊕ *www.taillevent.com* ⌕ *Reservations essential. Jacket and tie* ▭ *AE, DC, MC, V* ⊙ *Closed weekends and Aug.* Ⓜ *Charles-de-Gaulle–Étoile* ✚ *1:D4.*

# 9ᴱ ARRONDISSEMENT

**$$**
BISTRO

✕ **Bistrot des Deux Théâtres.** This theater-lover's bistro with red-velour banquettes, black-and-white photos of actors, and a giant oil painting depicting celebrities, is always packed, and with good reason. The great-value prix-fixe menu for €38 (there's no à la carte) includes a *kir royale* (sparkling white wine with cassis), three courses, half a bottle of unpretentious wine, and coffee. This isn't a place for modest eaters, so have foie gras or escargots to start, a meaty main such as the crackly crusted rack of lamb, and a potent baba au rhum or rustic lemon meringue tart for dessert. Waiters are jokey, English-speaking, and efficient. ✉ *18 rue Blanche, Montmartre* ☎ *01–45–26–41–43* ⊕ *www.bistrocie.fr* ▭ *AE, MC, V* Ⓜ *Trinité* ✚ *2:A2.*

**¢–$**
BISTRO
☺

✕ **Chartier.** This classic *bouillon* (a term referring to the Parisian soup kitchens popular in the early 20th century) is a part of the Gérard Joulie group of bistros and brasseries, which discreetly updated the menu without changing the fundamentals. People come here more for the bonhomie and the stunning 1896 interior than the cooking, which could be politely described as unambitious—then again, where else can you find a plate of foie gras for €6.90? This cavernous restaurant—the only original fin-de-siécle *bouillon* to remain true to its mission of serving cheap, sustaining food to the masses—enjoys a huge following, including one regular who has come for lunch nearly every day since 1946. You may find yourself sharing a table with strangers as you study the old-fashioned menu of such standards as pot-au-feu and blanquette de veau. ✉ *7 rue du Faubourg-Montmartre, Opéra/Grands Boulevards* ☎ *01–47–70–86–29* ⊕ *www.restaurant-chartier.com* ⌕ *Reservations not accepted* ▭ *AE, MC, V* Ⓜ *Montmartre* ✚ *2:C4.*

**17**

**$–$$**  ✕ **Le Ch'ti Catalan.** Run by two friends, one from northern France (best
BISTRO  known for its potent cheeses and creative use of Belgian endive) and the
other from the Catalan-influenced southwest, this bistro has a unique
mission in Paris: to combine the two seemingly incompatible styles.
Though the restaurant looks a bit scruffy from the outside, the interior
is painted in warm ocher tones and the chatty English-speaking staff
will put you at ease. Among the seasonal dishes on the handwritten
chalkboard menu, you might come across a wonderful starter of roasted
red peppers and fresh anchovies, delicious pork simmered with white
beans, Catalan-style salt cod, and steak with potent Maroilles cheese.
At lunch there is a bargain two-course menu for €13.50. ⊠ *4 rue de
Navarin, Montmartre* ☎ *01–44–63–04–33* ▭ *MC, V* ☉ *Closed Sun. and
Christmas wk. No lunch Sat.* Ⓜ *Notre-Dame-de-Lorette* ✛ *2:B2.*

**$**  ✕ **Rose Bakery.** On a street lined with French food shops selling produce,
BRITISH  fish, baguettes, and monastery cheeses, this British-run café-restaurant
Fodor's Choice  might easily go unnoticed—if it weren't for the frequent line out the
★  door. Whitewashed walls, childlike art, and concrete floors provide the
decor, and organic producers supply the ingredients for food so fresh
and tasty it puts most Paris lunch spots to shame. French office workers
and the area's Anglos fill the room at lunch to feast on salads, soups,
and hot dishes such as delicious risotto, followed by carrot cake, sticky
toffee pudding, or comically large lemon tarts. The nostalgic can buy
homemade granola, British marmalade, or baked beans to take home.
And should you find that you can't live without the food here, Rose
Bakery has its own cookbook in English, plus a second branch at 30
rue Debelleyme in Le Marais. Weekend brunch is popular, so plan to
arrive early. ⊠ *46 rue des Martyrs, Montmartre* ☎ *01–42–82–12–80*
⌲ *Reservations not accepted* ▭ *AE, MC, V* ☉ *Closed Mon. and 2 wks
in Aug. No dinner* Ⓜ *Notre-Dame-de-Lorette* ✛ *2:C2.*

**$$**  ✕ **Villa Victoria.** The restaurant formerly known as Velly has changed
BISTRO  owners and name, but the kitchen continues to turn out some of the best
bistro food in the neighborhood. In a timeworn setting—including a
lovely Art Deco bar—happy regulars tuck into updated French fare such
as squid-topped risotto, beef fillet in green mustard sauce with sautéed
potatoes, or sea bass with spinach and chanterelles. The chalkboard
selection changes constantly, and three courses are a bargain at €32,
though you can also order individual dishes at slightly stiffer à la carte
prices. Seating is elbow-to-elbow and the atmosphere is convivial, aided
by the well-priced wines. ⊠ *52 rue Lamartine, Montmartre* ☎ *01–48–
78–60–05* ⊕ *www.la-villa-victoria.com* ▭ *AE, MC, V* ☉ *Closed Sun.
and Aug.* Ⓜ *Notre-Dame-de-Lorette* ✛ *2:C3.*

## 10ᴱ ARRONDISSEMENT

**$**  ✕ **Chez Casimir.** Thierry Breton's bright, easygoing bistro is popular
BISTRO  with polished Parisian professionals, for whom it serves as a sort of
canteen—why cook when you can eat this well so affordably? The €29
dinner menu (€22 for two courses at lunch) covers lentil soup with fresh
croutons, braised endive and andouille salad, and roast lamb on a bed
of Paimpol beans, and there are 12 cheeses to choose from. Good, if
not exceptional, desserts include *pain perdu*, a dessert version of French

toast—here it's topped with a roasted pear or whole cherries. Drop in at lunchtime on Saturday or Sunday for the great-value €25 buffet. ✉ 6 *rue de Belzunce, Opéra/Grands Boulevards* ☎ *01–48–78–28–80* 🖃 *MC, V* ⊘ *Closed 3 wks in Aug. and 1 wk at Christmas. No dinner weekends* Ⓜ *Gare du Nord* ✛ *2:E2.*

**$$**
HAUTE FRENCH
✕ **Julien.** Famed for its 1879 decor—think Art Nouveau stained glass and *La Bohème*–style street lamps hung with vintage hats—this Belle Époque dazzler in the up-and-coming neighborhood near Gare de l'Est certainly lives up to its oft-quoted moniker, "the poor man's Maxim's." Look for smoked salmon, stuffed roast lamb, cassoulet, and, to finish, profiteroles or the *coupe Julien* (ice cream with cherries). The crowd here is lots of fun, and the restaurant has a strong following with the fashion crowd, so it's mobbed during the biannual fashion and fabric shows. Food is served until midnight, and there are various prix-fixe menus that start at €18.50 for a main course with *café gourmand* (coffee and sweets). ✉ *16 rue du Faubourg St-Denis, Opéra/Grands Boulevards* ☎ *01–47–70–12–06* ⊕ *www.julienparis.com* 🖃 *AE, MC, V* Ⓜ *Strasbourg St-Denis* ✛ *2:E4.*

**$–$$**
NORTH AFRICAN
✕ **Le Martel.** Of the scads of neighborhood couscous joints in Paris, a few have become fashionable thanks to their host's magnetic personality and their stylish setting—and this converted bistro ranks among the more recent of that set. It's crowded, but the clientele of fashion designers, photographers, models, and media folk is as cool as it gets in this up-and-coming quartier. Everyone digs in to a mix of French standbys (such as artichokes with vinaigrette) and more exotic fare like lamb tagine with almonds, prunes, and dried apricots. ✉ *3 rue Martel, République* ☎ *01–47–70–67–56* 🖃 *MC, V* ⊘ *Closed Sun. and 2 wks in Aug. No lunch Sat.* Ⓜ *Château d'Eau* ✛ *2:E4.*

## 11ᴱ ARRONDISSEMENT

**$$**
BISTRO
✕ **Astier.** There are three good reasons to go to Astier: the generous cheese platter plunked on your table atop a help-yourself wicker tray, the exceptional wine cellar with bottles dating back to the 1970s, and the French bistro fare, even if portions seem to have diminished over the years. Dishes like marinated herring with warm potato salad, sausage with lentils, and baba au rhum are classics on the frequently changing set menu for €32, which includes a selection of no less than 20 cheeses. The vintage 1950s wood-paneled dining room attracts plenty of locals and remains a fairly sure bet in the area, especially since it's open every day. ✉ *44 rue Jean-Pierre Timbaud, République* ☎ *01–43–57–16–35* ⊕ *www.restaurant-astier.com* ⌕ *Reservations essential* 🖃 *MC, V* ⊘ *Closed weekends and Mon. in Aug.* Ⓜ *Parmentier* ✛ *2:H5.*

**¢**
VIETNAMESE
✕ **Dong Huong.** Dong Huong isn't a secret, but you wouldn't find it by accident. These two undecorated dining rooms on a Belleville side street are where the local Chinese and Vietnamese come for a reassuring bowl of *pho* (noodle soup) or plate of grilled lemongrass-scented meat with rice. Spicy, peanut-y *saté* soup is a favorite, and at this price (€6.50) you can also spring for a plate of crunchy imperial rolls, to be wrapped in accompanying lettuce and mint. Try one of the lurid nonalcoholic drinks; they're surprisingly tasty. ✉ *14 rue Louis-Bonnet, Père*

17

**CLOSE UP**

# A Cheese Primer

Their cuisine might be getting lighter, but the French aren't ready to relinquish their cheese. Nearly every restaurant, humble or haute, takes pride in its odorous offerings. Some present a single, lovingly selected slice, whereas the more prestigious restaurants wheel in a trolley of specimens aged on the premises. Cheese always comes after the main course and before—or instead of—dessert.

Among the best bistros for cheese are **Astier,** where a giant basket of oozy wonders is brought to the table, and **Le Comptoir,** where a dazzling cheese platter is part of the five-course prix-fixe dinner. A few *bars à fromages* are springing up, too: devoted to cheese the way *bars à vins* are dedicated to wine. **La Fromagerie 31** (⊠ *64 rue de Seine* ☎ *01–43–26–50–31*) is a terrific example.

Armed with these phrases, you can wow the waiter and work your way through the most generous platter.

**Avez-vous le Beaufort d'été?** (Do you have summer Beaufort?)

Beaufort is similar to Gruyère, and the best Beaufort is made with milk produced in summer, when cows eat fresh grass. Aged Beaufort is even more reminiscent of a mountain hike.

**Je voudrais un chèvre bien frais/ bien sec.** (I'd like a goat cheese that's nice and fresh/nice and dry.)

France produces many goat cheeses, some so fresh they can be scooped with a spoon, some tough enough to use as doorstops. It's a matter of taste, but hard-core cheese eaters favor drier specimens, which stick to the roof of the mouth and have a frankly goaty aroma.

**C'est un St-Marcellin de vache ou de chèvre?** (Is this St-Marcellin made with cow's or goat's milk?)

St-Marcellin is a more original choice than ubiquitous *crottin de chèvre* (poetically named after goats' turds). Originally a goat cheese, today it's more often made with cow's milk. The best have an oozy center, though some like it dry as a hockey puck.

**C'est un Brie de Meaux ou de Melun?** (Is this Brie from Meaux or Melun?)

There are many kinds of Brie; Brie de Meaux is the best known, with a smooth flavor and runny center; the much rarer Brie de Melun is more pungent and saltier.

**Je n'aime pas le Camembert industriel!** (I don't like industrial Camembert!)

Camembert might be a national treasure, but most of it is industrial. Real Camembert has a white rind with rust-color streaks and a yellow center.

**Avez-vous de la confiture pour accompagner ce brebis?** (Do you have any jam to go with this sheep's cheese?)

In the Basque region berry jam is the traditional accompaniment for sharp sheep's-milk cheeses like Ossau-Iraty.

**C'est la saison du Mont d'Or.** (It's Mont d'Or season.)

This potent mountain cheese, also known as Vacherin, is produced only from September to March. It's so runny it's eaten with a spoon.

—*Rosa Jackson*

*Lachaise* ☎ *01–43–57–18–88* ▤ *MC, V* ⊘ *Closed Tues. and 3 wks in Aug.* Ⓜ *Belleville* ✛ *2:H4.*

**$–$$**
**BISTRO**

╳ **La Table de Claire.** Just the kind of neighborhood bistro everyone wishes they had around the corner, La Table de Claire is inviting with its vintage tiles, Formica bar, contemporary light fixtures, and clientele of locals who invariably greet the owners with handshakes or kisses. Serge Haguenauer runs the dining room while Claire Seban watches over bistro dishes such as rabbit confit in the style of duck, steamed cod with ginger butter and four vegetables, and blanc manger with berries. Once a month, Claire and Serge host a chef d'un soir, usually a gifted amateur who, for two days, presents a menu of French or international dishes alongside the usual kitchen offerings. ✉ *30 rue Émile Lepeu, Bastille/Nation* ☎ *01–43–70–59–84* ⊕ *www.latabledeclaire.fr* ▤ *AE, MC, V* ⊘ *Closed Sun.–Tues. and Aug.* Ⓜ *Charonne* ✛ *2:H5.*

**$$**
**BISTRO**
**Fodor's Choice**
★

╳ **Le Bistrot Paul Bert.** Faded 1930s decor: check. Boisterous crowd: check. Thick steak with real frites: check. Good value: check. The Paul Bert delivers everything you could want from a traditional Paris bistro, so it's no wonder its two dining rooms (one recently added) fill every night with a cosmopolitan crowd. Some are from the neighborhood, others clutch weathered copies of *Gourmet* or the *Financial Times*, but they've all come in search of the elusive balance of ingredients that makes for a feel-good experience every time. The impressively stocked wine cellar helps a lot, as do the laid-back yet efficient staff and hearty dishes such as monkfish with white beans and duck with pears—the reasonable prix fixe is three courses for €34, or you can order à la carte. If you're looking for an inexpensive wine, choose from the chalkboard rather than the wine list. ✉ *18 rue Paul Bert, Bastille* ☎ *01–43–72–24–01* ✍ *Reservations essential* ▤ *MC, V* ⊘ *Closed Sun., Mon., and Aug.* ✛ *4:H3.*

**$$**
**BISTRO**

╳ **Le Chateaubriand.** A chef who once presented a single, peeled apple pip (really) on a plate (at the museum restaurant Le Transversal outside Paris) has no ordinary approach to food. Self-taught Basque cook Inaki Aizpitarte is undeniably provocative, but he gets away with it because (a) he's young and extremely cool and (b) he has an uncanny sense of which unexpected ingredients go together, as in a combination of oysters and lime zest in chicken stock. Simple, home-style French dishes are served at lunch, but at dinner the cooking gets far more modern and deconstructed, and the vintage dining room buzzes with an artsy, black-dressed crowd. ✉ *129 av. Parmentier, Oberkampf* ☎ *01–43–57–45–95* ✍ *Reservations essential* ▤ *AE, MC, V* ⊘ *Closed Sun. and Mon.* Ⓜ *Goncourt* ✛ *2:H5.*

**$$–$$$**
**BISTRO**

╳ **Le Repaire de Cartouche.** In this split-level, dark-wood bistro between Bastille and République, chef Rodolphe Paquin applies a disciplined creativity to earthy French regional dishes. The menu changes regularly, but typical options are a salad of haricots verts topped with tender slices of squid; scallops on a bed of diced pumpkin; juicy lamb with white beans; game dishes in winter; and old-fashioned desserts like baked custard with tiny shell-shaped madeleines. In keeping with cost-conscious times, he whips up a bargain three-course lunch menu for €16 that doesn't skimp on ingredients—expect the likes of homemade pâté to

17

start, followed by fried red mullet or hanger steak with french fries, and chocolate tart. The wine list is very good, too, with some bargain wines from small producers. ⊠ *8 bd. des Filles du Calvaire, Bastille/Nation* ☎ *01–47–00–25–86* ⚆ *Reservations essential* ☰ *MC, V* ⊗ *Closed Sun., Mon., and Aug.* Ⓜ *Filles du Calvaire* ✛ *4:G1.*

**$$**
LATIN AMERICAN

✕ **Unico.** An architect and a photographer, both Parisians born in Argentina, teamed up to open one of Bastille's hottest restaurants—literally hot, too, since the Argentinean meat served here is grilled over charcoal—and good-looking young locals pile into the orange-tiled, vintage 1970s dining room or the covered terrace to soak up the party vibe. Whichever cut of beef you choose (the ultimate being *lomo*, or fillet), it's so melt-in-your-mouth that the sauces served on the side seem almost superfluous. Dessert probably won't be necessary, but banana in dulce de leche could satisfy the strongest sweet craving. Be sure to order an Argentinean wine, the perfect accompaniment for this bold cuisine. ⊠ *15 rue Paul-Bert, Bastille/Nation* ☎ *01–43–67–68–08* ⊕ *www. resto-unico.com* ☰ *MC, V* ⊗ *Closed Sun. No lunch Mon.* Ⓜ *Faidherbe-Chaligny* ✛ *4:H3.*

# 12ᴱ ARRONDISSEMENT

**$$$**
BISTRO

✕ **Au Trou Gascon.** This classy establishment off Place Daumesnil—well off-the-beaten tourist track but worth the trip—is overseen by celebrated chef Alain Dutournier, while his wife runs the dining room, which combines contemporary furnishings and beautiful ceiling moldings. Dutournier does a refined take on the cuisine of Gascony—a region renowned for its ham, foie gras, lamb, and duck. Most popular with the regulars are the surprisingly light cassoulet (all the meats are grilled before going into the pot) with big white Tarbais beans and a superb duck or goose confit. You can also try an ethereal dessert of raspberries, ice cream, and meringue. Prices are steep, but there is a limited-choice lunch menu for €38 and a five-course tasting menu at dinner for €49. With some 1,100 wines and 130 Armagnacs to choose from, this is the place to splurge on vintage. ⊠ *40 rue Taine, Bastille/Nation* ☎ *01–43–44–34–26* ⊕ *www.autrougascon.com* ☰ *AE, DC, MC, V* ⊗ *Closed weekends, Aug., and 1 wk at Christmas* Ⓜ *Daumesnil* ✛ *4:H4.*

**$$–$$$$**
ITALIAN

✕ **Sardegna a Tavola.** Paris might have more Italian restaurants than you can shake a noodle at, but few smack of authenticity like this out-of-the-way Sardinian spot with peppers, braids of garlic, and cured hams hanging from the ceiling. Dishes are listed in Sardinian with French translation—*malloredus* is a gnocchi-like pasta; Sardinian ravioli are stuffed with cheese and mint. Perhaps best of all are the clams in a spicy broth with tiny pasta and the orange-scented prawns with tagliatelle, though the choice of dishes changes with the seasons and the chef's imagination. ⊠ *1 rue de Cotte, Bastille/Nation* ☎ *01–44–75–03–28* ☰ *AE, MC, V* ⊗ *Closed Sun. and Aug. No lunch Mon.* Ⓜ *Ledru-Rollin* ✛ *4:H4.*

## ON THE RUN

Eating on the run doesn't come naturally to the French, and you can easily spend two hours, albeit pleasantly, having lunch in a Paris café. If you're looking for something quicker, there's no point in trying to make a Parisian waiter move faster than he wants to; instead, head to a new breed of snack shop that puts speed first, without sacrificing quality. Prices can be high for what you get (expect to spend €10–€15 for a meal), but it's still a lot cheaper than most bistros.

**Be.** Star chef Alain Ducasse and wizard baker Eric Kayser make sandwiches a luxury item here; snag one of the handful of tables amid the heavenly bakery aromas. (⊠ 73 bd. de Courcelles, 17ᵉ ☎ 01–46–22–20–20).

**Bioboa.** Famed for its veggie burger, this organic café also serves seasonal salads, soups, sandwiches, and hot dishes, alongside freshly squeezed juices, milk shakes, and almost-virtuous homemade cakes. It's mobbed with office workers at lunch, so come early. (⊠ 3 rue Danielle Casanova, 1ᵉʳ ☎ 01–48–04–52–56).

**Bob's Juice Bar.** If you're strolling along Canal St-Martin, stop into this funky juice bar run by American Marc Grossman, aka Bob, for juices, organic salads, and muffins. Bob's also has a northern Marais offshoot called Kitchen (⊠ 74 rue des Gravilliers, 3ᵉ). (⊠ 15 rue Lucien Saimpax, 10ᵉ ☎06–82–63–72–74).

**Cojean.** This French-run chain takes an Anglo approach to healthful eating, with salads and sandwiches plus quick dishes available at the counter.

**Cosi.** This Italian sandwich shop in St-Germain piles fillings onto delicious crusty bread. (⊠ 54 rue de Seine, 6ᵉ ☎ 01–46–33–35–36).

**Le Pain Quotidien.** Part bakery, part café, this Belgian chain with locations throughout the city serves fresh salads and sandwiches at lunch and is great for breakfast. It tends to be overrun with office workers at peak times.

**Oh Poivrier!** Specializing in open-face sandwiches, this is a long-established chain with several locations; some have terraces.

**Scoop.** Linger in the comfy upstairs room or perch at the counter of this cheerful Anglo-inspired café near the Louvre to tuck into inventive wraps and salads. (⊠154 rue St-Honoré, 1ᵉʳ ☎ 01–42–60–31–84).

**17**

## 13ᴱ ARRONDISSEMENT

§ ✕ **L'Avant-Goût.** Christophe Beaufront belongs to a generation of gifted
BISTRO  bistro chefs who have rejected the pressure-cooker world of haute cui-
☺  sine for something more personal and democratic. The result: delighted and loyal customers. The three-course dinner prix-fixe costs €31; there's also a lunch menu for €14 (soup, main course, glass of wine, and coffee) and a more elaborate tasting menu for €40. Typical of his market-inspired cooking is his signature pot-au-feu *de cochon aux épices*, in which spiced pork stands in for the usual beef, and the bouillon is served separately. Homemade desserts and a good-value wine list round off a satisfying experience; children get an especially warm welcome here.

Drop into his épicerie across the street to browse the wine selection or order dinner to go, complete with a returnable cast-iron pot. ✉ *26 rue Bobillot, La Butte aux Cailles* ☎ *01–53–80–24–00* ⊕ *www.lavantgout. com* ⚒ *Reservations essential* ▭ *MC, V* ⊘ *Closed Sun., Mon., and 3 wks in Aug.* Ⓜ *Place d'Italie* ✛ *4:G6.*

$   ✕ **L'Ourcine.** Sylvain Danière knows just what it takes to open a wildly
BISTRO   popular bistro: choose an obscure location in a residential neighborhood, decorate it simply but cheerfully, work extremely hard, set competitive prices (€32 for three courses, €24 for two courses at lunch), and constantly reinvent your menu. The real key ingredient is talent, though, and Danière has plenty of it, as demonstrated by his updated duckling *au sang* (in blood sauce) with celery root puree, and a popular *crémeux au chocolat* (chocolate pudding) to finish things off. Locals mingle with well-informed tourists from Texas or Toulouse in the red-and-cream dining room, and you can watch the chef hard at work in his small kitchen. The only flaw is the inconsistent service, but one of the small producers' wines should make that go down more easily. ✉ *92 rue Broca, Les Gobelins* ☎ *01–47–07–13–65* ▭ *MC, V* ⊘ *Closed Sun., Mon., and 3 wks in Aug.* Ⓜ *Les Gobelins* ✛ *4:D6.*

$   ✕ **La Chine Massena.** With wonderfully overwrought rooms that seem
CHINESE   draped in a whole restaurant-supply catalog's worth of Asiana (plus
☾   four monitors showing the very latest in Hong Kong music videos), this is a fun place. Not only is the pan-Asian food good and moderately priced, but the place itself has a lot of entertainment value—wedding parties often provide a free floor show, and on weekends Asian disco follows variety shows. Steamed dumplings, lacquered duck, and the fish and seafood you'll see swimming in the tanks are specialties. For the best value come at noon on weekdays for the bargain lunch menus, starting at €11, or drop in for dim sum on weekends. ✉ *Centre Commercial Massena, 13 pl. de Vénétie, Chinatown* ☎ *01–45–83–98–88* ⊕ *www.chone-massena.fr* ▭ *AE, MC, V* Ⓜ *Porte de Choisy* ✛ *4:F6.*

¢   ✕ **Le Bambou.** The line-up outside this restaurant anytime after 7 PM is a
VIETNAMESE   sure sign that something exciting is going on in the kitchen. The small dining room is crowded and noisy and service is more than brisk—the only thing missing is an eject button on your seat but it's well worth it for some of the cheapest and most authentic Vietnamese food in town. If you find yourself in doubt about how to eat some of the dishes that involve wrapping meat and herbs in transparent rice paper or lettuce leaves, just spy on the regulars, many of them Vietnamese. Otherwise, go for one of the huge bowls of soup: tripe is popular, though there are plenty of other meat and seafood variations. ✉ *70 rue Baudincourt, Chinatown* ☎ *01–45–70–91–75* ▭ *MC, V* ⊘ *Closed Mon. and 3 wks in Aug.* Ⓜ *Tolbiac or Olympiades* ✛ *4:F6.*

---

## 14ᴱ ARRONDISSEMENT

$$   ✕ **L'Assiette.** David Rathgeber spent 12 years working for Alain Ducasse
BISTRO   as chef of Aux Lyonnais and then Benoît before taking over this landmark restaurant, where he has created a new menu and welcomed a new clientele. Expect bourgeois classics with a subtle modern touch, perhaps white tuna steak with spinach, lemon, capers, and croutons, and crème

caramel with salted butter—all executed with the precision you would expect of a Ducasse veteran. There is a two-course lunch menu with coffee for €23. ⊠ *181 rue du Château, Montparnasse* ☎ *01–43–22–64–86* ⊕ *www.restaurant-lassiette.com* ⊟ *AE, MC, V* ☉ *Closed Mon., Tues., and Aug.* Ⓜ *Pernety, Mouton-Duvernet* ✛ *3:H6.*

**$**
BISTRO
✕ **La Cerisaie.** Cyril Lalanne belongs to a breed of young chefs who like to cook for a privileged few. And if you're clever enough to nab a seat in this unremarkable yellow-and-red dining room (be sure to call ahead), you'll be rewarded with food whose attention to detail restores your faith in humanity. Foie gras makes several appearances on the chalkboard menu, since Lalanne is from southwest France, but you can also find freshly caught fish and perhaps farmer's pork from Gascony, a rarity in Paris. Lalanne does his own variation on baba au rhum—with Armagnac, another nod to his native region—and the wine list is strong on southwestern French bottles. ⊠ *70 bd. Edgar Quinet, Montparnasse* ☎ *01–43–20–98–98* ⌂ *Reservations essential* ⊟ *MC, V* ☉ *Closed weekends, mid-July–mid-Aug., and 1 wk at Christmas* Ⓜ *Edgar Quinet* ✛ *4:A6.*

**$$**
BRASSERIE
✕ **La Coupole.** This world-renowned cavernous spot with Art Deco murals practically defines the term *brasserie.* La Coupole might have lost its intellectual aura since it was restored by the Flo restaurant group, which has put its rather commercial stamp on many historic Paris brasseries, but it's been popular since Jean-Paul Sartre and Simone de Beauvoir were regulars, and it's still great fun. Today it attracts a mix of bourgeois families, tourists, and lone diners treating themselves to a dozen oysters. Recent additions to the classic brasserie menu are a tart of caramelized apple and panfried foie gras, beef fillet flambéed with cognac before your eyes, and profiteroles made with Valrhona chocolate. You usually can't make reservations after 8 or 8:30, so be prepared for a wait at the bar. ⊠ *102 bd. du Montparnasse, Montparnasse* ☎ *01–43–20–14–20* ⊕ *www.flobrasseries.com* ⊟ *AE, DC, MC, V* Ⓜ *Vavin* ✛ *4:A6.*

**$$$$**
BRASSERIE
✕ **Le Dôme.** Now a fancy fish brasserie serving seafood delivered fresh from Normandy every day, this restaurant began as a dingy meeting place for exiled artists and intellectuals like Lenin and Picasso. Try the *sole meunière* or the *bouillabaisse,* the ingredients of which are on display in their raw form in the restaurant's sparkling fish shop next door. You can still drop by the covered terrace for just a cup of coffee or a drink. ⊠ *108 bd. Montparnasse, Montparnasse* ☎ *01–43–35–25–81* ⊟ *AE, DC, MC, V* ☉ *Closed Sun. and Mon. in July and Aug.* Ⓜ *Vavin* ✛ *4:A6.*

## 15ᴱ ARRONDISSEMENT

**$$**
BISTRO
✕ **Afaria.** This otherwise unexciting arrondissement has become home to yet another promising young chef: Julien Duboué, who worked with fellow Basque Alain Dutournier at Le Carré des Feuillants and Daniel Boulud in New York before settling into this high-ceiling space near Porte de Versailles. Basque cooking is known for its bold flavors and generosity, and the choices at Afaria are no exception: crisp-skinned duck breast with balsamic-fig vinegar (for two) is served dramatically,

inside a roof tile, with the accompanying potato gratin perched on a bed of twigs, and big chunks of spoon-tender slow-cooked pork from Gascony come in an earthenware dish with cubes of roasted celery root. Another signature dish consists of slices of blood sausage layered with apple and topped with grainy mustard. Tapas are served at a high table near the entrance, and there's a large-screen TV for rugby matches. ✉ *15 rue Desnouettes* ☎ *01–48–56–15–36* ▭ *MC, V* ◷ *Closed Sun., Mon., 3 wks in Aug., and 2 wks in Feb.* Ⓜ *Convention* ✛ *3:C6.*

**$$–$$$**  ╳ **Jadis.** There's something very grown-up about the cooking of young
**BISTRO**  chef Guillaume Delage, which isn't so much of a surprise when you learn that he trained with the likes of Michel Bras, Frédéric Anton (of Le Pré Catelan), and Pierre Gagnaire. It's worth making your way to what seems like the middle of nowhere to taste his nostalgic bistro cooking with a modern touch: you might find pâté en croûte among the chef's suggestions, but there are also dishes like the shrimp with saté spices, creamed black rice, and spinach. The best value is the €32 set menu (€25 for two courses), with several choices for each course; tasting menus are €45 and €65. Though simple, the gray-and-burgundy dining room decorated with mirrors and vintage posters has charm. Convention or Porte de Versailles. ✉ *208 rue de la Croix-Nivert* ☎ *01–45–57– 73–20* ⊕ *www.bistro-jadis.com* ⌕ *Reservations essential* ▭ *AE, MC, V* ◷ *Closed weekends, 1 wk in May, 3 wks in Aug., 1 wk at Christmas.* Ⓜ *Convention or Porte de Versailles* ✛ *3:B6.*

**$**  ╳ **L'Os à Moelle.** Come for the early sitting at this little bistro on the edge
**BISTRO**  of town and you'll often discover the dining room filled with English and Japanese tourists (the waiters speak English automatically). The €35 multicourse dinner menu accounts for the restaurant's popularity—there are two, sometimes three, dinner sittings each night. Of six courses, at least four are likely to be fine—but not all his ideas work, such as warm oysters in herb butter that fail to preserve the taste of the sea. Waiters plunk even the higher-priced bottles of wine on the table without waiting for the customer to swill and slurp. Still, these problems are nothing that couldn't be fixed with a little more attention from the chef. ✉ *3 rue Vasco-de-Gama, Trocadéro/Tour Eiffel* ☎ *01–45–57–27– 27* ⌕ *Reservations essential* ▭ *AE, MC, V* ◷ *Closed Sun., Mon., Aug., 1 wk in spring, and 1 wk at Christmas* Ⓜ *Balard* ✛ *3:A6.*

**$$$–$$$$**  ╳ **Le Troquet.** A quiet residential street shelters one of the best-value bis-
**HAUTE FRENCH**  tros around: prix-fixe menus start at €26 at lunch and rise to €42 for a six-course tasting menu (there is no à la carte), but it's the quality, not quantity, that counts. Chef Christian Etchebest sends out a changing roster of dishes from the Basque and Béarn regions of southwestern France, and a typical meal might include vegetable soup with foie gras and cream, panfried scallops in crab sauce or *axoa de veau* (a Basque veal sauté), and a vanilla soufflé with cherry jam. Béarn red wine fills the glasses and happy regulars fill the dining room. ✉ *21 rue François-Bonvin, Trocadéro/Tour Eiffel* ☎ *01–45–66–89–00* ▭ *MC, V* ◷ *Closed Sun., Mon., 3 wks in Aug., 1 wk in May, and 1 wk at Christmas* Ⓜ *Sé-gur* ✛ *3:E5.*

# 16ᴱ ARRONDISSEMENT

**$$$$**
FRENCH FUSION
Fodor'sChoice
★

✕**Hiramatsu**. In this Art Deco dining room near Trocadéro, Hajime Nakagawa continues his variations on the subtly Japanese-inspired French cuisine of restaurant namesake Hiroyuki Hiramatsu, who still sometimes works the kitchen. Luxury ingredients feature prominently in dishes such as thin slices of lamb with onion jam and thyme-and-truffle-spiked jus, or an unusual pot-au-feu of oysters with foie gras and black truffle. For dessert, a mille-feuille of caramelized apples comes with rosemary sorbet. Helpful sommeliers will guide you through the staggering wine list, with more than 1,000 different bottles to choose from. There's no way to get away cheaply, so save it for a special occasion, when you might be tempted to order a tasting menu for €95 or €130 (lunch menus start at €48). ⊠ *52 rue de Longchamp, Trocadéro/Tour Eiffel* ☎ *01–56–81–08–80* ⊕ *www.hiramatsu.co.jp/fr* ⌕ *Reservations essential* ▤ *AE, DC, MC, V* ⊘ *Closed weekends, Aug., and 1 wk at Christmas* Ⓜ *Trocadéro* ✛ *1:B6.*

**$$$$**
HAUTE FRENCH
Fodor'sChoice
★

✕**L'Astrance**. Granted, Pascal Barbot rose to fame thanks to his restaurant's amazing-value food and casual atmosphere, but after the passage of several years, Astrance has become resolutely haute, with prices to match. With no à la carte, you can choose from a lunch menu for €70, a seasonal menu for €120, or the full tasting menu for €190 (this is what most people come for)—the latter two are available at lunch and dinner. Barbot's cooking has such an ethereal quality that it's worth the considerable effort of booking a table—you should start trying at least two months in advance. His dishes often draw on Asian ingredients, as in grilled lamb with miso-lacquered eggplant and a palate-cleansing white sorbet spiked with chili pepper and lemongrass. Each menu also comes at a (considerably) higher price with wines to match each course. ⊠ *4 rue Beethoven, Trocadéro/Tour Eiffel* ☎ *01–40–50–84–40* ⌕ *Reservations essential* ▤ *AE, DC, MC, V* ⊘ *Closed Sat.–Mon., 1 wk in Feb., 1 wk in late Oct./early Nov., and Aug.* Ⓜ *Passy* ✛ *1:B6.*

**$$$$**
MODERN FRENCH
Fodor'sChoice
★

✕**La Table de Joël Robuchon**. Chef David Alvès keeps up the lofty standard that was set here by star chef Joël Robuchon, with dishes like quail stuffed with foie gras, served with truffled potato puree. As at Robuchon's L'Atelier, you'll find a selection of small plates alongside more substantial dishes, but the seating arrangement is more conventional (no bar, just tables and chairs) and the food is generally even better. Unlike L'Atelier, La Table accepts reservations even for peak times—in fact, you should book well in advance for a seat in this small dining room that is somewhat disconcertingly decorated in gold leaf. The "menu club" set menu for €59 at lunch is a relative bargain. ⊠ *16 av. Bugeaud, Trocadéro/Tour Eiffel* ☎ *01–56–28–16–16* ⊕ *www.joel-robuchon.com* ⌕ *Reservations essential* ▤ *MC, V* Ⓜ *Victor-Hugo* ✛ *1:A5.*

**$$–$$$$**
BISTRO
Fodor'sChoice
★

✕**La Table Lauriston**. Serge Barbey has developed a winning formula in his chic bistro near the Trocadéro: top-notch ingredients, simply prepared and generously served. To start, you can't go wrong with his silky foie gras *au torchon*—the liver is poached in a flavorful bouillon—or one of the seasonal salads, such as white asparagus in herb vinaigrette; his trademark dish, a gargantuan rib steak, is big enough to silence even the hungriest Texan. Given the neighborhood you might expect

**17**

a businesslike setting, but the dining room feels cheerful, with vividly colored walls and velvet-upholstered chairs, and there is a 16-seat terrace. Don't miss the giant baba au rhum, which the waiters will douse in a choice of three rums. ⊠ *129 rue de Lauriston, Trocadéro/Tour Eiffel* ☎ *01–47–27–00–07* ⊕ *www.restauranttablelauriston.com* ⚑ *Reservations essential* ▭ *AE, MC, V* ☉ *Closed Sun., 3 wks in Aug., and 1 wk at Christmas. No lunch Sat.* Ⓜ *Trocadéro* ✛ *1:A6.*

**$$$$** ✕ **Le Cristal Room.** The success of this restaurant in the Baccarat museum-

HAUTE FRENCH boutique stems not only from the stunning decor by Philippe Starck—mirrors, patches of exposed-brick wall, and a black chandelier—but also from the culinary stylings of chef Guy Martin. The menu provides a taste of his ultra-refined style with dishes such as green asparagus soup with a lemon-poached egg, and sole meunière with grapefruit and an arugula flan. Plan on reserving a week or two ahead for dinner; lunch requires little advance notice now that the initial feeding frenzy has died down. ⊠ *11 pl. des États-Unis, Trocadéro/Tour Eiffel* ☎ *01–40–22–11–10* ⊕ *www.baccarat.fr* ⚑ *Reservations essential* ▭ *AE, DC, MC, V* ☉ *Closed Sun.* Ⓜ *Kléber* ✛ *1:C5.*

**$$** ✕ **Le Petit Rétro.** A diverse clientele (men in expensive suits at noon, well-

BISTRO dressed locals in the evening) frequents this little bistro with Art Nouveau tiles and bentwood furniture. You can't go wrong with the daily specials, which are written on a chalkboard presented by one of the friendly servers: perhaps crisp-skinned blood sausage with apple-and-honey sauce, *blanquette de veau,* and a crêpe mille-feuille with orange and Grand Marnier. Arrive with an appetite as the food is hearty. There are several prix-fixe menus to choose from, starting at €25 at lunch (two courses). ⊠ *5 rue Mesnil, Trocadéro/Tour Eiffel* ☎ *01–44–05–06–05* ⊕ *www.petitretro.fr* ▭ *AE, MC, V* ☉ *Closed weekends and 3 wks in Aug.* Ⓜ *Victor-Hugo* ✛ *1:A5.*

**$$$$** ✕ **Le Pré Catelan.** Live a Belle Époque fantasy by dining beneath the

HAUTE FRENCH chestnut trees on the terrace of this fanciful landmark *pavilion* in the Bois de Boulogne. Each of chef Frédéric Anton's dishes is a variation on a theme, such as *l'os à moelle:* bone marrow prepared two ways, one peppered and the other stuffed with porcini and cabbage, both braised in a concentrated meat jus. For a taste of the good life at a (relatively) gentle price, order the €85 lunch menu and soak up the opulent surroundings along with service that's as polished as the silverware. ⊠ *Rte. de Suresnes, Bois de Boulogne* ☎ *01–44–14–41–14* ⊕ *www.restaurant-precatelan.com* ⚑ *Reservations essential. Jacket and tie* ▭ *AE, DC, MC, V* ☉ *Closed Sun. and Mon., 2 wks in Feb., 3 wks in Aug., and 1 wk in late Oct./early Nov.* Ⓜ *Porte Dauphine* ✛ *1:A3.*

## 17ᴱ ARRONDISSEMENT

**$** ✕ **Au Petit Verdot du 17e.** Sandwich bars might be threatening the tradi-

BISTRO tional two-hour lunch, but that doesn't stop this old-fashioned neighborhood bistro with a freshly painted facade and wine-theme dining room from flourishing—even though it's open only at lunch, except Thursday and Friday. Businessmen loosen their neckties to feast on homemade pâté, plate-engulfing steak for two, or guinea hen with cabbage, along with one of 40 or so small producers' wines, which are delivered directly to the restaurant. ✉ *9 rue Fourcroy, Champs-Élysées* ☎ *01–42–27–47–42* 🞸 *MC, V* 🕑 *Closed weekends. No dinner Mon.–Wed.* Ⓜ *Charles-de-Gaulle–Étoile* ✛ *1:C2.*

**$$–$$$**
BISTRO
✕ **Goupil le Bistro.** The best Paris bistros emit an air of quiet confidence, and this is certainly the case with Goupil, a triumph despite its out-of-the-way location not far from the Porte Maillot conference center. The dining room attracts dark suits at lunch and a festive crowd in the evenings, with a few well-informed English-speakers sprinkled into the mix. The tiny open kitchen works miracles with seasonal ingredients, transforming mackerel into luxury food (on buttery puff pastry with mustard sauce) and pan-frying monkfish to perfection with artichokes and chanterelles. Friendly waiters are happy to suggest wines by the glass. ✉ *4 rue Claude Debussy, Parc Monceau* ☎ *01–45–74–83–25* 🍽 *Reservations essential* 🞸 *AE, MC, V* 🕑 *Closed weekends and 3 wks in Aug.* Ⓜ *Porte de Champerret* ✛ *1:B1.*

**$$$$**
HAUTE FRENCH
**Fodor's**Choice
★
✕ **Guy Savoy.** Revamped with dark African wood, rich leather, cream-color marble, and the chef's own art collection, Guy Savoy's luxury restaurant doesn't dwell on the past. Come here for a perfectly measured haute-cuisine experience, since Savoy's several bistros have not lured him away from his kitchen. The artichoke soup with black truffles, sea bass with spices, and veal kidneys in mustard-spiked jus reveal the magnitude of his talent, and his mille-feuille is an instant classic. If the waiters see you're relishing a dish, they won't hesitate to offer second helpings. Generous half portions allow you to graze your way through the menu—unless you choose a blowout feast for set menus of €275 or €345—and reasonably priced wines are available (though beware the cost of wines by the glass). Special promotions are sometimes available on the Web site. Best of all, the atmosphere is joyful, because Savoy knows that having fun is just as important as eating well. ✉ *18 rue Troyon, Champs-Élysées* ☎ *01–43–80–40–61* 🌐 *www.guysavoy. com* 🍽 *Reservations essential. Jacket required* 🞸 *AE, MC, V* 🕑 *Closed Sun., Mon., Aug., and 1 wk at Christmas. No lunch Sat.* Ⓜ *Charles-de-Gaulle–Étoile* ✛ *1:C3.*

**$$–$$$**
JAPANESE
✕ **Kifune.** It's rare to see a non-Japanese face in the bistrolike dining room of Kifune, where you can sit at the bar and admire the sushi chef's lightning-quick skills or opt for a more intimate table. The crab-and-shrimp salad is a sublime starter, and the miso soup with clams is deeply flavored. To follow, you can't go wrong with the sashimi. A meal here will leave a dent in your wallet (though there is a €30 set menu at lunch), but some expats say you won't find anything closer to authentic Japanese cooking in Paris. With only 20 seats they often turn away would-be customers, so be sure to book. ✉ *44 rue St-Ferdinand, Champs-Élysées* ☎ *01–45–72–11–19* 🍽 *Reservations essential* 🞸 *MC, V* 🕑 *Closed Sun. and Mon., 3 wks in Aug., 1 wk in Dec., and 2 wks in May* Ⓜ *Argentine* ✛ *1:A3.*

**$$$**
SEAFOOD
✕ **L'Huîtrier.** If you have a single-minded craving for oysters, this is the place for you. The friendly owner will describe the different kinds available and you can follow with any of several daily fish specials—or opt for a full seafood platter for around €50. Blond-wood and cream

tones prevail in the dining room. If you have trouble getting a table, L'Huîtrier also runs the Presqu'île next door. ⌧ *16 rue Saussier-Leroy, Parc Monceau* ☎ *01–40–54–83–44* ☰ *AE, MC, V* ☉ *Closed Sun., and Mon. May–Aug.* Ⓜ *Ternes* ✚ *1:C2.*

**$**    ✕ **Le Hide.** Hide Kobayashi, known as "Koba," is one of several Japa-
HAUTE FRENCH nese chefs in Paris who trained with some of the biggest names in French cuisine before opening their own restaurants. With stints at Lenôtre, the Louis XV in Monaco, and Joël Robuchon under his belt, Koba had the brilliant idea of opening a great-value bistro near the Arc de Triomphe (the three-course prix fixe costs €29). Not surprisingly, this little din-ing room with cream-color walls and red banquettes became instantly popular with locals as well as visiting Japanese and Americans who follow the food news. Generosity is the key to the cooking here, which steers clear of haute cuisine flourishes: both the monkfish fricassee with anchovy-rich tapenade and a classic veal kidney in mustard sauce, for instance, come with a heap of mashed potatoes. For dessert try the stunning *île flottante* (floating island), made with oven-baked meringue. Wines by the glass start at €2, and a beer is €2.50—unheard-of in this area. ⌧ *10 rue du Général Lanzerac, Champs-Élysées* ☎ *01–45–74– 15–81* ⊕ *www.lehide.fr* ✍ *Reservations essential* ☰ *AE, DC, MC, V* ☉ *Closed Sun. and 2 wks in Aug. No lunch Sat.* Ⓜ *Charles de Gaulle– Étoile* ✚ *1:B3.*

**$$$**    ✕ **Rech.** Having restored the historic Paris bistros Aux Lyonnais and
SEAFOOD Benoît to their former glory, star chef Alain Ducasse has turned his
Fodor'sChoice piercing attention to this seafood brasserie founded in 1925. His wis-
★ dom lies in knowing what not to change: the original Art Deco chairs in the main floor dining room; seafood shucker Malec, who has been a fixture on this chic stretch of sidewalk since 1982; and the XL éclair (it's supersized) that's drawn in locals for decades. Original owner Auguste Rech believed in serving a limited selection of high-quality products—a principle that suits Ducasse perfectly—and legendary 60-year-old chef Jacques Maximin is now in the kitchen, turning out Med-inspired dishes such as tomato cream with crayfish and fresh almonds or Niçoise-style sea bass with thyme fritters. Save room for the whole farmer's Cam-embert, another Rech tradition. A great-value €30 menu is available at lunch. ⌧ *62 av. des Ternes, Champs-Élysées* ☎ *01–45–72–29–47* ⊕ *www.rech.fr* ✍ *Reservations essential* ☰ *AE, DC, MC, V* ☉ *Closed Sun., Mon., late July–late Aug., and 1 wk at Christmas* ✚ *1:B3.*

## 18ᴱ ARRONDISSEMENT

**$$$**    ✕ **Guilo Guilo.** Already a star in Kyoto, Eiichi Edakuni has created a sen-
JAPANESE sation with his first Parisian restaurant, where 20 diners seated around
Fodor'sChoice the black bar can watch him at work each night. The no-choice, €45
★ set menu is a bargain given the quality and sophistication of the food: it changes every month, but you might come across dishes such as sea bream and wagyu beef on shiso leaves with ponzu sauce, or the chef's signature foie gras sushi, an idea that could easily fall flat but instead soars. If you can afford it, complement your meal with exceptional sakes by the glass, one of which is sparkling. This restaurant is no

secret, so reserve three weeks ahead. ✉ *8 rue Garreau, Montmartre* ☎ *01–42–54–23–92* ⊕ *www.guiloguilo.com* ⌕ *Reservations essential* ⊟ *MC, V* ☉ *Closed Sun. and Mon.* Ⓜ *Abbesses* ✛ *2:B1.*

**$$–$$$**
BRASSERIE

✕ **La Mascotte.** Though everyone talks about the "new Montmartre," exemplified by a wave of chic residents and throbbingly cool cafés and bars, it's good to know that the old Montmartre is alive and well at the untrendy-and-proud-of-it Mascotte. This old-fashioned café-brasserie—which dates from 1889, the same year that saw the opening of the Tour Eiffel and the Moulin Rouge—is where you can find neighborhood fixtures such as the drag queen Michou (of the nearby club Chez Michou), who always wears blue. Loyalists come for the seafood platters, the excellent steak tartare, the warming *potée auvergnate* (pork stew) in winter, and the gossip around the *comptoir* (bar) up front. There is a two-course lunch menu for €22, and nonstop service on weekends. ✉ *52 rue des Abbesses, Montmartre* ☎ *01–46–06–28–15* ⊕ *www.la-mascotte-montmartre.com* ⊟ *MC, V* Ⓜ *Abbesses* ✛ *2:B1.*

**$**
BISTRO
☪

✕ **Le Miroir.** Residents of Montmartre are breathing a sigh of relief: they no longer have to leave the neighborhood to find a good-value bistro. Run by a trio who honed their skills at Lavinia, La Tour d'Argent, and Aux Lyonnais, this red-and-gray bistro with a glass roof at the back serves just the kind of sophisticated comfort food everyone hopes to find in Paris. A meal might start with a plate of *cochonailles* (pâté, cured sausage, and deboned pig's trotter with onion jam) or perhaps a salad of whelks and white beans, before hearty main courses such as a stunning beef rib for two with sautéed potatoes or duck breast with chanterelle mushrooms and a slice of panfried foie gras. To finish, it's hard to choose between the aged Beaufort cheese or the vanilla pot de crème, served with shortbread and chocolate *financiers* (almond cakes). ✉ *94 rue des Martyrs, Montmartre* ☎ *01–46–06–50–73* ⌕ *Reservations essential* ⊟ *AE, MC, V* ☉ *Closed Mon. and 3 wks in Aug. No lunch Sun.* Ⓜ *Abbesses* ✛ *2:B1.*

## 19ᴱ ARRONDISSEMENT

**$–$$$**
BRASSERIE

✕ **Au Boeuf Couronné.** La Villette once housed the city's meat market, and this brasserie devoted to fine beef (whether French or Irish) soldiers on as if nothing has changed. If you're beginning to tire of the Flo brasserie formula (the Flo chain owns such historic brasseries as La Coupole, Le Balzar, and Brasserie Flo), it's worth the trek to this far-flung neighborhood to sample one of the 16 takes on the beef theme (plus a gargantuan marrow bone), or good fish and seafood dishes, such as sole or scallops (in season). You'll find bon vivants from all over Paris in the buzzy dining room. ✉ *188 av. Jean-Jaurès, La Villette* ☎ *01–42–39–44–44* ⊕ *www.gerard-joulie.com* ⊟ *AE, DC, MC, V* Ⓜ *Porte de Pantin* ✛ *2:H1.*

**17**

## 20ᴱ ARRONDISSEMENT

**$$**  ✕ **La Boulangerie.** In a former bakery spruced up with a bread-theme
BISTRO  mural, this bistro in the shabby-chic neighborhood of Ménilmontant
dishes up a great-value lunch menu for €15 (two courses) or €17 (three
courses). Dinner is a still-reasonable €32, and the quality of the ingre-
dients is admirable, even if the cooking can be inconsistent. Expect
seasonal dishes like squash soup with spice-bread croutons, pot-roasted
veal with root vegetables, and *cannelés* (eggy, caramelized cakes) with
jasmine ice cream made on the premises. If you're exploring the area
around Père Lachaise, it would be hard to find a better French eatery.
✉ *15 rue des Panoyaux, Père Lachaise* ☎ *01–43–58–45–45* ⌂ *Reser-
vations essential* 🖃 *MC, V* ⊘ *Closed Sun., Mon., 1 wk in July, 3 wks
in Aug., and 1 wk at Christmas. No lunch Sat.* Ⓜ *Ménilmontant*
✛ *2:H5.*

**$$**  ✕ **Le Baratin.** Le Baratin has been around for more than 20 years but that
BISTRO  hasn't stopped it from recently becoming one of the most fashionable
ℭ  out-of-the-way bistros in Paris. The key to its success is the combination
Fodor'sChoice  of inventive yet comforting cooking by Argentinean-born chef Raquel
★  Carena and a lovingly selected list of organic and natural wines from
small producers, courtesy of her partner Philippe Pinoteau. He might
seem brusque at first, but show an interest and he opens up like a vin-
tage wine. Carena learned the art of making bouillons from none other
than star Breton chef Olivier Roellinger, and uses them to bring out
the best in any ingredient from fish to foie gras. ✉ *3 rue Jouye Rouve,
Ménilmontant* ☎ *01–43–49–39–70* ⌂ *Reservations essential* 🖃 *MC, V*
⊘ *Closed Sun., Mon., and Aug.* Ⓜ *Pyrénées, Belleville* ✛ *2:H3.*

# Where to Eat and Stay in Paris

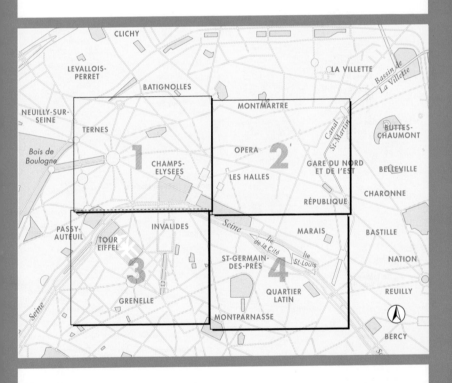

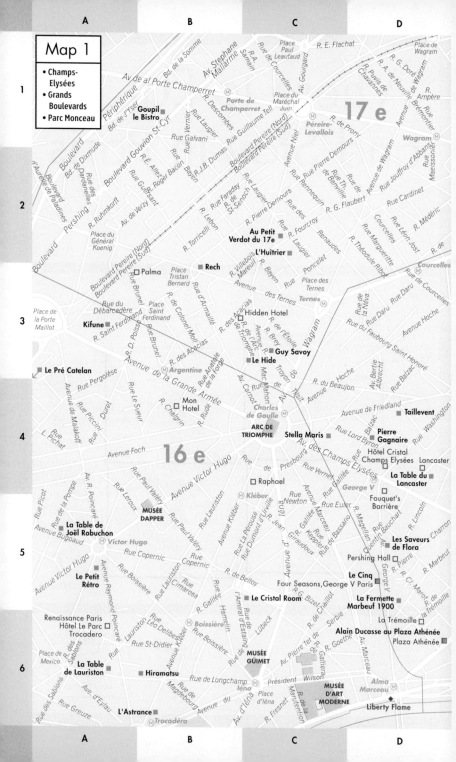

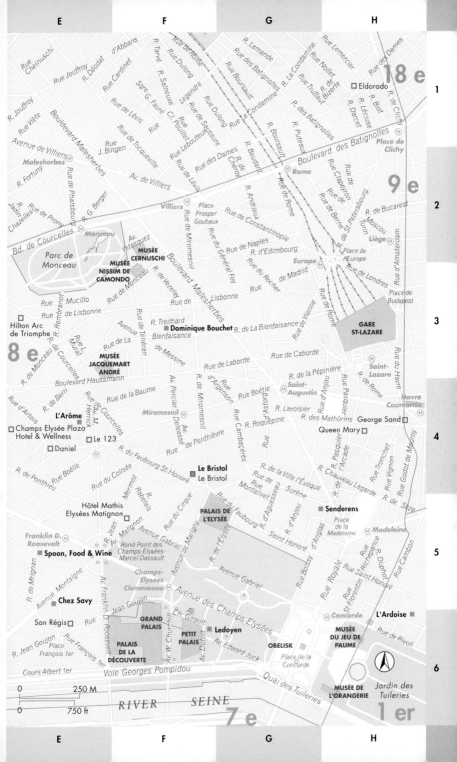

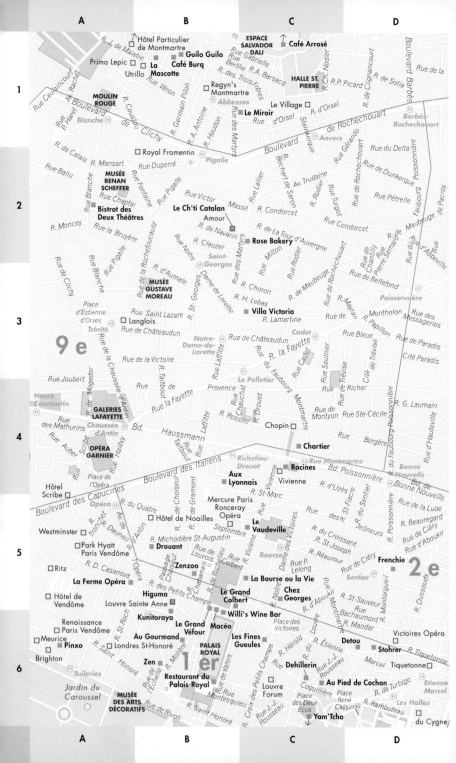

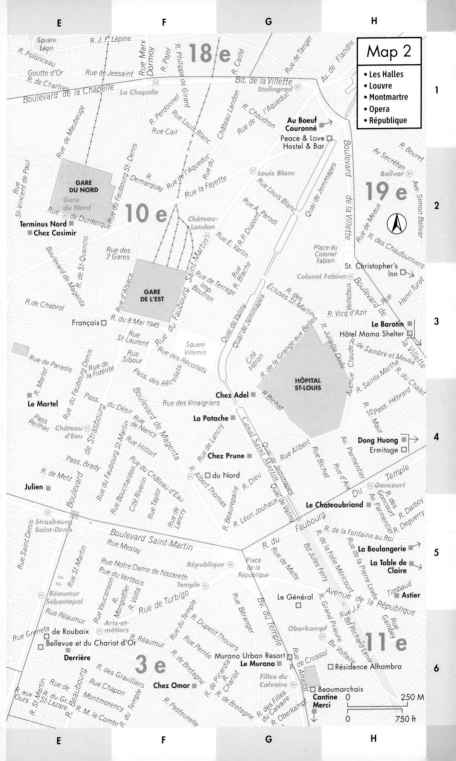

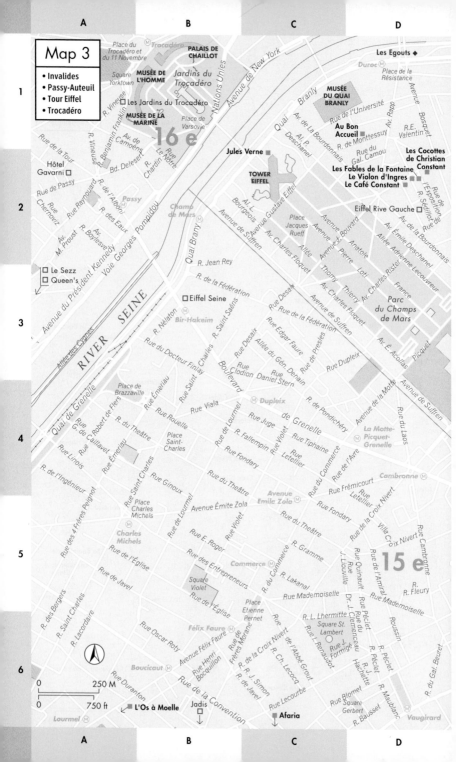

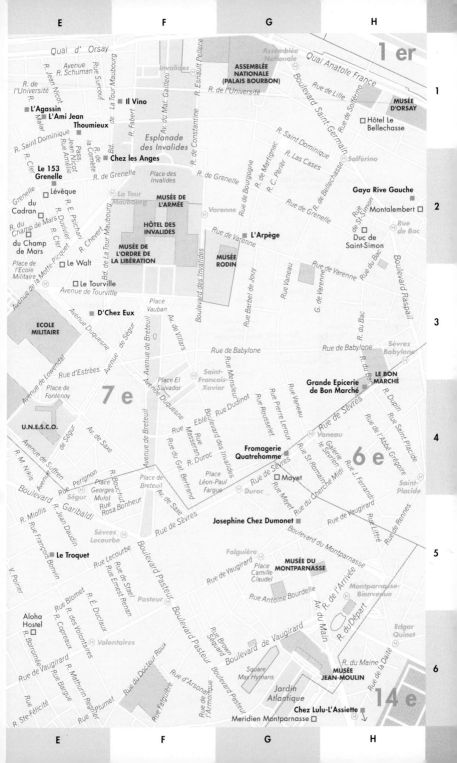

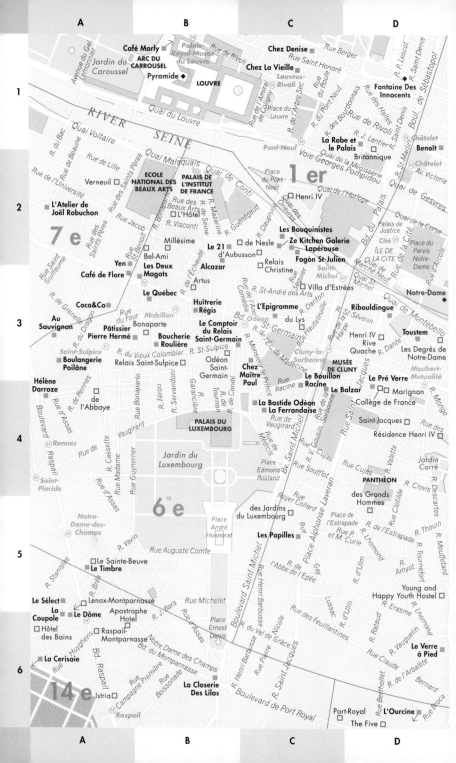

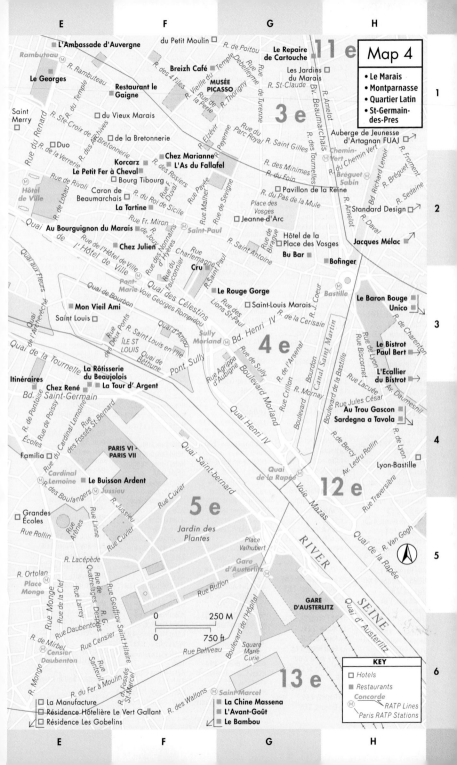

# Where to Stay

**WORD OF MOUTH**

"For a first time visit, the 4, 5,and 6th arrondissements I think would be best. This gives you access to lots of restos, and walking distance to some sites."

—Michel_Paris

Updated
by Heather
Stimmler-Hall

If your Parisian fantasy involves staying in a historic hotel with the smell of fresh-baked croissants gently rousing you in the morning, here's some good news: you need not be Ritz-rich to realize it. With more than 1,450 hotels, the City of Light gives visitors stylish options in all price ranges.

In terms of location, there are more hotels on the Rive Droite (the Right Bank) offering luxury—in terms of formality—than on the Rive Gauche (the Left Bank), where the hotels are frequently smaller and richer in old-fashioned charm. The Rive Droite's 1$^{er}$, 8$^e$, and 16$^e$ arrondissements are still the most exclusive, and the prices there reflect that. Some of these palatial hotels charge more than €500 a night without batting an eye. Less expensive alternatives on the Rive Droite can be found in the fashionable Marais quarter (3$^e$ and 4$^e$ arrondissements). The hotbed of chic hotels on the Rive Gauche is the 6$^e$ arrondissement; choices get cheaper in the 5$^e$ and 7$^e$. Some excellent budget deals can be found slightly off the beaten track in the 9$^e$ and 13$^e$ arrondissements. Wherever possible, we've located budget hotels in more expensive neighborhoods—check out the handful of budget-priced sleeps in the shadow of Notre-Dame, St-Germain-des-Prés, and the Louvre.

Although historic charm is a given, space to stretch out is not. Even budget travelers can sleep under 200-year-old wooden beams, but if you're looking for enough room to spread out multiple suitcases, better book a suite in a four-star palace hotel. Indoor spaces—from beds to elevators—may feel cramped to those not used to life on a European scale. The new no-smoking law went into effect in all public spaces in January 2008. Enforcement may not be perfect for the first few years, but at least now you'll have a valid complaint if your room smells like stale smoke. Amenities have also improved, with virtually every hotel now equipped with cable TV (meaning CNN and BBC news in English), minibars, in-room safes, and wireless Internet access (though not always free). Another recent change is the increasing availability of air-conditioning, which can be saintly in August.

## WHERE SHOULD I STAY?

| | NEIGHBORHOOD VIBE | PROS | CONS |
|---|---|---|---|
| St-Germain and Montparnasse (6$^e$, 14$^e$, 15$^e$) | The center of café culture and the emblem of the Rive Gauche, the mood is leisurely, the attractions are well established, and the prices are high. | A safe, historic area with chic fashion boutiques, famous cafés and brasseries, and lovely side streets. Lively day and night. | Expensive. Noisy along the main streets. The area around the monstrous Tour Montparnasse is a soul-sucking tribute to commerce. |
| The Quartier Latin (5$^e$) | The historic student quarter of the Rive Gauche, full of narrow, winding streets, and major parks and monuments such as the Panthéon. | Plenty of cheap eats and sleeps, discount book and music shops, and noteworthy open-air markets. Safe area for wandering walks. | Touristy. No métro stations on the hilltop around the Panthéon. Student pubs can be noisy in summer. Hotel rooms tend to be smaller. |
| Marais and Bastille (3$^e$, 4$^e$, 11$^e$) | Cute shops, museums, and laid-back bistros line the narrow streets of Le Marais, home to both the gay and Jewish communities. Farther east, ethnic eats, and edgy shops. | Generally excellent shopping, sightseeing, dining, and nightlife in the super-safe Marais. Bargains aplenty at Bastille hotels. Several modern-design hotels, too. | Le Marais's narrow sidewalks are always overcrowded, and rooms don't come cheap. It's noisy around the gritty boulevards of Place de la Bastille and Nation. |
| Montmartre and northeast Paris (18$^e$, 19$^e$, 20$^e$) | The Rive Droite's hilltop district is known for winding streets leading from the racy Pigalle district to the stark-white Sacré-Coeur Basilica. | Amazing views of Paris, romantic cobblestone streets, easy access to Roissy-Charles de Gaulle airport. | Steep staircases, few métro stations, and Pigalle can be too seedy to stomach, especially late at night, when it can also be unsafe. |
| Champs-Élysées and western Paris (8$^e$, 16$^e$, 17$^e$) | The world-famous avenue is lively 24/7 with cinemas, high-end shops, and nightclubs, all catering to the moneyed jet set. | The home to most of the city's famous palace hotels, there's no shortage of luxurious sleeps here on the Rive Droite. | The high prices of this neighborhood, along with its Times Square tendencies, repel Parisians but lure pickpockets. |
| Around the Eiffel Tower (7$^e$, 15$^e$) | The impressive Eiffel Tower and monumental Palais de Chaillot at Trocadéro straddle the Seine River. | Safe, quiet, and relatively inexpensive Rive Gauche area of Paris with green spaces and picture-perfect views at every turn. | With few shops and restaurants, this district is quiet at night; long distances between métro stations. |
| Louvre, Les Halles, Ile de la Cité (1$^e$, 2$^e$, 8$^e$) | The central Parisian district around the Tuileries gardens and Louvre museum is best known for shopping and sightseeing; Les Halles is a buzzing hub of commerce and mass transit. | Convenient for getting around Paris on foot, bus, or métro. Safe, attractive district close to the Seine and shops of all types. All the major métro and RER lines are right by Les Halles. | The main drag along Rue de Rivoli can be noisy with traffic during the day, and the restaurants cater mostly to tourists. Shops are tacky and fast food predominates around Les Halles. |

**18**

# WHERE TO STAY PLANNER

## Lodging Strategy

Where should we stay? With hundreds of Paris hotels, it may seem like a daunting question. But fret not—our expert writers and editors have done most of the legwork. The 100-plus selections here represent the best this city has to offer. Scan "Best Bets" on the following pages for top recommendations by price and experience. Or find a review quickly in the listings, which are arranged by arrondissement and then alphabetically.

## Reservations

Make reservations as far in advance as possible, especially for May, June, September, and October. Calling works, but e-mail (or fax) may be the easiest way to make contact, since hotel staff are probably more likely to read English than understand it over the phone. Specify arrival and departure dates; room size (single or double), room type (standard, deluxe, or suite); the number of people in your party; and whether you want a bathroom with a shower or bathtub (or both). Ask if a deposit is required, and what happens if you cancel.

## Checking In

Typical check-in and check-out times are 2 PM and noon, respectively, although some properties allow check-in as early as noon and require check-out as early as 11 AM. Many flights from North America arrive early in the morning, but having to wait six hours for a room after arriving jet-lagged at 8 AM isn't the ideal way to start a vacation. Alert the hotel of your early arrival; larger establishments can often make special early check-in arrangements, but don't expect more than baggage storage.

## Hotel Quality

Note that the quality of accommodations can vary from room to room. If you don't like the room you're given, ask to see another. The French star ratings can be misleading: official stars are granted for specific amenities and services rather than for ambience, style, or overall comfort, so you may find that a two-star hotel eclipses a three-star establishment. Many hotels prefer to remain "under-starred" for tax reasons.

## Children

Most hotels in Paris allow children to stay in their parents' room at no charge. Hotel rooms are often on the small side, so inquire about connecting rooms or suites. For more information about kid-friendly accommodations, consult the "With Kids?" feature in this chapter.

## Breakfast

Almost all Parisian hotels charge extra for breakfast, with per-person prices ranging from €5 to more than €30. Continental breakfast—coffee, baguette, croissant, jam, and butter—is sometimes included in the hotel rate. We denote this with a CP, for Continental Plan. If you decide to eat elsewhere, inform the staff so breakfast won't be charged to your bill.

## Hotel Features

Unless stated in the review, hotels have elevators, and all guest rooms have air-conditioning, TV, telephone, and a private bathroom. In France the first floor is the floor above the ground floor, or *rez-de-chaussée*. Note that we use "Internet" to designate the presence of genuine high-speed lines and mention wireless access where available (otherwise, expect escargot-pace Web surfing). The number of rooms listed at the end of each review reflects those with private bathrooms (which means they have a shower or a tub, but not necessarily both). Tubs don't always have fixed curtains or showerheads; how the French rinse themselves with the handheld nozzle without flooding the entire bathroom remains a cultural mystery. It's rare to find moderately priced places that expect guests to share toilets or bathrooms, but be sure you know what facilities you are getting when you book a budget hotel.

## What It Costs

Often a hotel in a certain price category will have a few less-expensive rooms; it's worth asking. In the off-season—mid-July, August, November, early December, and late January—rates can be considerably lower. You should also inquire about specials and weekend deals, and you may be able to get a better rate per night if you're staying a week or longer. There's a nominal city *taxe de séjour* ranging between €0.20 and €1.20 per person, per night, based on the hotel's star rating. Sometimes this tax is included in the room price, sometimes not.

If you're staying in Paris for more than just a few days, you might want to look into the increasingly popular option of renting an apartment. Check out the Lodging Alternatives feature in this chapter. Not only does this often save in nightly costs, but with your own kitchen you can save by living like a local and cooking some of your own meals.

## In this Chapter

**18**

| WHAT IT COSTS | | | | | |
|---|---|---|---|---|---|
| | ¢ | $ | $$ | $$$ | $$$$ |
| FOR TWO PEOPLE | under €80 | €81–€120 | €121–€175 | €176–€250 | over €250 |

Prices are for two people in a standard double room in high season, including tax (19.6%) and service charge

# BEST BETS FOR PARIS LODGING

Fodor's offers a selective listing of high-quality lodging experiences at every price range, from the best budget options to the most sophisticated grande-dame hotel. Below are our top recommendations by price and experience.

# HOTELS

*(Alphabetical by arrondissement; use the coordinate (⊕ 1:B2) at the end of each listing to locate a site on the corresponding map.)*

## 1<sup>ER</sup> ARRONDISSEMENT

It simply doesn't get any more central than the Louvre/Tuileries neighborhood. It's a five-minute walk to major sights such as the Louvre, les Jardins des Tuileries, Notre-Dame, and Sainte-Chapelle. Also nearby are two major shopping streets—Rue de Rivoli and Rue St-Honoré—and the Forum des Halles shopping mall. The central bus, RER, and métro stations will get you around the rest of Paris effortlessly.

$$$ **Hôtel Brighton.** Many of Paris's most prestigious palace hotels face the Tuileries or Place de la Concorde, and while the Brighton breathes the same rarified air under the arcades, it does so for a fraction of the price. Smaller rooms look onto a courtyard; street-facing ones have balconies and a royal view of the gardens and Rive Gauche. Extensive renovations updated all the rooms, with the newest ones featuring flat-screen TVs and heated towel racks. First-floor rooms have high ceilings. **Pros:** great views; central location in a prestigious neighborhood; free Wi-Fi. **Cons:** the busy street can make rooms with a view a bit noisy; variable quality in decor between rooms. ⊠ *218 rue de Rivoli, Louvre/Tuileries* ☎ *01–47–03–61–61* ⊕ *www.paris-hotel-brighton.com* ↘ *61 rooms* ⚿ *In-room: safe, Wi-Fi. In-hotel: laundry service* ▤ *AE, DC, MC, V* Ⓜ *Tuileries* ⊕ *2:A6.*

$$$ **Hôtel Britannique.** Open since 1861 and a stone's throw from the Louvre, the Britannique blends courteous English service with old-fashioned French elegance. Take the winding staircase to rooms done in a mix of attractive repro furniture and antiques. Wi-Fi and in-room flat-screen TVs lend an air of modernity. In World War I, the hotel served as headquarters for a Quaker mission. **Pros:** one of the city's most charming hotels, on a calm side street less than a block from the métro/RER station; attentive staff. **Cons:** smallish rooms; soundproofing between rooms could be better. ⊠ *20 av. Victoria, Beaubourg/Les Halles* ☎ *01–42–33–74–59* ⊕ *www.hotel-britannique.fr* ↘ *38 rooms, 1 suite* ⚿ *In-room: safe, Wi-Fi. In-hotel: bar, laundry service* ▤ *AE, DC, MC, V* Ⓜ *Châtelet* ⊕ *4:1D.*

$ **Hôtel du Cygne.** Passed down from mother to daughter, "the Swan" is decorated with homey touches like hand-sewn curtains, country quilts, and white wood furniture. Bathrooms are marble; older ones have mosaic tiling. Book early for the larger rooms, which include Nos. 16, 26, 35, and 41. Ancient wood beams run the length of the two stairwells, which makes for uneven stepping that challenges even the most agile guests. **Pros:** spotless rooms and bathrooms; central location on a pedestrian street; good value. **Cons:** old building with small rooms; no elevator; not the most attractive area of central Paris; can be intimidating after dark. ⊠ *3 rue du Cygne, Beaubourg/Les Halles* ☎ *01–42–60–14–16* ⊕ *www.cygne-hotel-paris.com* ↘ *20 rooms* ⚿ *In-room: no a/c, safe, Internet* ▤ *MC, V* Ⓜ *Étienne Marcel, Les Halles* ⊕ *2:D6.*

**18**

¢   🖭 **Hôtel Henri IV**. When tourists think of staying on one of the islands, it's usually Ile St-Louis, not Ile de la Cité, but the overlooked isle shelters one of the city's most beloved budget-priced sleeps. The 17th-century building that once housed King Henri IV's printing presses offers few comforts: the narrow staircase (five flights, no elevator) creaks and the rooms have few amenities. Recent renovations, however, have added showers and toilets in almost every room. The payoff is a location overlooking the oasislike Place Dauphine, just a few steps from the Pont Neuf and Sainte-Chapelle. **Pros:** very quiet, central location; breakfast included. **Cons:** steep stairs and no elevator; few services or amenities; no e-mail or online reservations. ⊠ *25 pl. Dauphine, Ile de la Cité* ☎ *01–43–54–44–53* ⊕ *www.henri4hotel.fr* ↪ *15 rooms, 11 with bath* ⚱ *In-room: no a/c, no phone, no TV* ⊟ *MC, V* ⦿⦿ *CP* Ⓜ *Cité, St-Michel, Pont Neuf* ✛ *4:C2.*

$$   🖭 **Hôtel Londres St-Honoré**. An appealing combination of character and comfort distinguishes this small, inexpensive hotel a five-minute walk from the Louvre. Exposed oak beams, statues in niches, and rustic stone walls give the place an old-fashioned air. Most rooms have floral bedspreads and standard hotel furniture, though bathrooms are refreshingly modern, with real hair dryers. Note that elevator service begins on the second floor, so some stairs are guaranteed. **Pros:** within walking distance of major sites; free Wi-Fi. **Cons:** small elevator that doesn't go to ground floor; small beds; upper rooms can get very hot in summer (fans are available). ⊠ *13 rue St-Roch, Louvre/Tuileries* ☎ *01–42–60–15–62* ⊕ *www.hotellondresthonore-paris.com* ↪ *21 rooms, 4 suites* ⚱ *In-room: a/c (some), safe, Wi-Fi. In-hotel: Internet terminal, some pets allowed* ⊟ *AE, DC, MC, V* Ⓜ *Pyramides* ✛ *2:A6.*

$$   🖭 **Hôtel Louvre Forum**. This hotel near the Louvre, Les Halles, and Palais-Royal is a find, with modern, spotless rooms that are well equipped for the price. Furniture is of the Ikea genre, and the baths are simple white tile, but bonuses include a bright sitting area and a stone-cellar breakfast room, both with murals. **Pros:** clean and comfortable with elevator; in the center of Paris. **Cons:** rooms and elevator are small; not much character. ⊠ *25 rue du Bouloi, Louvre/Tuileries* ☎ *01–42–36–54–19* ⊕ *www.paris-hotel-louvre-forum.com* ↪ *27 rooms* ⚱ *In-room: safe, Wi-Fi. In-hotel: bar* ⊟ *AE, MC, V* Ⓜ *Louvre* ✛ *2:C6.*

$$   🖭 **Hôtel Louvre Sainte Anne**. This small but modern hotel between the Opéra and the Louvre has bright rooms decorated in a country theme, with little extras like heated towel racks. The two spacious triples on the top floor cost a bit extra but have small terraces with views of Sacré-Coeur. Breakfast is served in a stone-vaulted cellar, and the exceptionally friendly staff can recommend plenty of noteworthy nearby restaurants. **Pros:** central location; free Wi-Fi; helpful staff. **Cons:** smallish rooms and dull decor; "Japanese" district can feel very un-Parisian. ⊠ *32 rue Ste-Anne, Louvre/Tuileries* ☎ *01–40–20–02–35* ⊕ *www.louvre-ste-anne.fr* ↪ *20 rooms* ⚱ *In-room: safe, Wi-Fi. In-hotel: room service, Internet terminal, some pets allowed* ⊟ *AE, MC, V* Ⓜ *Pyramides* ✛ *2:B5.*

$$$$   🖭 **Hôtel Meurice**. Since 1835, the Meurice has welcomed royalty and
☾   celebrities, from the Duchess of Windsor to Salvador Dalí. In late 2007

the lobby, bar, and restaurant were given a swanky makeover by French designer Philippe Starck. Rooms have a gilded Louis XVI or Napoleonic Empire style, with antique furnishings covered in sumptuous French and Italian brocades. Most rooms have a Tuileries/Louvre or Sacré-Coeur view, but the massive Royal Suite takes in a 360-degree panorama. Bathrooms are marble, with deep, spacious tubs. The spa includes Swiss Valmont facials, Thermes Marins de St-Malo body treatmenrts, and "By Terry" makeovers; children are pampered with their own Meurice teddy bear and tot-size slippers and bathrobe. **Pros:** views over the gardens; central location, trendy public spaces. **Cons:** on a noisy street; popularity makes the public areas not very discreet. ⊠ *228 rue de Rivoli, Louvre/Tuileries* ☎ *01–44–58–10–09* ⊕ *www.lemeurice.com* ⤿ *160 rooms, 36 suites* ⍾ *In-room: safe, Wi-Fi. In-hotel: 2 restaurants, room service, bar, gym, spa, laundry service, Internet terminal, some pets allowed* ⊟ *AE, DC, MC, V* Ⓜ *Tuileries, Concorde* ✛ *2:A6.*

$$$$ 🏨 **Renaissance Paris Vendôme.** Hiding behind a classic 19th-century facade is a fresh, contemporary hotel with subtle 1930s influences. Under a huge atrium skylight, the lobby's polished black-marble floors, hardwood furnishings, neutral fabrics, and decadent antiques set the mood. The small library has free Wi-Fi and a wood-burning fireplace, and the intimate Bar Chinois is decorated with elaborate Chinese wallpaper. Imported woods and black slate accent the hotel's sauna, steam room, and countercurrent swimming pool. Rooms have modern amenities like flat-screen TVs and free high-speed Internet. The marble bathrooms feature Bulgari toiletries and heated towel racks. Contemporary French and Basque-style cuisine are served in the hotel's Pinxo Restaurant. **Pros:** posh location; trendy restaurant. **Cons:** as part of the Marriott group it can feel a bit lacking in character. ⊠ *4 rue du Mont Thabor, Louvre/Tuileries* ☎ *01–40–20–20–00* ⊕ *www.renaissanceparisvendome. com* ⤿ *82 rooms, 15 suites* ⍾ *In-room: safe, DVD, Internet. In-hotel: restaurant, room service, bar, pool, gym, spa, laundry service, parking (paid)* ⊟ *AE, DC, MC, V* Ⓜ *Tuileries* ✛ *2:A6.*

$$$$ 🏨 **Ritz.** Ever since César Ritz opened the doors of his hotel in 1898, the ☾ mere name of this venerable institution has become synonymous with luxury. The famed Ritz Escoffier cooking school, where you can learn the finer points of *gateaux*, is here, as is the new Ritz Lounge Bar and the Hemingway Bar. There's also a Greek-temple-style subterranean spa and swimming pool. Guest rooms match this level of luxe; even the humbler spaces have every modern doodad, cleverly camouflaged with the decor of gleaming mirrors, chandeliers, and antiques. (Think marble baths with gold pull chains that summon the valet or maid.) The most palatial suites are named after famous Ritz residents: Coco Chanel, the Prince of Wales, and Elton John. **Pros:** spacious swimming pool; selection of bars and restaurants; top-notch service. **Cons:** can feel stuffy and old-fashioned; easy to get lost in the vast hotel; paparazzi magnet. ⊠ *15 pl. Vendôme, Louvre/Tuileries* ☎ *01–43–16–30–30* ⊕ *www. ritzparis.com* ⤿ *106 rooms, 56 suites* ⍾ *In-room: safe, Wi-Fi. In-hotel: 3 restaurants, room service, bars, pool, gym, spa, children's programs (ages 6–12), laundry service, Internet terminal, parking (paid)* ⊟ *AE, DC, MC, V* Ⓜ *Opéra* ✛ *2:A5.*

18

## 2ᴱ ARRONDISSEMENT

Posh boutiques, 24-hour brasseries, and bustling boulevards define this lively neighborhood, at the center of which are the Opéra Garnier and the historic department stores of the Boulevard Haussmann. The Montorgueil market street is now also home to several trendy bars and vintage clothing shops, and the clubs and cinemas around the métro Grands Boulevards attract a boisterous nightlife crowd.

¢ **Hôtel Bellevue et du Chariot d'Or.** This Belle Époque time traveler is proud to keep its dingy chandeliers and faded gold trimming. Budget groups from France and the Netherlands come for the clean, sans-frills rooms; some units sleep four. Halls are lined with stamped felt that helps muffle sounds trickling up from the marble-floor lobby and bar. There may be some quirks, like the hefty old-fashioned room keys and the bathtub/showers without curtains, but you're just a few blocks from hipper addresses in the heart of Le Marais. **Pros:** large rooms great for families; easy walk to Le Marais and Les Halles districts. **Cons:** busy, noisy street; not the most attractive part of central Paris; drab decor. ⊠ *39 rue de Turbigo, Beaubourg/Les Halles* ☎ *01–48–87–45–60* ⊕ *www.hotelbellevue75.com* ⤳ *59 rooms* ⚿ *In-room: no a/c, Wi-Fi. In-hotel: bar, Wi-Fi hotspot* ⊟ *AE, DC, MC, V* ⍁ *CP* Ⓜ *Réaumur-Sébastopol, Arts et Métiers* ✛ *2:E6.*

$$$ **Hôtel de Noailles.** With a nod to the work of postmodern designers like Putman and Starck, this style-driven boutique is both contemporary and cozy. Rooms are sleek and streamlined, with backlit, custom-built cabinets, glassed-in bathrooms, and fabric or faux-leather wall coverings. A spacious outdoor terrace is off the breakfast lounge. **Pros:** a block from the airport bus; easy walk to the Louvre and Opéra. **Cons:** small elevator; no interesting views. ⊠ *9 rue de Michodière, Opéra/Grands Boulevards* ☎ *01–47–42–92–90* ⊕ *www.hoteldenoailles.com* ⤳ *58 rooms* ⚿ *In-room: safe, Wi-Fi. In-hotel: room service, bar, laundry service, some pets allowed* ⊟ *AE, DC, MC, V* Ⓜ *Opéra* ✛ *2:B5.*

¢ **Hôtel Tiquetonne.** Just off the Montorgueil market and a short hoof from Les Halles (and slightly seedy Rue St-Denis), this is one of the least expensive hotels in the city center. The so-old-fashioned-they're-vintage-cool rooms aren't much to look at and have few amenities, but they're clean, and some are spacious. Cheaper rooms are available with just a sink (toilets and pay showers are in each hall). **Pros:** dirt-cheap rooms in the center of town; in a newly trendy shopping and nightlife area. **Cons:** minimal service and no amenities; noise from the street. ⊠ *6 rue Tiquetonne, Beaubourg/Les Halles* ☎ *01–42–36–94–58* ⤳ *45 rooms, 33 with bath* ⚿ *In-room: no a/c, no TV. In-hotel: some pets allowed* ⊟ *AE, MC, V* ⊘ *Closed Aug. and last wk of Dec.* Ⓜ *Étienne Marcel* ✛ *2:D6.*

$ **Hôtel Vivienne.** The decor is a bit schizoid: some guest rooms have chandeliers, others have fuzzy brown rugs and busy bedspreads, and another is fashionably minimalist. Rooms Nos. 39, 40, and 41 are blessed with large rooftop balconies. The location near the Opéra Garnier and Grands Boulevards department stores make this a good bet in this price range. **Pros:** good value for central Paris; a block from the métro station. **Cons:** a noisy street and late-night bar across the road can make it hard to keep windows open in summer; some rooms are small and ugly. ⊠ *40 rue Vivienne, Opéra/Grands Boulevards* ☎ *01–42–33–13–26* 🖷 *01–40–41–98–19* ⊕ *www.vivienne.com* ⇆ *45 rooms, 35 with bath* ♿ *In-room: no a/c, Wi-Fi. In-hotel: Internet terminal, some pets allowed* ⊟ *MC, V* Ⓜ *Bourse, Richelieu-Drouot* ✛ *2:C4.*

**$$$$**  🖫 **Hôtel Westminster.** On one of the most prestigious streets in Paris between the Opéra and Place Vendôme, this former inn was built in the mid-19th century. Even now that Wi-Fi has arrived, the public areas and rooms happily retain their period furniture, marble fireplaces, crystal chandeliers, and piped-in classical music. Duke's piano bar is a pleasant, popular rendezvous spot, and the hotel's gourmet restaurant, Le Céladon, serves outstanding French cuisine. The fitness center has a Moorish-inspired steam room and views over Paris's rooftops. **Pros:** prestigious location; good-value promotional rates on the Web site; popular jazz bar. **Cons:** not trendy; some views of air shaft; location makes the price higher than expected. ⊠ *13 rue de la Paix, Opéra/Grands Boulevards* ☎ *01–42–61–57–46* ⊕ *warwickwestminsteropera.com* ⇆ *80 rooms, 21 suites* ♿ *In-room: safe, Wi-Fi. In-hotel: restaurant, room service, bar, gym, spa, laundry service, Internet terminal, parking (paid), some pets allowed* ⊟ *AE, DC, MC, V* Ⓜ *Opéra* ✛ *2:A5.*

**$$$$**  🖫 **Park Hyatt Paris Vendôme.** Understated luxury with a contemporary Zen vibe differentiates this Hyatt from its more classic neighbors between the Place Vendôme and Opéra Garnier. Five Haussmann-era office buildings have been converted into a showcase for polished beige limestone, mahogany veneer surfaces, and bronze sculptures. The minimalist cool vibe in the rooms extends to the Japanese-inspired spalike baths, under-floor heating, and spacious dressing area. Spa treatments feature French Carita products, and the entire hotel is Wi-Fi accessible. **Pros:** the latest hotel technology and stylish design; spa suites; popular bar and restaurant. **Cons:** as part of the Hyatt chain, can feel anonymous. ⊠ *3–5 rue de la Paix, Opéra/Grands Boulevards* ☎ *01–58–71–12–34* ⊕ *www.paris.vendome.hyatt.com* ⇆ *132 rooms, 36 suites* ♿ *In-room: safe, DVD (some), Internet. In-hotel: 2 restaurants, room service, bar, gym, spa, laundry service, Internet terminal, parking (free), some pets allowed* ⊟ *AE, DC, MC, V* Ⓜ *Concorde, Opéra* ✛ *2:A5.*

**18**

## 3ᴱ ARRONDISSEMENT

The north end of Le Marais is still an up-and-coming district of art galleries and hip cafés mixed with traditional bistros and unrenovated *hôtels particuliers* (town houses). At the south end are the Picasso Museum and easy access to the many other museums and shopping streets of Le Marais. The busy Place République and the colorful Enfants Rouges covered market are to the northeast.

**¢**  🖫 **Hôtel de Roubaix.** Although this faded ghost hasn't updated its grandmotherly decor or creaky elevator in recent decades, it conveys an amiable coziness and charges unbeatable prices, especially given the location five minutes from Le Marais and the Centre Pompidou. Rooms are bright but basic, with large beds. **Pros:** centrally located on a not-so-busy side street; typical old-fashioned Parisian character; good value.

Cons: old and outdated decor; no bathtubs; no air-conditioning. ⊠ *6 rue Greneta, Beaubourg/Les Halles* ☎ *01–42–72–89–91* ⊕ *www.hotel-de-roubaix.com* ↻ *53 rooms* ⟳ *In-room: no a/c, Internet* ⊟ *MC, V* ⟦○⟧ *CP* Ⓜ *Réaumur-Sébastopol, Arts et Métiers* ✛ *2:E6.*

$$$  🛏 **Hôtel du Petit Moulin**. French designer Christian Lacroix personally decorated each of the 17 rooms in this former bakery dating back to the reign of Henri IV. Opened as a hotel in 2005, the historic facade and elegant lobby retain the historic architectural elements, and the lounge, halls, and rooms are an explosion of styles and colors that define Lacroix's fashions: shag carpeting and clay tiles, pink pop-art walls and *toile de Jouy f*abric, antique furnishings, and contemporary light fixtures. The result is a comfortable, discreet hotel without the flash of its trendy boutique competitors. **Pros:** unique hotel with historical character and contemporary style in a trendy neighborhood. **Cons:** the nearest métro station is a few blocks away; rooms have minimal amenities; bar is not open to the public. ⊠ *29–31 rue de Poitou, Le Marais* ☎ *01–42–74–10–10* ⊕ *www.hotelpetitmoulinparis.com* ↻ *12 rooms, 5 suites* ⟳ *In-room: safe, Wi-Fi. In-hotel: room service, bar, laundry service, some pets allowed* ⊟ *AE, MC, V* Ⓜ *Filles-du-Calvaire* ✛ *4:F1.*

$$$$  🛏 **Murano Urban Resort**. As the epicenter of Parisian cool migrates eastward, it's no surprise that a design-conscious hotel has followed. On the trendy northern edge of Le Marais, this cheeky hotel that dares to call itself a resort combines Austin Powers playfulness with serious 007-inspired gadgetry. A psychedelic elevator zooms guests to ultraviolet-lighted hallways, where they enter pristine white rooms via fingerprint sensor locks. White shag carpeting, black-slate bathrooms, pop-art furniture, and bedside control panels that change the color of the lighting keep guests amused, until it's time to go downstairs for cocktails. Stylish Parisians pack the hotel's vodka bar and sleek restaurant, where a DJ holds court. Two suites have private terraces with heated, countercurrent pools. **Pros:** high-tech amenities and funky style; trendy bar attracts stylish locals; brunch served until 5 PM on Sunday. **Cons:** at the far edge of Le Marais on a noisy, busy boulevard; dark hallways can make it difficult to find your room; the white carpeting quickly shows wear and tear. ⊠ *13 bd. du Temple, République* ☎ *01–42–71–20–00* ⊕ *www.muranoresort.com* ↻ *43 rooms, 9 suites* ⟳ *In-room: safe, DVD, Wi-Fi. In-hotel: restaurant, room service, bar, pool, gym, laundry service, parking (paid), some pets allowed* ⊟ *AE, DC, MC, V* Ⓜ *Filles du Calvaire* ✛ *2:G6.*

$$$$  🛏 **Pavillon de la Reine**. This enchanting countrylike château is hidden off the regal Place des Vosges behind a stunning garden courtyard. Gigantic beams, chunky stone pillars, original oils, and a weathered fireplace speak to the building's 1612 origins. The hotel has large doubles, duplexes, and suites decorated in either contemporary or 18th-century-style wall fabrics. Many rooms look out on the entry court or an interior Japanese-inspired garden. **Pros:** typically Parisian historic character; proximity to the Place des Vosges without the noise. **Cons:** expensive for Le Marais and the size of the rooms; the nearest métro is a few blocks away. ⊠ *28 pl. des Vosges, Le Marais* ☎ *01–40–29–19–19; 800/447–7462 in U.S.* ⊕ *www.pavillon-de-la-reine.com* ↻ *30 rooms,*

26 suites ☾ In-room: safe, Wi-Fi. In-hotel: room service, bar, laundry service, parking (free), some pets allowed ▭ AE, DC, MC, V Ⓜ Bastille, St-Paul ✛ 4:G2.

## 4ᴱ ARRONDISSEMENT

Le Marais and the neighboring Ile St-Louis are two of the most charming neighborhoods for shopping and architecture in Paris, although their old streets are better reached on foot than by métro (the central location helps). Between them is the busy Rue St-Antoine/Rue de Rivoli east–west shopping artery. Le Marais is also known for its many museums, lively nightlife, and quirky but harmonious mix of the city's gay and Jewish communities.

$ **Grand Hôtel Jeanne-d'Arc.** You can get your money's worth at this hotel in an unbeatable location off the tranquil Place du Marché Ste-Catherine, one of the city's lesser-known pedestrian squares. The 17th-century building has been a hotel for more than a century, and the recently renovated rooms are well maintained, with spotless tiled bathrooms and cheery, if somewhat mismatched, colors (some rooms facing the back are more muted). The welcoming staff is informal and happy to recount the history of this former market quartier. **Pros:** charming street close to major sites; good value for Le Marais; lots of drinking and dining options nearby. **Cons:** late-night revelers on the square can be noisy after midnight; minimal amenities; rooms have varying quality and size. ✉ 3 rue de Jarente, Le Marais ☎ 01–48–87–62–11 ⊕ www. hoteljeannedarc.com ⟿ 36 rooms ☾ In-room: no a/c. In-hotel: Wi-Fi hotspot, some pets allowed ▭ MC, V Ⓜ St-Paul ✛ 4:G2.

$$$ **Hôtel Bourg Tibourg.** Scented candles and subdued lighting announce designer-du-jour Jacques Garcia's mix of haremlike romance and Gothic contemplation. Royal-blue paint and red velvet line the claustrophobic halls, and Byzantine alcoves hold mosaic-tile tubs. Rooms are barely bigger than the beds, and every inch has been upholstered, tasseled, and draped in a cacophony of stripes, florals, and medieval motifs. A pocket garden has room for three tables, leafy plants, and a swath of stars above. **Pros:** quiet side street in central Paris; luxurious style at moderate prices; great nightlife district. **Cons:** rooms are small and ill equipped for those with large suitcases; no hotel restaurant. ✉ 19 rue Bourg Tibourg, Le Marais ☎ 01–42–78–47–39 ⊕ www.hotelbourgtibourg.com ⟿ 29 rooms, 1 suite ☾ In-room: safe, Wi-Fi. In-hotel: room service, laundry service ▭ AE, DC, MC, V Ⓜ Hôtel de Ville ✛ 4:E2.

$$ **Hôtel Caron de Beaumarchais.** The theme of this intimate, romantic hotel is the work of former next-door neighbor Pierre-Augustin Caron de Beaumarchais, supplier of military aid to American revolutionaries and playwright who penned *The Marriage of Figaro* and *The Barber of Seville*. First-edition copies of his books adorn the public spaces, and the salons reflect the taste of 18th-century French nobility—down to the wallpaper and 1792 pianoforte. Richly decorated with floral fabrics and period furnishings, the rooms have original beams and hand-painted bathroom tiles, as well as flat-screen TVs and Wi-Fi. **Pros:** cozy, historic Parisian decor; central location within easy walking distance to

**18**

major monuments. **Cons:** small rooms; busy street of bars and cafés can be noisy. ✉ *12 rue Vieille-du-Temple, Le Marais* ☎ *01–42–72–34–12* ⊕ *www.carondebeaumarchais.com* ⌤ *19 rooms* ⌂ *In-room: safe, Wi-Fi. In-hotel: laundry service* ▭ *AE, DC, MC, V* Ⓜ *Hôtel de Ville* ✛ *4:F2.*

**$$** 🛌 **Hôtel de la Bretonnerie.** This small hotel is in a 17th-century *hôtel particulier* (town house) on a tiny street in Le Marais, a few minutes' walk from the Centre Pompidou and the bars and cafés of Rue Vieille du Temple. Choose either *chambres classiques* or *chambres de charme*; the latter are more spacious (and pricier), with more elaborate furnishings like Louis XIII–style four-poster canopy beds and marble bathtubs. Overall, the establishment is spotless, and the staff is welcoming. Breakfast is served in the vaulted cellar. **Pros:** central location and comfortable decor at a moderate price; typical Parisian character. **Cons:** quality and size of the rooms vary greatly; the in-your-face gay district location may not be to everyone's taste. ✉ *22 rue Ste-Croix-de-la-Bretonnerie, Le Marais* ☎ *01–48–87–77–63* ⊕ *www.bretonnerie.com* ⌤ *22 rooms, 7 suites* ⌂ *In-room: no a/c, safe, Wi-Fi. In-hotel: laundry service* ▭ *MC, V* Ⓜ *Hôtel de Ville* ✛ *4:E1.*

**$** 🛌 **Hôtel de la Place des Vosges.** Despite a lack of some expected comforts and an elevator that doesn't serve all floors, a loyal clientele swears by this small, historic hotel. The Louis XIII–style reception area and rooms with oak-beam ceilings, rough-hewn stone, and a mix of rustic finds from secondhand shops evoke the Old Marais. The lone top-floor room, the hotel's largest, has a Jacuzzi and a view over Rive Droite rooftops. Other, considerably smaller rooms are cheaper. Fans are provided in summer. **Pros:** excellent location; fans on request; historic Parisian decor; good value rates for the amenities. **Cons:** no air-conditioning; most rooms are very small; street-facing rooms can be noisy. ✉ *12 rue de Birague, Le Marais* ☎ *01–42–72–60–46* ⊕ *www.hotelplacedesvosges. com* ⌤ *16 rooms* ⌂ *In-room: no a/c, safe, Wi-Fi* ▭ *AE, DC, MC, V* Ⓜ *Bastille* ✛ *4:G2.*

**$$$** 🛌 **Hôtel Duo.** The former Axial Beaubourg hotel doubled in size and changed its name in 2006. It now has a fresh, contemporary style with bold colors and dramatic lighting, particularly in the newer wing; the original 16th-century beams add character to the older rooms. Amenities include a small fitness area, a sauna, and a stylish bar and breakfast lounge that fits in perfectly with the hip design vibe of the Marais district. **Pros:** trendy Marais location; walking distance to major monuments; choice of two different room styles. **Cons:** noisy street; service not always delivered with a smile. ✉ *11 rue du Temple, Le Marais* ☎ *01–42–72–72–22* ⊕ *www.duoparis.com* ⌤ *58 rooms* ⌂ *In-room: safe, Wi-Fi. In-hotel: room service, bar, gym, laundry service* ▭ *AE, DC, MC, V* Ⓜ *Hôtel de Ville* ✛ *4:E1.*

**$$** 🛌 **Hôtel du Vieux Marais.** A great value for the money in one of the most popular neighborhoods in Paris, this pleasingly minimalist hotel with a *fin-de-siècle* facade is on a quiet street in the heart of Le Marais. Rooms are bright and impeccably clean, with contemporary oak furnishings, burgundy-leather seating, and velour curtains. Bathrooms are immaculately tiled in Italian marble, with walk-in showers or combination shower/tubs. If you prefer a bit of extra space, ask about special rates on the triple rooms. The staff is exceptionally friendly, and the lobby has Wi-Fi. **Pros:** quiet side street location in central Paris; good value for the size and comfort. **Cons:** some rooms are very small and face a dark inner courtyard; decor lacks character. ✉ *8 rue du Plâtre, Le Marais* ☎ *01–42–78–47–22* ⊕ *www.vieuxmarais.com* ➳ *30 rooms* ⚒ *In-room: safe, Wi-Fi* ▤ *MC, V* Ⓜ *Hôtel de Ville* ✚ *4:E1.*

$$ ⊞ **Hôtel Saint Louis.** The location on the Ile St-Louis is the real draw of this modest hotel, which retains many of its original 17th-century stone walls and wooden beams. Tiny balconies on the upper levels have Seine views. Number 51 has a tear-shaped tub and a peek at the Panthéon. Breakfast is served in the vaulted stone cellar. **Pros:** romantic location on the tiny island Ile St-Louis; ancient architectural details; air-conditioning. **Cons:** the location makes the price high; métro stations are across the bridge; small rooms. ✉ *75 rue St-Louis-en-l'Ile* ☎ *01–46– 34–04–80* ⊕ *www.saintlouisenisle.com* ➳ *19 rooms* ⚒ *In-room: safe, Wi-Fi. In-hotel: some pets allowed* ▤ *MC, V* Ⓜ *Pont Marie* ✚ *4:E3.*

$$ ⊞ **Hôtel Saint Merry.** Due south of the Centre Pompidou is this small and stunning Gothic hideaway, once the presbytery of the adjacent St-Merry church. Inside the 17th-century stone interior you can gaze through stained glass, relax on a church pew, or lean back on a headboard recycled from an old Catholic confessional. Room No. 9 is bisected by stone buttresses still supporting the church. The Saint Merry's lack of elevator and modern temptations like TV are in keeping with its ascetic past (and keeps the place monkishly quiet). **Pros:** unique medieval character; central location on a pedestrian street full of cafés and shops. **Cons:** no amenities; street-facing rooms can be too noisy to open windows in summer. ✉ *78 rue de la Verrerie, Beaubourg/Les Halles* ☎ *01–42–78– 14–15* ⊕ *www.hotelmarais.com* ➳ *11 rooms, 1 suite* ⚒ *In-room: safe, no TV (some), Wi-Fi. In-hotel: room service, laundry service, some pets allowed* ▤ *AE, MC, V* Ⓜ *Châtelet, Hôtel de Ville* ✚ *4:E1.*

## 5ᴱ ARRONDISSEMENT

The Quartier Latin is the historic center of Parisian learning, and a large student population still frequents the cheap eateries and chain clothing shops around the Sorbonne and the Musée Cluny. The narrow streets along the Seine hide many ancient churches and bookshops, and the hillside leading up to the Panthéon is full of casual bars and colorful food markets at Place Maubert and Rue Mouffetard.

$$ ⊞ **The Five Hôtel.** Small is beautiful at this tiny design hotel on a quiet street near the Mouffetard market. Rooms combine cozy and high-tech features such as fiber-optic fairy lights above the beds and in the bathrooms, fluffy duvet comforters, original Chinese lacquer artworks, and 400 satellite channels on flat-screen TVs. All rooms have free Wi-Fi and L'Occitane toiletries; the ground-floor suite has a private Jacuzzi patio. The One by the Five apartment-hotel across the street provides a luxurious getaway for a romantic weekend. **Pros:** stylish design; personalized welcome; quiet side street. **Cons:** most rooms are too small for excessive baggage; the nearest métro is a 10-minute walk. ✉ *3 rue Flatters, Quartier Latin* ☎ *01–43–31–74–21* ⊕ *www.thefivehotel.com*

18

🛏 *24 rooms* ♿ *In-room: safe, Wi-Fi. In-hotel: room service, laundry service* ▭ *AE, DC, MC, V* Ⓜ *Gobelins* ✣ *4:D6.*

$ ⛱ **Hôtel Collège de France.** Exposed-stone walls, wooden beams, and medieval artwork echo the style of the Musée Cluny, two blocks from this small, family-run hotel. Rooms convey a less elaborate, more streamlined aesthetic than the lobby and are relatively quiet owing to the side-street location. Number 62, on the top floor, costs a bit more but has a small balcony with superb views. **Pros:** walking distance to major Rive Gauche sights and the islands; free Wi-Fi; ceiling fans. **Cons:** big difference between renovated and unrenovated rooms; no air-conditioning; thin walls between rooms. ✉ *7 rue Thénard, Quartier Latin* ☎ *01–43–26–78–36* ⊕ *www.hotelcdf.com* 🛏 *29 rooms* ♿ *In-room: no a/c, safe, Wi-Fi. In-hotel: room service* ▭ *AE, DC, MC, V* Ⓜ *Maubert-Mutualité, St-Michel–Cluny–La Sorbonne* ✣ *4:D4.*

$$ ⛱ **Hôtel des Jardins du Luxembourg.** Blessed with a personable staff and a smart, stylish look, this hotel on a calm cul-de-sac a block away from the Jardin du Luxembourg is an oasis for contemplation. The welcoming hardwood-floor lobby with a fireplace leads to smallish rooms furnished with wrought-iron beds, contemporary bathrooms, and Provençal fabrics. Ask for one with a balcony, or request one of the larger ground-floor rooms with private entrance onto the street. A hot buffet breakfast is served in the cheerful dining room. It's an easy commute to either the airport or the Eurostar via the RER train that stops at the end of the street. **Pros:** quiet street close to gardens and RER station; nice decor; hot buffet breakfast. **Cons:** extra charge to use Wi-Fi; some very small rooms; air-conditioning not very strong. ✉ *5 impasse Royer-Collard, Quartier Latin* ☎ *01–40–46–08–88* ⊕ *www.les-jardins-du-luxembourg.com* 🛏 *26 rooms* ♿ *In-room: safe, Wi-Fi. In-hotel: laundry service* ▭ *AE, DC, MC, V* Ⓜ *RER: Luxembourg* ✣ *4:C5.*

$ ⛱ **Hôtel Familia.** Owners Eric and Sylvie continue to update and improve

Fodor's Choice their popular budget hotel without raising the prices. They've added
★ custom-made wood furniture from Brittany, new carpeting, and antique tapestries and prints on the walls. The second and fifth floors have balconies (some with views of Notre-Dame), and all rooms are perfectly soundproofed from traffic below. **Pros:** attentive, friendly service; great value; has all the modern conveniences. **Cons:** on a busy street; some rooms are small; noise between rooms can be loud. ✉ *11 rue des Ecoles, Quartier Latin* ☎ *01–43–54–55–27* ⊕ *www.hotel-paris-familia. com* 🛏 *30 rooms* ♿ *In-room: Wi-Fi. In-hotel: laundry service, parking (paid)* ▭ *AE, DC, MC, V* ⦿ *CP* Ⓜ *Cardinal Lemoine* ✣ *4:E4.*

$$ ⛱ **Hôtel Grandes Ecoles.** Guests enter Madame Lefloch's country-style domain through two massive wooden doors. Distributed among a trio of three-story buildings, rooms have a distinct grandmotherly vibe with flowery wallpaper and lace bedspreads, but are downright spacious for this part of Paris. The Grandes Ecoles is legendary for its cobbled interior courtyard and garden, which becomes the second living room and a perfect breakfast spot, weather permitting. Rooms in the "garden" wing are coolest in summer. **Pros:** large courtyard garden; close to Quartier Latin nightlife spots; good value. **Cons:** uphill walk from the métro; outdated decor; few amenities. ✉ *75 rue du Cardinal Lemoine*

☎ *01–43–26–79–23* ⊕ *www.hotel-grandes-ecoles.com* ⇱ *51 rooms* ⅏ *In-room: no a/c, no TV, Wi-Fi. In-hotel: room service, parking (paid), some pets allowed* ☰ *MC, V* Ⓜ *Cardinal Lemoine* ✛ *4:E5.*

$$$ ⛨ **Hôtel Henri IV Rive Gauche.** From the ashes of the legendary dive bar Polly Magoo rose this smart new hotel back in 2003; it's 50 paces from Notre-Dame and the Seine. The identical, impeccable rooms have beige and rose blossom–print linens and framed prints of architectural drawings. Street-side rooms get a bit of traffic noise, but views of the 15th-century Église St-Severin make up for it. The lobby has pleasing terra-cotta floor tiles, pale green walls, and a stone fireplace. (Note: Don't confuse this with other Henri IV hotels in the area.) **Pros:** elegant, comfortable decor; central location close to major sights and RER station. **Cons:** on a busy street full of late-night bars; some rooms are small. ✉ *9–11 rue St-Jacques, Quartier Latin* ☎ *01–46–33–20–20* ⊕ *www. henri-paris-hotel.com* ⇱ *23 rooms* ⅏ *In-room: safe, Wi-Fi. In-hotel: Internet terminal, some pets allowed* ☰ *AE, DC, MC, V* Ⓜ *St-Michel* ✛ *4:D3.*

$ ⛨ **Hôtel Marignan.** Paul Keniger, the energetic third-generation owner,
☖ has cultivated a convivial atmosphere for independent international travelers. Not to be confused with the hotel of the same name near the Champs-Élysées, this Marignan lies squarely between budget-basic and youth hostel (no TVs or elevator) and offers lots of communal conveniences—a fully stocked kitchen, free laundry machines, and copious tourist information. Rooms are modest (some sleep four or five) but generally large, and bathrooms are clean. It's a good choice for families. The least expensive rooms share toilets and/or showers. **Pros:** great value for the location; kitchen and laundry; free Wi-Fi. **Cons:** no elevator; room phones only take incoming calls; has a bit of a youth-hostel atmosphere. ✉ *13 rue du Sommerard, Quartier Latin* ☎ *01–43–54–63–81* ⊕ *www.hotel-marignan.com* ⇱ *30 rooms, 12 with bath* ⅏ *In-room: no a/c, no TV, Wi-Fi. In-hotel: laundry facilities* ☰ *MC, V* �ⓞⅼ *CP* Ⓜ *Maubert-Mutualité* ✛ *4:D4.*

$$$ ⛨ **Hôtel Résidence Henri IV.** Sometimes travelers, especially those with
☖ children, need a home base where they can kick back and make their own meals, and this is a good option. The elegant rooms here have molded ceilings, marble mantelpieces, and kitchenettes equipped with two-burner stoves, dorm-size fridges, sinks, and basic dishware. Apartments have space for up to four guests. Free Wi-Fi is available in the lobby. The location on a quiet cul-de-sac is steps from the Panthéon and the Sorbonne. **Pros:** kitchenettes; close to Quartier Latin sights. **Cons:** closest métro is a few blocks away. ✉ *50 rue des Bernardins, Quartier Latin* ☎ *01–44–41–31–81* ⊕ *www.residencehenri4.com* ⇱ *8 rooms, 5 apartments* ⅏ *In-room: safe, kitchen, Wi-Fi. In-hotel: laundry service, some pets allowed* ☰ *AE, DC, MC, V* Ⓜ *Maubert-Mutualité* ✛ *4:D4.*

$$ ⛨ **Hôtel Saint-Jacques.** Nearly every wall in this bargain hotel is bedecked with faux-marble and trompe-l'oeil murals. As in many old, independent Paris hotels, each room is unique, but a general 19th-century theme of Second Empire furnishings and paintings dominates, with a Montmartre cabaret theme in the new breakfast room. Wi-Fi is available in the lounge bar. About half the rooms have tiny step-out balconies

18

that give a glimpse of Notre-Dame and the Panthéon. Room 25 has a long, around-the-corner balcony, and No. 16 is popular for its historic ceiling fresco and moldings. Repeat guests get souvenir knickknacks or T-shirts. **Pros:** unique Parisian decor; close to Quartier Latin sights. **Cons:** very busy street makes it too noisy to open windows in summer; thin walls between rooms. ⊠ *35 rue des Ecoles, Quartier Latin* ☎ *01–44–07–45–45* ⊕ *www.hotel-saintjacques.com* ➲ *38 rooms* ⊘ *In-room: safe, Wi-Fi. In-hotel: bar, Internet terminal* ⊟ *AE, DC, MC, V* Ⓜ *Maubert-Mutualité* ✛ *4:D4.*

**$$** 🛏 **Les Degrés de Notre-Dame.** On a quiet lane a few yards from the Seine, this diminutive budget hotel is lovingly decorated with the owner's flea-market finds. Number 23 is the largest of the lower-price rooms, whereas the more costly No. 24 has more space, wooden floors, and particularly appealing antique furnishings. The most expensive room, No. 501, occupies the entire top floor, with views of Notre-Dame and space for four guests. There's no elevator, but colorful murals of Parisian scenes decorate the winding stairwell. The shabby-chic Parisian character of the hotel and its French-Moroccan restaurant-bar make this unique establishment charming and unforgettable. **Pros:** within walking distance of Notre-Dame and Ile St-Louis; attractive location in quiet part of Quartier Latin; popular locals' restaurant. **Cons:** no air-conditioning; outdated decor; no elevator. ⊠ *10 rue des Grands Degrés, Quartier Latin* ☎ *01–55–42–88–88* ⊕ *www.lesdegreshotel.com* ➲ *10 rooms* ⊘ *In-room: no a/c, safe, Wi-Fi. In-hotel: restaurant, bar, no kids under 12* ⊟ *MC, V* ⦿❘ *CP* Ⓜ *Maubert-Mutualité* ✛ *4:D3.*

FodorsChoice
★

¢ 🛏 **Port-Royal Hôtel.** The spotless rooms and extra-helpful staff at the Port-Royal are well above average for this price range. Just below the Rue Mouffetard market at the edge of the 13ᵉ arrondissement, it may be somewhat removed from the action, but the snug antique-furnished lounge areas, garden courtyard, and rooms with wrought-iron beds, mirrors, and armoires make it worth the trip. Rooms at the lowest end of the price range are equipped only with sinks (an immaculate shared shower room is in the hallway). **Pros:** excellent value for the money; attentive service; typical Parisian neighborhood close to two major markets. **Cons:** not very central; on a busy street; few amenities. ⊠ *8 bd. de Port-Royal, Les Gobelins* ☎ *01–43–31–70–06* ⊕ *www.hotelportroyal. fr* ➲ *46 rooms, 20 with bath/shower* ⊘ *In-room: no a/c, no TV* ⊟ *No credit cards* Ⓜ *Les Gobelins* ✛ *4:C6.*

## 6ᴱ ARRONDISSEMENT

The 6ᵉ is a popular Rive Gauche area, known for the chic boutiques around St-Germain-des-Prés. The streets are more tranquil near the elegant Jardin du Luxembourg, and the nightlife is liveliest around Odéon and Place St-André-des-Arts. In addition to the well-known boutique hotels, some excellent budget sleeps can be found here—but what you gain in location you lose in size and comfort.

**$$** 🛏 **Apostrophe Hotel.** Those enamored with the artistic and literary history of Paris's Left Bank will appreciate this whimsical family-run hotel between Montparnasse and Luxembourg Gardens. The unique decor was created by local artists and each room has a different theme, screen-printed curtains, ceiling-mounted artwork, and hand-painted walls. Rooms are small but well equipped with a flat-screen TV and CD/DVD player, free Wi-Fi, luxury bedding, and open-plan bathrooms with rain shower and separate toilet. Some rooms have views of the Eiffel Tower and Jacuzzi tubs. **Pros:** friendly service; charming neighborhood close to the métro; free laptop and bike loans. **Cons:** limited closet space; the open bathroom plan offers little privacy from roommates. ⊠ *3 rue de Chevreuse, Montparnasse* ☎ *01–56–54–31–31* ⊕ *www. apostrophe-hotel.com* ⇗ *16 rooms* ⚏ *In-room: safe, DVD, Wi-Fi. In-hotel: room service, Internet terminal, Wi-Fi hotspot* ▭ *AE, D, DC, MC, V* ✣ *4:A6.*

$$$$ ⌂ **Artus Hôtel.** One of the best things about the Artus, aside from the sleek look, is the fact that it's smack in the middle of Rue de Buci. This means you can breakfast at Paul, shop at the wonderful street market, then have an espresso at Bar du Marché. Contemporary rooms have dark-wood furnishings and whitewashed, wood-beamed ceilings that complement brightly colored walls and bedspreads. Bathrooms are in marble and chrome. The more spacious duplex suite under the roof, No. 140, has a small bathroom loft with a shower, makeup table, and freestanding bathtub; the street-facing top-floor suite has a patio with a table and chairs, perfect for people-watching. **Pros:** attentive service; excellent location on a market street; stylish design. **Cons:** rooms are small for the price; neighborhood is quite busy and at times noisy. ⊠ *34 rue de Buci, St-Germain-des-Prés* ☎ *01–43–29–07–20* ⊕ *www. artushotel.com* ⇗ *25 rooms, 2 suites* ⚏ *In-room: safe, Wi-Fi. In-hotel: room service, gym, laundry service, Internet terminal, some pets allowed* ▭ *AE, DC, MC, V* ⍩ *CP* Ⓜ *Mabillon* ✣ *4:B3.*

$$$$ ⌂ **Hôtel Bel-Ami.** Just a stroll from Café de Flore, the Bel-Ami hides its past as an 18th-century textile factory behind veneer furnishings and crisply jacketed staff. You're immediately hit by the Conran Shop–meets–espresso bar lobby, with club music and a sleek fireplace lounge to match. There's Wi-Fi throughout, and the fitness center includes a sauna and Tibetan massage treatment rooms. Rooms lean toward minimalist chic in soothing colors but are transformed often to keep up with the hotel's young and trendy clientele. It fills up fast when the fashion circus comes to town. **Pros:** upscale, stylish hotel; central St-Germain-des-Prés location; spacious fitness center and spa. **Cons:** some guests report loud noise between rooms; some very small rooms in lower price category. ⊠ *7–11 rue St-Benoît, St-Germain-des-Prés* ☎ *01–42–61–53–53* ⊕ *www.hotel-bel-ami.com* ⇗ *113 rooms, 2 suites* ⚏ *In-room: safe, Wi-Fi. In-hotel: room service, bar, gym, spa, laundry service* ▭ *AE, DC, MC, V* Ⓜ *St-Germain-des-Prés* ✣ *4:B2.*

$$ ⌂ **Hôtel Bonaparte.** The congenial staff makes a stay in this intimate hotel a special treat. Old-fashioned upholsteries and 19th-century furnishings make the relatively spacious rooms feel comfortable and unpretentious. Services may be basic, but the location in the heart of St-Germain is fabulous. Light sleepers should request rooms overlooking the courtyard. **Pros:** upscale shopping neighborhood; large rooms for the Rive Gauche, newly upgraded air-conditioning. **Cons:** outdated decor and

18

Hôtel d'Aubusson.

Hôtel Odéon Saint-Germain

Les Degrés de Notre-Dame.

some tired mattresses. ✉ *61 rue Bonaparte, St-Germain-des-Prés* ☎ *01–43–26–97–37* ⊕ *www.hotelbonaparte.fr* ⤳ *29 rooms* ⌂ *In-room: safe, refrigerator, Wi-Fi (some)* ▭ *MC, V* ⍾ *CP* Ⓜ *St-Sulpice* ⊹ *4:B3.*

**$$$$**

Fodor's Choice

★

▦ **Hôtel d'Aubusson.** The staff greets you warmly at this 17th-century town house and former literary salon. The showpiece is the stunning front lobby spanned by massive beams and headed by a gigantic fireplace. Decked out in rich burgundies, greens, or blues, the bedrooms are filled with Louis XV– and Regency-style antiques and Hermès toiletries; even the smallest rooms are a generous size by Paris standards. Behind the paved courtyard is a second structure with three apartments, which are ideal for families. The hotel's Café Laurent hosts jazz musicians Thursday through Saturday evenings, and piano on Wednesdays. All returning guests (and new guests who book at least three nights) get VIP treatment such as champagne and flowers on arrival. **Pros:** central location near shops and market street; live jazz on weekends; personalized welcome. **Cons:** some of the newer rooms lack character; busy street; bar can be noisy on weekends. ✉ *33 rue Dauphine, St-Germain-des-Prés* ☎ *01–43–29–43–43* ⊕ *www.hoteldaubusson.com* ⤳ *49 rooms* ⌂ *In-room: safe, DVD (some), Wi-Fi. In-hotel: room service, bar, laundry service, parking (paid), some pets allowed* ▭ *AE, DC, MC, V* Ⓜ *Odéon* ⊹ *4:C2.*

**$$$**

▦ **Hôtel de l'Abbaye.** This hotel on a tranquil side street near St-Sulpice welcomes you with a cobblestone ante-courtyard and vaulted stone entrance. The lobby's salons have vestiges of the original 18th-century convent, with a breakfast room overlooking the spacious garden. Rooms are a mix of floral and striped fabrics with period furnishings, or are contemporary minimalist with wood paneling and modern art. All have flat-screen TVs; upper-floor accommodations have oak beams and sitting alcoves. Duplexes (split-level suites) have lovely private terraces. **Pros:** tranquil setting; upscale neighborhood; good value for price. **Cons:** rooms differ greatly in size and style; some are quite small. ✉ *10 rue Cassette, St-Germain-des-Prés* ☎ *01–45–44–38–11* ⊕ *www.hotel-abbaye.com* ⤳ *42 rooms, 4 suites* ⌂ *In-room: safe, Wi-Fi. In-hotel: room service, bar, laundry service, Internet terminal* ▭ *AE, MC, V* ⍾ *CP* Ⓜ *St-Sulpice* ⊹ *4:A4.*

**$**

▦ **Hôtel de Nesle.** This one-of-a-kind budget hotel is like a quirky, enchanting dollhouse. Services are bare-bones—no elevator, phones, or breakfast—but the payoff is in the snug rooms cleverly decorated by theme. Sleep in Notre-Dame de Paris, lounge in an Asian-style boudoir, spend the night with Molière, or steam it up in Le Hammam. Decorations include colorful murals, canopy beds, or clay tiles. Most rooms overlook an interior garden, and the dead-end-street location keeps the hotel relatively quiet. If you book one of the 11 rooms without a shower, you'll have to share the one bathroom on the second floor. **Pros:** unique, fun decor; good value for chic location; small garden. **Cons:** few amenities or services; reservations by phone only. ✉ *7 rue de Nesle, St-Germain-des-Prés* ☎ *01–43–54–62–41* ⊕ *www.hoteldenesleparis.com* ⤳ *20 rooms, 9 with bath* ⌂ *In-room: no a/c, no phone, no TV, Wi-Fi (some). In-hotel: Internet terminal, some pets allowed* ▭ *MC, V* Ⓜ *Odéon* ⊹ *4:C2.*

**18**

**$** ⬚ **Hôtel du Lys.** To jump into an inexpensive Parisian fantasy, just climb the stairway to your room (there's no elevator) in this former 17th-century royal residence. Well maintained by Madame Steffen, the endearingly odd-shape guest rooms have tiny nooks, weathered antiques, and exposed beams. It may be modest, but it's extremely atmospheric. Breakfast is served in the lobby or in your room. **Pros:** central location on a quiet side street; historic character. **Cons:** old-fashioned decor is decidedly outdated; perfunctory service, no air-conditioning. ✉ *23 rue Serpente, Quartier Latin* ☎ *01–43–26–97–57* ⊕ *www.hoteldulys. com* ⇨ *22 rooms* ♿ *In-room: no a/c, safe. In-hotel: some pets allowed* ⊟ *MC, V* ⎮◎⎮ *CP* Ⓜ *St-Michel, Odéon* ✛ *4:C3.*

**$$** ⬚ **Hôtel Le Sainte-Beuve.** On a tranquil street between the Jardin du Luxembourg and Montparnasse's timeless cafés and brasseries is the pleasant Sainte-Beuve. The spacious lobby and breakfast area are bathed in light, showcasing a wood-fire hearth and Greek Revival columns. White and beige tones dominate the uncluttered rooms, with wooden period furnishings. Extras include bathrobes and a laptop that you can borrow for free (though you can't take it out of the hotel). **Pros:** stylish decor; upscale location without tourist crowds; close to major métro lines. **Cons:** a good 10-minute walk to the Quartier Latin or St-Germain-des-Prés; small rooms and elevator. ✉ *9 rue Ste-Beuve, Montparnasse* ☎ *01–45–48–20–07* ⊕ *www.parishotelcharme.com* ⇨ *22 rooms* ♿ *In-room: safe, Wi-Fi. In-hotel: room service, bar, laundry service, Internet terminal, some pets allowed* ⊟ *AE, DC, MC, V* Ⓜ *Vavin* ✛ *4:A5.*

**$$** ⬚ **Hôtel Mayet.** This fresh, quirky hotel a few blocks from the Bon Marché department store feels a bit like an art-school dormitory: the identical rooms are decorated in battleship gray and maroon, with big aluminum wall clocks, chunky propellerlike ceiling fans, and metal storage containers. The basement breakfast room blasts you with primary colors, and a canvas by the graffitist André hangs in the entry. **Pros:** funky, artistic atmosphere; free Wi-Fi; close to two main métro stations and an English bookshop. **Cons:** not very central; decor can feel almost dormlike; closed in August. ✉ *3 rue Mayet, Montparnasse* ☎ *01–47–83–21–35* ⊕ *www.mayet.com* ⇨ *23 rooms* ♿ *In-room: no a/c, Wi-Fi. In-hotel: Internet terminal, some pets allowed* ⊟ *AE, DC, MC, V* ⊘ *Closed Aug. and Christmas wk* ⎮◎⎮ *CP* Ⓜ *Duroc* ✛ *3:G4.*

**$$$** ⬚ **Hôtel Millésime.** Step through the doors of this St-Germain-des-Prés hotel and you'll feel transported to the sunny south of France. Rooms in this 17th-century city mansion are decorated in warm reds, yellows, and royal blues, with rich fabrics and sparkling tiled bathrooms. The centerpiece is the gorgeous Provençal courtyard with ocher walls and wrought-iron balconies (Room 15 has direct access). Friendly service and a bountiful buffet breakfast make this a great find. **Pros:** upscale shopping location; young, friendly staff; well-appointed rooms. **Cons:** ground floor rooms can be noisy; larger rooms are significantly more expensive. ✉ *15 rue Jacob, St-Germain-des-Prés* ☎ *01–44–07–97–97* ⊕ *www.millesimehotel.com* ⇨ *20 rooms, 1 suite* ♿ *In-room: safe, Wi-Fi. In-hotel: room service, bar, laundry service, Internet terminal, some pets allowed* ⊟ *AE, MC, V* ⎮◎⎮ *CP* Ⓜ *St-Germain-des-Prés* ✛ *4:B2.*

**$$$$** ⬛ **Hôtel Odéon Saint-Germain.** The exposed stone walls and original
**Fodor'sChoice** wooden beams give this 16th-century building typical Rive Gauche
★ character, and designer Jacques Garcia's generous use of striped taffeta
curtains, velvet upholstery, and plush carpeting imbues the family-run
hotel with the distinct luxury of St-Germain-des-Prés. Several small
rooms decorated with comfy armchairs and Asian antiques make up the
lobby, where guests can help themselves to a Continental buffet breakfast in the morning and an honesty bar throughout the day. Rooms are
decorated in eggplant and caramel, with flat-screen TVs and designer
toiletries. The ones overlooking the street have more space and double
windows for soundproofing. **Pros:** warm welcome; free Internet; luxuriously appointed, historic building in an upscale shopping district. **Cons:**
small rooms aren't convenient for those with extra-large suitcases. ✉ *13
rue St-Sulpice, St-Germain-des-Prés* ☎ *01–43–25–70–11* ⊕ *www.paris-
hotel-odeon.com* ⤵ *22 rooms, 5 junior suites* ⟁ *In-room: safe, Wi-Fi.
In-hotel: room service, bar, laundry service, Internet terminal, some pets
allowed* ▭ *DC, MC, V* Ⓜ *Odeon* ✛ *4:B3.*

**$$$** ⬛ **Hôtel Relais Saint-Sulpice.** A savvy clientele frequents this fashionable
little hotel sandwiched between St-Sulpice and the Jardin du Luxem-
bourg. Eclectic art objects and furnishings, some with an Asian theme,
oddly pull off a unified look. A zebra-print stuffed armchair sits beside
an Art Deco desk, and an African mud cloth hangs above a neo-Roman
pillar. The rooms themselves, set around an ivy-clad courtyard, are
understated, with Provençal fabrics, carved wooden furnishings, and
sisal carpeting. Downstairs there's a sauna and a glass-roofed break-
fast salon. Room 11 has a terrific view of St-Sulpice. **Pros:** chic loca-
tion; close to two métro stations; bright breakfast room and courtyard;
good value. **Cons:** smallish rooms in the lower category; noise from
the street on weekend evenings. ✉ *3 rue Garancière, St-Germain-des-
Prés* ☎ *01–46–33–99–00* ⊕ *www.relais-saint-sulpice.com* ⤵ *26 rooms*
⟁ *In-room: safe, Wi-Fi. In-hotel: laundry service* ▭ *AE, DC, MC, V*
Ⓜ *St-Germain-des-Prés, St-Sulpice* ✛ *4:B3.*

**$$$$** ⬛ **L'Hôtel.** Why do rock stars love this eccentric and opulent boutique
hotel? Though sophisticated in every way, there's something just a bit
naughty in the air. Is it its history as an 18th-century *pavillion d'amour*
(inn for trysts)? Is it that Oscar Wilde permanently checked out in Room
16, back in 1900? Or is it Jacques Garcia's makeover—rooms done in
yards of thick, rich fabrics in colors like deep red and emerald green? We
say all of the above, plus the intimate bar and restaurant allows guests
to mingle with the Parisian *beau monde.* A grotto holds a countercur-
rent pool and a steam room. **Pros:** luxurious decor; elegant bar and
restaurant; walking distance to the Orsay and the Louvre. **Cons:** some
rooms are very small for the price; closest métro station is a few blocks'
walk. ✉ *13 rue des Beaux-Arts, St-Germain-des-Prés* ☎ *01–44–41–99–
00* ⊕ *www.l-hotel.com* ⤵ *16 rooms, 4 suites* ⟁ *In-room: safe, Wi-Fi.
In-hotel: restaurant, room service, bar, pool, laundry service, some pets
allowed* ▭ *AE, DC, MC, V* Ⓜ *St-Germain-des-Prés* ✛ *4:B2.*

**$$$$** ⬛ **Relais Christine.** This exquisite property was once a 13th-century
abbey, but don't expect monkish quarters. You enter from the impressive
stone courtyard into a lobby and fireside honor bar decorated with rich

**18**

fabrics, stone, wood paneling, and antiques. The cavernous breakfast room and adjacent fitness center feature vaulted medieval stonework. Spacious, high-ceilinged rooms offer a variety of classical and contemporary styles: Asian-theme wall fabrics, plain stripes, or rich aubergine paint. Split-level lofts sleep up to five people, and several ground-level rooms open onto a lush garden with private patios and heaters. **Pros:** quiet location while still close to the action; historic character; luxuriously appointed rooms. **Cons:** some guests report noise from doors on the street; no on-site restaurant. ⊠ *3 rue Christine, St-Germain-des-Prés* ☎ *01–40–51–60–80; 800/525–4800 in U.S.* ⊕ *www.relais-christine.com* ⤳ *33 rooms, 18 suites* ⟁ *In-room: safe, DVD (some), Wi-Fi. In-hotel: room service, bar, gym, spa, laundry service, Internet terminal, parking (free), some pets allowed* ⊟ *AE, DC, MC, V* Ⓜ *Odéon* ✛ *4:C2/3.*

## 7ᴱ ARRONDISSEMENT

The wide, tree-lined avenues of the 7ᵉ are home to several of the city's immense monuments, including the Eiffel Tower and Les Invalides. In between are mostly residential streets dotted with embassies and other government buildings. Evenings tend to be quiet, and shopping streets are sparse, with the exception of the charming Rue Cler food market and its many cafés.

$ **Grand Hôtel Lévêque.** The Eiffel Tower is around the corner, but the real draw here is the bustling pedestrian street market, one of the city's finest, just outside the hotel's front door. Staff are friendly and helpful, and the bistro-style breakfast room next to the reception desk has hot- and cold-drink machines. Rooms have simple furnishings and ceiling fans. **Pros:** prime location on a popular market street; budget singles if you don't mind a shared shower. **Cons:** only superior rooms have been recently renovated; air-conditioning only available from June to September. ⊠ *29 rue Cler, Invalides* ☎ *01–47–05–49–15* ⊕ *www.hotel-leveque. com* ⤳ *50 rooms, 45 with bath/shower* ⟁ *In-room: safe, Internet* ⊟ *AE, MC, V* Ⓜ *École Militaire* ✛ *3:E2.*

$$$ **Hôtel du Cadran.** Completely redesigned in 2009, the sleek minimalist lines are punctuated by bright shots of color and vintage clocks— "cadran" means clock. Rooms have flat-screen TVs and large beds with fluffy duvet comforters. The Cadran, however, may be best known for its Christophe Roussel chocolate bar, which serves colorful *macarons* and chocolates throughout the day. **Pros:** easy walk to Eiffel Tower, Les Invalides, and the market; free Wi-Fi; queen- and king-size beds. **Cons:** small rooms; prices at the high end for this area. ⊠ *10 rue du Champ de Mars, Invalides* ☎ *01–40–62–67–00* ⊕ *www.cadranhotel.com* ⤳ *40 rooms, 1 suite* ⟁ *In-room: safe, Wi-Fi. In-hotel: room service, bar, laundry service* ⊟ *AE, DC, MC, V* Ⓜ *École Militaire* ✛ *3:E2.*

$ **Hôtel du Champ de Mars.** This hotel just off Rue Cler has an appealing down-home feel, with a vibrant Provençal-inspired lobby and huge picture windows overlooking the street. Country-style wood furnishings and crisp fabric chair covers decorate each room. The two on the ground floor open onto a leafy private courtyard. **Pros:** cozy country decor; good value; walking distance to Eiffel Tower and Les Invalides. **Cons:** smallish rooms; no air-conditioning. ⊠ *7 rue du Champ de*

# Apartment Rentals

Many Fodorites rent apartments in Paris because they favor extra space plus that special sense of living like a local. Rentals can also offer savings, especially for groups.

Check out the **Paris Tourism Office** Web site (⊕ www.parisinfo.com) for reputable agency listings. Policies differ, but you can expect a minimum required stay from three to seven days; a refundable deposit payable on arrival; possibly an agency fee; and maid service. A great Web site with unbiased ratings of agencies and listing services is **Paris Apartment Info** (⊕ www.paris-apartment-info.com).

The following is a list of good-value residence hotels and apartment services: **Ah! Paris** (☎ 01–40–28–97–96 ⊕ www.ahparis.com) offers a large selection of rentals with reasonable all-inclusive rates and no additional fees. **Citadines Résidences Hôtelières** (☎ 08–25–33–33–32 ⊕ www.citadines.fr) is a chain of apartment-style hotel accommodations. They're somewhat generic, but offer many services and good value for short stays. **Lodgis Paris** (☎ 01–70–39–11–11 ⊕ www.lodgis.com) has one of the largest selections in Paris; however, the agency fee makes it cheaper to rent for more than one week. **Paris Vacation Apartments** (☎ 06–12–44–64–78 ⊕ www.parisvacationapartments.com) specializes in luxury rentals, with all-inclusive prices by the week. Agencies based in the United States can also help you find an apartment in Paris: **Rendez-vous à Paris** (✉ 1220 N. Market St., Suite 606, Wilmington, DE ⊕ www.rendez-vousaparis.com) has just a few properties, but all are in prime locations and are top quality at a reasonable price. **Rentals in Paris**

(☎ 516/977–3318 ⊕ www.rentals-in-paris.com) has two dozen centrally located rentals with all-inclusive weekly rates and last-minute special offers.

Additionally, **Fodorites** recommend these rental services:

"I rented . . . from **Rent Paris** (⊕ www.rentparis.com) last summer and had a great experience." —slangevar

"I always rent from **Paris Perfect** (⊕ www.parisperfect.com). All of their places are lovely." —gracejoan3

"**Vacation in Paris** (⊕ www.vacationinparis.com) is a great company and service, and one can pay in U.S. dollars. . . . One also gets the apartment keys mailed . . . no need to meet an agent to let one into the apartment." —Guenmai

"We rented from **Guest Apartment Services** (⊕ www.guestapartment.com) . . . Superlative experience. I stayed there with my mother and she is picky!" —Leely2

"We have rented three apartments in recent years from **Rothray** (⊕ www.rothray.com). I can't tell you how completely reliable Ray is and how nice his apartments are. . . . Look at his website and know he will help you with everything and is 100% honest." —MAP

"The English speaking owners are a pleasure to deal with, and seem to have thought of everything. . . . See for yourself at **Rental Apartment Paris** (⊕ www.RentalApartmentParis.com)." —lregeo

"We have rented twice from Thierry at **Paris Best Lodge** (⊕ www.parisbestlodge.com). He is great . . . I would definitely trust him." —emsmom

18

Mars, Invalides ☎ *01–45–51–52–30* ⊕ *www.hotelduchampdemars. com* ⇄ *25 rooms* ♿ *In-room: no a/c, safe, Wi-Fi* ☰ *MC, V* Ⓜ *École Militaire* ✛ *3:E2.*

$$$$ 🔑 **Hôtel Duc de Saint-Simon.** If it's good enough for the notoriously choosy Lauren Bacall, you too may fall for the Duc's charms. Its hidden location between Boulevard St-Germain and Rue de Bac is just one of many pluses. Four of the antique-filled rooms have spacious terraces overlooking the courtyard. The 16th-century basement lounge is a warren of stone alcoves with a zinc bar and plush seating. **Pros:** upscale neighborhood close to St-Germain-des-Prés; historic character. **Cons:** rooms in the annex are smaller and have no elevator; no air-conditioning; some worn decor. ⊠ *14 rue St-Simon, St-Germain-des-Prés* ☎ *01–44–39–20–20* ⊕ *www.hotelducdesaintsimon.com* ⇄ *29 rooms, 5 suites* ♿ *In-room: a/c (some), safe, Wi-Fi. In-hotel: room service, bar, laundry service, parking (paid), no kids under 10* ☰ *AE, DC, MC, V* Ⓜ *Rue du Bac* ✛ *3:H2.*

$$ 🔑 **Hôtel Eiffel Rive Gauche.** On a quiet street near the Eiffel Tower, this bright, welcoming hotel is a good budget find. Rooms are small but comfortable, with modern wood furnishings and orange and gold walls; many open directly onto the Tuscan-style patio with its verdigris railings and terra-cotta tiles. Fans are available in the summer. The owner, Monsieur Chicheportiche, is a multilingual encyclopedia of Paris. **Pros:** close to the Eiffel Tower; bright, cheery decor. **Cons:** no air-conditioning; some noise between rooms; big difference in room sizes. ⊠ *6 rue du Gros Caillou, Trocadéro/Tour Eiffel* ☎ *01–45–51–24–56* ⊕ *www.hotel-eiffel.com* ⇄ *29 rooms* ♿ *In-room: no a/c, safe, Wi-Fi. In-hotel: laundry service, Internet terminal* ☰ *MC, V* Ⓜ *École Militaire* ✛ *3:D2.*

$$$ 🔑 **Hôtel Le Tourville.** This is a rare find: a cozy upscale hotel that doesn't cost a fortune. Each room has crisp, milk-white damask upholstery set against pastel or ocher walls, a smattering of antique bureaus and lamps, original artwork, and fabulous old mirrors. The junior suites have hot tubs, and the superior room has its own private garden terrace. The staff couldn't be more helpful. **Pros:** close to the Eiffel Tower and Les Invalides; attentive service; soundproofed windows. **Cons:** no shower curtains for the bathtubs; air-conditioning works only during summer months. ⊠ *16 av. de Tourville, Invalides* ☎ *01–47–05–62–62* ⊕ *www. hoteltourville.com* ⇄ *27 rooms, 3 suites* ♿ *In-room: safe (some), Wi-Fi. In-hotel: room service, bar, laundry service, some pets allowed* ☰ *AE, DC, MC, V* Ⓜ *École Militaire* ✛ *3:E3.*

$$$$ 🔑 **Le Bellechasse.** French designer Christian Lacroix helped decorate all 34 rooms of Le Bellechasse, which is just around the corner from the popular Musée d'Orsay. Guests enter a refreshingly bright lobby of black slate floors, white walls, and mismatched velour and leather armchairs. Floor-to-ceiling windows overlook the elegant patio courtyard. Each room design is unique, but all have an eclectic mix of fabrics, textures, and colors, as well as Lacroix's whimsical characters screened on the walls and ceilings. Most guest rooms have an open-concept bathroom, with the bathtub and sink in a corner and a separate toilet. Four rooms have doors leading to the patio courtyard. **Pros:** central location near top Paris museums; unique style; spacious and

bright; Anne Semonin toiletries. **Cons:** street-facing rooms can be a bit noisy. ✉ *8 rue de Bellechasse, Invalides* ☏ *01–45–50–22–31* ⊕ *www. lebellechasse.com* ⤴ *34 rooms* ⚏ *In-room: safe, Internet, Wi-Fi* ▭ *AE, DC, V* Ⓜ *Solferino* ✛ *3:H1.*

## 8ᴱ ARRONDISSEMENT

For those seeking the city's glitz and glamour, it's hard to beat the 8ᵉ arrondissement. From the cafés and shops of the lively Champs-Élysées to the couture boutiques and clubs of Avenue George V and Avenue Montaigne, there are plenty of opportunities to whip out the platinum card. Prices come down to earth a bit on the quiet side streets.

**$$$$** 🏨 **Champs-Elysées Plaza Hotel and Wellness.** Discreet, contemporary elegance, just steps from the hustle-and-bustle of the Champs-Élysées is what you'll find at this gracious seven-floor town house. No detail has been overlooked, from sumptuous fabrics in plums, browns, and grays—Marie-Antoinette would have lusted after these silks for her dresses—to Hermès toiletries, fresh flowers, and jazz on the in-room stereo. Rooms and bathrooms are more than spacious, and higher floors have lovely views of the city. Great care has been taken to make the gym, hammam, and sauna areas fresh and welcoming with plants, mirrors, and spaces that aren't claustrophobic. **Pros:** extremely comfortable spaces; attentive service; central location. **Cons:** neighborhood is too chichi to have much character; small (but charming) elevator. ✉ *35 rue de Berrii* ☏ *01–53–53–20–20* ⊕ *www.champs-elysees-plaza.com* ⤴ *6 rooms, 29 suites* ⚏ *In-room: safe, refrigerator, Wi-Fi. In-hotel: restaurant, room service, bar, gym, spa, laundry service, Internet terminal* ▭ *AE, MC, V* Ⓜ *George V, St-Philippe-du-Roule* ✛ *1:E4.*

**$$$$** 🏨 **Four Seasons Hôtel George V Paris.** The George V is as poised and polished as the day it opened in 1928: the original Art Deco detailing and 17th-century tapestries have been restored, the bas-reliefs regilded, and the marble-floor mosaics rebuilt tile by tile. Rooms are decked in fabrics and Louis XVI trimmings but have homey touches like selections of CDs and French books. Le Cinq restaurant is one of Paris's hottest tables. The low-lighted spa and fitness center pampers guests with 11 treatment rooms, walls covered in toile de Jouy fabrics, and an indoor swimming pool. A relaxation room is available for guests who arrive before their rooms are ready. Even children get the four-star treatment, with personalized T-shirts and portable DVD players to distract them at dinnertime. **Pros:** in the couture shopping district; courtyard dining in summer; guest-only indoor swimming pool. **Cons:** several blocks from the nearest métro; lacks the intimacy of smaller boutique hotels. ✉ *31 av. George V, Champs-Élysées* ☏ *01–49–52–70–00; 800/332–3442 in U.S.* ⊕ *www. fourseasons.com/paris* ⤴ *184 rooms, 61 suites* ⚏ *In-room: safe, kitchen (some), DVD, Internet, Wi-Fi. In-hotel: 2 restaurants, room service, bar, pool, gym, spa, children's programs (ages 1–12), laundry service, some pets allowed* ▭ *AE, DC, MC, V* Ⓜ *George V* ✛ *1:D5.*

Ⓒ

FodorśChoice

★

**$$$** 🏨 **Hidden Hotel.** The rough-hewn wood facade heralds the nature-friendly theme of this boutique hotel a block from the Arc de Triomphe, and the interior follows through with handcrafted glass, wood, stone,

**18**

and ceramic decor in materials. Rooms have open-plan bathrooms in black slate and marble, and 100% organic Coco-Mat bed mattresses with pure linen sheets. Friendly service and a gourmet-but-healthful breakfast buffet have already given this new hotel a loyal following. **Pros:** organic toiletries in recycled packaging; free Wi-Fi; a block from main métro line and Champs-Élysées. **Cons:** rooms on the small side; open-plan bathrooms have little privacy for roommates. ⊠ *28 rue de l'Arc de Triomphe, Champs-Élysées* ☎ *01–40–55–03–57* ⊕ *www. hiddenhotelparis.com* ➪ *23 rooms* ⚲ *In-room: safe, Wi-Fi. In-hotel: room service, bar, Wi-Fi hotspot, parking (paid), some pets allowed* ▭ *AE, D, DC, MC, V* ✛ *1:B3.*

**$$$$** ⬚ **Hôtel Cristal Champs Elysées.** Opened in the fall of 2009 just off chi-chi avenue des Champs-Élysées, this contemporary hotel is minimalist from the outside but makes use of real quartz crystals in the interior design scheme. The white marble lobby, crystal frieze, and asymmetrical mirrors are softened by plush carpeting in the rooms, custom-made hardwood furnishings by baroque designer Mattia Bonetti, and bright splashes of hot pink, orange, red, and purple throughout. Rooms have free Wi-Fi, ADSL connections, and queen-size beds. Deluxe rooms have freestanding claw-foot tubs or one-way glass walls separating the bathroom. **Pros:** laptop rental; central location; central atrium courtyard. **Cons:** not child-friendly; expensive neighborhood. ⊠ *9 rue Washington, Champs-Élysées* ☎ *01–45–63–27–33* ⊕ *www.hotel-le-cristal.com* ➪ *24 rooms, 2 suites* ⚲ *In-room: safe, Internet, Wi-Fi. In-hotel: room service, bar, Internet terminal, Wi-Fi hotspot* ▭ *AE, D, DC, MC, V.*

**$$$$** ⬚ **Hôtel Daniel.** A contemporary antidote to the minimalist trend, the Daniel is decorated in sumptuous fabrics and antique furnishings from France, North Africa, and the Far East. The lobby feels like a living room, with deep sofas covered in colorful satin pillows, dark hardwood floors, and delicate Chinese floral wallpaper. Rooms have toile de Jouy fabrics, free Wi-Fi, and flat-screen TVs. Little luxuries include lavender sachets and padded hangers in the closets, and glass jars of sea salts in the marble or Moroccan-tile bathrooms. Room No. 601, under the roof, has a huge claw-foot bathtub. **Pros:** intimate, homey atmosphere; free Wi-Fi; close to the Champs-Élysées. **Cons:** across from a noisy bar; no fitness center. ⊠ *8 rue Frédéric Bastiat, Champs-Élysées* ☎ *01–42–56–17–00* ⊕ *www.hoteldanielparis.com* ➪ *17 rooms, 9 suites* ⚲ *In-room: safe, DVD, Wi-Fi. In-hotel: restaurant, room service, bar, laundry service, parking (paid), some pets allowed* ▭ *AE, DC, MC, V* Ⓜ *St-Philippe-du-Roule* ✛ *1:E4.*

**$$$$** ⬚ **Hôtel Fouquet's Barrière.** This luxury hotel opened in 2006 above the legendary Fouquet's Brasserie at the corner of the Champs-Élysées and Avenue George V. The design, by Jacques Garcia, is more refined retro than opulent, with a rich neutral palette in silk, mahogany, velvet, and leather. The hotel competes with Parisian palaces by offering 24-hour butler service and plasma TV screens hidden behind mirrors and above bathtubs. Le Diane restaurant offers a more feminine atmosphere than the brasserie, and the teak- and red-walled spa claims to have the largest indoor pool in Paris. **Pros:** many rooms overlooking the Champs-Élysées; bathroom TVs; métro right outside. **Cons:** anonymous decor;

busy street can be noisy; expensive part of town. ⊠ *46 av. George V* ☎ *01–40–69–60–00* ⊕ *www.fouquets-barriere.com* ⤳ *107 rooms, 40 suites* ♿ *In-room: safe, DVD, Internet, Wi-Fi. In-hotel: 2 restaurants, room service, bar, pool, gym, spa, laundry service, parking (paid), some pets allowed* ▭ *AE, DC, MC, V* Ⓜ *George V* ⊹ *1:D4.*

$$$$ 🖼 **Hôtel Lancaster.** Contemporary flourishes like perfume-bottle lamp bases and a Japanese garden give this former Spanish nobleman's town house a refreshing, modern atmosphere. Not everything is contemporary, though: room keys and doorbells are vintage, and there are more than 1,000 antiques and 18th-century paintings throughout the hotel. Free Wi-Fi and iPod docking stations in every room cater to high-tech travelers. Rooms are elegant—the Emile Wolf Suite has a baby grand—with a mix of antiques and updated fabrics, marble bathrooms, and walk-in closets. The fitness room has a splendid view of Sacré-Coeur. **Pros:** Sunday brunch with organic farm products; just steps away from the Champs-Élysées. **Cons:** street-facing rooms can be noisy; size of rooms varies greatly. ⊠ *7 rue de Berri, Champs-Élysées* ☎ *01–40–76–40–76; 877/757–2747 in U.S.* ⊕ *www.hotel-lancaster.fr* ⤳ *46 rooms, 11 suites* ♿ *In-room: safe, DVD, Wi-Fi. In-hotel: restaurant, room service, bar, gym, laundry service, parking (paid), some pets allowed* ▭ *AE, DC, MC, V* Ⓜ *George V* ⊹ *1:D4.*

$$$$ 🖼 **Hôtel Le Bristol.** The Bristol ranks among Paris's most exclusive hotels and has the prices to prove it. Some of the spacious and elegant rooms have authentic Louis XV and Louis XVI furniture and marble bathrooms in pure 1920s Art Deco; others have a more relaxed 19th-century style. A new wing added in 2009 has suites overlooking avenue Matignon, as well as a second gourmet brasserie with contemporary floral decor. The public salons are stocked with old-master paintings and sculptures, and sumptuous carpets and tapestries. The huge interior garden restaurant and monthly fashion shows in the bar draw the posh and wealthy. **Pros:** large interior garden; luxury shopping street. **Cons:** a few blocks from the nearest métro; old-fashioned atmosphere may not be for everyone. ⊠ *112 rue du Faubourg St-Honoré, Champs-Élysées* ☎ *01–53–43–43–00* ⊕ *www.hotel-bristol.com* ⤳ *109 rooms, 78 suites* ♿ *In-room: safe, DVD, Internet, Wi-Fi. In-hotel: 2 restaurants, room service, bar, pool, gym, spa, laundry service, parking (free), some pets allowed* ▭ *AE, DC, MC, V* Ⓜ *Miromesnil* ⊹ *1:F4.*

$$$$ 🖼 **Hôtel Mathis Elysées Matignon.** Each room in this boutique hotel has been lovingly decorated with antiques and artworks. Leopard-print carpets, rich aubergine, slate, and mustard walls, and Baroque mirrors make for an eclectic look. Room 43 has a sexy boudoir style, and the top-floor suite has a modern pop-art look. The Mathis's restaurant is owned separately from the hotel, but shares an entrance. **Pros:** a block from the Champs-Élysées and Faubourg St-Honoré; large choice in decor of rooms; free Wi-Fi. **Cons:** some noise from street and bar downstairs; small closets; few services. ⊠ *3 rue de Ponthieu, Champs-Élysées* ☎ *01–42–25–73–01* ⊕ *www.paris-inn.com* ⤳ *23 rooms* ♿ *In-room: safe, Wi-Fi. In-hotel: room service, laundry service, some pets allowed* ▭ *AE, DC, MC, V* Ⓜ *Franklin-D.-Roosevelt* ⊹ *1:F5.*

**18**

**$$$$** Hôtel Plaza Athénée. Prime-time stardom as Carrie Bradshaw's Parisian pied-à-terre in the final episodes of *Sex and the City* boosted the street cred of this 1911 palace hotel. Its revival as the city's lap of luxury, however, owes more to the meticulous attention of the renowned chef Alain Ducasse, who oversees everything from the hotel's flagship restaurant and restored 1930s Relais Plaza brasserie to the quality of the breakfast croissants. Rooms have been redone in Regency, Louis XVI, or Art Deco style, with remote-control air-conditioning, mini hi-fi/CD players, and even a pillow menu. The trendy bar has as its centerpiece an impressive Bombay glass comptoir glowing like an iceberg. **Pros:** on a luxury shopping street; new Dior spa; Eiffel Tower views; special attention to children. **Cons:** vast difference in style of rooms; easy to feel anonymous in such a large hotel. ✉ *25 av. Montaigne, Champs-Élysées* ☎ *01–53–67–66–65; 866/732–1106 in U.S.* ⊕ *www.plaza-athenee-paris.com* ⇥ *145 rooms, 43 suites* ♿ *In-room: safe, DVD, Internet. In-hotel: 3 restaurants, room service, bar, spa, laundry service, some pets allowed* ⊟ *AE, DC, MC, V* Ⓜ *Alma-Marceau* ✛ *1:D6.*

Fodor's Choice ★

**$$$** Hôtel Queen Mary. This cheerfully cozy hotel is two blocks from Place de la Madeleine and Paris's famous department stores. Sunny yellow walls, plush carpeting, and fabrics in burgundy, gold, and royal blue soften the regal architectural detailing and high ceilings. Rooms are handsomely appointed with large beds and such thoughtful extras as trouser presses, Roger & Gallet toiletries, and decanters of sherry. Guests mingle in the bar during happy hour and, in good weather, enjoy breakfast in the garden courtyard. **Pros:** close to high-end shopping streets and department stores; large beds; extra-attentive service. **Cons:** some rooms are quite snug; ones on the ground floor and facing the street can be noisy. ✉ *9 rue Greffulhe, Opéra/Grands Boulevards* ☎ *01–42–66–40–50* ⊕ *www.hotelqueenmary.com* ⇥ *35 rooms, 1 suite* ♿ *In-room: safe, Wi-Fi. In-hotel: room service, bar, laundry service, some pets allowed* ⊟ *MC, V* Ⓜ *Madeleine, St-Lazare, Havre Caumartin* ✛ *1:H4.*

**$$$$** Hôtel San Régis. On a quiet side street near tony Avenue Montaigne, this discreet hotel walks softly but wields huge snob appeal (the same family that opened it once owned the Tour d'Argent and the George V). All guest rooms and suites have carefully chosen antiques, embroidered silks and brocades, and richly patterned Pierre Frey wall fabrics; bathrooms are done in Italian marble, with Hermès toiletries. Top-floor suites have balcony views of the Eiffel Tower, Grand Palais, Opéra Garnier, and Madeleine. The elegant wood-paneled Boiseries Lounge leads to the tiny English Bar and a dining room that serves traditional French cuisine. **Pros:** on a quiet street; authentic old Parisian feel; personalized service. **Cons:** old-fashioned decor can feel outdated; no fitness facilities. ✉ *12 rue Jean-Goujon, Champs-Élysées* ☎ *01–44–95–16–16* ⊕ *www.hotel-sanregis.fr* ⇥ *33 rooms, 11 suites* ♿ *In-room: safe, Wi-Fi. In-hotel: restaurant, room service, bar, laundry service, Internet terminal* ⊟ *AE, DC, MC, V* Ⓜ *Franklin-D.-Roosevelt* ✛ *1:E6.*

**$$$$** La Trémoille. La Trémoille offers business travelers a trendy home base, with Haussmann-era marble fireplaces and plaster moldings that have been given a shot of style by contemporary armoires, furniture

Hôtel Plaza Athénée

Hôtel Langlois

Four Seasons Hôtel George V Paris

upholstered in fake fur, and funky mohair curtains. Unique to this hotel is the "hatch," a butler closet by each door where meals and laundry can be delivered without disturbing the guests. The Louis II restaurant and piano lounge bar features French Mediterranean cuisine and a trendy-but-cozy setting of black lacquer tables, silver beaded curtains, and beige and eggplant fabrics. **Pros:** piano bar frequented by locals; spa and fitness facilities. **Cons:** a few blocks from the nearest métro; expensive neighborhood. ⊠ *14 rue de La Trémoille, Champs-Élysées* ☎ *01–56–52–14–00* ⊕ *www.hotel-tremoille.com* ↘ *88 rooms, 5 suites* ⚘ *In-room: safe, DVD, Internet, Wi-Fi. In-hotel: restaurant, room service, bar, gym, spa, laundry service, parking (paid), some pets allowed* ⊟ *AE, DC, MC, V* Ⓜ *Alma-Marceau* ✛ *1:D6.*

$$$$ ⬚ **Pershing Hall.** Formerly an American Legion hall, this circa-2001 boutique hotel quickly became a must-stay address for the dressed-in-black pack. Designed by Andrée Putman, Pershing Hall champions masculine minimalism, with muted surfaces of wood and stone and cool attitudes to match. Rooms have stark white linens, slender tubelike hanging lamps, and tubs perched on round marble bases. The only trace of lightheartedness is the free minibars. Deluxe rooms and suites face the courtyard dining room, whose west wall is a six-story hanging garden with 300 varieties of plants. The lounge bar serves drinks, dinner, and DJ-driven music until 2 AM. **Pros:** prime shopping and nightlife district; bar and restaurant frequented by hip locals; in-room DVD players. **Cons:** bar noise can be heard in some rooms; expensive neighborhood. ⊠ *49 rue Pierre-Charron, Champs-Élysées* ☎ *01–58–36–58–00* ⊕ *www.pershinghall.com* ↘ *20 rooms, 6 suites* ⚘ *In-room: safe, DVD, Internet, Wi-Fi. In-hotel: restaurant, room service, bar, gym, spa, laundry service, some pets allowed* ⊟ *AE, DC, MC, V* Ⓜ *George V, Franklin-D.-Roosevelt* ✛ *1:D5.*

# 9ᴱ ARRONDISSEMENT

Ideal if you're seeking good deals near Montmartre and central Paris, the 9ᵉ arrondissement has several distinctly different neighborhoods. To the southwest is the busy Opéra district with the historic department stores of the Grands Boulevards. To the north, at the foot of Montmartre, are the neon-lighted sex shops and clubs of the infamous Pigalle district. In between are the pleasant residential districts of Nouvelle Athènes and Rue des Martyrs.

$$ ⬚ **Best Western Ronceray Opéra.** On one of Haussmann's Grands Boulevards between a historic covered shopping passage and the Grévin Wax Museum, the Ronceray Opéra is convenient for exploring Montmartre, browsing department stores, or enjoying local nightlife. The hotel's original 19th-century architecture has been preserved in the elegant Rossini bar and ballroom, where breakfast is served under crystal chandeliers. Comfortably modern rooms glow with wood-paneled walls, warm red fabrics, and marble baths. Rooms 319 and 419 have views of Sacré-Coeur. **Pros:** unique location; historic architecture; central nightlife district. **Cons:** decor in rooms lacks character of public areas; noisy neighborhood. ⊠ *10 bd. Montmartre, Passage Jouffroy Opéra/*

*Grands Boulevards* ☎*01–42–47–13–45* ⊕*www.bestwestern.com* ⤶*130 rooms, 1 suite* ⌂*In-room: safe, Wi-Fi. In-hotel: room service, bar, laundry service, some pets allowed* ▭*AE, DC, MC, V* Ⓜ*Grands Boulevards* ✛*2:C4.*

**$$$** ⊞ **Hôtel Amour.** The hipster team behind this designer boutique hotel just off the trendy Rue des Martyrs already count among their fiefdoms some of the hottest hotels, bars, and nightclubs in Paris. But despite the cool factor and the funky rooms individually decorated by Parisian avant-garde artists, the prices remain democratically bohemian. Of course, there are few amenities, but there is a 24-hour retro brasserie and garden terrace in the back where locals come to hang out in warmer weather. The hotel is not designed for children; vintage nudie magazines decorate, and the sex shops of Pigalle are blocks away. **Pros:** hip clientele and locals at the brasserie; close to Montmartre; garden dining in summer. **Cons:** few amenities; a few blocks from the nearest métro; close to red-light district. ⊠*8 rue Navarin, Montmartre* ☎*01–48–78–31–80* ⊕*www.hotelamourparis.fr* ⤶*20 rooms* ⌂*In-room: no a/c, no phone, no TV, Wi-Fi. In-hotel: restaurant, room service, bar, laundry service, some pets allowed* ▭*AE, DC, MC, V* Ⓜ*Pigalle* ✛*2:B2.*

**$** ⊞ **Hôtel Chopin.** The Chopin recalls its 1846 birth date with a creaky-floored lobby and aged woodwork. The basic but comfortable rooms overlook the Passage Jouffroy's quaint toy shops and bookstores or the rooftops of Paris, but none face the busy nearby streets. The best rooms end in "7" (No. 407 overlooks the Grévin Wax Museum's ateliers), whereas those ending in "2" tend to be darkest and smallest (but cheapest). **Pros:** unique location; close to major métro station; great nightlife district. **Cons:** neighborhood can be noisy; some rooms are dark and cramped; few amenities. ⊠*10 bd. Montmartre, 46 passage Jouffroy, Opéra/Grands Boulevards* ☎*01–47–70–58–10* ⊕*www.hotelchopin.com* ⤶*36 rooms* ⌂*In-room: no a/c, safe* ▭*AE, MC, V* Ⓜ*Grands Boulevards* ✛*2:C4.*

**$$$** ⊞ **Hôtel George Sand.** This family-run boutique hotel where the 19th-century writer George Sand once lived is fresh and modern, while preserving some original architectural details. Rooms have tea/coffee-making trays and high-tech comforts such as complimentary high-speed Internet and cordless phones. Bathrooms are decked out in yacht-inspired wood flooring, with Etro toiletries. **Pros:** next door to two department stores; historic atmosphere. **Cons:** noisy street; some rooms are quite small. ⊠*26 rue des Mathurins, Opéra/Grands Boulevards* ☎*01–47–42–63–47* ⊕*www.hotelgeorgesand.com* ⤶*20 rooms* ⌂*In-room: safe, Internet, Wi-Fi. In-hotel: room service, laundry service* ▭*AE, MC, V* Ⓜ*Havre Caumartin* ✛*1:H4.*

**$$**
**Fodor's Choice**
★ ⊞ **Hôtel Langlois.** After starring in *The Truth About Charlie* (a remake of *Charade*), this darling hotel gained a reputation as one of the most atmospheric budget sleeps in the city. Rates have crept up, but the former circa-1870 bank retains its beautiful wood-paneled reception area and wrought-iron elevator. The individually decorated and spacious rooms are decked out with original glazed-tile fireplaces and period art. Some rooms, such as Nos. 15, 21, and 41, have enormous retro bathrooms. **Pros:** excellent views from the top floor; close to department stores and

18

Opéra Garnier; historic decor. **Cons:** noisy street; off the beaten path; some sagging furniture. ✉ *63 rue St-Lazare, Opéra/Grands Boulevards* ☏ *01–48–74–78–24* ⊕ *www.hotel-langlois.com* ⤧ *24 rooms, 3 suites* ⟁ *In-room: Wi-Fi. In-hotel: Internet terminal, some pets allowed* ⊟ *AE, MC, V* Ⓜ *Trinité* ✛ *2:A3.*

$　　🚼 **Hôtel Royal Fromentin.** At the border of Montmartre's now tamed red-light district sits this former cabaret with much of its Art Deco wood paneling and theatrical trappings intact. Prices are at the low end of its category. The hotel has dark, rich decor, with green walls, red armchairs, an antique caged elevator, and vaudeville posters in the stained-glass-ceiling lounge. Reproduction furniture, antique prints and oils, and busy modern fabrics fill out the larger-than-average rooms. Some windows face Sacré-Coeur. Guests receive a complimentary book illustrating the history of absinthe, which is once again served in the hotel's historic bar. **Pros:** spacious rooms for the price; historic absinthe bar; close to Sacré-Coeur. **Cons:** some guests may find neighborhood peep shows and sex shops disturbing; far from the center of Paris. ✉ *11 rue Fromentin, Montmartre* ☏ *01–48–74–85–93* ⊕ *www.hotelroyalfromentin.com* ⤧ *47 rooms* ⟁ *In-room: no a/c, Wi-Fi. In-hotel: room service, bar, laundry service, some pets allowed* ⊟ *AE, DC, MC, V* Ⓜ *Blanche* ✛ *2:B2.*

$$$$　🚼 **Le Scribe.** This historic property has housed numerous illustrious tenants and events since it opened in 1861, and now each floor is themed to celebrate those occupants and moments, ranging from the Salon Indien—where the Lumière brothers debuted the cinematograph (film camera) in 1895—to Jazz Age icon Josephine Baker, who once lived at the property. Rooms are spacious with rich fabrics and modern amenities like Jacuzzis and flat-screen TVs. New additions to the property include the upscale restaurant, Le Café Lumière, a spa, and La Maison de Thé, an elegant tearoom. **Pros:** incredibly plush bedding; central, easily accessible location. **Cons:** understaffed concierge; tiny fitness center. ✉ *1 rue Scribe* ☏ *01–44–71–24–24* ⊕ *www.hotel-scribe-paris.com* ⤧ *200 rooms, 4 suites* ⟁ *In-room: safe, DVD, Internet, Wi-Fi. In-hotel: 2 restaurants, room service, bar, gym, spa, parking (paid)* ⊟ *AE, MC, V* Ⓜ *Opéra, RER Auber* ✛ *2:A5.*

## 10ᴱ ARRONDISSEMENT

As one of the latest up-and-coming districts of Paris, the multicultural 10ᵉ attracts many students, artists, and young professionals, particularly around the Canal St-Martin to the east and the Rue du Faubourg St-Denis to the west. In between are two of the city's busy train stations, Gare de l'Est and Gare du Nord, home of the Eurostar. Nightlife is concentrated around the Bonne Nouvelle métro station.

¢　🚼 **Hôtel du Nord.** Behind the rustic facade of this budget hotel that's just around the corner from Place de la République is a charming little lobby with clay-tile floors, exposed stone walls, and wooden beams. There are few perks, but the hotel does have bikes available free to guests, perfect for a ride down to the nearby Marais district or a cruise along the tree-lined Canal St-Martin. **Pros:** bike rental; close to East Paris nightlife districts. **Cons:** few amenities; busy Place de la République is quite noisy. ✉ *47 rue Albert Thomas, République* ☎ *01–42–01–66–00* ⊕ *www.hoteldunord-leparivelo.com* ⇆ *24 rooms* ⌂ *In-room: no a/c. In-hotel: bicycles, Wi-Fi hotspot* ▭ *MC, V* Ⓜ *République* ✛ *2:F4.*

$ ⊞ **Hôtel Français.** This Haussmann-era budget hotel faces historic Gare de l'Est and is two blocks from Gare du Nord and the popular Canal St-Martin district. The decor isn't memorable, but it's still rare to find air-conditioning, elevators, hair dryers, free Wi-Fi, and trouser presses in rooms of this price, so fussing over the color of the curtains seems pointless. Some rooms overlook the charming indoor patio breakfast room. The busy neighborhood isn't very attractive, but the métro station across the street is a direct line to Notre-Dame, the Quartier Latin, St-Germain-des-Prés, and the Marché aux Puces. **Pros:** convenient for Eurostar travelers; many amenities for the price. **Cons:** noisy street; unattractive neighborhood. ✉ *13 rue du 8 Mai 1945, République* ☎ *01–40–35–94–14* ⊕ *www.hotelfrancais.com* ⇆ *71 rooms* ⌂ *In-room: safe, Wi-Fi. In-hotel: room service, bar, parking (paid), some pets allowed* ▭ *AE, MC, V* Ⓜ *Gare de l'Est* ✛ *2:E3.*

# 11ᴱ ARRONDISSEMENT

This East Paris neighborhood became a popular new district for artists and "bourgeois bohemians" in the late 1990s with its laid-back bars, cheap clubs, and funky boutiques along Rue Oberkampf and Rue Méilmontant. There are no museums or monuments, but the relaxed atmosphere, relatively low prices, and proximity to the Bastille and Marais make it popular.

$$ ⊞ **Hôtel Beaumarchais.** This bold hotel straddles the fashionable Marais district in the 3ᵉ and the hip student and artist neighborhood of Oberkampf in the 11ᵉ. Brightly colored vinyl armchairs, an industrial metal staircase, and glass tables mark the lobby, which hosts monthly art exhibitions. Out back, a small courtyard is decked in hardwood, a look you'll rarely see in Paris. The rooms hum with primary reds and yellows, some with Keith Haring prints. Kaleidoscopes of ceramic fragments tile the bathrooms. **Pros:** free Internet; popular nightlife district; bright and colorful. **Cons:** smallish rooms; off the beaten tourist track. ✉ *3 rue Oberkampf, République* ☎ *01–53–36–86–86* ⊕ *www.hotelbeaumarchais.com* ⇆ *31 rooms* ⌂ *In-room: safe, Internet, Wi-Fi. In-hotel: room service, some pets allowed* ▭ *AE, MC, V* Ⓜ *Filles du Calvaire, Oberkampf* ✛ *2:G6.*

$ ⊞ **Hôtel Résidence Alhambra.** The white facade, rear garden, and flower-filled window boxes brighten this lesser-known neighborhood between Le Marais and Rue Oberkampf. Rooms are smallish (splurge for a triple, just €116), with modern furnishings and run-of-the-mill bedspreads and drapes. Some overlook the flowery courtyard. There's a free Internet station in the lobby, and five métro lines are around the corner at Place de la République. **Pros:** bright and colorful; popular nightlife district. **Cons:** small doubles; long walk to the center of town; no air-conditioning. ✉ *13 rue de Malte, République* ☎ *01–47–00–35–52* ⊕ *www.hotelalhambra.fr* ⇆ *58 rooms* ⌂ *In-room: no a/c. In-hotel:*

18

*Internet terminal, Wi-Fi hotspot* ▤ *AE, DC, MC, V* Ⓜ *Oberkampf* ✛ *2:H6.*

$$$  Le Général Hôtel. Designer Jean-Philippe Nuel's sleek hotel was one of Paris's first budget design hotels. The daring interior splashes fuchsia on the walls, though rooms are more subdued in cream, chocolate, and chestnut. Clever elements include clear-plastic desk chairs and silver rubber duckies to float in the tubs. The fifth- and sixth-floor rooms facing the street have balconies with chimney-pot views to the west. One of the hotel's two seventh-floor suites has a bathtub right in the bedroom. **Pros:** free Wi-Fi; coffee/tea-making facilities in the room; in popular nightlife district. **Cons:** smallish rooms; not within easy walking distance of major tourist sights. ⊠ *5–7 rue Rampon, République* ☎ *01–47–00–41–57* ⊕ *www.legeneralhotel.com* ⇱ *45 rooms, 2 suites* ⌂ *In-room: safe, Wi-Fi. In-hotel: bar, gym, laundry service, Internet terminal, some pets allowed* ▤ *AE, DC, MC, V* Ⓜ *République* ✛ *2:G5.*

$$$  Les Jardins du Marais. Behind an unassuming facade on a narrow street, this rambling hotel's nine historic buildings (including Gustave Eiffel's old workshop) surround a spacious sculpture-garden courtyard. The Art Deco rooms overlook the garden, where meals are served in summer. In cooler weather you can still enjoy garden views from the glass conservatory restaurant and bar. **Pros:** historic building; easy walk to Le Marais and Bastille; all rooms face garden courtyard. **Cons:** often booked by groups; big difference between room decor and public areas; some rooms in these odd old buildings have a pillar in the center. ⊠ *74 rue Amelot, Bastille/Nation* ☎ *01–40–21–20–00* ⊕ *www.homeplazza. com* ⇱ *201 rooms, 64 suites* ⌂ *In-room: safe, Wi-Fi. In-hotel: restaurant, room service, bar, parking (paid)* ▤ *AE, DC, MC, V* Ⓜ *St-Sébastien-Froissart* ✛ *4:H1.*

$$  Standard Design Hôtel. It was about time for a design hotel to open in this alternative hipster corner of the Bastille district. Its sleek black facade and black-and-white interior reflect the mood of its fashion-forward clientele, and the fairly affordable rates don't clash with the neighborhood's funky boutiques and retro bistros. In-room stylings include black duvets, flat-screen TVs, and white lacquered furnishings. A bright breakfast room is on the top floor. Massage and manicures are available in the guest rooms. **Pros:** trendy design style; free Wi-Fi; funky shopping and nightlife district. **Cons:** can be noisy; some rooms very small. ⊠ *29 rue des Taillandiers, Bastille* ☎ *01–48–05–30–97* ⊕ *www. standard-hotel.com* ⇱ *36 rooms* ⌂ *In-room: Wi-Fi. In-hotel: room service, Internet terminal* ▤ *AE, DC, MC, V* Ⓜ *Bastille* ✛ *4:H2.*

## 12ᴱ ARRONDISSEMENT

The Bastille district remains a beacon for night owls with its cinemas, late-night bars, and nightclubs spread along the Rue de Lappe and Rue du Faubourg St-Antoine. During the day people come for the two colorful markets on the north end of Place de la Bastille and at Place d'Aligre. The Viaduc des Arts, home to craft boutiques, artisans, and art galleries, stretches from the Opéra Bastille to the Gare de Lyon.

**$$** ⊞ **Hôtel Lyon-Bastille.** This cozy, family-run hotel is a block from the Gare de Lyon and has been open since 1903. Its turn-of-the-20th-century pedigree shows up in its curves and alcoves, and tall French windows let in plenty of light. The rooms have been done up in pale blues and lilacs, and have satellite TV and free Wi-Fi. The Marché Aligre and Viaduc des Arts artisan boutiques are just a few blocks away. **Pros:** easy access to major métro and train lines; friendly welcome. **Cons:** outdated decor; noisy traffic area; tiny elevator. ⊠ *3 rue Parrot, Bastille/Nation* ☎ *01–43–43–41–52* ⊕ *www.hotellyonbastille.com* ⤳ *47 rooms, 1 suite* ⎈ *In-room: safe, Wi-Fi* ⊟ *AE, DC, MC, V* Ⓜ *Gare de Lyon* ✛ *4:H4.*

## 13ᴱ ARRONDISSEMENT

The 13ᵉ is often dismissed as a "new" district of high-rise apartments—which is true in the Chinatown area east of Place d'Italie—but the historic Gobelins district blends seamlessly with the Mouffetard market and Jardin des Plantes of the neighboring 5ᵉ, without the steep prices. The 13ᵉ is also home to the charming Butte-aux-Cailles hilltop and the contemporary Rive Gauche district along the Seine.

**$$** ⊞ **Hôtel La Manufacture.** Just behind Place d'Italie and a short stroll from both the Jardin des Plantes and Rue Mouffetard, La Manufacture's lesser-known location makes you feel like a *vrai* (real) Parisian. The lobby has oak floors, subtle lighting, a wooden bar, and a cozy breakfast room. Rooms are decorated in clean lines and natural colors; options include triples and eight sets of connecting rooms for families. The most expensive top-floor rooms are more spacious and have Eiffel Tower or Panthéon views. **Pros:** easy access to major métro and bus lines; safe nontouristy district; bright breakfast room. **Cons:** street noise; a long stroll to the center of Paris; small rooms. ⊠ *8 rue Philippe de Champagne, Les Gobelins* ☎ *01–45–35–45–25* ⊕ *www.hotel-la-manufacture.com* ⤳ *57 rooms* ⎈ *In-room: Internet, Wi-Fi. In-hotel: bar, laundry service, some pets allowed* ⊟ *AE, DC, MC, V* Ⓜ *Place d'Italie* ✛ *4:E6.*

**$$** ⊞ **Résidence Hôtelière Le Vert Galant.** In a little-known neighborhood west of Place d'Italie awaits a sincere welcome from Madame Laborde, the proprietress. More like her own house, this plain but proper hotel encloses a peaceful green garden. Eight of the rooms have kitchenettes, which can reduce dining-out costs, unless the hotel's pricey L'Auberge Etchegorry restaurant lures you in. Victor Hugo was known to take a glass or two at this outstanding Basque dining spot. **Pros:** quiet location with a garden; kitchenettes in some rooms; safe residential district. **Cons:** not very central; no air-conditioning; some noise between rooms. ⊠ *41–43 rue Croulebarbe, Les Gobelins* ☎ *01–44–08–83–50* ⊕ *www.vertgalant.com* ⤳ *15 rooms* ⎈ *In-room: no a/c, safe, kitchen (some), Wi-Fi. In-hotel: restaurant, laundry service, parking (paid)* ⊟ *AE, DC, MC, V* Ⓜ *Les Gobelins* ✛ *4:E6.*

**$** ⊞ **Résidence Les Gobelins.** Wicker furniture and sunny colors warm up this small, simple hotel on a quiet side street between Place d'Italie and the Quartier Latin, not far from the market street Rue Mouffetard. Some rooms overlook a small flower-filled garden, as does the lounge–breakfast room. Jamaican expat Jennifer Poirier runs the Résidence with

**18**

her French husband, Philippe. Their wholehearted welcome is a big part of this hotel's draw. **Pros:** close to major métro and bus lines; friendly welcome. **Cons:** 20-minute walk to the center of Paris; few amenities; no air-conditioning. ⊠ *9 rue des Gobelins, Les Gobelins* ☎ *01–47–07–26–90* ⊕ *www.hotelgobelins.com* ⇱ *32 rooms* ⌂ *In-room: no a/c, Wi-Fi. In-hotel: Internet terminal* ☰ *AE, MC, V* Ⓜ *Les Gobelins* ✣ *4:E6.*

## 14ᴱ ARRONDISSEMENT

Once the stomping ground of artists and writers, Montparnasse is still a lively area of Paris, separated from the more upscale 6ᵉ arrondissement by the busy Boulevard du Montparnasse. Although the area around the hulking Tour Montparnasse, train station, and commercial center looks a bit like Times Square, with billboards and cinemas, the area around the cemetery has more of a Parisian village atmosphere, particularly on the Rue Daguerre market street near Denfert-Rochereau.

$ ⊡ **Hôtel des Bains.** In a charming neighborhood, this hidden find has tastefully decorated rooms, satellite TV, and air-conditioning. Prices are excellent, especially for the family-friendly two-room suites (€105–€155), one with a terrace, in a separate building off the courtyard garden. Local artists contributed different pieces to each room. **Pros:** close to Jardin du Luxembourg and St-Germain-des-Prés; garden courtyard; typical Parisian character. **Cons:** decor may seem a bit outdated; streets can be noisy; some rooms very small. ⊠ *33 rue Delambre, Montparnasse* ☎ *01–43–20–85–27* ⊕ *www.hotel-des-bains-montparnasse.com* ⇱ *35 rooms, 8 suites* ⌂ *In-room: safe, Wi-Fi. In-hotel: parking (paid)* ☰ *MC, V* Ⓜ *Vavin, Edgar Quinet* ✣ *4:A6.*

$ ⊡ **Hôtel Lenox-Montparnasse.** Parisians know this hotel near the Jardin du Luxembourg for its monthly live-music concerts in the cozy bar. Tourists appreciate the extra amenities such as free Wi-Fi. The largest (and best) rooms have fireplaces and exposed beams; in the standard-size rooms, there's barely a suitcase-width between the wall and the foot of the bed. **Pros:** close to Montparnasse and St-Germain-des-Prés; lively music bar. **Cons:** standard rooms are small; noisy street. ⊠ *15 rue Delambre, Montparnasse* ☎ *01–43–35–34–50* ⊕ *www.paris-hotel-lenox.com* ⇱ *46 rooms, 6 suites* ⌂ *In-room: safe, Wi-Fi. In-hotel: room service, bar, laundry service, Internet terminal, parking (paid)* ☰ *AE, DC, MC, V* Ⓜ *Vavin* ✣ *4:A6.*

$$ ⊡ **Hôtel Raspail-Montparnasse.** Rooms are named after the artists who made Montparnasse the art capital of the world in the 1920s and '30s—Picasso, Chagall, and Modigliani. Pay a bit extra—and reserve well in advance—for one of the three deluxe corner rooms, which have windows facing the Eiffel Tower. All are soundproofed, but none completely drown out the traffic below. **Pros:** convenient to métro and bus; many markets and cafés nearby; friendly staff. **Cons:** traffic noise; some smallish rooms. ⊠ *203 bd. Raspail, Montparnasse* ☎ *01–43–20–62–86* ⊕ *www.hotelraspailmontparnasse.com* ⇱ *38 rooms* ⌂ *In-room: safe, Wi-Fi. In-hotel: room service, bar, laundry service, Internet terminal, parking (paid)* ☰ *AE, DC, MC, V* Ⓜ *Vavin* ✣ *4:A6.*

# 15ᴱ ARRONDISSEMENT

If your ideal Paris hotel is within walking distance of the Iron Lady, the 15ᵉ won't disappoint. There are few other monuments or sights, but this residential district has plenty of bistros, boutiques, cafés, and, beneath the elevated métro line, a popular street market.

**$$$**

Fodor's Choice
★

🏨 **Eiffel Seine Hôtel.** Opened in 2006, this stylish hotel mixes contemporary amenities and custom Art Nouveau decor. Directly across from the Eiffel Tower's métro station, it's hard to believe this independently owned hotel doesn't cost twice as much. Thoughtful extras include the hearty buffet breakfast, free Wi-Fi, and free public parking. **Pros:** next door to the Eiffel Tower; easy métro access. **Cons:** not an easy walk to the center of town; some street noise. ⊠ *3 bd. de Grenelle, Trocadéro/ Tour Eiffel* ☎ *01–45–78–14–81* ⊕ *www.eiffelseine.com* 🛏 *45 rooms* ♨ *In-room: safe, Wi-Fi. In-hotel: room service, laundry service, parking (free)* ▤ *AE, DC, MC, V* Ⓜ *Bir Hakeim* ✛ *3:B3.*

# 16ᴱ ARRONDISSEMENT

The 16ᵉ arrondissement is so large that it has two postal codes. Considered one of the poshest residential districts in Paris, it's a good destination for travelers interested in sightseeing during the day and getting a good night's sleep in a safe, quiet neighborhood. Museums are concentrated on the northern end around Trocadéro, and luxury shopping streets are found closer to the Arc de Triomphe. Nature lovers may want to stay close to the Bois de Bologne, the city's largest park.

**$$**

🏨 **Hôtel Gavarni.** With the traditional, verging on old-fashioned Parisian decor, it may come as a surprise to learn that this property in a chic residential neighborhood is one of the first certified ecohotels in Paris. The Gavarni's dedication to the environment is more than skin deep, though, and they use energy- and water-saving fixtures, and carbon-offsetting practices. Rooms have carpeting, tiled bathrooms and flat-screen TVs. **Pros:** organic breakfast; charming Parisian neighborhood; friendly welcome. **Cons:** a few blocks to the nearest métro; outdated decor. ⊠ *5 rue Gavarni, Passy/Western Paris* ☎ *01–45–24–52–82* ⊕ *www.gavarni.com* 🛏 *21 rooms, 4 suites.* ♨ *In-room: safe, Wi-Fi (some). In-hotel: room service, bar, Internet terminal, Wi-Fi hotspot, some pets allowed* ▤ *AE, D, DC, MC, V* ✛ *3:A2.*

**$$$$**
♨

🏨 **Hôtel Raphael.** This discreet palace hotel was built in 1925 to cater to travelers spending a season in Paris, so every space is generously sized for long, lavish stays. The closets, for instance, have room for ball gowns and plumed hats. Guest rooms, most with king-size beds and 6-foot windows, are decorated with 18th- and early-19th-century antiques, Oriental rugs, silk damask wallpaper, and ornately carved wood paneling. Bathrooms are remarkably large, and most have claw-foot tubs. The roof terrace, home to a restaurant in summer, has panoramic views. Parents will find a friend in the concierge, who can arrange bilingual babysitters, and offers recommendations on kid-friendly restaurants and entertainment. **Pros:** a block from the Champs-Élysées and Arc de Triomphe; rooftop garden terrace; cozy hotel bar frequented by locals. **Cons:** old-fashioned Parisian decor won't impress fans of minimalism;

**18**

the neighborhood can have a majestic yet cold atmosphere. ⊠ *17 av. Kléber, Trocadéro/Tour Eiffel* 🕾 *01–53–64–32–00* ⊕ *www.raphael-hotel.com* ⮑ *52 rooms, 38 suites* ⟁ *In-room: safe, DVD (some), Wi-Fi. In-hotel: 2 restaurants, room service, bar, gym, laundry service, some pets allowed* ☰ *AE, DC, MC, V* Ⓜ *Kléber* ✛ *1:C4.*

$$$$ 🔟 **Le Sezz.** Created by French furniture designer Christophe Pillet, Le Sezz mixes rough stone walls with flashes of bright color. One-way glass walls separate the sleeping areas from the bathrooms, many of which have tubs big enough for two. The owner has pushed the trend of scaled-down reception desks even further by not having one at all. All paperwork is done in advance, so you can go directly to your room without having to stand around the lobby. A champagne bar and *Espace Bien-Être* ("well-being center," or spa) cater to jet-setters. **Pros:** sexy designer decor; huge bathtubs; quiet location. **Cons:** residential district far from the center; the hotel bar is a bit too quiet; services are limited for a hotel in this price range. ⊠ *6 av. Frémiet, Passy-Auteuil* 🕾 *01–56–75–26–26* ⊕ *www.hotelsezz.com* ⮑ *13 rooms, 14 suites* ⟁ *In-room: safe, DVD, Wi-Fi. In-hotel: room service, bar, spa, laundry service, Internet terminal* ☰ *AE, DC, MC, V* Ⓜ *Passy* ✛ *3:A3.*

$$$ 🔟 **Les Jardins du Trocadéro.** This hotel near the Trocadéro and the Eiffel Tower blends old-style French elegance (period antiques, Napoleonic draperies, classical plaster busts) with modern conveniences (DVDs, flat-screen TVs, free Wi-Fi). Wall paintings of genies and dressed-up monkeys add a fanciful dash. Beds are large—either kings or queens—and have hypoallergenic bedding and mattresses. Marble bathrooms have whirlpool tubs. **Pros:** hillside views over the Eiffel Tower; upscale residential district. **Cons:** not an easy walk to the center of town; some rooms are rather small and cramped; room service doesn't always speak English. ⊠ *35 rue Benjamin-Franklin, Trocadéro/Tour Eiffel* 🕾 *01–53–70–17–70; 800/246–0041 in U.S.* ⊕ *www.jardintroc.com* ⮑ *20 rooms* ⟁ *In-room: safe, Wi-Fi. In-hotel: restaurant, room service, bar, laundry service, parking (paid)* ☰ *AE, DC, MC, V* Ⓜ *Trocadéro* ✛ *3:A1.*

$$$$ 🔟 **Mon Hotel.** Contemporary design and modern comforts, just two blocks from the Arc de Triomphe and Champs-Élysées, are big draws for this stylish boutique hotel. The lobby is dramatic, but the rooms are more comforting with chamois wall coverings, neutral tones, and black-and-white portraits of famous personalities. High-tech amenities include MP3 docking stations and Nespresso machines, and more than 1,000 satellite TV stations. A sexy new bar-restaurant serving fusion cuisine opened in 2009. **Pros:** free Wi-Fi; unique contemporary decor; convenient to the Champs-Élysées. **Cons:** some rooms have limited closet space; no extra beds for children; inconvenient for walking to the center of Paris. ⊠ *1 rue Argentine, Champs-Élysées* 🕾 *01–45–02–76–76* ⊕ *www.monhotel.fr* ⮑ *37 rooms* ⟁ *In-room: safe, Wi-Fi. In-hotel: restaurant, room service, bar, spa* ☰ *AE, MC, V* Ⓜ *Argentine* ✛ *1:B4.*

$$ 🔟 **Queen's Hôtel.** One of only a handful of hotels in the tony residential district near the Bois de Boulogne, the Queen's is a small, comfortable, old-fashioned place with a high standard of service. It bills itself a hôtel-musée, because it contains works by contemporary French artists such as René Julian and Maurice Friedman, whose paintings hang in

Eiffel Seine Hôtel

St. Christopher's Inn

Hôtel Mama Shelter

the rooms and public areas. Guest rooms pair contemporary and older furnishings and have large mirrors and spotless tiled bathrooms, many with jetted tubs. **Pros:** unique artsy atmosphere; charming shopping street; friendly welcome. **Cons:** not so convenient for getting around the city on foot; vast difference in quality of room decor. ⊠ *4 rue Bastien-Lepage, Passy-Auteuil* ☎ *01–42–88–89–85* ⊕ *www.hotel-queens-hotel. com* ⟿ *21 rooms, 1 suite* ⚒ *In-room: safe, Wi-Fi. In-hotel: some pets allowed* ⊟ *AE, DC, MC, V* Ⓜ *Michel-Ange Auteuil* ✛ *3:A3.*

**$$$$** 🖼 **Renaissance Paris Hôtel Le Parc Trocadéro.** Spacious and elegant, this historic urban retreat was once the home of Alfred Nobel, whose will established the Nobel Prizes. It has a contemporary-classic Parisian decor of neutral fabrics and whitewashed wooden furnishings. Just a short stroll from the bustling Place du Trocadéro (overlooking the Eiffel Tower), the leafy garden courtyard gives it the feel of a country hideaway. **Pros:** large beds with plush comforters; historic building in upscale neighborhood; 24-hour fitness center. **Cons:** conference hotel hosts large groups; inconvenient for walking to the center of Paris. ⊠ *55–59 rue Raymond-Poincaré, Trocadéro* ☎ *01–44–05–66–66* ⊕ *www.parisrenaissance.com* ⟿ *116 rooms, 20 suites* ⚒ *In-room: safe, DVD, Internet, Wi-Fi. In-hotel: restaurant, room service, bar, gym, laundry service, Internet terminal, parking (paid), some pets allowed* ⊟ *AE, MC, V* Ⓜ *Trocadéro* ✛ *1:B4.*

## 17ᴱ ARRONDISSEMENT

In the 17ᵉ you can find both an upscale residential district, between the Arc de Triomphe and the pretty Parc Monceau, and a more artsy, bohemian flavor in the former working-class districts of Batignolles and Place de Clichy. Still relatively undiscovered by tourists, it's an area of Paris with many excellent hotel deals.

**¢** 🖼 **Hôtel Eldorado.** The unpretentious Eldorado, just west of Montmartre, is perfect for guests who are happy lying low without room phones, TVs, or an elevator. Each room has its individual distressed-chic charms—leopard spots and zebra stripes, knickknacks from Africa and the Far East, flea-market antiques, and club chairs. Many rooms face the garden courtyard, where artsy bohemian types from the hotel's wine bistro hang out on summer nights. Rooms No. 16 and No. 17 have their own little balconies. Ask for a room in the back building for a quiet night's sleep. **Pros:** budget decor with character; leafy garden courtyard; hipster locals' hangout. **Cons:** far from the center of Paris; few amenities; courtyard can be noisy in summer. ⊠ *18 rue des Dames, Montmartre* ☎ *01–45–22–35–21* ⊕ *www.eldoradohotel.fr* ⟿ *33 rooms, 23 with bath* ⚒ *In-room: no a/c, no phone, no TV, Wi-Fi. In-hotel: restaurant* ⊟ *AE, DC, MC, V* Ⓜ *Place de Clichy* ✛ *1:H1.*

**$$** 🖼 **Hôtel Palma.** This modest hotel in a small 19th-century building between the Arc de Triomphe and Porte Maillot is an exceptional deal considering its rather aristocratic neighbors. Cheerful and homey rooms have hand-painted wood furnishings, floral-motif fabrics, and tile bathrooms. Ask for one on an upper floor with a view across Rive Droite rooftops. There's air-conditioning on the sixth (top) floor only. **Pros:**

close to the Champs-Élysées; cozy decor; quiet location. **Cons:** a bit off the beaten track; no air-conditioning on lower floors; the only Internet access is with a modem. ✉ *46 rue Brunel, Champs-Élysées* ☎ *01–45–74–74–51* ⊕ *www.hotelpalma-paris.com* ⇨ *37 rooms* ♿ *In-room: a/c (some), Internet. In-hotel:* 🚫 *AE, MC, V* Ⓜ *Argentine* ✛ *1:A3.*

## 18ᴱ ARRONDISSEMENT

Home to the Moulin Rouge and the scene of Audrey Tatou's flights of fancy in the film *Amélie*, Montmartre inspires visitors with its narrow, cobbled streets and sweeping cityscape from the steps of Sacré-Coeur. The trade-offs for this old-village atmosphere are steep staircases and a location far from the heart of Paris.

$ 📶 **Ermitage Hôtel Sacré Coeur.** It's a bit of a hike from the nearest métro, but this family-run hotel in a Napoléon III–era building is friendly and filled with mirrored armoires, chandeliers, and other antiques. There's a private terrace for the two ground-level rooms, and all rooms have funky flowery decor. The building is only two stories high, and the highest-tech item is the fax machine. **Pros:** family-run atmosphere; charming Parisian neighborhood. **Cons:** not close to the métro station; no online reservations; minuscule bathrooms. ✉ *24 rue Lamarck, Montmartre* ☎ *01–42–64–79–22* ⊕ *www.ermitagesacrecoeur.fr* ⇨ *12 rooms* ♿ *In-room: no a/c, no TV. In-hotel: Internet terminal, some pets allowed* 🚫 *No credit cards* ℗ *CP* Ⓜ *Lamarck Caulaincourt* ✛ *2:H4.*

$$ 📶 **Hôtel Prima Lepic.** An impressive value, the Prima Lepic stands out among the mediocre traps in this tourist zone. Elements from the original 19th-century building remain, such as vintage tiling in the entry, while the bright rooms are full of spring colors and florals; the so-called Baldaquin rooms have reproduction canopy beds. Larger rooms are suitable for families but have little natural light. **Pros:** charming decor; surrounded by boutiques and cafés. **Cons:** no air-conditioning; thin walls; not convenient for getting to the center of town on foot. ✉ *29 rue Lepic, Montmartre* ☎ *01–46–06–44–64* ⊕ *www.hotelparislepic.com* ⇨ *38 rooms* ♿ *In-room: no a/c, safe, Wi-Fi. In-hotel: room service, laundry service* 🚫 *AE, DC, MC, V* Ⓜ *Blanche* ✛ *2:A1/B1.*

$ 📶 **Hôtel Regyn's Montmartre.** Lots of folks book the tiny Regyn's for the out-of-*Amélie* Place des Abbesses location; they're also pleased to find bright, warm colors and rooms with modern bathrooms, hair dryers, radios, and Wi-Fi. Ask to stay on one of the two top floors for great views of either the Eiffel Tower or Sacré-Coeur. Overall, courteous service and a relaxed charm make this an attractive low-budget choice. **Pros:** métro station right outside; great views over Paris; new mattresses. **Cons:** no air-conditioning; some street noise; tiny elevator. ✉ *18 pl. des Abbesses, Montmartre* ☎ *01–42–54–45–21* ⊕ *www.hotel-regyns-paris. com* ⇨ *22 rooms* ♿ *In-room: no a/c, safe, Wi-Fi. In-hotel: some pets allowed* 🚫 *AE, MC, V* Ⓜ *Abbesses* ✛ *2:B1.*

$ 📶 **Hôtel Utrillo.** This very likable hotel is on a quiet side street at the foot of Montmartre, near colorful Rue Lepic. The tired old decor is slowly being replaced by a more contemporary style with bold colors and artworks. Two rooms (Nos. 61 and 63) have views of the Eiffel

Tower. In the lobby are two free Internet stations, and the sauna is a luxury at this price. **Pros:** family-run feel; some Eiffel Tower views. **Cons:** no air-conditioning; some street noise. ⊠ *7 rue Aristide-Bruant, Montmartre* ☎ *01–42–58–13–44* ⊕ *www.hotel-paris-utrillo.com* 🛏 *30 rooms* ⟺ *In-room: no a/c, Wi-Fi. In-hotel: Internet terminal, some pets allowed* ⊟ *MC, V* Ⓜ *Abbesses, Blanche* ✛ *2:B1.*

# 19ᴱ ARRONDISSEMENT

Northeast Paris is a culturally diverse, up-and-coming area full of artists' ateliers, edgy nightlife venues, and good-value bistros. Prices are the lowest in Paris, though it's best for those who are comfortable with taking public transportation, since it's too far to walk to most sights.

¢
Fodor's Choice
★

**St. Christopher's Inn.** Overlooking the canal, near the Parc de la Villette, this British-run hostel is the first purpose-built hostel in Paris, and opened in 2008. The spacious rooms have individual lockers, linens, curtained beds, and the women's-only floor includes towels. There's a large bar and restaurant open to the general public, an Internet room, and free Wi-Fi throughout. **Pros:** spanking-new facilities; bike rentals; 24-hour reception. **Cons:** a bit far from the major sights; can be noisy since it attracts groups of young travelers. ⊠ *68 Quai de la Seine, Buttes-Chaumont* ☎ *01–40–34–34–40* ⊕ *www.st-christophers.co.uk* 🛏 *175 rooms* ⟺ *In-room: no a/c, no phone, safe, no TV, Wi-Fi. In-hotel: restaurant, bar, Internet terminal* ⊟ *MC, V* Ⓜ *Riquet* ✛ *2:H3.*

# 20ᴱ ARRONDISSEMENT

The 20ᵉ is another of Paris's culturally diverse eastern districts, known for Père Lachaise Cemetery and the artists' ateliers. This is a great location for business travelers who need to be close to the airport.

$
Fodor's Choice
★

**Hôtel Mama Shelter.** The heir to the Club Med empire decided to do for the hotel industry what jeans did for fashion: democratize style. Opened in 2008 in the up-and-coming 20ᵉ district close to Père Lachaise, this new hotel is immense by Paris standards, with a fun and funky interior designed by Philippe Starck. Rooms have kitchenettes with microwave, Kiehl's toiletries and wireless Internet via flat-screen TVs; many have huge balconies. The spacious restaurant-bar-lounge is open to the public, and guests can rent electric scooters and cars. The popular Fleche d'Or nightclub is across the street and Roissy-CDG airport just a quick drive. **Pros:** trendy design; easy access to airport; good value. **Cons:** on the edge of Paris; club across the street can be noisy. ⊠ *109 rue de Bagnolet, Saint Blaise* ☎ *01–43–48–48–48* ⊕ *www.mamashelter.com* 🛏 *172 rooms* ⟺ *In-room: safe, kitchen, DVD, Internet, Wi-Fi. In-hotel: restaurant, bar, laundry service, Internet terminal, parking (paid), some pets allowed* ⊟ *AE, MC, V* ✛ *2:H3.*

# Side Trips from Paris

**WORD OF MOUTH**

"Even though Versailles is more crowded on weekends, I would make a point of going then to see the fountains. They are only on Sat. and Sun. and at specific times. The grounds are so large that it doesn't feel crowded at all. I can't imagine NOT seeing the fountains. We enjoyed them more than the interior of the palace."

—Connie

# SIDE TRIPS PLANNER

## Train versus Car

Traveling to Chartres, Disneyland Paris, and Versailles from Paris is easy. Although each side trip is within an hour's drive, we *strongly* recommend taking the train from the city rather than renting a car. If Disneyland is your destination and you don't plan to visit Paris, there are shuttle buses that will take you directly from the airports to the park.

## Tour Options

**Cityrama** (☎ *01-44-55-60-00* ⊕ *www.cityrama.com*) and **Paris Vision** (☎ *01-42-60-30-01* ⊕ *www.parisvision.com*) run half- and full-day trips to Versailles (€54–€115). **Paris Euroscope** (☎ *01-56-03-56-81* ⊕ *www.euroscope.fr*) operates half-day guided excursions to Chartres (€88).

## Planning Tips

The château of Versailles is closed on Monday.

Disneyland Paris gets extremely crowded on summer weekends, so plan your trip during the week, and early, if possible.

## Getting Out of Town

**Versailles:** Three train routes connect Paris and Versailles (25–40 minutes each way, round-trip fare €16). The RER-C to Versailles-Rive Gauche takes you closest to the château. The other SNCF trains run from Paris's Gare St-Lazare to Versailles-Rive Droite (closer to the Trianons and town market but ½ mi from the château) and from Paris's Gare Montparnasse to Versailles-Chantiers (also about ½ mi from the château via Rue des Etats-Généraux and Avenue de Paris). Some trains continue on to Chartres from Versailles-Chantiers.

**Chartres:** Trains depart hourly from Paris's Gare Montparnasse to Chartres (50–70 minutes, round-trip fare about €27). The cathedral is a ¼-mi uphill walk from the station.

**Disneyland Paris:** Shuttle buses run to the park from Charles de Gaulle and Orly airports. Trip time is 45 minutes; the fare is €17 one-way. Disneyland's train station (Marne-la-Vallée–Chessy) is right outside the park. Trains run every 10–20 minutes from RER-A stations in central Paris. Trip time is 40 minutes and costs €16 round-trip.

**Train Information Gare de Fontainebleau-Avon** (✉ *Pl. de la Gare, Avon* ☎ *01-64-22-38-57*). **Gare de Versailles Chantiers** (✉ *Cour de la Gare, 4 rue de l'Abbé Rousseau, Versailles* ☎ *36-35 [€0.34 per min]*). **SNCF** (☎ *08-91-36-20-20 [€0.23 per* ⊕ *www.transilien.com*). **TGV** (⊕ *www.tgv.com*).

### WHAT IT COSTS

|  | ¢ | $ | $$ | $$$ | $$$$ |
|---|---|---|---|---|---|
| Restaurants | under €12 | €12–€17 | €18–€24 | €25–€32 | over €32 |
| Hotels | under €50 | €50–€80 | €80–€120 | €120–€190 | over €190 |

Restaurant prices are per person for a main course at dinner, including tax (19.6%) and service. Hotel prices are for a standard double room in high season, including tax (19.6%) and service charge.

Updated by Mary Papenfuss

With so much to see in Paris, it may seem hard to justify a side trip. But just outside the city is the rest of the fabled region known as Ile-de-France, where, along with gorgeous countryside and quiet towns, you can find spectacular Versailles, the immense Chartres cathedral, and a little region unto itself where a mouse named Mickey is king.

Plan to spend an entire day at **Versailles** (at least), enjoying the gorgeously manicured gardens—one of the largest parks in Europe—as well as touring the palace, which includes the Hall of Mirrors, and Marie-Antoinette's private retreat in an enclave of the royal park. **Chartres** is a charming town that makes a lovely day or half-day side trip from Paris. Its main attraction is Cathédrale de Chartres, an awe-inspiring Gothic cathedral that looms like a great fantasy ship on the horizon, and is world-renowned for its stained-glass windows. **Disneyland Paris** arrived in 1992, but the magic was slow to take effect. The resort opened with the uninspiring name of EuroDisney and further baffled the French, for whom no meal is complete without wine, with its ban on alcohol. After the ban was lifted in the park's sit-down restaurants and the park's name was changed, Disneyland Paris became France's leading tourist attraction, drawing sellout crowds of Europeans seeking a kitschy glimpse of the American Dream—and of American families stealing a day from their museum schedule. A second park, Walt Disney Studios, opened in 2002.

**19**

## VERSAILLES

*16 km (10 mi) west of Paris via A13.*

### EXPLORING

Fodor'sChoice
★
The Sun King would be so proud to see the thousands of people that still stream to gaze, agog, at the splendors of his **Château de Versailles**—the world-famous palace that housed Louis XIV and 20,000 of his courtiers—just as stunned visitors did centuries ago. The grandest palace in France remains one of the marvels of the world and its full story

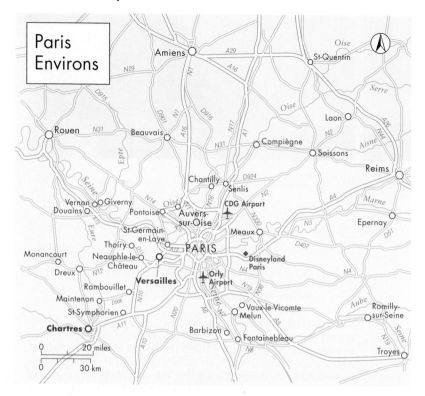

Paris
Environs

is covered in the special photo feature on the château in this chapter, "Gilt Trip: A Tour of Versailles." This edifice was not just home to Louis XIV, it was to be the new headquarters of the French government capital (from 1682 to 1789 and again from 1871 to 1879). To accompany the palace, a new city—in fact, a new capital—had to be built from scratch. Tough-thinking town planners took no prisoners, dreaming up vast mansions and avenues broader than the Champs-Élysées, presented in a stunning, geometric starburst. If you have any energy left after exploring Louis XIV's palace and park, a tour of Versailles—a textbook 18th-century town—offers a telling contrast between the majestic and the domestic.

For a glimpse of the burg, when you exit the front gate of the palace turn left onto the Rue des Resérvoirs and walk over to Rue Carnot past the stately Écuries de la Reine, once the queen's stables, now the regional law courts, then down Carnot to octagonal Place Hoche. Down Rue Hoche to the left on Rue de la Paroisse is the powerful Baroque facade of **Notre-Dame**, built from 1684 to 1686 by Jules Hardouin-Mansart as the parish church for Louis XIV's new town.

Around the back of Notre-Dame, on Boulevard de la Reine (note the regimented lines of trees), are the elegant Hôtel de Neyret and the **Musée Lambinet**, a sumptuous mansion from 1751, furnished with paintings, weapons, fans, and porcelain. ✉ *54 bd. de la Reine, Versailles* ☎ *01–39–50–30–32* 🕭 *€5.50* 🕙 *Tues., Thurs., and weekends 2–6, Wed. 1–6, Fri. 2–5.*

Take a right onto Rue le Nôtre, then go left and right again into Passage de la Geôle, a cobbled alley, lined with quaint antiques shops, which climbs up to **Place du Marché-Notre-Dame,** whose open-air morning market on Tuesday, Friday, and Sunday is famed throughout the region (note the four 19th-century timber-roof halls).

Cross Avenue de St-Cloud and walk to **Avenue de Paris;** its breadth of 120 yards makes it wider than the Champs-Élysées, and its buildings are just as grand and even more historic. Cross the avenue and head back toward the château. Avenue de Paris leads to Place d'Armes, a vast sloping plaza usually filled with tourist buses. Facing the château are the Trojan-size royal stables.

The **Grande Écurie** *(Grand Stable),* to the right, houses the **Musée des Carrosses** (Carriage Museum), open April through October, weekends only (€2), and the **Manège,** where you can see 30 white horses and their riders, trained by the equine choreographer Bartabas, which practice every morning. ✉ *1 av. de Paris, Versailles* ☎ *01–39–02–07–14* 🕭 *€6 for a visit, €12 to watch morning practice* 🕙 *Weekends and some Thurs. 11:15–12:30.*

Turn left from the Grande Écurie, cross Avenue de Paris and Avenue de Sceaux, pass the imposing chancellery on the corner, and take Rue de Satory—a cute pedestrian shopping street—to the domed **Cathédrale St-Louis,** with its twin-towered facade, built from 1743 to 1754 and enriched with a fine organ and paintings.

Rue d'Anjou leads down to the historic 6-acre **Potager du Roi,** the lovingly restored, split-level royal fruit-and-vegetable garden created in 1683 by Jean-Baptiste de La Quintinye. ✉ *Entrance at 4 rue Hardy, Versailles* ☎ *01–39–24–62–62* ⊕ *www.potager-du-roi.fr* 🕭 *€6.50* 🕙 *Apr.–Oct., Tues.–Sun. 10–6; Nov. and Dec., Tues., Thurs. 10–6, Sat. 10–1; Jan.–Mar., Tues., Thurs. 10–1.*

**19**

## WHERE TO EAT AND STAY

$$–$$$ ✕**Au Chapeau Gris.** This bustling wood-beamed restaurant just off
FRENCH Avenue de St-Cloud, overlooking elegant Place Hoche, offers hearty selections of meat and fish, ranging from boeuf rossini with wild mushrooms to salmon and scallops marinated in lime and the top-price lobster fricasseed in Sancerre. The wine list roams around the vineyards of Bordeaux and Burgundy, while desserts include crème brûlée with lemon zest, and apricot and caramel tart. The €21 ("for queens") and €28 ("for kings") prix-fixe menu makes a filling lunchtime option. ✉ *7 rue Hoche, Versailles* ☎ *01–39–50–10–81* ▤ *AE, MC, V* 🕙 *Closed Wed. No dinner Tues. and late July–late Aug.*

$$$$ ▨**Trianon Palace.** A modern-day Versailles, this deluxe hotel is in a turn-
★ of-the-20th-century, creamy white creation of imposing size, filled with soaring rooms (including the historic Salle Clemenceau, site of the 1919 Versailles Peace Conference), palatial columns, and with a huge garden close to the château. Once faded, the hotel, now part of the Westin chain, is aglitter once again with a health club (the pool idles beneath

*Continued on page 427*

# GILT TRIP
## A TOUR OF VERSAILLES

Louis XIV's Hall of Mirrors

A two-century spree of indulgence in the finest bling-bling of the age by the consecutive reigns of three French kings produced two of the world's most historic artifacts: gloriously, the Palace of Versailles and, momentously, the French Revolution.

Less a monument than an entire world unto itself, Versailles is the king of palaces. The end result of 380 million francs, 36,000 laborers, and enough paintings, if laid end to end, to equal 7 miles of canvas, it was conceived as the ne plus ultra expression of monarchy by Louis XIV. As a child, the king had developed a hatred for Paris (where he had been imprisoned by a group of nobles known as the Frondeurs), so, when barely out of his teens, he cast his cantankerous royal eye in search of a new power base. Marshy, inhospitable Versailles was the stuff of his dreams. Down came dad's modest royal hunting lodge and up, up, and along went the minion-crushing, Baroque palace we see today.

Between 1661 and 1710, architects Louis Le Vau and Jules Hardouin Mansart designed everything his royal acquisitiveness could want, including a throne room devoted to Apollo, god of the sun (Louis was known as *le roi soleil*). Convinced that his might depended upon dominating French nobility, Louis XIV summoned thousands of grandees from their own far-flung châteaux to reside at his new seat of government. In doing so, however, he unwittingly triggered the downfall of the monarchy. Like an 18th-century Disneyland, Versailles kept its courtiers so richly entertained they all but forgot the murmurs of discontent brewing back home.

As Louis XV chillingly foretold, "After me, the deluge." The royal commune was therefore shocked— shocked!—by the appearance, on October 5, 1789, of a revolutionary mob from Paris ready to sack Versailles and imprison Louis XVI. So as you walk through this awesome monument to splendor and excess, give a thought to its historic companion: the French Revolution. A tour of Versailles's grand salons inextricably mixes pathos with glory.

# CROWNING GLORIES:
# TOP SIGHTS OF VERSAILLES

Versailles from the outside

Seducing their court with their self-assured approach to 17th- and 18th-century art and decoration, a trinity of French kings made Versailles into the most vainglorious of châteaux.

**Galerie des Glaces (Hall of Mirrors).** Of all the rooms at Versailles, none matches the magnificence of the Galerie des Glaces (Hall of Mirrors). Begun by Mansart in 1678, this represents the acme of the Louis Quatorze (Louis-XIV) style. Measuring 240 feet long, 33 feet wide, and 40 feet high, it is ornamented with gilded candlesticks, crystal chandeliers, and a coved ceiling painted with Charles Le Brun's homage to Louis XIV's reign.

Detail of the ceiling

In Louis's day, the Galerie was laid with priceless carpets and filled with orange trees in silver pots. Nighttime galas were illuminated by 3,000 candles, their blaze doubled in the 17 gigantic mirrors that precisely echo the banner of windows along the west front. Lavish balls were once held here, as was a later event with much greater world impact: the signing of the Treaty of Versailles, which put an end to World War I on June 28, 1919.

Hall of Mirrors

**The Grands Appartements (State Apartments).** Virtual stages for ceremonies of court ritual and etiquette, Louis XIV's first-floor state salons were designed in the Baroque style on a biceps-flexing scale meant to one-up the lavish Vaux-le-Vicomte château recently built for Nicolas Fouquet, the king's finance minister.

Inside the Apollo Chamber

Flanking the Hall of Mirrors and retaining most of their bombastic Italianate Baroque decoration, the Salon de la Guerre (Salon of War) and the Salon de la Paix (Salon of Peace) are ornately decorated with gilt stucco, painted ceilings, and marble sculpture. Perhaps the most extravagant is the Salon d'Apollon (Apollo Chamber), the former throne room.

Hall of Battles

**Appartements du Roi (King's Apartments).** Completed in 1701 in the Louis-XIV style, the king's state and private chambers comprise a suite of 15 rooms set in a "U" around the east facade's Marble Court. Dead center across the sprawling cobbled forecourt is Louis XIV's bedchamber—he would awake and rise (just as the sun did, from the east) attended by members of his court and the public. Holding the king's chemise when he dressed soon became a more definitive reflection of status than the possession of an entire province. Nearby is Louis XV's magnificent Cabinet Intérieur (Office of the King), shining with gold and white boiseries; in the center is the most famous piece of furniture at Versailles, Louis XV's roll-top desk, crafted by Oeben and Riesener in 1769.

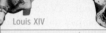

Louis XIV

King's Apartments

**VINTAGE BOURBON**

Versailles was built by three great kings of the Bourbon dynasty. Louis XIV (1638–1715) began its construction in 1661. After ruling for 72 years, Louis Quatorze was succeeded by his great grandson, Louis XV (1710–74), who added the Royal Opera and the Petit Trianon to the palace. Louis XVI (1754–93) came to the throne in 1774 and was forced out of Versailles in 1789, along with Marie Antoinette, both guillotined three years later.

**Chambre de la Reine (Queen's Bedchamber).** Probably the most opulent bedroom in the world, this was initially created for Marie Thérèse, first wife of Louis XIV, to be part of the Queen's Apartments. For Marie Antoinette, however, the entire room was glammed up with silk wall-hangings covered with Rococo motifs that reflect her love of flowers. Legend has it that the gardens directly beyond these windows were replanted daily so that the queen could enjoy a fresh assortment of blossoms each morning. The bed, decked out with white ostrich plumes *en panache*, was also redone for Louis XVI's queen. Nineteen royal children were born in this room.

Queen's Bedchamber

**Petits Appartements (Small Apartments).** As styles of decor changed, Louis XIV's successors felt out of sync with their architectural inheritance. Louis XV exchanged the heavy red-and-gilt of Italianate Baroque for lighter, pastel-hued Rococo. On the top floor of the palace, on the right side of the central portion, are the apartments Louis XV commissioned to escape the wearisome pomp of the first-floor rooms. Here, Madame de Pompadour, mistress of Louis XV and famous patroness of the Rococo style, introduced grace notes of intimacy and refinement. In so doing, she transformed the daunting royal apartments into places to live rather than pose.

**Parc de Versailles.** Even Bourbon kings needed respite from Versailles's endless maze, hence the creation of one of Europe's largest parks. The sublime 250-acre grounds (☎ 01–30–83–77–88 for guided tour) is the masterpiece of André Le Nôtre, presiding genius of 17th-century classical French landscaping. Le Nôtre was famous for his "green geometries": ordered fantasies of clipped yew trees, multicolored flower beds (called *parterres*), and perspectival allées cleverly punctuated with statuary, laid out between 1661 and 1668. The spatial effect is best admired from inside the palace, views about which Le Nôtre said, "Flowers can only be walked on by the eyes."

Ultimately, at the royal command, rivers were diverted—to flow into more than 600 fountains—and entire forests were imported to ornament the park, which is centered around the mile-long Grand Canal. As for the great fountains, their operation costs a fortune in these democratic days, and so they perform only on Saturday and Sunday afternoons (☉ 3:30–5:30) from mid-April through mid-October; admission to the park during this time is €6. The park is open daily 7 AM–8 PM or dusk.

**LIGHTING UP THE SKY**

The largest fountain in the Versailles park, the Bassin de Neptune, becomes a spectacle of rare grandeur during the Fêtes de Nuit (☎ 01-30-83-78-88 for details), a light-and-fireworks show held on ten nights (usually Saturday) between late July and early September. The spectacle begins at 10:30 PM, and also features some 200-plus actors costumed in knee-breeches wigs. The 90-minute show is well worth the ticket admission of €16 to €48.

Dauphin's Apartments

Bassin de Neptune

**Chapel and Opéra Royal:** In the north wing of the château are three showpieces of the palace. The solemn white-and-gold Chapelle was completed in 1710—the king and queen attended daily mass here seated in gilt boxes. The Opéra Royal (Opera House), entirely constructed of wood painted to look like marble, was designed by Jacques-Ange Gabriel for Louis XV in 1770. Connecting the two, the 17th-century Galeries have exhibits retracing the château's history.

Opéra Royal

## VERSAILLES: FIRST FLOOR, GARDENS & ADJACENT PARK

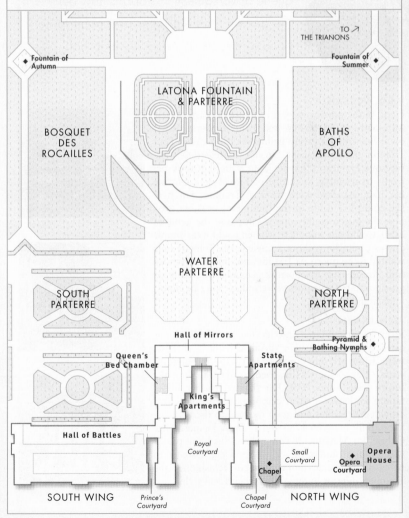

TO ↗
THE TRIANONS

Fountain of
Autumn

Fountain of
Summer

LATONA FOUNTAIN
& PARTERRE

BOSQUET
DES
ROCAILLES

BATHS
OF
APOLLO

WATER
PARTERRE

SOUTH
PARTERRE

NORTH
PARTERRE

Hall of Mirrors

Pyramid &
Bathing Nymphs

Queen's
Bed Chamber

State
Apartments

King's
Apartments

Hall of Battles

Royal
Courtyard

Small
Courtyard

Opera
House

Chapel

Opera
Courtyard

SOUTH WING

Prince's
Courtyard

Chapel
Courtyard

NORTH WING

## LET THEM EAT CRÊPE:
## MARIE ANTOINETTE'S ROYAL LAIR

Was Marie Antoinette a luxury-mad butterfly flitting from ball to costume ball? Or was she a misunderstood queen who suffered a loveless marriage and became a prisoner of court etiquette at Versailles? Historians now believe the answer was the latter and point to her private retreats at Versailles as proof.

### R.F.D. VERSAILLES?

Here, in the northwest part of the royal park, Marie Antoinette (1755–93) created a tiny universe of her own: her comparatively dainty mansion called Petit Trianon and its adjacent "farm," the relentlessly picturesque Hameau ("hamlet"). In a life that took her from royal cradle to throne of France to guillotine, her happiest days were spent at Trianon. For here she could live a life in the "simplest" possible way; here the queen could enter a salon and the game of cards would not stop; here women could wear simple gowns of muslin without a single jewel. Toinette only wanted to be queen of Trianon, not queen of France. And considering the horrible, chamber-pot-pungent, gossip-infested corridors of Versailles, you can almost understand why.

### TEEN QUEEN

From the first, Maria-Antonia (her actual name) was ostracized as an outsider, "l'Autrichienne"—the Austrian. Upon arriving in France in 1770—at a mere 15 years of age—she was married to the Dauphin, the future King Louis XVI. But shamed by her initial failure to deliver a royal heir, she grew to hate overcrowded Versailles and soon escaped to the Petit Trianon. Built between 1763 and 1768 by Jacques-Ange Gabriel for Madame de Pompadour, this bijou palace was a radical statement: a royal residence designed to be casual and unassuming. Toinette refashioned the Trianon's interior in the sober Neoclassical style.

Hameau

Queen's House

Temple of Love

Petit Trianon

## "THE SIMPLE LIFE"

Just beyond Petit Trianon lay the storybook Hameau, a mock-Norman village inspired by the peasant-luxe, simple-life daydreams caught by Boucher on canvas and by Rousseau in literature. With its water mill, thatched-roof houses, pigeon loft, and vegetable plots, this make-believe farm village was run by Monsieur Valy-Busard, a farmer, and his wife, who often helped the queen—outfitted as a Dresden shepherdess with a Sèvres porcelain crook—tend her flock of perfumed sheep.

As if to destroy any last link with reality, the queen built nearby a jewel-box theater (open by appointment). Here she acted in little plays, sometimes essaying the role of a servant girl. Only the immediate royal family, about seven or so friends, and her personal servants were permitted entry; disastrously, the entire official-dom of Versailles society was shut out—a move that only served to infuriate courtiers. This is how fate and destiny close the circle. For it was here at Trianon that a page sent by Monsieur de Saint-Priest found Marie-Antoinette on October 5, 1789, to tell her that Paris was marching on an already half-deserted Versailles.

Was Marie Antoinette a political traitor to France whose execution was well merited? Or was she the ultimate fashion victim? For those who feel that this tragic queen spent—and shopped—her way into a revolution, a visit to her relatively modest Petit Trianon and Hameau should prove a revelation.

Marie Antoinette

### THE GRAND TRIANONS

A mile from the château, the Grand Trianon was created by Hardouin Mansart in 1687 as a retreat for Louis XIV; it was restored in the early 19th century, with Empire-style salons. It's a memorable spot often missed by foot-weary tourists exhausted by the château, but well worth the effort. A special treat is Marie Antoinette's hideaway nearby, the Petit Trianon, presumably restored to how she left it before being forced to Paris by an angry mob of soon-to-be revolutionaries.

# TAKING ON VERSAILLES (WITHOUT LOSING YOUR HEAD)

Statue of King Louis XIV

✉ Place d'Armes, Versailles

🌐 www.chateauversailles.fr

☎ 01-30-83-78-00

💶 A €20 day pass will get you into almost all of the sites, with audio-guide, on weekdays, €25 on weekends.

Château only is €13.50. Petit and Grand Trianons (joint ticket) €9; Parc de Versailles free; Grand Eaux Musicale fountain show's €6; Fêtes de Nuit €16–€48.

🕐 The château is open Apr.–Oct., Tues.–Sun. 9–6:30; Nov.–Mar., Tues.–Sun, 9–5:30. Trianons Tues.—Sun. noon—5, Nov.–Mar. Park open daily dawn–dusk.

Ⓜ RER Line C from Paris to Versailles–Rive Gauche station (closest to the Palace) or SNCF trains from Paris's Gare St-Lazare to Versailles–Rive Droite and Gare Montparnasse to Versailles.

Tickets are €16. The best bargain (and a line-dodging time saver) is to buy a Forfait Loisirs Château de Versailles ticket (€19.40) that includes round-trip transportation from Paris and entrance to the main Versailles sights. Tickets are available at SNCF transilien train stations.

## TOURING THE PALACE

The army of 20,000 noblemen, servants, and syco-phants who moved into Louis XIV's huge Château de Versailles is matched today by the battalion of 3 million visitors a year. You may be able to avoid the modern-day crowds (and lines for tours) if you arrive here at 9 AM and buy your ticket in advance at FNAC or SNCF or online. The main entrance is near the top of the courtyard to the right; there are different lines depend-ing on tour, physical ability, and group status. Frequent English guided tours visit the private royal apartments. More detailed hour-long tours explore the opera house or Marie Antoinette's private parlors. You can wander the grandest rooms—including the Hall of Mirrors and Marie Antoinette's stunningly opulent bed chamber—without a group tour. To figure out the system, pick up a brochure at the information office for details.

## TOURING THE PARK

If the grandeur of the palace begins to overwhelm, the Parc de Versailles is the best place to come back down to earth. The distances of the park are vast—the Trianons themselves are more than a mile from the château—so you might want to climb aboard the train (🎟 €6 round-trip, ☎ 01–39–54–22–00), or rent a bike from Petite-Venise (🎟 €5.20 per hr or €26 for 6 hrs, ☎ 01–39–66–97–66). You can hire a rowboat on the Grand Canal (🎟 €8.50 per hr) or drive to the Trianons and canal through the Grille de la Reine (🎟 €5.50 per car).

a glass pyramid) and a refurbished lobby with Murano chandeliers and high-back, green-leather armchairs. Try to avoid the newer annex, the Pavillon Trianon, and insist on the main building (ask for one of the even-numbered rooms, which look out over the woods near the Trianons; odd-numbered rooms overlook the modern annex). The hotel features the mouthwatering fare of the first restaurant in France to be run by charismatic British chef and television personality Gordon Ramsay. **Pros:** palatial glamour; wonderful setting right by château; views of sheep grazing, right out the windows. **Cons:** it's expensive to stay in a palace. ⊠ *1 bd. de la Reine* ☎ *01–30–84–50–00* ⊕ *www.trianonpalace. fr* ⤴ *199 rooms, 27 suites* ⌂ *In-room: safe, refrigerator, Wi-Fi. In-hotel: 2 restaurants, room service, bar, pool, gym, spa, Wi-Fi hotspot, parking, some pets allowed* ⊟ *AE, DC, MC, V* ⦿ *BP.*

### NIGHTLIFE AND THE ARTS

Directed by Bartabas, the **Académie du Spectacle Equestre** (☎ *01–39–02–07–14* ⊕ *www.acadequestre.com*) stages hour-long shows on weekend afternoons and evenings of horses performing to music—sometimes with riders, sometimes without—in the converted 17th-century Manège (riding school) at the Grande Écurie opposite the palace. The **Centre de Musique Baroque** (☎ *01–39–20–78–10* ⊕ *www.cmbv.com*) often presents concerts of Baroque music in the château opera and chapel. The **Mois Molière** (☎ *01–30–21–51–39* ⊕ *www.moismoliere.com*) in June heralds a program of concerts, drama, and exhibits inspired by the famous playwright.

### SHOPPING

**Aux Colonnes** (⊠ *14 rue Hoche, Versailles*) is a highly rated *confiserie* (candy shop) with a cornucopia of chocolates and candies; it's closed Monday. **Fromagerie Legall** (⊠ *Pl. du Marché, Versailles*) has a huge choice of cheeses; it's closed Sunday afternoon and Monday.

**19**

## CHARTRES

*88 km (55 mi) southwest of Paris.*

### EXPLORING

If Versailles is the climax of French secular architecture, perhaps Chartres is its religious apogee. All the descriptive prose and poetry that have been lavished on this supreme cathedral can only begin to suggest the glory of its 12th- and 13th-century statuary and stained glass, somehow suffused with burning mysticism and a strange sense of the numinous. Chartres is more than a church—it's a nondenominational spiritual experience. If you arrive in summer from Maintenon across the edge of the Beauce, the richest agrarian plain in France, you can see Chartres's spires rising up from oceans of wheat. The entire town—with its old houses and picturesque streets—is worth a leisurely exploration. From Rue du Pont-St-Hilaire there's an intriguing view of the rooftops below the cathedral. Ancient streets tumble down from the cathedral to the river, lined most weekends with *bouquinistes* selling old books and prints. Each year on August 15 pilgrims and tourists flock here for the *Procession du Voeu de Louis XIII*, a religious procession through the streets commemorating the French monarchy's vow to serve the Virgin Mary.

Fodor's Choice
★

Worship on the site of the **Cathédrale Notre-Dame,** better known as Chartres Cathedral, goes back to before the Gallo-Roman period; the crypt contains a well that was the focus of druid ceremonies. In the late 9th century Charles II (known as the Bald) presented Chartres with what was believed to be the tunic of the Virgin Mary, a precious relic that drew hordes of pilgrims to the church. The current cathedral, the sixth church on the spot, dates mainly from the 12th and 13th centuries and was erected after the previous building, dating from the 11th century, burned down in 1194. A well-chronicled outburst of religious fervor followed the discovery that the Virgin Mary's relic had miraculously survived unsinged. Princes and paupers, barons and bourgeois gave their money and their labor to build the new cathedral. Ladies of the manor came to help monks and peasants on the scaffolding in a tremendous resurgence of religious faith that followed the Second Crusade. Just 25 years were needed for Chartres Cathedral to rise again, and it has remained substantially unchanged since.

The lower half of the facade survives from the earlier Romanesque church: this can be seen most clearly in the use of round arches rather than the pointed Gothic type. The **Royal Portal** is richly sculpted with scenes from the life of Christ—these sculpted figures are among the greatest created during the Middle Ages. The taller of the two spires (380 feet versus 350 feet) was built at the start of the 16th century, after its predecessor was destroyed by fire; its fanciful flamboyant intricacy contrasts sharply with the stumpy solemnity of its Romanesque counterpart (access €3, open daily 9:30–noon and 2–4:30). The **rose window** above the main portal dates from the 13th century, and the three windows below it contain some of the finest examples of 12th-century stained-glass artistry in France.

As spiritual as Chartres is, the cathedral also had its more earthbound uses. Look closely and you can see that the main nave floor has a subtle slant. This was built to provide drainage as this part of the church was often used as a "hostel" by thousands of overnighting pilgrims in medieval times.

Your eyes will need time to adjust to the somber interior. The reward is seeing the gemlike richness of the stained glass, with the famous deep Chartres blue predominating. The oldest window is arguably the most beautiful: **Notre-Dame de la Belle Verrière** (Our Lady of the Lovely Window), in the south choir. The cathedral's windows are being gradually cleaned—a lengthy, painstaking process—and the contrast with those still covered in the grime of centuries is staggering. It's worth taking a pair of binoculars with you to pick out the details. If you wish to know more about stained-glass techniques and the motifs used, visit the small exhibit in the gallery opposite the north porch. For even more detail, arrange a tour (in English) with local institution Malcolm Miller, whose knowledge of the cathedral's history is formidable. (He leads tours twice a day Monday through Saturday; the cost is €10. You can reach him at the telephone number below.) The vast black-and-white labyrinth on the floor of the nave is one of the few to have survived from the Middle Ages; the faithful were expected to travel along its entire length (some 300 yards) on their knees. Guided tours of the **Crypte** start from the Maison de la Crypte opposite the south porch. You can also see a 4th-century Gallo-Roman wall and some 12th-century wall paintings. ⊠ *16 cloître Notre-Dame, Chartres* ☎ *02–37–21–75–02* ⊠ *Crypt €2.70, cathedral €6.20* ⊙ *Cathedral 8:30–7:30, guided tours of the crypt Apr.–Oct., daily at 11, 2:15,*

GET ENLIGHTENED

*Vitrail* (stained glass) being the key to Chartres's fame, you may want to visit the **Galerie du Vitrail** (⊠ *17 cloître Notre-Dame, Chartres* ☎ *02–37–36–10–03* ⊕ *www.galerie-du-vitrail.com*), which specializes in the noble art. Pieces range from small plaques to entire windows, and books on the subject are available in English and French.

*3:30, and 4:30, with an added 5:15 tour from mid-June to mid-Sept. Nov.–Mar., daily at 11 and 4:15.*

The **Musée des Beaux-Arts** *(Fine Arts Museum)* is in a handsome 18th-century building just behind the cathedral that used to serve as the bishop's palace. Its varied collection includes Renaissance enamels, a portrait of Erasmus by Holbein, tapestries, armor, and some fine (mainly French) paintings from the 17th, 18th, and 19th centuries. There's also a room devoted to the forceful 20th-century landscapes of Maurice de Vlaminck, who lived in the region. ⊠ *29 cloître Notre-Dame, Chartres* ☎ *02–37–90–45–80* ⊠ *€3* ⊙ *Wed.–Sat. and Mon. 10–noon and 2–5, Sun. 2–5 (2–6 May–Nov.).*

The Gothic church of **St-Pierre** (⊠ *Rue St-Pierre, Chartres*), near the Eure River, has magnificent medieval windows from a period (circa 1300) not represented at the cathedral. The oldest stained glass here, portraying Old Testament worthies, is to the right of the choir and dates from the late 13th century.

Exquisite 17th-century stained glass can be admired at the church of **St-Aignan** (⊠ *Rue des Grenets, Chartres*), around the corner from St-Pierre.

## WHERE TO EAT AND STAY

$$–$$$
FRENCH
Fodor's Choice
★

✕ **Moulin de Ponceau.** Ask for a table with a view of the River Eure, with the cathedral looming behind, at this 16th-century converted water mill. Better still, on sunny days you can eat outside, beneath a parasol on the stone terrace by the water's edge—an idyllic setting. Choose from a regularly changing menu of French stalwarts such as rabbit terrine, trout with almonds, and tarte tatin, or splurge on "la trilogie" of scallops, foie gras, and langoustine. ⊠ *21 rue de la Tannerie, Chartres* ☎ *02–37–35–30–05* ▭ *AE, MC, V* ⊙ *Closed Mon. and 2 wks in Feb. No dinner Sun.*

$$–$$$
FRENCH

✕ **La Vieille Maison.** Just 100 yards from the cathedral, in a pretty 14th-century building with a flower-decked patio, this restaurant is a fine choice for either lunch or dinner. Chef Bruno Letartre changes his menu regularly, often including such regional specialties as asparagus, rich duck pâté, and superb homemade foie gras along with fish, seafood, and game in season. Prices, though justified, can be steep, but the €20 lunch menu served on summer weekdays is a good bet. ⊠ *5 rue au Lait* ☎ *02–37–34–10–67* ⊕ *www.lavieillemaison.fr.st* ⊟ *MC, V* ⊘ *Closed Mon. No dinner Sun. No lunch Tues.*

$$–$$$    ⌂ **Le Grand Monarque.** Set on Chartres's main town square not far from
★    the cathedral, this is a delightful option with decor that remains seductively and warmly redolent of the 19th century. Built originally as a coaching inn (and today part of the Best Western chain), the hotel has numerous rooms, many attractively set with brick walls, wood antiques, lush drapes, and modern bathrooms; the best are in a separate turn-of-the-20th-century building overlooking a garden, while the most atmospheric are tucked away in the attic. Downstairs, the stylishly decorated Georges restaurant serves such delicacies as pheasant pie and scallops with lentils and has prix-fixe menus starting at €29.50. It's closed Monday and there's no dinner Sunday, but the hotel's Madrigal brasserie is open daily. **Pros:** old-fashioned charm; good restaurant. **Cons:** best rooms are in an annex; stiff uphill walk to the cathedral. ⊠ *22 pl. des Épars* ☎ *02–37–18–15–15* ⊕ *www.bw-grand-monarque. com* ⊃ *55 rooms* ⌂ *In-room: no a/c (some), refrigerator, Wi-Fi. In-hotel: restaurant, bar, public Wi-Fi hotspot, parking (fee), some pets allowed* ⊟ *AE, DC, MC, V* ⦿ *BP.*

# DISNEYLAND PARIS

🕒 *38 km (24 mi) east of Paris via A4.*

### EXPLORING

**Disneyland Paris** is probably not what you've traveled to France to experience. But if you have a child in tow, the promise of a day here may get you through an afternoon at Versailles or Fontainebleau. There's also something curiously sublime about sitting on "Main Street" USA, in Paris, listening to the ersatz barking of a dog. If you're a dyed-in-the-wool Disney fan, you'll want to make a beeline for the park to see how it has been molded to appeal to the tastes of Europeans (Disney's "Imagineers" call it their most lovingly detailed park). And if you've never experienced this particular form of Disney showmanship, you may want to put in an appearance if only to see what all the fuss is about. When it opened, few turned up to do so; today the place is jammed, and Disneyland Paris is here to stay—and grow, with **Walt Disney Studios** opened alongside it in 2002.

**Disneyland Park,** as the original theme park is styled, consists of five "lands": Main Street USA, Frontierland, Adventureland, Fantasyland, and Discoveryland. The central theme of each land is relentlessly echoed in every detail, from attractions to restaurant menus to souvenirs. The park is circled by a railroad, which stops three times along the perimeter. **Main Street USA** goes under the railroad and past shops and restaurants toward the main plaza; Disney parades are held here every afternoon and, during holiday periods, every evening.

Top attractions at **Frontierland** are the chilling Phantom Manor, haunted by holographic spooks, and the thrilling runaway mine train of Big Thunder Mountain, a roller coaster that plunges wildly through floods and avalanches in a setting meant to evoke Utah's Monument Valley. Whiffs of Arabia, Africa, and the West Indies give **Adventureland** its exotic cachet; the spicy meals and snacks served here rank among the best food in the park. Don't miss the Pirates of the Caribbean, an exciting mise-en-scène populated by eerily humanlike, computer-driven figures, or Indiana Jones and the Temple of Doom, a breathtaking ride that re-creates some of this hero's most exciting moments.

> ## PUTTING THE PARIS IN DISNEYLAND PARIS
>
> The following are quirks unique to Mickey's European pied-à-terre. Wine is served in the park (they changed their no-alcohol policy in the 1990s) and there's no Mickey walking around—he was too mobbed by kiddies; now he stays in one spot, and you line up to see him.

**Fantasyland** charms the youngest park goers with familiar cartoon characters from such classic Disney films as *Snow White, Pinocchio, Dumbo,* and *Peter Pan.* The focal point of Fantasyland, and indeed Disneyland Paris, is Le Château de la Belle au Bois Dormant (Sleeping Beauty's Castle), a 140-foot, bubblegum-pink structure topped with 16 blue-and-gold-tipped turrets. Its design was allegedly inspired by illustrations from a medieval *Book of Hours*—if so, it was by way of Beverly Hills. The castle's dungeon conceals a 2-ton, scaly, green dragon that rumbles in its sleep and occasionally rouses to roar—an impressive feat of engineering, producing an answering chorus of shrieks from younger children. **Discoveryland** is a futuristic eye-knocker for high-tech Disney entertainment. Robots on roller skates welcome you on your way to Star Tours, a pitching, plunging, sense-confounding ride based on the *Star Wars* films. In Le Visionarium, a simulated space journey is presented by 9-Eye, a staggeringly realistic robot. The Jules Verne–inspired **Space Mountain Mission 2** pretends to catapult *exploronauts* on a rocket-boosted, comet-battered journey through the Milky Way.

**19**

**Walt Disney Studios** opened next to the Disneyland Park in 2002. The theme park is divided into four "production zones." Beneath imposing entrance gates and a 100-foot water tower inspired by the one erected in 1939 at Disney Studios in Burbank, California, **Front Lot** contains shops, a restaurant, and a studio re-creating the atmosphere of Sunset Boulevard. In **Animation Courtyard,** Disney artists demonstrate the various phases of character animation; Animagique brings to life scenes from *Pinocchio* and *The Lion King*; while the Genie from *Aladdin* pilots flying carpets over Agrabah. **Production Courtyard** hosts the Walt Disney Television Studios; Cinémagique, a special-effects tribute to U.S. and European cinema; and a behind-the-scenes Studio Tram tour of location sites, movie props, studio decor, and costuming, ending with a visit to Catastrophe Canyon in the heart of a film shoot. **Back Lot** majors in stunts. At Armageddon Special Effects you can confront a flaming meteor shower aboard the Mir space station, then complete your visit at the giant outdoor arena with a Stunt Show Spectacular involving cars, motorbikes, and Jet Skis. ☎ 01–60–30–60–30 ⊕ *www.disneylandparis. com* ✉ *Prices range from €67 (for adults, €57 for children) for a one-day, one-park pass to €178 for a 3-day, 2-park pass that covers Disneyland*

*and Walt Disney Studios* ⏲ *Hrs vary: Disneyland: mid-Sept.–mid-June, generally 10–7 weekdays with many weekends 10–9 and 10–10; July and Aug., daily 10–11. Walt Disney Studios generally open daily 10–6* ▭ *AE, DC, MC, V.*

> **WORD OF MOUTH**
>
> "In the Disneyland park . . . there's enough to see for a good two days, depending on crowds and your endurance. The stage shows are quite good . . . Don't forget the little-known places like the upper floors of Sleeping Beauty's castle, the fort at Frontierland, the huge dragon in the dungeon under the castle, the Nautilus, Casey Junior's train, the spooking tunnels and rickety bridges on Adventure Island and the Swiss Family Robinson's tree." —AnthonyGA

## WHERE TO EAT AND STAY

¢–$$$ ECLECTIC ✕ **Disneyland Restaurants.** Disneyland Paris is peppered with places to eat, ranging from snack bars and fast-food joints to five full-service restaurants—all with a distinguishing theme. In addition, Walt Disney Studios, Disney Village, and Disney Hotels have restaurants open to the public, outside the park. ☎ *01–60–30–40–50* ▭ *AE, DC, MC, V.*

$$$–$$$$ **Disneyland Hotels.** The resort has 5,000 rooms in seven hotels, all a short distance from the park, ranging from the luxurious Disneyland Hotel to the not-so-rustic Davy Crockett Ranch. Free transportation to the park is available at every hotel. Packages including Disneyland lodging, entertainment, and admission are available through travel agents in Europe. *Centre de Réservations, B.P. 100, 77777 Marne-la-Vallée Cedex 4 France* ☎ *01–60–30–60–53, 407/934–7639 in U.S.* *www.disneylandparis.com* ☞ *All hotels have at least 1 restaurant, café, indoor pool, health club, sauna, bar, Wi-Fi* ▭ *AE, DC, MC, V* *FAP.*

## NIGHTLIFE AND THE ARTS

Nocturnal entertainment outside the park centers on **Disney Village,** a vast pleasure mall designed by American architect Frank Gehry. Featured are American-style restaurants (crab shack, diner, deli, steak house), including **Billy Bob's Country Western Saloon** (☎ *01–60–30–40–50*). Also in Disney Village is **Buffalo Bill's Wild West Show** (☎ *01–60–45–71–00 for reservations*), 1½-hour dinner extravaganza with a menu of sausages, spare ribs, and chili; performances by a talented troupe of stunt riders, bronco busters, tribal dancers, and musicians; plus some 50 horses, a dozen buffalo, a bull, and an Annie Oakley–style sharpshooter, with a golden-maned "Buffalo Bill" as emcee. It's corny but great fun. There are two shows nightly, at 6:30 and 9:30; the cost is €74.80 for adults, €56.80 for children under 12.

# UNDERSTANDING
# PARIS

Books and Movies

Vocabulary

# BOOKS AND MOVIES

## Books

**Fiction.** Think of writers in Paris, and the romanticized expat figures of the interwar "lost generation" often come to mind: Ernest Hemingway (*The Sun Also Rises*), F. Scott Fitzgerald, Ezra Pound, and Gertrude Stein just to name a few. Further back in time are classics like Charles Dickens's *A Tale of Two Cities*, set during the Revolution, and Henry James's novels *The American* and *The Ambassadors*, both tales of Americans in Europe. The expats of World War II set the scene for future Americans in Paris: James Baldwin's life in the city in the 1950s informed novels such as *Giovanni's Room*, and the denizens of the so-called Beat Hotel (Allen Ginsberg, William Burroughs, and Henry Miller) squeezed in some writing among their less salubrious activities. The Canadian writer Mavis Gallant, who published many stories in *The New Yorker*, also began her tenure in Paris in the '50s; her collection *Paris Stories* is a delight.

Recent best sellers with a Paris setting include, of course, Dan Brown's *The Da Vinci Code*, as well as Diane Johnson's *Le Divorce* and *Le Mariage*, Anita Brookner's *Incidents in the Rue Laugier*, and Patrick Suskind's *Perfume: The Story of a Murderer*. Paul LaFarge's *Haussmann, or the Distinction* spins historical detail about the ambitious city planner into a fascinating period novel. For literary snacking, *Paris in Mind* pulls together excerpts from books by American authors.

**For Children.** Who doesn't remember Miss Clavel and her 12 young students in two straight lines? Ludwig Bemelmans's beloved *Madeleine* series about the namesake heroine is also illustrated with the author's drawings of Paris landmarks such as the Opéra and the Jardins du Luxembourg. *Eloise in Paris*, by Kay Thompson, also has illustrations, these by Hilary Knight (look for his take on Christian Dior). The *Anatole* books by Eve Titus are classics, starring a Gallic mouse. Playful, bright illustrations drive Maira Kalman's *Ooh-la-la (Max in Love)*; the singsong language, smattered with French, is perfect for reading aloud. Joan MacPhail Knight wrote a pair of books about an American girl visiting France in the late 1800s: *Charlotte in Giverny* and *Charlotte in Paris*.

**History.** Recent studies devoted to the capital include Philip Mansel's *Paris Between Empires: Monarchy and Revolution*; Jill Harsin's *Barricades: War on the Streets in Revolutionary Paris*; and Johannes Willms's *Paris: Capital of Europe*, which runs from the Revolution to the Belle Époque. Simon Schama's *Citizens* is a good introduction to the French Revolution. Alistair Horne's *Seven Ages of Paris* skips away from standard historical approaches, breaking the city's past into seven eras and putting a colorful spin on the Renaissance, the Revolution, Napoléon's Empire, and other periods.

Biographies and autobiographies of French luminaries and Paris residents can double as satisfying portraits of the capital during their subjects' lifetimes. Works on Baron Haussmann are especially rich, as the 19th-century prefect so utterly changed the face of the city. For a look at American expatriates in Paris between the wars, pick up *Sylvia Beach and the Lost Generation*, by Noel R. Fitch. Tyler Stovall's *Paris Noir: African-Americans in the City of Light* examines black American artists' affection for Paris during the 20th century; *Harlem in Montmartre*, by William A. Shack, homes in on expat jazz culture. Walter Benjamin's *The Arcades Project* uses the 19th century as a point of intersection for studies on advertising, Baudelaire, the Paris Commune, and other subjects.

**Memoirs, Essays, and Observations.** Ernest Hemingway's *A Moveable Feast*, the tale of his 1920s expat life in Paris as a struggling writer, grips from its opening lines. Gertrude Stein, one of Hemingway's friends, gave her own version of the era in *The Autobiography of Alice B. Toklas*. In *The Secret Paris of the '30s*, Brassaï put into words the scenes he captured in photographs. Joseph Roth gave an exile's point of view in *Report from a Parisian Paradise*. Art Buchwald's funny yet poignant *I'll Always Have Paris* moves from the postwar GI Bill days through his years as a journalist and adventurer. Stanley Karnow also drew on a reporter's past in *Paris in the Fifties*. Henry Miller's visceral autobiographical works such as *The Tropic of Cancer* reveal a grittier kind of expat life. Janet Flanner's incomparable *Paris Journals* chronicle the city from the 1940s through 1970, and no one has yet matched A.J. Liebling at table, as described in *Between Meals*.

More recent accounts by Americans living in Paris include Edmund White's *Our Paris: Sketches with Memory* (White is also the author of a brief but captivating wander through the city in *The Flâneur*), Alex Karmel's *A Corner in the Marais: Memoir of a Paris Neighborhood*, Thad Carhart's *The Piano Shop on the Left Bank*, and the very funny *Me Talk Pretty One Day*, by David Sedaris. Adam Gopnik, a *New Yorker* writer who lived in Paris in the 1990s, intersperses articles on larger French issues with descriptions of daily life with his wife and son in *Paris to the Moon*. Gopnik also edited the anthology *Americans in Paris*, a collection of observations by everyone from Thomas Jefferson to Cole Porter.

**Works in Translation.** Many landmarks of French literature have long been claimed as classics in English as well—Victor Hugo's great 19th-century novels, including *The Hunchback of Notre-Dame* and *Les Misérables*, spin elaborate descriptions of Paris. Other 19th-century masterpieces include Gustave Flaubert's *Sentimental Education*, set against the capital's 1848 uprisings, and Honoré de Balzac's *Human Comedy*, a series of dozens of novels, many set in Paris.

Marcel Proust's masterpiece *À la Recherche du Temps Perdu* (*In Search of Lost Time*) describes fin-de-siècle Paris's parks, glittering aristocratic salons, and dread during the Great War. Colette was another great chronicler of the Belle Époque; her short works include *Chéri* and the Claudine stories.

Simone de Beauvoir's *The Prime of Life*, the second book in her autobiographical trilogy, details her relationship with the existentialist philosopher Jean-Paul Sartre in the context of 1930s and '40s Paris, when the Rive Gauche cemented its modern bohemian reputation in its cafés and jazz clubs.

## Movies

**Drama.** One of the most talked-about movies of 2006 was Sofia Coppola's lavish *Marie Antoinette*; it might not have been a box office hit, but it's an interesting take on life at Versailles. Previous to that, the film version of *The Da Vinci Code* (2006), starring Tom Hanks and Audrey Tautou, was talked about for months preceding its release, although some were disappointed. The heist film *Ronin* (1998) pairs Robert De Niro and Jean Reno with a hyperkinetic chase through the streets of Paris, and in *Frantic* (1987) Harrison Ford plays an American doctor visiting Paris when his wife disappears and director Roman Polanski shoots the city to build suspense and dread. The Palais-Royal gets an equally tense treatment in the Audrey Hepburn–Cary Grant thriller *Charade* (1963); the 2002 remake, *The Truth About Charlie*, doesn't hold a candle to the original. In *Before Sunset* (2004), Ethan Hawke meets Julie Delpy in Paris in the sequel to *Before Sunrise*.

**French Films.** One of the biggest hits out of France was *Amélie* (2001), which follows a young woman determined to change people's lives. There's a love angle, *bien sûr*, and the neighborhood of Montmartre is practically a third hero, although

Parisians sniffed that it was a sterilized version of the raffish quartier.

Jean-Luc Godard's *Breathless* (1960) and François Truffaut's *The 400 Blows* (slang for "raising hell"; 1959) kicked off the New Wave cinema movement. Godard eschewed traditional movie narrative techniques, employing a loose style—including improvised dialogue and hand-held camera shots—for his story about a low-level crook (Jean-Paul Belmondo) and his girlfriend (Jean Seberg). Truffaut's film is a masterwork of innocence lost, a semiautobiographical story of a young boy banished to juvenile detention.

Catherine Deneuve is practically a film industry in and of herself. Her movies span the globe; those shot in Paris range from *Belle de Jour* (1967)—Luis Buñuel's study of erotic repression—to *Le Dernier Métro* (1980), a World War II drama.

Classic film noir and contemporary crime dramas are also highlights of French cinema: for a taste, rent *Rififi* (1955), with its excruciatingly tense 33-minute heist scene; *Le Samouraï* (1967), in which Alain Delon plays the ultimate cool assassin; or Robert Bresson's *Pickpocket* (1959). *La Casque d'Or* (1952) looks back to the underworld of the early 1900s, with Simone Signoret as the title irresistible blond. French director Luc Besson introduced a sly female action hero with *Nikita* (1990), in which Jean Reno chills as the creepy "cleaner" you don't want making house calls.

Filmed during the Occupation, *The Children of Paradise* (1945) became an allegory for the French spirit of resistance: the love story was set in 1840s Paris, thereby getting past the German censors. Other romantic films with memorable takes on Paris include *Cyrano de Bergerac* (1990), with Gérard Depardieu as the large-schnozzed hero; the comedy *When the Cat's Away* (1996); the talk-heavy films of Eric Rohmer; *Camille Claudel* (1988), about the affair between Rodin and fellow sculptor Claudel; and the gritty *The Lovers on the Bridge* (1999), the flaws balanced by the bravado of Juliette Binoche waterskiing on the Seine surrounded by fireworks. *The Red Balloon* (1956) is also a love story of a sort: a children's film of a boy and his faithful balloon.

**Musicals.** Love in the time of Toulouse-Lautrec? Elton John songs? Baz Luhrmann's *Moulin Rouge* (2001) whirls them together and wins through conviction rather than verisimilitude. John Huston's 1952 film of the same name is also well worth watching. Gene Kelly pursues Leslie Caron through postwar Paris in *An American in Paris* (1951); the Gershwin-fueled film includes a stunning 17-minute dance sequence. Caron reappears as the love interest—this time as a young girl in training to be a courtesan—in *Gigi* (1958). *Funny Face* (1957) stars Fred Astaire and Audrey Hepburn, and there's an unforgettable scene of Hepburn descending the staircase below the *Winged Victory* in the Louvre.

# VOCABULARY

One of the trickiest French sounds to pronounce is the nasal final n sound (whether or not the n is actually the last letter of the word). You should try to pronounce it as a sort of nasal grunt—as in "huh." The vowel that precedes the n will govern the vowel sound of the word, and in this list we precede the final n with an h to remind you to be nasal.

Another problem sound is the ubiquitous but untransliterable eu, as in bleu (blue) or deux (two), and the very similar sound in je (I), ce (this), and de (of). The closest equivalent might be the vowel sound in "put," but rounded. The famous rolled r is a glottal sound. Consonants at the ends of words are usually silent; when the following word begins with a vowel, however, the two are run together by sounding the consonant. There are two forms of "you" in French: vous (formal and plural) and tu (a singular, personal form). When addressing an adult you don't know, vous is always best.

| ENGLISH | FRENCH | PRONUNCIATION |
| --- | --- | --- |
| **BASICS** | | |
| Yes/no | Oui/non | wee/nohn |
| Please | S'il vous plaît | seel voo play |
| Thank you | Merci | mair-**see** |
| You're welcome | De rien | deh ree-**ehn** |
| Excuse me, sorry | Pardon | pahr-**don** |
| Good morning/afternoon | Bonjour | bohn-**zhoor** |
| Good evening | Bonsoir | bohn-**swahr** |
| Good-bye | Au revoir | o ruh-**vwahr** |
| Mr. (Sir) | Monsieur | muh-**syuh** |
| Mrs. (Ma'am) | Madame | ma-**dam** |
| Miss | Mademoiselle | mad-mwa-**zel** |
| Pleased to meet you | Enchanté(e) | ohn-shahn-**tay** |
| How are you? | Comment allez-vous? | kuh-mahn-tahl-ay **voo** |
| Very well, thanks | Très bien, merci | tray bee-ehn, mair-**see** |
| And you? | Et vous? | ay voo? |
| **NUMBERS** | | |
| one | un | uhn |
| two | deux | deuh |
| three | trois | twah |

| ENGLISH | FRENCH | PRONUNCIATION |
|---|---|---|
| four | quatre | **kaht**-ruh |
| five | cinq | sank |
| six | six | seess |
| seven | sept | set |
| eight | huit | wheat |
| nine | neuf | nuf |
| ten | dix | deess |
| eleven | onze | ohnz |
| twelve | douze | dooz |
| thirteen | treize | trehz |
| fourteen | quatorze | kah-**torz** |
| fifteen | quinze | kanz |
| sixteen | seize | sez |
| seventeen | dix-sept | deez-**set** |
| eighteen | dix-huit | deez-**wheat** |
| nineteen | dix-neuf | deez-**nuf** |
| twenty | vingt | vehn |
| twenty-one | vingt-et-un | vehnt-ay-**uhn** |
| thirty | trente | trahnt |
| forty | quarante | ka-**rahnt** |
| fifty | cinquante | sang-**kahnt** |
| sixty | soixante | swa-**sahnt** |
| seventy | soixante-dix | swa-sahnt-**deess** |
| eighty | quatre-vingts | kaht-ruh-**vehn** |
| ninety | quatre-vingt-dix | kaht-ruh-vehn-**deess** |
| one hundred | cent | sahn |
| one thousand | mille | meel |

## COLORS

| | | |
|---|---|---|
| black | noir | nwahr |
| blue | bleu | bleuh |

| ENGLISH | FRENCH | PRONUNCIATION |
|---------|--------|---------------|
| brown | brun/marron | bruhn/mar-**rohn** |
| green | vert | vair |
| orange | orange | o-**rahnj** |
| pink | rose | rose |
| red | rouge | rouge |
| violet | violette | vee-o-**let** |
| white | blanc | blahnk |
| yellow | jaune | zhone |

## DAYS OF THE WEEK

| Sunday | dimanche | dee-**mahnsh** |
|--------|----------|----------------|
| Monday | lundi | luhn-**dee** |
| Tuesday | mardi | mahr-**dee** |
| Wednesday | mercredi | mair-kruh-**dee** |
| Thursday | jeudi | zhuh-**dee** |
| Friday | vendredi | vawn-druh-**dee** |
| Saturday | samedi | sahm-**dee** |

## MONTHS

| January | janvier | zhahn-vee-**ay** |
|---------|---------|------------------|
| February | février | feh-vree-**ay** |
| March | mars | marce |
| April | avril | a-**vreel** |
| May | mai | meh |
| June | juin | zhwehn |
| July | juillet | zhwee-**ay** |
| August | août | ah-**oo** |
| September | septembre | sep-**tahm**-bruh |
| October | octobre | awk-**to**-bruh |
| November | novembre | no-**vahm**-bruh |
| December | décembre | day-**sahm**-bruh |

| ENGLISH | FRENCH | PRONUNCIATION |
|---------|--------|---------------|

## USEFUL PHRASES

| ENGLISH | FRENCH | PRONUNCIATION |
|---------|--------|---------------|
| Do you speak English? | Parlez-vous anglais? | par-lay **voo** ahn-**glay** |
| I don't speak . . . | Je ne parle pas . . . | zhuh nuh parl pah . . . |
| French | français | frahn-**say** |
| I don't understand | Je ne comprends pas | zhuh nuh kohm-**prahn** pah |
| I understand | Je comprends | zhuh kohm-**prahn** |
| I don't know | Je ne sais pas | zhuh nuh say **pah** |
| I'm American/ British | Je suis américain/ anglais | zhuh sweez a-may-ree-**kehn**/ahn-**glay** |
| What's your name? | Comment vous appelez-vous? | ko-mahn vooz a-pell-ay-**voo** |
| My name is . . . | Je m'appelle . . . | zhuh ma-**pell** . . . |
| What time is it? | Quelle heure est-il? | kel air eh-**teel** |
| How? | Comment? | ko-**mahn** |
| When? | Quand? | kahn |
| Yesterday | Hier | yair |
| Today | Aujourd'hui | o-zhoor-**dwee** |
| Tomorrow | Demain | duh-**mehn** |
| Tonight | Ce soir | suh **swahr** |
| What? | Quoi? | kwah |
| What is it? | Qu'est-ce que c'est? | kess-kuh-**say** |
| Why? | Pourquoi? | poor-**kwa** |
| Who? | Qui? | kee |
| Where is . . . | Où est . . . | oo ay |
| the train station? | la gare? | la gar |
| the subway station? | la station de métro? | la sta-**syon** duh may-**tro** |
| the bus stop? | l'arrêt de bus? | la-ray duh booss |
| the post office? | la poste? | la post |
| the bank? | la banque? | la bahnk |

| ENGLISH | FRENCH | PRONUNCIATION |
|---------|--------|---------------|
| the . . . hotel? | l'hôtel . . .? | lo-**tel** |
| the store? | le magasin? | luh ma-ga-**zehn** |
| the cashier? | la caisse? | la **kess** |
| the . . . museum? | le musée . . .? | luh mew-**zay** |
| the hospital? | l'hôpital? | lo-pee-**tahl** |
| the elevator? | l'ascenseur? | la-sahn-**seuhr** |
| the telephone? | le téléphone? | luh tay-lay-**phone** |
| Where are the | Où sont les | oo sohn lay |
| restrooms? | toilettes? | twah-**let** |
| (men/women) | (hommes/femmes) | (**oh**-mm/**fah**-mm) |
| Here/there | Ici/là | ee-**see**/la |
| Left/right | A gauche/à droite | a goash/a draht |
| Straight ahead | Tout droit | too drwah |
| Is it near/far? | C'est près/loin? | say pray/lwehn |
| I'd like . . . | Je voudrais . . . | zhuh voo-**dray** |
| a room | une chambre | ewn **shahm**-bruh |
| the key | la clé | la clay |
| a newspaper | un journal | uhn zhoor-**nahl** |
| a stamp | un timbre | uhn **tam**-bruh |
| I'd like to buy . . . | Je voudrais acheter . . | zhuh voo-**dray ahsh**-tay |
| cigarettes | des cigarettes | day see-ga-**ret** |
| matches | des allumettes | days a-loo-**met** |
| soap | du savon | dew sah-**vohn** |
| city map | un plan de ville | uhn plahn de **veel** |
| road map | une carte routière | ewn cart roo-tee-**air** |
| magazine | une revue | ewn reh-**vu** |
| envelopes | des enveloppes | dayz ahn-veh-**lope** |
| writing paper | du papier à lettres | dew pa-pee-**ay** a **let**-ruh |
| postcard | une carte postale | ewn cart pos-**tal** |

| ENGLISH | FRENCH | PRONUNCIATION |
|---|---|---|
| How much is it? | C'est combien? | say comb-bee-**ehn** |
| A little/a lot | Un peu/beaucoup | uhn peuh/bo-**koo** |
| More/less | Plus/moins | plu/mwehn |
| Enough/too (much) | Assez/trop | a-say/tro |
| I am ill/sick | Je suis malade | zhuh swee ma-**lahd** |
| Call a . . . | Appelez un . . . | a-play uhn |
| doctor | docteur | dohk-**tehr** |
| Help! | Au secours! | o suh-**koor** |
| Stop! | Arrêtez! | a-reh-**tay** |
| Fire! | Au feu! | o fuh |
| Caution!/Look out! | Attention! | a-tahn-see-**ohn** |

## DINING OUT

| | | |
|---|---|---|
| A bottle of . . . | une bouteille de . . . | ewn boo-**tay** duh |
| A cup of . . . | une tasse de . . . | ewn tass duh |
| A glass of . . . | un verre de . . . | uhn vair duh |
| Bill/check | l'addition | la-dee-see-**ohn** |
| Bread | du pain | dew panh |
| Breakfast | le petit-déjeuner | luh puh-**tee** day-zhuh-**nay** |
| Butter | du beurre | dew burr |
| Cheers! | A votre santé! | ah **vo**-truh sahn-**tay** |
| Cocktail/aperitif | un apéritif | uhn ah-pay-ree-**teef** |
| Dinner | le dîner | luh dee-**nay** |
| Dish of the day | le plat du jour | luh plah dew **zhoor** |
| Enjoy! | Bon appétit! | bohn a-pay-**tee** |
| Fixed-price menu | le menu | luh may-**new** |
| Fork | une fourchette | ewn four-**shet** |
| I am diabetic | Je suis diabétique | zhuh swee dee-ah-bay-**teek** |
| I am vegetarian | Je suis végétarien(ne) | zhuh swee vay-zhay-ta-ree-**en** |

| ENGLISH | FRENCH | PRONUNCIATION |
|---|---|---|
| I cannot eat . . . | Je ne peux pas manger de . . . | zhuh nuh puh pah mahn-**jay** deh |
| I'd like to order | Je voudrais commander | zhuh voo-**dray** ko-mahn-**day** |
| Is service/the tip included? | Est-ce que le service est compris? | ess kuh luh sair-**veess** ay comb-**pree** |
| It's good/bad | C'est bon/mauvais | say bohn/mo-**vay** |
| It's hot/cold | C'est chaud/froid | say sho/frwah |
| Knife | un couteau | uhn koo-**toe** |
| Lunch | le déjeuner | luh day-zhuh-**nay** |
| Menu | la carte | la cart |
| Napkin | une serviette | ewn sair-vee-**et** |
| Pepper | du poivre | dew **pwah**-vruh |
| Plate | une assiette | ewn a-see-**et** |
| Please give me . . . | Donnez-moi . . . | doe-nay-**mwah** |
| Salt | du sel | dew sell |
| Spoon | une cuillère | ewn kwee-**air** |
| Sugar | du sucre | dew **sook**-ruh |
| Waiter!/Waitress! | Monsieur!/ Mademoiselle! | muh-**syuh**/mad-mwa-**zel** |
| Wine list | la carte des vins | la cart day vehn |

# MENU GUIDE

| FRENCH | ENGLISH |
|---|---|
| **GENERAL DINING** | |
| Entrée | Appetizer/Starter |
| Garniture au choix | Choice of vegetable side |
| Plat du jour | Dish of the day |
| Selon arrivage | When available |
| Supplément/En sus | Extra charge |
| Sur commande | Made to order |

| FRENCH | ENGLISH |
|---|---|
| **PETIT DÉJEUNER (BREAKFAST)** | |
| Confiture | Jam |
| Miel | Honey |
| Oeuf à la coque | Boiled egg |
| Oeufs sur le plat | Fried eggs |
| Oeufs brouillés | Scrambled eggs |
| Tartine | Bread with butter |
| Poissons/Fruits de Mer | Fish/Seafood |
| Anchois | Anchovies |
| Bar | Bass |
| Brandade de morue | Creamed salt cod |
| Brochet | Pike |
| Cabillaud/Morue | Fresh cod |
| Calmar | Squid |
| Coquilles St-Jacques | Scallops |
| Crevettes | Shrimp |
| Daurade | Sea bream |
| Ecrevisses | Prawns/Crayfish |
| Harengs | Herring |
| Homard | Lobster |
| Huîtres | Oysters |
| Langoustine | Prawn/Lobster |
| Lotte | Monkfish |
| Moules | Mussels |
| Palourdes | Clams |
| Saumon | Salmon |
| Thon | Tuna |
| Truite | Trout |

| FRENCH | ENGLISH |
| --- | --- |
| **VIANDE (MEAT)** | |
| Agneau | Lamb |
| Boeuf | Beef |
| Boudin | Sausage |
| Boulettes de viande | Meatballs |
| Brochettes | Kabobs |
| Cassoulet | Casserole of white beans, meat |
| Cervelle | Brains |
| Chateaubriand | Double fillet steak |
| Choucroute garnie | Sausages with sauerkraut |
| Côtelettes | Chops |
| Côte/Côte de boeuf | Rib/T-bone steak |
| Cuisses de grenouilles | Frogs' legs |
| Entrecôte | Rib or rib-eye steak |
| Épaule | Shoulder |
| Escalope | Cutlet |
| Foie | Liver |
| Gigot | Leg |
| Porc | Pork |
| Ris de veau | Veal sweetbreads |
| Rognons | Kidneys |
| Saucisses | Sausages |
| Selle | Saddle |
| Tournedos | Tenderloin of T-bone steak |
| Veau | Veal |
| **METHODS OF PREPARATION** | |
| A point | Medium |
| A l'étouffée | Stewed |
| Au four | Baked |
| Ballotine | Boned, stuffed, and rolled |

| FRENCH | ENGLISH |
| --- | --- |
| Bien cuit | Well-done |
| Bleu | Very rare |
| Frit | Fried |
| Grillé | Grilled |
| Rôti | Roast |
| Saignant | Rare |

## VOLAILLES/GIBIER (POULTRY/GAME)

| | |
| --- | --- |
| Blanc de volaille | Chicken breast |
| Canard/Caneton | Duck/Duckling |
| Cerf/Chevreuil | Venison (red/roe) |
| Coq au vin | Chicken stewed in red wine |
| Dinde/Dindonneau | Turkey/Young turkey |
| Faisan | Pheasant |
| Lapin/Lièvre | Rabbit/Wild hare |
| Oie | Goose |
| Pintade/Pintadeau | Guinea fowl/Young guinea fowl |
| Poulet/Poussin | Chicken/Spring chicken |

## LÉGUMES (VEGETABLES)

| | |
| --- | --- |
| Artichaut | Artichoke |
| Asperge | Asparagus |
| Aubergine | Eggplant |
| Carottes | Carrots |
| Champignons | Mushrooms |
| Chou-fleur | Cauliflower |
| Chou (rouge) | Cabbage (red) |
| Laitue | Lettuce |
| Oignons | Onions |
| Petits pois | Peas |
| Pomme de terre | Potato |
| Tomates | Tomatoes |

| FRENCH | ENGLISH |
|--------|---------|

## FRUITS/NOIX (FRUITS/NUTS)

| FRENCH | ENGLISH |
|--------|---------|
| Abricot | Apricot |
| Amandes | Almonds |
| Ananas | Pineapple |
| Cassis | Black currants |
| Cerises | Cherries |
| Citron/Citron vert | Lemon/Lime |
| Fraises | Strawberries |
| Framboises | Raspberries |
| Pamplemousse | Grapefruit |
| Pêche | Peach |
| Poire | Pear |
| Pomme | Apple |
| Prunes/Pruneaux | Plums/Prunes |
| Raisins/Raisins secs | Grapes/Raisins |

## DESSERTS

| FRENCH | ENGLISH |
|--------|---------|
| Coupe (glacée) | Sundae |
| Crème Chantilly | Whipped cream |
| Gâteau au chocolat | Chocolate cake |
| Glace | Ice cream |
| Tarte tatin | Caramelized apple tart |
| Tourte | Layer cake |

## DRINKS

| FRENCH | ENGLISH |
|--------|---------|
| A l'eau | With water |
| Avec des glaçons | On the rocks |
| Bière | Beer |
| Blonde/brune | Light/dark |
| Café noir/crème | Black coffee/with steamed milk |
| Chocolat chaud | Hot chocolate |
| Eau-de-vie | Brandy |

| FRENCH | ENGLISH |
| --- | --- |
| Eau minérale | Mineral water |
| gazeuse/non gazeuse | carbonated/still |
| Jus de . . . | . . . juice |
| Lait | Milk |
| Sec | Straight or dry |
| Thé | Tea |
| Au lait/au citron | with milk/lemon |
| Vin | Wine |
| Blanc | white |
| Doux | sweet |
| Léger | light |
| Brut | very dry |
| Rouge | red |

# Travel Smart
# Paris

## WORD OF MOUTH

"I like riding the bus, I got to see parts of Paris I
have never seen while riding #95."

—cafegoddess

# GETTING HERE AND AROUND

Addresses in Paris are fairly straightforward: there's the number, the street name, and the zip code designating one of Paris's 20 *arrondissements* (districts); for instance, Paris 75010 (the last two digits, "10") indicates that the address is in the 10*e*. The large 16*e* arrondissement has two numbers assigned to it: 75016 and 75116. For the layout of Paris's arrondissements, see the What's Where map in the *Experience* chapter.

The arrondissements are laid out in a spiral, beginning from the area around the Louvre (1*er* arrondissement), then moving clockwise through Le Marais, the Quartier Latin, St-Germain, and then out from the city center to the outskirts to Ménilmontant/Père-Lachaise (20*e* arrondissement). Occasionally you may see an address with a number plus *bis*—for instance, 20 bis, rue Vavin. This indicates the next entrance or door down from 20 rue Vavin. Note that in France you enter a building on the ground floor, or *rez-de-chaussée* (RC or 0), and go up one floor to the first floor, or *premier étage*. General address terms used in this book are *av.* (avenue), *bd.* (boulevard), *carrefour* (crossway), *cours* (promenade), *passage* (passageway), *pl.* (place), *quai* (quay/wharf/pier), *rue* (street), and *sq.* (square).

## ▌ BY AIR

Flying time to Paris is 7 hours from New York, 9½ hours from Chicago, and 11 hours from Los Angeles. Flying time from London to Paris is 1½ hours.

The French are notoriously stringent about security, particularly for international flights. Don't be surprised by the armed security officers patrolling the airports, and be prepared for very long check-in lines. Peak travel times in France are between mid-July and September, during the Christmas–New Year's holidays in late December and early January, and

during the February school break. During these periods airports are especially crowded, so allow plenty of extra time. Never leave your baggage unattended, even for a moment. Unattended baggage is considered a security risk and may be destroyed.

**Airline and Airport Links.com** (⊕ *www. airlineandairportlinks.com*) has links to many of the world's airlines and airports.

**Airline Security Issues** Transportation Security Administration (⊕ *www.tsa.gov*) has answers for almost every question that might come up.

### AIRPORTS

The major airports are Charles de Gaulle (CDG, also known as Roissy), 26 km (16 mi) northeast of Paris, and Orly (ORY), 16 km (10 mi) south of Paris. Both are easily accessible from Paris. Whether you take a car or bus to travel from Paris to the airport on your departure, always allot an extra hour because of the often horrendous traffic tie-ups in the airports themselves (especially in peak seasons and at peak hours). Free light rail connections (Orlyval and CDGval) available between the major terminals are one option for avoiding some of the traffic mess, but still give yourself enough time to navigate your way through these busy airports.

**Airport Information** Charles de Gaulle/ Roissy and Orly (☎ 3950* in English; outside of France, 0033–1–70–36–39–50 ⊕ www.adp.fr).

### GROUND TRANSPORTATION

**By bus from CDG/Roissy:** Roissybus, operated by the RATP (Paris Transit Authority), runs between Charles de Gaulle and the Opéra every 20 minutes from 6 AM to 11 PM; the cost is €9.10. The trip takes about 45 minutes in regular traffic, about 90 minutes in rush-hour traffic.

**By shuttle from CDG/Roissy:** The Air France shuttle service is a comfortable option to get to and from the city—you don't need to have flown the carrier to use it. Line 2 goes from the airport to Paris's Charles de Gaulle Etoile and Porte Maillot from 5:45 AM to 11 PM. It leaves every 20 minutes and costs €15, which you can pay on board. Line 4 goes to Montparnasse and the Gare de Lyon from 7 AM to 9 PM. Buses run every 30 minutes and cost €16.50. Passengers arriving in Terminal 1 need to take Exit 34; Terminals 2A and 2C go to exit C2; 2B and 2D take exit B1; Terminals 2E and 2F, Exit 3.

A number of van services serve both Charles de Gaulle and Orly airports. Prices are set so there are no surprises even if traffic is a snail-pace nightmare. To make a reservation, call or fax your flight details at least one week in advance to the shuttle company and an air-conditioned van with a bilingual chauffeur will be waiting for you upon your arrival. Confirm the day before. These vans sometimes pick up more than one party, though, so you may have to share the shuttle with other passengers. Likewise, when taking people to the airport these shuttles usually pick up a couple of groups of passengers. This adds at least 20 minutes to the trip.

**By taxi from CDG/Roissy:** Taxis are generally the least desirable mode of transportation into the city. If you're traveling at peak hours, journey times (and prices) are unpredictable. At best, the journey takes 30 minutes, but it can be as long as one hour.

**By train from CDG/Roissy:** The least expensive way to get into Paris from CDG is the RER-B line, the suburban express train, which runs from 5 AM to 11:30 PM daily. There are two RER stations at CDG "RER B Aéroport Charles de Gaulle 1" for Terminals 1 (via CDGval) and 3 (via

**NAVIGATING PARIS**

Paris is a walker's city, but public transportation is excellent when your feet get tired. The métro and bus systems are extensive and easy to use.

There are many landmarks in Paris to orient yourself—churches, the Opéra, the Tour Eiffel, etc. Choose one near your hotel, for example, and if you get lost, it'll be easy to get back on track.

As with any city that's not laid out in a numbered grid, it can be confusing to find what you're looking for—especially in a foreign language; don't hesitate to ask for help. Most people are happy to give assistance, especially if you try out some French (like bonjour).

a covered walkway). "RER B Aéroport Charles de Gaulle 2" serves Terminal 2, accessible via walkways or by the free N1 shuttle. Trains to central Paris (Les Halles, St-Michel, Luxembourg) depart every 15 minutes. The fare (including métro connection) is €8.50, and journey time is about 45 minutes.

**By bus from Orly:** Air France buses run from Orly to Les Invalides, Charles de Gaulle Etoile, and Montparnasse; these run every 15 minutes from 6 AM to 11 PM. (You need not have flown on Air France to use this service.) The fare is €11.50, and journey time is between 30 and 45 minutes, depending on traffic. To find the bus, take Exit L if you've arrived in Orly South, or Exit B-C from Orly West. RATP's Orlybus is yet another option; buses leave every 15 minutes for the Denfert-Rochereau métro station in Montparnasse from Exit H in Orly South and Exit G in Orly West. The cost is €6.40. The cheapest bus is the RATP city bus 183, which shuttles you from Metro Porte de Choisy (Line 7) to Orly South for just €3.70, every 30 minutes from 5:30 AM to 8:30 PM. Travel time is approximately 50 minutes.

**By train from Orly:** The cheapest way to get into Paris by train is to take the shuttle bus from Exit F at Orly South or Exit G at Orly West to the station RER-C Pont de Rungis–Aéroport d'Orly into Paris. Trains to Paris leave every 15 minutes. The fare is €2.60 (Shuttle) plus €3.60 (RER), and journey time is about 35 minutes. Another slightly faster option is to take RATP's monorail service, Orlyval, which runs between the Antony RER-B station and Orly Airport daily every four to eight minutes from 6 AM to 11 PM. Passengers arriving in the South Terminal should use Exit K; take Exit W if you've arrived in the West Terminal. The fare to downtown Paris is €9.85 and includes the RER transfer.

| TRAVEL TO CENTRAL PARIS | | |
| --- | --- | --- |
| From | Orly | CDG |
| Taxi | 20 mins–45 mins; €30–€50 | 45 mins–75 mins; €40–€70 |
| Bus | 30 mins–50 mins; €3.70–€11.50 | 45 mins–90 mins; €9.10–€16.50 |
| Airport Shuttle | 45 mins–90 mins; €25–€45 | 1 hr–2 hrs; €25–€45 |
| RER | 25 mins–40 mins; €6.20 | 45 mins–1 hr; €8.50 |

**TRANSFERS BETWEEN AIRPORTS**

To transfer between Paris's airports, there are several options. See the "By Train" options above: the RER-B travels from CDG to Orly with Paris in the middle, so to transfer, just stay on. Travel time is about 50–70 minutes and costs €18.20. The Air France Bus line 3 also runs between the airports for €19 one way, every 30 minutes, with about 50 minutes travel time. Taxis are available but expensive: from €60 to €80, depending on traffic.

**Contacts Air France Bus** (☎ 08–92–35–08–20 recorded information in English, €0.34 per min ⊕ www.cars-airfrance.com). **Airport Connection** (☎ 01–43–65–55–55 🖷 01–43–65–55–57 ⊕ www.airport-connection.com). **Paris Airports Services** (☎ 01–55–98–10–80

☎ 01–55–98–10–89 ⊕ www.parisairportservice. com). **RATP (including Roissybus, Orlybus, Orlyval)** (☎ 08–92–68–77–14, €0.34 per min ⊕ www.ratp.com).

**FLIGHTS**

As one of the premier destinations in the world, Paris is serviced by a great many international carriers and a surprisingly large number of U.S.-based airlines. Air France (which partners with Delta) is the French flag carrier and offers numerous direct flights (often several per day) between Paris's Charles de Gaulle Airport and New York City's JFK Airport; Newark, New Jersey; Washington's Dulles Airport; and the cities of Boston, Philadelphia, Atlanta, Cincinnati, Miami, Chicago, Houston, Seattle, San Francisco, Los Angeles, Toronto, Montréal, and Mexico City. Most other North American cities are served through Air France partnerships with Delta and Continental Airlines. American-based carriers are usually less expensive but offer, on the whole, fewer nonstop direct flights. United Airlines has nonstop flights to Paris from Chicago, Denver, Los Angeles, Miami, Philadelphia, Washington, and San Francisco. American Airlines offers daily nonstop flights to Paris's Charles de Gaulle Airport from numerous cities, including New York City's JFK, Miami, Chicago, and Dallas/Fort Worth. Northwest has a daily departure to Paris from its hub in Detroit. In Canada, Air France and Air Canada are the leading choices for departures from Toronto and Montréal; in peak season departures are often daily. From London, Air France, British Airways, and British Midland are the leading carriers, with up to 15 flights daily in peak season. In addition, direct routes link Manchester, Edinburgh, and Southampton with Paris. Ryanair, easyJet, CityJet, and BMI Baby offer direct service from Paris to Dublin, Birmingham, London, Glasgow, Amsterdam, Cardiff, Zurich, and Brussels, to name just a few. Tickets are available on the Web only and need to be booked well in advance to get the best prices—a one-way ticket from Paris to Dublin costs a mere €45, for example.

**Airline Contacts** Air Canada (☎ *888/247–2262 in U.S. and Canada, 0825–882–900 in France* ⊕ *www.aircanada.com*). **Air France** (☎ *800/237-2747 in U.S., 3654 [€0.34/min]* ⊕ *www.airfrance.com*). **American Airlines** (☎ *800/433-7300, 01-55-17-43-41 in France* ⊕ *www.aa.com*). **British Airways** (☎ *800/247–9297 in U.S., 08–25–82–54–00 in France [€0.15/min]* ⊕ *www.britishairways.com*). **Continental Airlines** (☎ *800/523–3273 for U.S. and Mexico reservations, 800/231–0856 for international reservations, 01–71–23–03–35 in France* ⊕ *www.continental.com*). **Delta Airlines** (☎ *800/221–1212 for U.S. reservations, 800/241–4141 for international reservations, 08–11–64–00–05 in France* ⊕ *www.delta.com*). **Northwest Airlines** (☎ *800/225–2525, 00–890–710–710 in France* ⊕ *www.nwa.com*). **United Airlines** (☎ *800/864–8331 for U.S. reservations, 800/538–2929 for international reservations, 08–10–72–72–72 in France* ⊕ *www.united.com*). **USAirways** (☎ *800/428–4322 for U.S. and Canada reservations, 800/622–1015 for international reservations, 08–10–63–22–22 in France* ⊕ *www.usairways.com*).

**Discount Airlines** BMI Baby (☎ *01–41–91–87–04 in France* ⊕ *www.bmibaby.com*). **easy-Jet** (☎ *08–26–10–26–11 in France* ⊕ *www.easyjet.com*). **Ryan Air** (☎ *08–92–78–02–10 in France* ⊕ *www.ryanair.com*). **CityJet** (☎ *0820–320–820 in France* ⊕ *www.cityjet.com*).

**Within Europe** Air France (☎ *0845/242–9242 in U.K., 08–25–86–48–64 in France* ⊕ *www.airfrance.com*). **British Airways** (☎ *0870/850–9850 in U.K., 08–25–82–54–00 in France* ⊕ *www.britishairways.com*). **British Midland** (☎ *01623/724–099 in U.K., 01–41–91–83–04 in France* ⊕ *www.flybmi.com*).

## ▌ BY BOAT

Linking France and the United Kingdom, a boat or ferry trip across the Channel can range from 35 minutes (via hovercraft) to 95 minutes (via ferryboat). Trip length also depends on departure point: popular routes link Boulogne and Folkestone,

Le Havre and Portsmouth, and, the most booked passage, Calais and Dover. DirectFerries.fr groups the sites for several ferry–land hovercraft crossings to make reservations more streamlined.

P&O European Ferries links Dover, England, with Calais (75 minutes). P&O has up to three sailings a day. Seafrance operates up to 15 sailings a day from Dover to Calais; the crossing takes 70 or 90 minutes, depending on the ship.

The driving distance from Calais to Paris is 290 km (180 mi). The fastest routes to Paris from each port are via N43, A26, and A1 from Calais and the Channel Tunnel; and via N1 from Boulogne.

**Information** P&O European Ferries (☎ *0870/598–0333 in U.K., 0825/120–156 in France* ⊕ *www.poportsmouth.com*). **Seafrance** (☎ *+44845/458–0666 from France* ⊕ *www.seafrance.net*). **DirectFerries.fr** (⊕ *www.directferries.fr*).

## ▌ BY BUS

### ARRIVING AND DEPARTING PARIS

The excellent national train service in France means that long-distance bus service in the country is practically nonexistent; regional buses are found where train service is spotty. Local bus information to the rare rural areas where trains do not have access can be obtained from the SNCF (⇨ *see By Train, below*).

The largest international operator is Eurolines France, whose main terminal is in the Parisian suburb of Bagnolet (a half-hour métro ride from central Paris, at the end of métro Line 3). Eurolines runs international routes to more than 1,500 cities in Europe.

It's possible to take a bus (via ferry) to Paris from the United Kingdom; just be aware that what you save in money will almost certainly cost you in time—the bus trip takes about seven hours as opposed to the three it takes on the Eurostar train line (St-Pancras Station–Gare du Nord).

In general, the price of a round-trip bus ticket is 50% less than that of a plane ticket and 25% less than that of a train ticket, so if you have the time and the energy, this is a good way to cut the cost of travel. Eurolines also offers a 15-day (€175–€310) or 30-day (€240–€410) pass if you're planning on doing the grand European tour. Ask about one of the Circle tours that depart from Paris (for example, via London, Amsterdam, then back to Paris again). Eurolines operates a service from London's Victoria Coach Station, via the Dover-Calais ferry, to Paris's Porte de Bagnolet. There's an 8 AM departure that arrives in Paris at 4:30 PM, a noon departure that arrives at 9:30 PM, and the overnight trips at 9:30 PM, which arrive in Paris at 7:15 AM, and the 10:30 PM departure, which arrives at 7:30 AM. Fares are €57 round-trip (an under-25 youth pass is €53). Other Eurolines routes include Amsterdam (7 hours, €67), Barcelona (15 hours, €139), and Berlin (10 hours, €137). There are also international-only arrivals and departures from Avignon, Bordeaux, Lille, Lyon, Toulouse, and Tours.

Eurolines accepts all major credit cards but does not accept traveler's checks.

Reservations for an international bus trip are essential. Be sure to check the Eurolines Web site for special discounts or incentives. Avoid buying your ticket at the last minute, when prices are highest.

### IN PARIS

With dedicated bus lanes now in place throughout the city—allowing buses and taxis to whiz past other traffic mired in tedious jams—taking the bus is an appealing option. Although nothing can beat the métro for speed, buses offer great city views, and the new ones are equipped with air-conditioning—a real perk on those sweltering August days.

Paris buses are green and white; route number and destination are marked in front, major stopping places along the sides. Brown bus shelters contain timetables and route maps; note that buses must be hailed at these larger bus shelters, as they service multiple lines and routes. Smaller stops are designated simply by a pole bearing bus numbers.

More than 200 bus routes run throughout Paris, reaching virtually every nook and cranny of the city. On weekdays and Saturday, buses run every five minutes (as opposed to the 15- to 20-minute wait you'll have on Sunday and national holidays). One ticket will take you anywhere within the city and is valid for one transfer within 90 minutes.

A map of the bus system is on the flip side of every métro map, in all métro stations, and at all bus stops. Maps are also found in each bus. A recorded message announces the name of the next stop. To get off, press one of the red buttons mounted on the silver poles that run the length of the bus, and the *arrêt demandé* (stop requested) light directly behind the driver will light up. Use the rear door to exit.

The Balabus, an orange-and-white public bus that runs on Sunday and holidays between mid-April and September, gives an interesting 50-minute tour around the major sights. You can use your Paris-Visite or Mobilis pass *(⇨ by Métro)*, or one to three bus tickets, depending on how far you ride. The route runs from La Défense to the Gare de Lyon.

The RATP has also introduced aboveground tram lines: two (T-1 and T-2) operate in the suburbs, and the new T-3 tram, which connects the 13$^e$, 14$^e$, and 15$^e$ arrondissements, running from the Porte d'Ivry (Chinatown) to the Parc Montsouris, Porte d'Orléans, and the Paris Expo–Porte de Versailles. Trams take the same tickets as buses and the métro, with one ticket good for the entire line.

Regular buses accept métro tickets. Your best bet is to buy a *carnet* of 10 tickets for €11.60 at any métro station, or you can buy a single ticket on board (exact change appreciated) for €1.70. If you have individual tickets, you should be prepared to punch your ticket in the red-and-gray machines at the entrance of the bus. You need to show (but not punch) Paris-Visite/Mobilis tickets to the driver. Tickets can be bought on buses, in the métro, or in any bar–tabac store displaying the lime-green métro symbol above its street sign.

Most routes operate from 7 AM to 8:30 PM; some continue to midnight. After midnight you must either take the métro or one of the 35 Noctilien lines (indicated by a separate signal at bus stops). These bus lines operate every 10–60 minutes (12:30 AM–5:30 AM) between Châtelet, major train stations, and various nearby suburbs; they can be stopped by hailing them at any point on their route. The Noctilien uses the same tickets as the métro and regular bus.

**Bus Information** Euroline**s** (☎ 08-92-89-90-91 in France, 08705-808080 in U.K. ⊕ www.eurolines.fr or www.eurolines-pass.com). Noctilien (⊕ www.noctilien.fr). RATP (☎ 08-92-68-77-14 €0.35 per min ⊕ www.ratp.com).

# ▌ BY CAR

We can't say it too many times: unless you have a special, compelling reason, do yourself a favor and **avoid driving in Paris.** But if you've decided to do it anyway, there are some things to know. France's roads are classified into five types; they are numbered and have letter prefixes: A (*autoroute*, expressways), N (*route nationale*), D (*route départmentale*), and the smaller C or V. There are excellent links between Paris and most French cities. When trying to get around Ile-de-France, it's often difficult to avoid Paris—just try to steer clear of rush hours (7–9:30 and 4:30–7:30). A *péage* (toll) must be paid on most expressways outside Ile-de-France: the rate varies but can be steep. Certain booths allow you to pay with a credit card.

The major ring road encircling Paris is called the *périphérique*, with the *périphérique intérieur* going counterclockwise

around the city, and the *périphérique extérieur,* or the outside ring, going clockwise. Up to five lanes wide, the périphérique is a major highway from which *portes* (gates) connect Paris to the major highways of France. The names of these highways function on the same principle as the métro, with the final destination as the determining point in the direction you must take.

Heading north, look for Porte de la Chapelle (direction Lille and Charles de Gaulle Airport); east, for Porte de Bagnolet (direction Metz and Nancy); south, for Porte d'Orléans (direction Lyon and Bordeaux); and west, for Porte d'Auteuil (direction Rouen and Chartres) or Porte de St-Cloud.

### GASOLINE

There are gas stations throughout the city, but they can be difficult to spot; you can often find them in the underground tunnels that cross the city and in larger parking garages. Gas is expensive and prices vary enormously, ranging from about €1.35 to €1.70 per liter. If you're on your way out of Paris, save money by waiting until you've left the city to fill up. All gas stations accept credit cards.

### PARKING

Finding parking in Paris is tough. Both meters and parking-ticket machines use parking cards (*cartes de stationnements*), which you can purchase at any café posting the red TABAC sign; they're sold in two denominations: €10 and €30. Parking in the capital runs €2.10 per hour. Insert your card into the nearest meter, choose the approximate amount of time you expect to stay, and receive a green receipt. Place it on the dashboard on the passenger side; make sure the receipt's clearly visible to the meter patrol. Parking tickets are expensive, and there's no shortage of blue-uniformed parking police. Parking lots, indicated by a blue sign with a white P, are usually underground and are generally expensive (charging €1.20 to €3 per hour, or €9 to €23 per day). One bright spot: you can park for free on Sunday, national holidays, and in certain residential areas in August. Parking meters with yellow circles indicate the free parking zone during August.

## ROAD CONDITIONS

Chaotic traffic is a way of life in Paris. Some streets in the city center can seem impossibly narrow; street signs are often hard to spot; jaded city drivers often make erratic, last-minute maneuvers without signaling; and motorcycles often weave around traffic. Priority is given to drivers coming from the right, so watch for drivers barreling out of small streets on your right. Traffic lights are placed to the left and right of crosswalks, not above, so they may be blocked from your view by vehicles ahead of you.

There are a few major roundabouts at the most congested intersections, notably at *L'Étoile* (around the Arc de Triomphe), the Place de la Bastille, and the Place de la Concorde. Watch oncoming cars carefully and stick to the outer lane to make your exit. The *périphériques* (ring roads) are generally easier to use, and the quais that parallel the Seine can be a downright pleasure to drive when there's no traffic. Electronic signs on the périphériques and highways post traffic conditions: *fluide* (clear) or *bouchon* (jammed).

Some important traffic terms and signs to note: *sortie* (exit), *sens unique* (one way), *stationnement interdite* (no parking), *impasse* (dead end). Blue rectangular signs indicate a highway; triangles carry illustrations of a particular traffic hazard; speed limits are indicated in a circle, with the maximum speed circled in red.

## ROADSIDE EMERGENCIES

If your car breaks down on an expressway, pull your car as far off the road as quickly as possible, set your emergency indicators, and, if possible, take the emergency triangle from the car's trunk and put it at least 30 yards behind your car to warn oncoming traffic; then go to a roadside emergency telephone. These phones put you in direct contact with the police,

automatically indicating your exact location, and are available every 3 km (2 mi). If you have a breakdown anywhere else, find the nearest garage or contact the police. There are also 24-hour assistance hotlines valid throughout France (available through rental agencies and supplied to you when you rent the car), but do not hesitate to call the police in case of any roadside emergency, for they are quick and reliable and the phone call is free.

**Emergency Services Police** (☎ 17).

## RULES OF THE ROAD

You must always carry vehicle registration documents and your personal identification. The French police are entitled to stop you at will to verify your ID and your car—such spot checks are frequent, especially at peak holiday times. In France you drive on the right and give priority to drivers coming from the right (this rule is called *priorité à droite*).

The driver and all passengers in vehicle must wear seat belts, and children under 12 may not travel in the front seat. Children under 10 need to be in a car seat or specific child-restraining device, always in the back seat. Speed limits are designated by the type of road you're driving on: 130 KPH (80 mph) on expressways (*autoroutes*), 110 kph (70 mph) on divided highways (*routes nationales*), 90 KPH (55 MPH) on other roads (*routes*), 50 kph (30 mph) in cities and towns (*villes et villages*). These limits are reduced by 10 kph (6 mph) in rainy, snowy, and foggy conditions. Drivers are expected to know these limits, so signs are generally posted only when there are exceptions to these rules. Right-hand turns are not allowed on a red light.

The use of handheld cellular phones while driving is forbidden; the penalty is a €60 fine. Alcohol laws have become quite tough—a 0.05% blood alcohol limit (a lower limit than in the United States).

# ▮ BY MÉTRO

Taking the métro is the most efficient way to get around Paris. Métro stations are recognizable either by a large yellow *M* within a circle or by the distinctive curly green Art Nouveau railings and archway bearing the full title (Métropolitain). *See the Métro map on the inside back cover of this book.*

Fourteen métro and five RER (Réseau Express Régional, or the Regional Express Network) lines crisscross Paris and the suburbs, and you are seldom more than 500 yards from the nearest station. The métro network connects at several points in Paris with the RER, the commuter trains that go from the city center to the suburbs. RER trains crossing Paris on their way from suburb to suburb can be great time-savers, because they make only a few stops in the city (you can use the same tickets for the métro and the RER within Paris).

It's essential to know the name of the last station on the line you take, as this name appears on all signs. A connection (you can make as many as you like on one ticket) is called a *correspondance*. At junction stations, illuminated orange signs bearing the name of the line terminus appear over the correct corridors for each correspondance. Illuminated blue signs marked *sortie* indicate the station exit. Note that tickets are valid only inside the gates, or *limites*.

Access to métro and RER platforms is through an automatic ticket barrier. Slide your ticket in and pick it up as it pops out. **Keep your ticket during your journey;** you'll need it to leave the RER system and in case you run into any green-clad ticket inspectors, who will impose a hefty fine if you can't produce your ticket.

Métro service starts at 5:30 AM and continues until 1 AM Sunday through Thursday, and until 2 AM on Friday and Saturday, when the last train on each line reaches its terminus. Some lines and stations in Paris are a bit risky at night, in particular lines 2 and 13, and the mazelike stations at Les Halles and République. But in general, the métro is relatively safe throughout, providing you don't travel alone late at night or walk around with your wallet hanging out of your back pocket.

| TICKET/ PASS | PRICE |
|---|---|
| Single Fare | €1.60 (€1.70 if purchased on bus) |
| Daily Mobilis Pass | €5.90 |
| Paris Visit One-Day Pass | €8.80 |
| 10-Ticket Carnet | €11.60 |
| Paris Visit Two-Day Pass | €14.40 |
| Paris Visit Three-Day Pass | €19.60 |
| Paris Visit Five-Day Pass | €28.30 |
| Pass Navigo Découverte Weekly | €17.20 |
| Pass Navigo Découverte Monthly | €56.60 |

All métro tickets and passes are valid not only for the métro but also for all RER, tram, and bus travel within Paris. Métro tickets cost €1.60 each; a *carnet* (10 tickets for €11.60) is a better value. The *Carte Navigo* replaced the weekly Carte Orange in March 2008. Receive a Pass Navigo Découverte at any ticket window for €5 plus the subscription for weekly (€17.20, valid Monday–Sunday) or monthly (€56.60, beginning the first of the month) service. Be sure to immediately attach a passport-size photo and sign your name. This magnetic swipe card allows you to zoom through the turnstiles and can be kept for years; just recharge it at any purple kiosk in the métro stations. Visitors can also purchase the one-day (Mobilis) and two- to five-day (Paris-Visite) tickets for unlimited travel on the entire RATP (Paris transit authority) network: métro, RER, bus, tram, funicular (Montmartre), and Noctilien (night bus). The Mobilis and Paris-Visite passes are valid starting any day of the week. Paris-Visite also gives you discounts on a few museums and attractions, too. Mobilis tickets cost €5.90. Paris-Visite is €8.80 (one day), €14.40 (two days), €19.60 (three days), and €28.30 (five days) for Paris only.

**Métro Information.** Any RATP window in the métro sells tickets and provides maps, but if you're looking to purchase RATP souvenirs, you can find them at the main office near the Gare de Lyon. **RATP** (⊠ *54 quai de la Rapée, 12ᵉ* ⊕ *www.ratp.fr*), open daily 9–5.

## ∎ BY TAXI

Taxi rates are based on location and time. Daytime rates, denoted A (7 AM–7 PM), within Paris are €0.89 per kilometer (½ mi), and nighttime rates, B, are €1.14 per kilometer. Suburban zones and airports, C, are €1.38 per kilometer. There's a basic hire charge of €2.20 for all rides, a €1 supplement per piece of luggage, and a €0.70 supplement if you're picked up at an SNCF (the French rail system) station. Waiting time is charged at €27.90 per hour. The easiest way to get a taxi is to ask your hotel or a restaurant to call one for you, or go to the nearest taxi stand (you can find one every couple of blocks)—they're marked by a square, dark blue sign with a white T in the middle. ∎TIP→ **People waiting for cabs often form a line but will jump at any available taxi; be firm and don't let people cut in front of you.** A taxi is available when the entire sign is lighted up, and taken when just the little bulb at the bottom of the sign is lighted. They'll accept a fourth passenger for an average supplement of €2.95. It's customary to tip the driver about 10% (⇨ *Tipping*).

**Taxi Companies Airport Taxi** (☎ *0825–560–320*). **Taxis Bleus** (☎ *0891–70–10–10*). **Taxi G7** (☎ *01–47–39–47–39*).

## ∎ BY TRAIN

The SNCF, France's rail system, is fast, punctual, comfortable, and comprehensive. There are various options: local trains, overnight trains with sleeping accommodations, and the high-speed TGV, or Trains à Grande Vitesse (averaging 255 kph [160 mph] on the Lyon/southeast line and 300 kph [190 mph] on the Lille and Bordeaux/southwest lines).

The TGVs, the fastest way to get around the country, operate between Paris and Lille/Calais, Paris and Lyon/Switzerland/Provence, Paris and Angers/Nantes, Paris and Tours/Poitiers/Bordeaux, Paris and Brussels, and Paris and Amsterdam. As with other mainline trains, a small supplement may be assessed at peak hours.

Paris has six international rail stations: Gare du Nord (northern France, northern Europe, and England via Calais or Boulogne); Gare St-Lazare (Normandy, England via Dieppe); Gare de l'Est (Strasbourg, Luxembourg, Basel, and central Europe); Gare de Lyon (Lyon, Marseille, Provence, Geneva, Italy); Gare d'Austerlitz (Loire Valley, southwest France, Spain); and Gare Montparnasse (Brittany, Aquitaine, TGV-Atlantique service to the west and south of France, Spain). Until 2005 there were smoking and no-smoking cars on the trains, including the TGVs, but smoking is now prohibited on all trains in France.

There are two classes of train service in France: *première* (first class) or *deuxième* (second). First-class seats have 50% more legroom and nicer upholstery than those in second class, and the first-class cars tend to be quieter. First-class seats on the TGV have computer connections. First-class fares are nearly twice as much as those for second-class seats.

Fares are cheaper if you avoid traveling at peak times (around holidays and weekends), purchase tickets at least 15 days in advance (look for the *billet Prem's*), or find your destination among the last-minute offers online every Tuesday.

You can call for train information or reserve tickets in any Paris station, irrespective of destination, and you can access the multilingual computerized schedule information network at any Paris station. You can also make reservations and buy your ticket while at the computer. Go to the Grandes Lignes counter for travel within France and to the Billets Internationaux desk if you're heading out of the country. Note that calling the SNCF's 08 number costs €0.35 per minute; to save this cost, go to the nearest station and make the reservations in person or visit the SNCF Web site, ⊕ *www.sncf.fr*.

If you plan to travel outside Paris by train, consider purchasing a France Rail Pass, which allows three days of unlimited train travel in a one-month period. If you travel solo, first class will run you $305 and second class is $261; you can add up to six days on this pass for $46 a day for first class, $39 a day for second class. For two people traveling together on a Saver Pass, the first-class cost is $259, and in second class it's $224; additional days (up to six) cost $40 each for first class, $33 each for second class. Other options include the France Rail 'n Drive Pass (combining rail and rental car).

France is one of 17 countries in which you can use EurailPasses, which provide unlimited first-class rail travel in all the participating countries for the duration of the pass. If you plan to rack up the miles, get a standard pass. These are available for 15 days ($767), 21 days ($994), one month ($1,235), two months ($1,744), and three months ($2,151). If your travels will be more limited, the Eurail Selectpass gives you first-class travel over a two-month period in three to five bordering countries in 22 Eurail network countries. The Selectpass starts at $484 for five days of travel within three countries. Another option is the Regional Pass, which covers rail travel in and between pairs of bordering countries over a two-month period. Unlike most Eurail passes, Regional Passes are available for first- or second-class travel. Costs begin at $371 (first class) and $296 (second class) for four days of travel; up to six extra days can be purchased.

In addition to standard EurailPasses, there are the Eurail Youthpass (for those under age 26, with second-class travel), the Eurail Saver Pass (which gives a discount for two or more people traveling together), the Eurail Flexipass (which allows a certain number of travel days within a set period), and the Euraildrive Pass (train and rental car). ■TIP→ Remember that you must purchase your Eurail passes at home before leaving for France. You can purchase Eurail passes through the Eurail Web site as well as through travel agents.

Another option is to purchase one of the discount rail passes available for sale only in France from SNCF.

When traveling together, two people (who don't have to be a couple) can save money with the Prix Découverte à Deux. You'll get a 25% discount during *périodes bleus* (blue periods: weekdays and periods not on or near any holidays). Note that you have to be with the person you said you would be traveling with.

Reduced fares are available if you're a senior citizen (over 60), for children under 12, and up to four accompanying adults, and if you're under 26.

If you purchase an individual ticket from SNCF in France and you're under 26, you automatically get a 25% reduction (a valid ID such as an ISIC card or your passport is necessary). If you're going to be using the train quite a bit during your stay in France and if you're under 26, consider buying the Carte 12–25 (€49), which offers unlimited 50% reductions for one year (provided that there's space available at that price; otherwise you'll just get the standard 25% discount).

If you don't benefit from any of these reductions and you plan on traveling at least 200 km (132 mi) round-trip and don't mind staying over a Saturday night, look into the Prix Découverte Séjour. This ticket gives you a 25% reduction.

■ TIP➜ A rail pass does not guarantee you a seat on the train you wish to ride. You need to book seats ahead even if you have a pass.

Seat reservations are required on TGVs and are a good idea on trains that may be crowded—particularly in summer and during holidays on popular routes. You also need a reservation for sleeping accommodations.

## THE CHANNEL TUNNEL

Short of flying, taking the Channel Tunnel is the fastest way to cross the English Channel: 35 minutes from Folkestone to Calais, 60 minutes from motorway to motorway, or 2 hours and 15 minutes from London's St. Pancras Station to Paris's Gare du Nord. The Belgian border is just a short drive northeast of Calais. High-speed Eurostar trains use the same tunnels to connect London's St. Pancras Station directly with Midi Station in Brussels in around 2 hours.

There's a vast range of prices for Eurostar—round-trip tickets range from €450 for first class (with access to the Philippe Starck–designed Première Class lounge) to €78 for second class, depending on when you travel. It's a good idea to make a reservation if you're traveling with your car on a Chunnel train; cars without reservations, if they can get on at all, are charged 20% extra.

British Rail also has four daily departures from London's Victoria Station, all linking with the Dover–Calais/Boulogne ferry services through to Paris. There's also an overnight service on the Newhaven–Dieppe ferry. Journey time is about eight hours. Credit-card bookings are accepted by phone or in person at a British Rail Travel Centre.

**Information Rail Europe** (☏ 800/622–8600 in U.S. ⊕ www.raileurope.com). **SNCF** (✉ 88 rue St-Lazare, Paris ☏ 08–92–35–35–35 €0.35 per min ⊕ www.Voyages-sncf.fr).

**Channel Tunnel Car Transport Eurotunnel** (☏ 0870/535–3535 in U.K., 0810/630304 in France ⊕ www.eurotunnel.com). **French Motorail/Rail Europe** (☏ 08448/484–051 ⊕ www. raileurope.co.uk/frenchmotorail).

**Channel Tunnel Passenger Service BritRail Travel** (☏ 866/274–8724 in U.S. ⊕ www. britrail.com).

**Eurostar** (☏ 08–92–35–35–39 in France, 0870/518–6186, in U.K. ⊕ www.eurostar. co.uk). **Rail Europe** (☏ 888/382–7245 in U.S., 0870/584–8848 in U.K. inquiries and credit-card bookings ⊕ www.raileurope.com).

# ESSENTIALS

## ■ COMMUNICATIONS

### INTERNET

If you use a major Internet provider, getting online in Paris shouldn't be difficult. Call your Internet provider to get the local access number in Paris. Many hotels have business services with Internet access, in-room modem lines, or high-speed wireless access. ■TIP➜ You will, however, need an adapter for your computer for the European-style plugs. If you're traveling with a laptop, carry a spare battery and adapter. Never plug your computer into any socket before asking about surge protection. A few of the more conveniently located Internet cafés are listed below.

Cybercafes La Baguenaude (✉ 30 rue Grande-Truanderie, 1ᵉʳ, Beaubourg/Les Halles ☎ 01-40-26-27-74 ⊕ pagesperso-orange. fr/baguenaude.cafe/). Cybersquare (✉ 1 pl. République, 3ᵉ, République ☎ 01-48-87-82-36 ⊕ www.cybersquare-paris.com). Milk (✉ 53 rue de la Harpe, 5ᵉ, Quartier Latin ☎ 01-44-07-38-89 ⊕ www.milklub.com). Sputnik (✉ 14 rue Butte-aux-Cailles, 13ᵉ, Les Gobelins ☎ 01-45-65-19-82).

### PHONES

The good news is that you can now make a direct-dial telephone call from virtually any point on earth. The bad news? You can't always do so cheaply. Calling from a hotel is almost always the most expensive option; hotels usually add huge surcharges to all calls, particularly international ones. In some countries you can phone from call centers or even the post office. Calling cards usually keep costs low, but only if you buy them locally. And then there are mobile phones (⇨ *below*), which are sometimes more prevalent than landlines; as expensive as mobile phone calls can be, they are still usually a much cheaper option than calling from your hotel.

The country code for France is 33. The first two digits of French numbers are a prefix determined by zone: Paris and Ile-de-France, 01; the northwest, 02; the northeast, 03; the southeast, 04; and the southwest, 05. Pay close attention to numbers beginning with 08. Calls that begin with 08 followed by 00 are toll-free, but calls that begin with 08 followed by 36—like the information lines for the SNCF, for example—cost €0.35 per minute. Numbers that begin with 06 are reserved for cell phones.

Note that when dialing France from abroad, you should drop the initial 0 from the telephone number (all numbers listed in this book include the initial 0, which is used for calling *from within* France). To call a number in Paris from the United States, dial 011–33 plus the phone number, but minus the initial 0 listed for the specific number in Paris. In other words, the local number for the Louvre is 01–40–20–51–51. To call this number from New York City, dial 011–33–1–40–20–51–51. To call this number from within Paris, dial 01–40–20–51–51. To call France from the United Kingdom, dial 00–33, then dial the number in France minus the initial 0 of the specific number.

### CALLING CARDS

French pay phones are operated by *télécartes* (phone cards), which you can buy from post offices, tabacs, magazine kiosks, and any métro station. The ones you insert into pay phones have a "puce" microchip—a small copper square—that you can see on the card. There are as many phone cards these days as bakeries, so to be safe, request the *télécarte international,* which, despite its name, allows you to make either local or international calls and offers greatly reduced rates. Instructions are in English, and the cost is €9 for 60 units and €18 for 120 units. You may also request the simple *télécarte,* which allows you to make calls in France (the cost is €8 for 50 units, €15 for 120 units). You can use your credit card in much the same way as a télécarte, but there's a minimum €20 charge. You have 30 days after the first call on your credit card to use the €20 credit.

There are also international calling cards that work on any phone (including your hotel phone) because you dial a free number and punch in a code; these do not have the "puce" microchip. Don't hesitate to invest in one if you plan on making calls from your hotel, as hotels often levy service charges and also have the most expensive rates.

### CALLING OUTSIDE FRANCE

Good news—telephone rates are actually decreasing in France because the France Telecom monopoly now has some stringent competition. As in most countries, the highest rates fall between 8 AM and 7 PM and average out to a hefty €0.22 per minute to the United States, Canada, and the closer European countries, including Germany and Great Britain. Rates are greatly reduced from 7 PM to 8 AM, costing an average of €0.10 per minute.

To make a direct international call out of France, dial 00 and wait for the tone; then dial the country code (1 for the United States and Canada, 44 for the United Kingdom, 61 for Australia, and 64 for New Zealand) and the area code (minus any initial 0) and number.

To call with the help of an operator, dial the toll-free number 08–00–99–00 plus the last two digits of the country code. Dial 08–00–99–00–11 for the United States and Canada, 08–00–99–00–44 for England, and 08–00–99–00–61 for Australia.

**Access Codes AT&T Direct** (☎ 08–00–99–00–11 or 08–00–99–01–11, 800/222–0300 for information). **MCI WorldPhone** (☎ 08–00–99–00–19, 800/444–4444 for information). **Sprint International Access** (☎ 08–00–99–00–87, 800/793–1153 for information).

### CALLING WITHIN FRANCE

For telephone information in France, you need to call one of the dozen or so six-digit *renseignement* numbers that begin with 118. Some of the better-known ones

are 118–008 for the Pages Jaunes, or 118–711 for France Telecom. The number 118–247 is a bilingual option, run in partnership with the Paris tourism office. The average price for one of these calls is about €1.

Since all local numbers in Paris and the Ile-de-France begin with a 01, you must dial the full 10-digit number, including the initial 0. A local call costs €0.15 for every three minutes.

To call from region to region within France, dial the full 10-digit number, including the initial 0.

Public telephone booths can almost always be found in post offices, métro stations, bus stops, and in some cafés, as well as on the street.

### MOBILE PHONES

If you have a multiband phone (some countries use different frequencies than what's used in the United States) and your service provider uses the world-standard GSM network (as do T-Mobile, Cingular, and Verizon), you can probably use your phone abroad. Roaming fees can be steep, however: 99¢ a minute is considered reasonable. And overseas you normally pay the toll charges for incoming calls. It's almost always cheaper to send a text message than to make a call, since text messages have a very low set fee (often less than 5¢).

If you just want to make local calls, consider buying a new SIM card (note that your provider may have to unlock your phone for you to use a different SIM card) and a prepaid service plan in the destination. You'll then have a local number and can make local calls at local rates. If your trip is extensive, you could also simply buy a new cell phone in your destination, as the initial cost will be offset over time.

■TIP➜ If you travel internationally frequently, save one of your old mobile phones or buy a cheap one on the Internet; ask your cell phone company to unlock it for you, and take it with you as a travel phone, buying a

# LOCAL DO'S AND TABOOS

## CUSTOMS OF THE COUNTRY

The French like to look at people—that's half the point of cafés and fashion, so get used to being looked at; it's as natural here as breathing. They'll look at your shoes or your watch, check out what you're wearing or reading. What they will not do is maintain steady eye contact or smile. If a stranger of the opposite sex smiles at you, it's best to do as the French do and return only a blank look before turning away. If you smile back, you might find yourself in a Pepé Le Pew–type situation.

Visitors' exuberance—and accompanying loud voices—may cause discreet Parisians to raise their eyebrows or give a deep chesty sigh. They're not being rude, but they're telling you that they think you are. Be aware of your surroundings and lower your voice accordingly, especially in churches, museums, restaurants, theaters, cinemas, and the métro.

When entering and leaving a shop, greet and say good-bye to the staff. A simple *bonjour, monsieur/madame* and *au revoir, merci* are considered a virtual necessity for politeness. Other basic pleasantries in French include *bonne journée* (have a nice day); *bonne soirée* (have a nice evening); *enchanté* (nice to meet you); *s'il vous plaît* (please); and *je vous en prie* (you're welcome). When asking for directions or other help, be sure to preface your request with a polite phrase such as *excusez-moi de vous déranger, madame/monsieur* (excuse me for bothering you, ma'am/sir).

## GREETINGS

When meeting someone for the first time, whether in a social or a professional setting, it's appropriate to shake hands. Other than that, the French like to kiss. For the Parisians, it's two *bisous*, which are more like air kisses with your cheeks touching lightly—don't actually smack your lips onto the person's face!

## OUT ON THE TOWN

When visiting a French home, don't expect to be invited into the kitchen or to take a house tour. The French have a very definite sense of personal space, and you'll be escorted to what are considered the guest areas. If you're invited to dinner, be sure to bring a gift, such as wine, flowers, or chocolates.

Table manners are often considered a litmus test of your character or upbringing. When dining out, note that the French fill wineglasses only until half full—it's considered bad manners to fill it to the brim. They never serve themselves before serving the rest of the table. During a meal, keep both hands above the table, and keep your elbows off the table. Bread is broken, never cut, and is placed next to the plate, never on the plate. When slicing a cheese, don't cut off the point (or "nose"). Coffee or tea is ordered after dessert, not with dessert. (In fact, coffee and tea usually aren't ordered with any courses during meals, except breakfast.) Eating on the street is generally frowned on—though with the onslaught of Starbucks you can sometimes see people drinking coffee on the go.

## LANGUAGE

One of the best ways to avoid being an Ugly American is to learn a bit of the local language.

The French may appear prickly at first to English-speaking visitors, but it usually helps if you make an effort to speak a little French. A simple, friendly *bonjour* (hello) will do, as will asking if the person you're greeting speaks English (*parlez-vous anglais?*). Be patient, and speak English slowly—but *not* loudly. *See the French Vocabulary and Menu Guide at the back of the book.*

A phrase book and language-tape set can help get you started. *Fodor's French for Travelers* (available at bookstores everywhere) is excellent.

new SIM card with pay-as-you-go service in each destination.

Cell phones are called *portables* and most Parisians have one. British standard cell phones work in Paris, but for North Americans only triband phones work. If you'd like to rent a cell phone for your trip, reserve one at least four days before your departure, as most companies will ship it to you before you travel. Cellular Abroad rents cell phones packaged with prepaid SIM cards that give you a French cell-phone number and calling rates. Planetfone rents GSM phones, which can be used in more than 100 countries, but the per-minute rates are expensive.

Contacts **Cellular Abroad** (☎ 800/287–5072 ⊕ www.cellularabroad.com). **Mobal** (☎ 888/888–9162 ⊕ www.mobalrental.com) rents mobiles and sells GSM phones (starting at $49) that will operate in 140 countries. Per-call rates vary throughout the world. **Planet Fone** (☎ 888/988–4777 ⊕ www.planetfone. com).

# ∎ CUSTOMS AND DUTIES

You're always allowed to bring goods of a certain value back home without having to pay any duty or import tax. But there's a limit on the amount of tobacco and liquor you can bring back duty-free, and some countries have separate limits for perfumes; for exact figures, check with your customs department. The values of so-called "duty-free" goods are included in these amounts. When you shop abroad, save all your receipts, as customs inspectors may ask to see them as well as the items you purchased. If the total value of your goods is more than the duty-free limit, you'll have to pay a tax (most often a flat percentage) on the value of everything beyond that limit.

If you're coming from outside the European Union (EU), you may import the following duty-free: (1) 200 cigarettes or 100 cigarillos or 50 cigars or 250 grams of tobacco; (2) 2 liters of wine and, in addition, (a) 1 liter of alcohol over 22% volume (most spirits) or (b) 2 liters of alcohol under 22% volume (fortified or sparkling wine) or (c) 2 more liters of table wine; (3) 50 ml of perfume and 250 ml of toilet water; (4) 200 grams of coffee, 100 grams of tea; and (5) other goods to the value of about €182 (€91 for ages 14 and under).

If you're arriving from an EU country, you may be required to declare all goods and prove that anything over the standard limit is for personal consumption. But there is no limit or customs tariff imposed on goods carried within the EU except on tobacco (800 cigarettes, 200 cigars, 1 kg of tobacco) and alcohol (10 liters of spirits, 90 liters of wine, with a maximum of 60 liters of sparkling wine, 110 liters of beer).

Any amount of euros or foreign currency may be brought into France, but foreign currencies converted into euros may be reconverted into a foreign currency only up to the equivalent of €769.

Information in Paris **Direction des Douanes** (☎ 01–40–40–39–00 ⊕ www.douane.gouv.fr).

U.S. Information **U.S. Customs and Border Protection** (⊕ www.cbp.gov).

# ∎ ELECTRICITY

The electrical current in Paris is 220 volts, 50 cycles alternating current (AC); wall outlets take Continental-type plugs, with two round prongs.

Consider making a small investment in a universal adapter, which has several types of plugs in one lightweight, compact unit. Most laptops and mobile phone chargers are dual voltage (i.e., they operate equally well on 110 and 220 volts), so require only an adapter. These days the same is true of small appliances such as hair dryers. Always check labels and manufacturer instructions to be sure. Don't use 110-volt outlets marked FOR SHAVERS ONLY for high-wattage appliances such as hair dryers.

# ▌ EMERGENCIES

The French National Health Care system has been organized to provide fully equipped, fully staffed hospitals within 30 minutes of every resident in Paris. A sign of a white cross in a blue box appears on all hospitals. This book does not list the major Paris hospitals, as the French government prefers an emergency operator to assign you the best and most convenient option for your emergency. Note that if you're able to walk into a hospital emergency room by yourself, you are often considered "low priority," and the wait can be interminable. So if time is of the essence, it's best to call the fire department (☎ 18); a fully trained team of paramedics will usually arrive within five minutes. You may also dial for a Samu ambulance (☎ 15); there's usually an English-speaking physician available who will help you assess the situation and either dispatch an ambulance immediately or advise you about your best course of action. Be sure to check with your insurance company before your trip to verify that you are covered for medical care in other countries.

In a less urgent situation, do what the French do and call SOS Doctor or SOS Dental services; like magic, in less than an hour a certified, experienced doctor or dentist arrives at the door, armed with an old leather doctor case filled with the essentials for diagnosis and treatment (at an average cost of €65). The doctor or dentist may or may not be bilingual but, at worst, will have a rudimentary understanding of English. This is a very helpful 24-hour service to use for common symptoms of benign illnesses that need to be treated quickly for comfort, such as high fever, toothache, or upset stomachs (which seem to have the unfortunate habit of announcing themselves late at night).

The American Hospital and the Hertford British Hospital both have 24-hour emergency hotlines with bilingual doctors and nurses who can provide advice. For small problems go to a pharmacy, marked by a green neon cross. Pharmacists are authorized to administer first aid and recommend over-the-counter drugs, and they can be very helpful in advising you in English or sending you to the nearest English-speaking pharmacist.

Call the police (☎ 17) if there has been a crime or an act of violence. On the street, some French phrases that may be needed in an emergency are *Au secours!* (Help!), *urgence* (emergency), *samu* (ambulance), *pompiers* (firemen), *poste de station* (police station), *médecin* (doctor), and *hôpital* (hospital).

A hotline of note is SOS Help for English-language crisis information, open daily 3 PM–11 PM.

**Doctor and Dentist Referrals** SOS Dentiste (☎ 01–43–37–51–00). SOS Médecin (☎ 01–47–07–77–77).

**Foreign Embassies** U.S. Embassy Consular Section ✉ 4 av. Gabriel, 8ᵉ, Paris ☎ 01–43–12–22–22, appointments required (online form) except for lost/stolen passports and emergencies Ⓜ Concorde.

**General Emergency Contacts** Ambulance (☎ 15). Fire Department (☎ 18). Police (☎ 17). These numbers are toll-free and can be dialed from any phone.

**Hospitals and Clinics** The American Hospital (✉ 63 bd. Victor-Hugo, Neuilly ☎ 01–46–41–25–25). The Hertford British Hospital (✉ 3 rue Barbès, Levallois-Perret ☎ 01–46–39–22–22).

**Hotline** SOS Help (☎ 01–46–21–46–46).

**Pharmacies** Dhéry (✉ Galerie des Champs, 84 av. des Champs-Élysées, 8ᵉ ☎ 01–45–62–02–41) is open 24 hours. Pharmacie des Arts (✉ 106 bd. Montparnasse, 14ᵉ ☎ 01–43–35–44–88) is open daily until midnight. Pharmacie Internationale (✉ 5 pl. Pigalle, 9ᵉ ☎ 01–48–78–38–12) is open Monday–Saturday until midnight. Pharmacie Matignon (✉ 2 rue Jean-Mermoz, at Rond-Point de Champs-Élysées, 8ᵉ ☎ 01–45–62–79–16) is open daily until 2 AM.

# ∎ HOLIDAYS

With 11 national holidays (*jours fer-iés*) and five weeks of paid vacation, the French have their share of repose. In May there's a holiday nearly every week, so be prepared for stores, banks, and museums to shut their doors for days at a time. If a holiday falls on a Tuesday or Thursday, many businesses *font le pont* (make the bridge) and close on that Monday or Friday as well. Some exchange booths in tourist areas, small grocery stores, restaurants, cafés, and bakeries usually remain open. Bastille Day (July 14) is observed in true French form. Celebrations begin on the evening of the 13th, when city fire fighters open the doors to their stations, often classed as historical monuments, to host their much-acclaimed all-night balls and finish the next day with the annual military parade and air show.

Note that these dates are for the calendar year 2011: January 1 (New Year's Day); April 24–25 (Easter Sunday/Monday); May 1 (Labor Day and Ascension); May 8 (VE Day); June 12 (Pentecost Sunday); July 14 (Bastille Day); August 15 (Assumption); November 1 (All Saints' Day); November 11 (Armistice); December 25 (Christmas).

# ∎ HOURS OF OPERATION

On weekdays banks are open generally 9–5 (note that the Banque de France closes at 3:30), and some banks are also open Saturday 9–5. In general, government offices and businesses are open 9–5. *See Mail, below, for post office hours.*

Most museums are closed one day a week—usually Monday or Tuesday—and on national holidays. Generally, museums and national monuments are open from 10 to 5 or 6. A few close for lunch (noon–2) and are open only in the afternoon on Sunday. Many of the large museums have one *nocturne* (nighttime) opening per week, when they are open until 9:30 or 10. Pharmacies are generally open Monday–Saturday 8:30–8. Nearby pharmacies

that stay open late, for 24 hours, or Sunday, are listed on the door.

Generally, large shops are open from 9:30 or 10 to 7 or 8 Monday to Saturday and remain open through lunchtime. Many of the large department stores stay open until 10 on Wednesday or Thursday, and new laws passed in 2009 allow them to open on Sunday. Smaller shops and many supermarkets often open earlier (8 AM) but take a lengthy lunch break (1–3) and generally close around 8 PM; small food shops are often open Sunday morning 9–1. There is typically a small corner grocery store that stays open late, usually until 11, if you're in a bind for basic necessities like diapers, bread, cheese, and fruit. Note that prices are substantially higher in such outlets than in the larger supermarkets. Not all shops stay open on Sunday, except in Le Marais, where shops that stand side by side on Rue des Francs Bourgeois, from antiques dealers to chic little designers, open their doors to welcome hordes of Sunday browsers. The Bastille, the Quartier Latin, the Champs-Élysées, Ile St-Louis, and the Ile de la Cité also have shops that open Sunday.

# ∎ MAIL

Post offices, or PTT, are scattered throughout every arrondissement and are recognizable by a yellow LA POSTE sign. They're usually open weekdays 8–7, Saturday 8–noon. Airmail letters or postcards usually take at least five days to reach North America. When shipping home antiques or art, request assistance from the dealer, who can usually handle the customs paperwork for you or recommend a licensed shipping company.

Airmail letters and postcards to the United States and Canada cost €0.85 for 20 grams, €1.70 for 50 grams, and €2.30 for 100 grams. Stamps can be bought in post offices and cafés displaying a red TABAC sign.

If you're uncertain where you'll be staying, have mail sent to American Express (if you're a card member) or to "poste restante" at any post office.

**Main Branches Main office** (✉ *52 rue du Louvre, 1ᵉʳ*), open 24 hours, 7 days a week. **Champs-Élysées office** (✉ *10 rue Balzar, 8ᵉ*), Monday to Saturday, open until 7 PM.

### SHIPPING PACKAGES

Sending overnight mail from Paris is relatively easy. Besides DHL, Federal Express, and UPS, the French post office has an overnight mail service called Chronopost that has special prepaid boxes for international use (and also boxes specifically made to mail wine). All agencies listed can be used as drop-off points, and all have information in English.

**Express Services DHL** (✉ *6 rue des Colonnes, 2ᵉ* ☎ *08–20–20–25–25* ⊕ *www.dhl.com* ✉ *59 av. Iéna, 16ᵉ* ☎ *08–20–20–25–25*). **Federal Express** (✉ *63 bd. Haussmann, 8ᵉ* ☎ *01–40–06–90–16* ⊕ *www.fedex.com/fr*). **UPS** (✉ *34 bd. Malesherbes, 8ᵉ* ☎ *08–21–23–38–77* ✉ *107 rue Réaumur, 2ᵉ* ☎ *08–00–87–78–77* ⊕ *www.ups.com*).

## ▌ MONEY

Although a stay in Paris is far from cheap, you can find plenty of affordable places to eat and shop, particularly if you avoid the obvious tourist traps. Prices tend to reflect the standing of an area in the eyes of Parisians; the touristy area where value is most difficult to find is the 8ᵉ arrondissement, on and around the Champs-Élysées. Places where you can generally be certain to shop, eat, and stay without overpaying include the St-Michel/Sorbonne area on the Rive Gauche; the mazelike streets around Les Halles and Le Marais in central Paris; in Montparnasse south of the boulevard; and in the Bastille, République, and Belleville areas of eastern Paris.

In cafés, bars, and some restaurants you can save money by eating or drinking at the counter instead of sitting at a table. Two prices are listed—*au comptoir* (at the counter) and *à salle* (at a table)—and sometimes a third for the terrace. A cup of coffee, standing at a bar, costs from €1.50; if you sit, it will cost €2 to €7. A glass of beer costs from €2 standing and from €2.50 to €7 sitting; a soft drink costs between €2 and €5. A ham sandwich will cost between €3 and €6.

Expect to pay €7–€10 for a short taxi ride. Museum entry is usually between €4 and €11.50, though there are hours or days of the week when admission is reduced or free.

Prices throughout this guide are given for adults. Substantially reduced fees are almost always available for children, students, and senior citizens.

### ATMS AND BANKS

Your own bank will probably charge a fee for using ATMs abroad; the foreign bank you use may also charge a fee. Nevertheless, you can usually get a better exchange rate at an ATM than at a currency-exchange office. And extracting funds as you need them is a safer option than carrying around a large amount of cash.

ATMs are one of the easiest ways to get euros. Although transaction fees may be higher abroad than at home, banks usually offer excellent wholesale exchange rates through ATMs. You may, however, have to look around for Cirrus and Plus locations; it's a good idea to get a list of locations from your bank before you go. Note, too, that you may have better luck with ATMs if you're using a credit card or debit card that is also a Visa or MasterCard rather than just your bank card.

▌TIP➔ To get cash at ATMs in Paris, your PIN must be four digits long. If yours has five or more, remember to change it before you leave. If you're having trouble remembering your PIN, do not try more than twice, because at the third attempt the machine will eat your card, and you will have to go back the next morning to retrieve it.

## CREDIT CARDS

Throughout this guide, the following abbreviations are used: **AE**, American Express; **DC**, Diners Club; **MC**, MasterCard; and **V**, Visa.

It's a good idea to inform your credit-card company before you travel, especially if you're going abroad and don't travel internationally very often. Otherwise, the credit-card company might put a hold on your card owing to unusual activity—not a good thing halfway through your trip. Record all your credit-card numbers— as well as the phone numbers to call if your cards are lost or stolen—in a safe place, so you're prepared should something go wrong. Both MasterCard and Visa have general numbers you can call (collect if you're abroad) if your card is lost, but you're better off calling the number of your issuing bank, since MasterCard and Visa usually just transfer you to your bank; your bank's number is usually printed on your card.

If you plan to use your credit card for cash advances, you'll need to apply for a PIN at least two weeks before your trip. Although it's usually cheaper (and safer) to use a credit card abroad for large purchases (so you can cancel payments or be reimbursed if there's a problem), note that some credit-card companies *and* the banks that issue them add substantial percentages to all foreign transactions, whether they're in a foreign currency or not. Check on these fees before leaving home, so there won't be any surprises when you get the bill.

■TIP➔ Before you charge something, ask the merchant whether he or she plans to do a dynamic currency conversion (DCC). In such a transaction the credit-card *processor* (shop, restaurant, or hotel, not Visa or Mas-terCard) converts the currency and charges you in dollars. In most cases you'll pay the merchant a 3% fee for this service in addition to any credit-card company and issuing-bank foreign-transaction surcharges.

**Reporting Lost Cards American Express** (✆ 800/528-4800 in U.S., 336/393-1111 collect from abroad ⊕ www.americanexpress. com). **Diners Club** (✆ 800/234-6377 in U.S., 0810-314-159 in France ⊕ www.dinersclub. com). **MasterCard** (✆ 800/627-8372 in U.S., 0800-90-1387 in France ⊕ www.mastercard. com). **Visa** (✆ 800/847-2911 in U.S., 0800-90-1179 in France ⊕ www.visa.com).

## CURRENCY AND EXCHANGE

In 2002 the single European Union (EU) currency, the euro, became the official currency of the 12 countries participating in the European Monetary Union (with the notable exceptions of Great Britain, Denmark, and Sweden). The euro system has eight coins: 1 and 2 euros, plus 1, 2, 5, 10, 20, and 50 cents. All coins have one side that has the value of the euro on it, whereas the opposite side is adorned with each country's own unique national symbol. There are seven colorful notes: 5, 10, 20, 50, 100, 200, and 500 euros. Notes have the principal architectural styles from antiquity onward on one side and the map and the flag of Europe on the other and are the same for all countries. Also be aware that because of their high nickel content, euro coins can pose problems for people with an allergic sensitivity to the metal.

If you've brought some rumpled francs from home this trip, you can still exchange them. You have until midnight February 17, 2012, to change notes at the Banque de France. A fixed rate of exchange was established: 1 euro equaling 6.55957 French francs. After this date, however, you may as well frame those remaining francs and hang them on the wall for posterity, not prosperity.

At this writing, 1 euro equaled approximately US$1.48 and 1.59 Canadian dollars.

The easiest way to get euros is through ATMs; you can find them in airports, train stations, and throughout the city. ATM rates are excellent because they are based on wholesale rates offered only by major banks. ■TIP→ It's a good idea to bring some euros with you from home so you don't have to wait in line at the airport. At exchange booths always confirm the rate with the teller before exchanging money. You won't do as well at exchange booths in airports or rail and bus stations, in hotels, in restaurants, or in stores. French banks only exchange the money of their own clients.

## ▌PACKING

You'll notice it right away: in Paris the women dress well to go shopping, to go to the cinema, to have a drink; the men look good when they're fixing their cars. The Parisians still wear hats to the races and well-cut clothes for fine meals; you will not see them in sweats unless they're doing something *sportif*. So, don't wear shorts, sweats, or sneakers if you want to blend in. Good food in good settings deserves good clothing—not necessarily a suit and tie, but a long-sleeved shirt and pants for him, something nice for her. Trendy nightclubs usually refuse entrance to men who are wearing sandals.

Be sure to bring rain gear, a comfortable pair of walking shoes, and a sweater or shawl for cool churches and museums. You can never tell about the weather, so a small, foldable umbrella is a good idea. If you'd like to scrutinize the stained glass in churches, bring a pair of small binoculars. A small package of tissues is always a good idea for the occasional rustic bathroom in cafés, airports, and train stations. An additional note: if you're the kind of person who likes a washcloth in the bathroom, bring your own; they're not something you'll find in Paris hotels.

## ▌PASSPORTS AND VISAS

All citizens of Canada and the United States, even infants, need only a valid passport to enter France for stays of up to 90 days. If you lose your passport, call the nearest embassy or consulate and the local police immediately.

## ▌RESTROOMS

Use of public toilet facilities in cafés and bars is usually reserved for customers, so you may need to buy a little something first. Bathrooms are often downstairs and are unisex, which may mean walking by a men's urinal to reach the cubicle. Turkish-style toilets—holes in the ground with porcelain pads for your feet—are still found (though they are becoming scarcer). Stand as far away as possible when you press the flushing mechanism to avoid water damage to your shoes. In certain cafés the lights will not come on in the bathroom until the cubicle door is locked. These lights work on a three-minute timer to save electricity. Simply press the button again if the lights go out. Clean public toilets are available in fast-food chains, department stores, and public parks. You can also find free toilet units on the street, in the larger métro stations, town halls, and in all train stations.

There are restroom attendants in train and métro stations and some of the nicer restaurants and clubs, so always bring some coins to the bathroom. Attendants in restaurants and clubs are in charge of cleaning the bathrooms and perhaps handing you a clean towel; slip some small change into the prominently placed saucer.

Find a Loo The Bathroom Diaries (⊕ www. thebathroomdiaries.com) is flush with unsanitized info on restrooms the world over—each one located, reviewed, and rated.

## ▌SAFETY

Paris is one of the safest big cities in the world, but as in any big city be streetwise and alert. Certain neighborhoods are more seedy than dangerous, thanks to the night trade that goes on around Les Halles and St-Denis and on Boulevard Clichy in Pigalle. Some off-the-beaten-path neighborhoods—particularly the outlying suburban communities around Paris—may warrant extra precaution. When in doubt, stick to the boulevards and well-lighted, populated streets, but keep in mind that even the Champs-Élysées is a haven for pickpockets.

The métro is quite safe overall, though some lines and stations, in particular lines 2 and 13, get dodgy late at night. Try not to travel alone late at night, memorize the time of the last métro train to your station, ride in the first car by the conductor, and just use your common sense. If you're worried, spend the money on a taxi. Pickpocketing is the main problem, day or night. Be wary of anyone crowding you unnecessarily or distracting you. Pickpockets often work in groups; on the métro they usually strike just before a stop so that they can leap off the train as it pulls into the station. Be especially careful if taking the RER from Charles de Gaulle/Roissy airport into town; disoriented or jet-lagged travelers are vulnerable to sticky fingers. Pickpockets often target laptop bags, so keep your valuables on your person.

A tremendous number of protest demonstrations are held in Paris—scarcely a week goes by without some kind of march or public gathering. Most protests are peaceful, but it's best to avoid them. The CRS (French riot police) carefully guard all major demonstrations, directing traffic and preventing violence. They are armed and use tear gas when and if they see fit.

Report any thefts or other problems to the police as soon as possible. There are three or four police stations in every arrondissement in Paris and one police station in every train station; go to the police station in the area where the event occurred. In the case of pickpocketing or other theft, the police will give you a Déclaration de Perte ou de Vol (receipt for theft or loss). Police reports must be made in person, but the process is generally quite streamlined. In the case of theft, valuables are usually unrecoverable, but identity documents have been known to resurface. You may need a receipt of theft or loss to replace stolen train or plane tickets, passports, or traveler's checks; the receipts may also be useful for filing insurance claims.

Although women traveling alone sometimes encounter troublesome comments and the like, *dragueurs* (men who persistently profess their undying love to hapless female passersby) are a dying breed in this increasingly politically correct world. Note that smiling automatically out of politeness is not part of French culture and can be quickly misinterpreted. If you encounter a problem, don't be afraid to show your irritation. Completely ignoring the *dragueur* should be discouragement enough; if the hassling doesn't let up, don't hesitate to move quickly away.

■TIP➔ Distribute your cash, credit cards, IDs, and other valuables between a deep front pocket, an inside jacket or vest pocket, and a hidden money pouch. Don't reach for the money pouch once you're in public.

# ■ TAXES

All taxes must be included in affixed prices in France. Prices in restaurants and hotel prices must by law include taxes and service charges. ■TIP➔ If these appear as additional items on your bill, you should complain.

V.A.T. (value-added tax, known in France as TVA) at a standard rate of 19.6% (33% for luxury goods) is included in the price of many goods, but foreigners are often entitled to a refund. To be eligible for V.A.T. refund, the item (or items) that you have purchased must have been bought in a single day in a participating store (look for the "Tax-Free" sticker on the door) and must equal or exceed € 182. The V.A.T. for services (restaurants, theater, etc.) is not refundable.

When making a purchase, ask for a V.A.T. refund form and find out whether the merchant gives refunds—not all stores do, nor are they required to. Have the form stamped like any customs form by customs officials when you leave the country or, if you're visiting several European Union countries, when you leave the EU.

After you're through passport control, take the form to a refund-service counter for an on-the-spot refund (which is usually the quickest and easiest option), or mail it to the address on the form (or the envelope with it) after you arrive home. You receive the total refund stated on the form, but the processing time can be long, especially if you request a credit-card adjustment.

Global Refund is a Europe-wide service with 225,000 affiliated stores and more than 700 refund counters at major airports and border crossings. Its refund form, called a Tax Free Check, is the most common across the European continent. The service issues refunds in the form of cash, check, or credit-card adjustment.

**V.A.T. Refunds Global Refund** (☎ 800/566–9828 ⊕ www.globalrefund.com).

# ▌ TIME

The time difference between New York and Paris is six hours (so when it's 1 PM in New York, it's 7 PM in Paris). The time difference between London and Paris is one hour.

The European format for abbreviating dates is day/month/year, so 7/5/06 means May 7, not July 5.

# ▌ TIPPING

Bills in bars and restaurants must by law include service (despite what entrepreneurial servers may tell you), but it is customary to round your bill with small change unless you're dissatisfied. The amount varies—from €0.20 for a beer to €1–€2 after a meal. In expensive restaurants it's common to leave an additional 5% on the table.

Tip taxi drivers and hairdressers 10% of the bill. Give theater ushers €0.50. In some theaters and hotels cloakroom attendants may expect nothing (watch for signs that say *pourboire interdit*—tipping forbidden); otherwise, give them €0.75.

Washroom attendants usually get €0.30, though the sum is often posted.

If you stay more than two or three days in a hotel, leave something for the chambermaid—about €1.50 per day. Expect to pay €1.50 (€0.75 in a moderately priced hotel) to the person who carries your bags or hails a taxi for you. In hotels providing room service, give €1 to the waiter (unless breakfast is routinely served in your room). If the chambermaid does pressing or laundering for you, give her €1.50–€2 on top of the bill. If the concierge has been helpful, leave a tip of €8–€16.

Museum guides should get €1.50–€3 after a guided tour. It's standard practice to tip long-distance bus drivers about €2 after an excursion.

| TIPPING GUIDELINES FOR PARIS | |
| --- | --- |
| Bellhop | €1–€2, depending on the level of the hotel |
| Hotel Concierge | €5 or more, if he or she performs a service for you |
| Hotel Doorman | €1–€2 if he helps you get a cab |
| Hotel Maid | €1–€2 a day (either daily or at the end of your stay, in cash) |
| Hotel Room-Service Waiter | €1–€2 per delivery, even if a service charge has been added |

| TIPPING GUIDELINES FOR PARIS | |
|---|---|
| Taxi Driver | 10%, or just round up the fare to the next euro amount |
| Tour Guide | 10% of the cost of the tour |
| Valet Parking Attendant | €1–€2, but only when you get your car |
| Waiter | Just small change (up to a euro or two) to round out your bill. Service is included |
| Restroom Attendant | Restroom attendants in more expensive restaurants expect small change or €1 |

# ▎ TOURS

Guided tours are a good option when you don't want to do it all yourself. And not all guided tours are an if-it's-Tuesday-this-must-be-Belgium experience. A knowledgeable guide can take you places that you might never discover on your own, and you may be pushed to see more than you would have otherwise. Tours aren't for everyone, but they can be just the thing for trips to places where making travel arrangements is difficult or time-consuming (particularly when you don't speak the language). Whenever you book a guided tour, find out what's included and what isn't. Also, in most cases prices in tour brochures don't include fees and taxes. And remember that you'll be expected to tip your guide (in cash) at the end of the tour.

## BIKE AND SEGWAY TOURS

Cycling is a wonderful way to get a different view of Paris and work off all those three-course "snacks." A number of companies organize bike tours around Paris and its environs (Versailles, Chantilly, and Fontainebleau); these tours always include bikes, helmets, and an English-speaking guide. Costs start at around €25 for a half day; reservations are recommended.

Fat Tire Bike Tours is the best-known anglophone group. In addition to a general orientation bike tour, they organize a nighttime cycling trip that includes a boat cruise on the Seine. Paris à Vélo, C'est Sympa offers thematic tours; the Paris Wakes Up tour, for instance, is a unique spin through Montmartre at 6 AM.

**Information Fat Tire Bike Tours** (✉ *24 rue Edgar Faure, 15ᵉ* ☎ *01–56–58–10–54* ⊕ *www. FatTireBikeToursParis.com*). **Paris à Vélo, C'est Sympa** (✉ *37 bd. Bourdon, 4ᵉ* ☎ *01–48–87– 60–01* ⊕ *www.parisvelosympa.com*).

## BOAT TOURS

There are several boat tour companies operating cruises of one hour to a half day of sightseeing (and even dining) on the Seine. See the In-Focus on the Seine for more information. Canauxrama organizes leisurely tours year-round in flat-bottom barges along the Canal St-Martin in east Paris. There are four daily departures; the trips last about 2½ hours and have live commentary in French and English. Reservations are required. Paris Canal runs 2½-hour trips with live bilingual commentary between the Musée d'Orsay and the Parc de La Villette from April to mid-November. Reservations are required. Yachts de Paris organizes romantic 2½-hour "gourmand cruises" (for about €165) year-round. Yachts set off every evening at 7:45; you'll be served a three-course meal.

**Information Canauxrama** (☎ *01–42–39– 15–00* ⊕ *www.canauxrama.com*). **Paris Canal** (☎ *01–42–40–96–97* ⊕ *www.pariscanal.com*). **Yachts de Paris** (☎ *01–44–54–14–70* ⊕ *www. yachtsdeparis.fr*).

## BUS TOURS

The two largest bus-tour operators are Cityrama, with 90-minute double-decker tours for €24, and Paris Vision, a two-hour luxury coach tour for €24. Both have headsets for commentary in more than a dozen languages. For a more intimate—albeit expensive—tour of the city, Paris Vision also runs minibus excursions with a multilingual tour operator from €61. Paris L'OpenTour gives tours in a London-style double-decker bus with English or French commentary over individual headsets. You can catch the bus at any of 50 pickup points; tickets cost €29 for one day, €32 for unlimited use for two days. Les Cars Rouges also has hop-on–hop-off tours on double-decker London-style buses, but with only 10 stops. A ticket good for two consecutive days costs €24.

For a more economical and commentary-free trip, take a regular Parisian bus for a mere €1.70 per ticket. A special Montmartrobus (€1.80) runs from the Anvers métro station to the top of Montmartre's winding streets. The RATP's Balabus goes from Gare du Lyon to the Grand Arche de la Défense, passing by dozens of major sights on the way. The Balabus runs from mid-April through September; tickets are €1.70 each, with one to three tickets required, depending on how far you travel.

**Information** Les Cars Rouge (☏ 01–53–95–39–53 ⊕ www.carsrouges.com). **Cityrama** (✉ 4 pl. des Pyramides, 1ᵉʳ ☏ 01–44–55–61–00 ⊕ www.ecityrama.com). **Paris L'OpenTour** (☏ 01–42–66–56–56 ⊕ www.paris-opentour. com). **Paris Vision** (✉ 214 rue de Rivoli, 1ᵉʳ ☏ 01–42–60–30–01 ⊕ www.parisvision.com). **RATP** (☏ 08–92–68–41–14 €0.35 per min ⊕ www.ratp.fr).

## MINIBUS TOURS

Paris Trip and Paris Major Limousine organize tours of Paris and environs by limousine, Mercedes, or minibus (for 4–15 passengers) for a minimum of four hours. Chauffeurs are bilingual. The price varies from €260 to €400.

**Information** Paris Major Limousine (✉ 6 pl. de la Madeleine, 8ᵉ ☏ 01–44–52–50–00 ⊕ www.1st-limousine-services.com). **Paris Trip** (✉ 2 Cité de Pusy, 17ᵉ ☏ 01–56–79–05–23 ⊕ www.paris-trip.com).

## SPECIAL-INTEREST AND WALKING TOURS

Has it been a while since Art History 101? Paris Muse can help guide you through the city's museums; with its staff of art historians (all native English-speakers) you can crack the Da Vinci code or gain a new understanding of hell in front of Rodin's sculpted gates. Rates run from €90 to €280, including museum admission.

If you'd like a bit of guidance flexing your own artistic muscles, catch a themed photography tour with Paris Photo Tours. Run by the transplanted Texan Linda Mathieu, these relaxed tours are perfect for first-time visitors and anyone hoping to improve their photography abilities.

Sign up with Chic Shopping Paris to smoothly navigate the city's shopping scene. You can choose a set tour, such as Shabby Chic (vintage–secondhand places) or Made in France (unique French products), or ask for an itinerary tailor-made to your interests. Tours start at €100.

Edible Paris, the brainchild of food writer and Fodor's updater Rosa Jackson, is a customized itinerary service for food-oriented visitors. Submit a wish list of your interests and guidelines for your tastes, and you'll receive a personalized itinerary, maps, and restaurant reservations on request. Prices start around US$100 per half day. If you'd like a behind-the-scenes look at food in the capital, contact Culinary Concepts; Stephanie Curtis's tours will take you to Rungis, the gigantic professional food market on the outskirts of Paris, at €120 per person. The Rungis trip starts at 5 AM and must be booked a month ahead with a minimum of three people. Or try the bread, cheese, and wine walking tour for €120, which takes you into cheese and wine cellars and to the wood-burning ovens at the celebrated Poîlane bakery.

The team at Paris Walking Tours offers a wide selection of tours, from neighborhood visits to museum tours and theme tours such as Hemingway's Paris, and the Marais, Montmartre, and Latin Quarter itineraries. The guides are knowledgeable, taking you into less trammeled streets and divulging interesting stories about even the most unprepossessing spots. A two-hour group tour costs €12. For a more intimate experience, Context

Paris offers specialized in-depth tours of the city's art and architecture by English-speaking architects and art historians. Prices range from €35 per person for a two-hour general tour, to €75 per person for a three-hour Medieval Architecture tour; private tours range from €170 per group (maximum five people) for a two-hour Introductory Paris walk, to €1,100 for a four-hour gourmet lunch and history of French gastronomy tour.

Black Paris Tours offers tours exploring the places made famous by African-American musicians, writers, artists, and political exiles. Tours include a four- to five-hour walking-bus-métro tour (€90) that offers first-time visitors a city orientation and a primer on the history of African-Americans in Paris. For those interested in getting behind the scenes at the Château de Versailles, French Links has more than 150 fully customizable themed tours, including Jewish Paris, Normandy Beaches, and Champagne Houses, from $550 per half day. Secrets of Paris offers a Naughty Paris theme tour for ladies, with visits to female-friendly adult toy and racy lingerie boutiques, erotic art galleries, the city's sexiest cocktail bars, and recommendations for naughty cabarets and couples-only clubs.

A list of walking tours is also available from the Caisse Nationale des Monuments Historiques, in the weekly magazine *Pariscope,* and in *L'Officiel des Spectacles,* which lists walking tours under the heading "*Conférences*" (most are in French, unless otherwise noted). The magazines are available at the press kiosk.

**Information Black Paris Tours** (☎ 01–46–37–03–96 ⊕ www.tomtmusic.com/id24.htm). **Caisse Nationale des Monuments Historiques** (✉ Bureau des Visites/Conférences, Hôtel de Sully, 62 rue St-Antoine, 4e ☎ 01–44–61–21–70). **Chic Shopping Paris** (☎ 06–14–56–23–11 ⊕ www.chicshoppingparis. com). **Context Paris** (☎ 06–13–09–67–11 ⊕ www.contextparis.com). **Culinary Concepts** (✉ 10 rue Poussin ☎ 01–45–27–09–09 ✎ stecurtis@aol.com). **Edible Paris** (⊕ www.

edible-paris.com). **French Links** (☎ 01–45–77–33–63 ⊕ www.frenchlinks.com). **Paris Muse** (☎ 06–73–77–33–52 ⊕ www.parismuse. com). **Paris Photo Tours** (☎ 01–44–75–83–80 ⊕ parisphototours.com). **Paris Walking Tours** (☎ 01–48–09–21–40 ⊕ www.paris-walks.com). **Secrets of Paris** (☎ 01–43–36–69–85 ⊕ www. secretsofparis.com).

# ▌ VISITOR INFORMATION

The Maison de la France is the international arm of the French tourism ministry; through its newsletters, brochures, and Web site you can pick up plenty of information on Paris attractions, special events, promotions, and more.

Once you're in Paris, you can turn to the branches of the tourist information office. The longtime main tourist office that was on the Champs-Élysées moved to Rue des Pyramides (near the Opéra) in 2004, and a half dozen visitor bureaus are stationed at the city's most popular tourist sights. It's often easier to visit one of these branches in person than to call the hotline, because on the phone you'll have to wait through long stretches of generic recorded information at €0.34 per minute. Most are open daily; the Gare de Lyon and Opéra–Grands Magasins branches, however, are open Monday through Saturday. The tourism bureaus have friendly, efficient, and multilingual staff. You can gather info on special events, local transit, hotels, tours, excursions, and discount passes. The branch in the Carrousel du Louvre specializes in information on the Ile-de-France (the region around Paris).

**Contacts Maison de la France** (☎ 514/288–1904 or 310/271–6665 in U.S. ⊕ www. franceguide.com).

**Local Tourism Information Espace du Tourisme d'Ile-de-France** (✉ Carrousel du Louvre, 99 rue de Rivoli ☎ 08–92–68–30–00 ⊕ www.pidf.com Ⓜ Palais-Royal Musée du Louvre). **Office du Tourisme de la Ville de Paris Pyramides** (✉ 25 rue des Pyramides ☎ 08–92–68–30–00 [€0.34 per min]

Ⓜ *Pyramides*). **Office du Tourisme de la Ville de Paris Gare du Lyon** (✉ *Arrivals, 20 bd. Diderot* Ⓜ *Gare du Lyon*). **Office du Tourisme de la Ville de Paris Gare du Nord** (✉ *18 rue de Dunkerque* Ⓜ *Gare du Nord*). **Office du Tourisme de la Ville de Paris Opéra–Grands Magasins** (✉ *11 rue Scribe* Ⓜ *Opéra*). **Office du Tourisme de la Ville de Paris Tour Eiffel** (✉ *Between east and north legs of Eiffel Tower* Ⓜ *Champs de Mars/Tour Eiffel*).

## ONLINE RESOURCES
### ALL ABOUT PARIS

Besides the tourist office Web sites, ⊕ *en. parisinfo.com* and ⊕ *www.PIDF.com*, there are several other helpful government-sponsored sites. The Paris mayor's office site, ⊕ *www.paris.fr*, covers all kinds of public cultural attractions, student resources, park and market info, and more. On the French Ministry of Culture's site, ⊕ *www.culture.fr*, you can search by theme (contemporary art, cinema, music, theater, etc.) or by region (Paris is in the Ile-de-France). The Réunion des Musées Nationaux (RMN), a consortium of public museums, hosts a group site for 32 national institutions: ⊕ *www.rmn.fr*. Fourteen of these museums are in Paris proper, including the Louvre, the Musée Rodin, and the Musée d'Orsay. The site has visitor info and an exhibition calendar for current and upcoming shows.

A useful Web site for checking Paris addresses is the phone and address directory, Les Pages Jaunes (⊕ *www. pagesjaunes.fr*). Input a specific address, and you get not just a street map but a photo.

For food-related info, make a beeline for Alexander Lobrano's site (⊕ *www. hungryforparis.com*). It covers the food journalist's latest dining reviews, his articles published in *Gourmet* magazine, and his favorite Paris food links. Dining-infrance.com (⊕ *www.dininginfrance. com*) has a special section on Paris, with a selection of recent newspaper and magazine articles published on the capital's food scene.

Secrets of Paris (⊕ *www.secretsofparis. com*) is a free online newsletter of tips on dining, nightlife, accommodations, and sightseeing off the beaten path put together by Fodor's updater Heather Stimmler-Hall.

Paris-Anglo.com (⊕ *www.paris-anglo. com*) includes directories of cooking schools, galleries, language classes, and more, plus a biweekly column on various *la vie parisienne* topics. Though not entirely dedicated to Paris, the journal *France Today* (⊕ *www.francetoday.com*) often covers Paris-related news, arts events, and the like. And of course there are all sorts of Paris-related blogs that can be great sources of information and travel inspiration. Some of our faves are Paris Daily Photo (⊕ *www.parisdailyphoto. com*), a fun blog with cool photos from around the city, and Do It in Paris (⊕ *www.doitinparis.com*), a bilingual site covering fashion, shopping, dining, and fun things to do in Paris. French Word-a-Day (⊕ *www.french-word-a-day.typepad. com*) is an engaging slice-of-life, with a vocabulary bonus.

# INDEX

## PHOTO CREDITS

1, *Sam Gillespie/Alamy*. 2, *Jon Arnold/age fotostock*. 5, *SuperStock/age fotostock*. **Chapter 1: Experience:** 8-9, *Bildarchiv Monheim/age fotostock*. 10-15 (all) and 16 (left), *Joanne Rosensweig*. 16 (top center), *Bryan Busovicki/Shutterstock*. 16 (bottom center), *Bensliman/Shutterstock*. 16 (top right), *Jan Kranendonk/Shutterstock*. 16 (bottom right), *Ferenc Cegledi/Shutterstock*. 17 (top left), *wikipedia.org*. 17 (bottom left), *José Fuste Raga/age fotostock*. 17 (top center), *Jan Kranendonk/Shutterstock*. 17 (bottom center), *Joanne Rosensweig*. 17 (right), *travelstock44/Alamy*. 18, *Rob Knight/iStockphoto*. 19 (left), *Joanne Rosensweig*. 19 (right), *Steven Allan/iStockphoto*. 20, *Jan Kranendonk/Shutterstock*. 21 (left), *Photofrenetic/Alamy*. 21 (right), *Jochem Wijnands/age fotostock*. 24, *Francesco Dazzi/Shutterstock*. 25 (left), *Joanne Rosensweig*. 25 (right), *alysta/Shutterstock*. 26 and 27, *Joanne Rosensweig*. 28, *hsinli wang/iStockphoto*. 29 (left), *Joanne Rosensweig*. 29 (right), *claude thibault/Alamy*. 30, *Joseph Cesare/wikipedia.org*. 31 (left), *Fpinault/wikipedia.org*. 31 (right), *Raphael Frey/wikipedia.org*. 32, *Franck Chazot/Shutterstock*. 33 (top), *Paul Hahn/laif/Aurora Photos*. 33 (bottom), *SuperStock/age fotostock*. 34 (top), *Galina Barskaya/Shutterstock*. 34 (bottom), *Renaud Visage/age fotostock*. 35 (top left), *Stevan Stratford/iStockphoto*. 35 (top right), *Robert Haines/Alamy*. 35 (bottom), *Paul Hahn/Laif /Aurora Photos*. 36 (left), *Renaud Visage/age fotostock*. 36 (right), *Carsten Madsen/iStockphoto*. 37 (top left), *xc/Shutterstock*. 37 (top right), *Mehdi Chebil/Alamy*. 37 (bottom), *Corbis*. 38, *Elena Elisseeva/Shutterstock*. **Chapter 2: Ile de la Cité and Ile St-Louis:** 39, *Jonathan Larsen/Shutterstock*. 41, *ImageGap/Alamy*. 42, *ImageGap/Alamy*. 45, *SuperStock/age footstock*. 47, *Ewan Chesser/Shutterstock*. 48, *Fabien1309/wikipedia.org*. 49, *Renaud Visage/age fotostock*. 50, (left), *Frank Peterschroeder/Bilderberg/Aurora Photos*. 50, (right), *ostill/Shutterstock.*. **Chapter 3: La Tour Eiffel and Les Invalides:** 51, *Sean Nel/Shutterstock*. 53, *Patrick Hermans/Shutterstock*. 54, *Cristina CIOCHINA/ Shutterstock*. 55, *tkachuk/Shutterstock*. 58, *Pline/wikipedia.org*. 60, *Directphoto.org/Alamy*. 62, and 63, (left), *Directphoto.org/Alamy*. **Chapter 4: The Champs-Elysées:** 65, *Art Kowalsky/Alamy*. 67, *Clay McLachlan/Aurora Photos*. 68, *dalbera/Flickr*. 69, *fabio chironi/age fotostock*. 71, *Lazar Mihai-Bogdan/Shutterstock*. 75, *dalbera/Flickr*. **Chapter 5: The Faubourg St-Honoré and Les Halles:** 79, *blickwinkel/Alamy*. 81, *Sylvain Grandadam/age fotostock*. 82, *David A. Barnes/Alamy*. 84, *Travel Pix Collection/age fotostock*. 86, *pandapaw/Shutterstock*. 90-91, *Fischer/Bilderberg/Aurora Photos*. 91 (top), *Public Domain*. 92 (top left, top right, bottom left, bottom 2nd from left, bottom 3rd from left, and right), *Public Domain*. 92 (4th from left), *Toño Labra/age fotostock*. 93 (top left), *Visual Arts Library (London)/Alamy*. 93 (top right), *SPC 5 James Cavalier, US Military/wikipedia.org*. 93 (bottom left), *Hideo Kurihara/Alamy*. 93 (bottom 2nd from left), *Directphoto.org/Alamy*. 93 (bottom 3rd from left, bottom 4th from left, and bottom right), *Public Domain*. 94, *Rough Guides/Alamy*. 95 (top), *Peter Horree/Alamy*. 95 (2nd from top), *Public Domain*. 95 (3rd from top), *Timothy McCarthy/Art Resource*. 95 (bottom), *INTERFOTO Pressebildagentur/Alamy*. 96, *PCL/Alamy*. 97 (top), *The Bridgeman Art Library*. 97 (2nd from top), *Toño Labra/age fotostock*. 97 (3rd from top), *legge/Alamy*. 97 (bottom), *Public Domain*. 98, *SuperStock/age fotostock*. 99 (top, 2nd from top, and bottom), *Public Domain*. 99 (3rd from top), *Hideo Kurihara/Alamy*. **Chapter 6: Les Grand Boulevards:** 105, *Kevin George/Alamy*. 107, *Tristan Deschamps/Alamy*. 108, *iStockphoto*. 110, *Frank Herholdt/Alamy*. 111 (top left), *Luciana Pampalone/age fotostock*. 111 (center left), *Repetto*. 111 (bottom left), *Directphoto.org/Alamy*. 111 (top right), *eddie linssen/Alamy*. 111 (center right), *Vanessa Bruno*. 111 (bottom right), *keith van-Loen/ Alamy*. 112 (top left), *Cartier*. 112 (center left), *Lamarthe*. 112 (bottom left), *Oliver Knight/Alamy*. 112 (top right), *Agnes B.* 112 (center right), *Longines*. 112 (bottom right), *Cacharel*. 113 (top left), *Cartier*. 113 (center left), *Directphoto.org/Alamy*. 113 (bottom left), *Roger Vivier*. 113 (top right), *Kevin George/Alamy*. 113 (bottom right), *Cartier*. 114 (bottom left), *PCL/Alamy*. 114 (bottom right), *Jean-Luc Morales/Alamy*. **Chapter 7: Montmartre:** 121, *Hemis/Alamy*. 123, *Matthew Bergheiser/Shutterstock*. 124, *Jon Arnold Images/Alamy*. 125, *rfx/SHutterstock*. 128, *L F File/Shutterstock*. 129, *Rough Guides/Alamy*. **Chapter 8: Le Marais:** 133, *Oliver Knight/Alamy*. 135, *Berndt Fischer/age fotostock*.

136, *David Jordan/age fotostock*. 138-39, *Marisa Allegra Williams/iStockphoto*. 142, *M & M Valledor/ age fotostock*. 146, *tbkmedia.de/Alamy*. 149, *Timothy Ball/iStockphoto*. **Chapter 9: Canal St-Martin,Bastille, and Oberkampf:** 151, *Bob Handelman/Alamy*. 153, *Berndt Fischer/age fotostock*. 154, *f1 online/Alamy*. 156-57, *tbkmedia.de/Alamy*. 160, *Alex Segre/Alamy*. **Chapter 10: The Quartier Latin:** 167, *Danita Delimont/Alamy*. 169, *AA World Travel Library/Alamy*. 170, *Renaud Visage/age fotostock*. 171, *adam eastland/Alamy*. 174, *Aschaf/Flickr*. **Chapter 11: St-Germain:** 179, *Robert Harding Picture Library Ltd/Alamy*. 181, *Robert Harding Picture Library Ltd/Alamy*. 182, *Ian Dagnall/Alamy*. 183, *David Noton Photography/Alamy*. 186, *Sylvain Grandadam/age fotostock*. 188, *Scott Warren/ Aurora Photos*. 190, *Public Domain*. **Chapter 12: Montparnasse:** 193, *Berndt Fischer/age fotostock*. 195 and 196, *Berndt Fischer/age fotostock*. **Chapter 13: Western Paris:** 201, *Eddie Gerald/Alamy*. 203, *Brian Yarvin/age fotostock*. 204, *tbkmedia.de/Alamy*. 206, *Directphoto.org/Alamy*. **Chapter 14: Nightlife:** 209, *Marco Cristofori/age fotostock*. 212, *cgo2/Flickr*. 213, *Oliver Knight/Alamy*. 221, *Paradis Latin Cabaret*. 229, *Linda Sole/Alamy*. **Chapter 15: Performing Arts:** 231 and 233, *Directphoto.org/ Alamy*. 234, *365photos.free.fr/Flickr*. 239, *Bruce Bi/age fotostock*. **Chapter 16: Shopping:** 243, *PCL/ Alamy*. 246, *Directphoto.org/Alamy*. 247, *David A. Barnes/Alamy*. 248, *sebastien Baussais/Alamy*. 249, *Directphoto.org/Alamy*. 250, *Robert Harding Picture Library Ltd/Alamy*. 251, *Cephas Picture Library/Alamy*. 252, *Alex Segre/Alamy*. 253, *Jean-Marc Charles/age fotostock*. 254 and 255, *Rough Guides/Alamy*. 256, *Croixboisee, Fodors.com member*. 257, *Oliver Knight/Alamy*. 271, *Directphoto. org/Alamy*. **Chapter 17: Where to Eat:** 295, *Directphoto.org/Alamy*. 296, *Dana Ward/Shutterstock*. 300 and 301, *La Coupole*. 302, *Les Deux Magots*. 303 (top), *La Coupole*. 303 (bottom), *Poilâne*. 304, *P. Narayan/age fotostock*. 305 (top), *Monkey Business Images/Shutterstock*. 305 (bottom), *Neil Rouse/ Alamy*. 306 and 307 (top), *Petit Fer à Cheval*. 307 (bottom), *Andrea Matone/Alamy*. 308, *Directphoto. org/Alamy*. 309 (top), *Madeleine Openshaw/Shutterstock*. 309 (bottom), *P. Narayan/age fotostock*. 310, *Laurence MOUTON*. 311 (top), *Tomo Jesenicnik/Shutterstock*. 311 (bottom), *Directphoto.org/ Alamy*. 312, *L'Atelier de Joël Robuchon*. 313 (top), *Shebeko/Shutterstock*. 313 (bottom), *Sylvain Grandadam/age fotostock*. 314, *Steve Silver/age fotostock*. 315 (top), *Clive Sawyer/Alamy*. 315 (bottom), *Robert Fried/Alamy*. **Chapter 18: Where to Stay:** 369, *Four Seasons Hotels and Resorts*. 370, *The Leading Hotels of the World*. 373, *Terrass Hotel*. 388 (top), *Fabrice Rambert*. 388 (bottom left), *Hôtel Odéon Saint-Germain*. 388 (bottom right), *Les Degrés de Notre Dame*. 399 (top), *The Leading Hotels of the World*. 399 (bottom left), *Hôtel Langlois*. 399 (bottom right), *Jaime Ardiles-Arce/Four Seasons Hotels and Resorts*. 409 (top), *Hôtel Eiffel Seine*. 409 (bottom left), *St. Christopher's Inns*. 409 (bottom right), *Francis Amiand*. **Chapter 19: Side Trips from Paris:** 413, *Wojtek Buss/age fotostock*. 415, *Photodisc*. 418, *AM Corporation/Alamy*. 420 (top), *Elias H. Debbas II/Shutterstock*. 420 (2nd from top), *Jason Cosburn/Shutterstock*. 420 (3rd from top), *Public Domain*. 420 (4th from top and bottom), *Michael Booth/Alamy*. 421 (top), *Public Domain*. 421 (center), *Jens Preshaw/age fotostock*. 421 (bottom), *The Print Collector/Alamy*. 422 (top), *michel mory/iStockphoto*. 422 (center), *Mike Booth/ Alamy*. 422 (bottom), *Tommaso di Girolamo/age fotostock*. 423, *Hemis/Alamy*. 424 (top), *Public Domain*. 424 (2nd from top), *Jason Cosburn/Shutterstock*. 424 (3rd from top), *Guy Thouvenin/age fotostock*. 424 (bottom), *Visual Arts Library (London)/Alamy*. 425 (top), *Guy Thouvenin/age fotostock*. 425 (bottom), *Public Domain*. 426, *Jim Tardio/iStockphoto*.

# NOTES

# ABOUT OUR WRITERS

When writer-editor **Jennifer Distler-Ladonne** decided it was time to leave her longtime home, Manhattan, there was only one place to go: Paris. Her insatiable curiosity—which earned her a reputation in New York for knowing just the right place to get just the right anything—has found the perfect home in the inexhaustible streets of Paris. If you're looking for rare medieval arcana or Paris's wild edible mushrooms, she's the person to call, as we did for our shopping update.

Since moving to Paris from New York in 2004, journalist/photographer **Linda Hervieux** has explored most corners of city while covering assignments ranging from the French presidential election to the search for the perfect hot chocolate. Her writing has appeared in publications including the *New York Daily News*, the *New York Times*, and the *International Herald Tribune*. Paris is perfect base to pursue two of her favorite hobbies: studying art history at the Louvre school and mastering the French language, a battle that never ends.

**Rosa Jackson's** love affair with French cooking began at age 4, when she spent her first year in Paris before returning to the Canadian north. Early experiments with éclairs and croissants led her to the Paris Cordon Bleu where, while working as an interpreter, she learned that even great chefs make mistakes. A France-based food writer for more than a decade, Rosa also creates personalized food itineraries via ⊕ *www.edible-paris.com*, teaches cooking in Nice (⊕ *www.petitsfarcis.com*), and has her own food blog (⊕ *www.rosajackson.com*). She has eaten in hundreds of Paris restaurants—and always has room for dessert.

**Heather Stimmler-Hall** came to Paris as a university student in 1995 and was almost immediately put to work by family and friends back home who were asking for hotel recommendations. A decade later she's made a career out of reading between the lines of glossy hotel brochures and talking even the grumpiest receptionist into letting her poke around their rooms. She's reviewed hundreds of hotels for international publications such as *France* magazine, *Hotelier International*, her own monthly e-newsletter, ⊕ *www.secretsofparis.com*, *Naughty Paris: A Lady's Guide to the Sexy City*. Although she's not too jaded to appreciate the city's gorgeous five-star palace and design-boutique hotels, what really gets her excited are the hidden budget hotels with a uniquely Parisian character.